TWO HUNDRED YEARS OF

THE AMERICAN CIRCUS

TWO HUNDRED YEARS OF

THE AMERICAN CIRCUS

FROM ABA-DABA TO THE ZOPPE-ZAVATTA TROUPE

TOM OGDEN

Foreword by Albert F. House

Facts On File

Two Hundred Years of the American Circus:
From Aba-Daba to the Zoppe-Zavatta Troupe

Copyright © 1993 by Tom Ogden

Facts On File, Inc.
460 Park Avenue South
New York NY 10016
USA

Library of Congress Cataloging-in-Publication Data
Ogden, Tom.
Two hundred years of the American circus : from Aba-Daba to the
Zoppe-Zavatta Troupe / Tom Ogden.
p.   cm.
Includes bibliographical references and index.
ISBN 0-8160-2611-4
1. Circus—United States—Encyclopedias.   2. Circus—United
States—History.   I. Title.
GV1815.033   1993
791.3'03—dc20

92-31880

A British CIP catalogue record for this book is available from the British Library.

Facts On File books are available at special discounts when purchased in bulk quantities for businesses, associations, institutions or sales promotions. Please call our Special Sales Department in New York at 212/683-2244 or 800/322-8755.

Text design by Ron Monteleone
Jacket design by Ellie Nigretto
Composition and manufacturing by the Maple-Vail Book Manufacturing Group
Printed in the United States of America

10 9 8 7 6 5 4 3 2 1

This book is printed on acid-free paper.

In Loving Memory of
Mom
Who Allowed Me to "Run Away with the Circus"
and to
Dr. Charles W. "Doc" Boas
Who Gave Me Somewhere to Run

CONTENTS

FOREWORD

When I first met Tom Ogden in Freehold, New Jersey in 1973, he was a young college student appearing on Circus Kirk, an all-student circus. I was a high school history teacher and a booking agent for the Circus Kirk in the New York City–New Jersey area. Eager and outgoing, Tom was driven to become a top-notch performer. In the sideshow he performed hand tricks with balls, rope and rings. In the big show he was ringmaster, performed illusions and did a straightjacket escape routine in which he hung upside down from the top of the Big Top. Tom worked with a sense of pride and showmanship. Here, I decided, was a young man who would make his mark on the circus.

After four seasons on Circus Kirk, Tom became the sideshow magician and inside talker on the Clyde Beatty-Cole Bros. Circus. Performing there for one year, he honed his skills, learning new routines and gaining valuable life experience.

Tom left the circus business in 1975 to try other entertainment fields; and, just like Harry Houdini, his circus experience provided him with a set of credentials. Moving to the West Coast, he worked club and industrial dates, parties and cruise ships, establishing himself as a professional entertainer.

In 1990 we met again at the 20-Year Circus Kirk Reunion in Harrisburg, Pennsylvania. Tom had organized this reunion of people formerly involved with the show; the weekend was a rousing success, with about 25% of the former Kirk personnel attending.

After the dinner and formalities were over, I spoke with Tom because I was especially curious about him. He told me he was compiling an encyclopedia of the American circus. I was impressed because there was no such circus reference source available. Although good histories, biographies and autobiographies on the circus existed, the definitive circus encyclopedia was missing. Tom's book, I could see, would fill a definite gap in circus literature.

Tom continued working during the ensuing two years to compile this wonderful book. After contacting many sources and spending much time writing and editing, he has produced this volume—a welcome addition to any private or public library.

For casual researchers, *Two Hundred Years of the American Circus* gives enough detail to answer questions about the major circus personalities, the top circuses and the unique jargon of the circus world. Historically, the book covers over 3,600 years of circus tradition and, in specific detail, the 200 years of American circus history.

For circus historians, this book provides a starting point for extended research; however, details, facts and pertinent information about all of the circus subjects are covered. Although not every name can be mentioned, the major ones are. Some, such as Buffalo Bill Cody of Wild West fame, are long dead. Others, such as Art Concello, former general manager of the Ringling show, are contemporary. Circus titles, animals with their supporters and detractors, clowns and towns—they're all in here.

For circus fans of all ages, this volume is on the must-have list. It is full of choice material that cannot be found elsewhere, except perhaps in scattered libraries around the nation. Now fans have their own ready reference source to answer those perplexing questions that pop up at the most unusual times.

For readers who are interested in joining circus activities and meeting like-minded people, here are four organizations to which I belong and recommend: the Circus Fans Association of America, the Circus Historical Society, the Circus Model Builders and the Windjammers, Inc.

> — Albert F. House, President, Circus Fans
> Association of America, 1982–83
> February 10, 1992

INTRODUCTION

"**S**tep right up, ladies and gentlemen, boys and girls!"

Although the circus traces its roots all the way back to the time of the Roman Colosseum, up through the equestrian shows of Philip Astley in 18th-century England and on to the American colonies, the American circus as we know it today is only two centuries old. On April 3, 1993 we celebrated the 200th anniversary of the first complete circus performance in the United States by John Bill Ricketts, the "Father of the American Circus."

Interest in the circus remains unabated. Record crowds at recent tours of the Ringling Bros. and Barnum & Bailey Circus indicate that the love of the circus grows each year, as does the demand for books on the history and lore of the subject.

Of the more than 1,250 books listed in the Library of Congress under the general heading of circus, only a few dozen specifically provide a historical overview of the circus. Even fewer address the unique qualities, contributions and history of the American circus. None of the volumes is a "user-friendly" reference work that could be utilized by researchers and casual readers in order to know more about the fascinating history of circusdom.

Then what do all of the other books contain? Classics such as Connie Clausen's *I Love You Honey, But the Season's Over* and Fred Prowledge's *Mudshow* deal with one person's anecdotal tale of a season or two on the road with a single show. There are also the "star" autobiographies, from the numerous Clyde

Beatty books up to the recently published Gunther Gebel-Williams tome (see bibliography). Some chronicle a famous circus personage—such as Irving Wallace's P.T. Barnum bio (see bibliography)—or a well-known family—such as *The Cristianis* by Hubert Miller. It is hoped that this book will fill the void in the volumes written on the American circus.

My own circus story starts in the winter of 1969–70 when I was enrolled as a freshman at Pennsylvania State University. I was passing by the job placement board of the student affairs office when a notice caught my eye:

WANT TO GET INTO SHOW BIZ? JOIN THE CIRCUS!

The poster was from Circus Kirk, a small circus that employed college students and had its winter quarters in York, Pennsylvania. It listed more than two dozen jobs and performance skills—from electricians to wire walkers—that were needed for the following season. Of course, the only acts I could perform—magic and ventriloquism—were not on the board.

Nevertheless, I wrote the owner/manager of the show, Dr. Charles W. Boas, who was then a geography professor at York College. Much to my surprise, he called only a few days later and asked me to drive out to York for an interview.

It was almost a five-hour trip in those pre-expressway days and, at the age of 18, I had never driven that far before. I threw a few tricks and my dummy in a trunk, however, and took off.

I didn't know at the time that, according to circus jargon, when a circus goes back to quarters at season's end it is sometimes said to be put "in the barn"; I was surprised, therefore, to learn that "Doc" lived on a farm and quite literally had his equipment from the first season stored in his barn. As we walked the grounds, he told me about the show's mission and showed me some of the trucks and equipment. Then he ushered me into the barn.

There he displayed several major illusions—a Tabouret (used to make a girl disappear from a cage in midair) and Houdini's Metamorphosis (a trunk escape). The previous year the magician had gotten them half built but never put them into the show. Doc said he would allow me to perform them in the center ring if I finished building them. (I had never even driven a nail into a piece of wood other than in shop class in high school.) Boas proudly showed me an antique set of Punch & Judy puppets he had been given as a gift. If I wished, I could also perform Punch & Judy in the sideshow.

A few hours later, as I was about to leave, I asked Doc if he wanted to see me "do" anything. So far he had only taken my word that I could perform magic and ventriloquism.

"No," he said, "if you say you can do it I believe you can. I interview people more to find out whether they can fit into a circus family."

"When will I know," I asked, "whether I am hired?"

"Why? Did you see something here you don't like?"

Thus I started my rocky road from "First of May" to "trouper."

Traveling for four seasons with Circus Kirk, its offshoot (the Boas Bros. Circus) and then the Clyde Beatty-Cole Bros. Circus for the full 1974 season certainly gave me a behind-the-scenes look at the tinsel-and-sawdust view the audience has of the circus world.

At the time, however, it was only a job to me. I didn't come from a circus family. I hadn't seen many (if any) circuses as I was growing up. I didn't grow up with the dream of wanting to run away with the circus.

Mine was a true love/hate relationship with the circus. As much as I enjoyed performing in front of hundreds or a thousand people, as much as I re-

lished the challenge of entertaining under sometimes seemingly impossible conditions, as much as I loved making new friends and seeing new places on the road, I did not appreciate the rigors of the outdoor amusement industry. I didn't enjoy performing in a sweaty tuxedo. I didn't enjoy helping to drop and roll the big top during Hurricane Agnes. I didn't enjoy the amount of hard, grueling physical labor that was often necessary to drive stakes, lace canvas, repair props, set rigging, wash in cold water out of a bucket before performing two shows—only to reverse the actions during tear down to put the show to bed at night.

And I had no interest in the past glory of the circus. So what could conceivably prompt this admitted nonhistorian to write a reference book on the American circus?

Skipping a few years to 1989—I am on the beach in Santa Monica attending a performance of the celebrated Cirque du Soleil, and I am hating it. I can't understand why. The show is exceptional in its theatricality and the performances are thrilling. Yet throughout the entire first half I am sitting in the blues writhing in pain.

During intermission I walk the lot, trying to sort out the emotions I am feeling; suddenly it hits me. I am jealous. I am envious of the artists, their sense of community and their shared pride in the show. I realize that I am angry and resentful that I am not "with it" any more; for the first time in 16 years—perhaps for the first time ever—I want to run away and join the circus.

It was then that I decided I wanted to know *about* the circus. I wanted to understand its past, its history and its traditions. Perhaps if I learned the legends and legacy the circus had to offer, then I could once again feel that shared spirit and sense of family; I could once again be not only "with it" but also "for it."

When I set out to write this book, the task seemed simple enough. Certainly, I thought, all of the facts must be matters of public record. What I didn't realize was how gargantuan (if I may use a term associated with the famous Ringling gorilla) a job it would be to sort through the centuries of legend and lore.

Consider the case of A.F. Wheeler who, from

1928 through 1933, operated his circus under as many different names as there were touring seasons. Or the deliberate exaggeration of circus press agents to glorify their shows. Or the thousands of artists who appeared, sometimes for only a single season, under the big tops and open-air arenas of the American circus. How can all of this be chronicled in a one-volume historical encyclopedia?

The unfortunate answer is: It can't. While every attempt has been made to be as complete as possible, a single book by its very nature cannot constitute a full "who's who" of the circus. That Herculean task, although it would be invaluable to historians, is beyond the scope of this book. Unfortunately, it was necessary to make constant decisions during the writing and editorial process as to not only what was essential from a historical standpoint, but also what might be of significant interest to a noncircus person.

It is, therefore, unavoidable that many noteworthy entries have been omitted. In no way should a performer's or show's exclusion be considered a measure of talent or historical importance. Sometimes the reason is as simple as sufficient biographical information not being available to me. Every possible effort has been made to cover the most important and fascinating subjects in the circus world. Since all inclusions were necessarily quite subjective decisions, any suggestions for additions in future volumes—or corrections to these entries—are certainly welcomed.

In addition, a great deal of material has been included that, while not having taken place under a Big Top, is still of significant peripheral interest to the circus aficionado. The origin of the Flea Circus, the song "The Flying Trapeze" and the cast of the film *Berserk!* might fall under this category.

A great deal of circus jargon—or slang—is included as entries. While it was tempting to list all of these terms in a separate glossary, many are so seminal to the understanding of circus life that I felt they warranted their own entries. Many common phrases in everyday American language, such as "hold your horses!" "let's get this show on the road!" and "rain or shine," can be traced directly back to their uses in early circuses. The terms "jumbo," "white elephant" and "gargantuan" also have circus roots. In his bid to be reelected, Woodrow Wilson literally "threw his hat into the ring" when he visited the Barnum & Bailey Circus in Washington, D.C. in 1916. Supposedly Dan Rice called to Zachary Taylor to "get on the bandwagon" during a street parade so that the candidate could be seen better.

Circus jargon has been sprinkled through the articles so that the reader may gain a feel for how the phrases are actually used in context by troupers. The jargon also has been cross-referenced in case its meaning is not immediately or completely clear.

Occasionally, due to conflicting reference materials, it was necessary to make educated guesses at such seemingly obvious "facts" as the spelling of names and important dates. For example, three different books supply different spellings of "Hagenbeck." (A poster from the Hagenbeck-Wallace Circus confirmed the spelling used here.) Various sources list the death of Charles Ringling as having occurred in 1925, 1926 and 1927! Every attempt has been made to ensure the accuracy of spellings, dates and other facts, but again, any corrections or clarifications are certainly welcome for inclusion in subsequent editions.

To avoid duplication of information, I have used an extensive cross-referencing system for many entries. Small capitalization within the text indicates that another entry by that name appears elsewhere in the book. If another closely related article might be of interest but is not directly named in the entry, a "see also" cross-reference is used. Thus, if on first glance the entry on the Ringling Bros. and Barnum & Bailey Circus seems shorter than it should be, it is because much of the early history of the show is covered in the associated articles on P.T. Barnum, the Ringling Brothers, the Ringling Bros. Circus, James A. Bailey and the Barnum & Bailey Circus. Occasionally the cross-reference does not exactly match the second entry's headword (this is especially true in the case of singular/plural forms), but this small discrepancy has been allowed to avoid redundancy.

With apologies for the limitations of the English language, I have tried to avoid becoming entangled in the controversy over sexist versus non-gender-specific terms. In most cases throughout the book, I have used the male gender pronoun form. It should be understood that virtually any job or position on the circus—from lion trainer to show owner—can be, and probably has been, performed by a member of either sex.

Many of the circus acts mentioned in this book are in the "daredevil" category; and certainly all of them require great skill, practice and care. Even with all necessary precautions, many circus acts are inherently dangerous—the thrill of danger being part of its audience appeal—and accidents, often tragic, do happen. The reader is cautioned not to try the stunts in this book without a personal, professional circus trainer and supervision. In no way should a description of an act, gag, routine or stunt in these pages be inferred to be complete or adequate instructions to attempt any of them.

As the United States becomes more and more aware of its past, assumed truths are being reinvestigated and much of its history—including that of the circus—is being rewritten. As this book was being written, John Ringling and his wife Mable were *literally* out of their graves as courts finally granted permission for their bodies to be entombed on their former estate in Sarasota. Recently the identity of one of the last unknown victims of the great Ringling fire in Hartford was discovered. And, just as circus traditions continue (such as head bull handler Fred Logan's signing on for his 22nd consecutive season on the Clyde Beatty-Cole Bros. Circus), each year sees the beginning of a whole new generation of young performers in the circus ring and new fans in the circus tents and arenas.

A work of this magnitude would be impossible without the assistance and support of many people. Primary thanks and credit must be given to many true circus historians, authors and fans who have so diligently attempted to document and chronicle the sweeping panorama of the American circus. Also, I must thank the cooperative personnel in all of the winter quarters offices and circus press departments who have been so generous with their time and promotional materials.

On a personal level, I want to thank the following: For assistance in securing unusual and often never-before-seen photographs—Keith Allen, Andy Bakner, Bill Biggerstaff of Graphics 2000, Claire Brandt, Walter Heist, Betty and Tom Hodgini of Circus City Photo Supplies, Al House, Roger Lai at Sunset Photo Lab, Mark Willoughby and Mary K. Witkowski (head of the Historical Collections, Bridgeport Public Library); for research assistance—Judd Walson and Timothy Ludin; for interviews, articles, videos and circus support—Dr. Charles W. Boas, Chuck Burnes and Bambi Aurora Burnes of Periwinkle Productions, Dr. Maurice A. Crane of the MSU Voice Library, Art and Randy Concello, Mary Dierickx, Eugene Earl, Ruth Epstein, Frank Felt, Chappie Fox, Dave Fulton, Jeff Gabel, Harry L. Graham, Kevin Guilfote, Bob Hannigan, the Rev. L. David and Trudy Harris, James Judkins, Larry Marthaler and the Sarasota Convention & Visitors Bureau, Florrie Steven McGarrity, D.R. Miller, Bob Pelton (curator of the Barnum Museum in Bridgeport, CT), Penn & Teller, Tim Spindler (archivist, Circus World Museum), Middy Streeter, Gudrun Strong, Franz Unus and Alberto Zoppe; my book agent and my contract consultant—Sharon Jarvis and Laurie Feigenbaum; my editor, Gary M. Krebs, and his predecessors—Kate Kelly (who so enthusiastically first brought the project to Facts On File) and Neal Maillet; the first published author that I personally knew—Patrick A. Kelley; and, of course, my family. Most of all I want to thank Michael Kurland for his friendship and daily assistance, and for literally walking me through the book-writing process from first the proposal to final proofs. Without his help this project would never have gotten beyond the dream stage.

— Tom Ogden
Hollywood, California
February 17, 1992

A

AARON TURNER CIRCUS One of the first tented circuses in America, the Aaron Turner Circus was founded in the 1830s. For his first circus experience, P.T. BARNUM joined Aaron TURNER's traveling circus as a ticket taker in 1836.

Another young man on the show that season was George F. BAILEY, who became Turner's son-in-law and went on to own the circus. It was George Bailey who renamed the show the George F. Bailey Circus and ultimately linked it with the FLATFOOTS.

ABA-DABA Circus jargon for any dessert that is served in the COOKHOUSE.

ACME CIRCUS CORPORATION See BEATTY, CLYDE; CLYDE BEATTY-COLE BROS. CIRCUS; COLE BROS. CIRCUS.

ACROBATS Modern circus acrobats can trace their roots to at least 2,400 years before Christ. Immortalized on frescoes discovered by Sir Arthur Evans in Cnossus on the island of Crete, bull leaping was a popular and daring circuslike gymnastic stunt.

The sport was performed in an arena, with violent bulls charging at near-naked young men and women. As the animal approached, a youth would literally grasp the bull by the horns, swing upward and turn a full somersault over the bull's back. Once on the ground, the acrobat would turn and catch the next leaper.

Hieroglyphics from the same period show that contortionists and acrobatics such as building human pyramids were popular in ancient Egypt as well. Among the more dangerous feats was leaping headfirst between two rows of upraised swords.

Gymnastic exhibitions continued to be popular through the Roman Empire, and were part of the otherwise bloodthirsty entertainment in the CIRCUS MAXIMUS and the COLOSSEUM. Medieval tumblers continued the tradition as part of roving troupes of entertainers during the Middle Ages.

The first existing—and extremely rare—text demonstrating the art of leaping was written in France by Archange Tuccaro in 1599. Illustrations show not only flying somersaults but also leapers jumping through a series of hoops.

Acrobatics finally entered the circus ring when Philip ASTLEY, Father of the Modern Circus, added gymnasts to his show to augment his trick-riding routines in the late 1760s. Among the many acts he featured throughout his career was "The Egyptian Pyramids—an Amusing Performance of Men Piled upon Men," an act so popular he highlighted it in a large painting over the entrance to his London open-air arena.

Leaping was accomplished by running up an inclined board, jumping onto a springboard and flying onto a landing pad at the other end. Leapers who appeared during the heyday of the American tented circus—the 40 years or so beginning in the 1880s—included Frank A. Gardiner, William H. Batcheller and John Worland, all of whom were able to turn double somersaults as they jumped over rows of ELEPHANTS.

A new genre of acrobatics was created when a TEETERBOARD was substituted for the springboard. A gymnast stands at one end of the board, and one or more members of the troupe jump onto the other end, sometimes from a high platform. The force thrusts the acrobat into the air. The acrobat performs one or several tricks, such as somersaults or pirouettes, before landing upon the shoulders of a BOTTOM MAN, or "understander," waiting to catch him a few feet away from the board.

The tower created by one performer standing on another's shoulders is called a TWO HIGH. Much more difficult to achieve—but the minimal determinant of real circus skill—is the THREE HIGH, a vertical tower of three people. Acrobatic balancing troupes constantly seek to increase the number of performers in the tower as well as to create more difficult aerial tricks. The higher the tower, the more important that a MECHANIC is used, not only in rehearsal, but often in performance.

Sometimes, instead of hurling onto a tower of performers, the somersaulting aerialist will fly from the teeterboard and land in a seated position in a chair at the end of a PERCH balanced on the shoulders of the bottom man. Once the tower goes beyond a three high, or a perch is involved, a "spotter" is almost invariably used as well. It is the spotter's job to catch or break the fall of the top acrobat in case of a miss or a loss of balance.

Typical of the acrobatic troupes of the turn of the century was the Diericks Brothers. Joseph Phillip Diericks, his brother and a friend came from Antwerp, Belgium to the United States to present their strong man and vaulting act on the Orpheum Circuit and HAGENBECK-WALLACE CIRCUS. Diericks was onboard when the great train wreck occurred on June 22, 1918, in which at least 85 people died. He survived, however, and married the nurse who rescued him.

(See also VAULTING; YI, LU.)

ADAM FOREPAUGH & SELLS BROS. CIRCUS
Following the death of Adam FOREPAUGH in 1890, James E. COOPER and James A. BAILEY purchased the title and equipment of the ADAM FOREPAUGH CIRCUS, which had toured since 1866. Cooper and Bailey toured the circus under its own name through 1894.

Most of the circus's rolling stock was then moved over to supplement their BUFFALO BILL'S WILD WEST. Meanwhile, in 1896, Bailey teamed the Forepaugh title with the holdings of the SELLS BROTHERS CIRCUS to form a new show, the Adam Forepaugh & Sells Bros. Circus, often simply called the Forepaugh-Sells Circus. WINTER QUARTERS for the combined circus was on the old Sells grounds in Columbus, Ohio.

Among the show's many performers were "The Great and Only Troupe of Marvelously Educated Sea Lions and Seals Trained by Captain Woodward" and Madame Yucca, the "Female Hercules, the Strongest Woman on Earth—Handsome, Modest and Genteel, in the Costume of the Parlor She Performs Feats of Strength Never Attempted by Any Other Man or Woman."

Under the management of Cole and Lewis Sells, one of the new show's missions was to hold the northeastern territory against competition, such as the encroaching Ringling Bros. Circus, while Bailey had his BARNUM & BAILEY CIRCUS touring Europe for five years.

When Bailey returned in November 1902, he clearly saw that his plan was not working. In 1903 the Barnum & Bailey Circus had to stage its most extravagant STREET PARADE ever in New York City to revitalize interest in the show. In 1905 Bailey captured full ownership of the Forepaugh & Sells Circus; he immediately sold a half share in the show to the Ringlings. In the middle of the 1907 season the RINGLING BROTHERS purchased the other half of the show, but they continued to tour the Forepaugh & Sells Circus as its own unit through the end of the year.

The show remained in winter quarters in 1908 and 1909, but it hit the road for 1910 and 1911 before being retired forever. The title, however, had one last hurrah: In 1935 the Forepaugh name was added for legal and tax purposes to a Ringling holding, the Hagenbeck-Wallace & Forepaugh-Sells Bros. Circus.

ADAM FOREPAUGH CIRCUS
Adam FOREPAUGH, a predominant circus force in the second half of the 1800s, entered outdoor amusements in 1863. The Adam Forepaugh Circus operated from 1867 through 1894, and Forepaugh personally toured with it through 1889.

The Adam Forepaugh Circus was a major show converting from wagons to rail after the 1878 season. By 1881 it was as big as the BARNUM & BAILEY CIRCUS. One of the major innovations of the Forepaugh show was the introduction of the first regular COOKHOUSE for circus employees in 1871.

Like all good showmen, Forepaugh understood the public and the value of hoopla. In 1881 he had already created a sensation by sponsoring a beauty contest (perhaps the nation's first) and adding the winner, Louise Montague, to his troupe.

In early June of the following year, the show arrived at Grinnell, Iowa on a Sunday for a Monday stand. Forepaugh immediately heard that for weeks the local preachers had been speaking out in the pulpit against the evils of the circus; so, when everyone arrived on the LOT early Sunday morning to watch the SET UP, Forepaugh called the TOWNERS together and shepherded them down to the nearest church to attend services. It quieted the preachers, news spread among the townsfolk, and both shows on Monday played to STRAWHOUSES.

From 1880 through 1885 the Forepaugh and Barnum shows exchanged a notorious series of RAT SHEETS. In 1884 Forepaugh waged a highly publicized "war" against P.T. BARNUM, claiming that he—not Barnum—had the only true WHITE ELEPHANT on the road. Nevertheless, in 1887 the Forepaugh and Barnum circuses called a temporary truce to merge into a combined show for one major stand at MADISON SQUARE GARDEN.

Also in the late 1880s, as a result of the enormous popularity of the new vogue in entertainment, Forepaugh added a Wild West CONCERT to the "4 Paw Show," as the circus was often abbreviated in advertising posters. Star of the aftershow was Champion Wing Shot of America, Captain Adam H. BOGARDUS.

When Forepaugh died of pneumonia in his Philadelphia home in 1890, his show was bought by James E. COOPER and James A. BAILEY, who toured the Forepaugh show as a separate unit through 1894. It was one of the largest circuses on tour, second only to the BARNUM & BAILY CIRCUS; in 1891 it traveled on 52 rail cars.

After 1894, Bailey moved most of the equipment to augment his BUFFALO BILL'S WILD WEST, then combined the Forepaugh title with another of his holdings, the SELLS BROTHERS CIRCUS.

ADLER, FELIX (1898–1960)
Born on a small farm outside of Clinton, Iowa, Felix Adler ran away from home at the age of 12 or 13 to join the Ringling Brothers Circus. His father agreed to allow the boy to travel with the circus during the summer provided he stuck to his school books the rest of the year.

Adler's first job was as a water boy for the MENAGERIE and training dogs, ponies and monkeys; but he soon became fascinated by the CLOWNS. John RINGLING insisted that he receive some basic circus training first, however, so Adler began to work with a Chinese acrobatic team. His natural comedic clumsiness made him a born candidate for CLOWN ALLEY.

The day he graduated from high school, Felix applied to Charles Ringling for a full-time position and was hired as a clown. He floated in and out of the circus as he completed his studies at Iowa State College, served in World War I and spent time working in his father's construction business.

Eventually Adler realized that the circus was in his blood, and he returned to The BIG ONE for the rest of his career.

Felix Adler became famous for his trademark white costume, often spotted, with its padded hips and rear end. His white face was topped with a white pate, surrounded by scruffs of red hair. He wore tiny hats—often a crown—and carried a small umbrella. At one point in his career he wore a gem, the birthstone appropriate to the month in which he was performing, on the end of his putty nose.

Like Dan RICE before him, Adler was well known for his comic routines with a baby pig. One of these gags was having the pig climb the steps of a sliding board and slip down the other side, then rewarding the pig with a slurp from a baby bottle.

Billed as "King of Clowns," for 50 years Felix Adler was a featured clown with the RINGLING BROS. AND BARNUM & BAILEY CIRCUS. Known as the "White House Clown," Adler appeared before Presidents Coolidge, Harding and Franklin Delano Roosevelt. In 1932 he made history by becoming the first clown to appear on a television program.

ADVANCE
As generally used in show business, the advance is jargon to indicate the amount of ticket sales or monies collected in the box office before the play date of the show, as in—"What is the advance?"

Knowing the advance of the show allows a shrewd circus manager to calculate the additional box office receipts possible the day of show. If the advance is bad, the manager can then alert his advance crew to change advertising strategies or attempt to cut expenses to meet the show's daily NUT.

(See also ADVANCE CLOWN; ADVANCE MAN.)

ADVANCE CLOWN   Traveling several weeks ahead of "circus day" (the first day of the circus), the advance clown makes public appearances on behalf of his show.

As opposed to the ADVANCE MAN, the advance clown does not usually make the initial contacts with the press or coordinate the sponsor/circus needs. The main duties of the advance clown are to be available for "photo opportunities" and to spread good words about the circus. Since this work also often involves visiting hospitals, nursing homes and other charity events, the advance clown is sometimes referred to—especially in the case of The BIG ONE— as the "Goodwill Ambassador" for the show.

ADVANCE MAN   Any circus veteran will tell you that the day's business is only going to be as good as the ADVANCE.

The advance men are those who travel from a day up to several weeks in advance of the circus to ensure good box office business and facilitate the show's arrival. Anyone who is sent out ahead of the show is said to be "on the advance."

Although technically referring to the agent who up to a year in advance contracts or signs the date the circus will come into town, the term advance man is reserved for those who travel ahead of the show once the circus season has begun.

In the early days of the American circus, the advance crew consisted of a single man who had the overall responsibility of preparing a town for the circus's arrival. Often he was also the bill poster. The best in the field were those advance crews who could find the most eye-catching venues for the outdoor sheets and who could convince the town's important merchants to display cards in their windows. The advance man's job could also include organizing press releases, articles and interviews; checking on sponsors; arranging the delivery of local supplies, such as food and water for the cast and the animals; obtaining necessary permits and sometimes even filling in last-minute bookings for the tour.

As circuses grew in size and competition from other shows increased, additional advance men were needed and their duties became more specific. To-day the advance men include—but are not limited to—the BILLING CREW, the PRESS AGENT and the 24-HOUR MAN.

During the heyday of the great rail shows, the banner brigade was the first part of the circus to appear in town. These men traveled on scheduled trains and posted cloth BANNERS on the sides of buildings. Next came the Number One advertising car, carried as one coach on a regular train, with a crew of 30 or more billposters who covered every-thing within a 100-mile radius of the town. The advertising car even carried its own boiler to make the paste necessary to glue the LITHOGRAPHS onto the buildings' walls. Also traveling on the Number One car were the press agents or agents who han-dled the local newspapers.

The larger shows sent out a Number Two bill (advertising) car as well. This second wave count-ered any negative press or RAT SHEETS generated by rival shows in the territory, restored torn paper and coddled the press closer to the show date. The day before the show, the 24-hour man arrived to do a final check of the LOT, to finalize contracts and licenses and to arrange for food and water for the cast and animals.

ADVERTISING BANNER   See BANNER.

AERIAL ACTS   Although not a part of the first cir-cuses in the United States, aerial acts are among the most thrilling acts currently seen in the modern American circus.

The invention of each new piece of aerial appa-ratus creates a new type of act, but certain ones have been staples, regularly—if not always—seen in a typical circus show. Most of the rigging of any of the acts is attached to a heavy metal CRANE BAR, which often stretches between the CENTER POLES at the roof of the BIG TOP. Thus, the terms aerial act and aerialist are never used by show folk to refer to performances on the high wire (including SKY-WALKS) or even the SWAY POLE. The word aerial requires that either the apparatus or artist *hangs* from overhead rigging, not simply that the act is performed high off the ground.

Two of the first routines learned by a showgirl or BALLY BROAD are the WEB and LADDERS. The Spanish web, as it is sometimes known, is a canvas rope, stuffed with cotton, that hangs all of the way from the tent dome to the ground. The showgirl climbs the rope, places her hand or foot through a canvas loop for safety and assumes various graceful positions as part of an ensemble display. The routine usually ends with the web being swung in a large circle by the WEB SITTER as the girl spins, dangling by one wrist from the rope.

The Roman or swinging ladders are just that: ladders that swing. A metal rectangle, approximately five feet by two feet, with several "rungs" welded into shape, is flown into the air. The aerialist climbs onto this small ladder by way of a web. As the ladder is swung back and forth, the showgirl performs elegant poses across, through and around the rungs.

Also learned by many of the women on the show, although often a featured solo turn, are the IRON JAW and the HAIR HANG. The iron jaw, performed as its own number or as the "blow off"—or big finish—to another aerial act is, quite literally, hanging onto a rope solely by the teeth. While this is accomplished with the aid of a piece of oral apparatus, the feat is nonetheless miraculous to watch. The girl performing the iron jaw has a plaster cast taken of her mouth, jaw and teeth; a large leather piece is formed that fills the entire mouth cavity. This piece is attached by a hook to the web, or other piece of equipment, from which the artist will spin.

The illusion of the hair hang is that a girl's hair is tied to a rope, and she is hoisted into the air. In fact, this speculation is not that far from the truth. The showgirl *does* hang from her real hair, but tied into the braiding is a metal ring. The hook that lifts the girl is slipped through the ring, and she is raised through a pulley system, controlled by men on the ground. While in the air, the showgirl often juggles as well, adding another circus skill to this already unbelievable sight.

A recent entry into the field is the aerial straps. As performed by Vladimir Kekhaial on the 1991 American tour of CIRQUE DU SOLEIL, the artist wraps two long lengths of leather stretching from the top of the tent, one around each wrist. The straps, which are connected to a rope through a pulley and back down to the ground, pull the acrobat up into the air. The gymnastics performed are similar to the somersaults, turns and displays that are possible on

the ROMAN RINGS and the TRAPEZE; but, because of the absence of apparatus or a bar, the act seems to be exclusively strength-oriented. In the 1990 edition of The BIG APPLE CIRCUS, the Panteleenko Brothers, also of the Soviet Union, performed a two-man version of the aerial straps.

Originally considered a "ground" exhibition act, Roman rings are now seen as a high aerial act. Two large metal rings, often canvas-padded, hang from separate straps from the overhead rigging or crane bar. The acrobat is pulled aloft by—or climbs a web to—the rings. Taking one in each hand, the artist performs a series of somersaults and other feats of strength.

Lillian LEITZEL was the most famous circus performer to perform on the rings in this century. After finishing her beautiful, balletic routine, she switched apparatus to perform an even more strenuous aerial exhibition, a series of one-arm PLANGES. Holding onto a web with only one hand, she would throw her body up and over itself, momentarily dislocating her shoulder on each swing in an awesome display of strength and agility.

The PERCH is also usually considered a ground act, because the person holding onto the perch (referred to as the BOTTOM MAN, regardless of sex) stands in the ring. One or more artists usually balance in midair at the top of the single pole, however. At the top of the perch pole, the gymnast might juggle or perform an iron jaw spin or any other aerial display.

An AERIAL PERCH is basically an upside-down perch pole. The long rod hangs from aerial rigging or the crane bar; one or more artists hang from it while performing aerial feats.

The CRADLE is an unusual-looking but increasingly popular aerial act in today's circuses. The cradle apparatus resembles two metal triangles that have been joined by long bars from point to point. The entire structure is flown high in the air, and a CATCHER wraps his feet around one of the bars and dangles downward. Another aerialist hangs from his arms and performs somersaults, spins and turns. Usually seen as a separate aerial act, the cradle apparatus is beginning to be used more often by the catcher in a FLYING TRAPEZE act.

The TRAPEZE is a single bar, held aloft by two cloth-covered ropes hanging from the loft of the tent or arena. Gymnastic poses and tricks are made even more difficult when the "still trap" becomes a "swinging trapeze."

To many, the ultimate in aerial acts is the flying trapeze, an act generally credited as having been invented by Jules LÉOTARD. The modern apparatus consists of at least three pieces: a platform from which the flyers take off; the swinging trapeze from which the artists make their somersaults and leaps; and a second trapeze (or cradle) from which the catcher hangs. Most of the amazing stunts, such as the TRIPLE SOMERSAULT, are performed by the artist between the swinging trapeze and the arms of the catcher.

Some say that Man is born with an inner longing to fly. If so, it explains why the great American aerial acts have become some of the most famous circus performers of all time.

AERIAL BALLET   See AERIAL ACTS; BALLY BROAD; LADDERS; WEB; WEB GIRL; WEB SITTER.

AERIAL CRADLE   See CRADLE.

AERIAL PERCH   Used for performances in midair at the top of the BIG TOP, the aerial perch (also known as a hanging perch) is a vertical pole suspended high above the performing arena. By holding onto the perch, or by being held to it by safety loops, acrobats can perform tricks. The creation of the apparatus spurred a whole new type of aerial act.

(See also AERIAL ACTS.)

AERIAL STRAPS   See AERIAL ACTS.

AERIALISTS   See AYALA, MARGARITA VAZQUEZ; BARBETTE; CODONA, ALFREDO; COLLEANO, WINNIE; CONCELLO, ANTOINETTE; CONCELLO, ART; FLYING CONCELLOS, THE; FLYING CRANES, THE; FLYING GAONAS, THE; FLYING VAZQUEZ, THE; GAONA, TITO; LEITZEL, LILLIAN; LÉOTARD, JULES; NAITTO, ALA; VAZQUEZ, MIGUEL.

A.F. WHEELER SHOWS   A.F. Wheeler formed his first show when he and Sam Dock left the WELSH BROS. CIRCUS in 1893. They joined Andrew DOWNIE, already a noted circus operator, to form the Downie & Wheeler Circus from 1911 to 1913.

Wheeler then went out on his own, eventually buying the Welsh Bros. Circus in 1915. Wheeler toured his Wheeler Bros. Circus from 1914 through 1916 and again from 1921 through 1922. He then owned or managed various shows through 1930 before remounting as the Al F. Wheeler Circus.

With various partners, Wheeler toured a succession of shows under his name, including the Wheeler & Sautelle Circus (1931–1932), the Al F. Wheeler Circus and Tiger Bill Wild West (1932) and the Wheeler & Almond Circus (1933).

(See also SAM DOCK CIRCUS.)

AFTERSHOW   See CONCERT.

AL G. BARNES CIRCUS   Alpheus George Barnes Stonehouse (Al G. Barnes) started his career as an animal trainer and owner of a wild animal circus and MENAGERIE.

In 1895 he opened his first one-wagon show, touring it among carnivals and small circuses. In 1906 he expanded the troupe into the Al G. Barnes Trained Wild Animal Circus. Known as a "western wonder," the ten-railroad-car circus toured the West, sometimes Canada, but seldom went east of Indiana. Noted for having the best trained animals in the business as well as for its variety of trained performing stock and large menagerie—including the infamously dangerous elephant, Tusko—the circus grew to travel on 30 cars.

In 1929 the Al G. Barnes Circus was sold to the AMERICAN CIRCUS CORPORATION, which operated it for a year before selling it—along with the rest of its assets—to John RINGLING.

Ringling ran the Al G. Barnes Circus through 1938, but in its last years the show toured under a variety of titles. Perhaps to increase marquee value, Ringling combined circus names from his holdings; and, in 1937 and 1938, the show traveled as the Al G. Barnes-Sells Floto Circus. In its last year it was also called the Al G. Barnes-Sells Floto & John Robinson Combined Circuses. Finally, after a workers' strike closed the RINGLING BROS. AND BARNUM & BAILEY CIRCUS, the show had its last tour as the Al G. Barnes-Sells Floto Circus with Ringling Bros. and Barnum & Bailey Stupendous New Features.

(See also ROTH, LOUIS; STARK, MABEL.)

AL G. KELLY & MILLER BROS. CIRCUS

Also known simply as the Kelly-Miller Bros. Circus, the Al G. Kelly & Miller Bros. Circus was founded in Missouri in 1938 by Obert Miller (11 January 1886–29 October 1969), along with his two sons, Kelly (5 March 1913–20 February 1960) and D.R. (see MILLER, DORY "D.R."). Not coming from a circus family and having limited circus experience, they taught themselves the circus business—even to the point of sewing their first BIG TOP by themselves. When the two sons married, their wives joined in, making the show a true family concern.

Originally a tiny truck show, the circus was still very small through 1944. After World War II Kelly and Dory returned to the show and helped to expand the circus. Constantly improving, the Kelly-Miller Circus became one of the most profitable on the road in the 1950s, rivaling or even exceeding the "take" of the RINGLING BROS. AND BARNUM & BAILEY CIRCUS.

Among the many circus "firsts" introduced by Kelly-Miller were new styles of motorized equipment, such as the first successful transport of GIRAFFES by truck and the initial use of airplanes for circus advertising. Kelly Miller, along with Wayne C. Saguin, is credited with having updated the SPOOL WAGON to the modern spool truck, a staple on every major circus lot. During its heyday, the Kelly-Miller show was renowned for the size of its MENAGERIE and elephant herd.

Also by the 1950s the show had moved its WINTER QUARTERS to Hugo, Oklahoma; and, when Kelly Miller died in 1959, most of the day-to-day management of the circus fell to his brother D.R. Obert Miller wanted the show to remain small, but D.R.'s dream was to build it even larger. D.R. was already part owner of the FAMOUS COLE CIRCUS as well as the CARSON & BARNES CIRCUS, the latter under the management of Jack Moore.

Obert Miller, maintaining that "smaller is better," put out his own show, the Fairyland Circus, around 1962 to 1965, to only modest success. Over at Kelly-Miller, D.R. Miller also had mixed results with his "bigger is better" show.

In 1969 Jack Moore died and D.R. took direct control of the Carson & Barnes Circus. He moved its quarters to Hugo, transferred most of the personnel of the Kelly-Miller show over to the Carson & Barnes show and retired the Kelly-Miller title.

In the fall of 1983, the John Strong Circus was put up for sale; D.R. Miller purchased the title, tent and gear. The equipment became the nucleus of a new circus under the management of a third-generation circus performer, David E. Rawls, as president. David Rawls's partners in the venture were Jess Jessen and D.R. Miller.

D.R. suggested resurrecting the old Kelly-Miller title for the new show. In the spring of 1984 the Al G. Kelly-Miller Bros. Circus reemerged. The title was soon shortened officially to the Kelly-Miller Bros. Circus.

Today the show and its 65- to 75-member troupe travel on 25 vehicles, setting up on an area of about 90,000 square feet. The blue-and-gold, three-ring Big Top—a new Italian Scola Teloni design—seats 1,500 and is made of waterproof vinyl rather than canvas. The tent is 80 feet wide, 200 feet long and 30 feet in height with four CENTER POLES. In addition to the ticket wagon and concessions, the MIDWAY also features a pony ride and a full combined SIDESHOW and menagerie. Due to safety and insurance concerns, there are no wild animal acts in the main show; likewise, the most dangerous animal in the menagerie is a declawed tiger.

The show tours mostly 15 states in the eastern half of the United States and made a trip to Ontario, Canada in 1991. The following season the circus performed in 14 states and three Canadian provinces from March 21 through October 25, 1992. Current owners are David and Carol Rawls, Lorraine Jessen (her husband Jesse died in 1987), D.R. and Isla Miller and Geary and Barbara Byrd.

Three generations of the Rawls family have been involved in the circus. Harry E. Rawls, a respected veteran showman who had traveled with James M. COLE and D.R. Miller, helped to start the new unit and serves as its contractor and office manager in Hugo. His five sons have all been active in the circus world.

David, Rawls's oldest son, acts as manager on tour; David's wife Carol is artistic director. Their daughter Sasha is an office assistant, and their young son is an occasional performer. Bobby, Harry's second son, used to manage the CLYDE BEATTY-COLE BROS. CIRCUS, but has given up the road to return to Mead, Oklahoma. There, in his AAA Sign Shop, he has become a talented circus and sign painter. A third son, Chris (Harry C.), now works in management

"Here Today Only."   (Photo by Tom Ogden)

for Beatty-Cole; his wife Maria works in the office. The fourth, Michael, is concessions manager; and the fifth, William, is now a Kelly-Miller announcer. Harry E. Rawls's three daughters have all opted not to go into entertainment.

ALFALFA   Circus jargon for any currency or paper money.

ALL OUT AND ALL OVER   Circus jargon meaning the entire performance is concluded and all of the audience has left the BIG TOP.

ALLAN C. HILL'S GREAT AMERICAN CIRCUS   See HILL, ALLAN C.

ALLEN BROS. CIRCUS   A modern truck show, the Allen Bros. Circus is owned and operated by Allen and Erlynn Bedford. Performing under canvas, the show's TERRITORY is the eastern United States. The MIDWAY supports concessions, a petting ZOO, a pony ride and one, sometimes two, MOON BOUNCES. The novelties' joint (or souvenir stand) and elephant ride are inside the BIG TOP.

The main show includes a Spanish web, a cat act, ground acrobatics, aerial cradle, a BULL act and CLOWNS.

ALLIED OWNERS, INC.   In the fall of 1929, John RINGLING bought the AMERICAN CIRCUS CORPORATION for $2 million, $1.7 of which was secured by a personal note with the Prudence Bond and Mortgage Company. The purchase gave Ringling control of every major circus title and operation in the United States.

After the Stock Market Crash in October 1929, revenues for the circus industry dropped immediately. Ringling, also hurting from his other lost investments, defaulted on the loan.

The note held by Prudence was bought by two separate groups of businessmen, the Allied Owners and the New York Investors, both headed by Samuel W. GUMPERTZ.

At the next meeting of the board of directors for the Ringling corporation, relatives and creditors turned show management and operation over to the Allied Owners, Inc., with Gumpertz as senior vice president and general manager. John Ringling, whose personal assets were held as collateral until the Ringling family could buy the note of obligation back from Allied Owners, retained the honorary title of president.

In one of the most notorious moments in the history of the RINGLING BROS. AND BARNUM & BAILEY CIRCUS, Gumpertz actually ordered John Ringling off the lot during the 1936 opening at MADISON SQUARE GARDEN, saying that Ringling no longer had any say in the operation of the show.

In 1938 John Ringling NORTH, a lawyer and nephew to John Ringling, arranged a loan from Manufacturers Trust to purchase the bank note back from the Allied Owners, Inc., returning the circus to the Ringling family.

ALPERT, "PRINCE" PAUL (1914–1987)   Beginning his circus career as a WHITEFACE CLOWN in one of the Paul JUNG troupes, Paul Alpert—also one of the LITTLE PEOPLE—went on to fame on his own.

A native of Bangor, Maine, Paul Alpert first clowned in 1933 and performed with the RINGLING BROS. AND BARNUM & BAILEY CIRCUS for over 50 years. He had the rare honor of being credited in the 1967 circus program for one of the major clown production numbers he originated for that season's show:

**Display 25
WILD WEST WHOOP-DE-DO
The Ringling Clowns' Hilarious Version
of the Early Frontier Days
(Wild West Number Produced by 'Prince'
Paul Alpert)**

Over the years Prince Paul Alpert was a frequent teacher at the Ringling CLOWN COLLEGE. He retired in 1980 and moved to Massachusetts to be near his sister.

ALZANA, HAROLD (1918–   )   A well-known wire walker, Alzana's claim to fame was an ascent of an inclined cable. For the climb the cord would be stretched from the ground to the tent's apex at a 45-degree angle.

Born Harold Davis in Yorkshire, England, he went to work in the coal mine fields at the age of 15. Charles, his father, was a frustrated acrobat who preferred a stable family life to touring. He trained and encouraged his son, however, and by the age of 20, young Harold had put together a tight wire act with his two sisters, Elsie and Hilda. Harold took his nickname "Al" and Elsie's middle name "Annie" and combined them into the exotic-sounding "Alzana." Years later he explained, "If you didn't sport a foreign name in England, you couldn't get a job." The Great Alazanas did get jobs—at fairs and celebrations all over the Sheffield area.

In 1939 he convinced a neighbor, Minnie, to sit on his shoulders as he walked a 50-foot wire in Kent. They married in 1941, and she became a permanent part of the act.

Their performance career stopped during World War II, when Harold Alzana contributed to the war effort by working in the mines. After the war they began anew and were soon working for the Blackpool Tower Circus. Alzana sent photos to John Ringling NORTH who, in turn, sent an agent, Hans Lederer, to see them. Although the makeshift audition was performed in a backyard, the Alzanas were signed on the spot. They joined The BIG ONE at the start of the 1947 season.

The act was breathtaking, beginning with the ascent up the incline wire to the high wire. Once there, Alzana danced a Charleston, performed cartwheels and spins around the wire. Partway through the season, he slipped while performing in Marion, Ohio and fell 40 feet to the ground. Within six weeks he was on his feet, and soon he was back on the wire.

At five foot four inches tall and 145 pounds, with a high-toned muscular body, Alzana often took risks on the wire; and his daredevilry almost caused his death on several occasions.

Around 1955, Alzana began to harbor doubts about his own ability and lived with constant fear of falling. During the MADISON SQUARE GARDEN opening in 1958 his right knee buckled and he fell. Again, in 1960, during the Miami opening he got tangled while skipping rope and fell. Both times,

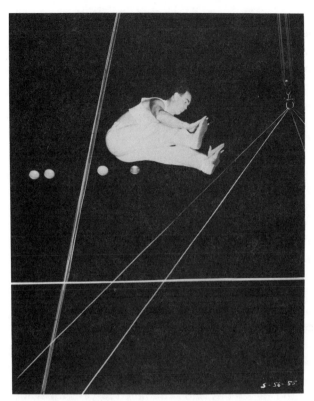

Harold Alzana, high wire artist with the Ringling Bros. and Barnum & Bailey Circus, makes a split after jumping from the high wire. (Author's collection)

spotters on the ground were able to break his fall, and he suffered only minor injuries.

He began to wind down his career in the late 1970s and was fully retired in SARASOTA, FLORIDA with his wife by the early 1980s. He sensibly left the ring because, in his words, "they don't want to pay you enough now to take the risks." He knew the eventual end to all wire walkers who continued to work past their prime: "You're gonna come down."

See also WIRE WALKING.

AMERICAN CIRCUS CORPORATION   Headed by Jeremiah "Jerry" MUGIVAN, Bert BOWERS and Ed Ballard, the American Circus Corporation—with its headquarters in PERU, INDIANA—owned five major shows at its zenith in the second decade of the 1900s. The circuses under their management were referred to as the "Corporation Shows."

Jerry Mugivan and Bert met as ticket sellers on the Sanger & Lentz show. In 1900 they moved over to work for Ben Wallace.

To start their own corporation in 1904, the partners used the name VAN AMBURGH CIRCUS for the first of their shows, although they had no connection to Isaac VAN AMBURGH. In the middle of the 1908 season, Mugivan and Bowers decided that the title had outlived its usefulness and changed the show's name to Howes' Great London Circus. The show toured under the new title until 1921, when the Van Amburgh title was revived briefly.

Following a flood in 1913, Ben Wallace sold his show, the HAGENBACK-WALLACE CIRCUS, to a syndicate that was soon headed by Peru's leading real estate broker, Ed Ballard. In 1920, after many years of negotiation, Mugivan and Bowers joined Ballard in purchasing for themselves the Hagenbeck-Wallace Circus, which was offered for only $36,000 after a devastating 1918 train wreck. In 1921 Mugivan, Bowers and Ballard became partners in the American Circus Corporation.

From 1921 until 1929, the American Circus Corporation also owned the SELLS-FLOTO CIRCUS. The show had a humble beginning in 1906 when the Floto Dog & Pony Show combined forces with Willie Sells, creating the Sells-Floto Circus.

The "Sells Bros. Circus" title was owned by the RINGLING BROTHERS, however, so in 1909 the Ringlings successfully sued to keep photos of the Sells brothers out of the Sells-Floto advertising.

In 1915 the Two Bills Show and Sells-Floto combined to form the Sells Floto-Buffalo Bill Circus, with William F. CODY as the featured star. When Cody was hired by the 101 RANCH WILD WEST the following year, the Sells-Floto Circus returned to its old name. It continued to tour under that title until 1929.

The American Circus Corporation bought the great AL G. BARNES CIRCUS in 1928 and operated it for two seasons. Barnes had started out as an animal trainer and expanded his act into a carnival show. By 1910 the show moved onto rails as a ten-car circus, eventually growing to 30 railroad cars. Especially noted for its large and varied MENAGERIE, the show carried two notoriously dangerous elephants, Tusko and Black Diamond. (The latter had to be executed as a ROGUE ELEPHANT in 1929.)

The American Circus Corporation also purchased the SPARKS CIRCUS in 1928. Begun as the John H. Sparks Old Virginia Shows in the 1890s, the circus was on two rail cars by 1900, seven cars by 1909 and 15 by 1916. Charles Sparks—the adopted son of John H. Sparks—became head of the show. Under his ideal management, the show traveled on 20 cars through the 1920s. When Charles sold the circus after 1928, he did not know that the true buyer was the American Circus Corporation.

The American Circus Corporation also owned—or claimed title to—the JOHN ROBINSON CIRCUS, the YANKEE ROBINSON CIRCUS, the Great Van Amburgh Circus, GOLLMAR BROS. CIRCUS and the Dide Fisk Circus.

In 1929 John RINGLING had a major dispute with the owners of MADISON SQUARE GARDEN over Friday-night performances. The Garden wanted to use the popular evening for prize-fighting, but Ringling refused to bring in his show if it meant the loss of weekend revenue. The Garden called Ringling's bluff and awarded its circus contract for the spring of 1930 to the American Circus Corporation, which promptly moved the Sells-Floto Circus into its rival's spot. To salvage his pride, Ringling bought out the Corporation for $2 million.

Although the American Circus Corporation was no more, its equipment, performers, animals and ownership of circus names was put under the Ringling banner. John Ringling owned a conglomerate of 240 rail cars, a huge menagerie and employed over 4,000 performers and workers, as well as having title to every railroad circus of note in America.

As an end note—only days after the deal was signed, the Stock Market Crash occurred. Ringling defaulted on his payments for the American Circus Corporation; ALLIED OWNERS, INC., took over ownership of the circus properties, making Sam W. GUMPERTZ the general manager.

AMERICAN MUSEUM   At the end of the 18th century, the Tammany Society in New York City started amassing a collection of natural-history curios that, beginning in 1790, they housed in City Hall. In 1795 the collection fell into private ownership; and shortly after 1800 John Scudder, a taxidermist, acquired it. He opened the display for public exhibition as Scudder's Museum, also known as the American Museum.

At the time of Scudder's death in 1821, the assortment included wax figures, stuffed animals, a machine run by a dog and dioramas. In 1830 Scudder's heirs moved the collection to a five-story building at the corner of Ann Street and Broadway, but by 1840 they were eager to sell. P.T. BARNUM was

Barnum's American Museum.   (Photo courtesy of Ronald W. Lackmann)

eager to buy but had no money. Through sheer charisma, Barnum convinced Francis Olmsted, the owner of the building, to purchase the collection on his behalf, using a piece of property that Barnum owned in Connecticut as collateral. Although Barnum claimed the tract—named Ivy Island—to be quite valuable, it was, in fact, little more than swampland.

John Heath, the administrator of Scudder's estate, still had control of the collection; and, despite a previous verbal offer to sell the assortment to Barnum, he decided to accept a rival offer from the New York Museum Company instead. Convinced that the company was planning to use the investment for a stock swindle, Barnum alerted the press. Confidence in the New York Museum Company plummeted; and when they didn't make the agreed payment on time, Heath sold the contents of the American Museum to Barnum.

Barnum was in business, and he quickly replaced the tired exhibits with more exciting displays. He added live shows, including magicians, ventriloquists, Punch & Judy puppeteers and knife throwers, all for the price of 25 cents admission. Gaudy posters were unfurled outside the museum to lure in the crowds, and deliberately bad musicians were sta-

tioned on the museum's outer balcony to drive passersby inside to escape the din. The logic worked. In fact, the museum became one of the most popular tourist attractions in the city. Some families entered when the doors opened at sunrise and spent the entire day there.

So large were the crowds that on one St. Patrick's Day customers lined the block to await their turn to view the wonders. Because the people inside were too slow to leave for Barnum's taste, he painted a sign that said "To The Egress." The patrons dutifully followed the arrow, hoping to see a new exotic wonder—only to find themselves outside on the street.

Among the well-known assortment of curiosities to be housed in Barnum's American Museum were an 18-inch mock-up of Niagara Falls—grandly advertised as "the Great Model of Niagara Falls"—and the FEEJEE MERMAID. Half monkey, half fish, the Feejee Mermaid attracted thousands of stunned onlookers, despite its dubious origin.

Soon human oddities were being added to Barnum's American Museum. The celebrated TOM THUMB, a 25-inch midget, first entered the museum at the age of five. Others included Anna Swan, a 7-foot-11 giant from Nova Scottia, and Madame CLOFULLIA, the bearded lady. Always an excellent promotor, Barnum himself instigated a lawsuit requiring Madame Clofullia to prove herself a female.

Perhaps the most unusual human attraction was CHANG AND ENG, called the Siamese Twins. Two brothers, inseparably joined at the chest, Chang and Eng had already been on international tour before agreeing to be exhibited at the American Museum.

Barnum sold the museum in 1855, but his personal bankruptcy forced him to resume management only a few years later. In 1864, in the middle of the Civil War, a firebomb destroyed part of the building; in July 1865 an accidental fire burned it to the ground.

On September 6, 1865, just two months later, Barnum reopened the New American Museum in a different location. He added a tented MENAGERIE next to the museum and boosted the size of the show with Van Amburgh's Menagerie (see VAN AMBURGH CIRCUS).

The New American Museum lasted only three years. In March 1868 the building was burned beyond repair in yet another fire. Although Barnum went on to many more great successes, the American Museum never opened its doors again.

ANGEVINE, CALEB S(UTTON) (1798–1859)
From SOMERS, NEW YORK, the "Cradle of the American Circus," Caleb S. Angevine was spurred on by the success of Nathan A. HOWES of nearby Brewster and became one of a number of farmers-turned-MENAGERIE owners. With his partners John J. JUNE and Lewis B. TITUS, Angevine formed Lewis, June, Angevine and Co., one of the strongest menageries of the early 19th century. Among their accomplishments was exhibiting the first live rhinoceros in America.

In January 1835 Angevine, along with most of the owners of the prominent American menageries, formed the ZOOLOGICAL INSTITUTE. While its stated purpose was to "to more generally diffuse and promote the knowledge of natural history and gratify rational curiosity," the Institute's true purpose was probably to attempt to control the exhibition of menagerie animals in the United States.

Following the close of the Institute on August 23, 1837, Angevine—as part owner of the Van Amburgh & Co. in addition to his own menagerie—became part of a separate group known as the FLATFOOTS, which from 1838 to 1842 also sought to form a monopoly over menagerie and circus animals. At the end of the 1842 season, June, Titus, Angevine and Co. went out of business. Angevine remained a partner in the Van Amburgh & Co. through at least 1847.

(See also VAN AMBURGH, ISAAC; VAN AMBURGH CIRCUS.)

ANIMAL ACTIVISTS
Ever since the exhibition of the first domesticated and exotic animals, there have been those who have claimed that all animals held in captivity are being unfairly and cruelly treated. While there have, indeed, been reported instances of unkind handling of animals by their trainers, circus managements strictly condemn and punish any such actions by employees or spectators on the LOT.

As early as the beginning of this century, newspaper editorials questioned the use of animals in circuses. A 1908 article by Maurice B. Kirby describes in detail methods used by an unscrupulous turn-of-the-century trainer to get a tiger to sit on a pedestal. The beast was jabbed with a steel fork, beaten on the nose with a whip, then tied and hoisted up by block and tackle. Jack London, the famous author, did much to flame the activist fires when he made Harris Collins, the protagonist of his 1917 book *Michael, Brother of Jerry*, a cruel and vicious animal trainer who delighted in torture-training his creatures.

In the June 30, 1923 issue of *BILLBOARD*, the first articles appeared refuting the claims of those who castigated the trainers without ever having seen their work and methods. In spite of these protests, arguments and name-calling from activists have continued up through today.

In the 1980s the American Society for the Prevention of Cruelty to Animals (ASPCA) and animal rights groups formed animal activist groups that began to picket and disrupt circus performances. They lobbied legislatures to pass unwise animal control acts and seriously challenged in courts a performer's right to use animals in the ring.

In late February 1991 activists actually succeeded in getting a Hollywood, Florida city council—in the heart of WINTER QUARTERS territory of the circus industry—to pass a law stating that:

No vertebrate animals shall be displayed for public enter-tainment or amusement on property owned by the city or in or on city owned property under lease, including but not limited to the exhibition of such animals in zoos, or farms, or during competitive races in arenas; however, animals may be displayed on public property for educational purposes so long as the care of such animals during their display conforms to guidelines established by the city in conjunction with the humane society of the country.

A permit might be obtained so long as "each animal to be displayed is not of an exotic, threatened or endangered species." In effect, circuses and their MENAGERIES were banned in that city. Other cities, including several in California, took note and began to pass similar regulations.

In his book *Circus Doctor*, J.Y. "Doc" HENDERSON, chief veterinarian of the RINGLING BROS. AND BARNUM & BAILEY CIRCUS and a great lover of animals, wrote: "Contrary to popular belief, seldom are animals beaten by a trainer. . . . Animals are hit, much in the same way that children are spanked, in order to show that certain behavior is unacceptable. This is a far cry from beating animals into submission."

Even the blank guns that many handlers carry are merely for show. They never carry live ammunition; even if a lion attacks, it is never in any danger of being shot. Alfred COURT, one of Ringling's premiere cat trainers, scoffed at the suggestion. "What would you do with a gun? With an audience completely surrounding you, if you missed the animal you would undoubtedly hit one or more spectators."

Many accidents on the circus lot involving members of the audience are the visitors' own fault. People often walk up from the rear without warning to pet the horses in the menagerie. The horse becomes startled; the animal's natural defense mechanism is to kick without looking first.

Circus visitors see the chains separating them from the cage wagons and the exotic animals. Every few years one hears an unfortunate story of a young child, not properly supervised by parents, who crawls under the PICKET LINE to try to pet the animals. The results are often tragic, and the media always seem to place the circus at fault.

Likewise, during the old STREET PARADES, spectators lining the route often dashed into the road to try to pet or feed the parading ELEPHANTS or other creatures. If the handler was not quick enough to stop the audience member, the animal often wound up tossing the person back into the amused patrons lining the way.

Doc Henderson pointed out that

apparently, a false impression exists in the public mind about circus animals. They see these animals in the show performing almost human and in some cases superhuman feats. Unconsciously, they reason that an animal with that skill and brains is not really wild . . . if he doesn't hurt the people whom they see handling him, then he won't hurt strangers. This false impression is very wrong, as I have proved by telling how even the best trainers are sometimes scratched, bitten, frequently mauled and occasionally killed by animals who know them well.

Damoo DHOTRE stated: "You can never, never, never tame a wild animal." Animals can only be trained.

Circuses have a strict rule that no one—not even the CAGE BOYS who give them the animals moment-to-moment care—are ever to hit an animal except in self-defense. Even when the animals must be poked, they are gently prodded to give them an idea of what the handler wants. Devices such as the ELEPHANT HOOK used by BULL HANDLERS do not hurt the jumbo beasts; although it looks menacing, the blunt instrument is merely a directional guide to the pachyderms.

Circus animals are kept in peak condition to keep them strong against changes in climate, food and water. On every circus, performers live night and day with their animals; each one is loved and cared for as a member of the family. On the Ringling show, for instance, a horse too old to perform was not sold. Rather it enjoyed a healthy "retirement" on the Ringling grounds until its death, and the carcass was never sold to butchers. It was buried on the property in an informal cemetery.

When on tour, Doc Henderson often invited the critics to really look at the animals on the lot. In addition, he asked the state veterinarian to examine his animals. "This," he wrote, "is the answer to those people who claim that the circus is cruel to its animals by making them perform; that shipping them constantly keeps them in a state of poor health."

Gunther GEBEL-WILLIAMS, perhaps the most famous all-around animal trainer in circus history, said:

There are people who believe that animal cruelty is part of the circus way of life. This is not true. I have never seen it where I worked in Europe or America.

I've always let people watch me train my animals. I have five or six tigers that aren't scared of fire. They are the ones I use to jump through a [flaming] hoop, not a cat that's scared. I never used a pistol or whip. I would never beat an animal. My tricks aren't harmful. You can't hurt an animal and have him give you his best performance.

As a reaction to the one-sided information being dispensed by the animal activist groups, an opposition group was formed in 1990. With offices located in Washington, D.C., Putting People First describes itself as pro-circus, pro-rodeo, pro-zoo *and* pro-animal. It seeks to disseminate the truth—that animals are being ethically treated when used in exhibition and performance in the United States.

ANIMALS AND ANIMAL TRAINERS See ANIMAL ACTIVISTS; BAUMANN, CHARLY; BEARS; BEATTY, CLYDE; BIG CAGE; BOLIVAR; BULL HANDLER; BULLS; CAGE BOY; CAMELS; CATS; CHIMPANZEES; CORNPLANTER; COURT, ALFRED; CRISTIANI, LUCIO; CRISTIANIS, THE; DHOTRE, DAMOO; DRESSAGE; ELEPHANT HOOK; ELEPHANTS; EN FÉROCITÉ; EQUESCURRICULUM; EQUESTRIAN DIRECTOR; EXCELSIOR; FLATFOOTS; FLEA CIRCUS; GARGANTUA; GAUTIER, AXEL; GEBEL-WILLIAMS, GUNTHER; GIRAFFES; GOLIATH; GORILLAS; HÄGENBACH, KARL; HANNEFORD, EDWIN "POODLES"; HANNEFORD, TOMMY; HANNEFORDS, THE; HANNIBAL; HENDERSON, J.Y. "DOC"; HERRIOTT, JOHN; HIGH SCHOOL HORSE; HORSES; JACOBS, CAPT. TERRELL; JUMBO; KING TUSK; LALLA ROOKH; LEAD STOCK; LIBERTY HORSES; LOGAN, FRED; LORD BYRON; LOYAL, GUISTINO; LOYAL-REPENSKY TROUPE, THE; MENAGERIE; MONKEYS AND APES; M'TOTO; OLD BET; PAD RIDING; PALLENBERG, EMIL; RING HORSE; RING STOCK; ROGUE ELEPHANTS; ROSINBACK; ROTH, LOUIS; STARK, MABEL; TIGERS; TOGNI, FLAVIO; TUBS, ELEPHANT; VAN AMBURGH, ISAAC; WHITE, PATRICIA; WHITE ELEPHANT; WIRTH, MAY; ZOOLOGICAL INSTITUTE; ZOPPE-ZAVATTA TROUPE, THE.

ANNIE GET YOUR GUN See THEATER.

ANNIE OAKLEYS Circus slang for free tickets or passes to the main show.

The origin of this term is directly traceable to a trick performed by Annie OAKLEY, the sharpshooter, during her tours with BUFFALO BILL'S WILD WEST. She had the uncanny ability of hitting the edge of a playing card at a distance of 90 feet and, as the card plummeted to the ground, puncturing it with several more shots. These cards, treasured by townsfolk as souvenirs, became known as "Annie Oakleys."

In time, any punched ticket used as a circus pass was referred to by that name. Today any free pass—holed or not—is known as an "Annie Oakley."

It has been suggested that the term grew in popularity due to zealous promoters who, in exchange for free advertising space in newspapers or for permission to place WINDOW CARDS or paste billboard sheets, would trade a genuine "Annie Oakley" card that could be presented as free admission at the gate. If this is true, there is no doubt that many merchants opted to keep their prized, authentic "Annie Oakleys" and pay the admission to see her in person rather than turn in the cards.

P.T. BARNUM, operating his BARNUM & BAILEY CIRCUS during the same years that Annie Oakley was performing on the Wild West, detested giving out free passes, even when it was necessary for press or public relations. At one point, to give to those who asked for "Annie Oakleys," Barnum had a card printed that read:

In those days there were no passes given. Search the Scriptures:
"Thou shalt not pass" Numbers XX, v. 18.
"Suffer not a man to pass" Judges III, v. 28.
"None shall pass" Mark XIII, v. 30.
"The wicked shall pass no more" Nathan I, v. 5.
"Beware that thou pass not" II Kings VI, v. 9.
"There shall no stranger pass" Amos III, v. 17.
"Neither any son of man shall pass" Jeremiah LI, v. 43.
"No man may pass through because of beasts" Ezekiel XIV, v. 15.
"Though they roar, yet they cannot pass" Jeremiah V, v. 22.
"So he paid the fare thereof and went" Jonah I, v. 3.

ANNOUNCER (See EQUESTRIAN DIRECTOR; RINGMASTER.)

ANTHONY, MARK "TONY" (1915–1990) Born Anthony Mark Galkowski in Norwich, Connecticut, on February 13, 1915, Mark Anthony became involved with circuses and clowning during his teenage years.

Anthony's parents were immigrants from Poland, and he had five brothers and sisters. Tragically, his mother died when he was only two years old. Anthony's father encouraged him to learn music and wanted him to be plumber, but he died when Mark was only 13 years old.

Raised by an older sister, Anthony picked cotton, sold junk and worked as a pin setter in a bowling alley at nights; he dropped out of school after the eighth grade. Feeling he was a burden to his sister, Anthony ran away from home at the age of 15.

Initially he wanted to become a comedian or a circus bareback rider. To try to learn the skills needed to become an equestrian, Anthony worked for a time as a farmhand. Then, still only 15 years old, he attempted to join the SELLS-FLOTO CIRCUS. He was turned down because of his age, but that didn't stop his interest in outdoor amusements.

During the Depression, he worked as a dancer and acrobat, traveling on the back of freight cars between dates. Eventually he was able to join the circus and, except for a brief turn in the Merchant Marines, Anthony spent his entire adult life touring with shows, including Sells Floto, the DAN RICE CIRCUS, the CLYDE BEATTY-COLE BROS. CIRCUS and, finally, the RINGLING BROS. AND BARNUM & BAILEY CIRCUS. His clowning career took him to Hawaii, Japan, Russia, Australia, England, Austria and most of Europe.

Beginning as a WHITEFACE CLOWN in 1937, he soon turned to the unique possibilities of the TRAMP CLOWN. His makeup featured a bald pate surrounded by red stringy hair and a red bulbous nose topped with a fly. He joined The BIG ONE in 1964 and remained with it until 1977. During his tenure with the Ringling show, he was also an instructor at the CLOWN COLLEGE. In 1987 he was invited to the Clown College Reunion as a guest clown.

In addition to his skills as a performer, Anthony was also a master prop builder and carver. His sculptures of animals and clowns made of wood, foam and papier-mâché are true collectibles. Like so many other circus performers, Anthony retired to southern Florida.

After his death on June 23, 1990, the Mark Anthony Memorial Scholarship Fund to the University of Wisconsin–La Crosse Clown Camp was set up in his name. The scholarship funds tuition for one person a year to the Clown Camp, which is held each summer on the university campus. Anthony was interred at Spring Grove Cemetery in Delavan,

Wisconsin, home of the CLOWN HALL OF FAME & RESEARCH CENTER.

(See also CIRCUS CAMPS.)

APES   See GARGANTUA; MONKEYS AND APES; M'TOTO.

ARLINGTON, EDWARD (fl. 1908–1917)   In 1908 Edward Arlington, already an experienced circus man, joined forces with the Miller family to create the Miller Bros. 101 Ranch Wild West.

Originally a 16-car rail show, the circus grew to almost twice the size; and, in 1915, one of its feature attractions was boxing champion Jess WILLARD.

In 1916 Arlington wooed Buffalo Bill away from the SELLS-FLOTO CIRCUS and renamed his show the BUFFALO BILL & 101 RANCH WILD WEST. At season's end, Arlington bought out the Millers' interest. When Arlington partnered with Willard in 1917, he transformed the 101 Ranch show into the BUFFALO BILL WILD WEST & JESS WILLARD SHOW, despite the recent death of Buffalo Bill. Not long thereafter, Willard bought out Edward Arlington and the show quickly folded.

(See also CODY, WILLIAM F.)

ARROW   Circus jargon for the small card, bearing a directional arrow, that is posted on poles along the route of the JUMP for the circus drivers to follow from one town to the next.

Arrowing can trace its history back to the earliest days of the American circus, long before motorized trucks or the rail show and even before the cardboard "arrow." Moving over dirt (or mud) roads in caravans of wagons, the first troupes might have covered only two or three miles per day, with a large jump being ten or 15 miles. Still, the route had to be marked. Today an ARROW MAN posts a cardboard sign at each turn, but on the early rural shows the ADVANCE MAN would "rail" every fork in the road so that the wagons would not make a wrong turn. This was done by literally taking a rail from a farmer's fence and placing it as a marker across the road that was not to be taken.

In modern times, the wooden posts have been replaced, in effect, by the cardboard arrows. Before the jump, each person with the MUD SHOW troupe receives a ROUTE CARD. Although it might be possible to plot a course to the next town, it would be impossible for drivers (especially during night jumps)

to locate the LOT or to anticipate difficult road conditions, such as construction, low-clearance overhangs and tunnels, bridges with weight restrictions and so on. To prevent losing half of the troupe, the circus always employs the arrow man to post the cards.

Along the route, a single arrow is tacked up every few miles to let the troupe know it is on course. Arrows cannot be posted more often because of the time it takes to stop at each location, jump out, staple or chalk up the arrow and get back on the road. Also, it is technically illegal to post arrows on many highways and even in some rural areas. Police tend to "look the other way" when they see these arrows to avoid the problem of having to assist in tracking down a fleet of lost circus trucks; however, the highway patrol cannot justify allowing too many arrows to be posted. They might follow the arrows to the lot and fine the circus or—worse yet—remove some of the arrows that could be crucial to the trucks trying to stay on course.

Normally, the arrow is posted vertically, with the point facing skyward. When a turn is upcoming, the arrow man has to warn the drivers. About a mile in advance of a right-hand turn, for example, a single arrow is posted with the point aiming at about a "two o'clock" position. Two or three arrows on the same pole and at the same angle let the driver know that the turn is imminent; and three arrows pointing at "three o'clock" signifies "turn here."

An arrow pointed downward at "six o'clock" means "stop." Arrow men also carry "SLO" arrows to warn of a dangerous road situation or a steep grade ahead.

The card that the arrow man posts, often a standard size of six by ten inches, shows a bold-colored arrow, usually red, blue or black. Often the card bears the initials of its circus. Each circus has a unique arrow; because many shows crisscross paths—especially during the busy summer season—drivers may confuse arrows from many shows posted on telephone poles.

The arrows are posted, usually by staple gun, on telephone or other wooden poles along the route. When an arrow must be posted and no wooden posts are available, masking tape is used to attach the cards to metal stands or highway signs. As a last

Arrows indicating that a left turn is coming up shortly.
(Photo by Tom Ogden)

resort, if there is absolutely no place to attach a card, colored chalk will be used to draw a large arrow on the roadway.

The arrows cannot be posted too long before the jump. To be effective, the arrows must stay on the poles; the weather, children, police officers, property owners and circus collectors are only a few of their natural enemies. Often the arrows are put up the day of that evening's jump, in which case posting the arrows may become a duty of the 24-HOUR MAN or the advance man.

Traveling at highway speeds, a driver must be able to instantly recognize and follow the arrows for his own show. Drivers who miss the signs, or "blow the arrows," may drive many miles out of the way before realizing it. Then they must rely on the route card and a map to try to find the way back to the correct destination.

(See also BOSS HOSTLER.)

ARROW MAN Circus jargon for the person who travels in advance of the show, posting the small directional cards for the drivers to follow during the JUMP.

(See also ARROW; 24-HOUR MAN.)

ASTLEY, PHILIP (1742–1814) Recognized as the "Father of the Modern Circus," Philip Astley was the son of a British cabinetmaker and a member of the 15th British Light Dragoons. Attaining the rank of sergeant-major, the six-foot Astley quit the army in 1766, got married and began an open-air equestrian show in London near Westminster Bridge.

Although trick riding was not new to England, Astley developed it to the finest art of the day. Before him, Thomas Johnson—the "Irish Tartar"— was able to ride bareback on one horse or two (ROMAN RIDING). His biggest crowd-pleaser, however, was straddling two horses, with a third galloping between the two steeds on which he balanced.

A skillful rider, Astley discovered that centrifugal force allowed him to stand without falling on the back of his horse Gibraltar as it galloped in a circle. This led to his designing the first ring and introducing it in a 1768 show. Another of his daring feats on horseback was riding with one foot on the saddle and the other on the horse's head while waving a sword. By 1770 the showgrounds was known as Astley's Riding School.

As success came his way, Astley fenced in his show field, constructed stands for the spectators and enclosed the entryway. In 1779 a roof was added, and the arena was renamed the Astley Royal Amphitheatre of Arts.

Over the next decade Astley augmented his show with musicians (two pipers and a drum), a strong man, a juggler, a tightrope walker, trained dogs, ACROBATS performing "The Egyptian Pyramid, an Amusing Performance of Men Piled Upon Men" and a famous clown act, "Billie Button, or the TAILOR'S RIDE TO BRENTFORD." Astley is credited with being the first to introduce comic dialogues between the RINGMASTER (himself) and the clown—later a staple of the American circus.

Astley took his company on tour to France in the 1780s and performed indoors. There an adversarial showman named Nicolai got a court injunction against Astley, based on an ancient law that prevented two stage shows from appearing simultaneously in Paris. As incredible as it sounds, Astley immediately placed a flat platform across the backs of several horses and played his acrobatic shows on top. Because his shows were not being presented on a permanent stage, Astley's performances were allowed. These concurrent shows may well be the first example of two circuses having the misfortune to DAY AND DATE.

Also while in France, Astley met Antoine Franconi, founder of the Cirque Olympic and member of the FRANCONI FAMILY. The two circus showmen became friendly rivals; the Franconis quickly incorporated Astley's style of horsemanship into their own performances.

In 1794 Astley's London indoor amphitheatre burned to the ground. Rebuilt the next year, the "New Astley's" was destroyed by flames in 1803. In that fire much of his livestock, as well as his mother-in-law, were lost. A showman to the end, Astley again rebuilt—this time without further incident. He died in 1814 at the age of 72.

Although Astley never traveled to the United States, his influence is felt to this day. His major contributions are the circus ring and the incorporation of gymnastic and variety acts among the displays of horsemanship. Also, the American circus, more than its European and Asian counterparts, still is based on equestrian talent.

ATTERBURY BROS. CIRCUS Robert L. Atterbury operated this circus for about 20 years, closing it in 1937. His children took over the show briefly after Atterbury's retirement; but, not inclined toward management, they soon dispersed to become headlined performers with other shows.

(See also LEE BROS. CIRCUS.)

AUGUSTE CLOWN One of the three main types of clowns, the auguste is a clumsy, slapstick comedian. Wearing no traditional costume, the auguste clown does not use white greasepaint as the makeup base.

Instead, a combination of color spots, swirls or decorations is used to accent the performer's face.

Tom Belling, an American performer working in Europe, is generally credited with the creation of the auguste clown character. Its actual origin, however, is steeped in myth and controversy.

One story (that may or may not be true) tells that Tom Belling created the character by accident. Belling was an American acrobat, appearing with a German circus. After missing a trick in the routine, he was disciplined by being confined to the PAD ROOM. As a spoof, he put on oversize clothing and a backward wig, impersonating the show's owner, Ernst Renz. The manager saw him and began to chase him. Belling inadvertently ran into the tent while the performance was still going on, tripping as he spilled over the RING CURB. The audience began yelling, "Auguste! Auguste!" (meaning "fool" in German) as it roared with laughter. The manager, delighted with the response, asked Belling to continue on in the character of "auguste."

A more probable explanation centers around Belling's earlier tour of Russia. A type of Russian clown—known as the "R'IZHII"—looked very much like the modern auguste; and it is widely believed that Belling merely copied and adapted the makeup for his own use. The English translation for "r'izhii" is "red-haired," a popular face and wig color for the modern auguste.

Regardless, Belling himself was not very successful as a clown and went on to a career as a magician. His contribution to the art of clowning, however, is undeniable.

The auguste clown needs several materials at hand to apply his makeup: white greasepaint, various colored greasepaints (always red, often pink or flesh, and black), various lining pencils, white or pink-tinted talc in a powder sock (simply a cupful of talc in a knotted men's white stocking) and makeup brushes.

To apply an auguste makeup, the performer must begin with a dry face, preferably clean-shaven. Many JOEYS like to start by spreading cold cream over the face, because colored paints are particularly difficult to get out of facial pores. If this base is used, it must be rubbed in, patted off and the excess wiped off with tissue or a towel.

The face is not given a complete painted base. Instead, using a pencil, the designs for the face are outlined first. This will divide the face into areas that will be colored.

Next is applied the color of greasepaint that takes up the greatest percentage of the face—usually red or pink. On some clowns this might be large red eyebrows; on others it might be huge pink cheeks. Greasepaint can be applied with sticks or brushes, but most professionals prefer to use their fingers.

The sock is used to "powder down" the makeup—that is, to "set it" and remove the gloss and streaks. Because additional greasepaints will be used, extra powder should be used on this first application to ensure a firm "set." Any excess should be brushed away so that it does not interfere with the next color of paint.

The second color is then applied. If two colored areas adjoin on the face, the paints must not be allowed to smear together. The two colors do not have to touch or meet exactly because a line separating the two will be drawn in later. Once again, the second color is powdered down.

Although it is unusual for more than two colors (red and pink) to be used on an auguste face, any other major areas of the face that need to be painted should be done next, followed by powdering. Then, all that is needed to complete the makeup are the final lines, color accents and character features. A nose and wig often complete the auguste face.

(See also JACOBS, LOU.)

AYALA, MARGARITA VAZQUEZ (1947–   )

Margarita Vazquez Ayala was born in Santiago, Nayarit, Mexico, on May 20, 1947, the daughter of Manuel Vazquez, patriarch of the famed FLYING VAZQUEZ troupe, and the sister of Miguel VAZQUEZ, the first to achieve the QUADRUPLE SOMERSAULT on the FLYING TRAPEZE.

Working in the aerial ballet from early childhood, she first performed the hair suspension act for which she is known today at 13 years old. Updating an act performed by Chinese acrobats on the BARNUM & BAILEY CIRCUS, Ayala is the circus performer most associated with the HAIR HANG today.

She first came to the United States in 1966, performing in a number of American circuses. On April 20, 1969 she married Miguel Ayala Leal, an exceptional low wire walker, in Philadelphia. The ceremony was renewed in a Catholic church in BARABOO, WISCONSIN, a few weeks later.

Appearing in the RINGLING BROS. AND BARNUM & BAILEY CIRCUS in the early 1980s, she began working under the professional name of Marguerite Michelle. On February 20, 1982, at the matinee performance of the Red Unit of the Ringling Bros. and Barnum & Bailey Circus at the Omni in Atlanta, Georgia, Ayala took a near-fatal fall while performing the hair hang. During her whirlwind pirouettes at the climax of her act, one of the ropes braided through her hair and the iron ring attached to the WEB broke. She flew from high over the CENTER RING down toward ring one and landed headfirst against the metal RING CURB.

Acting as her assistant, her husband was the first to reach her. She was rushed to Grady Memorial Hospital, where she remained in a coma for three weeks. After six weeks, she was returned to her home in SARASOTA, FLORIDA to recuperate. Upon leaving the hospital she vowed, "I'll be back. Right over the center ring at the Omni."

During her slow recovery, Ayala's daughter Michelle (b. January 31, 1970) asked her mother to teach her the hair hang. Although reluctant, Ayala finally consented; Michelle Ayala began performing the act within a year.

Eventually Margarita persuaded her husband to hoist her back up on the hair-hang rigging. By 1985 she was strong enough to alternate with Michelle in the ring. In 1987 the Ayalas performed in South Africa. Two years later they alternated their acts on Ringling's Gold Unit, the short-lived show that appeared under canvas in Japan.

That same year Ayala's daughter Andrea (b. April 15, 1973), learned the hair hang. Kenneth FELD signed all three to a 1990–1991 contract with the Blue Unit of The GREATEST SHOW ON EARTH. They would appear simultaneously over all three rings, claimed to be a circus first. Margarita and Michelle would alternate over the center ring and ring one, and Andrea would perform over ring three. As a result, Margarita Ayala was able to make her triumphant return, as promised, to the Omni in February 1990. The Ayalas, all still active, continue to perform separately on circuses internationally.

Their acts are identical and made up of several parts. First, they are hoisted aloft and remove their sequined jumpsuits while sailing through the air. They spin hoops on their legs as well as plates on sticks held in their mouths and hands. The women are lowered almost to the ground, where they switch their plates for more hoops. Once returned to the arena dome, they twirl three hoops on each arm (two in one direction, one in the other) and one hoop on a leg, with the center ring artiste spinning a hoop on each leg. The women are again lowered, and hoops are exchanged for flaming torches. They are pulled upward, then juggle the fire sticks. They descend to hand back the torches, then fly upward for their finale: three spinning women in whirling pirouettes. The entire act takes six minutes.

B

BACK DOOR Circus jargon for the performer's entrance to the BIG TOP.

On a one-ring circus, the back door is most often located directly across from the audience's entrance to the tent. On a three-ring circus, however, the back door is traditionally located at the middle of one of the tent's long sides. Flaps or a curtain cover the entranceway so that the audience cannot see the act preparing to go on.

The circuses that have a live band usually place the bandstand next to the back door, giving additional cover for the next performer. Often the RINGMASTER announces from a position next to the back door as well; from there he can easily be advised of any problem in the BACK YARD or can quickly send messages out to the awaiting cast.

BACK YARD Also backyard; circus jargon for the area in back of the BIG TOP reserved for use by the performers and crew. In addition to serving as the place where the performance is readied, the various dressing TENTS are also located there. On motorized tent shows, where the company does not return to a CIRCUS TRAIN after TEAR DOWN, the sleeping trailers are also positioned, or spotted, by the LAYOUT MAN in the back yard.

BAILEY, GEORGE F(OX) (1818–1903) George F. Bailey was born in North Salem, New York, the nephew of Hachaliah BAILEY. He first toured with the AARON TURNER CIRCUS in 1836. Among the troupe

that season, getting his first taste of circus life, was a young ticket taker named P.T. BARNUM.

Bailey married Aaron TURNER's daughter and eventually began to manage the show. He inherited it in the 1850s following Turner's death and toured the show as the George F. Bailey Circus.

In 1857 he toured a show throughout the Midwest with the elongated title of The Grand Metropolitan Quadruple Combination consisting of George F. Bailey & Co.'s Circus, Herr Driesbach's Menagerie, G.C. Quick's Colossal Hippopotamus, and Sands, Nathans & Co.'s Performing Elephants.

The hippopotamus trouped by Bailey and Quick was the first of its species to arrive in the United States. Using a water tank built into a strong wagon, they are credited with being the first to tour a hippopotamus in a MENAGERIE.

Around 1863, Bailey and several other showmen formed a second generation of FLATFOOTS, which were active until 1881. The George F. Bailey Circus became the syndicate's main attraction. Calling himself the Last of the Flatfoots, Bailey continued to tour his circus, finally retiring when the Flatfoots began operating Barnum's circus in 1875.

(See also SANDS & QUICK'S MENAGERIE.)

BAILEY, HACHALIAH (1775–1845) Although no relation to James A. BAILEY, Hachaliah Bailey was the first with the famous surname to be associated with circus attractions. Hachaliah (also seen as Hackaliah) Bailey purchased OLD BET—the second elephant to be brought to America—in 1815 for the princely sum of $1,000.

His exhibition of the beast in the environs of his home in SOMERS, NEW YORK, convinced many of his neighbors to enter the business of trouping MENAGERIES; among them were Aaron TURNER, John J. JUNE, Caleb S. ANGEVINE and Lewis B. TITUS; their names also became famous in the annals of the early American circus.

When Old Bet was shot by an irate farmer in Maine, Bailey raised a monument to the pachyderm's memory in front of his ELEPHANT HOTEL in Somers.

BAILEY, JAMES A(NTHONY) (1847–1906)

James A. Bailey was born James McGinnis, most probably on July 4, 1847 (although some historians claim it to have been 1845), in Detroit, Michigan. He ran away from the home of relatives after having been orphaned when he was about eight years of age. At the age of 12, while working at the Pontiac Hotel in Detroit, he met Frederick Harrison Bailey, who was on the ADVANCE for the Robinson & Lake Circus. Frederick Bailey gave the young boy a job; the lad never returned home, opting instead to adopt the name of his protector.

A quiet and dignified man, James A. Bailey grew to become one of the greatest managers in circus history. In 1873 he bought an interest in Hemmings & Cooper's Circus from James E. COOPER and changed the show's name to the COOPER & BAILEY CIRCUS. Under Bailey's leadership, the show became one of the largest railroad circuses in the country.

In 1876 Bailey took the Cooper & Bailey Circus to San Francisco, then on to Australia for two tours. With its two rings, a sizable MENAGERIE, a full SIDESHOW and a large cast, it was the biggest circus ever to perform in that country. The unit played throughout the South Pacific as well as at East Indian and South American stops. It returned triumphantly to New York on December 10, 1878.

Along with James E. Cooper and a new partner, James L. HUTCHINSON, Bailey purchased a bankrupt show formerly owned by Seth B. HOWES. For 1979 and 1880, the new merger operated as Howes' Great London Circus and Sanger's Royal British Menagerie, and Cooper and Bailey's International Allied Shows. The circus was the first to use electric lighting, a major point in their advertising.

An apocryphal story surrounds the beginning of the partnership of Bailey and P.T. BARNUM. On March 10, 1880 Bailey's WINTER QUARTERS was the site of the first ELEPHANT born in captivity in this country. Barnum was rumored to have attempted to purchase the baby and its mother for $100,000. Not only did Bailey refuse, but he used Barnum's telegram in his subsequent advertising. Realizing he had met a formidable opponent, Barnum suggested they join forces.

Cooper retired from the International Allied Shows in 1880, leaving only Bailey and James L. Hutchinson. Their new show in 1881 used all of the titles of their combined shows; thus P.T. BARNUM'S GREATEST SHOW ON EARTH, HOWES' GREAT LONDON CIRCUS AND SANGER'S ROYAL BRITISH MENAGERIE, also known as the BARNUM & LONDON CIRCUS, was born. To celebrate the opening, a spectacular circus STREET PARADE went down the streets of New York City on March 16, 1881, featuring 350 HORSES, 20 elephants, 14 CAMELS, four brass bands and close to 400 performers.

Bailey left the show in 1885, selling his interest to James E. Cooper and W.W. COLE. He began sole partnership with Barnum in 1888 to form a new show, the BARNUM & BAILEY CIRCUS. Bailey had been the true managerial strength of his shows; now he had an equal share in the profits with Barnum as well as full management. In 1891 P.T. Barnum died, giving Bailey complete control of the Barnum & Bailey Circus.

Three years later Bailey bought a controlling interest in BUFFALO BILL'S WILD WEST, then managed by partners William F. CODY and Nathan SALSBURY. By 1895 Bailey had the Wild West set for railroad travel, allowing one-night stands.

In 1896 Bailey joined up with W.W. Cole and two of the Sells brothers. They changed the title of their SELLS BROTHERS CIRCUS to the Great Adam Forepaugh and Sells Bros.' Shows Combined, also referred to as the ADAM FOREPAUGH & SELLS BROS. CIRCUS. In 1905 Bailey acquired full ownership, and he immediately sold a half interest to the RINGLING BROTHERS.

Meanwhile, in 1897 Bailey took his Barnum & Bailey Circus to Europe, returning at the end of the 1902 season. Reminiscent of his spectacular 1881 street parade, a magnificent procession in New York City also opened the 1903 season.

The innovative James A. Bailey died in his home near Mount Vernon, New York on April 11, 1906. In 1907 Bailey's remaining circus holdings were sold to the Ringlings.

Although James A. Bailey has been gone for almost a century, his name remains immortalized in circus history as part of the title of the RINGLING BROS. AND BARNUM & BAILEY CIRCUS.

BAILEY, JAMES AUGUSTUS "GUS" (1818–1896)

A musician with a traveling circus, Gus Bailey eloped with Mollie Kirkland in Mobile, Alabama in 1858. The couple set out on their own with a one-horse, one-wagon show throughout Alabama.

During the Civil War, they served together in Hood's Texas Brigade—he as a soldier-musician and she as a nurse. It was during this period that Bailey, seeing the comical antics of horses "drunk" on green corn, wrote the lyrics to the classic American song "The Old Gray Mare, She Ain't What She Used to Be."

After a year of touring their circus on a showboat following the war, Gus and Mollie founded the BAILEY CONCERT AND CIRCUS SHOW. The one-ring tented show played small towns throughout the South. In 1885 illness forced Gus to leave the road; but his wife continued to tour the show, renaming it the MOLLIE BAILEY CIRCUS.

Gus Bailey died in Houston in 1896 while Mollie was on tour.

BAILEY, MOLLIE (1841–1918)

Mollie Bailey has the unique distinction of being the first woman to have owned and operated her own circus in the United States.

Born Mollie Arline Kirkland to an English father and a French mother, she grew up in Mobile, Alabama, a beautiful and talented girl. She was trained in music and from early on she showed an ability for amateur theatrics.

At the age of 16, Mollie fell in love with James Augustus "Gus" BAILEY, a musician traveling with a circus that played Mobile. Since her father did not approve of the match, Mollie eloped with Bailey in 1858. The couple attempted a reconciliation with her father, but Mr. Kirkland disowned his daughter. Although she approached her parents many times throughout her life, Mollie's father never forgave her.

Faced with an uncertain future, Mollie took a horse and wagon from her father's plantation and set out on tour with her husband. Mollie and Gus Bailey traveled all through Alabama with their one-horse, one-wagon show, with Mollie performing skits and Gus playing various instruments. For years they toured throughout the South until the Civil War forced them to stop.

The couple joined Hood's Texas Brigade, leaving their one-year-old daughter with relatives. Gus became a soldier-musician and Mollie served as a nurse. In addition, Mollie occasionally sneaked across enemy lines—disguised as a local girl—to get needed supplies; on one occasion she dressed as an old woman selling cookies so that she could spy on a Yankee encampment.

For a short period after the Civil War the Baileys performed their circus on an old Mississippi River showboat. By this time the Baileys had four children—two girls and two boys—and Mollie wanted a place to call home. In 1867 "home" turned out to be all of Texas—after traveling all over the South with their wagon show for a year, they settled in Houston as a summer base.

The BAILEY CONCERT AND CIRCUS SHOW, "A Texas Show for Texas People," was a one-ring tented show. Seven wagons were needed to transport the troupe, which included Bailey's growing family of eight children.

Mollie became an expert at "following the crops"—that is, routing her show to match local prosperity. Still, the small MUD SHOW was plagued with bad weather, robbers and Indians. On one occasion, when Indians were set to attack their circled camp, Mollie began beating on a drum in her wagon. The Indians, thinking it was cannon from a neighboring fort, fled.

In the early 1880s Gus Bailey became sick and could no longer travel with the show. Tragedy struck when one of their young children died of food poisoning. Finally, in 1885 Gus's illness forced Mollie to take complete control of the show, and she decided to confine her touring to Texas.

Renamed the MOLLIE BAILEY CIRCUS, the modest show featured all of the Bailey children. One daughter performed a bird act; another performed as an equestrienne. The four sons played as musicians. Known as the "Circus Queen of the Southwest," Mollie annually brought a clean family show to town. Between performances she would shop or just walk through the village, greeting old friends and making new ones.

Mollie was a caring woman, and she possessed a keen business sense. As she toured, she bought vacant lots in the towns where her shows were given, and at one time she owned over 100 pieces of property. When the circus was not in town, the lots were given over to the town for baseball, recreation and community projects. School was canceled the day the circus came to town, and orphans and soldiers were always admitted to her show free of charge. The BIG TOP always flew three banners on its poles: the Union, the Confederate and the Texas flags.

Gus Bailey died in Houston in 1896 while the Mollie Bailey Show was on the road. Mollie carried on, moving her circus onto rail. The show grew again, with more ACROBATS, CLOWNS, tightrope walkers and animals, including a camel and BOLIVAR, an elephant.

At the age of 77, Mollie fell and broke her hip. On October 2, 1918, she died of complications. Her four sons tried to carry on the show, but the Mollie Bailey Circus—without her indomitable spirit—closed after two more seasons.

BAILEY CONCERT AND CIRCUS SHOW, THE   Mollie
BAILEY and James Augustus "Gus" BAILEY began touring with a two-person, one-horse, one-wagon show after their marriage in 1858. Following the Civil War, they traveled for one year with their circus on a showboat, then left because Mollie felt it was an unfit place to raise their four children.

The Bailey Concert and Circus Show, "A Texas Show for Texas People," was founded in Houston in 1867. It grew into a seven-wagon operation with a modest company. By then, the Bailey family had also grown to include eight children, four girls and four boys. The show toured throughout Texas until Gus became too ill to travel in 1885.

Mollie expanded the show and renamed it the MOLLIE BAILEY CIRCUS, touring it as sole owner and operator until her death.

BAKER, JOHNNY (fl. 1890–1920)   A young man
when he joined BUFFALO BILL'S WILD WEST, Johnny Baker was "adopted" by William F. CODY as his son

The bottom of a center pole surrounded by a bale ring. Note how the inner rings keep the lacings and other ropes from rubbing on the center pole as it is raised. Clyde Beatty-Cole Bros. Circus, 1989.   (Photo courtesy of Albert F. House)

when Cody's own boy, Kit Carson Cody, died at the age of six.

Born in North Platte, Nebraska, Baker developed a case of hero worship for Buffalo Bill while still a boy. Billed as "The Cowboy Kid," he had trained himself as a marksman so that Cody would accept him on the Wild West. Baker soon became Cody's chief assistant, helping to ready the great showman for his entrance into the arena. It was into Baker's arms that Cody fell, exhausted, after his last performance on November 11, 1916.

BALE, TREVOR (1913–   )   Born in Denmark on
June 13, 1913, animal trainer Trevor Bale first came to the United States to perform his tiger act on the RINGLING BROS. AND BARNUM & BAILEY CIRCUS in 1953. He appeared with the Big One on and off through 1964. During his career in the BIG CAGE, he worked

with more species of animals than any other trainer of his time, including ELEPHANTS, GIRAFFES, BEARS, llamas, zebras, HORSES, CAMELS, gorillas, dogs, a hippopotamus and CATS.

Born on the Circus Schumann to a circus family, Bale began his career in the circus at the age of three as a trick bicyclist. During his more than 40 years in the ring, Bale performed as a juggler, clown, acrobat, wire walker, flyer and, finally, a wild animal trainer. Especially known for his work with cats, Bale felt that tigers were the most dangerous, since they could turn faster and strike with less warning than any of the other big cats.

Trevor Bale is the father of daredevil Elvin Bale and two daughters, Gloria and Dawnita, who continue to perform his LIBERTY HORSES act.

BALE RING Circus jargon for the piece of equipment as well as the type of circus tent, named for the particular metal loop involved in the operation. As opposed to a PUSH POLE tent, in which the CENTER POLE is slid under the canvas and literally *pushed* upright into position, a bale ring operation, in a sense, *pulls* the canvas upward around the center poles. A bale ring set up is required because of the extreme weight of the massive expanse of canvas.

The LAYOUT MAN sets the position of the tent and then marks the location for the gigantic center poles. The base of the center pole is laid on the mark and the other end, perhaps 60 feet away, is raised on a small jack. The bale ring itself is a solid ring of steel an inch or two thick that has been welded into a circle, with the resulting loop being about twice the diameter of the center pole. A bale ring is slipped over the top and down to the bottom of each pole.

After the center poles are raised, the piles of canvas are unrolled, laced around the center poles and lashed to the bale rings. At the same time the canvas is being spread, blocks (for pulling up aerial rigging) and the light fixtures are attached to the bale ring.

Next the SIDEPOLES are raised. Ropes are run from the bale rings, up through pulleys at the tops of the tent poles and back down through pulleys at the bases of the poles, then out from under the canvas. By pulling on the ropes, the bale rings are raised by the pulley systems at the tops of the poles. This in turn lifts the heavy tarp to the tops of the center poles. As this is done, QUARTER POLES are added, and the GUY-OUT GANG works around the top.

BALLARD, ED See AMERICAN CIRCUS CORPORATION; GOLLMAR BROS. CIRCUS.

BALLOON ASCENSIONS Before the advent of the airplane, the daredevilry of hot-air balloon ascensions, coupled with Man's inner desire to fly, made them a popular part of some American circuses.

Balloon ascensions were not without their peril, however. At five o'clock on the afternoon of July 15, 1875 in Chicago, Illinois, "Professor" Washington H. Donaldson (along with Newton S. Grimwood of the Chicago *Journal*) took off from the grounds of the touring company of P.T. BARNUM'S GREAT ROMAN HIPPODROME.

Donaldson raised the hot-air balloon up and out over Lake Michigan, but by the time of the evening circus performance the balloon had not returned. A storm raged over the lake that night; the next morning Captain Anderson of an arriving schooner, *Little Guide,* announced that the day before, he had spotted the aircraft far out over Lake Michigan and heading north.

A month later, on August 18, Grimwood's body washed ashore at Stony Creek on the east shore of Lake Michigan. No trace of Donaldson or the balloon itself was ever seen again.

This well-publicized spectacle and the accompanying hoopla ending with a mysterious disappearance might well have been the inspiration for the Wizard character in L. Frank Baum's classic 1900 novel, *The Wonderful Wizard of Oz.*

BALLY The bally, sometimes known as the opening or BALLYHOO, is circus jargon for a talk given outside a tent—usually a SIDESHOW or MENAGERIE—to convince the customers to come inside while waiting for the DOORS of the BIG TOP to open and the main show to begin.

The person who gives the bally usually stands on a raised board, called the bally platform, to give his PITCH. A ticket box is located at one or both sides of the platform; on a busy day a third box might be placed in the center of the MIDWAY. At the end of the bally, the ticket sellers step up into the boxes and the GRIND begins.

The circus bally is a true art form in persuasive speaking. The LECTURER, or OUTSIDE TALKER, must stand on the platform to face a disinterested, possibly hostile audience—usually one that is hot and tired from standing in the unshaded midway waiting for the main show to start. First he must draw the crowd as close as possible to his tent. To do so, the bally master must entertain the crowd and disarm them into believing that he is there just to provide amusement while they are waiting, not to corral them into his attraction. To further put the crowd offguard, the ticket boxes are empty and no ticket takers are visible.

Part of the "free entertainment" that is promised, of course, is a preview of the human curiosities inside the sideshow or a lurid description of the unusual creatures in the menagerie. The most crucial moment—as in all sales pitches—is the closing. The circus bally equivalent of "closing a deal" is "turning the TIP."

As soon as it is announced that the boxes are open, the ticket sellers jump up into position and a rushed sale begins. Although the bally is officially over, the outside talker grinds on about the oddities to be seen inside the tent. The grind may or may not be continued by the same man who performed the bally. Because the bally is so important for bringing the crowds into the sideshow tent, an effective bally is literally worth its weight in gold.

One of the masters of the sideshow bally is Dr. Charles W. "Doc" BOAS, the former owner of CIRCUS KIRK. Here is a transcription of one of his typical ballys, as given on an average day, 30 minutes before the main show was ready to begin:

Now ladies and gentlemen, boys and girls, if everyone here on the circus grounds will come right over this way, we're gonna get the afternoon's entertainment under way. It's all free, and it takes place on this platform right over here.

What's that, young man? You say, "What's that hole in the platform?" There's no trapdoor in the platform, young man. You want the people to see the hole in the platform? Well, if you want to see it, folks, you'll have to come in nice and close.

Thanks for coming in real close, folks; but I told you, son: It's not a trapdoor. No, it's just a knot hole.

But thanks, folks, for coming in close, because we have a lot of information to give away before the big show begins. Those of you still in line, you might as well come over to hear. You're not going to lose your place in line.

In fact, when we open the doors to the big show, we open all the doors. Some of you may even be in the wrong line.

First of all, let me welcome you to the grounds of the circus. The big blue-and-white striped tent you see at the end of the midway, well, that's our main show. That's where you'll see all the acrobats, the animals and the funny old clowns. And we'll be starting that show at two o'clock or just as soon after that as we can get you all seated comfortably inside.

Now does everyone have a ticket? Because I've seen a lot of different colored tickets out here on the midway today, and I want to be sure everyone has a ticket. I've seen some red ones, some blue ones. Are there any brown ones? Because the brown ones were for yesterday. Everyone get out your tickets and check. Check your tickets. Good, good, no brown ones.

If you don't have a ticket yet, now listen close. Every day we have people come up to the gate and say, "Two, Mister." Well, we don't sell tickets at the door; we just take them there. If you don't have a ticket yet, then get out of line. There's only one place you can get a ticket, and that's at the big red wagon down at the end of the midway where you see the sign that says, oddly enough, "Tickets." Our friendly box office manager is waving his hand out the window now. He'll be happy to help you and your family right down there.

Across the way you see our concession wagon. That's where you get all the good things to eat and drink. The red-and-white striped tent down the way is our menagerie and petting zoo. You can go inside and see all the animals that will be performing in the big show. The kids can go right up and pet the llamas and the elephant. It's a big thrill for them. Don't fail to take them. Down there in the tent at the end you can get your souvenirs to help you remember your visit to the circus today.

I guess that explains everything except the big blue tent right behind me. Well, this is our circus sideshow, our museum of oddities and curiosities. Now I don't want to insult your intelligence. You can see for yourself the big banners displayed on the outside of the tent, all the way from one end to the other, from your right, my left to your left, my right, showing all ten of the strange and curious acts we have inside.

Now I don't have time to tell you about all of them, but I have time to tell you about four of the ten big acts we have on the inside. Let's bring them up on the platform for a little bit of free entertainment. Come right on in here, real close, so you can see them real good.

First of all, let me introduce our snake charmer. This is Miss Reptilia and one of her little friends. This is a six-foot boa constrictor, straight from the Amazon jungle. The boa constrictor captures its victim by literally squeezing her—I mean, it—to death. That's Miss Reptilia, and you'll see lots more of her friends inside.

Next we have the funny old magician, Mr. Mysto. The kids love him, he'll amaze and amuse you. It's lots of fun for the whole family.

There's another one I want to tell you about. But we haven't brought him out here today. It's the Human Pincushion. I never know what that guy is up to, but he tells me that today he is going to do the act—with the long, steel needle. Now all you ladies have a pincushion at home and know how to use it. When he takes that long, steel needle and aims it at his upper arm, well, if you don't like the sight of it, you can just turn your head.

Finally, let me introduce Flamo, the Fire-eater. He's the one who runs the red-hot flames up and down, all over his body. Yes, he places those red-hot gasoline-soaked torches straight into his mouth. You're thinking there's some salve or protection in his mouth. No. There's is no such salve or ointment. If there were such a salve, don't you think every fire company in our great nation would know about it and be using it today? Of course they would. This is the same act that came down to us from the times of the Pharaoh to the streets of New Delhi and Bombay. And it's here today, alive, alive, inside this very tent. Why not give them a little peek, Flamo? Eat just one of those torches out for the nice folks out on our midway today. Let's let our performers get ready and join all the other acts on the inside.

Now look, my time is up. Ladies and gentlemen, boys and girls. I'm gonna open the doors to the sideshow. There are three things I want you to remember, three things please. First, you do have time to see this show. By coming inside you don't miss a thing. We do not start any of the big show, we don't start a single note of the band's music, until this show is all out and all over and everyone is inside the main tent.

Next, there are plenty of seats in the Big Top. There are only about 700 people on the midway today, and there are more than one thousand soft pine wood seats on the inside. Everyone will get one.

Number three. The price. How much does it cost to go in to see the show? That's the smallest part of the whole circus. We've cut the price so everyone can afford to go. It's one price, and one price only. And the price is the same, man, woman, child or the family dog, if you happened to bring it. Are you ready? Can you stand it? All right, here it comes: fifty cents, one-half of a dollar.

The men are in the ticket boxes. The sideshow is open and ready.

BALLY BROAD   Bally broad is an affectionate (if disrespectfully sexist) name for a showgirl, either on the MIDWAY or in the main show. The term probably comes from the practice of employing real ballet dancers in the great circus SPECS from 1880 to 1910.

During the opening—or BALLY—outside the SIDESHOW tent, the TALKER usually brings several acts onto the platform to let the audience have a sample of what they could see inside. These performers might include the fire-eater or sword swallower; but the talker would almost always bring onto the platform one or two of the female performers, often clad in revealing wardrobe.

Few female performers find it financially rewarding to travel alone just to perform in the sideshow; rather, they are usually related to one of the other performers and are merely earning extra money by appearing in the sideshow. The acts that they present, such as the SNAKE CHARMER (who holds and displays a boa constrictor or two) and the contortionist (who curls in a box as the magician pushes blades around her), do not require a great deal of skill. Many times the attractive showgirls are just brought onstage to entice the men on the midway to come inside.

On most modern arena and tent circuses there are no midways, sideshows or ballys. In the main performance the term "bally broad" refers to a showgirl who works the opening spectacular (or the spec) and parades in the finale, styles other acts and takes part in the aerial production numbers.

To disassociate themselves from the midway, bally broads in the main show contend that "bally" is actually a vulgarization of "ballet," since the showgirls invariably take part in at least one "aerial ballet" during the show.

Lois Washburn, who was a showgirl on the Red Unit of the RINGLING BROS. AND BARNUM & BAILEY CIRCUS in 1972, describes the typical day of a bally broad:

We had been trained by the showgirls' instructor, Antoinette Concello, in every detail from proper styling in the ring to approved makeup. We took part in five numbers, the opening spec, the aerial Spanish web ballet, the first-half closing production parade, riding the elephants in the second act opening and the grand finale.

The show provided living quarters for the single showgirls, those not part of the other circus families; and we all lived on one train car. The car had two large suites in the middle, one of which was Antoinette's; and there were three private compartments at each end. My room had a single Murphy bed and a sink, and the three girls at each end shared a bathroom and a closet.

Of course there were no showers on the car, so we always cleaned up at the arena, which meant on our first bus trip in to the arena in the morning we all looked pretty bad— no makeup, hair undone, street clothes.

Our first day at a Boston arena, a catty usherette saw us dragging into the dressing room and said to one of her friends, "Well, I don't see what's so special about them!" *I turned to her and said, "Yeah? Well, listen, honey, let's* see *you* climb a forty-foot rope straight up, ride an elephant *and balance fifty pounds of feathers and sequins on your head; and I'll see if I can manage to handle your flash-light!"*

Once the performance begins, the showgirls provide much of the color and flash of the production. Without the glitter and sparkle supplied by the Ziegfeld-like parade of the bally broads, the circus would look sparse indeed.

(See also BALLYHOO.)

BALLYHOO
Circus jargon for the free show given outside the SIDESHOW tent to draw a crowd or TIP.

The term first came into existence at the 1893 Columbian Exposition in Chicago. The harem dancers and fakirs brought over from the Middle East spoke no English, only Arabic. An interpreter called the words *"dehalla hoon"* to bring the performers out front to the bally platform, on which an abbreviated performance was given. The American TALKERS misheard the expression as "ballyhoo," and from then on used this word when the interpreters were at dinner or on a break. Although the expression can still be heard, the shortened version, BALLY, is now more commonly used.

BANDWAGON
A highlight of the STREET PARADE, the bandwagon often held the honored spot at the front of the circus procession through the main avenue of town. The name "bandwagon" was quite literal, because it held the musicians whose merry music drew crowds to the city square. Usually the largest of the WAGONS in the parade, it was sometimes drawn by as many as 40 horses under rein.

The biggest bandwagon ever built was the TWO HEMISPHERES BANDWAGON. Created to lead the 1903 BARNUM & BAILEY CIRCUS parade in New York follow-

ing the circus's five-year European tour, the wagon was 28 feet in length and 10½ feet high. Although most wagons carry the same design on each side, the Two Hemispheres was different; one side represented the Eastern and the other the Western Hemisphere. Today the wagon is owned by John Zweifel and is housed at the CIRCUS WORLD MUSEUM in BARABOO, WISCONSIN.

Completely restored to its former glory and also maintained by the Circus World Museum is the famous Lion and Mirror Bandwagon, a unique white-and-gold–gilded cart with wood-carved figures and giant mirrors on the sides. Originally it was designed for the ADAM FOREPAUGH CIRCUS as a TELESCOPING TABLEAU WAGON, which could hoist statues of St. George and the Dragon into view. When it was bought by the Ringling Circus in late 1890 for use in its 1891 season, a platform and seats for musicians replaced the statues; it was used as their number-one bandwagon for 28 years.

Among the other original bandwagons owned and restored by the Circus World Museum—and which have been seen in modern times in the annual GREAT CIRCUS PARADE in Wisconsin—are the 1903 Pawnee Bill Bandwagon (also known as the Columbus-John Smith Bandwagon) and the 1902 Columbia Bandwagon.

Another of the great carriages, the white-and-gold Swan Bandwagon, built around 1905 by the MOELLER CARRIAGE AND WAGON WORKS, was subsequently owned by the CHRISTY BROTHERS CIRCUS and the Ringling Brothers Circus. The Columbus-John Smith Bandwagon, like the Two Hemispheres Bandwagon, is also unusual in that its two sides show completely different scenes: One side presents the arrival of Columbus in the New World, the reverse shows John Smith being saved by Pocohantas.

In 1878 the Fielding brothers of New York built the original wagon that was later converted into the Five Graces Bandwagon for the Adam Forepaugh Circus. Circus historians have argued over the carvings for years, because there are only three Graces in classical mythology. Many believe the central figure on the side of the wagon is actually that of Columbia ("Gem of the Ocean") surrounded by the Four Seasons. One of the most used and most variously owned of the great bandwagons, the Five Graces traveled with several circuses before it was with the Barnum & Bailey European Tour (1898–1902). Later it became the property of the combined RINGLING BROTHERS AND BARNUM & BAILEY CIRCUS; currently it is owned and displayed among the circus exhibits at the JOHN AND MABLE RINGLING MUSEUM OF ART in SARASOTA, FLORIDA.

BANDWAGON *Bandwagon* magazine, subtitled "The Journal of the Circus Historical Society," is the official publication of the fraternal historical organization, the CIRCUS HISTORICAL SOCIETY.

Edited for over 30 years by Fred Pfening, Jr., *Bandwagon* is a treasure trove of carefully researched articles on the American circus. Even a casual glance at some of the titles of recent articles—such as Joseph T. Bradbury's "M.L. Clark and Sons Circus: Season of 1945" and Stuart Thayer's "The Elephant in America 1840–1860"—shows that *Bandwagon* reflects the true historian's quest for separating circus fact from the PRESS AGENT's fancy.

Published bimonthly, the magazine's editorial offices are located at 2515 Dorset Road, Columbus, Ohio 43221.

BANNER Circus jargon for the paintings of the SIDESHOW attractions—done on large sheets of canvas—that are hung in front of the tent on a BANNERLINE to lure audiences inside. Real canvas banners are considered works of art. Perhaps the greatest painter of "rag banners" (as canvas banners are called) was Fred JOHNSON. In the late 1960s and 1970s those few motorized circuses that still carried sideshows began to paint their banners onto the sides of the trucks that hauled the tents.

Another type of "banner," an advertising banner, is sometimes seen inside the BIG TOP. Usually rectangular in shape and strung horizontally around the perimeter of the big top, these banners are made of paper or repainted canvas and display slogans or information from local merchants. The ADVANCE MAN for the show often has the job of "selling banners" before the show, agreeing to run them in exchange for advertising dollars.

BANNERLINE Circus jargon for the string of BANNERS that frame the front of the SIDESHOW tent, advertising the attractions within. Although the term suggests canvas and rope, they are referred to as a bannerline even when the paintings appear on trucks parked in front of the tent.

By parking a truck on each side of the entrance to the sideshow, the work crew avoids having to set up a line of poles and rigging every day. Also, it eliminates the worry about the safety of the banners, which tend to act like giant sails in even a modest breeze.

BARABOO, WISCONSIN The home of the RINGLING BROTHERS, Baraboo, Wisconsin served as their WINTER QUARTERS from their first variety shows in 1882 or 1883 until 1918. At the end of the 1918 season, the Ringling Bros. Circus returned to BRIDGEPORT, CONNECTICUT, the home of the BARNUM & BAILEY CIRCUS (another Ringling holding), rather than Baraboo. The shows merged into the RINGLING BROS. AND BARNUM & BAILEY CIRCUS in 1919, combining its permanent quarters at the Bridgeport location.

Baraboo also served as the site of the MOELLER CARRIAGE AND WAGON WORKS as well as the winter quarters of the GOLLMAR BROS. CIRCUS, advertised as "Gollmar Brothers, Greatest of American Shows."

Today the old Ringling winter quarters in Baraboo is the site of the CIRCUS WORLD MUSEUM, which operates the Robert L. Parkinson Library & Research Center, the largest circus archives in the world. Also on the grounds are many of the original buildings from the Ringling era.

BARBETTE (1902–1973) Somewhat of an anomaly in the circus world, Barbette was born Vander Clyde Broadway in Round Rock, Texas.

At the age of 14, his mother gave him permission to join an act known as the Alferetta Sisters, which was appearing in San Antonio 80 miles away. A female impersonator, he became a partner, billed as "America's Little Aerial Queen." A year and a half later, he learned an IRON JAW act to join another team of aerialists, Erford's Whirling Sensations. Soon, billed simply as "Barbette," he began to tour the Orpheum vaudeville circuit. In January 1923 he "played the Palace" in New York City when he was only 21 years old.

His next stop was Paris. With 25 trunks full of wigs, women's wardrobe, cosmetics and scenery, Barbette became the aerial sensation of Europe. At the finale of his act, he removed his wig, no doubt disappointing—or at least puzzling—the men in the

Bannerline trucks line the midway on the Clyde Beatty-Cole Bros. Circus.   (Photo courtesy of the Heist collection)

audience who had found his act erotically appealing. His acclaim led to tours through South America, Australia, the Middle East and Asia.

He appeared in films, including Scallera's *La Tosca* and Jean Cocteau's surrealistic *Blood of a Poet.* But in the early 1940s Barbette had to retire from performing when he was seriously injured in a fall.

He returned to the United States with a contract from John Ringling NORTH to stage his 60-girl aerial numbers. Other producers' requests followed. He worked with Billy Rose on his stage play *Seven Lively Arts* as well as on Orson Welles's *Around the World.* He supervised the circus aerial sequences for the American films *Till the Clouds Roll By, Jumbo* and others.

Even as the lavish spectacles of the railroad circus era were diminishing, Barbette continued to supervise the aerial ballets. He toured with the CLYDE BEATTY CIRCUS, the POLACK BROS. CIRCUS and, for three years beginning in 1969, the Australian tour of Disney on Parade.

The antics of the usually outspoken and often outrageous Barbette gave rise to a host of "Barbette-isms," witty comebacks and comic quotes attributed to him. One took place when Barbette was hired to be aerial director of the early Clyde Beatty Circus. Clyde BEATTY caught a glimpse of Barbette in the BACK YARD, burning all of the second-string aerial costumes in a big blaze. Astonished, Beatty complained, "Barbette, you're burning all of my rainy day wardrobe." Barbette replied succinctly, "Mr. Beatty, it *never* rains *that* hard!"

Unemployed and unable to cope with the disappointments of old age, Barbette ended his own life with an overdose of sleeping pills.

BAREBACK RIDING   See ROSINBACK; VAULTING.

BARKER   Contrary to common usage, the term "barker" has never been used in the circus world—or any other type of show in the outdoor amusement industry—to mean the TALKER, LECTURER, spieler or the person who performs a GRIND.

The word, apparently coined and connected to the circus by a misinformed author, is never used by a TROUPER; its use by a performer on the showgrounds would instantly point him out to be a FIRST OF MAY.

BARNES, AL G.   See AL G. BARNES CIRCUS; AMERICAN CIRCUS CORPORATION.

BARNETT BROS. CIRCUS   Founded in Canada in 1927, the Barnett Bros. Circus moved its WINTER QUARTERS to the United States in 1929. Operated for 16 years by Ray W. Rogers, the show was renamed the Wallace Bros. Circus for 1937 and for the war years 1941 through 1944.

Rogers died in 1943, but the cast and crew combined to keep the show open. It merged that same year with the CLYDE BEATTY CIRCUS, and in 1944 all of the remaining equipment was sold to Clyde BEATTY and to Floyd King to augment their shows.

BARNUM   See THEATER.

BARNUM, P(HINEAS) T(AYLOR) (1810–1891)   Phineas Taylor Barnum was born in Bethel, Connecticut, on July 5, 1810, the first of five children to Philo and Irena Barnum. His father, a farmer, died in poverty when Barnum was just 15 years old.

Taylor (as he was called) first worked on his father's farm, then as a clerk in a general store. Early on, he showed a facility for arithmetic as well as a keen business sense, and at the age of 18 he bought a small grocery. To transform it into a money-making operation, he recalled an incident when he was a clerk at a previous store: He had purchased a peddler's unwanted bottles and disposed of them—to a huge profit—in a lottery. Barnum set up his own store as a lottery headquarters until 1834, when lotteries were declared illegal in Connecticut.

On November 8, 1829 he married Charity Hallett, a seamstress from Bethel. Shortly thereafter Barnum started his own newspaper (the *Herald of Freedom*), with the first edition appearing on October 19, 1831. His business acumen did not include tact, however, and he was soon jailed for 60 days for libel. Many did not agree with the incarceration, and his release was cause for a huge parade and celebration in Danbury.

In 1834 Barnum sold the *Herald of Freedom* and moved to New York City with his wife and daughter. He began again in the grocery business, while Charity kept a boardinghouse.

In 1835 Barnum became a showman when he began exhibiting Joice HETH, an elderly black woman who claimed to have been George Washington's nursemaid and was supposedly 161 years old. This first foray into the world of entertainment lasted only until Heth's death in February of the following year.

Barnum's first association with a circus came in 1836 when he joined the AARON TURNER CIRCUS as a ticket collector. Although Phineas learned a valuable lesson in publicity from Aaron TURNER, it almost cost him his life. As a practical joke, Turner told a mob in Annapolis that Barnum was a wanted murderer. The rioters would have killed Barnum had Turner not stopped them. The circus owner laughed and said, "It's all for our good. The notoriety will fill our tent."

Barnum did not enter the world of the circus again until his partnership with William Cameron (W.C.) COUP and Dan CASTELLO in 1871.

It was in the 30 years beginning in 1841 that the Barnum legend began. That year, using an inherited worthless piece of Connecticut swampland named Ivy Island as collateral, Barnum persuaded the landlord and exhibit owners to lease him John Scudder's AMERICAN MUSEUM at the corner of Broadway and Ann Street in New York City.

The museum, run down after Scudder's death, held an unexciting collection of stuffed animals, waxworks and displays. Barnum immediately discarded old exhibits, added the bizarre and unusual, and reopened it as Barnum's American Museum on New Year's Day, 1842.

Magicians, ventriloquists, Punch and Judy shows and knife throwers were among the new attractions hired to entertain. One of the early novelty acts was a young Dan RICE performing a strongman routine. Six men lifted a heavy barrel seemingly filled with water and placed it onto his back. Following a salary dispute, Rice exposed the hoax: The barrel held only a bucket of water, which dripped from a secret compartment. Barnum, the master humbug, never forgave Rice for giving away the ruse.

P.T. Barnum. *(Photo courtesy of The Barnum Museum, Bridgeport, CT)*

Since "theater" was not considered a refined entertainment at that time, Barnum named a performance area the "Lecture Room," staging "refined amusements and moral dramas."

The FEEJEE MERMAID was one of Barnum's most successful hoaxes. Barnum leased the oddity from a Boston museum, which had gotten it from a Japanese fisherman in the Fiji Islands.

Thousands came to the museum the first year. Even though admission was only 25 cents, profits neared $30,000—three times the amount Scudder's Museum had grossed the year before. Barnum boasted that his museum drew more visitors daily than the free British Museum in London.

Barnum was the first showman to exhibit FREAKS and human oddities on a grand scale. Anna Swan from Nova Scotia was a giant at 7 feet 11 inches. A "fat boy" was billed as "Vantile Mack, the Giant Baby! Weighs 257 pounds! 7 years old, measures 38 inches around the leg!" Madame Josephine CLOFULLIA, the bearded lady from Switzerland, was the target of a lawsuit aimed at proving her sex. One of Barnum's most peculiar exhibits was the SIAMESE TWINS CHANG AND ENG. Born of Chinese parents in Siam, Chang and Eng were brothers inseparably joined at the chest. Probably the most famous attraction at the American Museum was Charles S. Stratton—who was renamed TOM THUMB. The 25-inch midget was so personable that when he toured following the close of the museum, he became a friend of royalty around the world.

Although P.T. Barnum was hugely successful—a master showman of hokum—he yearned for respectability. In 1850 he arranged for a European opera singer, JENNY LIND (billing her as "the Swedish Nightingale"), to tour the United States under his management. From her September 11, 1850 arrival until her departure in May 1852, Lind performed 60 concerts under Barnum's aegis, netting him a profit of more than $250,000.

A few months before Lind's arrival, Barnum—with partners Seth B. HOWES and Sherwood Stratton (Tom Thumb's father)—sent a ship to India to collect animals for his museum. Instead of placing them into the MENAGERIE in his museum, the men opened a canvas show, P.T. BARNUM'S GREAT ASIATIC CARAVAN, MUSEUM AND MENAGERIE in 1851. The show traveled for four years, when the partnership broke up.

Barnum was rich, famous and unrivaled as the top showman in the country. He stood 6 feet 2 inches tall, weighed 200 pounds, had curly brown hair, blue eyes, a bulbous nose and an announcer's voice. He was outgoing but not arrogant, to most a good-natured, if occasionally flamboyant, man. In 1855 he sold the American Museum for a huge profit and returned home to spend more time with his wife and three daughters.

Barnum's home outside Bridgeport, Connecticut, was a mansion that he had modeled after King George IV's Oriental pavilion in Brighton, England. With its overly ornate spires and domes, the gaudy residence was named IRANISTAN by Barnum. There, in semiretirement, he wrote his first autobiography, *The Life of P.T. Barnum, Written by Himself*, in 1854.

Whether actually "written by himself" or ghostwritten, the book was poorly received by the critics as well as readers. Many reviewers felt the book was an ill-conceived confessional that showed the ways Barnum—the self-admitted "Prince of Humbugs"—had deceived the public to make his fortune. Fifteen years later Barnum published a second, amended autobiography, *Struggles and Triumphs; or, Forty Years' Recollections of P.T. Barnum, Written by Himself.*

After purchasing land on the east side of the river opposite Bridgeport, Barnum laid out a model community and offered the acreage for sale in lots. The Jerome Clock Company of Bridgeport expressed an interest in moving its headquarters to East Bridgeport, and Barnum saw the change as a way to bring both business and a demand for housing to his new town. The company misrepresented its solvency to Barnum, and the great showman offered personal bonds of $110,000 to assist with the move. Within months it was discovered that the clock factory was not only bankrupt but in deep debt, and Barnum found himself personally responsible for the company's liabilities. Needless to say, the clock business venture was a complete failure, and Barnum had to tour with Tom Thumb to pay off over $500,000 in debts.

On the night of December 17, 1857 (through the next morning), while Barnum was in New York, his beloved Iranistan burned down. Barnum promptly built another large, if unpretentious, mansion, which he named Lindencroft, also in Bridgeport.

In 1860 Barnum returned as owner and director of the American Museum. The building was open "from sunrise to ten" at a ticket price of "thirty cents, with no extra charge, except for a few front seats and private boxes." On August 12, 1861 he opened the exhibition of "the first and only genuine hippopotamus that had ever been seen in America." To house two white whales from the St. Lawrence River, and later exotic fish from the Caribbean, Barnum installed the first indoor saltwater aquarium in the United States. The collection of curiosities grew so large that Barnum added an adjoining building, 40 by 100 feet large.

On Thanksgiving Day 1864, in the midst of the Civil War, a firebomb was tossed inside the American Museum, but it caused only slight damage. Just a year later, however, on July 13, 1865 the museum was burned to the ground by an accidental fire. On September 6 P.T. Barnum opened the doors to his New American Museum at a new location.

That same year Barnum entered politics, winning a Republican seat representing the city of Fairfield in the Connecticut legislature. Content, Barnum stayed in politics for a second term before losing a bid for the U.S. Congress in 1867.

Meanwhile, in 1866 Barnum consolidated with Van Amburgh's Menagerie and was chartered as the Barnum and Van Amburgh Museum and Menag-

erie Company in Connecticut. The summer touring show included lions, tigers, giraffes, bears and an elephant; during the winter, the animals were exhibited at the American Museum.

Only two years later, on the evening of March 3, 1868, his New American Museum burned to the ground. The cause of the fire was a defective flue in a restaurant in the basement of the museum. Johnny Denham, a fireman, was a hero in this fire; he killed an escaped tiger with an ax and carried a fat lady weighing 400 pounds out of the burning building.

Barnum was a fierce abolitionist, a teetotaler (and lecturer on temperance) and a Universalist thinker. Above all, however, he was a "museum man." Just three days after the fire that destroyed his first American Museum, Barnum wrote a private letter to Bayard Taylor dated July 16, 1865, in which he speculated about rebuilding his museum again. With help from a few letters of introduction and recommendation from friends in Washington, he might be able

to get presents for my new museum from all the public governmental museums in Europe. Thus a specimen or two or more from the Louvre & Versailles, labelled "Presented by Louis Napoleon, Emperor of France"; ditto museum at Kensington, presented by Queen Victoria . . . British Museum, East India Museum, London, and a score of other public and private institutions . . . Also from the Pope of Rome.

Six days later Barnum wrote another letter to Taylor, in which he mused: "I propose to erect a *National Free Museum* which shall contain specimens of *everything* presented by our govt. in any of its departments & everything presented by *anybody* in this or any other country."

Barnum did, in fact, suggest that the National Museum be open free to the public. Adjoining the National Museum, however, would be Barnum's American Museum, which would house his stage shows, menagerie, freaks and other curiosities.

"To this museum," he confided,

I charge an admission fee of 25 or 30 cts., children half price. Museum open from sunrise till 10 p.m. All Museum visitors admitted to National (concern) free at all hours from sunrise till 10 p.m. The public admitted to National concern free at fixed hours—same as in Europe—& fixed days—same as in Europe. At the division entrance between the free National & the paying Museum is a ticket seller who sells Museum tickets to such free visitors only *as happen to wish to visit the Museum. I suppose that 9/10ths of the National visitors will conclude to visit the Museum, but if they don't there's no harm done.*

Barnum had so many important and respected contacts both in the government and overseas—and the need for a national museum was so overwhelming—that he could very easily have succeeded in his plan. Soon after the project was conceived however, Mr. Smithson of Great Britain bequeathed his monies to form a national museum, in his name, for the United States. Thus, already endowed, the Smithsonian Institution was formed. A.H. Saxon, eminent Barnum scholar, notes: "The mind boggles at the prospect of what Barnum might have accomplished had he ever been offered the secretaryship of the Smithsonian."

This did not prevent Barnum from immediately cultivating a friendship with Joseph Henry, the first secretary of the Smithsonian, as well as with Professor Spencer F. Baird, his successor. For years Barnum had an unwritten understanding that the Smithsonian would send him copies of curiosities from casts (or duplicates from their collection) and Barnum would reciprocate with the carcasses of unusual beasts from his menagerie for the natural history branch of the national museum.

In later years Barnum also promised dead animals from his circus collection to his "pet" project, the Barnum Museum of Natural History at Tufts College. At one time or another he also had supposedly exclusive relationships with Moses Kimball of the Boston Museum and Henry A. Ward of Ward's Natural Science Establishment in Rochester, New York.

Some of these arrangements may have been covert, especially the one with the Smithsonian. In a January 9, 1884 letter to Henry A. Ward, Barnum apologized for not being able to turn over the dead bodies of half a dozen monkeys, then suggested that to Ward: "You can perhaps exchange [duplicate items] with Smithsonian for curiosities, duplicates, models &c." Frank A. Ward (Henry's son), who was assisting his father at the time, reported, "I shut my eyes when I came to this."

When the second American Museum burned on March 2–3, 1868, Barnum once again retired from show business. One of his first civic endeavors was campaigning for and establishing an oceanfront recreational area in Bridgeport that, upon its dedication on August 21, 1865, he called Seaside Park.

Additionally, Barnum opened several broad avenues across his own property, donating them for public use. This was, of course, not entirely altruistic: The property on both sides of the new streets skyrocketed in value.

In the summer of 1867, Charity Barnum's health declined noticeably, and her doctor suggested a move closer to the sea would be helpful. Phineas sold his beloved Lindencroft on July 1, 1867 and, after two years of temporary housing near Seaside Park, erected a luxurious but practical third Bridgeport estate, Waldemere ("Woods-by-the-Sea"), in June 1869. On the grounds he constructed two smaller houses, "Petrel's Nest" and "Wavewood," the latter of which was used by two of his daughters as a summer residence. Barnum took up the habit of spending the five summer months in Bridgeport and the remaining seven in New York City.

Barnum kept his hands in humbug, however. On October 16, 1869 a huge stone statue, reputed to be a fossilized man, was dug up on the farm of "Stub" Newell at Cardiff, a village near Syracuse, New York. Barnum viewed the CARDIFF GIANT, as it was known, and declared, "And they call *me* a humbug!" Even though he was sure it was a fake, Barnum offered the owners $60,000 for a three-month lease on the giant. They refused, having already opened their own concession; Barnum had an exact replica made in plaster and exhibited it in Brooklyn under canvas. When the owners brought the original statuary to New York for display, they took Barnum to court; but the judge ruled that there was no law preventing the exhibition of a fake of a fake. Each operator made a fortune with his respective "One and Only Original Cardiff Giant."

W.C. Coup, a former sideshow manager, and Dan Castello, an ex-clown, asked Barnum to join them in forming a new circus. Coup reasoned that their expertise, coupled with the Barnum name, would prove unbeatable. On April 10, 1871 Barnum officially entered the circus world when his tented show BARNUM'S GREAT TRAVELING MUSEUM, MENAGERIE, CARAVAN, HIPPODROME AND CIRCUS opened in Brooklyn. The first season, touring under three acres of canvas—the most mammoth expanse ever seen to that time—grossed more than $400,000.

The show traveled successfully for four years. In 1872, possibly at Coup's suggestion, it embarked on its first railroad tour, grossing $1 million in six months. By 1873 it had a daily NUT of $5,000.

In 1873, while Barnum was out of the country purchasing wild animals for the menagerie, Charity, his wife of 44 years, died. They had raised a family of four daughters, one of whom had died in childhood at the age of two. The others were married, with the eldest living on the old property of Iranistan and the others living in New York City and summering in Bridgeport.

Within ten months, Barnum was remarried to Nancy Fish, a young English lady. He remained happily married to her until the end of his life.

In the meantime, Coup had plans to take their show indoors. Barnum's winter programs had taken place in the HIPPOTHEATRON on 14th Street in New York, but it was destroyed by fire in 1872. The loss of his exotic menagerie cost the showman $300,000. While Barnum was in Europe, Coup leased the property at Madison Square (between 26th and 27th Street and Fourth and Madison Avenues) to move their giant show into an arena setting. He named the building P.T. BARNUM'S GREAT ROMAN HIPPODROME, which later became the original MADISON SQUARE GARDEN.

Some historians contend that, at first, Barnum denied ever having been consulted about the change to an arena show. When the Hippodrome turned out to be wildly successful, he claimed credit for its inception.

In April 1874 the largest crowd ever assembled in a New York structure up until that time (over 10,000 people) saw the first performance in the Hippodrome. The show consisted of a grand SPEC, the "Congress of Nations," which "required nearly 1,000 persons, several hundred horses, besides llamas, camels, ostriches, etc." Next came chariot races around the track, followed by the regular circus performance.

The Hippodrome show soon went on the road. Barnum's Great Traveling World's Fair, as it was sometimes known, gave three performances a day following a morning STREET PARADE. Coup added a second circus ring to the gas-lit tent show, and the circus was advertised as "Two Separate Rival Rings under a vast center-pole pavillion [sic] with seats for 14,000." Other attractions included "The Fiji Cannibals, Admiral Dot, An Endless Corps of Male and Female Riders," and "The Wonderful Talking Machine That Laughs, Sings and Talks in All Languages."

W.C. Coup was in large part responsible for the show's enormous success. He priced regular tickets at 50 cents; children under nine went in for half price; and clergy had free admission. Posters advertised the circus up to 75 miles from town; Coup even had railroads run excursion trains to the circus grounds the day of show. His moving the show onto rails and his method of end-loading CIRCUS TRAINS were to become industry standards, which allowed the performers to travel farther overnight and with a larger show.

In 1875 Barnum's partnership with Coup dissolved. Castello had already retired, and in 1874 Barnum had leased his name and Traveling World's Fair to John V. "Pogey" O'BRIEN, a notorious grifter (see GRIFT). Eventually Barnum turned over active management of the Great Traveling Museum to the powerful circus syndicate, the FLATFOOTS.

Even during his semiretirement and a term as mayor of Bridgeport in 1875, Barnum added new attractions to his namesake show. In 1880 these included a tattooed lady, a hairy-faced boy and "Mlle. ZAZEL, the First Human Cannonball." Also with the show was a new musical instrument, the gigantic ORCHESTMELOCHOR. Quoting Barnum, it was "of such immense volume and power that its melodious strains can be heard for a distance of over five miles, giving the effect of a full orchestra."

Throughout his middle and late life, Barnum held a warm friendship and correspondence with Samuel "Mark Twain" Clemens. An incident paralleling Twain's famous "Reports of my death have been greatly exaggerated" retort occurred to Barnum when he received a letter from J.A. McGonagle in 1880. McGonagle, of Cherokee, Iowa, wrote to say that in his part of the country it was commonly believed that the great showman was dead and that a letter from him would prove otherwise. P.T. promptly shot back this July 21, 1880 reply from Bridgeport: "Dear Sir, Your letter of inquiry is received. My impression is that I am not dead. P.T. Barnum."

At the age of 70, P.T. Barnum entered into the association that would ensure his name's immortality. In 1880 he joined forces with James A. BAILEY, who was a partner with James E. COOPER and James L. HUTCHINSON in the Great London Circus, sometimes called the International Allied Shows. The first elephant born in captivity in the United States took place at the Bailey WINTER QUARTERS on March 10,

1880. Barnum is reported to have sent a telegram to Bailey, offering to purchase the pachyderm and its mother for $100,000. Bailey not only refused, he printed Barnum's wire with the advertisement "What Barnum Thinks of the Baby Elephant."

Barnum realized he had met his match and suggested they become partners. Cooper had already retired from the merger; but the other three teamed as P.T. BARNUM'S GREATEST SHOW ON EARTH, HOWES' GREAT LONDON CIRCUS AND SANGER'S ROYAL BRITISH MENAGERIE. A huge parade in New York on March 16, 1881, featuring hundreds of animals and performers, celebrated their union.

It is generally thought that—due to his advanced age—Barnum was more or less a "silent" partner, merely lending his money and name to the enterprise while allowing his partners, especially Bailey, to do the hands-on management. Certainly Barnum drew his own weight in the merger, however, especially in terms of publicity and understanding the public. Barnum also had a long and healthy relationship with all of the newspapers in the country, and he was able to attract endorsements from prominent citizens and artists. He was an astute businessman, watching competitors and, if possible, buying them out. When he was on the circus LOT, Barnum was often one of his own prime attractions, riding the hippodrome in a carriage and saluting the audience; but he also continued to scout for new novelties and attractions to add to the show.

It was to the GREATEST SHOW ON EARTH that Barnum first brought the famous elephant JUMBO. Its purchase in England had caused an international incident, which only added to its value. Jumbo first arrived on American shores on Easter Sunday 1882.

Bailey, a frequent victim of "mental distress," was once again ailing at the end of the 1885 season. Barnum and Hutchinson bought out Bailey's share in the show and brought in W.W. COLE and James E. Cooper as their new partners.

In 1887 James A. Bailey, fully recovered, returned as manager and as sole equal partner with Barnum in a reorganized show, the BARNUM & BAILEY CIRCUS. Although the show was afterward rebuilt and continued, Barnum was once again plagued by fire when the circus's winter quarters in Bridgeport partially burned down in 1887. The damage was estimated at $250,000.

In 1889 Barnum made one last amendment to his autobiography, adding in chapters on his involvement with the circus and further condensing and sanitizing the chapters detailing his early career.

In 1890 P.T. Barnum suffered a stroke. The following spring he planned his own funeral and asked to read his own obituary in advance in *The Evening Sun*. The Greatest Showman on Earth died on April 7, 1891.

His widow, Nancy Fish Barnum, eventually moved to Europe, where she died on June 23, 1927. (See also RINGLING BROS. AND BARNUM & BAILEY CIRCUS.)

BARNUM & BAILEY CIRCUS   The seeds of what was eventually to become the trailblazing Barnum & Bailey Circus were planted in 1881 when James A. BAILEY and his partners James E. COOPER and James L. HUTCHINSON, then owners of HOWES' GREAT LONDON CIRCUS AND SANGER'S ROYAL BRITISH MENAGERIE, first joined forces with P.T. BARNUM, combining their show with his. The resultant circus, P.T. BARNUM'S GREATEST SHOW ON EARTH, HOWES' GREAT LONDON CIRCUS AND SANGER'S ROYAL BRITISH MENAGERIE— more succinctly known as the BARNUM & LONDON CIRCUS—toured through 1887.

Among the many "firsts" introduced by Bailey was the three-ring circus, introduced at their MADISON SQUARE GARDEN date in 1881 or 1882. Three-ring circuses became the American staple and have been associated with the name Barnum & Bailey ever since. It was also during this period that Barnum acquired JUMBO in England. The mammoth pachyderm toured with the show from 1882 until 1885.

In 1885 Bailey left the partnership; but in 1887 he reteamed with Barnum alone and became an equal partner; they renamed the new show the Barnum & Bailey Circus. With Bailey's managerial skills and Barnum's flair for extravaganza, their show quickly earned the full motto: THE GREATEST SHOW ON EARTH.

After 1889 the circus packed up and moved to England. The brouhaha over the purchase of Jumbo was forgotten (or forgiven) and the tour was a triumph. That season the show played the cavernous Olympia in London. It required three ocean liners to bring the entire show back to the States in the spring of 1890. Barnum's circulars announced "This Ever-Growing Show IS NOW SO GREAT NO BUILDING IN AMERICA CAN HOLD IT . . . It

Must Exhibit Always Under Canvas In Far Bigger Tents than Ever."

Among the attractions in the 1890s was the Grand Ethnological Congress, a SIDESHOW featuring unusual humans and animals from all over the world. A separate "black tent" sideshow (so-called because of the coloring of the drapes and backdrops) recreated many of the illusions that were being performed on stages by contemporary magicians.

Barnum died on April 7, 1891; three years later Bailey became the sole owner. The Barnum & Bailey Circus was now the largest show in the country, touring with 65 rail cars.

The circus made a successful five-year tour of Europe from 1897 to 1902. During its time overseas, the show had two winter engagements in London; twice toured England, Scotland and Wales; then moved on to Germany, France and other countries on the continent. Always an innovator, Bailey solved many new logistical problems of touring in England, including loading the wagons onto smaller-gauge rail cars, as well as reducing the cars' height for lower British tunnels.

During the show's run in England, the "human oddities" in the sideshow rebelled, requesting that they be given a more humane name than FREAKS. Canon Wilberforce of Westminster Abbey suggested the more dignified word "prodigies"; and the term stuck until the circus returned to the United States in late 1902.

When the circus began its German tour in Hamburg on April 15, 1900, it billed itself as "Die Grosste Schaustellung Der Erde." The show staged the largest circus parade in Germany's history, including its new 40-horse BANDWAGON team; although it was Easter Sunday, the opening matinee was sold out. The Greatest Show on Earth stayed in Hamburg for four weeks before moving to Berlin for 28 performances.

It was during this tour of Europe that the original Siegrist-Silbon aerial team first trouped with the Barnum & Bailey Circus. Also during this time, the circus was closely watched by the German Army, which later incorporated many of the show's managerial principles into its own training. Vienna was the WINTER QUARTERS for the show in 1900.

Upon its return to the United States, the Barnum & Bailey Circus realized that the upstart Ringling Bros. Circus had grown into a formidable opponent.

The most spectacular STREET PARADE in circus history was staged in New York City to announce the return of the Barnum & Bailey Circus, and it was in this magnificent procession that the remarkable TWO HEMISPHERES BANDWAGON, drawn by 40 horses was unveiled. The "America" TABLEAU WAGON, sold to the COLE BROS. CIRCUS in 1935, was also built for that homecoming parade. Barnum & Bailey issued a special lithograph to advertise the parade, billing it as a "Colossal, New, Free Street Parade, The Biggest and Greatest Free Procession Ever Beheld."

The Greatest Show on Earth was not the first to use a 40-horse hitch: It had been used by the SPALDING & ROGERS CIRCUS in 1848, the YANKEE ROBINSON CIRCUS in 1866 and the DAN RICE CIRCUS in 1873. The Barnum & Bailey Circus itself had used such a team for the entire 1897 season in the States before traveling to Europe.

Pulling the Two Hemispheres Bandwagon, however, the 40-horse team seemed to be a new American sensation all over again. The team was usually driven by Jim Thomas with two assistants—one on the brakes and the other keeping the reins straight and taut. Holding ten reins in each hand, Thomas sat 80 feet behind the lead row of four horses.

The circus continued to come head-to-head with the Ringling show. James A. Bailey died in 1906, and the RINGLING BROTHERS managed to buy the show and title from his widow in 1907. The Barnum & Bailey Circus was toured as a separate unit through the 1918 season, until 1919 when it finally merged with the Ringling show to form the major force in the American circus in this century—the RINGLING BROS. AND BARNUM & BAILEY CIRCUS.

BARNUM & LONDON CIRCUS   The shortened name, or nickname, of the P.T. BARNUM'S GREATEST SHOW ON EARTH, HOWES' GREAT LONDON CIRCUS AND SANGER'S ROYAL BRITISH MENAGERIE, the Barnum & London Circus began in 1881 as a conglomerate of the shows owned by P.T. BARNUM, James A. BAILEY and James L. HUTCHINSON. Bailey left the organization for health reasons in 1885, and the show continued for two more years. In 1887 Bailey returned as the sole equal partner with Barnum. One year later the BARNUM & BAILEY CIRCUS was formed.

BARNUM MUSEUM, THE   The Barnum Museum, housed in the original headquarters of the Barnum

A one sheet lithograph advertising poster from Barnum and Bailey Circus. It was printed in 1897 by the Strobridge Litho. Co. (Photo courtesy of The Barnum Museum, Bridgeport, CT)

Institute of Science and History in BRIDGEPORT, CONNECTICUT, is a celebration of P.T. BARNUM's life and contributions to the American circus, as well as his adopted home.

During the 1880s, the Bridgeport Scientific Society and the Fairfield County Historical Society accumulated large collections and memberships; but neither group had a permanent home. Barnum suggested the construction of a single edifice that would house both associations; he offered to finance the construction of the museum that would posthumously bear his name.

In February 1893, a full two years after Barnum's death, the official opening of the Institute was held. The building was designed and built by Longstaff and Hurd, the same architects that designed Barnum's fourth and last Bridgeport mansion, Marina.

Located at 820 Main Street (at the corner of Gilbert) in downtown Bridgeport, the Institute is a mix of architectural styles. The exterior of the first floor is covered with red sandstone. The upper floors boast a terra-cotta frieze that contains five scenes depicting Bridgeport in different historical eras: Indian (1670), Early Settler (1760), Maritime (1840), Civil War (1861) and Industrial (1870). A huge, red-tile dome topped by an eagle rises above the main entrance. The rear of the building contains a small, round tower, which was planned as an observatory.

With one room specifically set aside for the Bridgeport Medical Society, Barnum foresaw that the first floor would be leased out to meet expenses. Since this plan was never carried out, the organizations never maintained financial stability; by the turn of the century, the societies' memberships were at an all-time low.

The first floor was finally rented out in the 1920s, but in the 1930s the city of Bridgeport foreclosed on the building for unpaid taxes. The Institute became an annex to City Hall, and the top floor was opened briefly in 1936 during the city centennial to display part of the stored collections.

The Institute was reopened in 1968 as the Barnum Museum, focusing not only on P.T. Barnum and the circus but on Bridgeport history as well. Many would argue that the two are inseparably linked.

From 1982 until 1984 major renovation was done on the original structure; shortly after, People's Bank of Connecticut located its new corporate headquarters, Bridgeport Center, next to the museum. The Barnum Museum Foundation was created; by linking the Bank and museum's resources with the community spirit, the museum was greatly enlarged.

The first floor exhibits Barnum family heirlooms as well as a faithful recreation of the library in Barnum's first Bridgeport mansion, IRANISTAN. A six-foot animated statue of Barnum introduces a time line of world events during the showman's life. An ongoing introductory videotape by John Goberman (the host of *Live from Lincoln Center*) includes segments from the 1986 made-for-TELEVISION movie *Barnum*, which starred Burt Lancaster. Also on the main floor is the entrance to a new wing of the museum, a 7,000-square foot addition built to house original and touring historical displays.

Visitors climb the original terra-cotta–lined, curved staircase to the second floor. Exhibits there illustrate Bridgeport life in the 1800s and Barnum's interac-

The Barnum Museum, once the Barnum Institute of Science and History, was a gift from the master showman to his adopted home of Bridgeport, Connecticut. (Photo by Tom Ogden)

tion with the city. The next gallery depicts, in order, Barnum's four great Bridgeport residences: Iranistan, Lindencroft, Waldemere and Marina.

The third and uppermost floor is devoted entirely to "Barnum: The Showman to the World." The first gallery is dedicated to Barnum's three museums, the AMERICAN MUSEUM and the rebuilt New American Museum (both in New York City) and the current Barnum Museum. Also in the room is a recreation of a Punch and Judy show, a British puppet classic that Barnum is credited with introducing into American SIDESHOWS.

Among other treasures that can be seen are antique circus BANNERS and recreations of famous Barnum hoaxes, such as the FEEJEE MERMAID, a two-headed calf and a fragment from Noah's Ark. Two major exhibits tout the careers of Jenny LIND (in-

cluding her contract with Barnum and the White House piano, which she used in her performance for President Milliard Fillmore) and TOM THUMB with his wife Lavinia WARREN (including some of their furniture, clothing, wedding certificate and carriages).

A final gallery honoring CLOWNS leads to a true masterpiece by William Brinley of Meriden, Connecticut—a complete circus, hand-carved in wooden miniature and covering 1,000 square feet.

The Barnum Institute of Science and History, now the modern Barnum Museum, survives as P.T. Barnum's last gift to his adopted city of Bridgeport.

BARNUM'S GREAT TRAVELING MUSEUM, MENAGERIE, CARAVAN, HIPPODROME AND CIRCUS Following the fire that destroyed his second AMERICAN MUSEUM in March 1868, P.T. BARNUM retired to his home in Connecticut.

His break from show business was short-lived, however; a former ROUSTABOUT and SIDESHOW manager, William Cameron COUP, and ex-clown Dan CASTELLO, persuaded Barnum to join forces with them in the creation of a new circus and MENAGERIE. The two men figured that their experience, coupled with Barnum's name, would guarantee success.

P.T. Barnum finally entered the world of circuses when Barnum's Great Traveling Museum, Menagerie, Caravan, Hippodrome and Circus opened under canvas on April 10, 1871 in Brooklyn, New York. Coup became general manager, Castello was director of amusements and Barnum was, of course, in charge of advertising and promotion.

In 1872 the show went on its first railroad tour. A method to expedite loading and unloading after long overnight hauls was needed, and W.C. Coup is generally credited with inventing the end-loading system of getting cars and wagons on and off the CIRCUS TRAINS.

The show itself opened with a grand SPEC, and each year it offered new attractions. The attached sideshow featured midgets, giants and the Fiji Cannibals. The menagerie boasted sea lions, in addition to the usual assortment of African wild beasts.

During the winter, shows were held in the HIPPOTHEATRON in New York City. The amphitheater was destroyed by fire in 1873, so to house his show the next year the showmen leased the property at 26th and Madison, calling it P.T. BARNUM'S GREAT

ROMAN HIPPODROME, later the first MADISON SQUARE GARDEN.

By the end of the 1875 season, Castello had already retired from the partnership. Coup also became unhappy with the alliance, arguing that Barnum was allowing his name to be used by other, disreputable circus owners.

Coup left the association; Barnum, anxious to find a new manager, turned over the circus operation to the FLATFOOTS, which handled the show until its dissolution in 1880. Barnum continued to add attractions to the show, however; as late as 1880 he introduced a tattooed lady, a hairy-faced boy and Mlle. ZAZEL, "The First Human Cannonball."

(See also AMERICAN MUSEUM.)

BARSTOW, RICHARD   See CHOREOGRAPHY, CIRCUS.

BARTON & BAILEY CIRCUS   See WIEDEMANN BROS. BIG AMERICAN SHOWS.

BASKET ANIMAL   A clown prop, a basket animal is a small, step-through frame with an attached head and body that resembles some sort of beast from the MENAGERIE. The "basket" is attached to the performer's waist and is usually held up by straps over the clown's shoulders. The molded body of the animal might be made of papier-mâché or, for durability, fiberglass.

Dummy legs nailed to the bottom of the basket make it look as if the clown is sitting on the animal. In truth, of course, the performer's legs extend down through the middle of the basket animal's body to the ground.

Basket animals are often seen in the SPEC or as a CLOWN WALKAROUND.

BATCHELOR & DORIS CIRCUS   John B. Doris and George F. Batchelor were concessions managers on various circuses in the late 1800s, and they were successful enough to team together in 1879 to form their own show, the Batchelor & Doris Circus.

After 1882 the show was changed to the John B. Doris Inter-Ocean Circus, but in 1888, operating costs and competition forced the show, by then operating as the Doris & Colvin Circus, to close.

BAUMANN, CHARLY (1928–   )   Charly Baumann spent 35 years as a trainer of wild tigers,

chronicled in his autobiography, *Tiger Tiger*, before becoming the executive PERFORMANCE DIRECTOR of the RINGLING BROS. AND BARNUM & BAILEY CIRCUS.

His father, a famous movie actor and stuntman in Germany, died at the Bergen-Belsen concentration camp in the Holocaust during World War II. Born in Berlin, Charly worked briefly as a stable boy for the ravaged postwar Circus Busch. Baumann's first real circus experience, however, was as an assistant to Harry Williams, the owner and equestrian of Hamburg's Circus Williams. For a time, one of his co-apprentices was the young Gunther Gebel. (See Gunther GEBEL-WILLIAMS.)

In 1950 Charly Baumann saved the life of cat trainer Jean Michon during a lion attack. Michon and the CATS had been leased to Circus Williams by Eric Klant, the owner of a Dutch zoo. Klant sent Baumann a reward of $50 for saving Michon's life, along with a contract as a wild animal trainer. With no previous experience with the giant felines and two weeks to learn the act, Charly Baumann began his career in the BIG CAGE.

Baumann took over an existing lion act, but his ambition was to work with tigers. In 1957 he had the opportunity to perform his eight-tiger act with various circuses all over Europe, including a tour into the Soviet Union.

Charly Baumann practiced the training methods espoused by Karl HÄGENBACH, that brute force couldn't achieve "one-hundredth part of what can be done by humane and intelligent methods." After joining THE BIG ONE in 1964 at the request of Irvin FELD, Charly Baumann perfected his trademark trick: the simultaneous roll-over of several tigers. The stunt is hard enough with one tiger; but, because tigers inherently dislike rubbing fur, training two or more to turn over while lying side by side is not only difficult but incredibly dangerous. Eventually, at the urging of Feld, Baumann worked the trick up to a five-tiger multiple roll-over. Another of Charly Baumann's unique stunts was coaxing two tigers to simultaneously jump through flaming hoops.

Irvin Feld rewarded Baumann's obvious knack for patience and attention to detail by naming him assistant performance director of the Blue Unit in 1969 and then performance director, beginning with the 1971 season. Not all of Baumann's peers welcomed the announcement: Baumann himself admitted, "I found my time in the tiger cage ten times easier than dealing with people as performance director." Nevertheless, he effectively worked in the dual capacity of trainer and performance director for 13 years. "Since I had spent my life performing," Baumann said, "I have the ability to understand our circus performers' needs and concerns."

Baumann retired from the steel arena in Cleveland in 1983, after giving 10,196 performances. He remained on as performance director. In 1989 Kenneth FELD named Charly Baumann executive performance director for both units, a position he held until his retirement from the show at the end of the 1991 season.

BEARDED LADY   See BARNUM, P.T.; CLOFULLIA, MADAME JOSEPHINE; FREAKS; SIDESHOW.

BEARS   Long before bears became a staple of the traveling MENAGERIE or of the circus ring, frontiersmen were returning from the forests in 18th-century colonial America with their captive creatures. The bears would be led to taverns and exhibited by the rustic entrepeneurs in exchange for money, food or a night's lodging.

In April 1733 in Boston the first exotic, nonnative bear (a polar bear dubbed the "ferocious Greenland bear") was exhibited in the American colonies. Following the lion (1716) and the CAMEL (1721), the polar bear was probably the third exotic animal to be exhibited in North America.

When bears were included in the touring zoos, it soon became apparent that they were the most unpredictable of all wild animals, even more so than lions and tigers. They were also the most ferocious and tenacious. While a cat launches a single attack or swipe at the trainer and retreats (or is repulsed), a bear continues to attack until killing its prey. Once a bear has set teeth into flesh, nothing can beat it off—not even a full stream of water from a water hose or blank pistols shot directly in the face. The roly-poly, jolly-looking bear is, at heart, a natural killer.

Perhaps this is one reason why bear acts are so popular. On the outside, the big balls of fur seem cute and cuddly; but everyone is aware of the darker, more dangerous side of the brute waiting to strike. The fact that bears always appear in the ring muzzled accentuates the two sides of their nature.

Polar bears, the most impulsive bruins, began to appear regularly in menageries during the time of the ZOOLOGICAL INSTITUTE in the mid-1830s. When seen on circuses, they are often advertised on posters as rare attractions. The bears seen in the BIG TOP are usually large Russian Kodiak bears. One of the earliest star trainers in the United States was Emil PALLENBERG, a German emigrant, who brought his act to the RINGLING BROS. AND BARNUM & BAILEY CIRCUS in 1914. Among the many tricks that trainers such as Pallenberg, Louis ROTH and Clyde BEATTY have taught their bears to perform are riding a bicycle, walking a tightrope, roller skating around the ring and turning somersaults.

BEATTY, CLYDE (1903–1965)   One of the premier animal trainers in circus history, Clyde (Raymond) Beatty saw his first circus, the SUN BROS. CIRCUS (also known as the Sun Brothers World Progressive Shows) in his hometown of Bainbridge, Ohio, at the age of nine. He was so impressed by the tiger act that he put on his own child's version of a wild animal show in his backyard with a MENAGERIE that included his household pets.

When he was 17, Beatty ran away from home to join Howes' Great London Circus, then a railroad circus owned by the AMERICAN CIRCUS CORPORATION. For $5 a month plus room and board, he was a CAGE BOY for the famous Hungarian animal trainer Louis ROTH. Finally, when the regular polar bear trainer left the show, Roth allowed Beatty to take over the act.

In 1922 Beatty moved to the GOLLMAR BROS. CIRCUS (actually the Howes' show under a different name), where he served under trainer John "Chubby" Guilfoyle and began work with four or five polar BEARS. When one of the bears grabbed him during a training session, Beatty instinctively punched him in the nose. The bruin somersaulted backward. Soon the somersault itself became a "trick" in Beatty's act. Beatty also taught the bears to march in a circle and ride bicycles, adding these unique tricks to the standard repertoire of the dancing bears. In 1923 the show combined with the JOHN ROBINSON CIRCUS; and Beatty began working with lion trainer Peter Taylor.

Beatty was traveling with his new mentor on the HAGENBECK-WALLACE CIRCUS in 1925 when Taylor suffered a nervous breakdown. Beatty, still in his 20s, filled in and became the youngest wild animal trainer in the country. In 1926 he became celebrated for putting 40 male and female lions and tigers into the cage at one time.

It was at this time that Beatty developed his trademark dress as a stereotypical African safari hunter—wielding a whip, carrying a revolver and wearing a pith helmet, white breeches and shirt, and black boots and belt. Beatty was aware of the fact that a cat became confused and would back away from a chair that had its legs directed at it, so a metal-reinforced chair also became part of the act.

Interestingly, while Beatty pronounced his own name "Bay-tee," circus people invariably pronounced it—and the later circuses bearing his name—"Bee-tee." Billed as "the youngest and most fearless wild animal trainer," Beatty appeared in 1931 at the MADISON SQUARE GARDEN and Boston stands only of the RINGLING BROS. AND BARNUM & BAILEY CIRCUS. Clyde Beatty was the first lion and tiger act to appear with The BIG ONE since John RINGLING stopped using cat acts in 1926.

In 1932 Beatty was seriously wounded when he was mauled by Nero, one of his most powerful lions. Beatty was close to death for several days, with a fever peaking at 106 degrees because modern antibiotics had not yet been developed. His recovery was slow, but he did manage to make his Garden dates for the 1933 and 1934 seasons.

By then Clyde Beatty was a "movie star," having made two films (see FILMS, CIRCUS), *The Big Cage* (1933) and *The Lost Jungle* (1934). Sam GUMPERTZ, manager of The Big One after the show's takeover by the ALLIED OWNERS, INC., felt that Beatty was giving too much time and attention to Hollywood. He didn't understand that Beatty's two films could only help to publicize the circus.

In 1935 Beatty was approached by Jess Adkins and Zack Terrell who were reviving the "Cole Brothers" title with equipment from the old CHRISTY BROS. CIRCUS and ROBBINS BROS. CIRCUS. When Beatty accepted their offer of performing in the CENTER RING as well as lending his name to the enterprise, the COLE BROTHERS & CLYDE BEATTY CIRCUS was formed.

Like many American shows in the economically disastrous year of 1938, the COLE BROS. CIRCUS closed early. Beatty, along with several other acts, moved over to Robbins Bros. Circus, another Adkins and Terrell show; but he soon decided to work independently. He worked the Steel Pier in Atlantic City, then opened his own Clyde Beatty Jungle Zoo in Fort Lauderdale, Florida. As that small community boomed into a tourist resort, neighbors complained about the compound, and Beatty was forced to close the zoo in 1945.

Beatty returned to the steel arena. The "magic" of his name, seen with the Cole Brothers show a decade earlier, was repeated again in 1944 when his name alone proved to be a major attraction. It was added to the title of another great show, the RUSSELL BROS. CIRCUS. The CLYDE BEATTY & RUSSELL BROS. CIRCUS toured for one season with Beatty as star and Art CONCELLO as manager.

In 1945 Beatty took out a motorized show under his own name, employing apparatus from the Wallace Bros. Circus. The next season, however, he formed a new rail show, the CLYDE BEATTY CIRCUS. Except for the Ringling show, the Clyde Beatty Circus was the largest on rails by 1950.

In 1956 bad weather, small audiences and a strike forced Beatty to CLOSE AHEAD OF PAPER in Burbank, California on May 9 after only 43 days on the road. Despite listing debts of $280,000 against $260 worth of assets, Beatty was able to reopen in August and tour successfully through November before returning to his new De Land, Florida WINTER QUARTERS.

The show was saved from bankruptcy by the Acme Circus Corporation, made up of a triumvirate of entrepreneurs—Frank McClosky, Walter Kernan and Jerry Collins. In 1957 they acquired the old Cole Bros. Circus title and recombined the two, this time as the CLYDE BEATTY-COLE BROS. CIRCUS. Beatty became the star of the show, and he remained with it until his death in 1965.

In his 1933 autobiography *The Big Cage,* in *Facing the Big Cats* and in his later books and interviews, Clyde Beatty discussed many of his discoveries and principles of working with CATS. According to Beatty, the secret to remaining unhurt was in always maintaining dominance, while at the same time showing care and respect for the animal. He felt mixed jungle cats made a more exciting show, and in the event of a free-for-all it would actually work to the trainer's advantage: The lions and tigers hated each other more than they hated man. Beatty claimed jungle cats were smarter than animals born in captivity, and the latter tended to be lazy, spoiled and more unruly. He preferred to work with jungle creatures rather than bottle-fed cats because the latter are pampered and seldom punished. By the time they are old enough to train, any punishment—however light—sends them into a ferocious attack.

Common sense seemed to dictate that cats should be fed before a performance so they wouldn't want to attack the trainer; but Beatty noticed that feeding only made them sleepy, not necessarily less menacing. He sensed that the cats not only enjoyed grinding bones in raw meat with their teeth, but they also seemed happier. Also, contrary to popular belief, Beatty knew cats did more damage with their teeth than with their claws—a fact he could attest to, having been mauled dozens of times.

Most important, Beatty realized that a wild animal can only be "trained," it can never be truly "tamed." His guiding principles were never turn your back on an angry cat and always keep a clear path between yourself and the cage door.

At the end of his career, Beatty continued to appear in many circus films as well as on TELEVISION and radio. He died of cancer on July 19, 1965.

BEERS-BARNES CIRCUS   Beginning as a tented repertoire show in 1932, the Beers-Barnes show eventually changed into a circus format. The motorized show was operated by Mrs. George Beers, her son Charles, her son-in-law Roger Barnes and their families.

BENSON BROS. CIRCUS   Formerly touring as the Kelly-Morris Circus, the Benson Bros. Circus traveled as a small, motorized tent show, operated by William Morris throughout the 1950s.

BENTLEY BROS. CIRCUS   An unlikely meeting between two men, Tom Bentley and Charles Clancy, resulted in one of the hardest-working arena three-ring circuses on the road today.

Bentley was born in West Virginia and ran away from home to join the circus. He became a top high wire walker, juggler, bareback rider, TRAPEZE artist, dog trainer and DRESSAGE rider. He even filled in for ailing elephant and lion trainers on occasion.

Clancy was a banker in Boston, Massachusetts; but when the bank cut back operations and wanted to move him to an undesirable department, Clancy left. He became an auditor for the East Coast office

of a California circus. The office was being managed by Bentley.

Bentley was, of course, not thrilled about seeing an auditor. When Clancy discovered that Bentley had overpaid the home office and owed himself $1,800 in commissions, however, the two men became friends. Clancy admired Bentley's honesty; Bentley respected Clancy's business sense. They formed M. Charles Productions, dba Bentley Bros. Circus.

Today Clancy is the administrator, watching expenses and serving as the authority on interstate travel. He also supervises the many regional offices and manages the books. Bentley has the hands-on experience. As executive producer, he stages the shows, hires the acts, writes the contracts and covers publicity.

Often setting up open-air in ballparks and stadiums, Bentley Bros. Circus's rigging is versatile enough to allow indoor theater dates and work under canvas. After years of blue-sky dates, in 1991 the Bentley Bros. Circus bought a BIG TOP from Vicki and George Hanneford, Jr. (see the HANNEFORDS), for selected dates. Their route has covered the country from California to Pennsylvania; their offices are now located in Gibsonton, Florida, the home of Tommy Bentley.

BERGERON, BEV   See CLOWNS, TELEVISION.

BIBLES   In the plural, the term "bibles" is circus jargon for programs or souvenir booklets.

The Bible, however, is circus slang for the *BILLBOARD*, once the most important and comprehensive industry newspaper for the outdoor amusement industry. A weekly magazine, *Billboard* lost its standing as the definitive source for circus news in 1960 when its focus began to shift to the recording industry.

BIG APPLE CIRCUS, THE   Almost simultaneous to the organization of the PICKLE FAMILY CIRCUS in 1974 on the West Coast, The Big Apple Circus was reintroducing the one-ring circus format under canvas to the East Coast. Although some single-ring DOG AND PONY SHOWS still performed here and there in the United States, The Big Apple Circus was the first since the days of the railroad shows to attempt to reach major eastern seaboard markets with a European-style under-canvas show.

Bentley Bros. Circus open-air stadium setup.   (Photo by Tom Ogden)

The circus performs in an intimate tent where no one sits more than 50 feet from the ring. Each year a totally new show is created around a theme; and the use of original music, lighting, CHOREOGRAPHY, sets and costumes blends with classical circus elements and acts to create a theatrical sensation. Every year The Big Apple Circus consists of veteran favorite performers as well as many new acts. Guest performers have come from 21 different countries.

The spectacular annual production had humble beginnings. In 1975 Paul BINDER and Michael Christensen took their comic JUGGLING act to Europe, joining the Nouveau Cirque de Paris. After a season with the show, they temporarily split; Binder returned to New York City with the idea of forming a one-ring circus in America. At his birthday party in mid-October 1976, he pitched an idea to his friends: "The New York School for Circus Arts Presents The Big Apple Circus!"

Binder's friends were mesmerized and galvanized. Karen Gersch, an artist living in a loft/studio on 17th Street, remembered seeing a poster on a newsstand three years earlier. It showed two Russian State Circus performers who had emigrated to the United States. Gersch tracked them down, and Gregory Fedin and Nina Krasavina became the two primary acrobatic trainers for the first season. Although at the time they lived in Hartford, Connecticut, they began to commute to the city four days a week to begin work with a few students—in Gersch's loft! Soon a regular rehearsal studio was rented on Spring Street in Soho.

Fedin and Krasavina were tireless as trainers and astounding in their performance technique. Gregory Fedin explained:

Would you like to know our great secret? We do not see acrobat, we see space. There's no difference between space and acrobat because we are absolutely dissolved in the space of the universe. And if you are able to see space, the acrobat has to go through it . . . go with the curves, like the tracks of a railway. When he does not fit the curves of space, he's not a good acrobat. If he follows the lines correctly, he's a good acrobat; he fits in. The curves of space are the rails for the acrobatic tricks.

Richard Levy, an economist and teacher, started canvassing New York in search of business donors and contributors from society. Another friend, Carol Brightman, helped write the official corporate proposal, and Levy convinced Chase Manhattan Bank to pay for printing it.

Meanwhile, Binder took a quick trip to Paris to bring his old partner on board. Michael Christensen agreed to perform a "trained mole act" for the circus. Amateur and seasoned performers gathered at the studio, including six black streetwise teenage gymnasts who put together an act called "The Back Street Flyers." Michael Moschen—whose artistic work is too extraordinary to be confined by the mundane word "juggling"—also joined the troupe.

A tentative ten-act show was set, including Paul and Michael's Comedy Juggling, Nina & Gregory's Clown Acrobatics and Perch-Pole Act, Michael Moschen's juggling and Fire Torches, Michael Christensen's imaginary trained moles, aerialist Susan Perry, Paul Lubera on TRAPEZE, "The Back Street Flyers," a learned dog and a group of Argentine dancers named Los Indianos.

Binder continued to make the rounds with Levy, trying to enlist contributors. At one of the meetings, they met Maggie Heimann, an enthusiastic patron who suggested they contact Alan Slifka, an investment banker, his wife and William Woodward, a community leader. The three were brought onto the board of directors, with Alan Slifka as chairman.

Meanwhile, the production manager, Michael Davidson, was attempting to get the required permits to put up the tent anywhere in the city. The possible site for the show LOT had been narrowed down to Battery Park or Battery City Park landfill, a barren stretch along the Hudson River. When permits were rejected for the former, the latter won by default. When they went to Queens a few days later to pick up the tent that had been ordered, the troupe discovered that only the aluminum poles were in New York. A "subcontractor" in Boston was still stitching the canvas. Finally, the top was delivered to the lot at 5:30 A.M. on July 9, 1977; but when they tried to erect the tent, it only went halfway up. Warren Bacon, a trained aerialist and experienced tent RIGGER who had returned from Taiwan to be

part of the troupe, made a scale drawing of the tent that had been delivered. The tent makers had cut the canvas too small—five feet were missing!

Philippe PETIT, who had made a famous walk on a wire strung between the twin towers of the World Trade Center in 1974, inspected the half-raised tent. A friend of Binder and Christensen from their days in Paris, Petit explained a way to "jimmy-rig" the equipment, shifting the tension to allow the deficient canvas to be raised. Raising the top, which should have taken five hours, took two weeks.

After a year of struggle, The Big Apple Circus had been established as a not-for-profit performing arts organization. On July 20, 1977 the first resident circus in New York City in 80 years called DOORS! for its first season. The total attendance for the summer run was 45,000 people.

Paul Binder was artistic director, manager and RINGMASTER for the circus. At first, Binder also worked in the ring with Christensen as a juggler and a clown (Binder was an AUGUSTE CLOWN; Christensen worked as a WHITEFACE CLOWN). Binder later focused his full attention on his work as an announcer, while Christensen switched his character to a TRAMP CLOWN, creating "Mr. Stubs."

With the help of Christensen and associate director Dominique Jando, Binder set out to develop an all-new show each season. Jando, a circus historian, had been general secretary to the Cirque Gruss in Paris for ten years and head of its circus school. Jando was appointed the first head of The New York School for Circus Arts, which also opened in 1977.

The other major event in the circus's history to take place that year was the establishment of The Big Apple Circus Ticket Fund, which provided tickets free of charge to senior citizens and disadvantaged or handicapped children. Since its inception, the fund has given away over 250,000 free tickets.

In 1978 a spring and summer edition of the show toured the outer boroughs of New York; for fall and winter the Manhattan location moved from Battery Park to Eighth Avenue and 50th Street. By the following year, the circus's Arts in Education program was introduced to provide inner-city teens with circus training skills as part of their in-school curriculum.

In early 1980 circus members, along with performers from the RINGLING BROS. AND BARNUM &

BAILEY CIRCUS, helped to train some of the cast from the Broadway musical *Barnum,* which opened that year on April 30 (see THEATER).

Also that year, Danish equestrienne Katja Schumann, born into one of the circus world's oldest and most celebrated families, joined the show. Circus Schumann was founded in 1870 and firmly established in Denmark in 1891. The daughter of *maître ecuyer* (master horseman) Max Schumann, and great-great-great-granddaughter of the circus's founder, Katja made her debut in the ring as a ballerina on horseback at the age of ten. Today, she is a renowned DRESSAGE rider and a trainer of LIBERTY HORSES. Before going to The Big Apple Circus, she had won the Prix de la Dame du Cirque at the International Circus Festival of Monte Carlo in 1974 and the gold medal at the Circus World Championships in London in 1976. In her private life, she married Paul Binder in 1985.

To close out 1980, Lincoln Center's Damrosch Park became the annual Christmas season location for The Big Apple Circus's holiday run. Within a decade, the December stand grew into an 11-week engagement of 111 performances, followed by a 20-week tour.

MUSIC, an essential ingredient to any successful circus, was at the forefront in 1981 when Big Apple became the first American circus to have a composer-in-residence to write original music for the show and individual acts. Beginning in late 1981, movie audiences were able to see the circus in sequences of the film version of *Annie* (see FILMS, CIRCUS).

In 1982 a Big Apple Circus tradition started when Barry Lubin first presented his "Grandma" character as part of the show. A 1975 graduate of CLOWN COLLEGE, Lubin first created "Grandma" at the Venice, Florida school and had clowned with The BIG ONE through 1979.

A special OBIE, off-Broadway's award for achievement in the theater, was given for artistic excellence to The Big Apple Circus in 1983. That spring and summer, the show left New York City for the first time to go on tour. The route included several New England towns.

In 1984 the offices of the Arts in Education program—which reaches 40 to 80 inner-city students between the ages of 12 to 15 in grades 7 to 9 annually—moved to Harbor Junior High School for the Performing Arts on 109th Street in East Harlem. The students learn acrobatics, juggling, tumbling, WIRE WALKING, clowning and the history of the circus. In 1990, 18-year-old Carlos Guity became the first Circus Arts student to graduate to become a full-time performer with the regular Big Apple Circus troupe.

In 1985 the circus—in collaboration with the Boston Pops Orchestra—was featured on a PBS-television special, *Pops Joins the Circus.*

Ever since the ground-breaking book *Anatomy of an Illness* by Norman Cousins first established a possible link between laughing and wellness, "humor therapy" has been a topic of discussion among health-care workers worldwide. In 1986 The Big Apple Circus joined the ranks of "health professionals" when Michael Christensen (founder and director) and Jeff Gordon—under the circus sponsorship and initial funding from the Altman Foundation—started the Clown Care Unit (CCU) at Babies Hospital of the Columbia-Presbyterian Medical Center. It became the first hospital to be staffed by "clown doctors"—Christensen's "Dr. Stubs," Gordon's "Disorderly Gordoon" and Lubin's "Grandma," among others.

Jeff Gordon had been one of the first clowns with The Big Apple Circus before concentrating his work on the CCU. His character, "Gordoon," is a well-intentioned "klutz." His best-known routine involves being covered head-to-toe in a shower of toilet tissue. "The great privilege of a clown is to transform an ordinary object into a magical one," Gordon observed. "Making the ordinary extraordinary—that's what I love about clowning."

The Big Apple Circus Clown Care Unit is a project that helps sick children by utilizing humor. Through their work, the clowns are able to bring joy, excitement and fun—at least for a short time—back into the lives of the children and families of the chronically ill. In many cases, the humor has been a pathway for a child to "open up" verbally to a clown, to discuss feelings or to give unexpected positive physical responses.

The year 1987 marked the tenth anniversary of The Big Apple Circus as a tented show, and real estate developer Donald Trump helped the celebration by donating a new blue-and-white BIG TOP, custom-made in Italy with an improved seating plan for 1,980 people. The five-story tent is 47 feet high,

137 feet in diameter and is actually heated in the winter season. The 1987 spring and summer tour included Boston, Philadelphia and Washington, D.C.

In 1988 members of the troupe took part in the Premiere Rampe Festival, a circus school competition, held annually in Monte Carlo. The circus's Student Troupe won a silver cup from the Monte Carlo's daily newspaper *Le Journal Nice Matin* and one from their peers, the Junior Jury.

That same year another member of the cast, Dolly Jacobs, an internationally acclaimed aerialist on the ROMAN RINGS and the daughter of famous clown Lou JACOBS, took home the Silver Clown Award from the International Circus Festival, also held in Monte Carlo. She had been introduced to the rings by her godmother, Margie Geiger (of the Flying WALLENDAS). Jacobs came to prefer the freedom of movement of the Roman rings over the solo trapeze. Her literally death-defying finale is a somersault release from the rings to a Spanish web. The trick had been perfected and last performed in the 1930s by Frank Shepherd. Her act had won her the Prix de la Dame du Cirque at the Monte Carlo Circus Festival in 1977.

In 1988 the Nanjing Acrobatic Troupe from China made their American debut with The Big Apple Circus. Their gymnastic performances, directed by Lu YI, were seen again in 1989.

Meanwhile, the work of the Clown Care Unit was growing; by 1989 the CCU was making rounds in eight New York City hospitals, with over 50,000 visits each year. "Clown rounds" gave patients such surprises as rubber nose transplants and chocolate milk transfusions.

That same year the Student Troupe was invited to perform as part of the International Children's Festival at Wolf Trap Farm Park, Vienna, Virginia before 35,000 people.

By 1989 The Big Apple Circus had become big business, with an annual fund-raising drive of $1.5 million and performing before more than 400,000 people. It had come a long way from its first small show on the Battery Park City landfill. To help guide it into the 1990s, James C. McIntyre was named executive director.

For the 1990–91 season, the Panteleenkos—famed Russian aerialists—became the first Soviet guest artists to perform with an American circus. The tour moved westward to include Pittsburgh, Columbus, Chicago and Cleveland, with a theme of "Ballerinas, Horses & Clowns: The Golden Age."

Among the many featured acts in the 1992 extravaganza "Goin' Places" were two extraordinary Russian acts, The Egorov Troupe (aerialists) and Vladimir Tsarkov (an acrobat, juggler and mime). Making his American debut, and appearing with daughter Katja and granddaughter Katherine Rose Binder, was the legendary equestrian Max Schumann.

Paul Binder has remained the guiding inspiration for the circus as artistic director as well as usually performing as ringmaster. Despite conceptual differences of opinion, he is nevertheless a big fan of the so-called rival new-vaudeville circuses. In a Glenn Collins interview for the *New York Times,* Binder said, "I loved Circus Oz. And I think Cirque du Soleil is an extraordinary show. But neither show had the elements of circus I deem essential." By that he meant animals—especially horses—and sawdust. "It's said they're reinventing the circus form, but they've really created a new form. They've taken variety arts and created exciting shows with new technology—and a new sensibility—but without the soul and heart and warmth of a circus."

Unlike the Pickle Family Circus, CIRCUS OZ and the more recent CIRQUE DU SOLEIL—to which it is invariably compared—The Big Apple Circus has always felt that animals are an essential part of the circus tradition. In the 1991 season alone the show featured: two ELEPHANTS (47-year-old Anna May and six-year-old Baby Ned, trained by Bill Woodcock Jr.—who since 1982 has trained all of The Big Apple Circus bulls, including 37-year-old Peggy, who is also frequently featured); three ponies; and 12 HORSES (under the guidance of Master Equestrienne Katja Schumann; and four trained pigs.

Despite the artful look and state-of-the-art sound and lighting used in The Big Apple Circus, Paul Binder has said the use of animals

represents our stubborn refusal to give in to high tech. High tech won't give you real people. Circus is about families in and out of the ring; it's about man's relationship to animals and man's closeness to nature and the earth. Circus is a ritual form, the closest of all modern theatrical forms to the original tribal rites that became theater.

In *The Magic Ring* by Hana Machotka, Binder expounded.

Like those rituals, we transform the audience, taking it to another dimension. We can see this happen in their faces. Even the performers are transformed. How do we do this? We create magic. We use natural forces to create extraordinary things. The ugliness of the everyday world is transformed. And by making what we do look easy, we show people that they can go on, survive, and conquer their difficulties.

BIG BERTHA Circus jargon, a nickname for the RINGLING BROS. AND BARNUM & BAILEY CIRCUS. (See also The BIG ONE.)

BIG BLOW-OUT See FIRE-EATING; HUMAN VOLCANO.

BIG CAGE Circus jargon for the caged arena in which the wild trainer works with the CATS.

Usually the cat act is performed immediately after SPEC at the beginning of the show or as the first act after intermission. That way, the big cage can be set and ready. Individual animal cages are set end to end to form a long tunnel through which the cats enter the arena. At the end of the act, the cats are driven down the chute individually, and as each lion gets into its respective cage, a barred door is dropped to separate it from the next. This chain of cages can then be pulled from the arena and separated for ease of handling and loading.

The Big Cage is also the title of Clyde BEATTY's first autobiography as well as a subsequent 1933 Universal movie vaguely based on it (see FILMS, CIRCUS).

BIG CAGE, THE See BEATTY, CLYDE; FILMS, CIRCUS.

BIG JOHN STRONG CIRCUS See STRONG, "BIG" JOHN.

BIG ONE, THE Circus jargon, a nickname for the RINGLING BROS. AND BARNUM & BAILEY CIRCUS. Less frequently used is the term "BIG BERTHA."

BIG TOP Circus jargon for the largest tent on the LOT, in which the main show is performed. (See also TENTS.)

BILLBOARD From 1894 until 1960, *Billboard* magazine was considered the "Bible" of the circus industry. Although a sister magazine established in 1894, *Amusment Business*, known as *AB*, also carried informative articles on the outdoor amusement trade, it was *Billboard* that catered more to needs and interests of the circus world. Together, they supplanted the NEW YORK CLIPPER, which from May 1853 to July 1924 also carried circus news.

The weekly *Billboard* printed a combination of news and reviews sent in by stringer correspondents across the country, along with press agents' puff pieces. It was from *Billboard* that acts learned what was going on in the circus world; the March issues would even be filled with listings that told acts and workingmen when and where to report for the beginning of the new season.

The circus industry (along with the entire world of outdoor amusements) declined as radio, recordings, film and television blossomed. *Billboard* reacted by changing its coverage in 1961, focusing more on the music industry; today the magazine gives only nominal space to circus and carnival news.

(See also CIRCUS REPORT.)

BILLING CREW Part of the team that came to town in advance of the circus, the billing crew has always had one of the most important jobs in advertising the show. Today's circuses tend to concentrate their advertising on newspaper space and radio spots, but before 1900 (and even into the first third of this century) the colorful display of LITHOGRAPHS throughout the town was essential to a big box office on circus day.

Timing was essential in the arrival of the billing crew to a town; usually it came two or three weeks before the show date. The posters that would be pasted on the walls of buildings—and the WINDOW CARDS left in merchants' shops—had to appear close enough to circus day for the event to be fresh in the minds of the townspeople, but not so far away that people might think the date had already past. A new display in an unexpected location piqued interest, but if it was seen too often the prospective patron would walk by, no longer noticing it. Also, if the bill was there too long, it ran the risk of being damaged by weather or torn down by mischievous children, disgruntled townsfolk or another organization that wanted the space to advertise its own event. Today's crews must be wary of circus collectors who sometimes remove PAPER before the show takes place, inadvertently hurting the circus's chance for successful business.

Eddie Schmitt in the big cage of the Bentley Bros. Circus in Harrisburg, Pennsylvania in 1990.   (Photo by Tom Ogden)

In the heydey of the tented show, many circuses would play the same town during the season. If the second show became aware of the first circus's routing, it would often send in its billing crew to destroy the competition's bills. Known as OPPOSITION PAPER, the second crew usually pasted *over* the first circus's bills rather than taking the time to remove the first. To this day, major circuses release their route only a few weeks in advance because another circus might try to book in ahead and repaper the town.

During the days of the rail shows, billers had their own car. The larger shows, which had to paper a wider territory to attract enough customers to fill their tents, sometimes sent out more cars. Until the 1930s, for example, RINGLING BROS. AND BARNUM & BAILEY CIRCUS sent three in advance of the show. Regardless of the number, the bill car acted as a combination home and office, with a portion of the rail car set aside for the storage of the lithographs

as well as the water and boiler tanks to make the billing paste.

The bill poster had to be agile and dexterous. Tacking or pasting one or more litho sheets into position often required working on high ladders or swinging from a scaffold.

When paste would not hold a poster, the BANNER man would ascend the ladder with a mouthful of nails, spit out a tack at the head of his magnetic hammer, then bang it into place, all in one motion. Men who were skilled at this were known as tack spitters. These workers always carried a fresh, moist loaf of bread up the ladder with them as well. If a man accidentally swallowed a tack, he would yank out a bit of the loaf's soft center and eat it as soon as possible. The tack would eventually pass safely— and usually with no discomfort—through the system. As dangerous as this practice sounds, it should be remembered that there were often SIDESHOW

Billposters on the advance crew make a hit.
(Photo courtesy of Robert Brummett)

people back on the LOT who swallowed nails, broken glass and other scrap metal for a living.

(See also ADVANCE MAN.)

BINDER, PAUL (1943–   )   Founder of The BIG APPLE CIRCUS in 1977, Paul Binder continues to serve as the circus's artistic director and RINGMASTER.

The son of a Brooklyn salesman, Binder graduated from Dartmouth College in 1963. He then worked briefly as a television stage manager for Julia Child as he earned his masters of business administration from Columbia University.

In 1967 he married Vivian Bachrach, a Bennington graduate; they had a son, Adam, the following year. The marriage ended in divorce in 1970. Then, after working for television personality Merv Griffin as a talent scout, Binder dusted off a stand-up comedy act and moved to the Bay area in California.

Shortly thereafter, he joined the San Francisco Mime Troupe.

While in San Francisco, he teamed up with Michael Christensen and formed a comedy JUGGLING act. They decided to play the streets of Europe and, with $125 between them, they left for the Continent. A stage performance at the Casino de Paris led to a spot on French television. Seen by Pierre Etaix and Annie Fratellini, the duo was asked to join their Nouveau Cirque de Pairs in 1975.

Binder had never enjoyed circuses as a child. "It seemed distant and smelly and seedy to me," he confessed. But in Paris he discovered the European circus.

The following year Binder returned to New York with the dream of establishing a one-ring circus in America. "I realized," he said, "America did not have a small, beautiful, little show like the ones in Paris."

In 1977, after attracting funding and support for his vision, The Big Apple Circus was established as a not-for-profit performing arts organization. Its first performance took place on July 20, 1977 in a small canvas top on the Battery Park City landfill.

In his current role as artistic director, Binder conceives, creates and directs a new thematic production each year. Binder also serves as ringmaster during the circus's 11 weeks of shows in New York around the December holidays and the 20 weeks on tour.

During the "off-season," Paul Binder travels around the world, finding the "new stars" for his next season. "Our acts are fine pieces of work built specifically for this circus," says Binder, "and we look for artists with natural gaiety and joy."

While using the newest state-of-the-art theatrical technologies to create a spellbinding show, Binder relies on the basic circus acts and skills for tradition. "Our vision," Binder explains, "is intimacy." One of the first to spark a modern American interest in the European-style one-ring circus format, Paul Binder is an acknowledged leader in his field; the Big Apple Circus continues to enjoy a well-earned reputation as one of the great American circuses.

In 1985 Paul Binder married Dutch equestrienne star Katja Schumann, who had joined the Big Apple troupe in 1980; they have two children, Katherine Rose and Max Abraham. In 1989 Paul Binder was presented with a Presidential Medal of Achievement by Dartmouth College, his alma mater, and an honorary Doctorate of Fine Arts from Pratt Institute.

BLACK DIAMOND See ELEPHANTS; ROGUE ELEPHANTS.

BLONDIN (1824–1897) Born Jean François Gravelet in Saint Omer, France on February 28, 1924, Charles Blondin was the first person to cross Niagara Falls on a tightrope. The son of a professional soldier, Blondin saw his first ropewalker when he was five years old. He was sent to the Ecole de Gymnase in Lyons and after only six months' training made his debut as "the Little Wonder." An accomplished low wire walker, Blondin first came to the United States in 1851 as part of the Ravels troupe.

The famous Niagara Falls walk of June 30, 1859 was made on a single three-inch hemp cord, 1,100 feet long and 160 feet above the falls at one side and 270 feet at the other. Starting on the United States side, Blondin walked halfway, then lay on his back. He stood, performed a back somersault, then completed the eight-minute walk. Blondin immediately returned to the rope, carrying a camera tripod on his back. He walked halfway, then walked backward to the Canadian shore. He crossed a third time that day, sitting, then standing, on a chair he balanced on the cord.

Blondin repeated the stunt on several occasions with many different variations, including walking blindfolded, on stilts and pushing a wheelbarrow. On September 2, 1860 he offered to carry the Prince of Wales across on his back but was politely refused. On September 15 he crossed while carrying Harry Colcord (his agent) on his shoulders.

Blondin gave his last performance in Belfast, Ireland, in 1896. On February 19, 1897 he died in London. One of the great FUNAMBULISTS of all time, Blondin no doubt took his stage name from the light yellow color of his hair.

BLOWDOWN Circus jargon for when the tent is collapsed by winds or a storm. Blowdowns are feared almost as much as fire, and are as dangerous and as constant a concern.

Because of the weight of the canvas and rigging, winds seldom blow TENTS flat, although this is possible during gale conditions. More frequently, the wind comes in and under the canvas top and lifts the tent up, pulling the stakes out of the ground. The poles collapse when the wind escapes, and the unsupported canvas falls.

To prevent this, the crew will GUY OUT the ropes, sliding the knotted ropes farther down the STAKES. If extreme wind is expected—or if the ground is soft—the tent is sometimes "double-staked." Two stakes are driven by each rope coming from the tent top, and the rope is laced and tied around both stakes. Harder to drive in than metal, wooden stakes are also more difficult to pull out of the ground but are therefore preferred on windy or wet days.

Rain can cause a blowdown, although this happens less frequently. If the tent is not taut, for instance, rain will form puddles and pockets in the top. When the water becomes too heavy, rather than pulling the top down, it will tear a hole in the canvas. The sheer weight of water without accompanying winds cannot blow down a tent.

Rain causes a real threat when it washes tent stakes out of the ground. An even greater danger from rain comes after the storm is over: The rain stretches the canvas, and as it dries the top becomes quite slack, increasing the risk of a blowdown from even a gentle breeze. After a rainstorm, the GUY-OUT GANG can be seen constantly circling the tents, tightening the ropes and the top.

BLOWOFF Circus jargon for the period in which the audience leaves the BIG TOP. It can also mean the special added attractions in a curtained-off portion of the SIDESHOW tent that can be seen for a additional fee. Occasionally, "blowoff" is used to mean the most spectacular trick at the grand finale of an act. The slang term is also sometimes, if infrequently, used in reference to extra pay.

Sometimes, immediately following the blowoff after the main show, an extra short performance, known as the CONCERT is given for an added fee in the Big Top. At the turn of the century and in the heyday of the railroad shows, this blowoff show was often comprised of Wild West acts not normally seen as part of the regular circus fare.

Often during the blowoff, as the crowds spill onto the MIDWAY, one more sideshow performance also takes place. There are many reasons why this late extra show might be given. Sometimes the sideshow cannot accommodate all of the potential customers before the main show has to begin. If patrons arrived very late to the LOT, they missed the BALLY; and the GRIND alone might not have been enough to draw them into the sideshow. Also, those who resisted the bally and grind may now wish to attend, having heard from friends (or those sitting near them) how fascinating the sideshow was. Since the sideshow performers usually do not earn extra money for an aftershow (unless they have something to PITCH), the deciding factor to give the performance may simply be the avarice of the sideshow manager.

BLUE UNIT, THE   See FELD, IRVIN; RINGLING BROS. AND BARNUM & BAILEY CIRCUS.

BLUES   Circus jargon for the general admission seats in the main show. Traditionally, both in the days of wooden plank seating and today's metal seat wagons, the general admission seats are painted blue. This separates them from preferred or reserved ringside seating areas that are often painted red. In a three-ring circus, the blues are located all around the tent while the reserved section, often comprised of STAR BACK chairs, is usually centrally located opposite the BACK DOOR.

On crowded days, when the ushers try to pack more people into the tent, the RINGMASTER and CLOWNS encourage people to move up and back in the bleacher seats for supposed better viewing. This technique is called "raising the blues."

BOAS, DR. CHARLES W. "DOC" (1926–   )   Dr. Charles Boas was the creator and owner/manager of CIRCUS KIRK (which toured the northeastern United States from 1969 through 1977), Boas Bros. Circus and the president of North American Operating Company, Inc.

Academically, Dr. Boas holds degrees from Lafayette College, the University of Virginia and a doctorate in geography from the University of Michigan. He has held teaching positions in geography at Michigan State University, Harrisburg Area Community College and the York College of Pennsylvania.

Born September 5, 1926 in Harrisburg, Pennsylvania, Charles Boas got so "hooked" on circuses when they toured through his state that he gave up a university teaching position to join a small tented

Charles W. "Doc" Boas, 1968.
(Charles Miles photo, courtesy of Dr. Charles Boas)

show, the Penny Brothers Circus. In June 1961 these experiences were featured in a five-page photo spread in *Life* magazine. Over the next several years Dr. Boas learned every aspect of the circus business, from performing and managing to booking, on such shows as Sells & Gray, CARSON & BARNES CIRCUS, CLYDE BEATTY-COLE BROS. CIRCUS and RINGLING BROS. AND BARNUM & BAILEY CIRCUS.

In 1968 he toured central Pennsylvania with his own show, Boas Bros. Circus. Then he formed Circus Kirk, the first all-student touring tented circus. The show became a family venture, as his first wife (Kathleen) traveled on tour and his children (Charles, Jr., Mary, Laura and Elizabeth) took part in the performance.

Dr. Boas has been the subject of countless newspaper articles and has been honored for his contributions to the American circus by the CIRCUS FANS ASSOCIATION OF AMERICA. He also received citations from the governor and the House of Representatives of the Commonwealth of Pennsylvania as well as from the President of the United States.

In 1986 he married Frances Alison; in 1991 he retired from York College of Pennsylvania.

BOAS BROS. CIRCUS See BOAS, DR. CHARLES W. "DOC"; CIRCUS KIRK.

BOGARDUS, CAPTAIN ADAM H. (1833–1913) Captain Adam H. Bogardus was head of a family of famous sharpshooters known as the Bogardus troupe, which traveled with several Wild West shows, including BUFFALO BILL'S WILD WEST. In 1985, when the Bogardus family retired from that show in Louisville, Kentucky, their marksman spot was filled by a young newcomer, Annie OAKLEY.

As a youth, Bogardus shot ducks for a living. His career as a professional marksman began when he competed at a social sports club. He invented an early form of skeet thrower that shot glass balls into the air rather than clay "pigeons," a device used in his act. His record was shooting 5,000 balls in 500 minutes using a double-barreled shotgun.

At just under 6 feet, with a goatee and mustache and immaculate dress, the captain earned the title of Champion Wing Shot of America in an 1871 competition, and he successfully defended the title for years. This led to his being featured as the star performer of the Wild West CONCERT of the ADAM FOREPAUGH CIRCUS in the late 1880s.

BOIL UP Due to the lack of plumbing and hot running water, sanitation was often very poor on early American MUD SHOWS. Any day that the circus didn't play, all of the workingmen and the unmarried bosses would strip naked, "boil up" their clothing and take sponge baths.

Those who were infected by body lice—a common problem—were forced to boil up to get rid of them. In circus jargon, such men were referred to as "crummy," which may be the origin of the modern military slang term "crum up" meaning "wash" or "clean up."

Boiling up became a Sunday ritual for circus performers, since most shows made a JUMP in the morning but didn't perform again until Monday. Dozens of small campfires would be set up on the LOT, creating makeshift bathhouses for the men.

BOILER ROOM Circus jargon for telephone solicitation outfit or operation. The origin of the expression might have come from the mistaken impression that the agents call from dark basement hideaways. Others feel the derivation of boiler room comes from the high pressure that the salesmen sometimes apply.

Many circuses come into town under the auspices of local groups or as completely sponsored engagements, such as the SHRINE CIRCUS dates. In such cases, the local club has as much interest in the advance sale of tickets as the circus itself, so some sort of presale is desired. Often a circus requires a minimum "guarantee" to come to town: This covers the daily cost to operate, or NUT.

When the sponsor has no idea how to proceed on phone sales or does not wish to become actively involved in the calling, it hires a team of professional telephone solicitors known as PHONE PROMOTERS. In exchange for the hours of long and thankless work, the telephone solicitors take a major percentage of the advance ticket sales.

To set up a boiler room, the sales team moves into one or more motel rooms, arranges for direct outside telephone lines and begins to canvas the community. Telephone selling is a perfectly legal, if tedious, method of selling tickets; success in the field is a real skill.

Some phone promoters, however, let greed ruin their art. The possible scams that have been used by phone men include: claiming sponsorship by civic organizations that are not involved in bringing the show to town; deliberately overselling the house with the hopes that not all of the ticket buyers show up at the performances; skimming money off the top by not reporting sales or even selling tickets to a nonexistent show.

BOLIVAR In an attempt to counteract the popularity of JUMBO on the P. T. BARNUM show, in 1883 Adam FOREPAUGH added a massive pachyderm to his own circus—Bolivar.

Forepaugh advertised Bolivar as the "largest and heaviest elephant in the world." Barnum, Bailey and Hutchinson offered a challenge of $10,000 to anyone who could prove that Bolivar was "larger and heavier" than Jumbo; but the ultimatum really wasn't necessary. The public—Jumbo-mad by this point—had no interest in seeing Bolivar.

Even after Jumbo's death, the exhibition of his carcass and skeleton in the Barnum MENAGERIE outdrew Bolivar. By the end of the decade Bolivar became difficult to handle. With his massive tusks, he was extremely dangerous, and he was eventually given to a zoo in Philadelphia.

In the late 1890s the Mollie Bailey Circus also carried an elephant named Bolivar. Though a different bull from the one owned by Forepaugh, the pachyderm's name may very likely have been chosen to trade on the well-publicized elephant war.

BOSS CANVASMAN
Also seen as "boss canvas man," circus jargon for the man who lays out the LOT, deciding where each tent will be located. On most shows he is also head of the work crew that sets up the BIG TOP.

(See also LAYOUT MAN; TENTS.)

BOSS HOSTLER
Circus jargon for the man whose stock of horses pulled the wagons from one town to the next on the first MUD SHOWS.

The more common and more modern usage refers to the man who was in charge of all the baggage (work) horses on the show. His horses would be used to spot the wagons onto the LOT. After the advent of the railroad show, his steeds would also pull the wagons back and forth from the rail yards.

On duty from the time the show started to move in the morning until it was put to bed at night, the boss hostler was often in the saddle 16 or more hours a day. Until the days of the motorized shows, this invaluable horseman really had the final say on the movement of equipment on the lot.

BOTTOM MAN
In an acrobatic troupe, the bottom man is, literally, the one who stands at the bottom or base of the tower or pyramid. He is also sometimes known as the "understander."

His main role in a gymnastics act is usually to hoist—or "pitch"—other ACROBATS up into the air; but he also supports them on his head, shoulders or feet.

In a ground PERCH act, the bottom man holds the pole on which the other gymnasts perform.

BOWERS, BERT (1874–1936)
With his partners, Jerry MUGIVAN and Ed Ballard, Bert Bowers built the AMERICAN CIRCUS CORPORATION, the strongest circus empire outside of the Ringling organization.

Bowers met Mugivan when they were ticket sellers together on the Sanger & Lent Circus in 1893. In 1900 they moved over to the Ben Wallace Circus.

Bowers and Mugivan started their own small show in 1904, for which they misappropriated the name the VAN AMBURGH CIRCUS. The name was changed to Howes' Great London Circus and was toured under that title until 1921.

By 1920 Bowers and his ever-present partner Mugivan also owned or claimed title to the JOHN ROBINSON CIRCUS, Dide Fisk Circus, SANGER'S GREAT EUROPEAN CIRCUS, GOLLMAR BROS. CIRCUS, the YANKEE ROBINSON CIRCUS, the SELLS-FLOTO CIRCUS and BUFFALO BILL'S WILD WEST.

Meanwhile, Ben Wallace had sold his show to Ed Ballard, a real estate investor in PERU, INDIANA, following a 1913 flood. Bowers and Mugivan took in Ballard as a third partner and investor, purchasing the HAGENBECK-WALLACE CIRCUS in 1920. The following year they formed the American Circus Corporation. By the time Bowers, along with his partners, sold the corporation to John RINGLING in 1929, they also owned the SPARKS CIRCUS and the AL G. BARNES CIRCUS.

BOZO THE CLOWN
See CLOWNS, TELEVISION.

BRADNA, ELLA (1879–1957)
A romantic meeting between Ella Bradna, equestrienne, and a cavalry officer led to a career of four decades with American circuses.

The daughter of Johan and Katha Bradna, Ella grew up in her father's circus as it toured Bohemia, Austria and Hungary in the late 19th century. The beautiful girl developed remarkable skills in ballet and as a wire walker and ROSINBACK rider. Her father withheld her debut as a bareback rider, however, until he knew she was ready to appear on the scene as a sudden sensation.

Her older sister Beata was the star equestrienne with the circus, but when she broke both her legs in a fall from her horse in Pilsen, Bohemia, her father allowed 11-year-old Ella to go on in her place. Her balletic training was not wasted, because her bareback work was not only exciting but also breathtakingly graceful.

As with any attractive star, she had her share of admirers. The elderly mayor of Newbyzow proposed marriage, but Ella's father felt the girl was too young. The mayor promised to wait a few years before pressing his suit again, but his death put an end to that.

In 1887, unable to cross borders easily due to political problems in Europe, Johan closed Circus Bradna. The various acts split up among different shows; Ella, with her father and brother Charles, moved to Circus Drexler, then onto Germany's Circus Schumann. In 1900 Ella joined her brother Josephy on the Circus Salamonsky. Josephy convinced Ella that to become a top-notch equestrienne it was necessary for her to learn to break and train her own HORSES.

In the spring of 1901, Ella Bradna made her debut performance as a bareback rider in the *Nouveau Cirque* in Paris. Near the end of the act, Ella's horse tossed her over the RING CURB and into the arms of Frederick Ferber, who was seated in a box seat.

They married two years later, and Ferber adopted Ella's surname. Ella was offered a position with the BARNUM & BAILEY CIRCUS, which was then touring Europe, and the couple moved to America when the show returned to the States in late 1902. Although she started as an equestrienne in ring three, Bradna was soon moved to the CENTER RING.

The equestrienne, trained in ballet, performed "on point" as part of her "Act Beautiful," as it was known. Dressed in white satin, Bradna appeared in the ring with horses, doves and dogs; and the routine was frequently backed by a singing WHITEFACE CLOWN, a Hungarian midget named Paul Horompo.

While touring with her husband on a one-ring circus in Central America, Ella began work with Fred Derrick, another former Barnum & Bailey performer. In 1906 all three returned to the Barnum & Bailey Circus, where she and Derrick were a center-ring attraction for 12 seasons. She last rode bareback in 1929 at the Hippodrome in New York City but continued as a coach and trainer.

After Fred Bradna was hurt in a 1945 BLOWDOWN, Ella Bradna retired with her husband to SARASOTA, FLORIDA, where she died in 1957.

BRADNA, FRED (1878–1955)

Born Ferderick Ferber, Bradna was a young cavalry officer in the German Army when, in the spring of 1901, he visited

Fred Bradna, the veteran ringmaster of the Ringling show. (Author's collection)

the *Nouveau Cirque* in Paris. There he met the equestrienne star, ELLA BRADNA. They were married in 1903, with Ferber taking his famous wife's last name. That same year Fred, as Ella's assistant, joined the BARNUM & BAILEY CIRCUS when it returned to America after a European tour.

Bradna accepted a position as EQUESTRIAN DIRECTOR with a small Central American circus, and Ella accompanied him.

When they returned to the Barnum and Bailey Circus in 1906, Fred Bradna became the chief assistant to ring announcer William Gorman. In 1915, John RINGLING chose Bradna to succeed Gorman; he stayed with the Ringling organization when the shows merged into the RINGLING BROS. AND BARNUM & BAILEY CIRCUS.

Bradna became the archetypical RINGMASTER, replete with red tails, white pants, black riding boots and black top hat. He described the duties of a ringmaster in his autobiography, *The Big Top:*

He must be at once a showman, a stage director, a martinet, a diplomat, a family counselor, a musician, a psychologist, an animal keeper and a weather prophet.

Since horses are the keystone of circus entertainment, he should be an accomplished equestrian. He must know sufficient about all circus techniques: tumbling, leaping, flying, catching, casting, juggling, clowning, ballet, animal training (which varies greatly between seals, bears, tigers, dogs, horses, chimpanzees and elephants), slack and tight wire and even being shot from a cannon, to discern at a glance whether specialists in these arts are shirking and, in the case of animal acts, whether the sin of commission or omission is the fault of the human or the animal star.

Fred Bradna was injured during a BLOWDOWN of the BIG TOP on September 12, 1945. After 42 years with the circus, 31 of them as equestrian director, Fred Bradna and his wife Ella retired to SARASOTA, FLORIDA in 1945. He died there in 1955.

During his long and eventful career, Fred Bradna had the opportunity of introducing the greatest circus talents of his generation.

BRIDGEPORT, CONNECTICUT

Approximately 60 miles northeast of New York City and situated along the Atlantic coast, Bridgeport, Connecticut, has had a central role in the development of the American circus.

It was in nearby Bethel that P.T. BARNUM was born on July 5, 1810. Barnum's lifelong association with Bridgeport itself began when he was introduced to one of its residents, young Charles Stratton. Barnum christened the Stratton lad "General TOM THUMB" and built him into one of the first international superstars.

Apparently Barnum liked what he saw on his visits to the area, because in 1846 he purchased land in Bridgeport to build IRANISTAN, the first of four mansions he would own there. He invested heavily in the area, helping to develop the real estate across the river in East Bridgeport.

After Iranistan burned, Barnum built his home Waldemere ("Woods by the Sea") closer to the ocean. With his associates, he founded Seaside Park for the town's residents and set aside land for the Bethel Cemetery.

On April 5, 1875 Barnum was elected mayor of Bridgeport; and in 1877 and 1879 he was elected to represent Bridgeport in the Connecticut General Assembly.

On November 12, 1881, following the close of their newly combined BARNUM & LONDON CIRCUS, Barnum, James A. BAILEY and James L. HUTCHINSON

brought the WINTER QUARTERS to Bridgeport. It was there that the second baby ELEPHANT was born in captivity in America.

Barnum describes the event in his autobiography *Struggles and Triumphs:*

On February 2, 1882, "Queen" one of my twenty-two elephants gave birth to a young one at our 'winter quarters' in Bridgeport. The event had long been anticipated and thoroughly published throughout America and Europe. . . . When the interesting event was imminent it was telegraphed through the associated press to all parts of the United States, and about sixty scientists, medical men and reports arrived in time to be present at the birth. The next morning more than fifty columns of details of the birth, weight and name of the Baby Elephant appeared in the American papers, and notices cabled to London and Paris appeared in the morning papers. As this was the second elephant ever born in captivity, either in America or Europe, it created a great sensation. Its weight was only one hundred and forty-five pounds at birth. We named it "Bridgeport" after the place of its nativity and of my residence.

Shortly before his death and subsequent interment in Bridgeport's Mountain Grove Cemetery, the great benefactor gave one last gift to his beloved adopted city: the Barnum Institute of Science and History. Today the building houses the BARNUM MUSEUM, which commemorates the contributions of P.T. Barnum, his circuses and the industries of Bridgeport.

Late in Barnum's life, his circus had been restructured into the BARNUM & BAILEY CIRCUS. Even after Barnum's death, the winter quarters were maintained in Bridgeport. The RINGLING BROTHERS bought the Barnum & Bailey Circus from the widow of James A. Bailey in 1908; however, they maintained the show and its winter quarters separate from their own Ringling Brothers Circus.

In 1919 John RINGLING combined the two shows into the RINGLING BROTHERS AND BARNUM & BAILEY CIRCUS and moved the Ringling winter quarters from BARABOO, WISCONSIN to merge with those of the Barnum show in Bridgeport. The offices of the BIG ONE remained there through 1926 when, after acquiring full control of the circus after his brother Charles's death, John Ringling moved the entire operation to SARASOTA, FLORIDA in 1927.

BRILL'S BIBLE

Technically entitled *A. Brill's Bible of Building Plans,* Brill's catalog of blueprints of

"Baby Bridgeport," the second elephant born in captivity in America. (Photo courtesy of The Barnum Museum, Bridgeport, CT)

circus, carnival, fair and other outdoor amusement industry equipment was available from 1946 through the mid-1970s. Published by A.B. Enterprises of Peoria, Illinois, Brill issued plans for everything from JACKS AND STRINGERS to the RING CURB.

A. Brill started out in journalism—a cub reporter at 17, an editor at 18, a publisher at 19, then the owner of three newspapers. After a stint as the advertising representative for a local distillery, Brill became involved with the punchboard industry, first sending out a monthly newsletter, then producing catalogs for the manufacturers and operators of the then-legal gambling device. He returned to advertising, designing the newspaper ads for several furniture and appliance stores.

Brill's first taste of show business came as the manager of a lion trainer in 1939 and helping to construct the performer's BIG CAGE and props. The next year Brill switched to carnival work and ride construction until World War II. Before going overseas, he photographed and measured every piece of circus apparatus he could find. When he returned from Europe, Brill again began building equipment and, in 1946, issued his first set of plans.

Catalogue 14 (catalogue 13 had been skipped due to superstition), issued in 1970, was the first to include blueprints for circus apparatus, although circus magicians had already been using his illusion plans for years. Among the blueprints offered, ranging in price from $3 to $10, were plans for bleachers (or BLUES), a stake driver (see STAKES), the front of the SIDESHOW (including the BALLY platform, BAN-NERLINE and ticket boxes), unicycles and a clown "bucking bronco" bicycle (see CYCLISTS), a clown

CALLIOPE made of bottles, various CLOWN WALKA-ROUNDS and complete rope spinning and plate spinning acts.

BROAD TOSSERS

Slang for the card cheats and con artists who performed the "Three Card Monte" on the LOT. A favorite form of GRIFT on the old MUD SHOWS, "Find the Lady" or "Chase the Ace" was usually played in the CONNECTION between the MENAGERIE and the BIG TOP.

By the 1930s the larger rail shows came to depend on their good names to represent wholesome family entertainment. In an attempt to establish their TERRITORIES and repeat dates, the circuses were run as SUNDAY SCHOOL SHOWS, and the broad tossers and other con men were themselves tossed from the circus grounds.

BROWN, J. PURDY (c. 1802–1834)

Born in Westchester County, New York, J. Purdy Brown with his partner, thought to be Lewis Bailey, forever changed the American circus when they became the first authenticated circus owners to place their show beneath a canvas tent. The exact date of the first tented performance, as well as Brown's reasons for going under canvas, are lost in antiquity.

In 1826 Brown became the first circus operator to tour Virginia. He traveled along the banks of the Mississippi River as early as 1828. Although his involvement with the development of the minstrel show is unknown, minstrel numbers were performed on his circus in 1831 by Samuel H. Nichols, the singer who introduced the number "Jim Crow."

A cousin of Hachaliah BAILEY, Brown is also credited with being the first to combine the circus and MENAGERIE into a single show. In 1828 he loaned one of his acts, an equestrian named Andrew Levi, to his cousin, Benjamin Brown, who was touring a menagerie in the Caribbean. Four years later J. Purdy Brown obtained a menagerie, probably leased, and added it to his own show, touring under the title "Brown's Circus and Menagerie."

Despite his major circus innovations and contributions, today J. Purdy Brown is largely forgotten. He died suddenly on June 6, 1834 following a performance in Mobile, Alabama. His brother, Oscar W. Brown, himself a circus owner, continued the show's operation until 1837.

BROWN & LENT CIRCUS

Traveling on the Mississippi River by steamboat from 1835 through 1839, the Brown & Lent Circus was the first show of Lewis B. LENT.

BUCK JONES WILD WEST SHOW

Although many cowboy movie stars toured with circuses or Wild West shows over the years, most joined on as part of the troupe. A few, however, also entered management. Buck Jones (1889–1942), one of the latter, was unfortunate: The Buck Jones Wild West Show, which he toured in 1929, was not a financial success.

But Jones went on to a lucrative career in films, becoming the number-one western star of 1936. Some of his more than 100 films include *The Last Straw*, *The Big Punch* and *Skid Proof*. He died in 1942 in a nightclub fire in Boston.

BUD E. ANDERSON SHOW

Operating for 30 years under a variety of titles, the Bud E. Anderson Show began as Indian Bud's Wild West around 1922 and became a circus in 1924. Originally trouping on wagons, it became a truck show in 1927.

Despite the Depression, the show made large profits in the West, operating as the Seal Bros. Circus. The 1940s brought another name change, this time to Bud E. Anderson's Jungle Oddities Circus. Anderson was killed in a truck accident on July 4, 1950, but his son carried on the show until 1952.

BUFFALO BILL

See CODY, WILLIAM F(REDERICK).

BUFFALO BILL & 101 RANCH WILD WEST

Formed by Edward ARLINGTON and the Miller brothers in 1908, the 101 RANCH WILD WEST (also known as the Miller Bros. 101 Ranch Wild West) began as a 16-car rail show. In 1915 it featured boxing champion Jess WILLARD; and in 1916 Arlington hired William F. CODY (Buffalo Bill) away from the SELLS-FLOTO CIRCUS.

To capitalize on the fame of his new star attraction, Arlington renamed the circus the Buffalo Bill & 101 Ranch Wild West. At the end of the season, while the show was in WINTER QUARTERS, Arlington bought out the Millers' share and brought in Willard as a partner. When Buffalo Bill died on January 10, 1917 his name was maintained in the overhauled show, which became known as the BUFFALO BILL WILD WEST & JESS WILLARD SHOW.

BUFFALO BILL WILD WEST & JESS WILLARD SHOW

This show is a descendant of the original 101 RANCH WILD WEST (also known as the Miller Bros. 101 Ranch Wild West).

In 1908 Edward ARLINGTON and the Miller brothers co-founded the 101 Ranch show, a 16-car rail show modeled after the Millers' Wild West, which had appeared at the previous year's Jamestown Exposition. In 1915 ex-boxing champion Jess WILLARD joined the troupe, and the following year William F. CODY (Buffalo Bill) also joined. Taking advantage of its new headliner, the show toured as the BUFFALO BILL & 101 RANCH WILD WEST SHOW for the 1916 season.

At season's end, however, Arlington bought out the Millers and brought in Willard as a partner. Even though Cody died while the circus was in WINTER QUARTERS, Arlington and Willard continued to use his name in their new 1917 edition, the Buffalo Bill Wild West & Jess Willard Show.

Arlington sold his part in the show to Willard at the end of the year. Willard was not a capable manager on his own, however, and the show quickly folded during the next season.

BUFFALO BILL WILD WEST AND PAWNEE BILL GREAT FAR EAST SHOW

In 1894 James A. BAILEY joined partners William F. CODY ("Buffalo Bill") and Nathan SALSBURY in modernizing the BUFFALO BILL'S WILD WEST, and the next year the show took to rails.

Bailey died in 1906, and his circus assets were sold to the RINGLING BROTHERS in 1907. They, in turn, sold the Wild West equipment back to Cody. In 1908 one of Cody's chief rivals, Major Gordon W. "Pawnee Bill" LILLIE, became his partner, and their combined shows were renamed the Buffalo Bill Wild West and Pawnee Bill Great Far East Show (nicknamed the Two Bills Show).

The program for the new show featured the following acts: Introduction of the Congress of Rough Riders of the World; a Review of various Indian tribes; the Occident meets the Orient; U.S. Cavalry veterans; Australian bushmen; Cossacks; Hindu Fakirs; A Buffalo Hunt; a Virginia reel on horseback; a marksmanship contest; and the Deadwood stagecoach sequence.

The show was not a financial success, however. Cody added more acts and advertised the next season as the farewell tour, but the show still lost money. With the turn of the century, the heyday of the Wild West show was over. The great Two Bills Show closed early in Colorado in 1913.

Cody himself was never to own another show, but he did briefly tour late in life with the SELLS-FLOTO CIRCUS, only to be hired by one of his imitators, the 101 RANCH WILD WEST. Edward ARLINGTON and the Miller brothers, owners of the circus, renamed their show the BUFFALO BILL & 101 RANCH WILD WEST to honor the new star attraction. This was to be Cody's last tour.

(See also BUFFALO BILL WILD WEST & JESS WILLARD SHOW.)

BUFFALO BILL'S WILD WEST

The first show of its kind, Buffalo Bill's Wild West was unique—a cavalcade, circus and spectacle all rolled into one. The show was widely copied, and its popularity spawned a host of imitators as well as the western-themed CONCERT, or aftershow, on many circuses. In time, this also led to some stars of western motion pictures joining circus companies between films.

Buffalo Bill, born William Frederick CODY, had already had a full career as an Indian fighter and frontiersman when Ned Buntline made him the hero of a series of dime novels. The fame took Cody onto the stage in a string of western melodramas, but he yearned for something more—and that "something" became the Wild West.

Devised with Buntline, press agent John M. Burke and veteran showman Nathan SALSBURY, Buffalo Bill's Wild West—also known as "The Wild West, Rocky Mountain and Prairie Exhibition"—opened on the Omaha, Nebraska, Fairgrounds on May 17, 1883. The more familiar name was officially adopted the following year. Cody never used the word "show" in the title, insisting that "Wild West" was a noun—a distinct entity in outdoor entertainment.

The Wild West program included trick riding, sharpshooting, pageants and parades of cowboys and Indians and re-creations of famous Indian battles and covered wagon attacks. One such Concord coach was set upon twice daily for 35 years during the sketch described in the program as "Attack on the Deadwood Mail Coach by Indians, Passengers and Mail by Buffalo Bill and his Attendant Cowboys, Scouts and Frontiersmen." Another spectacle was the "Attack on a Settler's Cabin and Rescue by Buffalo Bill and a Band of Cowboys."

In 1887, under the management of Salsbury, the show toured England and performed for Queen Victoria during her Golden Jubilee. Upon returning to the United States, the show had one of its longest engagements when it set up across the street from the main gates of the Chicago World's Fair in 1893.

At the end of the 1894 season, Salsbury became ill. In 1895 Cody brought in James A. BAILEY, who equipped and routed the show in exchange for a half interest. Bailey moved much of the Forepaugh-Sells Circus equipment onto the Wild West to keep it in operation. He immediately reframed the Wild West for rail travel and to be able appear under canvas.

In 1902 Buffalo Bill's Wild West began a four-year tour of Europe, during which time Annie OAKLEY was one of the star attractions of the show.

Bailey died in 1906. His interest in the show became part of the sale of his circus holdings to the RINGLING BROTHERS in 1907, but they allowed Buffalo Bill to regain management control. Another Bailey share was purchased by one of Cody's earlier competitors, Major Gordon "Pawnee Bill" LILLIE. In 1908 the revamped show began touring as the BUFFALO BILL WILD WEST AND PAWNEE BILL GREAT FAR EAST SHOW (nicknamed the Two Bills Show). By the early 1900s the Wild West show had become passé, however, and midseason 1913 the show decided to CLOSE AHEAD OF PAPER.

The show's fame was such, however, that its title has been incorporated into many western-themed circuses since. Among them were the Sells Floto-Buffalo Bill Circus, the BUFFALO BILL & 101 RANCH WILD WEST (on which Cody toured), the BUFFALO BILL WILD WEST & JESS WILLARD SHOW, and the Hagenbeck-Wallace Circus & Buffalo Bill Wild West as well as several overseas shows.

(See also ARLINGTON, EDWARD; BOGARDUS, CAPTAIN ADAM H.; 101 RANCH WILD WEST; SELLS-FLOTO CIRCUS.)

BUFFALO BILL'S WILD WEST AND CONGRESS OF ROUGH RIDERS OF THE WORLD

William F. CODY first took his BUFFALO BILL'S WILD WEST on a grand tour of Europe in 1887. When the troupe returned to the United States in 1892 in preparation for an appearance at the 1893 Chicago World's Fair, Cody had added horsemen and trick riders from all over the continent. To announce the enlarged show, he renamed it Buffalo Bill's Wild West and Congress of Rough Riders of the World.

BUG JUICE   See JUICE.

BUGS

A popular concession on the MIDWAY, "bugs" was circus jargon for anolis, which are usually miscalled chameleons. The pitchmen who sold them were known as "bug men."

The lizards were especially fascinating and appealing to children. Since the pitchman always kept one bug on a little string pinned to his lapel, mothers knew that the creatures were harmless as well.

While they were a cheap, easy sale, captive bugs, unfortunately, did not usually live very long after leaving the circus grounds. In part because the fad has passed and partly because of ANIMAL ACTIVISTS' questions regarding the animals' care, bugs are seldom seen as a concession on circuses today.

BULL HANDLER

Any person who is a trainer or leads the ELEPHANTS (or BULLS). Despite its directness, the jargon is actually a term of respect. Even the top trainer is known as the head bull handler.

BULLS

Circus jargon for the ELEPHANTS, male or female.

BUNCE

Circus jargon for profits.

BURGESS, HOVEY (1940–   )

As one of the premier teachers of circus skills in the United States, Hovey Burgess's techniques and students can be seen on circuses and on stage throughout America.

Born on September 8, 1940 in Middlebury, Connecticut, Burgess learned to juggle from his father at the age of 14. Soon after he was riding a unicycle as well.

At 17 he was hired as a ROUSTABOUT on the SIDESHOW canvas crew of the HAGEN BROS. CIRCUS, but soon he was performing in the show with a unicycle act. The first show that hired Burgess as a juggler and unicyclist was the Patterson Bros. Circus, an indoor Michigan circus owned by Jay C. Patterson.

In 1960 Burgess matriculated at the Florida State University and immediately began performing with its annual student circus. At about the same time, he was learning the technical side of trouping a tented show: He worked as an usher with the CLYDE BEATTY-COLE BROS. CIRCUS and as a prop man with the HUNT BROS. CIRCUS.

Residing in New York City, Burgess began his current position as a professor of circus skills at New York University in 1966. Teaching within the Department of Graduate Acting in the Tisch School of the Arts, Burgess stresses the theatrical and physical benefits of exercise to the actor. To further underscore the connection between theater and the circus—especially the CLOWNS—Burgess has also directed two Commedia dell' Arte shows at the university.

Among his many early influences, Burgess is quick to mention juggler Harry Lind. Burgess says, "Circus people were always kind and very willing to teach me. In fact, it was unusual when someone didn't want to share their knowledge."

Burgess has more than returned the favors. In 1977 he published *Circus techniques,* a masterwork that covers all forms of circus skills, from balancing to aerial acrobatics. He has had a particular influence on the art of American JUGGLING. One of his students was Larry Pisoni, a founder of the PICKLE FAMILY CIRCUS. Phil Marsh, who toured with the Pickles, fondly described Burgess as "the mother cockroach of jugglers. Cockroaches lay 600,000 eggs a year. If you see my point."

Active in fraternal juggling and circus organizations, Hovey Burgess is a past president of the International Jugglers Association.

BURN THE TERRITORY

To "burn the territory," a circus must be so offensive to the community and its standards that it cannot return to the town. This might be caused by giving an intolerably bad show for the price, illegal gambling practices (or other legal troubles) or causing disputes in the city. It sometimes occurs today when shows do not live up to their contracts with the sponsors.

The real trouble with burning a TERRITORY, LOT or a town is that the ill-will caused by the first show affects all other circuses that try to book into the area. Many times the town is "burned" not only for the offending circus but for all traveling shows.

BURNES BROS. CIRCUS

The Burnes Bros. Circus, owned and operated by Chuck and Bambi Burnes,

was first produced in 1989. Chuck and Bambi Burnes met when they were performing (as a CLOWN and aerialist, respectively) on the RINGLING BROS. AND BARNUM & BAILEY CIRCUS in the 1950s and 1960s. The Burnes Bros. Circus is named after their sons, Charles L. Burnes, III, a stand-up comic and writer (who performs as Chip Lowell) and Richard Warren Burnes (who performed as ventriloquist Richard Warren).

The Burnes Bros. Circus, scheduled through the offices of Periwinkle Productions in Anaheim, California was created especially for sponsored dates, major events and conventions. The show plays a variety of venues mainly in southern California, although it has also appeared in New Orleans and San Francisco.

(See also FLEA CIRCUS; IRON JAW.)

BUTCHER

Circus jargon for the person who sells refreshments, also sometimes known as the candy butcher. The term usually applies to those who hawk the PINK LEMONADE, soda, peanuts, popcorn, hot dogs, COTTON CANDY and other circus staples in the stands inside the BIG TOP; but it has come to mean those who sell from the wagon on the MIDWAY as well.

Circus legend has it that the first candy butcher was the person who was the actual butcher for animal meat on the old JOHN ROBINSON CIRCUS sometime before the Civil War. To make extra money on the show, he began to take candy and other concessions inside the tent to sell; he was so successful, he was able to give up his work as a meat carver.

The name butcher stuck, however, and that's how his circus friends continued to address him. Soon others began to sell items in the BLUES as well; and, by tradition, they also came to be known as butchers.

BUTLER, FRANK (1850–1926)

Frank E. Butler, an experienced marksman, was on tour with a team of professional riflemen and appearing at the Cincinnati Opera House when he was beaten in a sharpshooting contest by 15-year-old Annie OAKLEY. They fell in love and married a year later.

At first they toured vaudeville and variety houses as a double act, with Annie always receiving top billing. In later years Butler became an assistant in the act, then later her manager.

Truck and concessions trailer for the butchers on the D.B. Wharton Circus in Greencastle, Pennsylvania in 1971.
(Photo courtesy of Andy Bakner)

Frank Butler and Oakley joined the SELLS BROTH-ERS CIRCUS in 1884. There they developed Oakley's trademark act of riding on horseback and shooting glass balls thrown in the air by Butler. After meeting William F. CODY, they joined BUFFALO BILL'S WILD WEST.

Butler remained in the background on tour with Oakley throughout her long, successful career. A devoted husband, he died 18 days after her in November 1926.

BUTLER, ROLAND (1887–1961) Born in Wayland, Massachusetts on June 2, 1887, Roland Butler came from a journalistic background. His father, Harry, was the managing editor of the *New Bedford Standard* during Roland's boyhood. Roland would later claim he learned more at his father's shop than he ever did in public schools.

Roland entered the field of journalism as an illustrator, starting with a humble satirical sports cartoon. At 18, he moved to Boston, quickly gaining a post on the *Boston Globe*. When no photographs were immediately available, Butler sketched the devastation of the San Francisco earthquake on April 18, 1906 from his imagination. As his reputation for resourcefulness grew, he bounced from newspaper to newspaper and from art to editorials and advertising.

His first work for the circus came when Charles Sparks asked him to design a program cover for the SPARKS CIRCUS. He was soon doing copy as well. Butler gave the "circus truth" in his press releases, knowing from experience what editors would publish.

By the early 1920s, Charles and John RINGLING were the only surviving "founding five brothers" of the BIG ONE. Charles Ringling, the "hands-on" brother, traveled with the show full time. He was aware of Butler's fine work for Sparks and invited him to join the press staff for the RINGLING BROS. AND BARNUM & BAILEY CIRCUS in 1924. Butler worked with the show for two years until Charles's death in 1926. John, who had never really forgiven Butler for plagiarizing Ringling LITHOGRAPHS to help promote the Sparks Circus in 1922, let him go. For the rest of his life, Butler always insisted that he had resigned.

When John Ringling NORTH assumed control of the show after his uncle's death, Butler was brought back on board. North was no longer president, however, when the tragic HARTFORD FIRE occurred. Butler and his staff were blamed for not being able to counteract the extreme negative publicity from the devastating blaze. In 1944 Butler was fired again.

Eventually North regained his position as president of the Ringling organization and Butler was rehired. In addition to the press releases and advertising campaigns, Butler designed the show's letterheads and programs—even the circus's Christmas cards! Although not rare, their beauty alone makes them collector's items today.

Butler's position lasted until 1954. He had been with the Ringling show on and off for 30 years when, during political upheavals within the executive organization, it was publicly announced that Roland Butler had "retired."

Bitter about his rejection, he turned to the CLYDE BEATTY-COLE BROS. CIRCUS. By mid-1961 his eyesight was failing badly, however, and his general health was deteriorating.

Roland Butler, one of the greatest masters of circus hyperbole, was rushed to the hospital on October 9, 1961. He remained there—receiving circus friends from his years of being WITH IT—until his death from an embolism at 3:15 P.M. on October 20.

C

CA' D'ZAN   By 1926 when his brother Charles died, John RINGLING—the last of the original "five founding" RINGLING BROTHERS—was one of the 20 richest men in the world. He built a Venetian Gothic-style palace in SARASOTA, FLORIDA as a winter residence and called it Ca' d'Zan, or "House of John."

The house was intended to combine architectural features of two of Mrs. Mable Ringling's favorite buildings: the facade of the Doge's Palace in Venice, Italy and the tower of the old MADISON SQUARE GARDEN in New York. Besides the obvious Italian influence, the building also contained elements of the French Renaissance, Baroque and modern architecture. The final plans and actual construction were overseen by Dwight James Baum of New York, and the mansion was from built from 1924 until just before Christmas 1926.

Mrs. Ringling presided over details of the design. She personally visited the kilns making the bricks, terra-cotta blocks and concrete to be sure their colors—soft red, yellow, blue, green and ivory—were precisely correct.

No expense was spared to bring ornate furnishings from around the world to the estate. Thousands of red barrel tiles for the roof were imported from Barcelona, Spain. The house was topped by a 60-foot tower within which a light shone when the Ringlings were home. All of the windows in the mansion were handmade from Venetian tinted glass.

Today the building is 200 feet long. Inside, there is an immense two-and-a-half-story roofed court-yard that served as the main living room. Adjacent to this central area are 30 rooms and 14 baths, plus kitchens, pantries and servants' quarters in the south wing.

Outside, along the waterfront, is an 8,000-square-foot terrace made of variegated marble and enclosed by terra-cotta balustrades. Thirteen steps of English veined marble lead down to a dock on the waterfront where Mable Ringling docked her Venetian gondola.

Tragically, Mable Ringling lived for only three years after the mansion was completed.

Built on Sarasota Bay, the residence reportedly cost nearly $1.5 million, which included the seawall, swimming pool and adjoining buildings. While Ca' d'Zan was the Ringling home, the grounds also held the JOHN AND MABLE RINGLING MUSEUM OF ART, which housed John's enormous and spectacular art collection.

Patricia R. Buck, public relations director for the museum and a granddaughter of August Ringling, points out that many mistakenly assume the Ca' d'Zan and the galleries are one and the same, or that part of the galleries were used as the residence. The museum, however, had its own architect who designed it in an Italian style; the galleries were built from 1927 to 1929.

In his will, John Ringling left Ca' d'Zan and the art galleries to the state of Florida, collectively to be called the John and Mable Ringling Museum of Art. It is currently maintained as a public museum.

Ca' d'Zan. (Photo courtesy of the John and Mable Ringling Museum of Art, Sarasota, Florida)

CAGE BOY   Circus jargon for an assistant to the animal trainer. The cage boy for the wild CAT trainer usually cleans the cages, feeds and waters the animals and is a general gofer. During a performance he often stands by the chutes and works as a spotter outside the cage, assisting the trainer in case of emergency.

There are also cage boys in the MENAGERIE top who see to the needs of the animals on display. Cage boys assist with the animal-associated chores whether the animals in their charge are caged or not.

CAGE WAGON   A traditional part of the STREET PARADE, cage wagons carried part of the MENAGERIE, often some of the more exotic wild animals, such as the lions, tigers or BEARS. Some cages were even designed to display unusual birds.

One type of unusual cage wagon with glass-window sides carried the snakes, or "living serpents." Sometimes four or five of these "dens" would be in the street parade; and, like all of the animals in the

parade, the snakes would appear in the menagerie back at the LOT.

Boards were often placed over the sides of some of the cages, lettered with the names or types of the wild animals within. The crowds along the parade route, who could only guess what the beasts inside the cages looked like, would be lured to the showgrounds to see them in person.

Two fine examples of vintage cage wagons with sideboards are the 1915 Royal Bengal Tigers Den and the 1905 Black Maned Nubian Lions Den, which often appeared in Wisconsin's GREAT CIRCUS PARADE and are currently owned by CIRCUS WORLD MUSEUM.

CALLIOPE   Synonymous with circus music and the circus parade is the calliope, pronounced in three syllables, "Cow-lee-ope," by circus folks.

The word "calliope" is ironic, as it is based on two Greek words that mean "beautiful voice." Joshua C. STODDARD of Worcester, Massachusetts is generally given credit for the invention of the modern calliope

Calliope. (Photo by Harry Nelson, author's collection)

because of his October 9, 1855 U.S. Patent No. 13,668. His calliope was actually an improvement on an existing non-steam-driven instrument. William Hoyt of Dupont, Indiana was the first to detail a steam whistle organ in print, making the suggestion in the April 1, 1851 edition of the *Dayton* (Ohio) *Journal and Advertiser*.

The calliope, carried on a wagon (or in the case of the earliest calliopes, a separate wagon for keyboard and boiler), resembles a miniature pipe organ. Run by steam, it is played on pianolike keys, with the sound coming out of a series of steam whistles. As the valve on the pipe opens, a sharp whistle is produced. Although the whistles have a range of several octaves, the steam pressure—produced by a sometimes dangerous (or, in the case of an explosion, lethal) boiler located at the rear of the calliope—is not always constant. The resultant cacophony of dissonant tones makes the sound of a true steam calliope unique.

In the STREET PARADE, the calliope would always be the last carriage in the circus procession from the railroad to the LOT. Just as the musicians on the BANDWAGON at or near the front of the march would draw crowds to the center of town, the calliope would seduce the patrons into following the parade to the showgrounds and the matinee performance.

Among the first circuses to employ a calliope were Nixon & Kemp's Great Eastern Show and the SPALD-ING & ROGERS CIRCUS (traveling on the steamer *James Raymond*), both in 1857. The following year Levi J. NORTH's National Circus and Sands, Nathans & Co. each carried a calliope as well.

(See also TABLEAU WAGON; WAGONS.)

CAMELS   The first camel to come to the American colonies arrived in Boston in 1721 and was advertised in the October 2, 9 and 23 issues of the *Boston Gazette*. Arriving very soon after the first lion, the camel was probably the second exotic MENAGERIE animal to reach North American shores.

Although far from the most dangerous animals in the circus, camels are probably the most difficult to work with and the most unpleasant creatures in the menagerie and SPEC. They are certainly the least favorite creature of all animal handlers.

Camels are mean beasts that spit when angered. Gallons of acidic liquid are ever-present in their stomachs, and they will send sprays flying with the least provocation.

Both Arabian one-humped (known as dromedaries) and two-humped (Bactrian) camels are seen on the circus. Both are covered with wrinkled skin under layers of fat. Used to rugged climate, camels are generally quite healthy animals.

As uncontrollable as they are in their daily lives, camels are possibly the most civil at breeding. If a female in the pack goes into heat, the male camels will not fight for an opportunity to mount her. Rather, they will line up single file and, in an orderly fashion, "service" her. When his turn is done, a male will walk around to the end of the line.

Llamas, a member of the camel family, can also be vile creatures. Like their desert brothers, they are not particularly bright and are almost impossible to train. A typical llama act consists of having the Andes animal jump a few low hurdles or mount a small pedestal. Needless to say, llamas share the camels' spitting ability.

CAMPBELL BROS. CIRCUS   A typical example of the change and growth of the American circus at the turn of the century, the Campbell Bros. Circus started as a wagon show in 1893 and closed as a 20 railroad-car circus in 1912. The small tented show had its WINTER QUARTERS in Fairbury, Nebraska.

CANDY BUTCHER   See BUTCHER.

CANDY PITCH As an added source of revenue, the candy pitch is both commercial and theatrical. During a pause in the show, or to cover a slow change in rigging, BUTCHERS or CLOWNS enter the CENTER RING exhibiting small boxes of candy that resemble Cracker Jacks.

The pitchman, usually the RINGMASTER, extols the virtues of the candy and then closes the sale by explaining that inside many of the boxes is a special coupon that can be exchanged for a prize.

A clown or BALLY BROAD then enters the ring carrying a huge display of balloons, plush toys or other circus souvenirs. As an added incentive for the audience to buy, some shows flaunt one or two larger premiums that can be won by finding a specially marked billet in the candy box.

The ringmaster explains that only a few minutes can be allotted for the sale of the candy. He GRINDS for the next three to five minutes as butchers run into the stands selling the sweets. Winners are encouraged to go into the ring immediately to claim their prizes.

The secret to a successful candy pitch is threefold: First, the candy must be priced low enough so that a hurried, high-volume sale can be made. Second, while the prize may be attractive, audience members cannot feel cheated if they don't win. Third, to spur on rapid early sales, the audience must see lots of winners quickly.

This is accomplished by "stacking the deck," or boxes, so to speak. The billets are stuffed into the candy by the circus butchers after the cartons are received from the manufacturer; a few of those boxes are put on top and sold first during the pitch. When the audience sees many children running into the ring to claim their balloons, they figure the odds of their also winning a prize are very high. Even those who were not interested in the candy itself are often tempted to buy a box. Needless to say, the number of winners diminishes quickly; but by that time numerous sales have been made.

CARDIFF GIANT Displayed under canvas by P.T. BARNUM, the Cardiff Giant may have been the most popular hoax of the mid-1800s; but originally it was not even Barnum's hoax at all.

George Hull, a cigar manufacturer, visited his sister in Ackley, Iowa in the spring of 1868. He attended a tent revival in Fort Dodge where he heard the Reverend Turk talk about the ancient giants that had walked the earth in the time of Goliath. When the reverend claimed with biblical certainty that the giants had been twice the size of modern man, a scheme evolved in Hull's mind.

In a quarry nearby, Hull located a block of gypsum 12 feet long, four feet wide and two feet thick.

He shipped the block to a barn on North Clark Street in Chicago and hired an artist and a stonecutter to carve him a naked giant man—complete in anatomical detail—twisted, as if having died in agony.

After Hull swore the men to secrecy, the gypsum giant—crated as a piece of machinery—was shipped to Union, New York, outside of Binghamton. He convinced a near-bankrupt cousin, a farmer named William Newell, to plant the giant behind his barn in the dead of night; grass was seeded over the spot. Hull waited, as did his $2,200 investment.

The following autumn Hull instructed Newell to feign the need for a new well; and, on Friday, October 15, 1869, in the company of two well diggers, "Stub" Newell set across his property with a dowsing rod. The stick finally pointed downward—right at the spot at which a giant man was buried three feet down!

While the men went to work, Newell left under the pretense of attempting to secure a bank loan for the digging. When he returned to the farm, a crowd was already circling the unearthed giant, still in its grave. Newell pitched a tent and started charging 50 cents admission to see the Eighth Wonder of the World. Soon Hull arrived and raised the price to a dollar.

The inevitable press and profits piqued the interest of master showman P.T. Barnum. At 60 years of age, he had temporarily retired after his New American Museum on Broadway in New York City had burned to the ground in 1868. Ever the master of humbug, Barnum was fascinated by the Cardiff Giant and wanted to own it, even though he was convinced it was a hoax.

Barnum sent a representative to Syracuse to see the crowd's reaction. When he learned that in a six-hour period 3,000 people paid $1 each to see the statue, Barnum offered Newell $60,000 for a three-month lease of the Giant. Hull, through Newell, refused. Barnum was so desperate to obtain it he did the only logical thing: He contracted a Syracuse sculptor, Carl C.F. Otto, to make an exact replica of the giant.

In 1871 a syndicate of three men—among them Amos Westcott and David Hannum—convinced Newell to sell a three-quarters share of the giant for $37,500 in cash. Hannum shipped it to New York City for exhibition during the Christmas holidays. Imagine his surprise when he discovered that Barnum had just set up the "original Cardiff Giant" for display under a tent in Brooklyn for only 50 cents admission!

The syndicate took Barnum to court, but the judge would not issue an injunction against him. The judge, convinced that the Cardiff Giant was indeed a hoax, saw no legal problem in Barnum's exhibiting a fake of a fake. Barnum, of course, incorporated the details of the court hearing into his advertising.

Both Barnum and the syndicate profited, as customers demanded to see both giants to decide for themselves which was real—if either—and which was fake. In January the "original" Cardiff Giant, having recouped its syndicate's investment and more, was moved to Boston.

In an early example of investigative journalism, the press eventually decided to tackle the issue. As the story led back to Chicago, the artists—convinced that they might be jailed—told their part in the hoax. Newspapers even followed the story back to the quarry workers in Ackley, Iowa.

Confronted with the story, George Hull laughed and confessed. Newspapers across the country printed the story, and suddenly "Old Hoaxey" (as some were now calling the Cardiff Giant) was big business again.

The Cardiff Giant traveled on the carnival and fair circuit into the 1880s. In 1901 it was shown at the Pan American Exposition in Buffalo and, after several years in storage, the Giant was exhibited in 1934 at the New York State Fair in Syracuse. In 1935, owned by Gardner Cowles, Jr., the Cardiff Giant was shown at the Iowa State Fair.

In 1939 the New York State Educational Department placed markers in Cardiff, telling the story of the amazing hoax. Nine years later the New York State Historical Society purchased the statue and placed it in the Farmers' Museum in Cooperstown,

New York. It was displayed in an open grave as it was first discovered.

Of course, the end of the story concerns Barnum's hoax of a hoax. Where is the Barnum Cardiff Giant today? Bob Pelton, current curator of the new BARNUM MUSEUM in BRIDGEPORT, CONNECTICUT, suggests that "After the New York exhibition, Barnum might have toured the Giant in one his later sideshows. There is a more probable theory, however. Barnum was well known for getting full value out of an exhibition, after which he usually simply discarded it. That was most likely the fate of *his* Cardiff Giant." To this day the whereabouts of Barnum's statue are unknown.

CARL HAGENBECK WILD ANIMAL SHOW   See GREAT WALLACE SHOWS; HÄGENBACH, KARL; HAGENBECK-WALLACE CIRCUS.

CARNIVAL   See THEATER.

CARON, GUY   See CIRQUE DU SOLEIL.

CARPET CLOWN   Circus jargon for a clown who works the arena floor or up in the stands among the audience.

CARSON & BARNES CIRCUS   Begun by Jack Moore as a small motorized tent show shortly after World War II, the Carson and Barnes Circus toured the Midwest and the West. Today, it performs under the largest circus tent in the world, and it is the only show that can boast of having five full rings under the BIG TOP.

Two or three years after its inception, Dory "D.R." MILLER became a co-owner and placed an elephant in the show. His involvement in the show became full time in 1968. Moore died in the spring of 1969, and his widow and Miller ran the circus through 1970. In 1971, Miller bought Mrs. Moore out, becoming full owner. Although he now travels with the show for only a portion of the year, he is active in the offices at the WINTER QUARTERS in Hugo, Oklahoma, planning the route and working with the general agents. For more than 50 years, D.R. Miller has been more than ably assisted by his wife and partner, Isla.

Interior of the Carson & Barnes Circus Big Top during setup. Note the elephant helping to erect the mammoth tent. (Photo courtesy of Carson & Barnes Circus)

Interior of the Carson & Barnes 5-Ring Circus Big Top ready for performance. (Photo by Tom Ogden)

As the president and co-owner (with his wife and daughters) of Carson & Barnes, Geary Byrd is responsible for moving the show on schedule, as well as handling the people and problems on the road. He is married to Barbara J. Byrd, the Millers' daughter. A former performer and business school graduate, she hires the acts, themes the music within the context of the show and decides on the running order of the acts in the circus performance. They are assisted in the day-to-day management of the show on tour by the vice president and general manager of the operation, James K. Judkins.

The circus moves on more than 75 vehicles (44 show-owned transport wagons and over 30 private trucks and trailers). With two or three exceptions, the show plays only one-day stands. Visiting approximately 240 towns in the western United States

during its 38-week season, the well-organized troupe is divided into 22 departments, including crews for the tents, props, water, cookhouse, electric, mechanics and press.

The animal department includes a pack of 20 pachyderms; three of the ELEPHANTS, Barbara, Kay and Susie, have been with the Carson & Barnes Circus for over 40 years. More than a hundred more exotic and domesticated animals appear with the show, including a white rhino; many are displayed in the free MENAGERIE that exhibits in a sidewalled section between the MARQUEE and the FRONT DOOR to the BIG TOP. Also in this area is the main concessions wagon and, off to one side, the DONNIKER.

Before retiring at the end of the 1990 season, Patricia WHITE starred in the center ring for a decade as one of the few female cat trainers ever in the business. She worked with a mixed group of CATS—Nubian lions, Siberian tigers and a trained liger (from the rare breeding of a lion and a tiger).

The 95 performers for the show come from over 15 countries, although most are part of large family troupes. During the grand performance, for instance, three different sets of artists on the FLYING TRAPEZE appear simultaneously. Members of the famous LOYAL-REPENSKY TROUPE of comedy bareback riders have been featured on the show for many years.

The current MIDWAY has kiddie rides, a MOON BOUNCE, a novelties joint, a concessions stand and two or three PIT SHOWS.

The general office and winter quarters of the Carson & Barnes 5-Ring Circus are located at P.O. Box J, Hugo, Oklahoma 74743.

CARVER, DR. W.F. (1844–19??)

Born in New York State, W.F. Carver traveled west with his mother and sister when he was only four years old. After the women were killed by Sioux warriors, the Indians raised him. While he was still a boy, Carver was discovered by a white trader who took him back East.

With hardly any education—and certainly with no formal training to be a dentist—Carver conferred a D.D.S. on himself and headed back West to practice. There he became an excellent marksman: He claimed to have killed 5,700 buffalo in one winter. At one exhibition, he shattered 5,500 glass balls in seven hours using only 6,212 shots from six Winchester rifles. Later in his career, at an exhibition in New Haven, Connecticut, Carver hit 60,016 out of 64,888 targets over a six-day period. Dissatisfied, he made the same attempt on another occasion and succeeded in hitting 59,350 out of 60,000 targets.

On June 1, 1878 he returned to New York City and challenged Captain Adam H. BOGARDUS, the "Champion Wing Shot" marksman, to a competition; but the contest never took place.

Shortly thereafter Carver became involved with William F. CODY, although historians disagree as to the exact circumstances. Some claim that Carver put up the money for the Wild West, Rocky Mountain and Prairie Exhibition, the original BUFFALO BILL'S WILD WEST, which opened on May 17, 1883, and toured with the show for one season. Purportedly Cody had invited Salsbury, who co-conceived the idea of the Wild West, to join the partnership; but Salsbury dubbed Carver "a faker in the show business." Other sources contend that Carver did not join Buffalo Bill until the Wild West returned from its 1887–1893 European tour.

What is certain is that while he toured with the Wild West, Carver was a one of its featured performers, playing one of the two scouts (with Cody) who rescued the Deadwood stagecoach from an Indian attack. Carver was also an excellent showman, standing six feet two, with long wavy hair and a red mustache. His wardrobe consisted of gray trousers, a black velvet shirt, gloves and a sombrero.

As early as 1878, Carver had traveled the carnival and fair circuit with a "High Diving Horse" act. In the daredevil MIDWAY attraction, a HORSE gallops up a steep ramp. At the top, a rider (usually female) leaps onto the horse's back; and the pair jump from the tall platform into a pool of water far below.

After leaving the Wild West, Carver took his unusual equine exhibition back on the road, and he toured it until after the turn of the century. Among his riders over the years were Sonora Webster, who relearned and performed the act even after a bad jump left her blind, and Carver's daughter Lorena, who was performing the act as late as 1960.

CASTELLO, DAN (1834–1909) Although his name appears in all circus literature as Dan Castello, some circus historians believe his real name was John Costello. A former clown, he joined with W.C. COUP and P.T. BARNUM to form BARNUM'S GREAT TRAVEL-ING MUSEUM, MENAGERIE, CARAVAN, HIPPODROME AND CIRCUS, which opened under canvas in Brooklyn, New York on April 10, 1871.

Castello assumed the duties of director of amusements, while Coup was general manager and Barnum handled promotion.

The show began traveling by rail in 1872, and that winter performances were held at the HIPPOTHEATRON in New York. After that building was destroyed by fire in 1873, the Traveling Museum wintered in the new P.T. BARNUM'S GREAT ROMAN HIPPODROME.

Castello left the show in 1875, and Coup left during a disagreement soon thereafter. Barnum turned management of their show over to the FLATFOOTS, who handled the tours until 1880.

CASTLE, HUBERT (1912–c.1977) A master wire walker, Hubert Castle did not perform on a taut cord, or tightrope. His domain was the slack wire, which had about a ten-inch give under his weight.

He was born Hal Smith in Enid, Oklahoma. He first became interested in WIRE WALKING when he saw Bird MILLMAN play his hometown with the Ringling show in 1919. Within two months Castle had learned to walk a clothesline and even sit on a chair he had balanced on the cord. He enlisted a buddy, Bunny Dryden, into the act; soon the boys were playing local dates.

In the summer of 1926, Hubert and Bunny, aged 14 and 15 respectively, joined the ORTON BROS. CIRCUS for $60 a week. Billed as Smith and Dryden, they performed wire walking, acrobatics and strongman stunts.

In 1928 Smith's father bought a circus and the two young men joined. Unfortunately, the show went bankrupt within a season. Smith joined the John S. Silver Circus and changed his name to Hal Silver, feeling that the word "silver" reflected on his connection to the wire.

He bounced from circus to circus, finally winding up in the Al G. Barnes and Sells-Floto Circus. Because John RINGLING wanted to bill him as a star from England, Smith-Silver changed his stage name for a final time to the more British-sounding Hubert Castle.

In 1935 he toured with the Tom Mix Circus where he met and later married Mary Tanner. It was about this time that Castle and Dryden split up as a team.

By that time, Dryden had switched from the slack to the high wire. Unfortunately, not long after, Dryden fell to his death while performing spins over and under the wire.

While never reaching the fame and status of Bird Millman or Con COLLEANO, Hubert Castle was an esteemed and admired wire walker throughout his entire career.

CATCHER Circus jargon for the member of a trapeze team who, literally, catches the aerialist after he has jumped from the swinging bar in a flying act.

(See also AERIAL ACTS; FLYING TRAPEZE.)

CATS Circus jargon for all of the wild animals in the cat family, such as lions, tigers, leopards, panthers and cheetahs. They are also sometimes referred to as "big cats."

Each species has its unique temperament and abilities. In the minds of the public, the lion is, of course, the "King of the Beasts." "In my opinion it is," said Damoo DHOTRE, famed trainer of the RINGLING BROS. AND BARNUM & BAILEY CIRCUS. "First of all, he looks the part. He looks like a king. He has size; he has dignity; he has what appears to be great pride. Secondly, even though some of the smaller animals can attack faster than he can, the long hair around his neck usually prevents his getting killed."

Coming from Africa, the lion is the largest of the cat family. Only the male sports the golden mane around the head and neck. Although noisy and raucous, lions are highly intelligent and able to learn tricks when quite young.

Lions can be deadly, however. Lions do not pounce: They rush in short jumps and try to knock the victims down with their body or a paw. With its long, sharp claws, the paw is very heavy and can easily break a person's neck or back.

Lions are fiercest when males and females are mixed together in the ring. In the wild, lions travel in prides, or groups; when the female comes into heat, the males will fight over her until one is a clear victor. To avoid any such problems, circus trainers keep lionesses out of the ring when they are in heat.

Despite the more ferocious look of lions, the tigers are the most vicious and the least reliable of the cats. Almost as large as lions, the average tiger is 12 or 13 feet in length and weighs up to 450 pounds.

Indian tigers are only slightly less savage than its cousin, the Royal Bengal. They can be told apart by their stripes: An Indian tiger's stripes are not as sharp and blend more into the fur. Both animals are violent, fast and quick-tempered. Nevertheless, they are intelligent as well and can be taught many tricks.

Spotted leopards are much smaller, weighing in at about 150 pounds. Panthers are actually leopards that have an excess of pigmentation, causing them to appear black. Spotted leopards may produce black panthers in their litters, and vice versa. Panthers are not solid black, however: Their coats actually consist of varying dark spots against a black coat. Perhaps because the "freak" coat does not camouflage well in the jungle, panthers have become even faster than leopards.

Many trainers consider panthers the most dangerous animals to work with, because they are impossible to make into friends. They never pass through a playful "kitten" period. Surly almost from birth, they are the most difficult to train.

Spotted jaguars look like leopards but are indigenous to the Western Hemisphere, from Texas to Paraguay. They are larger and heavier than their Eastern Hemisphere counterpart, and their faces are larger and more triangular in shape. In fact, their heads and necks more closely resemble those of bulls than felines. Jaguars are not very intelligent—which makes them hard to train—and they are as mean as leopards.

Black jaguars are also "freaks" of nature. Like black panthers, they do not blend in well with the jungle and so have become one of the most violent, vicious cats.

Despite their seemingly impervious constitutions, wild cats have their weaknesses. The big cats, for instance, are prone to sinus trouble and can easily develop headaches.

The first exhibition of a lion (or "Lyon of Barbary," as it was advertised) in the American colonies took place in 1716. This was probably the first exhibition and tour of an exotic animal in North America. The first exhibition of a leopard in the colonies occurred in 1768.

Compared to these cats, the tiger was a relative latecomer to the shores of North America (with the CAMEL and BEAR having also preceded it). The first announcement of an exhibition of a tiger was in the

New York *Daily Advertiser* in May 16, 1789. Tigers were seen regular on tour and in MENAGERIES after 1805.

The first major American animal trainer was Isaac A. VAN AMBURGH; and it was Van Amburgh who devised the classic stunt of placing a head into a lion's mouth. He stunned audiences by entering a cage of mixed cats on the stage of the Richmond Hill Theatre, New York, in 1833. Before Van Amburgh stepped into the BIG CAGE during a performance, cats were seen only as menagerie animals for exhibition and not as a circus act. Van Amburgh became world famous as a trainer, earning up to $400 a week. Soon he had saved enough to open his own show. Van Amburgh died a rich man in 1865, and he was so famous that his name was used as a title on other shows up until 1908.

From the times of pioneering trainers such as Van Amburgh to modern masters of the big cage such as Gunther GEBEL-WILLIAMS, the artists in the steel arena have always thrilled and amazed American circus audiences.

(See also BAUMANN, CHARLY; BEATTY, CLYDE; CAGE BOY; COURT, ALFRED; EN FÉROCITÉ; HENDERSON, J.Y. "DOC"; JACOBS, CAPT. TERRELL; ROTH, LOUIS; STARK, MABEL; TOGNI, FLAVIO; WHITE, PATRICIA.)

CATTLE GUARD Circus jargon, mostly outdated, for a row of seats placed in front of the general admission seats for overflowing crowds.

(See also STRAWHOUSE.)

CENTER POLE As the name suggests, center poles are the main poles in the middle of the tent that hold up the canvas top. Smaller TENTS may have only one center pole, but the mammoth BIG TOPS sometimes require as many as six center poles. Holding up a peak of the tent, a center pole can weigh as much as a ton and be up to 60 feet high.

The first center pole to be raised on the Big Top has its own nickname, the "king pole." It is along this pole that all the rest of the poles are sighted.

CENTER RING The multiple-ring circus is a uniquely American invention, growing out of the single-ring European tradition. The circus ring was first established by Philip ASTLEY in his London riding academy as a means of controlling his horses' movements in a circular path. Many credited Laurent and Henri

Franconi, sons of Antoine Franconi (the owner of the Franconi Hippodrome) as having standardized the 13-meter (approximately 42.9 feet) diameter size.

Although historians debate the earliest experimentation with extra rings under a canvas BIG TOP, credit is often given to W.C. COUP for establishing them as standard practice when he and his partners Dan CASTELLO and P.T. BARNUM were touring Barnum's Great Traveling World Fair in about 1875. The men realized that by moving their circus onto rails, they could skip the smaller, less profitable towns. Larger crowds in the cities, augmented by additional customers brought in by special excursion trains, required a bigger tent. When patrons seated far away from the ring began to complain, the partners decided to add a second ring under the top, with two acts performing simultaneously.

Within a few years, most of the major shows carried two rings of entertainment. Adam FOREPAUGH, a Barnum rival, still had only two rings on his circus when the BARNUM & BAILEY CIRCUS premiered the first three-ring circus in MADISON SQUARE GARDEN in 1881.

Three rings soon became the industry standard. Many times all of the rings were filled with the same type of acts, such as jugglers or ACROBATS. The more spectacular acts of the circus stars, however, were given special attention. The CENTER RING was reserved for their solo spots, and an act asked to perform in the center ring was considered the best act of its kind in the show.

CHANDELIER See SHANTY.

CHANG AND ENG (1811–1874) Chang and Eng, one of the most unusual curiosities ever exhibited, were brought to the AMERICAN MUSEUM in October 1860 by P.T. BARNUM after they had already appeared all over the world.

Born of Chinese parents in Meklong, Siam on May 11, 1811, Chang and Eng Bunker (their names mean "Left" and "Right" in Thai) were inseparably joined at the lower chest by a thick tube of skin, known as a cartilaginous band. Over the years they consulted a number of surgeons, only to be told repeatedly that separation would certainly cause death to one or both of them.

The twins were of opposite temperament. Sometimes they argued and went weeks without speaking to each other. Chang was an inch shorter than Eng, had an angry temper and was a drinking man. Eng was quiet, unassuming and a tea drinker. Remarkably, Eng never felt the effects of his brother's use of alcohol.

The twins arrived in this country in 1829, moved to Wilkes County, North Carolina and soon became American citizens. In 1843 the twins entered semi-retirement in Mt. Airy, North Carolina and married Sarah and Adelaide Yates, the daughters of an Irish farmer. For half the week the twins stayed in one house with Chang's wife; for the rest of week they lived with Eng's wife. Chang and Sarah parented ten children, and the other couple 12 children.

Chang and Eng's common interest seemed to be hunting and fishing, as well as a dislike of P.T. Barnum. Even after they married, Chang and Eng occasionally went out on tour, and it was during this brief period that they appeared at the American Museum. The twins felt that Barnum did not pay them adequately, making too much money off of their misfortune.

Barnum did not particularly like Chang and Eng either. Some historians feel that he could never completely forget that he had not personally discovered them.

Chang died first on January 17, 1874 at the age of 62; Eng followed less than three hours later, before a doctor could arrive. Their notoriety lives on, however: Even though Chang and Eng were Chinese, to this day twins joined together at birth are referred to as SIAMESE TWINS.

See also FREAKS.

CHARACTER CLOWNS   Within the world of the circus, there are at least two major types or styles of CLOWNS. The first are the WHITEFACE CLOWNS, whose makeup and costumes are an outgrowth of the Italian Commedia dell' Arte and British pantomime. They worked in a white face, accented with colored markings and handsome costume, also often white; the comedy consisted of gentle gags and slapstick. As their "patron saint" they have Joseph GRIMALDI who, in developing his character, earned the title of "the father of clowning." Today all clowns are nicknamed JOEY in his honor.

Simultaneously, at the beginning of the 19th century, a more rugged clown was developing on the European continent. These were not "pretty" clowns, and their makeup consisted mainly of colored marks or designs drawn directly onto the flesh rather than a cover-all greasepaint base. Their wardrobe was usually standard clothing, but ill-fitting or badly matched or torn. Their style of comedy had a more physical, knockabout nature. Rather than "prank-pullers," these clowns were struggling at odds against the world or their peers, creating comedy through the frustration and obstacles they encountered. These became known as character clowns.

Although many types of clowns fall into this catch-all category, two major kinds of character clowns predominate. Over time they created a distinct "look" for each.

The most common character clowns are the AUGUSTE CLOWNS. Generally credited to Tom Belling, an American gymnast working in a German circus, the development of the auguste clown—with its pink face and red highlights—is most probably based on the earlier Russian R'IZHII clowns with which he was familiar.

The other kind of character clown is an American creation that is only about 100 years old. Its look and actions have been so firmly established by such masters as Emmett KELLY and Otto GRIEBLING that it is often considered to be in a category of its own—the TRAMP CLOWN.

Since character clowns depend as much on their individual personalities, physical traits and actions as they do on specific makeup, they can be as varied as the artists and the imaginations creating them.

CHARIVARI   Circus jargon, sometimes spelled "shivaree" or "chivaree." The charivari is the noisy, boisterous and chaotic entrance (and, occasionally, the exit) of the artists. While the charivari could include tumblers and jugglers, the image is primarily of the CLOWNS entering in madcap madness, merriment and confusion.

The term most likely comes from the Latin word *caribari*, which means "headache." Its circus use was probably adapted from a rustic ritual, a mock serenade with pots, pans and kettles given in honor of a married couple on their wedding night. (Theatergoers will remember just such a scene in Rodger and Hammerstein's *Oklahoma*.) Over time, any loud and grandiose celebration has come to be known as a charivari.

Some linguists trace the word to the name given to the loose pants worn by Arabian ACROBATS in the tenth century and earlier. Their acts of tumbling and other gymnastics usually ended with a free-for-all whirling dervish dance; and the air was filled with moving colors and ballooning "charivari."

CHERRY PIE Circus jargon for the extra pay received by regular circus employees for performing additional work. This work could be an added performance or help with the heavy labor, or CHINESE. The term is also used to refer to the work duties themselves, as in "He worked 'cherry pie' to earn more money."

CHIMPANZEES Chimpanzees are among the most popular animal actors of the circus. They are apes, classified in the Primate order.

Chimpanzees, probably the smartest of the Pongidae family, are the most adaptable and the most common of all apes. They are also meaner and cause more trouble than their cousins. Their arms are strong: If they grab hold, they can easily pull a captive up close to bite with their incredibly sharp teeth. With a patient trainer, however, they can be made quite friendly.

They are not much kinder to their peers than they are to humans. If one chimp in a pair is weaker or shyer, the stronger one will continually beat on it. If they are left alone to feed, the stronger will eat all of the food, or keep the timid one away from it until the weak chimp starves.

Despite their fur, chimps are frail and very susceptible to colds due to drafts and dampness. They love the water, though, and are excellent swimmers and divers.

Chimps make the best performers at the age of five, and they can do routines such as bicycle riding until the age of ten or 12. After that, they usually turn nasty and become unmanageable.

See also MONKEYS AND APES.

CHINESE Circus jargon for the regular heavy labor of setting up the TENTS and equipment, as well as the name given to the work crew. The term has a racist origin: At the turn of the century, many businesses, including most circuses, employed large work crews of immigrant Asians to do the physical labor for low wages.

CHOOSING DAY On some of the early MUD SHOWS, such as the GREAT WALLACE SHOWS, a particular day was designated early in the season for unmarried staff and management to choose their bunkmates of the opposite sex for the remainder of the tour. After that, no exchanges were allowed.

This arrangement—or any situation in which members of the opposite sex cohabitated without the benefit of a legal marriage—was known as a carny wedding.

By the 1920s most circuses, especially the SUNDAY SCHOOL SHOWS, had very strict sexual taboos and any such "agreements" were greatly frowned upon.

On the AMERICAN CIRCUS CORPORATION shows, for example, management staff members were fined $5 if they were caught speaking with a showgirl for any reason; "hoteling up" with one on a Sunday (or any non-show day) was grounds for instant dismissal.

CHOREOGRAPHY, CIRCUS Perhaps one of the most overlooked occupations in the modern circus is that of the choreographer. While trying to realize the original conception of the director and the rest of the production staff, the choreographer must work with many artists who, although skilled athletes, are not trained dancers.

Of course, movement and dance have always been important parts of the modern circus. Until recently, however, the job of putting together the SPECS, parades and displays on most circuses has been relegated to an overall show director who received a program credit such as "Entire production designed by . . ."

In the 1950s Richard Barstow was listed not only as the director and stager but also the choreographer of the RINGLING BROS. AND BARNUM & BAILEY CIRCUS. Assisted by his sister, Edith, the Barstows spent about four months planning the show around a theme, then went to SARASOTA, FLORIDA to train the company in WINTER QUARTERS.

Today's choreographers also bring years of dance training and experience to the circus ring. Carl Jablonski, for example, has been the choreographer for the Ringling show for the past three years, for both the 121st and 122nd editions. Born in Gary, Indiana on June 23, 1937, he began to perform acrobatics and floor tumbling at the age of four; he was in tap and ballet shoes by five. At 18, he danced in the original company of *My Fair Lady.*

Jablonski moved to France, where he danced for four years and served as assistant choreographer to a Parisian dance company. He learned how to stage large spectaculars, a skill that would be invaluable years later with the BIG ONE. He used this ability while working as an assistant to Donn Arden, who staged the Lido de Paris shows in Paris and at the Stardust in Las Vegas, as well as the Holiday on Ice arena tours.

Jablonski appeared as a dancer for six years on Carol Burnett's television series. Meanwhile, he had become a noted choreographer himself, working on the "Minsky's Burlesque" at the Hacienda in Las Vegas and the "Howdy Doody 40th Anniversary Reunion Special" on television in 1987.

In 1990 director/choreographer Walter Painter asked Jablonski to help him mount the Red Unit in Venice, Florida. Jablonski did so and returned a year later to work on the Blue Unit.

Carl Jablonski says:

We used every act in the show in the big production numbers and specs. In fact, in 1991, we needed to find translators for the Chinese, Mongolian and Russian performers so that they could understand our directions.

In addition to putting 200-plus people from the cast, including all of the Clown Alley, into the major numbers and parades, we also had to integrate 32 elephants, camels, llamas and horses. It's just a wonderful experience to work on such a grand scale and to truly be part of "The Greatest Show on Earth."

As shows such as CIRQUE DU SOLEIL, the PICKLE FAMILY CIRCUS, THE BIG APPLE CIRCUS and others shift more and more toward theatrical styles, the art of dance becomes an increasingly important ingredient in the mix of circus elements.

CHRISTY BROS. CIRCUS
Beginning in 1910 as a vaudeville and tented movie theater, Christy's Big Hippodrome Shows changed to a circus format in 1914. The owner, George W. Christy of Texas, started expanding his two railroad-car show in 1919, and by 1921 there were seven cars. Only four years later the Christy Bros. Circus boasted 20 cars. It was one of the few rail shows of its time to operate independent of the Ringling organization and the AMERICAN CIRCUS CORPORATION.

The Depression devastated the show, and half of the train was sent back to its Houston, Texas WINTER QUARTERS in 1930. The cuts were not enough to save the circus, however, and it closed forever in Greeley, Colorado on July 7 of that year. The remaining equipment was later sold to the COLE BROS. CIRCUS.

CIRCUS AMERICA
A one-season wonder owned by Abe Pollin, Circus America was really created as part of a feud between him and Ringling's Irvin FELD.

Pollin, a building contractor, was working on the Capital Centre in Washington, D.C., when he approached his then-friend Feld for assistance in securing a hockey franchise for the new arena. Feld agreed to help, asking in exchange for favorable booking terms for Ringling, exclusive concession rights and an option to buy shares in the new team.

After the franchise was granted, Pollin and Feld disagreed on the terms of their arrangement. The dispute caused Pollin to refuse to book the Ringling show into the arena at all.

In an attempt to prove he could produce a show every bit as glamorous as the Ringling show, Pollin hired Karl WALLENDA and Paul V. KAYE in 1974 to help create Circus America. To further upset Feld, Pollin filled the cast with former Ringling stars.

As soon as the Circus America dates were announced for the new Capital Centre, Feld booked Ringling into the nearby D.C. Armory to DAY AND DATE the show. His plan, of course, was to have the press favorably compare his show to Circus America; but it failed when critics praised both shows equally.

Pollin, having won a moral victory, decided not to tour the short-lived Circus America. Later, Ringling did play the Capital Centre, no doubt after many behind-the-scenes compromises on the part of both entrepreneurs.

CIRCUS CAMPS
Over the years, many summer camps have added the teaching of circus skills to their activities. Some of the performance-oriented camps have even made it a major part of their curriculum. Others may specialize in one or more circus skills, such as clowning or JUGGLING.

Clown Camp

Since 1982 the University of Wisconsin–La Crosse has been the site of CLOWN CAMP. The project was begun as the brainchild of continuing education director Richard Snowberg, himself a noted clown. Snowberg is a former WORLD CLOWN ASSOCIATION "Clown of the Year" recipient for his work as "Snowflake." He is a past president of the association and has chaired its international convention. In addition, he has written four books on clowning and has served on the board of directors of the CLOWN HALL OF FAME & RESEARCH CENTER since it was founded.

Clown Camp's four-week-long training sessions are held between the Saturday of Memorial Day weekend and midsummer each year; students are housed, double occupancy, in resident dormitories and eat on campus. Each morning has two periods of classes, followed by "Clown Alley Meetings," in which students convene in small, informal groups of their peers to discuss common concerns. After lunch and a chance to shop in the camp store, students apply their makeup in preparation for the third class of the day. After dinner there is an evening performance or activity.

Students may choose from six different subject areas each period taught by a staff of 30 professionals; classes have been structured for beginners to advanced clowns. Eighty percent of the classes, such as Balloon Sculpturing and Comedy Magic, are offered every week; but some, such as Nosemaking, are offered only certain weeks. Also, each week has a special theme, so even the regular classes are taught with a different emphasis from week to week. The themes include: Physical Comedy, Getting Your Act Together, the Caring Clown/Theraputic Humor, and Clown Education/Teaching.

Enrollment at the 1991 camp drew 1,500 registrants, which turned out to be too unwieldy. As a result, the 1992 camp limited each individual class within the weekly session to 165 persons.

Throughout the rest of the year, the University of Wisconsin–La Crosse offers "Clown Camp on the Road," weekend seminars conducted by master clowns and held regionally throughout the United States.

Circus Smirkus

Circus Smirkus was started in 1987 by Rob Mermin as a summer camp project located in Greensboro, Vermont. Each July approximately 20 youngsters aged 10 to 17 show up at Mermin's farm for two weeks of training in circus skills. A canvas tented, one-ring circus tour is then undertaken, traveling anywhere from 15 to 20 towns in Vermont, New Hampshire and Massachusetts. A not-for-profit organization, Circus Smirkus was at first partly funded by the Catamount Arts Foundation; but now it is mostly self-sustaining through ticket sales.

In 1990 Circus Smirkus traveled to the Soviet Union. Joining with students from the MOSCOW CIRCUS school under the direction of Alla Anatolevna Yudina, they formed the Soviet/American Youth Circus. The troupe sold out 2,000-seat houses and won top honors at the International Children's Performance Festival held on the Black Sea.

In 1991 Mermin, with the help of Vermont's Project Harmony, engineered an ambitious undertaking with Yudina: a Latvian/American circus exchange in which the Juaniba Troupe—ten teenagers from Riga, Latvia, plus adult support staff—joined the American troupers to make Circus Smirkus a truly international show.

Circus Smirkus currently performs under a 70-foot round BIG TOP and travels on four trucks, two vans and a dressing-room tent-and-food bus. The 1992 show brought members of Moscow Circus school to Vermont. Also joining the cast were performers from The Great All American Circus, a year-round circus club under the direction of Jan Garrett and sponsored by the Redlands Family YMCA of Redlands, California. Together the three companies formed the National Youth Circus.

Circus Smirkus can be contacted by writing its offices in Greensboro, Vermont 05841 or by telephoning (802) 533-7125.

Tannen's Magic Camp

While courses at Tannen's Magic Camp are not aimed specifically at developing circus performers, the magic classes teach routines that are commonly used by amateur as well as professional circus clowns. Sponsored by Tannen's Magic Company of New York City, the school is a one-week intensive camp for kids aged 12 to 19. The only professional camp geared solely to the art of magic, it is held on one of the last two weeks in August at the LaSalle Academy on Long Island.

Each year a lecture is given in general stage makeup, and often one is presented on clown makeup as well. Many of the students are jugglers, in addition to being magicians; when the instructors are not looking, balls, rings and pins are frequently seen zooming down the dormitory hallways. At least one instructor each year is qualified to teach JUGGLING, and he or she holds informal sessions in juggling and sometimes unicycling outside on the spacious grounds.

Circus of the Kids

Founded in 1982 by Bruce Pfeffer, Circus of the Kids started as part of the New England Experience summer camp. Pfeffer was quickly joined by Tammy Lutter, a fire-eater/clown/trick cyclist and elementary school teacher, who had been teaching circus skills at French Woods Festival of the Performing Arts located in Hancock, New York. Since its inception, over 50,000 students have been a part of Pfeffer's programs.

During the scholastic year, Pfeffer approaches a school system, offering one- and two-week training workshops to groups of students at all grade levels. The school system provides all props, wardrobe and safety equipment for the rehearsals. Pfeffer also aims to promote academics; along with associates at the University of Louisville, he created "Circus Across the Curriculum," a syllabus of circus-related studies within standard school subject areas. Separate training sessions are also available for parents and teachers. The workshops culminate in a circus recital-performance.

During the summer, Circus of the Kids becomes part of the performance schedule of French Woods.

Ringling Brothers and Barnum & Bailey Circus Camp

In 1991, for the first time, the BIG ONE teamed up with an ongoing summer camp, Youth World Camp, Inc., to produce the Ringling Bros. and Barnum & Bailey Circus Camp. In addition to regular camp activities, the camp teaches the students clowning, FLYING TRAPEZE, STILT WALKING, JUGGLING and other skills. More information on the camp is available by contacting Youth World Camps, 10 Old Court Road, Baltimore, Maryland 21208-9943, telephone (800) CIRCUS-0.

CIRCUS CIRCUS   In 1968, amid the glitter and neon of the Las Vegas strip, a casino hotel opened with the then-novel approach of attracting families—not just high-rollers—to its doors. A bold mixture of traditional family entertainment and adult gambling facilities, Circus Circus is considered to be the world's largest permanent circus.

Housed under a unique pink-and-white striped, 90-foot-high, Flexiglass tent-shaped roof are the casino, the dining facilities and the circus and carnival MIDWAYS. Outside on the Strip, a giant neon sign featuring an animated clown attracts passersby. The main doors to the BIG TOP are built marquee-style to resemble the main entrance of a tented show; visitors walk directly into the casino, located on ground level.

After passing through the casino, a circular ramp or stairs leads to an upper level that contains a carnival midway, with 39 games of chance, 300 video arcade games, kiddie rides, fast-food stations, a souvenir gift shop—and even a booth for face-painting where children can be made up to "be a clown."

The games circle the feature attraction of Circus Circus: free, continuous circus acts from around the world. Performing in a circus ring, ground and aerial acts rotate with only short breaks in between, giving the audiences virtual nonstop entertainment for 13 hours every day, from 11 A.M. until midnight.

Circus Circus opened on October 18, 1968, at a reported cost of $15 million. Covering 129,000 square feet, in addition to the tent-shaped main structure, the hotel features 2,800 rooms and a futuristic Circus Sky Shuttle and Circus Skywalk linking the 29-story Circus Skyrise with the Big Top. There is also a 421-space Circusland recreational vehicle park on the grounds.

In 1978 a sister casino, also named Circus Circus, opened in Reno, Nevada. Following the same architectural and entertainment concepts as the Las Vegas property, Circus Circus/Reno has grown from its original 104 rooms to a 27-story Circus Skyway Tower with 1,625 rooms.

Listed in the *Guinness Book of World Records*, Circus Circus/Reno is fronted by the world's most massive animated sign. The gigantic advertising board, featuring Topsy the Clown, is 127 feet high, weighs over 45 tons and contains more than 1.4 miles of neon tubing. It is so large that Topsy's smile is 14 feet long.

In addition to its two circus-themed casino hotels, Circus Circus Enterprises also owns and operates

Excalibur Hotel/Casino, Silver City Casino and Slots-A-Fun Casino in Las Vegas as well as the Edgewater Hotel & Casino and the Colorado Bell Hotel & Casino in Laughlin, Nevada.

CIRCUS FANFARE The official publication of WIND-JAMMERS UNLIMITED, INC., *Circus Fanfare* is dedicated to the preservation and proliferation of traditional as well as new circus music. Its articles range from the historical to the currently newsworthy, and they are of interest to musicians and lovers of show music alike.

The bimonthly magazine was founded in 1971 by Art Stensvad and Charles Bennett, Jr. The journal is free to members of the Windjammers society, which is located at 2500 Old Forest Road, Corydon, Indiana 47112.

CIRCUS FANS ASSOCIATION OF AMERICA Known simply as Circus Fans of America or CFA, the Circus Fans Association of America is the largest fraternal organization dedicated to the love and preservation of the circus in America. It was formally founded during a May 1926 meeting in Washington, D.C., by interested businesspeople and professionals. At the meeting, the members met with President Calvin Coolidge and John RINGLING.

The actual association dates back more than a year earlier, however; and 107 charter members were enlisted by the end of 1925. Two U.S. Senators were among the first members; the Roman Catholic Bishop of Iowa served as the initial chaplain.

The CFA motto became "We Pay As We Go," a credo that let circuses know that the members did not expect free passes or special favors just because of their affiliation. In 1927, at the national convention in West Baden, Indiana, the slogan was adapted to include the words—which have also since been modified—"We Stand Between the Grifting Circus and the Public and Between the Grafting Public and the Circus."

At the 1929 national convention in Chicago, the New York City members were upset that they were denied the honorary title "Tent #1," even though the name had already been bestowed on the Iowa state delegation. Later the title dispute was resolved when the national organization was divided into state organizations known as "Tops" and local city chapters known as "Tents," most of which are named after famous area circus professionals. At the time, however, the conflict caused a major rift, and the New York group split away from the CFA to form another club, eventually evolving into the CIRCUS SAINTS AND SINNERS.

The Circus Fans Association of America publishes a bimonthly magazine, *The WHITE TOPS,* which is filled with club news, circus reviews and historical articles. *The White Tops* began as a four-page magazine in May 1927. Before that, *BILLBOARD* carried a weekly column dedicated to CFA news.

Association members can now be seen on nearly every circus LOT in the United States, cutting up JACKPOTS with friends and circus performers and often assisting in the labor and daily gofer chores. Information on CFA can be obtained through its offices at P.O. Box 3187, Flint, Michigan 48502.

CIRCUS FLORA Circus Flora, which has WINTER QUARTERS in St. Louis and tours mostly the Midwest, is the performing unit of the Circus Arts Foundation of Missouri. Founded in 1985 by David Balding, Sheila Balding Jewell, her husband, Sam, and Sacha Pavlata, the foundation, a not-for-profit theatrical and educational corporation, has a threefold mission: to produce Circus Flora as the most interesting one-ring circus in America; to foster appreciation of circus as an art form to a diverse audience; and to teach circus arts. The Circus Arts School, aimed at developing skills of inner-city youth, is run by Pavlata and Jessica Hentoff.

The interior of Circus Flora's one ring is covered with real sawdust, and a clown acts as RINGMASTER for the show. Like the current editions of shows such as the CIRQUE DU SOLEIL, The BIG APPLE CIRCUS and the PICKLE FAMILY CIRCUS, the program tells a complete story. The plots are advanced by the use of circus skills. This is not surprising, since one of the main CLOWNS appearing with the 1990 edition of the Circus Flora was Larry "Lorenzo Pickle" Pisoni, one of the co-founders of the Pickle Family Circus.

CIRCUS GATTI See GATTI, "MAJOR" JOSEPH.

CIRCUS HISTORICAL SOCIETY A fraternal organization of fans, the Circus Historical Society (CHS) is dedicated to preserving the lore of the circus, even as it separates fact from fantasy.

In its bimonthly publication *BANDWAGON: The Journal of the Circus Historical Society,* the society offers detailed descriptions of performers, shows and seasons in carefully documented articles. The CHS also hosts an annual summer convention.

The offices of the Circus Historical Society change annually with the election of the secretary-treasurer. Information on the society may best be obtained through the offices for *Bandwagon* at 2515 Dorset Road, Columbus, Ohio 43221.

CIRCUS JAEGER After years of experience on circuses in the United States and Japan, Eric Jaeger opened his own show in 1986. With WINTER QUARTERS in Kansas, Circus Jaeger travels a TERRITORY that extends eastward to New York State, playing mostly one-nighters.

The circus is performed in a one-ring format under an 85-foot vinyl round top. The canvas is laced to a ridge beam that is suspended between two CENTER POLES. The BIG TOP holds 700 people on one side, with seven-row, grandstand-style seating next to a 39-foot ring.

The entire top folds to travel, along with the show's seat stringers, poles and other equipment, on a single trailer, all pulled by a truck that also carries the show's GENNIE.

A semi-trailer, pulled by a rented tractor, holds the sleeper for the ROUSTABOUTS, the concessions, the ticket window and, in the back, the seat jacks and planks. Lights and sound equipment travel in the concessions section of the trailer.

The show families own additional equipment to carry their own RING STOCK, apparatus and living quarters. Besides the concessions and ticket windows, the MIDWAY carries only a pony ride.

Despite its compact size, Circus Jaeger gives a full, family show, with more than a dozen displays, including LIBERTY HORSES, ROSINBACK riding, an elephant act, trained dogs, JUGGLING and aerial acts.

CIRCUS KINGDOM, THE Conceived, founded and directed by the Rev. Dr. L. David and Trudy HARRIS, The Circus Kingdom is a traveling youth project that—while entertaining with traditional circus acts in a ring format backed by live band music—stresses peace, brotherhood, cooperation and a commitment to God.

The Circus Kingdom has been David Harris's dream project as far back as 1962 when he was an Evangelical United Brethren pastor in Philadelphia. Despite several attempts, funding was initially unavailable for his "living example" of shared humanitarian values.

In 1969 Harris suggested that Dr. Charles W. BOAS seek church sponsorship for the CIRCUS KIRK. For several years Harris was on the advisory board of the Kirk; and, in 1971, he traveled with the show as chaplain with his wife, Trudy, acting as nurse.

Harris's work as a journalist, choir director, musician and teacher of communication and sociology after the Kirk season were all to come into play in 1973. It was then that The Circus Kingdom finally became a reality. Loans and gifts from the Central Pennsylvania United Methodist Conference and the John Schmidt Foundation, coupled with the support of the Otterbein United Methodist Church in Dover, Pennsylvania (where Harris was current minister), made the circus possible. The first summer consisted of a troupe of 25 people all of whom, like people at Circus Kirk, were of college age. Playing indoor dates for five weeks in Pennsylvania, Maryland and Washington, D.C., the troupe gave 60 charity performances and 15 public shows.

Trudy Harris's work with the show was also of immense importance. Some even compared her drive and energy to Mollie BAILEY, the pioneer circus woman. Every day she would coordinate the schedules with sponsors, assist in meal planning, serve as nurse and help tend to the hundreds of other details of a touring show. In fact, her name became a running gag with the show. Those whose turn it was to assist in the day's chores—"Trudy helpers"—were said to have drawn "Trudy duty," which could mean anything from washing dishes to loading the "Trudy mobile" and transporting equipment to the next town.

The second season was expanded to 11 weeks in 12 states, but the number of public shows was increased to help pay for operating and equipment costs. The WINTER QUARTERS was also moved to Washington, D.C. because Harris was transferred there to be associate pastor of the Capitol Hill United Methodist Church. An official not-for-profit corporate status allowed The Circus Kingdom to receive funds from the National Endowment for the Arts.

Nine unicyclists in a row on The Circus Kingdom. (Photo courtesy of the Rev. Dr. L. David Harris, The Circus Kingdom)

There were two units in 1976. One performed daily in residence at Busch Gardens in Williamsburg, Virginia, while the other toured. By mid-1977 The Circus Kingdom had given over 2,000 performances in 30 states, the District of Columbia and Canada; more than 150 performers and musicians had gone through its ranks in all.

The show did not tour from 1978 to 1987 for a variety of reasons. David Harris changed home bases several times making it difficult to set up a practical circus office and winter quarters, and the show also had difficulty securing funding. Perhaps the primary cause, however, was Harris's constant battle with ill health.

Two cast reunions were held during the "hiatus" period. In 1983 there was a weekend retreat in Charleston, West Virginia, with the company giving two public shows. In 1987, during a reunion in Dallas, Texas, a small show was given at Dallas's Children's Hospital. It was discovered that many of The Circus Kingdom alumni had continued in the entertainment field: At least seven had "turned pro"

as performers; five had produced their own small indoor shows; several had run their own gymnastic schools or had become trainers; and even more had become involved in film or stage work.

In 1988, based at a new parish in Pennsylvania and with his health stabilized, David Harris was ready to tackle the complexities of running another tour. Trudy, a nurse at the Oakland Veterans Administration Medical Center in Pittsburgh, was also eager to "make it a go." They secured a promise from the officers of Calvary United Methodist Church in Pittsburgh (where David Harris was on the pastoral staff) to make the circus its youth ministries project. Gamma Phi Circus at Illinois State University loaned the equipment for the summer; and Lebanon Valley College, associated with the United Methodist Church in Annville, Pennsylvania offered academic credit in physical education for its college participants.

Since all of the performers on The Circus Kingdom must still be registered college or university students, the 1988 season started out with a whole new troupe from those who traveled WITH IT in the early 1970s. David Harris said:

The percentage of returning performers from year to year is pretty small. Back in the '70s the repeats were about one-third to one-half. Not any more. The performers this past summer numbered about 24 to 25, three of which were repeated from the previous summer.

Some graduate; some of them want to try something else. We only pay $100 a week, plus, of course, room and board. Some feel they can do better elsewhere; but [after] they have withholdings taken out and pay other expenses, they come out about the same. We've had two people, however, that have been with us three years; and one may be returning next summer. On the average, we will number three to six repeats each summer.

The Circus Kingdom remains closely affiliated with the church. "Most all of the kids are at least open to religion and there's a small percentage that are particularly religious," Harris said.

In the application, there's a pretty strong essay question that is designed to weed out those that might be hostile to religion and the church. I do that because on Sundays everybody goes to the local church where we're staying; and, of course, we stay in local churches all the time.

Religiously, I try for variety. Two summers ago I recruited heavily from a Seventh Day Adventist college in northern California that was heavy with gymnastics emphasis. I thought having the ultra-conservative Adventist kids on the show would be interesting—I thought they would try to convert everyone. It turned out they welcomed the time away from their religious school. If they were conservative Adventists no one knew it—at least, no one on the show! On the other hand, the really religious one on the show was a young Jewish man from New York who prayed in Hebrew before all or most of our meals. And I was glad for all of the above: They all got exposed to each other, from the very conservative to the very liberal to all points in between.

Harris finds recruitment is not difficult, however. "I don't recruit through the church. The Methodist denomination has several periodicals that reach college students, but I mostly recruit through coaches at the various colleges and circus training programs. They all know me, and several of them were with us themselves back in the '70s."

The 1990 tour traveled 6,000 miles for almost 12 weeks to 75 towns in 11 states throughout the Northeast and Midwest, giving more than 200 shows total. The cast was made up of 25 performers and musicians from over 20 universities, including two from Canada and two from the Soviet Union. David Harris's health problems returned, however; he was in the hospital all of June and most of July.

The 1991 summer tour was postponed because of sponsor cancellations and due to Harris's sudden hospitalization before planning was complete. The show did go out for the weekend of October 17–20, however, with two shows in Pennsylvania and one in West Virginia. From December 27, 1991–January 11, 1992, with a cast of 28, The Circus Kingdom went under canvas for its Florida tour. Although the show had been under canvas for its 1989 and 1990 dates for Boscov's department store in Reading and Pottsville, Pennsylvania, this was its first full tour under a BIG TOP. The show gave 23 public shows as well as its usual charity performances.

On January 2 and 3, 1992, The Circus Kingdom band played two concerts as part of the Sarasota Circus Festival. The summer tour opened in Pittsburgh on May 18 and closed in Newark, Ohio on August 16, having covered 8,000 miles in eight states. During that time, the 28 cast members performed 140 shows. In addition, The Circus Kingdom was the featured circus at the national convention of WINDJAMMERS UNLIMITED, the circus music society, at Chautauqua, New York. Also during the tour The Circus Kingdom brass band recorded over 50 selections for a 1993 double-CD release of circus music. From December 27, 1992 through January 9, 1993, The Circus Kingdom completed its second winter Florida tour. As in the previous tour, the show took part in the Sarasota International Circus Festival.

CIRCUS KIRK   Circus Kirk holds a unique place in circus history as first—and during its years on tour, the only—three-ring, touring, tented circus in which every cast and crew member was a high school, college or university student. Circus Kirk traveled for nine seasons (1969–77) and was all the dream of one man, Dr. Charles W. "Doc" BOAS.

Dr. Boas was trained as an educator, but left the teaching profession for several years in the mid-1950s to tour with shows such as CARSON & BARNES and Sells & Gray, learning all aspects of the business. His real ambition, though, was to have his own circus.

While a professor at York College in Pennsylvania in 1958, Dr. Boas located a small farm in nearby East Berlin and opened his WINTER QUARTERS.

The work of building a circus from scratch involved the construction of props, rigging, seating, tents and related equipment as well as restructuring vehicles to haul apparatus or act as sleeping units. Soon the entire Boas family was putting their lives into the project. The result was the Boas Bros. Circus, a small tented circus that played central Pennsylvania in the summer of 1968 and was a forerunner of Circus Kirk. On a modest budget, the Boas family pulled the one-ring show through two months of summer touring and got it "back in the barn" (a common circus phrase from mudshow days when farmers-turned-managers literally stored their show props in their barns).

During the winter of 1969 Dr. Boas met with the Rev. L. David HARRIS, an Evangelical United Brethren pastor in Philadelphia and a circus fan who shared Doc's vision. He recommended that Boas talk to the Central Pennsylvania Synod of the Lutheran Church in America (LCA): It might be interested in helping to support a circus as a summer youth project.

The Youth Ministries Division of the LCA liked the idea of Circus Kirk. The division, in effect, "sponsored" the first summer tour by loaning the project money to get it started. The Rev. Robert (Bob) Alexander was assigned as show pastor and church liaison.

There was never a mandate from the church indicating that Circus Kirk be anything more than a summer project that showed a healthy group of hardworking "kids" as an example to cities across America. Indeed, Doc Boas was adamant that the purpose of Circus Kirk was not, and would never be, to "witness in the center ring." Circus Kirk was to be exactly what its name implied—a circus. Unfortunately, the show's "mission" was unclear for years because of the other half of the circus's name: "kirk" is a Scottish word meaning "church."

Nevertheless, during the first season of 1969 (as chronicled in Carl T. Uehling's book *Blood, Sweat & Love*), Circus Kirk did close with a finale that included a parade of banners touting such slogans as "Peace," "Love" and "Celebrate Life." In addition, the Kirk presented several clown sketches with "morals," circus-style parables. One routine had two dissimilarly dressed sets of clowns building a bridge of paper plates through the center of the ring. The two groups of clowns fought over control of the ring, discovering that only through cooperation would they be able to "bridge a ring of brotherhood."

An early decision of Dr. Boas was that, other than those in his own family and the other adult sponsors, all members of the Kirk cast were to be currently registered college or university students. (In later years, this was amended to include some high school students with exceptional circus skills.) His call for performers brought in responses from students as far away as New Orleans (such as first and second season RINGMASTER and TRAPEZE artist Jeb Bourgoyne), as well as artists from the WENATCHEE YOUTH CIRCUS in Oregon. Eventually, a cast and crew of 35 took to the road in a one-state three-month tour.

In spite of Circus Kirk's aspirations, however, it was not yet a fully professional circus. Few of the students involved had true circus talents; rather, they had performance abilities that could be adapted to the circus ring. College gymnasts were transformed into ACROBATS. Theater majors became CLOWNS. Until joining the Kirk as ROUSTABOUTS, many crew members were unfamiliar with exotic tent rigging.

Also, none of the Kirk cast had ever endured the demands of rising before dawn, driving 50 to a 100 miles or more to the next town, raising the tents, setting rigging and props, doing two shows and tearing down by midnight, only to start the cycle of one-nighters again the next morning.

One of the weapons used most often to fight depression, frustration and burnout was frequent RING CURB MEETINGS, in which the company would sit around the curb of the CENTER RING and discuss the show and interpersonal problems. Part group therapy and part motivational seminar, the meetings did much to alleviate stress.

Another natural device to ease tensions was the ever-present sense of humor, often found in the most unlikely places. Every day the DONNIKER, or portable toilet, seemed to boast a new sign. During the run of the season such scatological gems as the following appeared: "Reserved Seats"; "Pay Toilet—Deposit 10 Cents in Slot"; "Please Don't Overload for a Brighter, Cleaner Wash"; and "Do Not Throw Cigarette Butts in Toilet—They Get Soggy and Wet and Are Hard to Light."

Circus Kirk, Ashland, Ohio in 1970. (Photo courtesy of Dr. Charles W. Boas)

The rolling stock of the first season was a veritable cacophony of vehicles. Their infamous donniker was a wood-framed oil drum pulled by the Boas family station wagon. A potato chip delivery truck became the advance wagon for the 24-HOUR MAN. One of the more creative conversions was turning old school buses, rigged with bunks and painted a bright silver to reflect heat, into sleeping quarters for the cast.

In its first season Circus Kirk achieved its goal—to prove that young people of different races and creeds could work and live harmoniously under seemingly impossible conditions. To relate this historically to the "outside" world, one has only to remember that 1969 was also the year of the first Vietnam War draft lottery.

Circus Kirk had forerunners in the field of youth circuses, but none was a touring show. The Wenatchee Youth Circus in Oregon operated as an open-air show, although Sarasota High School's SAILOR CIRCUS did work under canvas. Both had short runs

over a few weeks, however, and usually performed in only one location. Florida State University had its "Flying High" Circus, founded by Jack Haskin (d. 28 April 1993), which did not travel. The annual Circus Week Festival in PERU, INDIANA, encouraged the participation of youngsters from the town, but the Circus City Circus did not tour. As a result, most circus mavens felt that Kirk's success in 1969 could be attributed more to luck than skill and openly wondered if the show would reopen in 1970.

The second season began with an enlarged cast and a tour schedule from June 26 through August 29 that encompassed three states, adding Ohio and Maryland. A flow chart of department heads showed the new organization: North American Operating Co., Inc. (Dr. Boas, owner) and the Lutheran Church in America (Rev. Jim Percy, 1970 pastor/liaison) were now the co-directors of Circus Kirk. Boas was circus manager of six departments (band, business, operations, front end (MIDWAY), BACK YARD, performance), each with its own head. Boas was also manager of operations, with Larry French as superintendent, who in turn was responsible for the seven visible departments on the lot—the BIG TOP, the SIDESHOW, the RING STOCK, props, electrical, the COOKHOUSE and transportation. In addition, the Kirk front end carried two independent concessionaires, Len Knapp (the Reptilerama snake show) and Gene Earl (BUTCHER). The work details, which relied on town boys acquired by local sponsors to supplement labor, showed 14 assigned to the Big Top, four to the sideshow and two to the cookhouse.

The final program and running order of the 1970 Big Top show was representative of all of its seasons: Overture, Fanfare, Opening SPEC, Swinging LADDERS, Magic Act, Clowns, Tumblers, Clowns, Still Trapeze, Clowns, JUGGLING, Animal Menage, Plate Spinning, Clown Band, Low Wire, CLOWN WALKAROUND, Animal Fantasy, Fire Baton Juggling, Spanish WEB, CLOWN STOP, Balance Beam, Trampoline, Ascent of Incline Cable, Finale Parade.

By the middle of the 1970 season, an unfortunate financial reality had become obvious: The enormous setup costs for each season were constant whether the Kirk stayed out one week or 50 weeks. Certainly there were daily operating expenses such as salaries, gasoline and meals—in the '70 season the daily NUT was $750—which ended when the show closed; but many of the costs, such as insurance, vehicle registration, tent and prop purchases and office expenses were either ongoing or annual fees. Since at that point the performers' salaries were minimal ($50 per week), an extended season would go a long way toward amortizing those yearly expenses.

Midseason, Doc Boas announced a postseason tour of one additional week. A revised running order—for those cast members who did not have early university starts and could remain with the show—included a clown baseball sketch, a COLORING BOOK PITCH, the ROLLING GLOBE, a solo TRAMP CLOWN juggler, a single Spanish web, a comedy balance beam act and corporate sponsor announcements. This was the first of several attempts the Kirk made over the years to try to generate additional revenue.

The 1971 season toured the same states with a cast of 40 in 73 towns. They gave 146 performances from June 7 through September 4. Finally the Rev. Harris, so important in the creation of Kirk, was assigned show pastor by the LCA. At the end of the season, rather than continue the entire show for additional days, Boas decided to repackage just the Circus Kirk sideshow as a carnival ten-in-one (an enlarged sideshow that offers *ten* acts for *one* admission price).

For seven days (September 5–11), the Kirk sideshow played the Juniata County Fair in Port Royal, Pennsylvania, with four members of the Kirk cast, augmented with one new showgirl, or BALLY BROAD. Set up at one end of the fairgrounds, the sideshow was a ten-in-one in name only, because it only featured the same eight acts seen on the Kirk tour (Magic, Ventriloquism, Punch & Judy, the Human Blockhead, a SNAKE CHARMER, a Fire-eater, an Escape Artist and the Sword Box). The performance schedule was no longer two a day. The GRIND was constant, and a new BALLY was delivered whenever there were enough people to draw a TIP. The extension was not financially successful, and at week's end the tent was packed up in the rain for the barn.

Rain was not uncommon on the Kirk—indeed, on any mud show. The first postseason Circus Kirk ROUTE BOOK (published in 1972 by newcomer business manager James Kieffer, later on the volunteer board of directors at the CIRCUS WORLD MUSEUM) showed that rain fell on the Kirk for a quarter of its 86 days on the road, with 10 rain dates out of its first 15 days alone.

In fact, 1972 was memorable for the Kirk, as it was for all shows touring the northeastern United States that summer, as the year of Hurricane Agnes. Circus Kirk had endured wind and rainstorms before, and the crew had all been taught to GUY OUT the TENTS in the case of a midshow JOHN ROBINSON. All of the veterans remembered the sideshow tent blowdown of July 4th the previous year, but no one was prepared for the fury of Hurricane Agnes.

Rain began to fall on the show at suppertime on June 20 in Hershey, Pennsylvania, and continued throughout the evening. The next morning Kirk made a short JUMP to Elizabethtown and, after a LOT change, set up on a school athletic field in a valley. Rain poured throughout the day; but sellout crowds defied the storm, providing two STRAWHOUSES. By TEAR DOWN, a nearby creek had overflowed its banks; the water drained down onto the field, adding to the unrelenting downpour. When the tops were dropped that evening, the canvas sank completely beneath almost a foot of water.

Years later, Doc reminisced that his real concern that night was not for the equipment. The fact that lights, provided by the Kirk's own generator, had to remain on throughout tear down meant that there was a constant, though unvoiced, real danger of electrocution at all times.

By the next morning, swirling water had surrounded the trailers that had not driven or been pulled off by bulldozers; rain fell throughout the day, causing the worst area flooding in 30 years. When the storm finally abated, the Kirk had lost almost a week of dates, many of which could not be made up in the show's short summer schedule.

Despite this hardship, things had improved in several important areas in 1972. Virginia was added to its June 9–September 3 tour, for a total season distance of 2,835 miles. The cast and crew neared 50, including a full-time nurse, an 11-piece band, seven sideshow performers and an eight-member CLOWN ALLEY. The buses were retired and, for the first time, the truck fleet included four tractor-trailer semis, two of which became sleepers. The show had grown to boast a BALE RING big top with a 60-foot round and three 30-foot middles and a 30-by-70 PUSH POLE sideshow top.

The biggest change, however, was the break from the Lutheran Church in America. As late as January 1972, discussions were being held to move the show's jurisdiction from the Central Pennsylvania Synod to the Commission on Youth Activities of the LCA through its Philadelphia office. Negotiations did not result in any agreement; and, when the church loan was recalled, Kirk opened its 1972 season without church affiliation.

The Kirk had become increasingly secular with each year, having long abandoned "morality" clown sketches; but now even the finale banner parade was dropped in favor of a "Salute to Our Country," with the cast brandishing red, white and blue flags as a giant American flag was unfurled over the CENTER RING. Although still a SUNDAY SCHOOL SHOW according to circus jargon, Circus Kirk was no longer *literally* a "church show." Dr. Charles W. Boas finally had fulfilled his dream; in spite of its student-age performers, Circus Kirk was a professional show.

Circus Kirk opened its 1973 doors early on May 20 and toured for 15 full weeks, closing on September 3. Delaware and West Virginia were added to its list of seven states, and a new 40-foot middle replaced a center section of the big top. Road stock inventory showed six semi-trailers. With Doc Boas's time increasingly being taken up with routing and business needs, Stu Levens, the big top boss from the first Kirk season, was brought in as general superintendent. More and more, despite the age of its performers, Kirk became accepted in the circus world as a "real" circus.

Following the 1973 tour, Boas once again attempted to extend the season. He reframed the top as a one-ringer and sent it on a southern tour as Boas Bros. Circus—resurrecting the old name. Traveling with a cast and crew of 19, the new show toured from September 7 until October 27, going as far south as Lillington, North Carolina. The tour was not financially successful, and Kirk did not attempt another "southern tour" again until its final season in 1977.

By 1974 Circus Kirk was billing itself as "The All-American All-Student Show," touring six states and giving over 180 performances from May 25 through Labor Day. For the first time, the tour route was expanded into New Jersey and southern New England.

In 1975 the Central Pennsylvania Synod of the LCA reestablished ties with Circus Kirk, assigning a chaplain to its "summer youth project." By then, however, the new tone of Kirk was set; the show's program did not allow for parable sketches or parades of banners proclaiming universal brotherhood.

By 1976, for the Bicentennial Edition of Circus Kirk, the LCA was no longer affiliated with the show. Circus Kirk made history again that year when it became the first full tented circus to play on Martha's Vineyard. The entire convoy of trucks and equipment was ferried across to the island off the coast of Massachusetts to an enthusiastic response by the summer residents.

During much of 1976 and all of 1977 Dr. Boas was unable to tour with the Kirk for medical reasons; the show's financial woes, aggravated by its short season, escalated. In 1977 the decision was made to attempt a grand southern tour and continue Circus Kirk beyond its traditional Labor Day weekend closing date.

This extension had a twofold purpose: The primary objective was, of course, to close the show "in the black" with enough capital to continue operations into 1978. The "inside" word was that, because of Doc's health and the continuing money problems, Circus Kirk was on its last tour. The closer the Kirk got to Florida—the home for many in the circus industry—the more likely it would be to find a potential buyer.

Circus Kirk closed for the last time in early November 1977 in Florida, and the equipment was brought back to its quarters in East Berlin. Shortly thereafter, the North American Operating Company, the parent corporation of Circus Kirk, filed for bankruptcy; the following year a private investor purchased all of the Kirk inventory for approximately $45,000.

The legacy of Circus Kirk continues, however, as over 24 of the 500 veterans of the show went on— at least for a time—to professional circus or other performance careers. The last Kirk Big Top was still in use as late as the summer of 1989, when it was destroyed in a blowdown in Texas.

In September 1989 a reunion of the assembled casts and crews of the nine seasons of Circus Kirk met in Harrisburg, Pennsylvania, which is close to the show's original home. Dr. Charles W. Boas was honored there for his contributions to the American circus by the CIRCUS FANS ASSOCIATION OF AMERICA as well as by the State House of Representatives (which declared Labor Day 1989 as "Dr. Boas Day"), the Governor of Pennsylvania and the President of the United States.

CIRCUS MAXIMUS   The first use of the word "circus" in conjunction with outdoor "entertainment" was with the original Circus Maximus, built during the days of Imperial Rome. The U-shaped, roofless structure was 625 yards long with tiered seating for more than 150,000 spectators. The Latin word "circus" did not refer to the shape of the building but was applied because charioteers drove their horses round an arena track.

Essentially completed in 329 B.C. (although changes were made through A.D. 117), the arena was used primarily for chariot races—its most popular attraction—although it was also home to bloodthirsty events such as the slaughtering of animals (and men), which were later popularized in the COLOSSEUM.

Also known for the color, spectacle and excitement of its gymnastic exhibitions, ACROBATS, rope-dancing and equestrians, the Circus Maximus was in some ways a precursor of the modern circus. Admission was free, but local merchants did a brisk trade, perhaps as forerunners of today's candy BUTCHERS. Many times the spectacles began with an opening parade, similar to the SPEC in today's circuses.

Unfortunately, as the character of Rome changed, so did the shows in the Circus Maximus, with the wholesale killing of beasts and humans beginning about a century before the time of Christ.

CIRCUS MODEL BUILDERS, INC., INTERNATIONAL
A fraternal fan organization, Circus Model Builders International promotes one of the most fascinating hobbies in circusdom.

Circus model builders replicate, in exact miniature detail, the equipment, layout and often the performances of historical circuses. Many builders, of course, also build their own "dream" circuses using photographs or actual wagons, tents and other equipment as reference springboards to their fancy.

Founded in 1936, the group has regular memberships for those 16 or over and a separate junior division for those aged eight to 15. Although membership is open to women, there is also a separate Ladies Auxiliary for those women who are associated with the hobbyists but are not active model builders themselves.

The Circus Model Builders publishes its own monthly magazine, *LITTLE CIRCUS WAGON*. Membership information can be reached by writing Circus Model Builders, Inc., International at 347 Lonsdale Avenue, Dayton, Ohio 45419.

CIRCUS OF THE KIDS   See CIRCUS CAMPS.

CIRCUS OZ   Although not a frequent visitor, Circus Oz from Australia has appeared in the United States on a few occasions, usually in New York City or in the San Francisco Bay area.

The one-ring tented circus does not carry animals; rather, it stresses gymastic and aerial artists in the same fashion as the PICKLE FAMILY CIRCUS and CIRQUE DU SOLEIL.

CIRCUS REPORT   First issued on January 1, 1972 by Don Marcks, *Circus Report* has replaced *BILLBOARD* and *Amusement Business* as the true "Bible" of the circus industry. The weekly magazine contains approximately 30 pages in a 7- by 8½-inch format.

A labor of love, *Circus Report* has never emphasized the business aspect (such as grosses and attendance records) of the circuses on tour, although they are duly reported when available. Instead, through a network of regular columnists and frequent contributors, Marcks assembles up-to-date information on circus routes, personnel, performances and reviews, as well as articles of general interest to the circus community.

Among the many regular columnists is aerialist Billy Barton, billed as "Mr. Sensation," whose weekly column gives gossip and a behind-the-scenes look at all of the shows and personnel on tour. Each article signs off with his trademark, "See you down the road, luvs." Also appearing often is "News from So. California," by Chuck Burnes, a former Ringling clown and now director of his own production company and talent agency for showfolk, Periwinkle Productions, in Anaheim, California.

Subscriptions may be obtained by contacting editor Don Marcks at *Circus Report,* 525 Oak Street, El Cerrito, California 94530-3699. The phone number is (510) 525-3332.

CIRCUS SAINTS AND SINNERS   Founded by Freddie Benham, Circus Saints and Sinners is a fundraising organization for destitute circus workers.

The group can trace its beginnings to the 1929 Chicago convention of the CIRCUS FANS ASSOCIATION OF AMERICA. Many of the members of the New York City delegation, upset that their club was not designated the honorary title of "Tent #1," broke away from the national society. A portion of this association eventually evolved into the Circus Saints and Sinners.

CIRCUS SMIRKUS   See CIRCUS CAMPS.

CIRCUS TIHANY   Before making its first foray into the United States in 1989, Circus Tihany had already become an established institution in South and Central America.

The owner and star performer of Circus Tihany is Franz Czeisler, born in Tihany, Hungary, around 1910. As a boy, Czeisler saw his father perform small magic tricks; the art was to become a lifelong fascination.

After being orphaned in World War I, Czeisler stowed away on a ship bound for New York City. Once in the United States, he studied magic with Giovanni, Blackstone, Sr., Ufferini, Houdini, Chang and Zati Songar. Only 16 years old, he put together his own magic act and toured USO (United Service Organization) camps.

In 1952 he moved his family to Brazil. Within two years he had adopted "Tihany" as his stage name, bought a small tent and began to tour his first show through Latin America. The show grew rapidly. Part circus, part magical illusion show and part Las Vegas–style revue, Circus Tihany toured for over 30 years until Tihany's retirement to Florida in 1984.

After only one year, Tihany began to build a new circus; his dream was to bring his elaborately staged performance to the United States in a show that would outdo any of his former shows. In preparation, the new Circus Tihany began to travel throughout Mexico and farther south, with a cast and crew of over 200 performing on a platform stage viewed by over 4,000 spectators in unidirectional, theater-style seating.

Dates were set for Circus Tihany to begin "previews" in the United States at the Gulfgate Mall, Houston, Texas on September 29 through October 8, 1989, then continue to New Orleans City Park for an October 13–29, 1989 run. The official gala opening was set in Miami, Florida for November 3, 1989; the show was originally to continue with a 30-day stand.

Circus Tihany was a spectacular production and critically well received, but audiences did not fill the tent. Unfortunately, the show, with many of the crew demanding union wages, was just too large and too heavy to travel economically. The NUT could not be reduced; and, although the show rivaled many casino revue shows in quality, audiences expected ticket prices to be held to circus "family" prices.

After a several-month try at a U.S. tour, Circus Tihany returned south of the border, where it continues in 1993 as a major crowd pleaser and attraction.

CIRCUS TRAINS   Although other circus managers may have experimented with carrying stock by rail before him, W.C. COUP is generally credited with having begun the railroad era of circus transportation when he placed his show, BARNUM'S GREAT TRAVELING MUSEUM, MENAGERIE, CARAVAN, HIPPODROME AND CIRCUS, on rail in 1872. With the improvement and extension of rail service across the country, within a very few years all circuses of any size were traveling on rail cars.

Coup made circus trains practical by devising an "end-loading" method of hoisting the circus WAGONS up ramps at the back of the train and onto the flatcars. Metal and rope rigging then pulled the wagons forward the length of the cars, across metal plates set between them, to the front of the train until all of the flatcars were full.

Just as larger TENTS, wagons and MENAGERIES gave more status in the circus world, the number and variety of circus cars meant more prestige as well. The pinnacle of the railroad era came in 1911 when 32 shows were on rails, from the five cars of the Bulgar and Cheney Circus to the two behemoths, BARNUM & BAILEY CIRCUS and Ringling Brothers Circus, each with 84 cars.

As highways improved across the country and rail costs increased, truck transportation became more practical for many shows, especially the smaller circuses. In 1956, when the RINGLING BROS. AND BARNUM & BAILEY CIRCUS closed midseason and the CLYDE BEATTY CIRCUS left rails at the end of the year, the end of the railroad era had come. Although the Ringling show still travels by rail from one town to another, the true age of the circus train is a thing of the past.

During its heyday, however, the circus train was noted for its assortment and the practicality in the types of cars it carried. Flatcars carried stock wagons and parade wagons. Often the heavier flatcars were specially built to be double length—72 feet—instead of the usual 36 feet, because railroads charged by the length of the car, not by weight.

Before it went out from under canvas in 1956, the giant Ringling Bros. and Barnum & Bailey train traveled in four sections, leaving the LOT according to what order the cars needed to arrive at the other end. The first section contained the menagerie animals. Already caged, their wagons could be rolled directly onto the flatcars as soon as the menagerie top was dropped. If the weather was cold or damp, canvas was draped over the wagons to keep the animals warm and dry. Also setting out in the first section was the COOKHOUSE and all the personnel connected with it and the menagerie.

The second section carried the BIG TOP, along with the floats, wagons and props. Flatcars generally held four wagons each, but the wagon which carried the CENTER POLE for the big top took up half of a flatcar itself. The ROUSTABOUTS for the prop department, the big top and other tents traveled in this group, as did the work ELEPHANTS who assisted in putting up the tops.

Section three contained all of the seat wagons, HORSES and performing stock, as well as the animals' keepers. Animals were loaded on the stock cars sideways and packed tightly together: This saved space and helped prevent the animals from falling down. A full stock car could hold 13 or 14 elephants or over 30 horses.

The rest of the show personnel left last. They traveled on regular railroad coaches that had been emptied and refurbished as sleeping quarters, usually two or three bunks high. Management staff and star performers sometimes rated more comfortable staterooms; but the compartments were still far from elegant, and generally little time was spent in the railroad car once the train reached the show town.

Especially gruesome were the cars for the workingmen and roustabouts: Nicknamed CRUM CARS because of the rodents and body lice that infested them, the workingmen's cars provided little space, almost no ventilation and no sanitary facilities. Despite the danger, workers would often sleep directly on the flatcars under the wagons as the circus train moved between towns.

Every circus train also carried a dining car and a PIE CAR. Sometimes handled by the cookhouse and sometimes a separate concession, the pie car was a place where the cast and crew could meet informally after the show for good company, snacks, drinks and gambling.

Travel by rail allowed RED-LIGHTING, the undignified and disgraceful form of firing the hired help. The slang term referred to an unwanted member of the cast or crew who was tossed from the back of the moving train. When the person looked up in the darkness, all he could see was the red lights of the caboose disappearing into the darkness.

One of the real perils for the circus train, perhaps an inevitability, was the train wreck. Unlike the modern circus where one vehicle may be involved in a highway accident, a collision of two trains or a single railroad car jumping the tracks would involve the entire length of circus train. The most disastrous was surely that of the HAGENBECK-WALLACE CIRCUS on June 22, 1918, in which at least 85 people were killed and over 175 injured when an empty troop train slammed into the back of the circus train near Hammond, Indiana. The Hagenbeck-Wallace train had stopped on the tracks to investigate an overheated instrument on one of its cars, and flares were set at the rear of the train. The engineer of the approaching train was apparently asleep or did not see the flares, and the heavy troop train smashed through the circus caboose. The sleeping coaches were located directly in front of the caboose, and the troop train plowed through several of them before grinding to a halt.

Fifty-six of the dead, only 13 of whom were identified, were buried in a mass grave at the Showmen's League plot in Woodlawn Cemetery at Forest Park, Illinois.

The Ringling show offered its equipment and performers to help Hagenbeck-Wallace; only two dates were lost in the aftermath of the tragedy.

CIRCUS USA See Allan C. HILL.

CIRCUS VARGAS Started by Clifford E. VARGAS in 1969, Circus Vargas is the only major circus with its WINTER QUARTERS on the West Coast. With offices in Thousand Oaks, California, the show has been nicknamed "The Hollywood Circus."

Begun as a motorized show with three trucks and eight animals, Circus Vargas traveled as far east as New York in its early years. Cliff Vargas, the show's sole owner, came from a background as a PHONE PROMOTER for the Rudy Jacobi circus in northern California. When he started his own tented operation, Vargas became one of the pioneers of the use of shopping malls as tie-in sponsors. Before long, his show had grown into a three-ring format.

While the season usually begins in January and runs through November, Circus Vargas holds a record for playing an uninterrupted 56 weeks in 1974. According to Vargas, the headaches of running so long a season weren't worth it. "I had a theory at the time," he said, "I said to myself, 'Golly, you have to feed the animals, you have to keep your people

working—particularly the ROUSTABOUTS—or they'll go and get a job someplace else.' But it didn't really make sense."

By 1985, economics forced the show to cut back its route, touring only as far as Colorado. The longest single JUMP that season was 2,000 miles from Pendleton, Oregon to Colorado.

Meanwhile, Cliff Vargas, always a heavy smoker, had developed health problems. After recuperating from a heart attack and bypass surgery, he turned over day-to-day management of the show to his friend and colleague, Joe Muscarello. He frequently visited the LOT, however, and remained a familiar face to a generation of circus-goers. Clifford E. Vargas died in 1989.

In his will, Vargas left the show to Muscarello and Jack Bailey, longtime promoter and ADVANCE MAN for the circus. Muscarello, in turn, bought out Bailey's interest and brought in Roland Kaiser, Vargas's concessions manager for over 20 years, as co-owner.

Circus Vargas continued, touring in 1991 under a 300-by-200-foot BIG TOP. Consisting of 90,000 square feet of plasticized fabric, the top was supported by 24,478 feet of cable and rope, 485 STAKES and weighed more than 17 tons. The Big Top, the size of a football field and four stories high, could seat almost 5,000 people; at one time it was listed by the *Guinness Book of World Records* as the world's largest traveling top.

Circus Vargas was completed by a MIDWAY, consisting of a MOON BOUNCE, pony ride, elephant ride, concessions and a reptile SIDESHOW. The total value of the show's equipment was estimated at $20 million.

In an average season, the show moves two or three times a week, playing multiple-day stands on shopping-center parking lots or city recreational areas under local sponsors. During the year Circus Vargas and its crew of 400 give more than 600 performances in 90 to 100 towns, spending approximately three months of its annual tour in approximately 40 southern California cities. More than 2 million people see the show each year.

Most of the dozen or so acts are booked by September for the following season. Wardrobed in over 400 costumes, there are fourth- and fifth-generation circus families from over a dozen different countries. The blankets for the ELEPHANTS, valued at

Circus Vargas plays opposite the Hollywood Bowl in 1991.   (Photo by Tom Ogden)

close to $2 million, contain over 100,000 hand-sewn sequins; the show also features state-of-the art lighting as well as prerecorded music.

The year 1991 was the last three-ring season for Circus Vargas. By dropping sections from its old top, the show was able to perform its 1992 season in the popular European-style one-ring format. In 1993, Circus Vargas debuted its new, long-awaited round Big Top.

CIRCUS WORLD   The biggest financial fiasco of Irvin FELD's career was without a doubt Circus World. Conceived in 1970 as an extension of his RINGLING BROS. AND BARNUM & BAILEY CIRCUS, the complex was designed to draw the overflowing crowds from Disney World in nearby Orlando. The $100 million project was dubbed "The Greatest Place on Earth," and 750 acres were set aside for its expansion. Circus World featured daily circus performances, STREET PARADES, exhibitions of circus trains and even had a University of the Circus Arts on the grounds.

Mattel Toys, the major shareholder in the Ringling show and Circus World, was already burdened with $20 million in circus debts. Panicked when the park's opening weeks brought only 300 to 400 visitors a day, Mattel ordered a $3 million make-over. When the park reopened, Michael Downs—a former Opryland executive—had been brought in to replace Irvin Feld as director. Despite an enormous publicity campaign, Circus World never drew Florida tourists away from the many attractions already in the Orlando area; it closed within a few months at a tremendous monetary loss.

CIRCUS WORLD   See FILMS, CIRCUS.

CIRCUS WORLD MUSEUM   Located on the grounds of the WINTER QUARTERS of the original Ringling Bros. Circus (from 1884 to 1918) in BARABOO, WIS-

CONSIN, the Circus World Museum is dedicated to preserving the unique history of the American circus.

In 1954 John M. KELLEY, a former Ringling attorney, created Circus World Museum, Inc., as a fundraising and organizational vehicle to found a museum that could display props, costumes and equipment from the glamorous past—and present—of the circus. Just five years later, on July 1, 1959, the Circus World Museum opened to the public with the assistance of Charles Philip "Chappie" FOX. At the time, the museum occupied two of the original Ringling animal barns on Water Street with a few WAGONS and other memorabilia.

Today the complex takes up 50 acres, owned by the State Historical Society of Wisconsin and operated by the not-for-profit Historic Sites Foundation, Inc. In addition to funds from admission, the museum is supported by the dues of over 1,000 members as well as donations from friends and supporters. Among its 17 buildings is the new $1.6 million, 21,000-square-foot Irvin Feld Exhibit Hall & Visitor Center. Displays there include "The Ringling Bros. Story," the Howard Bros. Miniature Circus and a new movie highlighting the career of Gunther GEBEL-WILLIAMS. The Robert L. Parkinson Library & Research Center, named for its first curator, was founded in 1965. It is the largest archive and library and research facility dedicated exclusively to the circus.

The museum has an unparalleled collection that is constantly growing. As of 1989, an inventory of its holdings included the following: 175 antique circus wagons (including the famous TWO HEMISPHERES BANDWAGON); 44 historic circus railroad cars; 6,800 circus LITHOGRAPHS (c. 1835–1989); over 50,000 black-and-white photographic prints and an additional 21,000-plus black-and-white negatives; over 400 official circus ROUTE BOOKS; 1,800 programs, librettos and song sheets (1866–1989); over 12,000 circus newspaper advertisements (1793–1989); 1,700 HERALDS, couriers and broadsides (1816–1989); over 10,000 ROUTE CARDS (1988–1989); over 1,100 circus books; 380 pieces of original circus artwork; more than 5,600 tickets, passes, contracts and letterheads; over 1,500 advertising cuts and engravings; 5,850 band music portfolios and manuscripts; over 330 drawers of records, biographical and subject files and over 400 circus films and tapes (1904–89). The collection also includes woodcarvings, scale models, props, rigging, costumes, musical instruments, CALLIOPES and band organs.

The Exhibit Hall and selected displays (located at 426 Water Street) and the library and research facilities (at 415 Lynn Street), both in Baraboo, Wisconsin 53913, phone (608) 456-8341, are open year round. The rest of the Circus World Museum grounds are open only from early May until mid-September from early morning until late afternoon. Two circus performances are given daily under a circus tent during the summer months, and an additional "starlight show" is given under the BIG TOP from late July until mid-August, when the grounds are also open evenings. Performed along the same summer schedule is "The Mantle of Magic," a live illusion show. Also, the Circus World Museum annually produces the GREAT CIRCUS PARADE seen each July in Milwaukee. In order for the original wagons to be transported to the STREET PARADE, spectators along the rail route are treated each year to the Great Circus Train.

(See also PARKINSON, Robert Lewis.)

CIRQUE DU SOLEIL One of the newest entrants in the category of "circus-as-theater" is Montreal's celebrated Cirque du Soleil, begun in 1984 by Guy Laliberté, the founding president.

Born in 1960, Laliberté started out as a street performer. "As a child I went to the circus, but it didn't impress me at all. I never wanted to run off and join the circus," admits Laliberté. He left home as a teenager, leaving his parents a note with a quote from Kahil Gibran: "Your children are not your children. They are the sons and daughters of Life's longing for itself."

He told his folks that it was the first bit of philosophy he was able to comprehend. "I told them that's what I think, and when you are able to understand that, that's when we will be able to be close."

Laliberté became a juggler, accordion and harmonica player and magician, always working for a pass of the hat on street corners. He tried Europe, returned and added STILT WALKING and FIRE-EATING to his repertoire. By then, at the age of 24, he started to collect various street artists into a company. "I always had two sides in me. One was artistic," he points out. "One was business."

One of the performers in his first troupe was Guy Caron (1951–   ). Caron had been an actor for four years, then joined a clown troupe that toured Europe. Returning to Canada in 1981, he started a school simply named "Circus," which taught circus skills and techniques, in Montreal, Quebec. It was, and remains, a private school.

Laliberté proposed a provincial tour for his performance troupe to celebrate the 450th anniversary of Jacques Cartier's discovery of Canada. Originally known as Le Club de Talons Hauts ("The High-Heeled Club," a reference to stilt-walking), the company toured from 1982 to 1984.

Laliberté received an initial $1.5 million funding from the Quebec government to form the Cirque du Soleil and was able to attract corporate sponsors. Franco Dragone, the original and current director of the show, began shaping his spectacular company; and, as they performed 50 shows in less than three months, their unique blend of street performance, theater and circus was established.

Caron gives much of the credit of the circus's early success to the pool of performers available from his school. "I had this reservoir of artists in front of me, and I was able to say, 'This is a good one; this will be a great one soon.' I could think out the show one, two, three years ahead." In 1985 Caron changed the name of his academy to the National Circus School; coupled with the circus's acclaim, he was able to get an additional $5 million grant for the school.

By the end of its 1985 Canadian tour, the yellow-and-blue BIG TOP, a symbol for the artistic energy of the Canadian youth, had been set up for 150 shows. The national tour of 1986 including performing at the opening ceremonies of Expo 86 in Vancouver, had a company consisting of 77 cast and crew members.

Cirque du Soleil first appeared in the United States in 1987 as part of the Los Angeles Arts Festival, a forerunner of the Olympic Arts Festival. The show's theme that year was "We Reinvent the Circus"; eschewing such traditions as standard circus music and animal acts, it relied only on human performers. The show was such a success that it extended its run by moving from its downtown location to a LOT by the Pacific Ocean, adjacent to the Santa Monica pier.

Audiences immediately recognized that, unlike most American circuses, which are made up of a succession of "star turns," the Cirque du Soleil cast worked as a true ensemble. While the individual acts were some of the best of their kind in the world, they were meshed into a theatrical event, utilizing strikingly colorful costumes, nonstop choreography, smoke effects and state-of-the-art laser lighting. Even the most traditional of circus acts was clothed in layers of eccentricity: Members of the TEETERBOARD team entered the ring by waddling in penguin-style, carrying briefcases like so many junior executives on parade.

Also among the Cirque's performers was Denis Lacombe, one of the world's great young CLOWNS. An original member of the troupe in 1984, Lacombe won a bronze medal at the Festival Mondial du Cirque de Demain held in Paris. Then he moved over to the BIG APPLE CIRCUS, where he performed through August 1987.

Lacombe's most celebrated solo spot was called "The Maestro," in which he wildly caricatured the baton antics and body swaying of an orchestra conductor. His other popular routine was an elaboration of the pie-in-the-face gag, in which he joyfully smeared himself and covered the entire circus ring with the cream desserts.

The pulse of the show has always been the original hypnotic jazz/rock musical score by René Dupéré. "My challenge," explains Dupéré, "is to invent sounds that are perfectly suited to the performers' full range of movements and moods. When I'm composing for the TRAPEZE, I get so excited that I want to get up and fly!"

Much of the credit for the feel of Cirque du Soleil goes to Guy Caron. He compared a great circus show to going to the movies:

> It must be like going to a film; you enter into the screen, you forget about the camera, the actors, everything—you're lost in the story, and when you come out, it's like coming from a dream. In the traditional circus, the artistic technique is wonderful, but where is the show? It's just a succession of big acts. It's always in motion, that's why it pleases a child. They say the magic is there because they have 120 elephants, but that's not a show, it's a parade.

Despite Cirque du Soleil's sundry special effects, Caron insisted that his philosophy is "less is more." As artistic director, he focused on the action of the artists and the attention of the audience. He had attended his first circus at the age of eight and hated the show. Years later he decided to change that experience for new audiences. "I was in a huge crowd," he recalls. "I didn't know where to look. I heard a roar from the crowd, and I looked here, then the popcorn came, then I heard another roar, and I looked over there. I wasn't watching a show, but something that moved constantly. I didn't like it."

The Cirque's spectacular commercial success has not come without some criticism. Noting the definite minority of children in the audiences, some have called it the "circus for yuppies." Others complain that the steep prices prevent many families from attending. Circus traditionalists lament the absence of animals or a MIDWAY. Guy Caron answered his critics by saying "I don't forget tradition; I *use* tradition. . . . The old circus families, they were the first 'ensembles.' I use what they have forgotten to make something new. It's an old concept in a new style."

Cirque du Soleil's well-deserved popularity did not go unnoticed by other mainstream circuses: Even such precursor shows as the Big Apple Circus and the PICKLE FAMILY CIRCUS have subtly incorporated elements of Cirque into their work.

By the end of the 1987 tour, Guy Caron had parted paths with the Cirque du Soleil company. Many of the behind-the-scenes personnel remained WITH IT, however, maintaining the show's unique magic. In 1988 the circus returned to Los Angeles with an additional stop in San Francisco.

By 1989 the show had become an unqualified financial success, operating with a $16 million annual budget, only 3 percent of which was government funding. Its encore tour of the United States, adding Washington, D.C., New York City, Miami, Chicago and Phoenix to the route, was a fiscal sensation. Yet the show was not always well received critically; many felt it was merely a rehash and poor imitation of its former self. To some, the spark seemed gone.

After Guy Laliberté dispatched a unit of the 1987 original production to London, Cirque du Soleil's staff completely redesigned the 1989 show. The result was the "Nouvelle Experience." As part of a 20-month, 625-performance tour of the United States in its 1990–91 season, Cirque du Soleil played long

runs in Seattle, San Francisco, San Jose, Santa Monica, San Diego, Costa Mesa, New York City, Chicago, Washington, D.C. and Atlanta, in addition to the Canadian cities of Montreal, Ste.-Foy and Toronto. Playing to constant standing room only houses, Cirque du Soleil played to over 500,000 people within the first nine months of its North American tour.

Once again, the nearly two-and-a-half-hour show attempted to recapture the "child within" each of its adult audience members. Michel Crête, set designer, observed, "Our tools have always been our emotions, our spontaneity and our childlike imagination." Marking his fifth production for the Cirque, the new artistic director, Franco Dragone, reinforced the theatrical bent of the show: "Our reflections and perceptions help us create images that inspire us. We cannot work on a show without a purpose, a content vision of the world."

Beginning with the 1990 season, Cirque du Soleil welcomed artists from China, Europe, the Soviet Union and the United States to augment its Canadian cast. "There's one condition to work at Cirque du Soleil," Laliberté states. "You must have the passion, the love and the sense of pleasure in what you're doing."

International performers who met his standards included a company of Chinese-trained contortionists from Quebec, winners of the gold medal in the Festival du Cirque de L'avenir category of the Festival de Demain competition in Paris. During Cirque du Soleil's first visit to Monte Carlo's International Circus Festival, the Chinese troupe was awarded the 1992 Golden Clown Award.

Other 1991 featured performers were Zhao Liang, Wang Hong and Xu Hui-Man from China (FOOT JUGGLING umbrellas and circular mats); a trapeze act named Les Fous Volants ("The Flying Fools"); a French tightwire walker from France; and American clown David Shiner (replaced later in the season by Geoff Hoyle, whose Mr. Sniff character was one of the original trio of clowns in San Francisco's Pickle Family Circus).

David Shiner was one of three members of the troupe to come from the United States, even though his entry was by way of Germany. Shiner began working as a clown in 1978 and traveled to Europe in 1981. Beginning as a street performer, he ended up in Germany's Roncalli Circus and Switzerland's Knie Circus. Shiner was first seen by Cirque du

Cirque du Soleil's 1991 "Nouvelle Expérience." "Les flounes," from left to right: Christophe Lelarge, Cécile Ardail, Isabelle Chassé, Brian Dewhurst, Patrice Wojciechowski and David Lebel. (Photo by Al Seib, courtesy of Cirque du Soleil)

Soleil personnel in a Parisian circus festival in 1984. They kept in constant contact, but it was not until years later that he saw the show.

"When I finally saw Cirque du Soleil in 1988," Shiner admitted, "I was fascinated because it . . . combined so many things. It's not strictly circus, it's not strictly vaudeville. It's a combination of traditional skills with a modern concept. So I knew I could blend in very easily." Still, it was another two years until the show's theme and concept had a spot for his style. Working in pantomime in the "Nouvelle Experience," Shiner was given two long solo spots, one of which involved an extended slapstick walk through the audience and the other a comic spoof of silent movie-making that involved volunteers from the crowd.

The Soviet artists were guests from the Soviet National Circus Soyuzgoscirk; their performance in Cirque marked the first time the century-old circus allowed any of its performers to appear with a non-USSR show. Among them were three ACROBATS performing the Russian bar (a flexible pole, similar to a balance beam, held by a gymnast at each end of the bar) and the trampoline. Solo Russian equilibrist Vassiliy Demenchoukov built and ascended a sky-high tower of balancing chairs with one hand while holding a cake in the other.

The act that perhaps caused the greatest sensation and that closed the first half of the show was the muscular Soviet Vladimir Kekhaial, then 29 years old, performing the aerial straps (see AERIAL ACTS) while clad in only the briefest of costumes. Sylvie Drake, theater critic for the *Los Angeles Times,* for instance, described him as "a sort of Chippendale's meets Michelangelo. The Russian's self-awareness, brooding good looks, flowing black hair and Grecian designer jock strap are a curious paradox as they slice angelically and self-importantly through the air." Parenthetically, she added, "He'd make a fortune in Las Vegas"—which is where Vladimir (as he is now billed) has performed as part of the Stardust revue show, "Enter the Night," since December 1991.

Standouts among the Canadian-born performers were France La Bonté as a domineering ringmistress; the solo trapeze artist and silver medal winner Anne Lepage; and the unifying company of bizarre clownlike characters called "Flounes" (a combination of the words "clown" and "flo," a bastardization of French-Canadian slang for "children"). Dressed in some of the more exotic of the shows $200,000 worth of colorful costumes designed by Dominique Lemieux and working under the haunting masks of France Baillargeon and André Hénault, the Flounes appeared frequently throughout the madness of the circus, allowing audience members, by proxy, to enter the magical world of the unknown with them. This was enhanced by the Flounes's nonstop babbling of a language made up of comic gibberish.

Also on the 1990 tour, the one-ring format circus appeared under a new $1.2 million, fireproof, climate-controlled, trademark yellow-and-blue striped big top, custom made in France and Italy. The top seated 2,500 people; but the single-ring setup allowed a feeling of intimacy for the audience members. Also, the design had placed many tent poles away from the ring, minimizing view obstruction. The company consisted of 39 performers, 65 support staff and 650 tons of equipment, all carried on 65 vehicles, including a mobile COOKHOUSE, which served over 300 meals a day.

The enterprise has grown larger than even Guy Laliberté originally imagined. Laliberté has progressed from street artist to overseeing a $25 million company that includes not only the circus but a merchandising outfit, partnership in a ticketing outlet and a video production unit.

Just as concert musicians and entertainers have begun to look for corporate funds to help with touring expenses, so has Cirque du Soleil. AT&T was the presenting sponsor of the show for both its 1991–92 and 1992–93 U.S. tours.

The 1992–93 production was named "Saltimbanco," a title loosely derived from a 16th-century Italian word for street performers. The cast included 40 performers from 12 countries, including Cambodia, Cuba and China. The U.S. tour began in San Francisco in July, continuing on to San Jose, New York City, Chicago, Boston, Washington, D.C., Atlanta and Santa Monica, with its final run opening in Costa Mesa, California on January 30, 1993. The show, featuring an eccentric storyline and trademark outlandish makeup and wardrobe, was conceived by new artistic director Gilles Ste-Croix.

In an official press release on October 29, 1991, Cirque du Soleil announced that it would establish a permanent U.S. home at the Mirage Hotel in Las Vegas. Its first performance of a revised "Nouvelle Experience" at the hotel casino took place on October 6, 1992, commemorating the Mirage's third anniversary. A permanent tent-shaped building is the Cirque's home. Cirque du Soleil president Daniel Gauthier stated that the company had been "searching for a 'home' in Las Vegas" for some time and was "extremely pleased to have found it at the Mirage."

CLARABELL THE CLOWN   See CLOWNS, TELEVISION.

CLARKE, CHARLES (c. 1870s–d.) AND ERNEST (1876–1941)   Two of Britain's greatest aerialists, Charles F. and Ernest Clarke (b. 20n August 1876) first performed their FLYING TRAPEZE act in the United States in 1903. For their American debut they took the name "the Clarkonians" (also sometimes seen as The Great Clarkonian Aerial Act), and they worked together as a team until 1941.

The Clarke circus family dates back seven generations to Joseph Clark [sic], a 17th-century contortionist who performed in and around London before his death in 1690. Two generations later, John Clarke owned a London circus at the same time as Philip ASTLEY. Clarke's son, born in 1786, took control of the show as Old John Clarke. His sons, Alfred and Charles, started their own circuses.

Charles Clarke's show was titled Clarke's Continental Circus. The cast included his wife, Katherine Powell, three daughters (Laura, Bertha and Josephine, who worked as Venma) and three sons (Charles and Ernest—later the Clarkonians—and Percy).

Charles and Ernest Clarke were signed by BARNUM & BAILEY CIRCUS in Paris in 1901 and moved to the States with the show's return the following year. (Percy also joined the circus with his own act, a bareback equestrian company called The Clarke Family of Riders.)

In 1903 the Clarkonians premiered their flying act in Madison Square Garden and toured with the circus through 1904. During the winters they toured Cuba and with the ORRIN DAVENPORT CIRCUS in Mexico.

In 1905 the Clarkonians headlined at the New York Hippodrome and the next year joined the Ringling Bros. Circus (later the RINGLING BROS. AND BARNUM & BAILEY CIRCUS), where they stayed for 20 years. Other circuses with which they performed include the Tom Mix Circus, COLE BROS. CIRCUS, HAGENBECK-WALLACE CIRCUS, AL G. BARNES CIRCUS, SELLS-FLOTO CIRCUS, Gorman Bros. Circus and Patterson Circus.

In their act, Ernest was the FLYER and Charles was the CATCHER. Ernest was particularly impressive, regularly performing the TRIPLE SOMERSAULT; and in 1907 or 1908 he became the first to achieve a double somersault with a full pirouette. Because their flying act had only two members, precise timing was required to ensure that the swinging bar would be in the correct location for Ernest Clarke when he tried to make his return.

Ernest died on January 10, 1941 in Venice, California and is buried in Glendale Forest Lawn Cemetery; Percy retired. Charles continued to tour a juggling act with his wife and daughters for a few seasons. Ernest's daughter, Ernestine (born in 1924), performed with Guistino LOYAL on the Ringling Bros. and Barnum & Bailey Circus, then started her own a flying act with Willie Kaus. She traveled with her mother, Elizabeth Hanneford Clarke (1893–1975), who was the sister of George (Sr.) and Edwin "Poodles" HANNEFORD. During World War II Ernestine married Parley Baer, a journalist and actor.

Today there survive only two performers who flew or rode under the Clarkonian title: Ernestine and Charles Clarke's daughter Kay Clark Burslam.

In ceremonies during the 1992–93 Sarasota International Circus Festival and Parade (see SARASOTA, FLORIDA), the Clarkonians were inducted into the SARASOTA CIRCUS RING OF FAME.

CLARKONIANS, THE   See CLARKE, CHARLES AND ERNEST.

CLEM   Circus jargon for a fight on the LOT.

CLOFULLIA, MADAME JOSEPHINE FORTUNE (1831–18??)   P.T. BARNUM was the first showman to exhibit freaks and human oddities in large numbers. One of the most sensational attractions at the AMERICAN MUSEUM in New York City was Madame Josephine Clofullia.

In 1831, Josephine Boisdechines was born in Switzerland with a light fur all over her body. She was already married to Fortune Clofullia, Jr., before she began her career 1849. After exhibiting in England and France, she moved to Philadelphia in 1853. Barnum hired Clofullia and her son, Little Albert (who was also hirsute and was dubbed "Infant Esau" by the press).

Madame Clofullia, billed as the "Bearded Lady from Switzerland," became the object of a lawsuit in the early 1850s when it was claimed that she was not a woman at all, but a man in disguise. In court, three doctors testified that she was a woman; and her husband, the father of her two children, was also a witness.

New York City newspapers gave columns of space to the story, and the case was finally thrown out of court. The sordid affair astronomically increased business at the museum, and it should come as no surprise that Barnum himself had secretly arranged the trial as a publicity stunt.

Later in her career Madame Clofullia exhibited for other showmen, including, in 1859, a tour with DAN RICE'S ONE-HORSE SHOW.

CLOSE AHEAD OF PAPER   Circus jargon for returning to WINTER QUARTERS before the announced, or posted, end of the season. The reasons are almost always financial. No announcement was as dramatic as the one by John Ringling NORTH on July 16, 1956 in Pittsburgh, Pennsylvania. He declared that the days of the tented circus were over: Increased costs of fuel, insurance, rail charges, salary and maintenance for an outdoor show forced the RINGLING BROS. AND BARNUM & BAILEY CIRCUS to "close ahead of paper" and return to SARASOTA, FLORIDA midseason.

CLOUD SWING   One of the more unusual and seldom seen AERIAL ACTS, the cloud swing is a form of TRAPEZE.

Instead of a metal bar being strung between the two ropes that hang from the rigging or a CRANE

BAR at the top of the tent, a heavy cloth-covered, padded canvas cord—essentially a WEB—runs between them. The performer sits on the loose swing and performs the same graceful routines seen on the regular trapeze.

The cloud swing's side-to-side wobbly motion adds another dimension to the skilled performer's need for balance. Also, when the artist sits on the cloud swing, it becomes triangular in shape.

The cloud swing usually has hand loops attached to it, but the Mexican cloud swing does not; as it is little more than a bare slack rope, it is more difficult to perform.

CLOUD WALK

A unusual piece of aerial apparatus, the cloud walk is a series of padded foot loops, made of WEB material, hung from a CRANE BAR. The performer walks across the row of loops while hanging upside down, stepping on his instep with the feet very flexed.

CLOWN ALLEY

Circus jargon for the small tent, or portion of a tent, in which the CLOWNS put on their makeup and wardrobe and store their props.

The term originally referred to a walkway behind the BIG TOP. In case of emergency or an unexpected difficulty in rigging, the clowns would be sent in to relieve the audience's tension or stall for time. The clowns had to be close to the BACK DOOR of the top at all times, so their makeup tent was placed adjacent to the artists' entrance for convenience. The pathway between the two TENTS became known as Clown Alley, and the phrase soon came to refer to the clowns' tent itself.

CLOWN CAMP

See CIRCUS CAMPS.

CLOWN COLLEGE

Upon assuming the helm of the RINGLING BROS. AND BARNUM & BAILEY CIRCUS, Irvin FELD immediately noticed that the show's famed CLOWN ALLEY had dwindled to only 12 members with an average age of 60. Feld decided on a new program to refill the circus ranks with top-quality clowning talent; and, in 1968, he instituted the Ringling Bros. and Barnum & Bailey Clown College.

Clown College's first director was Melvin Miller, a one-season clown with the Ringling circus and then director of the John and Mable Ringling Circus Museum in SARASOTA, FLORIDA. His chief assistant was TRAMP CLOWN Danny Chapman. Miller taught

JUGGLING and makeup; Chapman added basic circus skills to the curriculum.

Although Miller and Chapman were the "heart and soul" of the first class at Clown College, they were actively assisted by master teachers Lou JACOBS, Otto GRIEBLING and Bobby KAY.

By 1984, when Glen "Frosty" LITTLE was added to the faculty as a master teacher, every clown on both touring units of The BIG ONE, with the exception of Jacobs and a few veteran clowns, were graduates of the Clown College. By 1992 over 1,000 students had passed through Clown College. The size of the Ringling Clown Alley had risen to over 50 JOEYS, with an average age of 23.

Located at the circus's WINTER QUARTERS, Clown College remains the only professional school in the world devoted entirely to the preservation and advancement of traditional circus clowning. Student indoctrination actually begins at the point of application, when they are asked everything from standard résumé questions to such queries as "When was the last time you cried?" and "What does it take to make you mad?" Because clown/actors must always be in touch with their own and the audience's feelings, the answers to these latter questions are often considered as or more important than the factual information.

Two to three thousand people apply each year for enrollment, and only about 60 are selected. Applicants range from high school graduates to oldsters looking to pursue a new career. So financial burden does not prevent talented newcomers from applying, Clown College has been tuition-free since its inception. Students do, however, pay their own room and board, plus wardrobe, materials and makeup fees.

Over a ten-week span students have an opportunity to see many professional workers go through their repertoires and dissect why gags are funny and how to build a character. In addition to the Master Teachers, "Deans" of Clown College regularly work with the troupe and other instructors. They emphasize developing a unique wardrobe and face as well as costume and prop construction. In addition, classes are taught in basic circus skills, including STILT WALKING, acrobatics, unicycling, JUGGLING, WIRE WALKING, choreography, improvisation and magic.

In 1970 the first seven female students enrolled at Clown College. Peggy Williams graduated and joined the Red Unit, becoming the first new female clown on the Ringling show in 20 years. Shortly thereafter, Maude Flippen was assigned to the Blue Unit. Williams went on to become an assistant performance director on the Red Unit. Bernice Collins became the first black female clown to appear with the Ringling Bros. and Barnum & Bailey Circus; and Ruth Chaddock, another graduate, became Ringling's top female stilt-walker.

In 1980, after five years with the Ringling Clown Alley, Ruth Chaddock began to work as an ADVANCE CLOWN and "Ambassador of Goodwill" for the circus. By 1992 her duties had expanded to include that of makeup instructor and stage manager at Clown College when it is in session. She is also audition coordinator and public relations liaison, working closely with the current Clown College director, Steve Smith (1951–   ).

Smith, whose professional clown name is T.J. Tatters, is himself a 1971 Clown College graduate. A six-year Ringling circus veteran, he is also a five-time Emmy award winner as host of *Kidding Around,* a Chicago-based children's variety television show. In 1993 Smith was inducted into the CLOWN HALL OF FAME in Delavan, Wisconsin.

Approximately one-third of the Clown College graduates are offered positions with the Ringling organization, either on one of the units or as advance clowns. Today, virtually every major circus on tour in the United States has at least one of Clown College's over-1,000 graduates in its troupe, all a result of Irvin Feld's desire to create a "renaissance in American clowning."

Clown College has even opened a second campus in Japan, although the faculty are all trained in Florida. The goals of the Japanese Clown College are more social in nature, to help graduates use humor in business and personal interactions as well as to build confidence.

CLOWN GAGS In CLOWN ALLEY, "gags" can take many forms. Among them are bits during the CLOWN WALKAROUND, the CLOWN STOP, antics by a CARPET CLOWN during COME-IN and entire sketches in the ring.

During a walkaround, a gag is presented in its most simple form: a "sight gag." As clowns stroll around the arena, they are seen holding comic props or outlandish signs intended to provoke laughter. A perfect example of this would be Lou JACOBS's parading the floor with a live Chihuahua stuck between giant hot-dog buns.

A gag during a clown stop entails a 30-second miniskit that sets up a premise, then delivers an immediate visual punch line. An example might be as follows: The clown stops in front of a section of the BLUES and hold up an attaché case. In large block letters, the suitcase says "First Dogs in Space." The clown gives time for everyone to read the message, then drops open the case. Inside are two rubber hot dogs dangling by invisible thread, seemingly floating "in space." As the laugh of recognition subsides, the clown closes the lid and moves on.

A carpet clown has longer to work with the crowds and can set up extended gags and bits of business. A standard clown gag involves the performer spying a pretty girl, going up to her and offering her a flower from a bouquet he is holding. When the girl takes the flower, she is left holding a soda straw that held the long-stemmed flower. The clown walks away smelling the rose.

Another favorite gag involves the clown following a patron as he finds his seat. Every so often, the clown tickles the back of the newcomer's neck with a long feather. The spectator will slap or rub his neck, thinking it is an insect; or, if he happens to turn around, the clown turns and walks away or innocently looks around. The seated audience, which has seen the whole scenario, laughs throughout the entire situation.

One of the most famous solo gags is the "spotlight gag." Made most famous by Emmett KELLY, the sketch involves a "poor soul" character trying to move or sweep up the spotlight, which takes on a life of its own. Many clowns over the years have presented variations of the gag, and it was used as the opening of the 1991 Red Unit show of the RINGLING BROS. AND BARNUM & BAILEY CIRCUS. Featured clown David LARIBLE finally captured the ball of light in his cap and, as he "tossed" it back into the air, the light broke into thousands of speckles of mirror-ball reflections.

The most involved gags take the form of an entire clown sketch, routine or act. Even a five- or ten-minute spot in the ring is often referred to as a gag. In a well-designed skit, every funny moment of each clown adds and builds to the BLOWOFF, or big finish, of the gag.

One of the most frequently seen of these gags is the "long shirt gag." One clown has been set up wearing a shirt that is a very long tube of cloth. The bottom, or excess, of the shirt is tucked into the clown's trousers. At the end of the gag, another clown grabs the first clown's shirt by the collar and runs with it. Other clowns often assist holding the cloth in the air, as the comedy shirt seems to stretch into yards of fabric.

The long shirt is often the final moment of another classic gag, the "clown boxing match." In the routine, clowns take the part of the standard participants in a boxing ring, including the two fighters, the referee, the corner managers, the girlfriend, the water boy and so on. The sketch involves the obvious knockabout of the various characters getting in the way and interfering with the fight. The gag is enhanced by having the "boxers" wear oversize boxing gloves, which are really giant flat mittens made of leather. As one clown swings at the other, the clown supposedly "receiving" the blow slaps his own gloves together, making a tremendous clap that can be heard in the far corners of the tent.

If the boxing match does not end in a free-for-all fight that culminates in the long shirt pull, it often ends with the "water gag." In a chase around the arena, at the tail end is the water boy, sloshing his full bucket. When he tosses it at a clown standing in front of the BLUES and accidentally misses, confetti, rather than water, flutters over the heads of the laughing audience.

Water also plays an important part in the "washerwoman gag." The sketch involves at least two male clowns, dressed in women's clothing, washing clothing in tubs of dirty, soapy water. As the clowns "accidentally" slash the water and slap the wet clothing against each other, they begin to fight. The gag usually ends in the chase and a bucket of confetti tossed into the audience.

The washerwoman gag is generally credited to Johnny Trippe and Bobby Kellogg (1926–   ) who created it during Kellogg's first season with the Ringling show in 1944. Kellogg toured with Ringling through 1948, then traveled two seasons with POLACK BROS. CIRCUS before retiring. He currently lives in Long Beach, California.

The water gag is almost always used within but is never the "blowoff" of the "clown firehouse gag." The firehouse gag is a complete one-act play, performed around a "burning building" constructed out of theatrical "flats" or lightweight plywood. Smoke

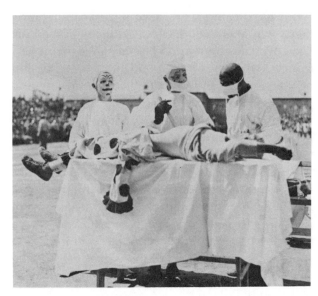

Prisoners at San Quentin perform the "clown doctor gag" during entertainment at their 1934 track meet. (Photo courtesy of the *Herald Examiner* collection/Los Angeles Public Library)

and flickering red cloth streamers that simulate fire shoot from the apartment, and a mother clutching her baby (a stuffed doll) is seen in an upper window. (The mother is usually played by a male midget, conforming to a basic law of clown comedy: Nothing is funnier than a clown in drag!)

The laughs come as the firemen stumble over one another trying to get to the building to put out the fire. All the while, the woman in the window keeps screaming "Save my baby!" At the end of the number, a firecracker explodes, and the doll (attached to a long rope looped over a pulley at the top of the BIG TOP) sails through the air, "saving the baby."

The "clown chase" is a staple gag seen in the circus. One version, the balloon chase, is especially popular, because the large colorful balloons are visible from anywhere in the house. In the gag, one clown runs by and steals a balloon from another. The first clown gives chase around the arena. A third clown steals the balloon from the second, and so on. Eventually whole groups of clowns are giving chase to each other around the rings.

Two other standard gags should also be mentioned. One, the "clown doctor gag," is a sketch in which a "patient" is, after much comic persuasion, placed on a gurney for an operation. The clown is covered with a cloth; the "doctor" and "nurse" (again, often a male clown in a woman's outfit) begin their procedure, using a giant rubber saw. All sorts of comic props are supposedly "removed" from the insides of the invalid.

In the very popular "clown levitation gag," the hypnotist/magician clown attempts to place another clown under a spell, but one of the observing clowns falls asleep instead. The mesmerist finally resorts to a gigantic rubber hammer to knock out the subject. The entranced clown is laid out on a low table, and he is covered with a cloth. The napping funster slowly appears to rise, floating horizontal to the ground. One of the other clowns provides the blow-off in which the sheet is accidentally removed, revealing the "sleeping" clown holding out a pair of stilts with shoes at arm's length.

Although solo gags are the invention and property of the individual clown, one of the jobs of the "producing" or head clown is to decide which gags the Clown Alley will perform for its full-cast sketches each year. The producing clown either invents a new gag or adapts one of the old standards, putting a modern twist on it. He and his crew then design, and perhaps even manufacture, the props necessary for the larger gags.

Just as certain personal gags become the "trademark" of an individual performer (such as Felix ADLER's carrying a baby pig during the walkaround and Otto GRIEBLING's attempting to deliver a melting block of ice), performers also can become associated with a large gag or prop. Lou Jacobs is best remembered for his "clown car" gag, in which the six-foot-one-inch clown was able to fit inside, drive and emerge from a two-foot-by-three-foot motorized car.

According to Fred BRADNA, longtime RINGMASTER with The GREATEST SHOW ON EARTH, Jacobs started working on the tiny car concept in 1944 and first introduced the gag in a regular show in the SPEC during Ringling's MADISON SQUARE GARDEN run in 1946. The car was unreliable, however, stalling or veering off the arena track; and it wasn't until the 1948 season that Jacobs perfected the car and routine that he performed for the rest of his career, as well as in Cecil B. deMille's film *The Greatest Show on Earth* (see FILMS, CIRCUS).

There have been many variations on the clown car gag. Otto Griebling is generally credited with

creating the gag in which dozens of clowns jump out of a miniature car. He asked Studebaker to modify one of their cars to his specifications so that 26 clowns could fit inside. When the car company said it was impossible, Griebling built his own. A combination of audience distance from the automobile (making the car appear smaller), careful loading of the clowns and clever contorting makes this incredible gag possible.

CLOWN HALL OF FAME & RESEARCH CENTER The Clown Hall of Fame & Research Center, located in downtown Delavan, Wisconsin, honors the tradition of clowning as well as famous members of the professional and hobbyist community.

Its single 15,000-square-foot building is open to the public every day, and it is supported by donations from four major clown organizations and from individual contributors. Every year several deserving CLOWNS of the past and present are inducted into the Hall of Fame; each of the four sponsoring organizations also gets to select a Clown of the Year from its current membership.

The Hall includes displays on the history of the art from the first clowns up to the most modern practitioners in the United States. The exhibits are changed frequently by a display director, currently Gene "Cousin Otto" LEE, also the editor of the WORLD CLOWN ASSOCIATION's monthly magazine, *CLOWNING AROUND*. Live shows presented by visiting and local performers augment the museum. The center is now in the process of creating a library and several workshop areas.

Since moving to Delavan in April 1991, the facility has been visited by over 20,000 people. The Clown Hall of Fame & Research Center is located at 114 North Third Street in Delavan, Wisconsin 53115.

CLOWN STOP Circus jargon for a short appearance of the CLOWNS rather than a prolonged sketch. Frequently this is done while props and rigging are being changed for the next feature act.

A clown stop can also be the pause a clown makes during a CLOWN WALKAROUND to present a sight gag. In current usage for a clown stop, especially on arena shows, is the phrase "track gag."

A classic example would be the clown who parades around the tent dressed as an artist in a smock, carrying a palate and canvas. He stops and seems to pick a member out of the audience as a model. He holds up his thumb to sight the subject, pretends to paint a bit, then repeats the action several times. Finally the clown turns around the canvas to show a painting of a giant thumb. Following the laugh, the clown moves farther down the track and repeats the gag for a new section of the audience.

(See also CLOWN GAGS.)

CLOWN WALKAROUND   Circus jargon for the clown act in which the members of CLOWN ALLEY get to show their individual turns in solo spots. The CLOWNS promenade around the rings, occasionally pausing to do a brief sketch for a section of the audience, or holding a sight gag as they walk along.

Each clown would have his own bit, some of which become an unofficial trademark of the creator over the years. An example of a classic walkaround gag would be Lou JACOB's parading around the arena holding a live Chihuahua in a giant hot-dog bun.

(See also CLOWN GAGS; CLOWN STOP.)

CLOWNFEST   An international conclave, Clownfest began in 1981 in Asbury Park, New Jersey. Since 1989 the annual weekend event has been held in nearby Seaside Heights. Anyone interested in the art of clowning, professional or amateur, may register for the get-together, which is advertised in circus and clown trade and fraternal periodicals.

The convention is sponsored each September by the National Clown Arts Council, Inc., an organization dedicated to clown awareness among the general public and to enhancing the image of CLOWNS and the artists who create them. The council has no separate membership per se but rather supports, and is supported by, other clown clubs.

Over a dozen lecturers each year speak on a variety of subjects at the Clownfest. Also each year a professional BIG TOP circus is in residency, set up right by the Boardwalk to perform shows for the public as well as convention registrants. During the 1991 convention VIDBEL'S OLD TYME CIRCUS was featured.

CLOWNING AROUND   *Clowning Around* is the official publication of the WORLD CLOWN ASSOCIATION. Since 1982 Gene LEE has been the editor of the periodical.

CLOWNS   P.T. BARNUM once said that "Elephants and clowns are the pegs upon which circuses are hung."

The beginning of clowns and clowning can be traced from the comic characters of the earliest theater, through the days of the court jester, all the way up to Tom SULLY who, in John Bill RICKETTS's 1793 circus, became the first circus clown to perform in the United States.

The most direct precursor of the modern "chalk-faced comedian" can be found in the plays of the Italian Commedia dell' Arte and in English pantomime.

The standard Commedia dell' Arte was, literally, an artful comedy of manners. Two young lovers were always opposed by Pantaloon, an old man. He, in turn, was always foiled by comic servants. One of those servants was HARLEQUIN, a "zanni" (from which we today get the word "zany"). Originally a victim of the pranks, his character has since turned into the perpetrator of the gags. Over the years one of the other zannis—known as Pedrolino—evolved in France from a victim to the romantic lead. His name was accordingly changed to Pierrot.

Besides their broad physical mannerisms, the characters were always distinguished by particular styles and colors of wardrobe and masks. This allowed unsophisticated audiences to follow the action of the play more easily. Pantaloon, for instance, was recognizable due to his wearing a red shirt, an unbuttoned black coat with a belt and pants resembling modern long johns.

Pierrot and his female counterpart Pierrette were always clothed in fancy, loose-fitting white costumes. Instead of the customary half-mask, the actor playing Pierrot powdered his face white, perhaps the beginning of the tradition of WHITEFACE CLOWNS.

In the late 18th century John Rich changed the Italian Commedia dell' Arte into the English pantomime in part by making Harlequin the central character of the story. The traditional harlequin costume was a loose jacket and pants, both decorated with multicolored, irregularly shaped patches.

In December 1800 James Byrne reduced the role of the harlequin and changed the wardrobe to white silk tights with diamond-shaped patches covered with spangles, a costume similar to what is worn by many whiteface clowns today. Though still a silent role, the character of harlequin also changed, becoming more sophisticated and elegant.

The mischievousness and comic bits in the pantomime were filled in by a character often simply called "clown." One of the first actors to play "clown" was Joseph GRIMALDI, who ushered in a new era by radically changing clown makeup and costumes. Venerated as the "Father of Clowning," all clowns are today known as JOEYS in his honor.

Existing side-by-side with the whiteface clowns are the CHARACTER CLOWNS. These can be further broken down into the types of characters or roles being portrayed, the most common of which are the AUGUSTE CLOWNS and TRAMP CLOWN.

The proliferation and arguments over "categories" of clowns are due more in part to competitions among hobbyists at conventions than to disagreements among professional circus performers. For many years Otto GRIEBLING and Emmett KELLY, both hobo types, appeared simultaneously with the RINGLING BROS. AND BARNUM & BAILEY CIRCUS without conflict, because each had a distinct characterization.

In today's circus, the performers in CLOWN ALLEY are as varied as their makeup. Like snowflakes, no two clowns look exactly alike. A professional clown goes to great pains to develop a unique face and costuming, and there is a moral code in clowndom not to copy another's look. Even trademarks such as CLOWN WALKAROUNDS and CLOWN STOP gags are jealously protected.

Larry Pisoni, one of the co-founders of the PICKLE FAMILY CIRCUS, explained how he designed the makeup for his unforgettable Lorenzo Pickle character:

The most important thing about clown makeup is that it not hide your face. People don't seem to understand that. Your face is your most important feature as a clown. If you paint a smile on your face, then you've got to be a character that smiles all the time, which is very limiting. Emmett Kelly, you know; the makeup around his mouth was just an oval; he didn't have a painted frown.

Clowns are possibly the hardest-working group of performers in the BIG TOP: They have at least five or six regular spots in the show, but they must be ready on a moment's notice to run into the ring to cover for prop changes, delays or other unexpected emergencies. Ironically, they are, as a group, the lowest-paid performers in the main show; and they are at the bottom of the Big Top caste system.

It takes a very special person, however, to be a clown: One who can make people laugh by causing them to recognize their own foibles. Pisoni explains why he entered the ring as Lorenzo Pickle:

I think the clown has a responsibility to present material that can act as a purge for a lot of things that are inside

us. *Through transference, someone in the audience can get nasty stuff out, purge it, transform it. The more open you are, the more childlike, the more effective that process can be.*

A clown character is really only a piece of canvas for the artist, for the individual who is presenting this piece of art. And it's a piece of art about the most important things in human life."

(See also ADLER, FELIX; ANTHONY, MARK "TONY"; CARPET CLOWN; CLOWN CAMP; CLOWNFEST; CLOWN GAGS; CLOWN HALL OF FAME & RESEARCH CENTER; CLOWNS INTERNATIONAL; CLOWNS OF AMERICA INTERNATIONAL, INC.; CLOWNS, TELEVISION; FOX, GEORGE L.; JACOBS, LOU; JAMES, JIMMY; KAY, BOBBY; LEE, GENE; LITTLE, GLEN "FROSTY"; MCBRYDE, LEON "BUTTONS"; POLAKOV, MICHAEL "COCO"; RICE, DAN; SALUTO, FRANKIE; SKELTON, RICHARD "RED"; WORLD CLOWN ASSOCIATION.)

CLOWNS, TELEVISION Nothing compares with experiencing the comic anarchy of the CLOWNS firsthand underneath the circus BIG TOP. For many people, however, their first experience of a chalk-faced comedian is seeing the JOEY on a television screen.

Clarabell the Clown

Not all of the clowns seen on television come from the tented arena. In fact, more than one has been drawn from the support staff of the variety show on which he is working, put into wardrobe, given a quick course in makeup and placed before the camera.

Such was the case with Clarabell the Clown who, appearing weekly on television's popular *The Howdy Doody Show* from 1947 until 1960, become one of the most beloved clowns in American history.

Clarabell was originally created by Bob Keeshan (1927–   ). After World War II, Keeshan began to do research work for Bob Smith's popular radio show at NBC, then assisted him on camera when Smith began work on *Puppet Playhouse*, one of television's first shows. *Puppet Playhouse* evolved into *The Howdy Doody Show*. Soon it was decided that a clown should become a permanent resident of "Doodyville." Bob Keeshan was sent to Brookes Costume House to be outfitted for a costume, with producer Roger Muir's admonition to "make it inexpensive." Brookes used a leftover bolt of green zebra-stripe material, added a yellow ruff around the neck, found a pair of oversize floppy shoes and attached a horn to a box at the belt.

Dick Smith, later to become one of Hollywood's top makeup men, was called in to design the clown's face and bald pate.

The head cap was ringed with red hair with a twisted, inverted ice-cream cone on the very top. The face was accented with large purple-and-white eyebrows high on the forehead; a red smile, outlined in white, took up most of the chin and cheeks. A bulbous red nose completed the AUGUSTE CLOWN face.

The name "Clarabell" was supplied by the show's writer, Eddie Kean.

Keeshan decided that Clarabell should follow in the great tradition of silent clowns, from Pierrot and HARLEQUIN to Joseph GRIMALDI, and remain silent. As a sort of "slapstick"—originally a jointed piece of wood that made a large crack, simulating a slap, when cracked across the leg or arm—Clarabell used his bicycle horn, honking for "yes" and "no." Keeshan also assumed Clarabell would always be able to attract enough comic attention with his ever-present bottle of seltzer water.

On December 22, 1952 Keeshan (along with three other actors) was unexpectedly fired during a rehearsal by Buffalo Bob's manager, Martin Stone, over a dispute regarding actor's representation. Keeshan was succeeded by Bobby Nicholson, a friend of Smith's. Nicholson was Clarabell for only a brief period, however, before moving over to play Doodyville's shopkeeper, Cornelius Cobby. For the remainder of the show's run until the last *Howdy Doody* telecast on September 30, 1960, Clarabell was played by the talented Lew Anderson.

Both Nicholson and Anderson continued Keeshan's original concept of Clarabell as a pantomime clown until the last program, in which the camera zoomed in for a close-up and Clarabell sadly whispered, "Good-bye, kids."

In 1955 Keeshan created and began playing his long-running character of Captain Kangaroo. In 1987 Lew Anderson re-created the role of Clarabell for a 40th Anniversary Howdy Doody Reunion, which was aired as a nationally syndicated television special.

In 1989 Keeshan published his autobiography, *Growing Up Happy: Captain Kangaroo Tells Yesterday's Children How to Nurture Their Own,* which included his insight into the creation of Clarabell.

Inducted into the Clown Hall of Fame in 1990 for his work as Clarabell the Clown, Bob Keeshan later served as honorary chairman for the CLOWN HALL OF FAME & RESEARCH CENTER's national fund drive.

Bozo the Clown

Bozo the Clown, created and originally portrayed by Larry Harmon for a local television series out of Hollywood, California in 1957, is one of the most famous and recognizable clown characters in the United States today. To fulfill obligations for personal appearances by Bozo, Harmon has trained over 200 people to portray his famous character. Most notable among those who have played Bozo is Willard Scott, the colorful weatherman on NBC's *Today Show.*

Instantly identifiable, Bozo the Clown wears a blue one-piece outfit with large white pom-poms on the front and a broad circular collar. With a face featuring exaggerated arched eyebrows and an oval mouth, Bozo's most outstanding feature is his twin tufts of orange hair, twirled and sharpened to a stiff point over each ear.

The Bozo Show is seen in 50 million homes daily as well as in locally produced overseas versions. Beginning in September 1990, *The Bozo Show* celebrated 30 years of transmission from Super Station WGN-TV in Chicago.

Perhaps the greatest testament to Bozo the Clown's popularity is the fact that his name has entered the English lexicon of American slang as anyone who acts silly or like a buffoon.

Rebo the Clown

Rebo the Clown was a creation for the first and only weekly network magic show ever to appear on national television. For five years Rebo, portrayed by Bev Bergeron (born Bevely [*sic*] Bergeron) (1930–   ), delighted millions as one of the main assistants to magician Mark Wilson on *The Magic Land of Allakazam.*

In 1957 Bergeron, already a seasoned magician himself, met Mark Wilson and began to work with him on Wilson's television magic show.

The following year Wilson began a new series, *Magic Circus,* and Wilson decided the format demanded a clown. He came up with the name "Rebo." Nani Darnelle, Wilson's wife and co-star, designed Rebo's clown costume, as she had all the show's wardrobe.

Television clown Rebo the Clown (center) with Nani Darnelle (left) and Mark Wilson (right), from "The Magic Land of Allakazam." Rebo is portrayed by Bev Bergeron. Nani Darnelle designed the costume, and Mark Wilson named the character.
(Photo courtesy of Mark Wilson, Magic Prods. International)

Bev Bergeron was left to create his own clown face and character. "Back then," said Bergeron, "it was easier to learn how to float a lady in the air than to put on clown makeup. Clowns simply wouldn't tell you . . . I designed my face the way kids draw clowns. With a pointed mouth."

Bergeron envisioned Rebo as a whiteface clown, with a red ball nose and high double-lined, two-toned arched eyebrows, red vertical lines through the eyes with black half-moons underneath and an "X" on each cheek.

In 1960 *The Magic Land of Allakazam* began airing nationally on CBS. As Rebo the Clown—Bergeron appeared for the next five years. The show continued on CBS every Saturday morning for two years, then moved over onto ABC for three more years.

As Bergeron refined his makeup, Nani Darnelle reworked his costume. Nani Darnelle recalls:

The original wardrobe for Magic Circus *was off-white with polka dots. You couldn't use pure white, of course,* on black-and-white television. For years I had to dye Mark's white tuxedo shirts gray! Rebo never had a ruffled collar, simply a straight collar.

For Allakazam, *I designed a bright-blue satin one-piece outfit decorated with gray stars. I had discovered on earlier shows that satin caught the light well and looked good on television as well as on stage. I had a duplicate costume made, but in red, so we could change them on personal appearances and fair dates. Rebo wore a large tie at his collar, and his hat was a derby that I decorated with silver store-bought stars. The blue jumpsuits had yellow collars; the red jumpsuits had blue collars.*

Bergeron described his Rebo character as a gentle pantomime clown, "basically a smart six-year-old who would probably follow a rolling ball out in the street, get hit by a car and not get hurt!"

Bev Bergeron built many of the props and illusions used on the *Allakazam* show, and over the years he has created hundreds of magical items and routines. Two "standards" still used by many clowns and comedy magicians are the "Hot Book" (when the cover of the hardbound book is opened, flames shoot out) and "Multiplying Wands" (a series of tubular wands, open at one end and nested inside one another).

Perhaps the greatest contribution of Bev Bergeron/Rebo the Clown to the industry is the "One Balloon Animal." Having seen Wally Boag—the original "Pecos Bill" in the Golden Horseshoe Revue in Disneyland—make an inflated animal out of several balloons in the 1940s, Bergeron worked at it until he created a dog that could be made quickly and easily with only one balloon. He estimates that the one-balloon doggie, including the pop-up poodle tail, was born around 1957. Bergeron admits that the invention was not entirely altruistic: After showing an audience onstage how easy it was to make a one-balloon doggie, he could PITCH a bag of balloons for 50 cents.

In 1959 Bergeron made the first one-balloon animal on television, and the response was immediate. Requests for instructions inundated the station. *Bob Follmer's Balloon Book,* which included Bergeron's drawings and directions for his one-balloon poodle, was published in the 1960s.

After finishing work as Rebo, Bergeron acted as gunslinger Pecos Bill at the Diamond Horseshoe Revue in Florida's Disney World from its opening in 1971 through 1986. In the 1990s he remains active as a magician, lecturer and author.

Ronald McDonald

The most famous television clown worldwide has never been a part of a regular series. Without a doubt, that honor goes to Ronald McDonald, the spokesman for McDonald's—the most popular fast-food chain on the globe. His trademark pantaloons, whiteface, red smile and orange wig are instantly recognizable anywhere on the face of the planet.

All of these clowns have made personal appearances, but none has toured with an American circus. Nevertheless, all of them have boosted the image of clowns and added to children's love of the circus comedians.

CLOWNS INTERNATIONAL The oldest existing fraternal organization for clowns in the world, Clowns International began in 1945 in England as the International Circus Clowns Club. Its quarterly magazine is called *The Joey*.

The club was founded by Stan Buit and Edward Graves—both circus fans—and Coco the Clown, a performer. Most of the early members were associated with Bertram Mills's Olympia Christmas Circus. In 1958 member Tommy Keele recommended the current name of the organization.

Catherine "Tootsie Mae" Linquist in a 1980 clown walka-round. (Photo courtesy of Charles A. DeWein)

CLOWNS OF AMERICA INTERNATIONAL, INC. Clowns of America International, Inc. is a worldwide fraternal organization dedicated to advancing the art of clowning for hobbyists as well as for professionals.

The organization holds an annual convention for its members and has an official publication, *The New Calliope*. Information on the club is available by writing P.O. Box 570, Lake Jackson, Texas 77566-0570.

CLYDE BEATTY & RUSSELL BROS. CIRCUS A merger of the two shows cited in its title, this tented operation toured for the 1944 season only.

(See also BEATTY, CLYDE; RUSSELL BROS. CIRCUS.)

CLYDE BEATTY CIRCUS After touring with a variety of circuses throughout his early career, the famous

wild animal trainer Clyde BEATTY formed the Clyde Beatty Circus in 1945, a motorized show utilizing equipment owned by the Wallace Bros. Circus.

Beatty toured with the Russell Brothers Pan-Pacific Circus for the 1946 season, then decided to open a new rail show with his Clyde Beatty Circus title. Second in size only to the Ringling show, the new Clyde Beatty Circus traveled on nine flatcars, two stock cars and four sleepers and extended its tours into the western United States and Canada. In the 1950s, due to the skyrocketing costs of railroad transportation, the show converted to trucks.

Although Beatty surrounded himself with superb performers, his own act remained the centerpiece of the show. Beatty toured the show until May 9, 1956 when a series of small audiences, bad weather and a strike forced him to CLOSE AHEAD OF PAPER in Burbank, California, after only 43 days on tour. At its bankruptcy hearing, the circus showed assets of only $260 against $280,000 in liabilities.

The circus was sold to the ACME CIRCUS CORPORATION, owned by Frank McClosky, Jerry Collins and Walter Kernan. They reorganized the show and reopened it in August with Beatty as the animal trainer. Since the Clyde Beatty Circus reopened after the RINGLING BROS. AND BARNUM & BAILEY CIRCUS had returned to WINTER QUARTERS, the Beatty show was the only rail unit on tour at the time. As a result, it had a highly successful fall tour through November, then returned to its new quarters in De Land, Florida. Nevertheless, the high costs of operating as a rail show convinced the show's managers to move back to a motorized circus.

In 1957 the Acme Circus Corporation acquired the Cole Brothers name, and the owners merged their two titles into the new CLYDE BEATTY-COLE BROS. CIRCUS, with Clyde Beatty as the star. Beatty remained with the show until his death in 1965.

CLYDE BEATTY-COLE BROS. CIRCUS
Carrying two of the most famous names in circus history, the Clyde Beatty-Cole Bros. Circus—or "Beatty-Cole" (or occasionally "CBCBC") as it is often referred to by showfolk—is a traditional, three-ring-under-canvas circus. Although Jess Adkins and Zack Terrell combined the "Cole Bros." title with CLYDE BEATTY's name for the 1935–38 circus seasons, the only connection their COLE BROS. & CLYDE BEATTY CIRCUS had to the current Clyde Beatty-Cole Bros. Circus was the star trainer.

After Clyde Beatty left the Adkins-Terrell show, he appeared with a variety of different circuses, eventually framing his own CLYDE BEATTY CIRCUS. After a disastrous 1956 season, the show limped back to Florida after only a few weeks on the road, rescued by the ACME CIRCUS CORPORATION. The corporation, owned by Frank McClosky, Walter Kernan and Jerry Collins, reorganized the show and put it back on rails in August for the remainder of the season.

McClosky and Kernan had been fired from the RINGLING BROS. AND BARNUM & BAILEY CIRCUS in 1955, and they were anxious to provide as much competition as possible for the BIG ONE. In 1957 they acquired the Cole title and recombined the two shows, this time as the new Clyde Beatty-Cole Bros. Circus. Once again Clyde Beatty was the star of the circus, which was now a motorized show. The next year they brought on Art CONCELLO (another former Ringling star) as manager.

Concello, who had been trying for years to convince John RINGLING to make his circus into an arena show, attempted to take Beatty-Cole into MADISON SQUARE GARDEN. Collins and McClosky, old MUD SHOW men, kept their show under canvas, however. Clyde Beatty remained their star until his death in 1965, when after a few interim performers (including Clyde Beatty, Jr.), David Hoover took over as trainer of the big cats. Hoover began as a CAGE BOY on the BEERS-BARNES CIRCUS, finally taking over the CAT act when it was sold to the show in 1954.

Over the years, economics forced Beaty-Cole to downsize, eventually dropping the SIDESHOW and PIT SHOWS from the MIDWAY. Although remaining a quality show, the number of acts was reduced, relying on larger families that could perform many routines, DOUBLING IN BRASS. Popular longtime clown Jimmy JAMES moved from WHITEFACE CLOWN to red tails to become one of the best RINGMASTERS under the BIG TOP. Another perennial, Fred LOGAN, became firmly established in charge of the BULLS.

Meanwhile, Johnny PUGH had moved from performer to front office to manager. The show was forced to rely more on sponsored dates, including buy-outs by shopping centers where the show set up on asphalt parking lots. When Frank McClosky died in 1979, the show was heavily in debt. In 1981 Pugh convinced Jerry Collins, a multimillionaire dog track owner and the last original partner in the Acme Circus Corporation, to give the circus to the state of Florida as a tax write-off. The show, put under the aegis of Florida State University, was appraised at $2.5 million.

In 1982 Pugh, along with E. Douglas Holwadel, acquired the Clyde Beatty-Cole Bros. Circus—along with its $600,000 in debts—for $2 million payable over 20 years at only 3% interest. Holwadel was a newcomer to the circus world. A former vice president of marketing of Santee Cement Company in South Carolina and a trader on the New York Stock Exchange, he had always loved circuses. His business background helped him to quickly earn the $200,000 capital needed to put the show back on the road. In 1985 Holwadel joined the show as the booking agent, bringing with him marketing expertise that included computerizing the office operation.

The show has rebounded, giving 486 shows in the eight months of its 1989 season, traveling 10,000 miles over 17 states along the eastern seaboard, with 170 performers and staff and 78 vehicles. The circus's WINTER QUARTERS is located in De Land, Florida.

CLYDE BROS. CIRCUS Owned and operated by Howard Suesz, the Clyde Bros. Circus began touring as a modern, indoor arena show in the mid-1950s. The show played under local sponsorship in the Midwest, Southwest and Ontario, Canada.

CODONA, ALFREDO (1883–1937) Handsome and talented, Alfredo Codona was known as the "King of the Flying Trapeze." Born in Sonora, Mexico, on October 7, 1883 of Irish, German and French extraction, his father Edward (who worked as Eduardo) was the leader of a TRAPEZE act—Los Cometos—that traveled through Mexico and Central America.

By the age of five Alfredo was in his father's act. His sister Victoria and brother Lalo performed a wire act, and the two were offered a CENTER RING position with the BARNUM & BAILEY CIRCUS in 1909. Alfredo was also offered a job, so the three children and their father traveled north. From 1909 through 1912 Alfredo built his reputation on the solo trapeze.

In 1911, with his brother Lalo, Steve Outch and Ruth Harris, Alfredo Codona formed a flying act. From 1913 through 1916 they toured with the Wirth Brothers Circus in Australia, finally returning to Barnum & Bailey in 1917.

Alfredo Codona entered circus history in 1920 when he became the first flyer to consistently achieve the elusive TRIPLE SOMERSAULT. The daring, if not reckless, aerialist continued to perform the stunt for over a decade. Others were able to duplicate Codona's stunts—the double somersault, the two-and-a-half somersault, and the double pirouette while returning from the CATCHER's hands to the trapeze. It was his flawless, crisp style and perfectionism that made Codona soar above all other flyers.

In 1927, after a volatile courtship, he married Lillian LEITZEL. Off-season the couple toured Europe and America. On Friday, February 13, 1931, while Codona was performing in Berlin, Leitzel's rigging snapped as she performed a PLANGE in a

performance in Denmark. Codona hurried to Copenhagen, but Leitzel assured him that she was fine and that he must return to Berlin. Two days later Leitzel died.

Codona commissioned a sculptor to build a monument to his wife. Placed over her grave in Inglewood, California is a statue of Leitzel clinging to a winged Codona (symbolizing flight). A pair of ROMAN RINGS, with a torn WEB, is etched into the base. The memorial is entitled "Reunion."

Codona subsequently became more foolhardy on the trapeze. In 1933 he was forced to retire from flying when he fell attempting a triple somersault and tore shoulder ligaments.

By this time Codona had married Vera Bruce, who was also an aerialist. It turned out to be an unhappy relationship. In 1937 she initiated divorce proceedings—charging cruelty and jealousy—and asked Alfredo to meet with her and her lawyer. Alone with his wife in the lawyer's office on July 31, 1937, Codona shot her to death, then killed himself, ending a flamboyant and troubled life in scandal.

A suicide note said, "I have no home. I have no wife to love me. I am going back to Leitzel, the only woman who ever loved me." On August 2, 1937 he was buried next to the ashes of his beloved Lillian Leitzel.

(See also FLYING TRAPEZE.)

CODY, WILLIAM FREDERICK (1846–1917) An army scout, buffalo hunter and pioneer for the first 26 years of his life, William F. Cody, the inventor of the Wild West show, endeared himself to audiences as "Buffalo Bill" for another 45 years.

Cody was born on a farm in Scott County, Iowa on February 26, 1846 and lived there for eight years until his family moved to Kansas. Cody's father was a trader with the local Indian tribe, and young William soon learned the customs and language of the Kickapoo.

As a boy, Cody was a messenger for a freight firm and a livestock tender on the Oregon Trail. At the age of 14 he worked for the Pony Express, once riding a continuous 300 miles when he discovered his scheduled stop-off station had been attacked by Indians.

During the Civil War, William F. Cody became a scout for the Union Army, joining the 4th Kansas Cavalry in 1863. In 1866 he married Louisa Frederici, a young St. Louis lass; but soon Cody was back on the frontier trail.

Cody's next Plains job was to supply buffalo meat for the workers laying the Kansas Pacific Railroad. Over the 17 months he worked for the railroad, Cody killed over 4,000 buffalo, earning him his famous nickname, "Buffalo Bill."

From 1868 to 1872 Cody fought Indians as a civilian scout for the western military. His heroism in a fight against the Indians on the Platte River earned him a Congressional Medal of Honor.

Ned Buntline (E.Z.C. Judson), a writer of paperback novels, saw a colorful hero in Cody, and published a story about Buffalo Bill in 1869. The book was dramatized as *Scouts of the Prairie,* and in 1872 Cody himself played the lead.

Although Cody worked on-and-off as an actor for 11 seasons, he rejoined the 5th U.S. Cavalry as chief scout in 1876, often serving under General George Armstrong Custer. A week after the Battle of Little Big Horn, Cody killed Chief Yellow Hand—a Cheyenne—in a duel.

Realizing that the days of the wild frontier were coming to an end, Cody conceived a circus-style show that would feature elements of the fabled Old West. In an open-air arena surrounded by grandstands, real-life cowboys and Indians would re-create their battles and stagecoach holdups as well as perform rodeo-style demonstrations of trick riding and shooting.

To assist him in his plans, Cody enlisted the aid of Buntline, press agent John M. Burke and Nathan Salsbury, also an experienced outdoor showman.

The first BUFFALO BILL'S WILD WEST, technically called "The Wild West, Rocky Mountain and Prairie Exhibition," opened on May 17, 1883 at the Fairgrounds in Omaha, Nebraska. An immediate success, the show featured Dr. W.F. CARVER, a trick shot artist, in addition to Cody. The Bogardus family, famous sharpshooters, headed by Captain Adam H. BOGARDUS, was also part of the company. Upon the Bogardus's retirement in 1885, a young girl named Annie OAKLEY joined the troupe. Another rifleman with the show was Johnny BAKER, whom Buffalo Bill took in as a foster son when his own boy, Kit Carson Cody, died at the age of six.

The Wild West traveled for three years, then planned a European tour at the suggestion of Samuel "Mark Twain" Clemens. Cody staged his first show in an English amphitheater in 1886, performing before royalty that included the Prince of Wales. At a later command performance, Chief Red Shirt— who considered himself Indian royalty—was introduced to Queen Victoria. Another command performance followed; Cody allowed the kings of Denmark, Belgium, Greece and Saxony to ride in the Deadwood stagecoach during the mock Indian attack.

Later European tours took Cody and his show to Spain, France, and Italy, where the show played before Pope Leo XIII. It was suggested that Cody might want to stage his Wild West in the ancient COLOSSEUM, but he claimed that it was too small.

Back in the United States, James A. BAILEY, who had just sold his interests in the Forepaugh-Sells Circus, joined Cody and Salsbury in 1895.

Bailey died in 1906, and his interest in the Wild West, purchased by the RINGLING BROTHERS in 1907, was sold back to Cody. A year later one of Cody's chief competitors, Major Gordon W. "Pawnee Bill" LILLIE, became a partner in the Wild West. With Lillie's help, the reorganized BUFFALO BILL WILD WEST AND PAWNEE BILL GREAT FAR EAST SHOW— nicknamed the Two Bills Show—hit its financial and artistic zenith.

Other shows soon rivaled Cody's Wild West, however. By 1911 revenues were at their lowest ebb, and the show finally closed in 1913. Cody further lost money trying to produce Indian war films; an attempt to sell mail-order prints of his portrait, done by Rosa Bonheur, failed. Once a hero, William F. Cody was financially—and possibly emotionally— bankrupt. He was forced to apply to the War Department for the $10-a-month allowance for those who held the Congressional Medal of Honor. As a final, posthumous blow, Cody's name was removed from the Medal of Honor roll: It was discovered that, although he had served in the military with distinction, Cody had been a civilian—not a soldier—when the medal was actually awarded.

Before his death, Cody toured briefly with the SELLS-FLOTO CIRCUS. At the age of 70, he was hired by the 101 RANCH WILD WEST. In Cody's honor—and to make full use of the feature attraction's name— Edward ARLINGTON and the Millers, owners of the 101 Ranch show, retitled their extravaganza the BUFFALO BILL & 101 RANCH WILD WEST.

This turned out to be Cody's final tour. Even after Cody's death the following year, however, Arlington continued to use the star's name in a restructured show, the BUFFALO BILL WILD WEST & JESS WILLARD SHOW.

William F. Cody died on January 10, 1917. He was entombed in solid rock on Lookout Mountain overlooking the Denver, Colorado plains.

COL. TIM MCCOY WILD WEST SHOW
The Col. Tim McCoy Real Wild West Show and Rough Riders of the World opened with high hopes in 1938, but failed financially after only 19 days of operation. It was notable in circus history as the last major attempt at producing a complete Wild West in the fashion of BUFFALO BILL'S WILD WEST.

Tim McCoy had been featured in the RINGLING BROS. AND BARNUM & BAILEY CIRCUS in 1936 and 1937, but he struck out on his own the following year. With 40 rail cars and a $400,000 investment (including a personal risk of $100,000), McCoy's Wild West had perhaps the sharpest and crispest look at the opening of any new show ever to tour.

The Number 1 ROUTE CARD showed dates booked from April 14 through May 14, beginning in Chicago. The McCoy Wild West appeared at the International Amphitheatre through April 23, but the stand was an economic disaster. Poor business followed in Columbus, Dayton and Cincinnati, Ohio; and in Parkersburg and Clarksburg, West Virginia; the show barely had enough funds to make its May 2 opening in Washington, D.C. The show folded there on May 4, never making it through the remainder of its first route sheet (Baltimore, Wilmington or Philadelphia), much less the remainder of the season.

While a major disappointment and a huge fiscal flop, the Col. Tim McCoy Wild West Show was certainly not alone. In 1938, the blackest economic year in American circus history, only one of the major rail shows (the Al G. Barnes-Sells Floto Circus) made it through the entire season. Even the Ringling show had to CLOSE AHEAD OF PAPER and wait for the spring of 1939 to reopen.

COLE, JAMES M. (1906–1992)
The great-great-nephew of W.W. "Chilly Billy" COLE, James M. Cole was born on January 11, 1906 in Penn Yan, New York. He saw his first circus, the JOHN ROBINSON CIRCUS, as a boy. His own entry into the circus world began when he worked in the office of the WALTER L. MAIN CIRCUS, followed by tours with the SELLS-FLOTO CIRCUS, the HAGENBECK-WALLACE CIRCUS and the RINGLING BROS. AND BARNUM & BAILEY CIRCUS.

In 1938 Cole opened his own indoor circus, the Cole All Star Circus. He operated the show, which played school gymnasiums in the winter months, under sponsored dates in New York and Pennsylvania for 50 years. During summer months the show toured under canvas as the Great James M. Cole Circus.

In 1957, he opened Circus Land, a small theme park, in Penn Yan, New York. In 1958, he became the manager of HAGEN BROS. CIRCUS and sold the show his herd of bulls. In the 1960s, Cole managed the KING BROS. CIRCUS.

A beloved showman in the industry, he was fondly known as "Mr. Cole" by friends as well as strangers. Upon his retirement to SARASOTA, FLORIDA in 1987, James Cole turned over the operation of the show to Billy Martin, his former RINGMASTER. Cole died on December 19, 1992.

COLE, W(ILLIAM) W(ASHINGTON) "CHILLY BILLY" (1847–1915)
Acknowledged as the first man to earn a $1 million in the circus business, W.W. Cole was born in New York, the son of William H. Cole, an English CLOWN and contortionist, and Mary Ann Cooke Cole, an equestrian and wire walker.

His grandfather was Thomas Taplin Cooke, a Scotsman, whose circus, Thomas Cooke's Royal Circus, was the first complete circus to travel to America from overseas. In addition to being the show's owner, Cooke was also a ropewalker, equestrian and strongman.

Sailing on the 3,000-ton *Royal Stuart* in 1836, the circus had a troupe of 120 people, along with 42 horses and 14 ponies. It arrived in New York, where Cooke built a 2,000-seat amphitheater for it in the Bowery.

Six months later the arena burned, so the circus moved briefly to Philadelphia, then Baltimore. An amphitheater was erected there, but it tragically burned too, killing all of Cooke's livestock. The company moved on to Boston before returning to Scotland.

W.W. Cole's parents decided to stay in America. After his father died in 1858, his mother married Miles Orton (1836–1903), a ROSINBACK rider with the ORTON BROS. CIRCUS.

In 1871 W.W. Cole partnered with his stepfather in the Cole & Orton Circus, with which he remained associated for at least two seasons. Cole founded his own first wagon show, W.W. Cole's New York and New Orleans Circus and Menagerie, in 1872 and moved it onto rails the following year.

His business plan was simple yet effective: His circus "followed the rail" into the western territories. As soon as the track was laid, Cole made certain that his was the first show into town. By 1884 the circus was a 31 railroad-car show, traveling out of St. Louis, Missouri. Also known as the W.W. Cole Circus, his show was the first to introduce a wild west sequence as part of the regular program. Dr. W.F. CARVER was one of the sharpshooters the circus featured.

Wishing to accept a managerial position with the BARNUM & BAILEY CIRCUS, Cole auctioned off his own show in 1886. Much of the equipment helped to form the LEMEN BROS. CIRCUS.

In 1896 he rescued a financially-strapped James A. BAILEY during the latter's European tour. Also partnered with Bailey and two of the Sells brothers, Cole reframed the SELLS BROTHERS CIRCUS into the ADAM FOREPAUGH & SELLS BROS. CIRCUS, generally referred to as the Forepaugh-Sells Circus. In 1905 Bailey acquired full ownership of the show from Cole and the Sells brothers.

W.W. Cole, one of the American circus's most notable entrepreneurs, left an estate of $5 million when he died. The Cole name was so associated with financial success that it was incorporated without permission into the titles of dozens of other circuses at the turn of the century. Among the many shows owing that debt of gratitude to "Chilly Billy" Cole were the COLE BROS. CIRCUS, the King Bros. & Cole Circus, the FAMOUS COLE CIRCUS and today's CLYDE BEATTY-COLE BROS. CIRCUS.

COLE ALL STAR CIRUCS See COLE, James M.

COLE & ORTON CIRCUS See COLE, W(ILLIAM) W(ASHINGTON) "CHILLY BILLY"; ORTON BROS. CIRCUS.

COLE BROS. CIRCUS When Martin J. Downs was looking for a name for his new 1906 circus, he remembered his circus history. W.W. "Chilly Billy" COLE, who had been the first man to make $1 million in the circus business, became his inspiration.

Downs adopted the name Cole Bros. Circus for his own use and toured his show through the 1908 season. Among the many other circus men to use the title on various shows were Al G. Campbell, Elmer Jones and John Pluto. For the 1929 and 1930 seasons, Floyd King (1888–1976) ran a Cole Bros. Circus as a ten-car rail operation.

With its WINTER QUARTERS in Rochester, Indiana, the new Cole Bros. Circus began in 1935. Built by Jess H. Adkins and Zack Terrell with equipment from the old Christy and Robbins shows, it was a powerful show traveling on 35 rail cars. Both Emmett KELLY and Otto GRIEBLING were in CLOWN ALLEY. For the first three years of its tour, the show starred Clyde BEATTY and, while the famous CAT trainer was with the show, it operated as the COLE BROTHERS & CLYDE BEATTY CIRCUS.

It was a comeback of sorts for Beatty: In 1932 he had been badly mauled by Nero, one of his lions, and this was his first full season back on the road. Although the act was his own, the cats he used were owned by the Ringling show; thus he had to quickly break in a new den of lions and tigers for the Cole show.

In 1939 the Cole Bros. Circus became the very last show to drop the tradition of the circus STREET PARADE as a regular feature. On February 20, 1940 the Cole Bros. Circus quarters was the site of one of the worst circus fires in history (see FIRES, CIRCUS). Despite the loss of all of the main buildings on the grounds and many of the MENAGERIE animals, the circus was able to open that same year with an even bigger show than the previous season.

Terrell toured the Cole Bros. Circus through 1948, when he sold it to Arthur M. Wirtz and associates. To boost attendance, Wirtz hired William "Hopalong Cassidy" Boyd for the 1949 season. Nevertheless, the tour was unsuccessful, and the Cole Bros. Circus closed on July 22, 1949.

The Cole title, however, remained in continuous use without authorization or any relation to the Downs/Adkins/Terrell/Wirtz show. In 1955, for instance, the KING BROS. SHOWS toured as the King Bros. & Cole Bros. Circus; and the FAMOUS COLE CIRCUS toured in the 1950s.

In 1957 the ACME CIRCUS CORPORATION—under the leadership of Frank McClosky, Walter Kernan and Jerry Collins—acquired the rights to the actual title and merged it with the Clyde Beatty title that they had secured the previous year; thus the CLYDE BEATTY-COLE BROS. CIRCUS was born.

COLE BROTHERS & CLYDE BEATTY CIRCUS

In 1935 Jess Adkins and Zack Terrell resurrected the COLE BROS. CIRCUS title, which had been toured by Martin Downs in 1906. As a special attraction, they convinced Clyde BEATTY, the famous animal trainer, to perform in the show and to lend his name to the circus as well. During the three seasons that Beatty was WITH IT, the show was known as the Cole Brothers & Clyde Beatty Circus. After Beatty left the show, it returned to its Cole Brothers title and toured continuously through 1950. An entirely different show was created in 1957 when the ACME CIRCUS CORPORATION acquired the two show names and once again linked them, this time as the CLYDE BEATTY-COLE BROS. CIRCUS.

COLLEANO, CON (1899–1973)

A renowned rope walker, Con Colleano was noted for performing a forward feet-to-feet somersault on the slack wire, a trick that he originated. The forward somersault is far more difficult than the backward leap, because in the forward somersault the legs are in front of the artist, blocking the performer's sight as the feet touch the wire.

Born in Australia, Colleano was of Spanish-Irish ancestry; by the age of 12 he was a ROSINBACK rider in his father's circus. Meanwhile, his sister Winnie COLLEANO developed a breathtaking TRAPEZE act. The climax of her act was a forward fall from a sitting position on the swinging trap to a heel catch. Although now a staple of single trapeze acts, Winnie did not attempt the stunt until she had spent nearly 20 years on the bar. In 1925 they both emigrated to the United States to join the RINGLING BROS. AND BARNUM & BAILEY CIRCUS.

Colleano soon moved from equestrian to wire walker. Always dressing as a matador, Colleano would execute a few bolero steps on the wire, making him literally a "rope dancer." In the middle of the act, he would throw himself into a backward somersault, removing his toreador pants in midair as he turned. Like Bird MILLMAN, he used no balancing umbrella—the first man to do so—but the loss of balance increased his flexibility.

Billed as "The Toreador of the Tight Wire," during the winter months Colleano would appear on the vaudeville circuit or, like many American circus acts, on British and European circus dates. He also occasionally performed with other circuses, such as his 1949 stint with the COLE BROS. CIRCUS and the Cristiani Bros. Circus in 1959.

Con Colleano retired at the age of 60, primarily due to failing eyesight brought on by cataracts. His last performance was in Honolulu in 1960 as part a major arena date put together by promoter E.K. Fernandez. As part of a three-ring low-wire display, one of the all-time greatest wire walkers was relegated to an end ring. No announcement was made of that fact that this was to be his final, farewell performance.

Colleano and his wife (coincidentally named Winnie) permanently retired to their home in Florida. In 1966 he was elected to the Circus Hall of Fame in SARASOTA, FLORIDA. Only two other Australians, his sister Winnie and May WIRTH, have also achieved that honor.

Con Colleano died of a heart attack November 12, 1973 at his home in South Miami. His widow died at a private hospital in Sydney, Australia on January 5, 1986.

(See also WIRE WALKING.)

COLLEANO, WINNIE (fl. 1915–1960)

Noted TRAPEZE artist and sister of circus star wire walker Con COLLEANO. Her most famous stunt was a heel catch from a seated position on a swinging solo trapeze.

COLORING BOOK PITCH

A children's coloring book is one souvenir that is always available at the circus.

As an extra source of revenue, many shows PITCH the book during the show while rigging is being set. Usually the RINGMASTER or one of the CLOWNS displays the coloring book, explaining how it was specially printed for that circus and contains line drawings of the most popular acts in the show. Providing an extra incentive to buy, the circus clowns distribute the books in the stands and often offer to autograph each copy. The coloring books are priced cheaply—usually at about $1 apiece—to sell quickly following the pitch.

In actuality, the coloring book *has* been specially printed, but usually only its cover. Major circus suppliers, such as Bill Biggerstaff at Graphics 2000 in Las Vegas and Spotlight Graphics in SARASOTA, FLORIDA, stock inexpensively printed books with generic drawings of a lion trainer, CLOWNS, a TRAPEZE artist and other common acts. These suppliers add colored covers made-to-order for bulk quantities, or are able to specially design a unique book for the show.

COLOSSEUM

Rome's Colosseum, also known as the Flavian Amphitheater, continued the spectacle tradition of the CIRCUS MAXIMUS.

Construction began between A.D. 70 and 72 during the reign of Vespasian. The Colosseum was dedicated by the Roman General Titus in A.D. 80, covering five acres with a seating capacity of 50,000 people. Two years later a final upper level was added, raising the seating to 87,000. According to the *Guinness Book of World Records,* its length of 612 feet and width of 515 feet made it the largest amphitheater on record in the world to this day.

Even so, the Colosseum's elliptical shape gave spectators a clear, close-up view of the shows and performers. Therefore, it was used more for "intimate extravaganzas," such as gladiator battles and unarmed Christians fighting lions and tigers. (Not surprisingly, Maccus, one of the earliest recorded CLOWNS, criticized the absence of humor in the Colosseum shows.) After the shows, the arena was often sprayed with perfumes and sand was spread over the floor.

On November 11, 1967—on the floor of the Colosseum amid the ruins of the ancient civilization—a new era was begun when John Ringling NORTH signed the agreement that turned his circus over to The Hoffeld Corporation, consisting of Irvin FELD, Israel FELD and Judge Roy HOFHEINZ.

COME-IN

Circus jargon for the time during which the audience enters the BIG TOP, or arena, until the show begins.

CONCELLO, ANTOINETTE (1912–c. 1984)

Born in Burlington, Vermont, one of six children to French-Canadian and English parents, Antoinette Cameau graduated from convent school at the age of 14. As she was preparing to go to college, she was invited by her sister and brother-in-law to join them on the SELLS-FLOTO CIRCUS.

Soon the diminutive Antoinette was amazing audiences with her presentation of the IRON JAW act, in which she would spin at the end of a hanging rope, holding on only by her teeth. It was during this period she met her future husband, the talented Art CONCELLO. When the Flying Wards (with whom he toured) moved to Sells-Floto from the HAGENBECK-WALLACE CIRCUS, he renewed the relationship.

Eddie and Mayme Ward of the Flying Wards trained Antoinette as a CATCHER; but she and Art soon married and formed their own act—the FLYING CONCELLOS—in 1929. When John RINGLING bought the Sells-Floto Circus in 1929, the Concellos became an end ring act with The GREATEST SHOW ON EARTH. Three years later Alfredo CODONA, a featured flyer with the show, was injured performing the TRIPLE SOMERSAULT; the Concellos were moved to the star spot in the CENTER RING, where they remained until their retirement in 1943.

Meanwhile, Art was grooming his wife as a FLYER. At a 1937 performance in Detroit, Antoinette Concello—already regularly performing the two-and-a-half—became the first female flyer to achieve the triple somersault. She remained the only woman to perform the stunt throughout the 1930s and '40s.

In 1943 Antoinette injured her shoulder and left the air. At the same time Art entered Ringling management. For six years Antoinette stayed in retirement, raising a son, then she resumed flying for several seasons. Finally, the greatest woman flyer in circus history retired as an active performer, assuming the role of aerial director of the RINGLING BROS. AND BARNUM & BAILEY CIRCUS. She died February 5, 1984.

(See also FLYING TRAPEZE.)

CONCELLO, ART (c. 1912–   )

Born on March 26, 1912 in Spokane, Washington to Portuguese parents, Arthur M. Concello moved to Bloomington, Illinois, home of the AMERICAN CIRCUS CORPORATION, when he was three years old. At the age of ten he attended a demonstration of the TRAPEZE at the local YMCA, and soon Art was taking to the air.

At 16 Concello joined the Flying Wards, a stellar act with the HAGENBECK-WALLACE CIRCUS, one of the corporation shows. Art seemed preoccupied or bored at rehearsals—when he attended them—but his undisciplined behavior was forgiven due to his extraordinary artistry when performing.

Concello moved with the Wards to the SELLS-FLOTO CIRCUS. While he was still with Hagenbeck-Wallace, Art had met his future wife, Antoinette Comeau, a daring performer of the IRON JAW. She trained with the Wards to become a CATCHER, and

Art and Antoinette soon married. In 1929 they formed the FLYING CONCELLOS.

The Concellos moved over to the RINGLING BROS. AND BARNUM & BAILEY CIRCUS when John RINGLING purchased the corporation shows. They were moved to the CENTER RING when Alfredo CODONA, the reigning "king of the flying trapeze," injured his shoulder performing a TRIPLE SOMERSAULT. The Flying Concellos remained the unquestioned star aerialists of the show until their retirement from the ring in 1943.

Concello was a superb FLYER himself, having been one of the first to perfect the triple somersault. Among the other amazing stunts he achieved included two backward somersaults with a half twist and a double horizontal pirouette.

Concello was well aware that flyers can perform for only a limited number of years. In 1933 he began coaching other flyers. He operated his own school; and when the new aerialists had completed their training, Concello booked them into Ringling or other shows internationally.

Short (five feet two inches tall) and vigorous, as well as a constant cigar smoker, Art Concello must have looked like a stereotypical manager when he was asked by John Ringling NORTH to join the Ringling front office in 1943. For years Art had studied every aspect of circus operations. Even during his act, Art often seemed disinterested in his work: His mind was busy trying to devise ways to improve the trapeze and other rigging or on methods to improve circus operations and efficiency.

Also in 1943, Concello accepted the offer of general manager of the Ringling show, even though he was also the owner of the RUSSELL BROS. CIRCUS that year. The next year Clyde BEATTY took over the Russell Bros. Circus, but Concello stayed involved with it, both in 1944 and again in 1946. Unable to divide his energies between the Ringling and Russell circuses, in 1947 Concello purchased the California-based Russell Bros. Circus and toured it for several seasons before rejoining The BIG SHOW.

In the next few years Concello continued to introduce new technologies to the circus world and tighten the burgeoning Ringling operations. He was responsible for one of the major innovations in circus history: In 1947 Concello perfected and patented the modern portable steel grandstand. Improving the seating design invented years before by "Cap"

Curtis for the HAGENBECK-WALLACE CIRCUS, Concello built the folding seats with stairways onto the sides of mechanical wagons. The 29 wagons the show used when it toured under canvas could be pulled into place within 45 minutes once the top was raised. The inside of the wagons, the space between them and under the bleachers, were then all used for dressing rooms.

Before this achievement, setting up wooden bleachers for the show took dozens of men as long as four hours; tearing them down took almost as long. The new arrangement also increased safety, totally eliminating the possibility of the grandstand seats collapsing due to too much weight or loose rigging. (As a side note, "Cap" Curtis went on to become Ringling's BOSS CANVASMAN under North's ownership and Concello's management.)

Concello also realized the potential for aluminum to replace heavy wooden QUARTER POLES and SIDE-POLES. The aluminum pole offered an extra safety factor: While the lightweight poles could become dented or bent, they would not snap unexpectedly like old wooden poles.

In the last years Ringling was under canvas, Concello recommended the elimination of the MENAGERIE—up to that point a circus staple—and lengthened the BIG TOP to accommodate the animals. When the show moved indoors, he devised a new tunnel wagon to move the beasts and equipment through the arena. Concello planned new productions, spruced up old numbers and, at one point, even made a monetary loan to the Ringling company.

Although Ringling remained Concello's main theater of operations, he was also associated with the CLYDE BEATTY-COLE BROS. CIRCUS during the 1950s and 1960s. In 1968 Art Concello, after an amicable divorce from Antoinette Concello, married a British ex-Ringling ballet dancer. He retired permanently from his circus associations and entered other business and real estate ventures.

(See also FLYING TRAPEZE.)

CONCERT   Also known as the aftershow, concert is circus jargon for an additional performance given in the BIG TOP for an extra fee after the main show is over.

The acts would usually consist of wild west numbers or novelty acts that were not seen in either the main performance or the SIDESHOW. Those who stayed would be moved from the BLUES, or general bleacher seating, closer to the CENTER RING where the aftershow acts would appear.

CONNECTION
While the term "connection" is used as circus jargon for a sidewalled walkway between any two tents, "the connection" was used to refer to the pathway between the MENAGERIE top and the BIG TOP on the major tented shows.

It was also in this area that the three-shell and three-card monte men performed their cons on the GRIFT shows that allowed it.

COOCH SHOWS
Performed as an extra added attraction for a small additional fee, cooch shows were frequently seen in the SIDESHOWS of the more disreputable circuses, especially the small GRIFT shows. The cooch shows were most often performed at night, after the BLOWOFF from the final BIG TOP show.

The INSIDE TALKER usually brought in audiences by saying that the show "separates the men from the boys."

It seldom did that, because neither the men nor the boys saw very much revealed: In fact, it is rumored that many of the most erotic cooch dancers on the early MUD SHOWS were actually female impersonators.

The term "cooch" is an abbreviation of the carnival slang "hootchy-kootchy," also sometimes seen as "hootchie-kootchie." Its derivation is most probably from the French *hocher*, meaning "to shake," or possibly from the Dutch *hotsen*, meaning "to jiggle." Its application to this supposedly Middle Eastern style of dancing is unknown.

COOK & WHITBY CIRCUS
Operating from 1892 through the 1894 season, the Cook & Whitby Circus was the retitled GREAT WALLACE SHOW. In 1895 the owner, Ben Wallace, returned to the original title before combining with the Carl Hagenbeck Wild Animal Show in 1907.

COOKHOUSE
One of the first wagons to be unloaded and set up from the circus train or caravan is the cookhouse. As soon as the dining tent is erected, a red flag is raised above its peak. The call of "FLAG'S UP" signals that a meal is ready to be served. ROUSTABOUTS who have been working since

dawn are among the first to enter the cookhouse dining tent for breakfast.

The first cookhouses, as well as circus-owned sleeping quarters, were started due to economic necessity. Before the Civil War, a performer on a small circus could be affordably housed in a local hotel, often for as little as 50 cents a day (including the cost of feeding and stabling his horse). As the size of casts and crew grew, it became less expensive to feed and house the troupe on the lot. In fact, this might be the origin of the nickname HOTEL often given the cookhouse.

While Adam Forepaugh is believed by some scholars to have had introduced the first *regular* cookhouse on his ADAM FOREPAUGH CIRCUS in 1871, it had been generally accepted that James E. COOPER had originated the use of an on-lot cookhouse tent in 1864. This fact was even noted in Cooper's obituary, albeit from information supplied by Cooper himself.

The most recent research of Stuart Thayer revealed that at least one other show, the Raymond & Van Amburgh Circus, experimented with feeding in the BACK YARD as early as 1851 (see Isaac VAN AMBURGH). William M. Davis, Jr. moved from that show to the MABIE BROS. CIRCUS in 1852 and convinced the Mabie brothers to purchase a tent for a cookhouse in 1857, although the dining tent probably did not go into operation until the 1858 season. Some claim it was actually circus man Walter Waterman, and not Davis, who was responsible for the addition.

Regardless, it was almost certainly the Mabie Bros. Circus, and not Cooper (who did not even begin his circus career until 1863), that introduced the daily use of a cookhouse tent to the circus lot. As late as the 1890s, however, the cookhouses were still usually set up in the open air, with food cooked in large kettles on open firepits.

By the 1920s the kitchens on cookhouses of the major shows used the most modern equipment; and the dining tent resembled huge restaurants, with tablecloths on the tables and service by waiters—another possible origin of the cookhouse nickname "hotel".

On almost every show, seating in the dining tent is neatly divided by rank and job description. On small family shows, the arrangement is informal and unspoken: Workers of similar tasks seem to congre-

Cookhouse crew cutting up jackpots on the Ringling Brothers and Barnum & Bailey Circus in Missoula, Montana on August 20, 1925.   *(Photo by Frank Updegrove, courtesy of the Heist collection)*

gate together in a particular, habitual area of the tent to be able to enjoy meals and talk over the day's events among colleagues and friends. On larger shows—especially during the heyday of the tented circus—the organization was much more formalized.

A curtain ran the length of the cookhouse, dividing it into the "long side" (for workingmen and their bosses) and the "short side" (for management, ticket sellers, candy BUTCHERS, front door men, ushers, performers, band and the SIDESHOW personnel). The two halves of the tent were the same size; "long" and "short" referred to the length of the tables that were used.

Each side tended to group itself into the caste system of the circus. On the "long side," for instance, management sat alone. Ticket sellers, front door men—in fact, anyone in a position of power or who handled money (and therefore might be promoted into the ranks of management)—formed a separate group. The band stayed as a unit, while the other performers sat in their own hierarchy. Most prestigious were the equestrians—the traditional backbone of the circus—followed by the aerialists and

wild animal trainers. Ground performers came next, with greater status accorded those with higher skill. First came the ACROBATS and tumblers, for example, followed by jugglers. Despite their contribution to the American circus, CLOWNS were the lowest rank performers.

These, of course, were only the BIG TOP performers. Also in the performers' area, but considered even lower in class, were the sideshow performers. The OUTSIDE TALKER and ticket sellers were considered, in a sense, middle management; but among the LITTLE TOP performers, the INSIDE TALKER or LECTURER was the most important.

Below the talker were the skilled performers (such as the magician, the ventriloquist, the sword-swallower and fire-eater), then the unskilled performers (for example, the SNAKE CHARMER), then the self-made and actual freaks (the Tattoed Man, the bearded lady, the SIAMESE TWINS). Again, the sideshow band—often a black or minstrel band—sat apart as its own entity.

Regardless of caste, everyone was served the same food and everyone got as much of it as desired. One of the maxims of outdoor amusements reads: "A circus moves on its stomach!" During its peak years as a tented circus, the RINGLING BROS. AND BARNUM & BAILEY CIRCUS customarily served over 4,000 meals a day to about 1,400 people.

Immediately after the evening meal (about 5:30 P.M.), the cookhouse tent was the first to be dropped. Along with the MENAGERIE and its working crews, the cookhouse was then sent aboard the FLYING SQUADRON, or first rail cars, to the next day's stand.

The term "cookhouse" refers to the entire complex used for feeding the show people on the circus. Those who are WITH IT, however, know that the word really means only the tent and the interior itself, never the kitchen. Every trouper has eaten meal after meal in the cookhouse; but nobody—other than, perhaps, the cookhouse staff itself—has ever eaten in the kitchen.

COOP & LENT CIRCUS

Begun as a rail show in 1916, the Coop & Lent Circus changed management after only one year. In 1918 it became one of the first circuses to make the transfer from railroad cars to tractor trailers. Ironically, the show closed because delivery on needed trucks was curtailed due to the United States' entry into World War I.

COOPER, JAMES E. (1832–1892)

James E. Cooper was the owner/manager of the Hemmings & Cooper's Circus in 1873 when James A. BAILEY bought in as a partner. The name was promptly changed to the COOPER & BAILEY CIRCUS.

Bailey moved the show onto rails in 1876, and the owners started the show on a two-year tour that took it as far as the South Pacific. Upon return to America in 1878, Bailey and a new partner, James L. HUTCHINSON, bought out Seth B. HOWES's bankrupt show to form Howes' Great London Circus, Sanger's Royal British Menagerie, and Cooper & Bailey's International Allied Shows, also known as the International Allied Shows.

In 1881 Cooper left the partnership, leaving the door open for P.T. BARNUM to join Bailey and Hutchinson. When Bailey retired at the end of the 1885 season, Cooper and W.W. COLE entered into the combine. Cooper remained with the show for two years, departing after the 1887 season.

On January 22, 1890 Adam FOREPAUGH died. Cooper, again with his old partner Bailey, bought the Forepaugh circus, increased its size and took it

on an 1891 cross-country tour, reaching the Pacific coast.

James E. Cooper died on January 1, 1892. James A. Bailey bought out Cooper's interest in the show, which continued to tour through the 1894 season.

COOPER & BAILEY CIRCUS

In 1873 James A. BAILEY bought into the Hemming & Cooper's Circus, which was owned by James E. COOPER. The two men promptly changed the title to the Cooper & Bailey Circus.

The unit moved onto rails in 1876 and left from San Francisco on November 8 for a two-year tour of Australia, New Zealand, the Netherlands East Indies and Java. To finish off that season, the circus performed throughout South America.

Returning to New York on December 10, 1878, Bailey and Cooper, with James L. HUTCHINSON, purchased the bankrupt show of Seth B. HOWES. Howes, having made a fortune with his circus, had turned it over to his nephews, Egbert and Elbert Howes, and James E. Kelley upon his retirement. Poor attendance and the 1873 depression, however, forced its closing.

The three new owners combined the titles to form Howes' Great London Circus, Sanger's Royal British Menagerie, and Cooper & Bailey's International Allied Shows, often referred to simply as the International Allied Shows.

The group was the first to use electricity to light its show—a benefit heavily advertised in the circus's promotion. Later in the same season, W.W. Cole also added electrical lights to his circus, but he charged an extra admission price to see the new wonder.

The International Allied Shows also claimed another circus landmark, having the first elephant born in captivity. P.T. BARNUM reportedly attempted to buy the baby Columbia and mother Hebe for $100,000 but the trio refused to sell. By the time negotiations with Barnum led to a merger of their shows in 1881, Cooper had departed from the partnership.

Although Cooper and Bailey were to become partners once more in 1890 when they each purchased part of the estate of Adam FOREPAUGH, the Cooper & Bailey Circus title was never revived again.

CORNPLANTER

Ricketts Circus, founded in 1793 by John Bill RICKETTS, offered a riding show that featured Cornplanter, Ricketts's personal steed. Ricketts performed the perilous feat of leaping from the horse's back 12 feet in the air—over a ribbon and cane—and down onto its back.

Cornplanter was further trained to leap over the back of another horse. Another trademark of Ricketts's performance was his assuming the pose of the Roman messenger god Mercury on Cornplanter's back, sometimes while carrying another performer on his shoulders.

COTTON CANDY Invented by Thomas Patton in 1900, cotton candy is the most popular confection sold at the circus. First called "fairy floss" in the United States, it is known as *"barbe de grandpere"* ("grandfather's beard") in France, *"pashmak"* in Persia and *"zuckerwolle"* ("sugar wool") in Germany.

Cotton candy is literally melted sugar, poured into a spinning drum. As it cools, it collects as long, weblike strands that are wound onto a paper cone.

By adding vegetable dyes to the sugar, candy BUTCHERS are able to change the colors of the cotton candy (sometimes to blue); but pink is still the preferred shade.

COUP, W(ILLIAM) C(AMERON) (1836–1895) Recognized as a circus innovator, W.C. Coup began his career in his native Wisconsin as a circus ROUSTABOUT, later graduating to the position of SIDESHOW manager.

On April 10, 1871, with Dan CASTELLO and P.T. BARNUM, Coup opened a new tented circus named BARNUM'S GREAT TRAVELING MUSEUM, MENAGERIE, CARAVAN, HIPPODROME AND CIRCUS. Coup became general manager, while Castello handled amusements and Barnum did promotion.

The circus played under almost three acres of canvas, a record at the time. The first season grossed $400,000, which encouraged Coup to move the show from wagons onto rail. Although there had been

Kids at the circus enjoy the Thomas Patton invention, cotton candy. (Photo by Tom Ogden)

early experiments with moving circus stock by rail, most historians agree that W.C. Coup began the era of the railroad circus when he put the Barnum show on rails in 1872. Coup is also credited with inventing the end-loading method of placing wagons onto CIRCUS TRAINS.

At the end of the 1873 season, while Barnum was in Europe purchasing wild animals, Coup took it upon himself to lease an indoor arena in New York City for winter performances. P.T. BARNUM'S GREAT ROMAN HIPPODROME, later called MADISON SQUARE GARDEN, opened in April 1874.

The Hippodrome show was soon put on the road. Barnum's Great Traveling World's Fair gave three performances daily following a morning STREET PA-RADE. On this show, Coup made the innovation of adding a second ring under the BIG TOP.

Although Barnum's name was a big draw, Coup, who traveled with the show, was greatly responsible for its success. He would HANG PAPER advertising the circus for 75 miles surrounding the showgrounds and arranged for excursion trains to bring far-flung patrons to the LOT.

The show and partnership prospered for four years, but by the end of the 1875 season Coup was dissatisfied. He was particularly upset that Barnum had allowed John V. "Pogey" O'BRIEN, a notorious circus owner who openly operated GRIFT shows, to join their corporation. Coup departed, and the show dissolved in 1880.

W.C. Coup took a two-year hiatus, then opened the $500,000 New York Aquarium with a German partner, Charles Reiche. He also operated the EQUESCURRICULUM, a tent show, advertised as "A College of Trained Animals and Cephalodian Monsters of the Deep from the New York Aquarium."

Splitting from Reiche in 1879, Coup founded the NEW UNITED MONSTER SHOWS. For the next few years, it was, indeed, monstrous—the largest combined circus and MENAGERIE on rails. Unfortunately, a tragic train wreck closed the show. Coup attempted many comebacks on a smaller scale, but none were successful. He retired to Florida and died in near poverty on March 4, 1895.

COURT, ALFRED (1883–1977)

One of the main animal trainers of the RINGLING BROS. AND BARNUM & BAILEY CIRCUS, Alfred Court performed with mixed CATS (lions, tigers, leopards, panthers, jaguars), polar BEARS and Great Danes, all in the same cage.

In 1926 John RINGLING decreed that exotic animal acts were cruel and improper for his show, but competition demanded that he occasionally allow a cat act to appear. Clyde BEATTY first performed on The BIG ONE in 1931 in New York and Boston only, but not on tour.

When John Ringling NORTH assumed control of the circus in 1938 he reversed the ban, and Alfred Court was the first great trainer to emerge. Born in Marseilles, France on January 1, 1883, Court came from aristocratic parents. At his strict Jesuit school, he became adept at gymnastics; so much so that when he ran away at 14 he was able to join a circus. Police returned him to school, but his escape the next year was permanent. In 1914 he went to the United States to perform as an ACROBAT with the Ringling Bros. Circus.

The next season he returned to Europe, touring most of the small circuses as a gymnast. By March 1917 he was director of a MUD SHOW in Mexico. He kept his eye on the lion trainer—who was prone to drink—fearing that he might have to replace him. When the trainer invited Court into the BIG CAGE, Court made his first move to be that replacement; a few days later, when the trainer was fired, Court was suddenly a lion trainer at the late age of 35.

His career as a circus performer was interrupted when he returned to his native France and, with his brother Jules, started a successful business in breeding and training wild animals. At one point he had placed five cat acts on circuses throughout Europe. At the start of World War II, however—and with an invitation from North to join The Big One—Court returned to the United States.

Court performed in a sophisticated European style, posing the wild animals into "tableaux." He shunned the Beatty-style dramatics—called EN FÉROCITÉ by the French—such as the use of whips, a chair and gun.

Although he possessed the iron nerve and physical dominance that all cat trainers require, the lean, gentlemanly Court never yelled his commands, performing with such élan and panache that he was regarded as a "trainer's trainer." He was almost courtly in his Old World courtesy to the beasts. For his loving efforts, Court was never seriously injured by his animals.

In 1945 he retired from Ringling. At the time of his departure, he was presenting a remarkable mixed menagerie in the steel arena of three polar bears, two black bears, eight lions, two leopards, two tigers, a jaguar, two wolves and two dogs. Court died on July 1, 1977.

(See also STOREY, WILSON F.)

CRADLE

One of the newer AERIAL ACTS, the aerial cradle is a piece of metal skyborne apparatus.

The simplest form of a cradle is two parallel TRAPEZE bars placed closely together. The CATCHER in a trapeze or cradle act sits on one bar, facing the other. He bends backward, hanging from the first trapeze bar by the knees, with feet hooked under the second stationary bar.

A more elaborate cradle consists of several metal rods, configured to look like two triangles joined by cross-bars. The apex of the triangles is upward, so the catcher sits across two bars on the bottom, or base, of the apparatus. The catcher wraps his legs around the padded bars, then hangs downward.

Another aerialist locks hands and wrists with the catcher and performs graceful poses, somersaults and other tricks. Meanwhile, the cradle itself may be fixed, hanging still or swinging.

The cradle is usually seen as its own feature act, but some catchers on the FLYING TRAPEZE have now begun to hang from cradles rather than a single bar.

A different type of apparatus, also called a cradle, is used in ground acts such as FOOT JUGGLING and RISLEY ACTS. In this case the cradle is the cushioned mat on which the artist lies to perform. The tailbone end is raised to a 30-degree angle to support the lower back as it raises the artist's legs perpendicular to the floor. Two shoulder pads help the performer remain in position and prevent his sliding off the front of the cradle while performing.

CRANE BAR

The crane bar, essential to all AERIAL ACTS, is a long metal rod suspended high above the ring at the top of the TENT. It is from this piece of heavy rigging that all of the aerial apparatus, such as the AERIAL PERCH, the ROMAN RINGS and the solo TRAPEZE, are hung.

CRISTIANI, LUCIO (1906–1992)

One of the greatest circus bareback riders in history, Lucio Cristiani was the patriarch of the clan that bears his name, the CRISTIANIS. He was the great-grandson of the first Cristiani to enter the European circus world.

He made his American debut in 1934 with the RINGLING BROS. AND BARNUM & BAILEY CIRCUS, then went on to travel with shows such as the HAGENBECK-WALLACE CIRCUS, the AL G. BARNES CIRCUS, the COLE BROS. CIRCUS and finally his own, the Cristiani Bros. Circus.

His feature trick was an incredible full backward twisting somersault from one horse, over another and onto the back of a third as all three galloped around the ring. In the usual horse-to-horse somersault, the performer curls into a ball but does not change axis. In the full twist, the body somersaults in an almost prone position, pirouetting before landing. Before Lucio Cristiani performed the stunt, it was thought to be impossible to do from horse to horse.

Multitalented, Cristiani also performed a LIBERTY HORSES and DRESSAGE act, and he was a talented clown.

Cristiani was honored in 1972 at the JOHN AND MABLE RINGLING MUSEUM OF ART in a special ceremony and was later added, along with the rest of his family, to the SARASOTA CIRCUS RING OF FAME on St. Armands Circle in SARASOTA, FLORIDA.

In the 1960s he started an uncaged leopard act for his wife, Gilda. The two continued to perform it for the rest of their careers. The routine was featured on TELEVISION's *Circus of the Stars*, with Juliet Prowse handling the CATS as Cristiani stood by.

The standard by which contemporary ROSINBACK riders are measured, Lucio Cristiani died in Sarasota on January 23, 1992.

(See also BAREBACK RIDING.)

CRISTIANI BROS. CIRCUS

See CRISTIANI, LUCIO; CRISTIANIS, THE.

CRISTIANIS, THE

The largest and most famous family of equestrians in circus history, the Cristiani family of Italy traces its beginnings in outdoor amusements back 150 years. Many feel that the Cristianis are also the most diversely talented, with members of this clan of 50+ artists performing on HORSES, as ACROBATS, as jugglers (see JUGGLING), BULL handlers and on the TRAPEZE. Troupes comprised of members of the extended family now appear on many different shows.

Known by many as the "Royal Family of the Circus," the Cristianis trace their circus roots back six generations. Emilio Cristiani (c. 1815–1906), an amateur gymnast from Pisa, Italy, was appointed royal blacksmith for King Victor Emmanuel II in or around 1862.

Emilio's son, Philade (c. 1854–1925), was an even more talented tumbler, as well as a trapeze artist and strongman. He fell in love with a circus equestrienne and aerialist, Anna Bottari, and followed her onto her show. His father, although a lover of the circus arts, was concerned about the family reputation: He felt that the son of someone on the royal staff should have his own show. Emilio, with King Victor Emmanuel's financial assistance, framed the first Cristiani circus, *Il Circo Cristiani*, in 1874.

Philade was married twice, producing 12 sons and 12 daughters, most of whom became involved in his circus. One son, Ernesto (1882–?), was an exceptional gymnast and a capable businessman—much more so that his father. After performing with several other circuses throughout Europe, Ernesto formed his own show in 1919. By 1930 his circus had become the biggest in Italy and one of the most successful in Europe.

In 1931, to escape the Mussolini regime, the Cristianis moved to Paris, performing for one season with the Cirque du Medrano. By this time Lucio CRISTIANI, Ernesto's son, was already performing his legendary backward somersault with a twist from one horse over a second and onto a third galloping behind.

Pat VALDO, ex-clown and talent scout for the RINGLING BROS. AND BARNUM & BAILEY CIRCUS, saw the Cristianis performing on the Circus Schumann in Belgium in the winter of 1933. They were brought to the United States for the first time in 1934, to perform with the Ringling-owned HAGENBECK-WALLACE CIRCUS. After two seasons on that show, the Cristianis moved over to another Ringling show, the AL G. BARNES CIRCUS. In 1938 the family appeared in a short film. It was seen by John Ringling NORTH, who immediately moved the Cristianis over to The BIG ONE.

Although they were truly star performers, the high-salaried clan grew in number to be too expensive for the Ringling show. They began to move from show to show, finally realizing it was necessary to either split into separate troupes or run their own circus.

In 1948, several members of the family moved into management with Floyd King and his KING BROS. CIRCUS, forming the King Bros. and Cristiani Circus the following year. The show opened its WINTER QUARTERS in Macon, Georgia.

In 1950 the show toured western Canada. The next year their TERRITORY switched to New England and the South. For the 1952 season, the circus carried 12 ELEPHANTS and featured Hugo ZACCHINI and a STREET PARADE. By 1953 the show was traveling on 54 trucks and regularly advertised a BALLOON ASCENSION as a free outdoor attraction.

The partnership with Floyd King ended after that season. In 1954 the Cristianis merged briefly with the small Bailey Bros. Circus, calling it, aptly enough, the Bailey Bros. and Cristiani Circus. The motorized show played open-air on football fields and ballparks rather than in a tent.

Setting out on July 1, 1954, and traveling by truck up the Alcan Highway, the Cristiani Bros. Circus became the first circus to appear in Alaska. To accomplish that milestone, the show made what was probably the longest single overland JUMP ever—from Casper, Wyoming to Anchorage, Alaska, a distance of 2,850 miles.

In 1955 the Cristiani Troupe performed for six months in England. The next year they visited France and Italy.

In 1956 the circus was revamped by patriarch Lucio Cristiani and placed back under canvas. Its quarters moved from Macon, Georgia to SARASOTA, FLORIDA, less than a mile down the road from those of the Ringling show.

This small unit quickly established its route on the eastern seaboard from Key West to Canada and was usually the first circus to go out on the road each year, starting in mid-March. The 1956 season, for example, began on March 12 in West Palm Beach, Florida, with a new BIG TOP measuring 245 by 115 feet that held 3,000 people. The SIDESHOW and MENAGERIE were combined under a separate tent on the MIDWAY. At least 30 trucks hauled the show 14,110 miles before it closed back in Sarasota on October 21. Of the 175 people in the cast and crew, 36 (or one-third of the performers) were Cristianis.

The undisputed head of the Cristiani Bros. Circus was Lucio Cristiani. In addition to managing the circus, he doubled as a bareback rider, still performing his horse-to-horse full-twist backward somersault.

Another Cristiani family specialty was a three-person simultaneous somersault from horse to horse. In the stunt, three horses gallop in a single file around the ring. Each ROSINBACK rider stands on his own horse. All three throw a backward somersault simultaneously, landing on the horse behind. The third rider lands on the ground, and the first horse continues at liberty.

In addition to their equestrian talents, the Cristianis were masters of the TEETERBOARD with which they were well-known for building a four-person tower. One member of the company, Ortans Cristiani, is the only woman to ever perform a triple somersault while being shot upward to the top of a "four-high."

Even Lucio's wife, Gilda, was actively involved in the show, as head of the COOKHOUSE.

By the late 1950s, the Cristiani Bros. Circus was showing limited returns, and many of the family members had to perform on other shows as well. The last full tour of the Cristiani Bros. Circus was the 1961 season, but members of the famed Cristiani family continue to appear on many other American circuses to this day.

CROWNINSHIELD, CAPTAIN JACOB (fl. 1790s)

On April 13, 1796 Captain Jacob Crowninshield, a Salem shipmaster, made circus history by importing the first ELEPHANT to the United States. The two-year-old pachyderm, probably female, but also occasionally reported as male, had sailed on his ship *America* from Bengal, where Crowninshield had paid $450 for her. The journey had taken four months. Crowninshield advertised the beast as being "upwards of 8 feet and weighing more than 5,700 pounds" and quickly sold it for $10,000 to a Philadelphia entrepreneur, a Welshman named Owen.

Billed only as "The Elephant," the animal was shown all over the eastern seaboard from upstate New York to South Carolina, leaving a trail of handbills and circulars behind. The elephant's first public appearance, in New York City, was advertised in the *Argus* on April 23, 1796 and her last documented exhibition was in York, Pennsylvania in July 1818.

CRUM CARS

Circus jargon for the railroad cars, or tractor trailers, that the workingmen and ROUSTABOUTS use as sleeping units and call home. The slang refers to the rodents and lice that frequented the cars due to overcrowding, poor ventilation and unsanitary conditions.

CULPEPPER-MERRIWEATHER GREAT COMBINED CIRCUS

With its WINTER QUARTERS in Queen Creek, Arizona, just outside Phoenix, the Culpepper-Merriweather Circus is one of the few circuses to be based west of the Mississippi River. Under the management of owner/RINGMASTER/fire-eater Red Johnson, the circus's one-ring tent holds 700 people.

Johnson became interested in the world of the circus as a young boy when the CLYDE BEATTY-COLE BROS. CIRCUS visited his home town of Pittsfield, Massachusetts. By 1977 Johnson was living in Quincy, California; he joined the Big John Strong Circus when it came to town that year.

Big John STRONG sold his show in 1983, but Johnson was determined to continue under the BIG TOP. In 1985, with a $10,000 personal donation from an executive of the CIRCUS FANS ASSOCIATION OF AMERICA, Johnson and four friends formed the Culpepper and Merriweather Great Combined Circus.

Johnson explains that "The first name came from a 1972 movie, *The Culpepper Cattle Company*. Merriweather was the maiden name of the our sponsor's mother. It sounded like an old English tea company, but it sounded right." Their first small shows were performed in the open air on Florida campgrounds. Soon a small tent was added, carried from town to town in the back of a pickup truck.

Four of the circus's founders remain with the show: In addition to Red Johnson is "Cap" Terrell Jacobs III (1957–), son of a FLYER and grandson of the famous CAT trainer, Capt. Terrell JACOBS, out of PERU, INDIANA. He began his circus career riding a pony in the ring at the age of six. His wife, Lynn Marie, also with the show from the beginning, is an ELEPHANT rider and popcorn BUTCHER, in addition to being the show's star aerialist. The fourth is the BOSS CANVASMAN, B.J. Herbert.

In 1992 the Culpepper and Merriweather Circus began its tour in Arizona in March. By the time it ended in El Paso, Texas 35 weeks later, it had visited 250 towns in 14 states, traveling over 11,000 miles. Its 90-minute show included a dog act, a bicycle act, a solo TRAPEZE, JUGGLING, a magician, Barbara the elephant and, of course, CLOWNS. In 1992 the show's NUT was approximately $2,000 per day, against ticket prices of $6 for adults and $4 for children.

The troupe consists of 35 people, 15 of them performers. FIRST OF MAYS earn approximately $10,000 per season, in addition to food and some travel expenses; veterans with four different acts can earn $20,000 or more.

According to Red Johnson, the circus survives because "it transports people into our nomadic lifestyle, which seems to be the problem-free world everyone wants."

CUSHING, "COLONEL" JOSEPH C. See HOWES, SETH B.; HOWES & CUSHING.

C.W. NOYES CRESCENT CITY CIRCUS See THAYER & NOYES CIRCUS.

CYCLISTS Bicycles, unicycles and motorcycles have been a part of the American circus for over a century.

The earliest bicycle acts were daredevil acts, including that of Leonati, a Frenchman, who toured with the ADAM FOREPAUGH CIRCUS in 1883. Billed as the "Spiral Ascensionist," Leonati rode a highwheeler—a strange-looking bicycle by today's standards, with an oversize front wheel and miniature rear wheel—up a spiral ramp to a small platform 50 feet in the air and then descended.

Another of the daring Forepaugh cyclists during the 1880s was Ella Zuila. Essentially a high wire artist, Zuila performed an amazing variety of stunts as she walked the tightrope: She could cross the wire with her feet laced into fruit baskets, on stilts made of iron, with her entire body in a potato sack, while carrying her husband on her shoulders, pushing her baby in a wheelbarrow or while pouring water from one urn to another over her head. Her bicycle was a wooden velocipede that she was advertised to be able to ride "on the aerial roadway . . . over a 3–4 inch wire, 100 feet in mid-air . . . backward and forward over a high wire." In 1899 she astounded crowds on the MIDWAY by whizzing down a ramp and jumping up and over the backs of six ELEPHANTS, landing on a ramp on the other side.

In the 1890s the pneumatic safety bike was invented, but circus daredevils became even more

reckless with their exhibitions. In 1903 on the ADAM FOREPAUGH & SELLS BROS. CIRCUS, a cyclist named Starr performed a straight plunge down a "triple extension ladder pitched at an acute angle of 52 degrees and 79 feet long but only two feet wide with the open rungs 10 inches apart." He descended with such speed that the momentum carried him all of the way around the hippodrome track.

The next year on the same show, Prodigious Porthos, "the Chasm-Vaulting Cyclist," emulated Ella Zuila by speeding down a ramp resembling a ski jump and flying over a 50-foot gap before landing on the far side.

A new act at the turn of the century was the "Loop the Loop." Performers raced down a long ramp that curled into a full loop. The daredevils spun a complete somersault, and they needed extreme speed to carry them all of the way around the loop by centrifugal motion. In 1904 stuntman Diavolo was one of the first to do this risky act, but others soon followed. The casualty rate among performers of the Loop the Loop became very high.

Several types of dramatic, if less dangerous, bicycle acts are still seen today. In one, riders wearing crash helmets and knee pads race back and forth between two almost-vertical curved walls, resembling skateboard courts, at tremendous speeds. When the bicycle reaches the top of the wall, the rider twists his vehicle in a midair somersault and rushes back down.

Bicycles have remained a staple of many high wire acts and had a featured spot in the performance of the WALLENDAS. Just as often today, bicycles are used in a form of acrobatic act reminiscent of an equestrian VAULTING act. The cyclist circles the interior of the ring at a steady speed, and other members of the company hop on and off the bicycle seat, bars and rider. Eventually a human pyramid is built, with performers hanging and balanced off both sides of the bicycle and the driver.

Many bicycle acts begin with or include a solo artist who is able to ride backward, perform "wheelies" or bounce the bicycle upright on the back wheel only. This type of act often concludes with a breakapart bike, leaving the performer sitting on a unicycle.

A unicycle consists of one wheel—usually 20 inches or 24 inches in diameter—two pedals, a pedal shank, a fork (the pole between the wheel and the seat)

The high unicycle is performed by "The 3 Shyrettos" on the 1942 edition of The Greatest Show on Earth.
(Author's collection)

and a seat perched on top. The length of the fork can vary considerably. Some performers use high unicycles, or "giraffes," as tall as ten feet; others ride on tiny midget unicycles only a few inches tall.

Similar to a ROLA BOLA or ROLLING GLOBE, a unicycle depends on balance; however, because the rider is almost standing, it is more of a cross between a rolling device and STILT WALKING. A logical extension of a unicycle act for the performer is JUGGLING rings, balls or clubs while teetering back and forth.

Minting (the "Australian Marvel"), one of the first unicyclists featured in a show, was also a daredevil. In 1902 he replicated the Leonati act of ascending

and descending a 20-inch-wide, 60-foot-high spiral—but on a unicycle. The Forepaugh-Sells show billed him as the "Only Unicycle Ascensionist in the World."

The unicycle is seen more often than the bicycle in today's circuses. While certain acts consist of the full company on unicycles (such as the King Charles Troupe of comedy unicyclist/basketball players), most unicyclists are solo performers.

Hobbyists and amateurs can join two different organizations dedicated to the art of unicycling. Both hold annual national and regional conventions and competitions, offer newsletters and magazines, and have offices in Redford, Michigan. The Unicycling Society of America can be reached at: P.O. Box 40534, Redford, Michigan 48240. Information on the International Unicycling Federation is available by writing: 16152 Kinloch, Redford, Michigan 48240.

Although not technically a bicycle or a motor bike, a related early daredevil stunt called the *L'auto Bolide* or the "Dip of Death" toured with the BARNUM & BAILEY CIRCUS in 1907. The driver, Isabella Butler, was harnessed into a vehicle that resembled an automobile. Starting on a high platform, the car sped down an incline, turned upside down and, while inverted, jumped "into space 40 feet away across a veritable chasm of death." Butler landed on an incline on the other side, looped around and ended the run on the hippodrome track.

A modern daredevil circus act is the "Globe of Death." Originally the routine was seen as an attraction on carnival midways; a man on a motorcycle would drive up the vertical walls of a circular room until he was eventually driving in a complete revolution on a horizontal plane to the ground.

The same stunt can be performed in a steel mesh "globe." The cyclist enters the open-wire ball through a trapdoor, which is then sealed. Spectators can see through the grid as the cyclist drives up and around in complete loops and in all directions. To make the act even more sensational, one or two more cyclists enter the globe; and they all circle at the same time. Some acts even have a person stand in the middle of the globe of death while three cyclists simultaneously zoom around the circumference of the ball's interior.

D

DAILEY BROS. CIRCUS Although many circuses made the change from railroad to truck shows in the second half of the 20th century, the Dailey Bros. Circus was the first show to make a complete switch from a motorized show to a rail circus.

Started by Benjamin C. Davenport, the Dailey Bros. Circus traveled on rails from 1944 until 1950, when it was financially forced to CLOSE AHEAD OF PAPER midseason. Joe LOUIS, the famous heavyweight boxer, was the star performer—or attraction—of that final tour. During that half decade, the Dailey Bros. Circus had grown from a 15-car show in 1945 to 25 rail cars in 1950.

Although the Dailey show never reorganized, Davenport was able to tour other truck shows in later years.

DAN RICE CIRCUS After gaining performance and touring experience with at least three different troupes (notably the NICHOLS CIRCUS, Nathan A. Howes Circus and the Rufus Welch Company), Dan RICE—the first great American clown—formed his own show in 1848, the Dan Rice Circus. Although some historians feel that the show was bankrolled at least in part by Rice's old nemesis "Dr." Gilbert R. SPALDING, clearly Rice was full manager and in complete control of his new circus.

The Dan Rice Circus consisted of a one-ring tented arena, with the clown as the focal point of the show. Finally Rice was able to give full rein to his talents—

dancing, singing and satirizing current affairs and people. Two of his popular songs were "Root Hog or Die" and "Red, White and Blue," the latter performed with Margaret Ann Curran, his wife at the time.

In addition to his own act, the circus also featured LORD BYRON, Rice's educated pig, and a new attraction, LALLA ROOKH, a rope-walking elephant that he named after the heroine of a Persian poem.

It was during this period that Dan Rice developed his distinctive appearance with chin whiskers, tall top hat and red-and-white striped costume. This image was caricatured as "Uncle Sam" in a *Harper's Weekly* illustration by Thomas Nast.

In 1848 Rice moved the circus onto *The Allegheny Mail* steamboat. For a year the Dan Rice Circus plied the waters of the Mississippi River, taking the show to river towns from New Orleans to St. Paul, Minnesota. Since the show played Hannibal, Missouri during this period, it is generally presumed that Samuel "Mark Twain" Clemens used it as a model when describing the circus in *Adventures of Huckleberry Finn:* "All the time that clown carried on so it most killed the people. The ringmaster couldn't ever say a word to him but he was back at him quick as a wink with the funniest things a body ever said; and how he ever *could* think of so many of them, and so sudden and so pat, was what I couldn't no way understand. Why, I couldn't 'a' thought of them in a year."

The Dan Rice Circus closed in 1850 when the

great clown was hospitalized for yellow fever. The show continued under its own and other names, including DAN RICE'S ONE-HORSE SHOW, throughout the 1850s.

Depending on his financial circumstances during the next two decades, Rice either ran his own circus or appeared as the star of another show. Among the featured performers on the Dan Rice Circus around 1860 were "Dr." James L. Thayer, also a successful clown, and Charles Noyes, an animal trainer. (The men would pair up later with the THAYER & NOYES CIRCUS.)

For some seasons the Dan Rice Circus was actually owned by others, but featured Rice as the main performer. In 1861, for instance, Noyes leased the Rice title, and Adam FOREPAUGH owned the Dan Rice name in 1865 and 1866. Rice toured with various partners until his alcohol and emotional problems ruined him in 1881.

The "Dan Rice Circus" title appeared on many unrelated shows after Rice's death in 1900. These shows, all unauthorized by his estate, included Dan Rice Circus (1901); the Rice Bros. Circus (1909–14); and other miscellaneous "Rice" shows in 1923, 1934–37 and 1945. A Dan Rice Circus carnival unit toured as late as 1954 and 1955.

DAN RICE'S ONE-HORSE SHOW
By the time Dan RICE opened Dan Rice's One-Horse Show, he had already toured under at least three other impresarios, the most famous having been "Dr." Gilbert R. SPALDING. His own legendary DAN RICE CIRCUS had come and gone, but by 1850 he was ready to start over.

The show got its name on November 9, 1950, in Cincinnati when Spalding (who had caused sheriffs to seize all but Rice's personal steed, Aroostook, earlier that day) stood at the performance and derisively yelled, "Dan Rice and his one-horse show." Rice replied, "The taking of Troy was strictly a one-horse show." News of the clever retort spread, and Dan Rice carried the new moniker with pride.

In December 1850 Aroostook was also confiscated. The following spring Rice purchased a new educated horse, EXCELSIOR. The steed had been trained to walk up and down stairs and was central to a new act that was to become a circus staple, the PETE JENKINS ACT. The "Pete Jenkins from Mud Corners" routine told the story of a tattered tramp who loses his clothing while trying to mount the horse, only to reveal his gorgeous, glittery undergarments.

The summer show was so successful that Rice opened a winter edition of Dan Rice's One-Horse Show indoors in a New Orleans amphitheater. For that engagement Mrs. Dan Rice was made the star equestrian. He also added a MENAGERIE and museum, more CLOWNS, tightrope walkers, rope dancers, pole balancers and LALLA ROOKH, a performing ELEPHANT, making it the largest circus of its time. Eventually the show settled into WINTER QUARTERS in Girard, Pennsylvania.

Rice continued his own set of satirical songs with current barbs, and by 1860 he was one of the most popular attractions on the road. Even in the midst of gathering war clouds, President Abraham Lincoln reportedly visited the show in the nation's capitol in 1861 or 1862.

Unfortunately, the war economy cut audience attendance; by the end of 1862 Rice lost his company and his circus.

DANCING BEARS
See BEARS; BEATTY, CLYDE; MOSCOW CIRCUS; PALLENBERG, EMIL.

DAUB
Circus jargon for the LOCATION in which the BILLING CREW pasted up the colorful advertising LITHOGRAPHS. Occasionally the PAPER itself was referred to as the "daub."

While WINDOW CARDS, HERALDS and even cloth BANNERS were hung, early circus men, and purists today, call the spot where one of these items was placed a HIT. Today the word "hit" is used commonly to mean the location where any circus advertising is posted.

Generally credited as being the first to use paste rather than tacks to post lithographs (in 1855) was Van Amburgh's Menagerie (see VAN AMBURGH CIRCUS).

DAVENPORT, ORRIN (1885–1962)
Orrin Davenport was a star equestrian, a bareback rider with the Ringling Bros. Circus. During his Ringling years he worked with the top female equestrienne of the day, May WIRTH, and taught her the backward somersault. Among Davenport's more spectacular stunts was a horse-to-horse somersault.

In 1906 he started producing indoor circuses during the winter off-season for Shrine sponsors. The route of the ORRIN DAVENPORT CIRCUS grew, and in 1937 Davenport eventually gave up his riding act to devote his entire attention to the management of his own show.

Over the years, the Orrin Davenport Circus toured mainly in Michigan, Ohio, Minnesota, the Dakotas and Canada, appearing under a different local sponsor's name in each city.

DAY AND DATE

Circus jargon. When two circuses perform in the same town at the same time, they are said to "day and date" each other.

In such cases, both circuses usually have lower attendance, because they have to share the prospective circus audience on that day. Some popular circuses have been known to try to day and date a smaller show deliberately to take away its business; this is why few circuses announce their route or publish ROUTE CARDS more than a month or two in advance.

DEADHEADS

Deadheads are extra show HORSES traveling with a circus that aren't being used in the program. Some are trained in the routines back in WINTER QUARTERS, while many are not.

Deadheads are not used as work horses, but are ready to be used at a moment's notice should any of the regular performing stock have to drop out of the show.

DEVIL STICKS

A form of gyroscopic JUGGLING apparatus, the devil stick is a cylindrical rod approximately 15 to 20 inches in length and tapered with a slightly smaller diameter in the middle. Two other dowel rods, one for each hand, complete the set.

Jugglers hold out both dowel sticks in front of themselves and rest the devil stick on the rods, horizontal and parallel to the floor. The left-hand rod pushes up and to the right, and the devil stick spins almost 180 degrees in a vertical plane. It is then struck by the right-hand dowel rod, up and to the left. The devil stick spins back toward its original position.

The rods click-clack the devil stick back and forth, keeping it from falling to the ground. Eventually the jugglers can add tricks, such as using only one handstick to hit back and forth on alternate sides of the devil stick. Quickly hitting one end of the devil stick over and over makes the stick spin into a type of propeller. The hands may also go under the leg or behind the back while doing the manipulations, and the devil stick could also be passed from partner to partner.

Although devil sticks have been known in the West for a long time, they actually originated in China. Even today they are common in Chinese acrobatic circuses.

DHOTRE, DAMOO (fl. 1940s–1950s)

From India, Damoo Dhotre was one of the featured CAT trainers with the RINGLING BROS. AND BARNUM & BAILEY CIRCUS in the middle part of the 20th century. Although a short man, Dhotre was powerfully built, strong and muscular.

From the age of ten he toured with his uncle's circus in India performing as an acrobat, clown and trick bicycle rider. He began his apprenticeship in handling the big cats at the age of 13; by the age of 17 he was known throughout India for his devil-may-care bicycle acrobatics and his equally daring animal handling. As a result, he was often attacked by the animals and suffered many narrow escapes. "I have been hurt many times," he was known to say, "and every time it was my own fault."

Damoo Dhotre explained that he didn't feel fear in the usual sense. He was always keenly aware of the danger; but since he knew exactly what each individual animal was likely to do in the ring, the fear was much more of a mental than a physical or emotional process.

By the time he began working with The BIG ONE, he had been handling cats for over 20 years. In the ring, he combined elements of the Hindu mystic and philosopher with the best qualities of a daredevil as he carefully studied and became familiar with his animals.

Although his formal education totaled less than five months, Dhotre was highly intelligent and well read, and his practical knowledge of animals was immense. His studies of animal psychology enabled him to know the creature's background, natural instincts and behavior patterns.

Damoo felt that training a cat was similar to working with a child. "The first step is to remove the animal's fear. An animal is instinctively afraid of a stranger; and, because he is afraid, he will attack."

When he started to work with a new animal, he spent many hours outside the cage, just getting the beast comfortable with his presence. He talked to the cat, calming it with his voice while feeding it as well.

Entering the cage for the first time, Dhotre made certain the cat was held taut by ropes. He played with the cat and again fed and talked to it. Eventually the cat was used to his presence and was somewhat friendly, and Damoo began teaching it simple tricks. After it performed each easy stunt, such as sitting on a pedestal, Damoo fed the feline. Finally he removed the training ropes.

Dhotre carried a large rod of bamboo in each hand when first working with a cat. That way, if the cat was looking for something to chew on, Damoo could offer it the stick. He carried a whip for signaling; but like all good trainers, he never beat the animal. A single crack might be used, the same way a parent might spank a child; but a heavy beating would only result in worse behavior down the line.

Dhotre summed up his philosophy of training this way:

If a child is allowed to do anything he likes and is never disciplined, he will have no respect for his parents and he will grow up to be a gangster. If, on the other hand, a child is beaten into submission at every point, he will have no respect but he will have fear and a grudge. He will wait for the chance to turn on his parents and if he can't turn on them, he will turn on someone else. He, too, is headed for gangsterdom. In animals, too, there must be both fear and respect. He is punished only for doing something wrong and he must know why *he is being punished each time. He must be rewarded for being good, and he must be made to understand what he has done to gain his trainer's favor. When you have this combination, you have a good animal. But he is still not* tamed. *He will never be tamed. You must watch yourself at every instant.*

DIBDEN AND HUGHES   The Royal Circus of Charles Dibden (the Elder) and Charles Hughes was one of the most important links between the English circus of Philip ASTLEY and the first American circus of John Bill RICKETTS. Although the *Oxford English Dictionary* dates the usage of "circus" in conjunction with an arena show only as far back as 1791, Charles Dibden (probably the first to use "circus" in its current connotation) was doing so by 1782.

Hughes was a trick horseman who worked briefly as Mr. Merrymen, a clown, for Astley in London in 1771. In 1772 he opened his own riding school in opposition; the two men feuded publicly for years. In 1782 Dibden, a composer, formed a partnership with Hughes to create an entertainment based on Hughes's work.

Because the term "circus" was commonly used at that time to describe a circular riding path for horses—then by 1771 a circular lane surrounded by houses, such as Piccadilly Circus and Oxford Circus—Dibden chose the word and applied it to his collection of equestrian acts, CLOWNS and jugglers. Dibden and Hughes' Royal Circus at Blackfriars, London was a direct rival to Astley's amphitheater, which was already presenting a similar show. The word "circus" caught the ear of the public, and it soon came generically to mean that unique blend of acts seen in the equestrian/variety shows.

Dibden soon left the partnership. His son, Charles Dibden (the Younger), remained in entertainment, becoming the manager of Sadler's Wells Theatre, and nurturing the career of Joseph GRIMALDI, the famous clown.

Charles Hughes traveled the continent and introduced the circus to the court of Catherine the Great in Russia, setting the stage for the eventual emergence of the MOSCOW CIRCUS. Hughes returned to London in 1793, but he could not match Astley's popularity. He lost his performance license and died penniless in 1797.

Hughes had unknowingly assisted in the germination of the circus in America, however. He was probably one of a group of British equestrians who traveled to the colonies in the 1770s; He performed with John Sharp and M.F. Foulks in Boston and with Thomas POOL and Jacob Bates in Philadelphia and New York. Bates first introduced Philip Astley's famous act "The TAILOR'S RIDE TO BRENTFORD" to America in 1772. That same year, John Bill Ricketts was learning his craft at Charles Hughes's riding academy back in London. Ricketts, of course, would go on to produce the first true circus performance in the United States on April 3, 1793.

As a postscript, Dibden and Hughes' Royal Circus was destroyed by fire in 1805. It was rebuilt, but five years later the ring was filled with benches, and it was transformed into a legitimate stage, the Surrey Theatre.

DIDE FISK CIRCUS   See SANGER'S GREAT EUROPEAN CIRCUS.

DOCK, SAM   See SAM DOCK CIRCUS.

DOG AND PONY SHOW   Circus jargon, generally a mocking term, for a small circus. The phrase implies that such a show is not large or spectacular enough to carry wild animals in its MENAGERIE or on its program; however, it probably carries ponies and domesticated pets. The term, no doubt, had its origin in fact.

Not all circuses and producers are embarrassed by the title, and some even use it proudly to let the public know what type of show they are going to see: a small, intimate family show. GENTRY BROS. CIRCUS was the first to use the phrase "Dog and Pony Show" in its name with great success.

DONA   Outdated circus jargon for a woman. The term is probably derived from the word *"doña"* (Spanish for "miss" or "madame") or *"donna"* (Italian for "woman" or "lady").

DONNIKER   Also spelled "donnicker" and "doniker," this is circus jargon for the portable rest rooms. Although most MUD SHOWS rely on local sponsors to provide portable toilets for the public on show days, the circus must still carry its own facilities for the troupe. These vary, of course, from the crudest form of dumpable barrels to the standard portable toilets set on trailers for hauling. Fortunately, due

White's Dogs enjoy a ride on Sparky, the educated pony, on the Polack Bros. Circus during a Shrine date.   (Author's collection)

A donniker on the Carson & Barnes Circus.   (Photo by Tom Ogden)

to more vigilant health inspectors, the facilities of most traveling shows are as sanitary as possible.

DOORS!   Circus jargon that is yelled across the circus LOT to warn the troupe that the BIG TOP is being opened and the audience is being admitted.

(See also FRONT DOOR.)

DOUBLE   Depending on the act involved, the term "double" has several meanings; it usually refers to a double somersault, whether on the ground, in acrobatics, or on the FLYING TRAPEZE. A double TRAPEZE act, on the other hand, is when two people work together on a single trapeze bar.

The "double double" (sometimes seen as "double-double") is a standard (but incredibly difficult) stunt first credited to Tito GAONA on the flying trapeze. It is a double somersault followed by a double pirouette, all of which occurs between the release of the trapeze bar and falling into the hands of the CATCHER.

To jugglers, a "double" is when a tossed object is flipped twice before it is caught.

The term "double" can also mean to perform two different jobs on the circus. For instance, an artist who can do two acts is said to "be able to double."

(See also DOUBLING IN BRASS.)

DOUBLING IN BRASS   This common expression, meaning to be able to do two or more jobs, is of circus origin.

In the old STREET PARADE, a clown band often rode on top of one of the TABLEAU WAGONS. The fact that a clown could legitimately play a musical instrument made the JOEY doubly valuable—and therefore more employable—to the circus. Since it was not their primary role in the show, however, when clowns played in a circus parade band they were said to be "doubling in brass."

DOWNIE, ANDREW (1863–1930)   Born Andrew Downie McPhee, Downie dropped his surname professionally when he became a pioneer showman. Beginning in 1884, he operated a series of circuses and tent shows by rail, wagon and riverboat.

Although usually touring his shows under some form of the "Downie" name, he also trouped with many different titles. Three of his rail shows were the Downie & Wheeler Circus (1911–13), La Tena Circus (1914–17) and the WALTER L. MAIN CIRCUS (1918–24).

From 1926 through 1930 he toured his last show, the Downie Bros. Circus, on trucks, pioneering the motorized circus. He sold the circus in 1930 to Charles Sparks, who operated the show under the Downie title through 1938. Sparks sold the Downie Bros. Circus in 1939, but the show soon folded and its equipment was scattered.

(See also A.F. WHEELER SHOWS.)

DOWNIE & WHEELER CIRCUS See A.F. WHEELER SHOWS; DOWNIE, ANDREW; SAM DOCK CIRCUS.

DOWNIE BROS. CIRCUS See DOWNIE, ANDREW.

DRESSAGE One of the most popular styles of showing trained HORSES, dressage refers to the type of equestrian performance in which the animal's paces are guided by small movements of the rider's body.

(See also HIGH SCHOOL HORSE.)

DRESSED Circus jargon, only rarely used today. When the sale of tickets has distributed the audience in such a way that no obvious sections of the arena are empty, the house is set to be "dressed."

DUCAT Circus jargon for the admission ticket. (See also DUCAT GRABBER.)

DUCAT GRABBER Circus jargon for the person who takes the admissions ticket or the door tender. (See also DUCAT.)

DUKEY Occasionally spelled "duckie," this is circus jargon for a box lunch.

A MUD SHOW must carry its own COOKHOUSE to feed the cast and crew, and early circus lingo dubbed the cookhouse the HOTEL. One of the first on the road was nicknamed the "Hotel du Quai." When pronounced quickly—if incorrectly—this sounded to the American ear like "dukey."

Somewhere, lost in tradition, the name transferred to the box lunches made by the cookhouse and distributed for long hauls.

(See also DUKEY RUN.)

DUKEY RUN Circus jargon for any JUMP longer than an overnight haul. The term also refers to the box lunch that the COOKHOUSE provides for such long runs, which is nicknamed a DUKEY.

In common usage, a dukey run is also any long distance. For instance, if the showgrounds are several blocks from the cookhouse or the rail yards, the crew might say, "It's a dukey run back to the train."

DUMBO See FILMS, CIRCUS.

E

EASTERN STATES CIRCUS See POLACK BROS. CIR-CUS.

ELDRED, GILBERT N. (1813–1885) A circus per-former and owner, Gilbert N. Eldred was involved in outdoor amusements from 1834 at least until his retirement around 1867.

The younger brother of Edward S. Eldred, who was himself a circus proprietor from 1832 to 1836, Gilbert began as a CLOWN in his sibling's show in 1834. By 1848 Gilbert had become a comic trick rider, and from 1853 through 1857 he performed an act (devised and performed elsewhere by Richard SANDS) in which he walked "upon a perfectly smooth ceiling, with his feet uppermost and his head down."

Eldred was a trick rider and "ceiling waker" on impressario John ROBINSON's first full circus, Robin-son & Foster, from 1842 to 1845. In 1846 he became Robinson's partner.

ROBINSON & ELDRED'S GREAT SOUTHERN SHOW toured for 11 successful seasons, building a large and ded-icated following in the South. The partnership came to an end on June 28, 1856 in Richmond, Virginia, with Eldred buying out Robinson's portion of the show.

Eldred continued to tour the show until the next season. On October 21, 1857 in Medina, Ohio, how-ever, a lien was placed on the circus by Quick, Nathans, Richard Sands and Avery Smith for non-payment for the SANDS & QUICK'S MENAGERIE, which had been leased to the operation. The show closed shortly thereafter.

Gilbert Eldred was on the road again in 1858 with G.N. Eldred's Great Rotunda Southern Circus and Menagerie, but it was at least partially owned by Sands, Nathans and Co. That same year the circus became one of the first American shows to travel into Mexico. One year later the show's title was changed to Franconi & Eldred.

In October 1859 Franconi & Eldred moved to Cuba, where the circus most likely merged with the remainder of Sands's show. Following its Cuba dates, Eldred left America for Europe in 1861 and never returned.

He was reported to have exhibited trained horses in England and other parts of Europe as late as 1867. Gilbert N. Eldred died in England in 1885.

ELEPHANT HOOK An elephant hook is a stick about one to two feet long with a small, dull hook at the end. It is used by BULL HANDLERS to lead the ELE-PHANTS.

Use of the hook doesn't hurt elephants. It merely tugs them in the direction the trainer wishes them to go, and the animals soon learn the commands.

ELEPHANT HOTEL Located in SOMERS, NEW YORK, the Elephant Hotel was owned by Hachaliah BAILEY and is the site of an obelisk monument to the mem-ory of OLD BET, the second elephant to be brought to the United States.

The Elephant Hotel was also where the most prominent MENAGERIE owners of the early 19th cen-

Captain Fred Logan, head bull handler on the Clyde Beatty-Cole Bros. Circus, prepares his herd for its thunderous entrance into the Big Top in Hagerstown, Maryland in 1988. Note the elephant hook in his right hand. (Photo courtesy of Walter G. Heist, Jr.)

tury met on January 14, 1835 to form the ZOOLOG-ICAL INSTITUTE.

ELEPHANTS Synonymous with the circus in the minds of the American public, elephants have been a part of the traveling MENAGERIE and the circus ever since the first pachyderm reached these shores in 1796.

Captain Jacob CROWNINSHIELD, from Salem, Massachusetts brought the first elephant to the United States on board his ship *America* on April 13, 1796. The creature, advertised merely as "the Elephant," was exhibited up and down the eastern seaboard, from South Carolina to upstate New York.

The second elephant to reach America, OLD BET, was of much greater historic interest. The profitable exhibition of Old Bet by her owner Hachaliah BAILEY of SOMERS, NEW YORK convinced several of his neighbors to change from farmers to showmen.

Somers and nearby Brewster became nicknamed the "Cradle of the American Circus," as such major circus figures as Aaron TURNER, John J. JUNE, Lewis B. TITUS, Caleb S. ANGEVINE, Seth B. HOWES and Nathan A. HOWES came from the region.

By the 1820s most of the touring museums as well as the ZOOLOGICAL INSTITUTE in New York were displaying elephants. They remained rare animals, however, because they all had to be imported from faraway India or Africa.

One of the great circus aphorisms came from the legendary P.T. BARNUM, who said, "Elephants and clowns are the pegs to hang a circus on." Barnum was certainly aware of the public's attraction to elephants. From the beginning, they were featured in the menagerie of his AMERICAN MUSEUM.

In 1850 Barnum partnered with Seth B. Howes and Sherwood Stratton (TOM THUMB's father), sending a ship to Ceylon to collect "twelve or more liv-

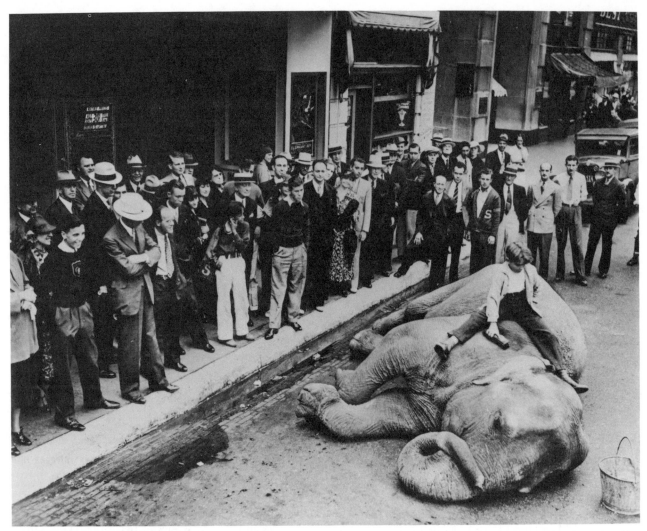

Teddy Metcalf washes elephant "Anna May" in this 1937 photo. (Photo courtesy of the *Herald Examiner* collection/Los Angeles Public Library)

ing elephants, besides such other wild animals as they could secure." Provisions of food and drink for the animals were left along the return route, and 13 pachyderms were actually captured. The seamen arrived back in New York in 1851 with ten elephants still living, and the pachyderms were harnessed in pairs to a chariot and paraded up Broadway.

In 1855 the partnership broke up and Barnum sold the entire show, including all but one of the elephants. Barnum put the single beast to plow his farm in Bridgeport, making sure that its keeper (dressed in Oriental garb) kept the elephant on the corner of the six-acre property within sight of the New York and New Haven railroad.

Every day hundreds of passengers gaped at the unexpected view, and newspapers circulated stories about the new beast of burden being used to plow fields in Connecticut.

Agricultural societies began to pummel Barnum with questions: "Is the elephant a profitable animal in the field?" "How much can it plow in a day?" "How much can it pull?" "Will it become 'generally useful' on the farm, adapting to other chores?" and, more practically, "How much does an elephant cost?" "How much does it eat?" and "Where do you buy one?"

Although Barnum had never meant to use the elephant as anything more than an underhanded advertisement for his American Museum, he an-

"Please do not feed the elephant little boys." Sid the pachyderm was part of the Clyde Beatty Circus menagerie in March 1952. (Photo courtesy of the *Herald Examiner* collection/Los Angeles Public Library)

swered all of these questions quite seriously. Imploring farmers not to rush into pachyderm plowing, he correctly pointed out that an elephant—if available at all in this country—would sell at that time for anywhere from $3,000 to $10,000. In cold weather it could not work at all, and even in the best of weather the animal would not earn more than half its keep.

When Barnum felt he had gotten as much promotional value as possible from the farm-broken elephant, he sold it to Van Amburgh's Menagerie.

Barnum's next major interest in elephants purportedly resulted in the formation of the BARNUM & BAILEY CIRCUS and his partnership with James A. BAILEY. On March 10, 1880 the birth of the first

elephant born in captivity in the United States occurred at the COOPER & BAILEY CIRCUS WINTER QUARTERS. Sensing its tremendous potential for exhibition, Barnum attempted to purchase both the baby Columbia and its mother Hebe for $100,000. Bailey refused. Taking a cue from the old master, Bailey used Barnum's telegram in his advertising, captioning it "What Barnum Thinks of the Baby Elephant."

Barnum realized he had finally met his match and suggested that he, Bailey and James L. HUTCHINSON join forces. The show they formed, P.T. BARNUM'S GREATEST SHOW ON EARTH, HOWES' GREAT LONDON CIRCUS AND SANGER'S ROYAL BRITISH MENAGERIE, became famous for introducing JUMBO. In 1882, when Jumbo became moody and hard to handle, Barnum was able to purchase him from his home at the Royal Zoological Gardens in London for $10,000. Jumbo arrived in New York on Easter Sunday, April 9, 1882 and became the country's most celebrated elephant, once again a gentle beast. Unfortunately, a speeding train ended his life in 1885. His skeleton remains in storage and on occasional display at the American Museum of Natural History in New York. His hide was destroyed in 1975 while on exhibition at Tufts University in Massachusetts.

Modern inspection of Jumbo's skull has uncovered that his violent behavior while in England can probably be attributed to unbearable pain he suffered due to impacted molars. Whether other elephant attacks are due to musth, injuries or illness or are outbursts against years of captivity is unknown; but there have been many well-documented cases of ROGUE ELEPHANTS in circus history, where a pachyderm suddenly "goes bad," becoming violent and injuring or killing innocent spectators or keepers. All trainers will tell you that elephants, like humans, have unique personalities and are affected by stress, overwork and pain. The most disturbing part of an elephant turning rogue is that such erratic behavior is usually sudden, unexpected and seemingly unprovoked.

Although ANIMAL ACTIVISTS would condemn the action by a modern circus, there have been several highly publicized elephant executions as a result of public outcry against a rogue's destructive tendencies. Among the more infamous have been Tops at Coney Island in 1903, "Murderous" Mary of the SPARKS CIRCUS in 1916, Black Diamond on the AL G. BARNES CIRCUS in 1929 and Janet on the Great American Circus in 1992.

Almost all of the elephants traveling with circuses and menageries come from India. African elephants, while larger with fanlike ears, are much more difficult to train and handle. They are usually used for exhibition only because of their unreliability in the ring.

The Indian elephants, on the other hand, are keen learners, even remembering tricks long after they have been dropped from their regular routines; often they seem genuinely to enjoy performing. Elephants are highly intelligent and, among mammals, are surpassed in wisdom only by chimpanzees, orangutans and, occasionally, humans. Legend has it that a pachyderm can hold grudges for years; this

Norman Torello, five, got a big assist from Minak, one of the trained elephants, when the Ringling Bros. and Barnum & Bailey Circus played the Hollywood Bowl in 1958. (Author's collection)

is perpetuated in such pithy quotes as the Saki witticism "Women and elephants never forget." It has been said that an elephant will wait years until just the right moment to seek revenge for a past injury, but the myth cannot be proved.

The average life span of an elephant equals that of a human. In fact, some BULLS have outlived the circuses on which they performed. Their usual shoulder height is from eight to ten feet, and the average bull eats 125 pounds of hay daily.

Despite the dry, wrinkled appearance of their hide, elephants actually have tender skin and are quite sensitive to touch. Walter McLain, longtime bull trainer with The BIG ONE, once noted, "They love a firm slap, but a fly or a tickle on their skin will drive them crazy!" Oddly, elephants will even allow a blowtorch to be used to burn off their long, hard hairs. The singeing is done to make the skin smoother; the elephants then can receive an oil rubdown, to preserve their skin.

To prevent drying and shedding and to avoid the blistering sun and to prevent the tickles of flies and mosquitoes, elephants constantly toss hay and dirt onto their backs. In fact, elephants whose backs are not covered with a thin layer of dust are only rarely seen.

The normal body temperature of elephants is 99 to 100 degrees Fahrenheit, but elephants frequently come down with chills. Although they do not often become seriously ill, they are frequently sick with other nuisances: They tend to bite each other's tails, partly out of nervousness and partly because "they just do"; often they are afflicted with broken tusks. Pachyderms are particularly prone to sore foot pads, broken cuticles and splintered toenails from walking on concrete roads and parking lots.

As elephants reach old age, their trunks tend gradually to become paralyzed, limiting flexibility and robbing them of their usual strength. While elephants can still feed themselves with hardened trunks, they have to toss the food up into the air and catch it in their mouths.

Most elephants used on circuses are female. Males generally tend to be more troublesome; and since elephants do not breed well in captivity, there is no advantage to having males as part of the herd.

Elephants remain a staple of the modern circus. Even the smallest MUD SHOWS try to troupe at least one pachyderm. Elephant rides on the MIDWAY or in the CENTER RING are always popular among children. Ring acts display groups of elephants sitting, standing and lifting BALLY BROADS in their mouths. Some elephants, such as the famous KING TUSK, also achieve singular fame and have to do little more than appear in the grand SPEC.

Nothing excites the tented audience, however, quite as much as the smell, sight and sound of a herd of ponderous pachyderms kicking up clouds of dust as it thunders down the hippodrome track. Suddenly the line of elephants stops its parade, stretching from one end of the arena to the other. The second elephant stands on its rear legs and places its front feet on the lead elephant's back. The third elephant follows suit, placing its feet up on the second elephant. Soon the entire line of pachyderms is standing in a LONG MOUNT, the most spectacular feat in the elephants' repertoire.

(See also BULL HANDLER; ELEPHANT HOOK; HANNEFORD, TOMMY; HANNIBAL; LALLA ROOKH; LOGAN, FRED;

Dick Walker, with the Rudy Bros. Circus, performing *en férocité* in the style of Clyde Beatty. (Author's collection)

TAIL UP; TRUNK UP; TUBS, ELEPHANT; WHITE ELEPHANT.)

EN FÉROCITÉ Circus jargon of French origin describing the type of wild animal acts in which the trainer seemingly battles the CATS, as opposed to the "tableau" acts in which the cats are made to assume poses. Clyde BEATTY, who worked in mock fight against the beasts, performed the most famous "en férocité" act of its time in the United States.

EQUESCURRICULUM Following the breakup of his partnership with P.T. BARNUM in 1874, W.C. COUP, a circus innovator and expert manager, took a two-year hiatus and then opened the New York Aquarium on his own.

The Equescurriculum was an outgrowth of the aquarium. It toured as a tented exhibition and was advertised as "A college of trained animals and Cephalodian monsters of the deep from the New York Aquarium."

The Equescurriuculum was on the road until 1879 when Coup began operation of his NEW UNITED MONSTER SHOWS.

(See also BARNUM'S GREAT TRAVELING MUSEUM, MENAGERIE, CARAVAN, HIPPODROME AND CIRCUS; CASTELLO, DAN; FLATFOOTS; MADISON SQUARE GARDEN; O'BRIEN, JOHN V. "POGEY"; P.T. BARNUM'S GREAT ROMAN HIPPODROME.)

EQUESTRIAN DIRECTOR

Circus jargon, today commonly used interchangeably with RINGMASTER.

The derivation of the phrase comes from the first 18th-century circuses in which the announcer/main performer usually presented an equestrian act. The actual equestrian director (that is, the director of the horses and horse acts) was not necessarily the announcer of the acts, nor the performance director who directed individual acts, decided on the show's running order and oversaw the overall flow of the show. Nor was the equestrian director originally the master of the ring, or ringmaster. That was usually a separate artist who would interact with the audience and the other performers in the ring.

Over the years, however, the distinctions between the titles blurred and they have become virtually synonymous.

EVANS, MERLE (1891–1987)

Born in Columbus, Kansas, Merle Evans joined his hometown band at the age of ten, playing his new John Slater cornet. He first toured professionally at 15 when he traveled with the S.W. Brundage Carnival. Evans left after one season when his duties expanded from playing cornet to also assembling and dismantling the carousel.

After working in a Salvation Army band and, nonmusically, as a pool hall sweeper and Victrola salesman, he joined a Dixieland band on a Mississippi steamboat, the *Cotton Blossom,* for one season. The next year he toured in a medicine show he formed with a friend, "Doc" Pullen, using his music to draw a crowd, or TIP, so that Pullen could present his PITCH. For the next several years he worked with a variety of local town bands and theatrical troupes. In 1916 Evans actually appeared with William F. CODY in a Wild West show band, one year before the legendary Buffalo Bill's death.

During these years Evans had seen a performance of the Ringling Bros. Circus when it played Sioux City, Iowa, and he applied to be a member of the band. In 1919 the news came from Charles Ringling: He was hired. Except for honoring the musicians' strike in 1942 and a four-year break when he toured with other shows from 1956 to 1960 (following an argument with John Ringling NORTH), Evans stayed with Ringling for the rest of his professional career.

When Evans first arrived in WINTER QUARTERS, however, John RINGLING wasn't sure about him. "I'm worried about that new band leader," he said. "He looks like a hayseed. Get some decent clothes on him." Properly suited up, the night of the first show Evans blared his cornet directly at the Ringling box by the bandstand. After the show, John Ringling came up to Merle Evans and confessed, "Son, you're all right. You damn near blew me out of the box tonight with that cornet."

While the show was in quarters, Evans traveled with an indoor circus owned by Fred BRADNA and put together his own tours. For three seasons Evans was the bandleader for the Mills Brothers Winter Circus in London, a show featuring an international cast of circus performers.

When Evans started with the Ringling circus, there were 36 musicians in the band. He became a personal favorite of Charles Ringling, often playing cornet duets with Ringling in the impresario's private rail car. At the end of each season, Ringling would ask Evans how he felt about that year's band. Each time Evans would say, "Well, I could use two more men. And maybe a ten-dollar raise." The frugal Charles would promise to bring it up with his brother John, and invariably Evans would start the new season with two more men and a 15-dollar raise.

Although John Ringling, like all of the RINGLING BROTHERS, was also a musician and music-lover, he slowly reduced the number of musicians in the band after Charles's death. By the end of Evans's tenure with the show, he had negotiated a 20-piece band with North.

As bandleader it was Merle Evans's job not only to locate appropriate songs for each act, but to create the overall theme and "feel" of that season's tour as well. He had to arrange the music to the act and be flexible enough to stretch, edit or change the music instantly as needed. Evans conducted with his left hand and played the cornet

Merle Evans, bandleader of the Ringling Bros. and Barnum & Bailey Circus. (Author's collection)

with his right, while standing with his back to the band.

Any act might have more than 20 quick cuts or cues, and a single performance of the full show might use portions of over 200 different songs, from marches to waltzes. It is, therefore, all the more amazing that during his 37-year period as leader, Evans led the band more than 18,000 times without missing an important cue. Evans said that the most difficult routine to conduct was the LIBERTY HORSES, because the dancing horses did not follow the music. He had to follow them!

From a musician's viewpoint, Evans was always most distressed by the adulation and applause given the trained seals as they honked horns in a horrendous rendition of "My Country 'Tis of Thee." Evans unequivocally stated, "Seals are tone-deaf. They play those damned horns for fish by means of signals from their trainers. You could send a seal to the Julliard School for ten years, and at the end of that time he couldn't blow his nose without assistance."

Evans also composed some of the original music needed for the show, including most of the circus world's now-standard fanfares as well as the "Fire Jump" GALOP and "Fredella," written for Fred and Ella BRADNA. He also created what he called his "Chicken Song," an improvised tune of a few bars when a flier took a bad fall. Although never written down, the vamp became well-known to his band and was used to cover myriad mistakes, from rigging stalls to acrobatic tumbles. Evans was also a master at giving chords, the traditional "ta-da" applause cues sprinkled throughout the acts. Each of the more than 40 chords, most of them B-flat concert chords, had a unique feel or sound.

On the tragic day of the HARTFORD FIRE in 1944, Merle Evans was one of the first to see flames licking the tent ropes of the BIG TOP. As circus tradition dictates, he immediately switched to "The Stars and Stripes Forever" to warn the ROUSTABOUTS and circus performers of the danger.

In 1930 Merle Evans and his band made the first phonograph record of circus music, and in the 1940s the group recorded the first complete album of circus songs. His own group, The Windjammers, were among the first circus musicians to appear on network radio.

Evans first left the Ringling bandstand in 1942. The musicians' union went on strike over a salary dispute; and, torn between his band and management, Evans stepped down for several months. Phonograph records were played in the band's absence.

Evans, however, continued working, becoming the band director at Hardin-Simmons University in Abilene, Texas. Although granted the honorary title of "Doctor," Merle Evans did not have the usual manner of college professors. Noting that the campus was overrun with jackrabbits, two of Evans's first acquisitions were a .410 shotgun and a pack of 15 hound dogs to hunt game.

In 1950 Merle Evans married Nina, a secretary for John Ringling North and Henry Ringling North. At the time she was handling payroll and other executive duties.

The bandleader was part of a cultural exchange between the United States and the Soviet Union in the mid-1960s. Evans had the opportunity to introduce many of the classic circus show tunes to his Soviet counterparts.

Merle Evans retired from the RINGLING BROS. AND BARNUM & BAILEY CIRCUS on December 4, 1969. For the rest of his life, the greatest circus bandmaster of modern times remained active musically, appearing as guest conductor at band concerts.

(See also MUSIC, CIRCUS.)

EXCELSIOR   The steed replacing Aroostook in DAN RICE'S ONE-HORSE SHOW. It was with Excelsior that Dan RICE developed a comic standard equestrian routine, the PETE JENKINS ACT, also known as "Pete Jenkins from Mud Corners."

Dan Rice purchased Excelsior for $200 in 1851 from William S. Thomas of Hawkesville, Kentucky. Although Excelsior went blind just over a year later, the horse continued to perform magnificently. He was injured in a fall in May 1859 in Buffalo, New York. Excelsior was taken to the show's WINTER QUARTERS in Girard, Pennsylvania, where he died a few days later and was quietly buried.

F

FAIRYLAND CIRCUS See AL G. KELLY & MILLER BROS. CIRCUS.

FAMOUS COLE CIRCUS Playing western and midwestern states under the management of Herb Walters in the 1950s, the Famous Cole Circus was one of dozens of shows that incorporated the name "Cole" as part of its title. W.W. "Chilly Billy" COLE had been the first outdoor showman to earn over $1 million in the circus business, so his name was frequently "borrowed" by other shows.

Even the Famous Cole Circus underwent a number of name changes; it opened in 1950 as the Cole & Walters Circus, then later toured as the George W. Cole Circus.

Though unrelated to the Walters show, the title is being used again today. Owned and operated by former booking agent and promoter Ron Bacon, the Famous Cole Circus plays indoor and arena dates primarily throughout the Atlantic seaboard and the Northeast. Its full title is the Famous Cole Indoor Variety Circus.

FAMOUS ROBINSON CIRCUS The Famous Robinson Circus was owned and operated by Dan ROBINSON for two seasons, 1910 through 1912. There was another Robinson Circus on the road, however, and that name was truly "famous"—the JOHN ROBINSON CIRCUS.

Circus entrepreneurs Jerry MUGIVAN and Bert BOWERS purchased the Famous Robinson Circus from Dan Robinson so that they could legitimately use the title in the same territory as the John Robinson show. They toured the circus only through 1915. At season's end, Mugivan and Bowers bought the actual John Robinson Circus and took the Famous Robinson Circus off the road.

FAT LADY See FREAKS.

FEEJEE MERMAID One of the greatest hoaxes ever presented by P.T. BARNUM was the "Feejee Mermaid," first shown by him at his AMERICAN MUSEUM in New York City.

Barnum leased the curiosity from a Boston museum that had gotten it from a Japanese fisherman in the Fiji Islands. The object was purported to be a true preserved mermaid, half woman, half fish. Very close examination was necessary to discover that the creature was actually the head and upper body of a monkey that had been carefully sewn to the tail and bottom half of a fish.

Barnum was, of course, aware of the deception; but he exhibited it with relish, making the Feejee Mermaid one of the most popular spectacles at the American Museum.

FEET JUMP Circus jargon. In bareback riding, the equestrian performs a "feet jump" by standing with his feet together and jumping from the ground or a springboard onto the back of a trotting horse.

(See also VAULTING.)

FELD, IRVIN (1916–1984) For two decades, Irvin Feld was the primary moving force of the new arena-style Ringling Bros. and Barnum & Bailey Combined Circus as well as a major producer of television, stage and other arena entertainments.

Irvin Feld saw his first circus in Hagerstown, Maryland at the age of five; at the age of 13 he followed carnivals with his brother Israel ("Izzy") (see FELD, ISRAEL S.), selling vanilla and lemon extract and "rattlesnake oil." This led into his ownership of a drug and variety store business in Washington, D.C. He expanded the record counter department of the operation into Super Music City, a chain of music stores.

Soon Feld entered the entertainment industry in full force. In 1944 he started his own record label, Super Discs. His first work as a music promoter was in 1946, and five years later he produced his first major touring arena music show, "The Biggest Show of Stars," featuring Nat King Cole and Sarah Vaughn.

Promoting special events and concerts, Irvin Feld worked with artists such as Andy Williams and Harry Belafonte and many early rock-and-roll legends, including Fats Domino and Bill Haley and the Comets. Having heard Buddy Holly and the Crickets on a demonstration tape, Feld mistakenly assumed that they were a black group and booked them into Harlem's Apollo Theatre. The appearance was a triumph, however, and its success remains a large part of the Buddy Holly legend.

Feld's natural bent toward management led to a long-term relationship with a young Canadian discovery, Paul Anka. Feld discovered the singer in Ottawa, Canada in 1956 and was his personal manager until 1966. Meanwhile, Feld's abilities and business acumen came in good stead as he took over direction of the federally owned Carter Barron Amphitheatre in Rock Creek Park near Washington, D.C., managing it from 1951 through 1974.

By 1955 Irvin Feld was a major force as a promoter of indoor arena entertainment. He attempted to persuade John Ringling NORTH to take his circus out from under canvas, but it was not until July 16, 1956—when the RINGLING BROS. AND BARNUM & BAILEY CIRCUS dropped its canvas for the last time— that Feld was to see his vision of the future of the American circus come true.

Feld's major mark in the entertainment world began in 1967 when, as part of a triumvirate that also included his brother Israel and Judge Roy HOFHEINZ, he became the principal buyer of the

Ringling Bros. and Barnum & Bailey Circus from John Ringling North.

With Judge Hofheinz increasingly involved in his own project, the Houston Astrodome, and Israel content in his background role as Ringling accountant, Irvin had a clear path to mold the flagship American circus.

Feld was well aware that to most Americans the word "circus" was synonymous with CLOWNS, and he noticed that few newcomers were being developed to fill in the ranks of the quickly retiring "old guard." In 1968 Irvin Feld opened his own CLOWN COLLEGE at the show's WINTER QUARTERS in Venice, Florida, to teach makeup, traditional clowning and standard circus skills to would-be clowns. Each year several of the graduates would be invited to join the Ringling ranks.

Feld's next, and perhaps most notable, innovation was to create an entirely new second touring show. For years Feld had been the promoter of the major portion of the Ringling arena dates, and he knew that many tour-worthy sites had to be given up simply because one circus could not logistically meet all possible dates. Hence, another show, the Blue Unit, was created to cover the new dates while the existing show, dubbed the Red Unit, continued to tour the usual route. Each year the units were to switch routes. The Blue Unit, centered around the talents of premier animal trainer Gunther GEBEL-WILLIAMS, opened in Hofheinz's Astrodome to great acclaim.

In 1969 Feld shocked the circus world by offering, for the first time, shares of Ringling stock to the general public on the New York Stock Exchange. The next year, when Judge Hofheinz gave up his option to buy the controlling shares of stock, Feld sold his $8 million investment to Mattel Toys for a reported $47 million. As part of the deal, Hofheinz was to remain the chairman of the board of directors of Ringling, Israel Feld was to remain as accountant (until his death in 1972) and Irvin Feld became president and chief executive officer of the circus.

Like all impresarios, Irvin Feld had his detractors as well as his admirers. In designing and casting his show, Feld imported many East European acts, many of whom, it was contended, relied too heavily on "MECHANICS"—the safety wires that prevented fatal falls from aerial equipment. Even when Feld did score a coup, such as snaring the remarkable Gunther

Gebel-Williams, some circus followers felt that the circus's showcasing of Gebel-Williams as the main attraction did a disservice to the other acts. Still others complained that the first-year graduates of the Clown College were not experienced enough to join the regular touring show and that the CLOWN ALLEY was soon filled with talented amateurs rather than seasoned professionals. Because of Feld's reliance on spectacle and parades, many suggested that the Ringling show had become nothing more than "an ice show without the ice."

Regardless, Feld had found a formula that worked, at least for his generation of circus-goers. In Ziegfeld tradition, he gave more flash and feathers, covering up a generally smaller cast with a show built around a featured solo "star." And everyone admitted that Feld was a master publicist, living up to *Time* magazine's inevitable comparison of him to P.T. BARNUM as "the Greatest Showman on Earth." The resemblance was not ill-founded. Feld's discovery and touring of MICHU as the world's smallest man, for instance, was a 20th-century update of TOM THUMB.

Beginning in April 1972, Irvin Feld had the biggest head-to-head fight of his career with another circus. When a disagreement arose over the terms of engagement for the Ringling show into the new Capital Centre in Washington, D.C., the arena's contractor, Abe POLLIN, framed his own show, CIRCUS AMERICA. After the press equally praised both shows, Pollin retired his one-season wonder and compromised with Feld over future appearances of The GREATEST SHOW ON EARTH.

The biggest fiasco of Feld's career was undoubtedly the CIRCUS WORLD complex near Orlando. The ill-conceived attempt to draw tourists from the huge Disney World crowds resulted in a multimillion-dollar loss for the Mattel corporation.

Late in his career, Irvin Feld commented that March 17, 1982, was "the happiest moment of my life." It was then that he and his son, Kenneth FELD, repurchased the Ringling Bros. and Barnum & Bailey Circus from Mattel, returning the show to family ownership.

Irvin Feld remained a producer and promoter of noncircus entertainments. In 1979 he and Kenneth took over management and production of the Ice Follies and Holiday on Ice Combined Shows, with his son as president. In 1981 the father-and-son team premiered Walt Disney Productions' World on Ice. Also in 1981, Irvin Feld became one of the co-producers of the Broadway hit musical *Barnum* (see THEATER) and began his association with illusionists Siegfried & Roy, opening their "Beyond Belief" show at the Frontier Hotel in Las Vegas. Three NBC TELEVISION specials featuring the two magicians also appeared under Feld's aegis. One of Feld's last projects was to co-produce the 1984 musical *The Three Musketeers*, which was in rehearsal at the time of his death.

Among his many awards, Irvin Feld received an honorary doctorate from Lehigh University and was named the 1984 Champion of Liberty by the Anti-Defamation League of B'Nai B'rith. It is his 16 years as the producer of "The Greatest Show on Earth" that has secured his legacy in the history of the American circus.

Irvin Feld died on September 6, 1984, in Venice, Florida after suffering a cerebral hemorrhage. Personally involved with his Clown College to his last days, Feld was in Venice to greet the 1984 class of aspiring clowns.

FELD, ISRAEL S. (1911–1972)

Israel Feld, brother of Irvin FELD, was one of the trio of men who purchased the RINGLING BROS. AND BARNUM & BAILEY CIRCUS from John Ringling NORTH in 1968, taking control of the circus out of the hands of the "Ringling" family.

From his home in Hagerstown, Maryland "Izzy" followed carnivals with his brother Irvin as a teenager, selling patent medicines. The brothers stayed partners through the ownership of a series of drug and variety stores, with Israel developing a talent in the financial and accounting end. A chain of music stores followed, which led Irvin into concert promotion.

The pair was ready by 1968, when the opportunity came to purchase the Ringling show. The third member of their triumvirate was Judge Roy HOFHEINZ. Israel quickly assumed a background role as Ringling accountant.

In 1969—on Israel's recommendation—Irvin Feld shocked the circus world by announcing their offer, for the first time, of shares of Ringling stock to the general public on the New York Stock Exchange.

In 1971 Judge Hofheinz gave up his option to buy the controlling shares of Ringling stock and Irvin sold his investment to Mattel Toys. As part of the deal, Israel Feld stayed on as accountant to the Ringling corporation for the remainder of his life. Israel Feld died of a heart attack on December 15, 1972.

FELD, KENNETH (1948–) Kenneth Feld, son of Irvin FELD, grew up amid the wonder of the RINGLING BROS. AND BARNUM & BAILEY CIRCUS. After he was graduated from Boston University in 1970, Kenneth quickly became his father's right-hand man, consulting with and assisting him in all major decisions affecting the circus. Upon Irvin's death in 1984, Kenneth Feld became owner, producer and president of the Ringling Bros. and Barnum & Bailey Combined Shows, Inc., as well as the head of Irvin Feld and Kenneth Feld Productions, Inc.

Even before assuming control, many of the innovations seen in the shows had been Kenneth's ideas. For instance, it was he who recommended to Gunther GEBEL-WILLIAMS that the trainer add a white tiger to his MENAGERIE of wild CATS. He also suggested the goat act that led to the debut of Gebel-Williams's son, Mark Oliver, with The GREATEST SHOW ON EARTH.

Feld immediately became immersed in his new role as impresario. He had been there when his father, in the P.T. BARNUM tradition, discovered and promoted MICHU, the smallest man alive. It was Kenneth Feld's own brand of "humbuggery," however, that introduced "The Living Unicorn" to the American public in 1985. The owner of four California Angora goats had surgically moved and merged their horn buds in a painless procedure shortly after the kids' birth. Feld heard of the goats following their exhibition at a San Francisco–area Renaissance Fair. The truth of the rumors surrounding the creatures' origin and Feld's find of the beasts were never revealed; and nothing more was required of the "unicorn" than to ride on a special chariot, being lovingly stroked by a fair damsel, during the grand SPEC. The major court cases filed by the American Society for the Prevention of Cruelty to Animals (ASPCA) only increased interest in the unicorn—as well as attendance at the circus—and it was discussed on television programs such as as *The Tonight Show* and the *CBS Early News*.

In 1986, in a move to placate ANIMAL ACTIVISTS and to showcase the work of conservationists, Feld toured a bison in the grand parade of the 113th edition of the circus. Also that year he imported the Shanghai Acrobatic Troupe to great BALLYHOO. Due to Kenneth Feld's agility in handling the press and ability at show production, between the last year of the reign of Irvin Feld and the second year of Kenneth's, attendance at the Ringling Bros. and Barnum & Bailey Circus rose from 8.5 million to 11.8 million.

Feld soon showed signs of merchandising prowess. Since 1970, his father had broadcast highlights of the circus on television at the beginning of each season. In 1987 Kenneth Feld began to sell videocassettes of the circus specials at the arenas following the end of each edition's run.

In 1987 Kenneth Feld introduced his answer to JUMBO: KING TUSK. Although somewhat shorter than Barnum's pachyderm, King Tusk was more massive and carried two of the most impressive tusks ever seen, one seven feet long and the other six feet six. Again, it was Feld's Barnumesque treatment that made it an overnight sensation.

In 1989 Kenneth Feld bought Circo Americano and merged its equipment and acts into the existing Ringling Blue Unit. The highest prize of the consolidation was the work of the Circo's owner and expert animal trainer Flavio TOGNI, along with his family.

A tireless businessman, Feld was responsible for the creation of a third unit of the Ringling show, the short-lived tented Gold Unit in Japan. Under his aegis, "Ringling Readers," an educational, entertaining series of circus-themed publications, were designed to help children learn to read.

Feld has also guided the Ringling corporation into expanded fields of merchandising. In autumn 1990 four Ringling Bros. Barnum & Bailey Circus Stores were opened, one each in Connecticut and New Jersey and two in Virginia, in addition to the one at the new Vienna, Virginia corporate headquarters. Under Feld's ownership, the entertainment conglomerate grossed $260 million in 1990, more than double the company's income the year he became president. Dubbed "America's Master Showman" by *Time* magazine, Kenneth Feld controls the world's largest entertainment empire, the Ringling Bros. and Barnum & Bailey Combined Shows, Inc., which employs over 2,500 performers and staff members who create attractions seen by an estimated 40 million people annually.

A "hands-on" manager, Kenneth Feld continues to move the circus in new directions. The 1991 edition of the Red Unit starred a clown, David LARIBLE, in a CENTER RING solo spot for the first time in Ringling history. For the all-new 122nd edition in 1992, Mongolian State Circus performers joined the troupe as did—in addition to the traditional circus band—a rock-and-roll style band, N/Motion.

As a supporter of circus arts, Kenneth Feld assists the efforts of the CIRCUS WORLD MUSEUM in BARABOO, WISCONSIN and the Circus Hall of Fame in PERU, INDIANA.

In addition to the circus units and his continued association with illusionists Siegfried & Roy in Las Vegas, Feld conceived and manages the five companies of Walt Disney's World on Ice, which tours worldwide to at least 15 countries on five continents. His newest entertainment project is the promotion of the American Gladiators 1992 Live Tour. Also seen in television syndication, the Gladiators tour as an arena attraction to approximately 100 cities in the United States, where local amateur athletes have the opportunity to challenge the "Gladiators" in national competition. Additionally, Kenneth Feld's business activities include a huge concessions operation, production of television specials and product licensing.

FILMS, CIRCUS

FILMS, CIRCUS If, as the philosophers say "art imitates life," then certainly the stories of courage and romance to be found in the mythology of the circus were bound to make their way to the silver screen.

Circus films have run the gamut from the poignantly cute (Dumbo), the sublime (Chad Hanna) and the epic (The Greatest Show on Earth) to the sleazy (Berserk!) and the bizarre (Chained for Life). Other films, such as Annie, while not being circus stories per se, have several sequences under the BIG TOP. From the famous to the obscure, American circus movies will always be an important part of the popular culture.

Annie

Columbia and Ray Stark, 1982; Metrocolor and Panavision; 128 minutes; produced by Joe Layton; directed by John Huston; screenplay by Carol Sobieski from the play with book by Thomas Meehan; music by Charles Strouse and lyrics by Martin Charnin

based on the Harold Gray comic strip; starring Albert Finney (Daddy Warbucks), Carol Burnett (Miss Hannigan), Aileen Quinn (Annie), Ann Reinking, Bernadette Peters, Tim Curry, Geoffrey Holder and Edward Herrman. This disastrous adaptation of a beloved stage musical did have one asset: It incorporated a circus scene in its climax that did not take place in the play. The sequences were shot under the Big Top of THE BIG APPLE CIRCUS.

Annie Get Your Gun

MGM, 1950; Technicolor; 107 minutes; produced by Arthur Freed; directed by George Sidney; screenplay by Sidney Sheldon from the Herbert and Dorothy Fields musical play; music and lyrics by Irving Berlin; starring Betty Hutton and Howard Keel. The film basically follows the musical play's story of the young hillbilly sharpshooter falling in love with Frank BUTLER, an expert marksman, when she joins BUFFALO BILL'S WILD WEST. Annie OAKLEY is played by Betty Hutton; Frank Butler is played by Howard Keel.

Of cinematic interest, the role of Annie Oakley was originally to have been played by Judy Garland, who was fired due to "artistic differences" early into the shoot. Footage of some numbers still exists. Others besides Betty Hutton considered for replacement include: Doris Day, Judy Canova and Betty Garrett. Also, Louis Calhern replaced Frank Morgan, who died during filming.

Annie Get Your Gun won an Academy Award for Adolph Deutsch's musical direction and an Academy Award nomination for Charles Rosher's photography.

Annie Oakley

RKO, 1935; black and white; 90 minutes; produced by Cliff Reid; directed by George Stevens; written by Joel Sayre; starring Barbara Stanwyck (as Annie Oakley), Preston Foster, Melvyn Douglas and Chief Thunderbird. The film is a historical story in typical Hollywood biographical fashion of Annie Oakley, the sharpshooter.

At the Circus

MGM, 1939; black and white; 87 minutes; produced by Mervyn LeRoy; directed by Edward Buzzell; written by Irving Brecher; starring the Marx Brothers (Groucho, Chico, Harpo), Margaret Dumont and

Eve Arden. The songs were written by Harold Arlen (music) and E.Y. Harburg (lyrics).

At the Circus is a standard Marx Brothers vehicle set against the backdrop of a circus. Highlights of the film include Groucho's singing "Lydia the Tattooed Lady," his seduction of Mrs. Dukesbury and the inevitable chaotic society party.

Battling with Buffalo Bill

Universal, 1931; 12-episode serial; black and white; directed by Ray Taylor and starring Tom Tyler. In *Battling with Buffalo Bill,* the sharpshooter fights a notorious gambler and savage Indians.

Behind the Make-up

Paramount, 1930; black and white; 65 minutes; directed by Robert Milton; screenplay by George Manker Watters and Howard Estabrook from a story by Mildred Cram; starring Hal Skelly, William Powell and Fay Wray. This melodrama tells the story of a talented clown and his conniving partner.

Berserk!

Columbia, 1967; Technicolor; 96 minutes; produced by Herman Cohen; directed by Jim O'Connolly; screenplay by Herman Cohen; starring Joan Crawford and co-starring Diana Dors.

A cult favorite due to its star, *Berserk!* featured Joan Crawford as a circus owner whose showgrounds are the site of several highly publicized murders.

The Big Cage

Universal, 1933; black and white; 71 minutes; directed by Kurt Neumann; screenplay by Edward Anthony and Ferdinand Reyher; starring Mickey Rooney and Andy Devine. The story concerns an orphan boy who idolizes a lion trainer, played by Clyde BEATTY.

The Big Circus

Allied Artists, 1959; Cinemascope and Technicolor; 109 minutes; produced by Irwin Allen; directed by Joseph Newman; screenplay by Irwin Allen, Charles Bennett and Irving Wallace; starring Victor Mature, Red Buttons, Rhonda Fleming, Kathryn Grant, Vincent Price, Peter Lorre, Gilbert Roland, David Nelson, Adele Mara and Steve Allen. The ex-partners of a destitute circus owner attempt to prevent him from taking his show back on tour. Irwin Allen won an Academy Award as producer.

The Big Show

API, 1961; De Luxe Cinemascope; 113 minutes; produced by Ted Sherdeman; directed by James B. Clark; screenplay by Ted Sherdeman; starring Esther Williams, Cliff Robertson, Nehemiah Persoff, Robert Vaughn, Carol Christensen, Margia Dean and David Nelson. The death of an overbearing circus owner results in his sons fighting for control of the tented show.

Big Top Pee-Wee

Paramount; 1988; 86 minutes; executive producers William E. McKuen and Richard Gilbert Abramson; produced by Paul Reubens and Debra Hill; directed by Randal Kleiser; screenplay co-authored by Paul Reubens; starring Paul ("Pee-Wee Herman") Reubens, Kris Kristofferson, Valeria Golina, Penelope Ann Miller and Susan Tyrrell.

When a small town refuses a circus permission to set up, the owner (played by Kristofferson) accepts Pee-Wee Herman's offer to let them quarter on his farm and perform in his backyard. Herman falls in love with the trapeze artist (Golina), much to the chagrin of his innocent girlfriend (Miller). Besides the colorful show folk and MENAGERIE of farm animals, including a talking pig, *Big Top Pee-Wee* is remembered for featuring the longest kiss in screen history.

Broadway Highlights of 1930

Collection of newsreels. National Telefilm Associates, 1930; produced by Adolph Zukor. Shown is the opening night of Billy Rose's musical play *Jumbo* at the legendary Hippodrome theater. Also seen is rare, archival footage of Jimmy Durante and other cast members in rehearsal, with part of the Rodgers and Hart score in the background.

Bronco Billy

Warner, 1980; De Luxe Panavision; 116 minutes; produced by Neal Dubrovsky and Dennis Hackin; directed by Clint Eastwood; screenplay by Dennis Hackin; starring Clint Eastwood, Sondra Locke, Scatman Crothers, Bill McKinney and Sam Bottoms. An East Coast shoe salesman (played by Eastwood) assumes command of a ragged Wild West show.

Buffalo Bill

20th Century-Fox; 1944; Technicolor; 89 minutes; produced by Harry Sherman; directed by William

Wellman; screenplay by Aeneas Mackenzie, Clements Ripley and Cecile Kramer; starring Joel McCrea, Maureen O'Hara, Edgar Buchanan and Anthony Quinn.

In a mostly factual film biography, Joel McCrea plays William Frederick CODY as he grows from buffalo hunter to Wild West owner. Maureen O'Hara's presence adds domestic interest to the western segments.

Buffalo Bill and the Indians

United Artists, 1976; Panavision; 118 minutes; produced and directed by Robert Altman; screenplay by Alan Rudolph and Robert Altman from the play *Indians* by Arthur Kopit; starring Paul Newman, Burt Lancaster, Joel Grey, Kevin McCarthy, Geraldine Chaplin, Harvey Keitel, John Considine and Denver Pyle.

Subtitled "Sitting Bull's History Lesson," *Buffalo Bill and the Indians* freely adapted Kopit's incisive play to a static talk piece. While the Wild West is in WINTER QUARTERS, William Cody and his friends sit around discussing his place in history and life in general.

Carnival

Columbia, 1934; black and white; 77 minutes; directed by Walter Lang; screenplay by Robert Riskin; starring Lee Tracy, Jimmy Durante, Dickie Walters and Lucille Ball. After a puppeteer is widowed, the maternal grandfather seeks custody of his child. To escape the authorities, the puppeteer takes refuge in a circus.

Carnival Story

King Brothers (a US/German co-production); 1954; Technicolor; 95 minutes; produced by Maurice and Frank King; directed by Kurt Neumann, screenplay by Kurt Neumann and Hans Jacoby; starring Anne Baxter. A poor waif becomes a trapeze star in a German circus, arousing envy within the troupe.

Chad Hanna

20th Century-Fox; 1940; Technicolor; 86 minutes; produced by Darryl F. Zanuck and Nunnally Johnson; directed by Henry King; screenplay by Nunnally Johnson from the novel *Red Wheels Rolling* by Walter D. Edmonds; starring Henry Fonda, Dorothy Lamour, Linda Darnell and John Carradine. A romantic drama from a best-selling book, *Chad Hanna* tells of circus life in New York in the 1840s.

Charlie Chan at the Circus

20th Century-Fox; 1936; produced by John Stone; directed by Harry Lachman; screenplay by Robert Ellis and Helen Logan. Charlie Chan, the Oriental detective, is played here by Warner Oland (who portrayed Chan from 1931 to 1937). Against the background of a circus, Chan solves a murder aided by his number-one son (played by Keye Luke).

The Chimp

Hal Roach Studios; 1932; black and white; 30 minutes; produced by Hal Roach; directed by James Parrott; screenplay by H. M. Walker; starring Laurel and Hardy. Stan and Oliver receive a CHIMPANZEE as their share of a bankrupt circus. Besides the comedic circus scenes, the funniest sequences involve the duo trying to check into their room without the landlord discovering that their "friend" is a monkey.

The Circus

United Artists; 1928; black and white; silent; 72 minutes; Charles Chaplin served as producer, director, writer and star. In this typical Chaplin piece the little tramp runs from the police and hides out in a circus. There he falls in love with the equestrienne star, played by Merna Kennedy. Chaplin received Academy Award nominations as actor and director.

Circus Clown

First National/Warner Bros.; 1934; black and white; 65 minutes; studio production directed by Ray Enright; screenplay by Burt Kalmar, Harry Ruby and Paul Gerard Smith; starring Joe E. Brown, Ernest Clarke (see CLARKE, CHARLES AND ERNEST) and Edwin "Poodles" HANNEFORD. Brown plays the double role of a young man (Happy Howard) and his father, an ex-circus performer, who doesn't want his son to join the show. In a comic misadventure, Howard falls in love with a female impersonator and follows him/her to the circus. Once he discovers the truth, Howard's attention quickly switches to the girl on the FLYING TRAPEZE. He is thrown off the LOT but returns to "save the day" when he fills in for the girl's brother who is too intoxicated to perform.

Circus Girl

Republic; 1937; black and white; 64 minutes; produced by Nat Levine; directed by John Auer; screenplay by Adele Buffington and Bradford Ropes, based on a story by Frank R. Adams; starring June Travis, Bob Livingston and Donald Cook. An average film involving a love triangle under the Big Top is made interesting to circus fans by the trapeze work of the Flying Escalante troupe.

The Circus Kid

Film Booking Office; 1928; black and white; 61 minutes; studio production directed by George B. Seitz; screenplay by Melville Baker and Randolph Bartlett, based on a story by James Ashmore Creelman; starring Joe E. Brown (King Kruger), Sam Nelson (Tad), Helene Costello (Trixie), Frankie Darro (Buddy) and Edwin "Poodles" HANNEFORD (Poodles). Buddy, an orphan boy joins the circus as an ACROBAT. Meanwhile, Kruger, a has-been lion trainer, and Tad, the up-and-coming CAT man, both fall in love with Trixie, the ROSINBACK rider. A lion escapes and begins to maul Tad. King Kruger fights the cat off but not before being mortally wounded. He blesses the two lovers' union, then dies.

The Circus Queen Murder

Columbia; 1933; black and white; 63 minutes; directed by Roy William Neill; screenplay by Jo Swerling from the novel by Anthony Abbott; starring Adolphe Menjou. Detective Thatcher Colt solves the murders plaguing a circus on tour.

Circus World

Bronston/Midway; 1964; Cinerama and Technicolor; 138 minutes; produced by Samuel Bronston; directed by Henry Hathaway; screenplay by Ben Hecht and Julian Halevy; starring John Wayne, Rita Hayworth, Claudia Cardinale and Lloyd Nolan.

The alcoholic ex-wife of an American circus owner flees to Europe when her lover falls to his death from a high TRAPEZE. Most of the circus spectacle takes place in the first hour of the film before the owner (played by Wayne) sets out in pursuit.

The Clown

MGM; 1952; black and white; 91 minutes; produced by William H. Wright; directed by Robert Z. Leonard; screenplay by Martin Rackin; starring Red SKELTON and Tim Considine. In a theme reminiscent of the film *The Champ*, the young son of an alcoholic clown dreams of his father regaining his stardom.

Dangerous Curves

Paramount; 1929; black and white; 75 minutes; directed by Lothar Mendes; screenplay by Donald David and Florence Ryerson; starring Clara Bow, Richard Arlen and Kay Francis. A star vehicle in this circus melodrama has a bareback rider falling in love with a tightrope walker.

Darkest Africa

Republic; 15-episode serial; 1936; black and white; produced by Barney Sarecky; directed by Breeves Easton and Joseph Kane; screenplay by John Rathmell, Barney Sarecky and Ted Parsons. On safari, a lion trapper meets a jungle boy and a beautiful woman, both of whom he saves from bat-people in a hidden city. The reels are of circus interest only for their star, Clyde BEATTY.

Dumbo

Walt Disney; 1941; Technicolor; 64 minutes; directed by Ben Sharpsteen; music by Frank Churchill and Oliver Wallace. One of the Disney animated "classics." An allegorical tale against prejudice, *Dumbo* tells the story of a baby elephant who is born with gigantic ears. At first the infant pachyderm is made an outcast, and his angry mother is wrongly accused of being a ROGUE ELEPHANT. Dumbo is consigned to CLOWN ALLEY where, during the "Firehouse CLOWN GAG," he discovers that he can fly. Dumbo, his rodent friend dressed as a RINGMASTER and his proud mother ultimately become the stars of the circus. *Dumbo* received an Academy Award for its musical score, plus an additional nomination for "Baby Mine" (Frank Churchill, music, Ned Washington, lyrics) for Best Song.

Fearless Fagan

MGM; 1952; black and white; 78 minutes; produced by Edwin H. Knopf; directed by Stanley Donen; screenplay by Charles Lederer; starring Carleton Carpenter, Janet Leigh, Keenan Wynn, Richard Anderson and Ellen Corby. In a comic farce, a circus clown enlists in the Armed Services and takes his pet lion with him.

The Flying Fontaines

Columbia; 1959; Eastmancolor; 73 minutes; directed by George Sherman; screenplay by Donn Mullally and Lee Erwin; starring Michael Callan, Evy Norlund, Joan Evans, Rian Garrick and Joe

DeSantis. Rivalry and jealousy cause trouble among a troupe of aerialists on the flying trapeze.

Freaks

MGM; 1932; black and white; 64 minutes; produced and directed by Tod Browning; screenplay by Willis Goldbeck and Leon Gordon from the Tod Robbins's novel *Spurs;* starring Wallace Ford, Olga Baclanova, Leila Hyams and Roscoe Ates. A classic cult film, *Freaks* tells the story of a gold-digging female trapeze star who marries a wealthy circus midget, then poisons him to inherit his fortune. His "peers" avenge his death by turning her into a freak as well. Overall, the film is maudlin; but many of the scenes are spellbinding, especially due to the cinematography of Merrit B. Gerstad. Nevertheless, because of the public's distaste for the subject material, MGM refused to acknowledge its own film.

Fun and Fancy Free

Disney; 1947; Technicolor; 73 minutes; produced by Ben Sharpsteen. One of the cartoon sequences told to Jiminy Cricket and Edgar Bergen involves "Bongo," a circus bear.

The Greatest Show on Earth

Paramount and Cecil B. de Mille; 1952; Technicolor; 153 minutes; co-produced by Henry Wilcoxon; directed by Cecil B. de Mille; screenplay by Frederic M. Frank, Theodore St. John, Frank Cavett and Barre Lyndon; directors of photography George Barnes, Peverell Marley and Wallace Kelley; music by Victor Young; starring Betty Hutton, Cornel Wilde, James Stewart, Charlton Heston, Dorothy Lamour, Gloria Grahame, Lyle Bettger, Henry Wilcoxon, Lawrence Tierney, John Kellogg as well as Emmett KELLY and John Ringling NORTH.

The Greatest Show on Earth's plot involves melodramatic love triangles, a clown hiding behind makeup to escape the law and subplots too numerous to mention. It is arguably the best circus movie ever made, faithful to the spirit of the BACK YARD and the circus sense of community. Long sequences of actual footage from the RINGLING BROS. AND BARNUM & BAILEY CIRCUS make this especially interesting to the circus historian, and the train wreck sequence is a harrowing reminder of the ever-present dangers of touring in the heyday of the American circus.

The Greatest Show on Earth received an Academy Award for Best Picture, with additional nominations for Best Original Screenplay and Best Director.

He Who Gets Slapped

MGM; 1924; black and white; silent; 80 minutes; directed by Victor Sjostrom; screenplay by Victor Sjostrom and Carey Wilson from the Leonid Andreyev play; stars Lon Chaney, Norma Shearer and John Gilbert. The plot involves a scientist who changes his career to begin anew as a circus clown. This is quite possibly the first film made with a circus theme, and it is definitely the first film feature of Metro-Goldwyn-Mayer.

Houdini

Paramount; 1953; Technicolor; 106 minutes; produced by George Pal; directed by George Marshall; screenplay by Philip Yordan; starring Tony Curtis as Harry Houdini and Janet Leigh as his wife, Bess. The movie accurately tells how Houdini began his performance career on a SIDESHOW platform. Although the movie shows it as a carnival, Houdini in fact traveled with the WELSH BROS. CIRCUS in 1898 and 1899. In typical film biography fashion, the screenplay takes great liberties with Houdini's life and career.

It's In The Bag

United Artists; 1945; black and white; 87 minutes; produced by Manhattan Productions; directed by Richard Wallace; screenplay by Jay Dratler and Alma Reville starring radio and film personalities Fred Allen, Binnie Barnes, Jack Benny, Richard Benchley, Don Ameche, Victor Moore, Rudy Vallee, William Bendix and Jerry Colonna. A fortune has been hidden in one of five chairs that have been sold to different people, and the operator of a FLEA CIRCUS must try to track them down.

Jumbo

MGM; 1962; Metrocolor and Panavision; 124 minutes; co-produced by Joe Pasternak and Martin Melcher; directed by Charles Walters; screenplay by Sidney Sheldon based on the stage play by Ben Hecht and Charles MacArthur; music by Richard Rodgers and lyrics by Lorenz Hart; choreography by Busby Berkeley; starring Doris Day, Jimmy Durante, Stephen Boyd, Martha Raye and Dean Jagger. Also known as *Billy Rose's Jumbo,* the film repeated the stage play's story: In 1910 the daughter of a down-on-his-luck circus owner tries to fend off potential buyers of the show. George Stoll received an Academy Award nomination for musical direction.

King of the Carnival

Republic; 12-episode serial; 1955; black and white; directed by Franklin Adreon; starring Harry Lauter; Fran Bennett, Keith Richards and Robert Shayne. Despite its title suggesting a carnival setting, this film is about gymnasts from a circus who work with the U.S. Treasury Department to flush out counterfeiters.

La Strada

Trans-Lux; 1954; black and white; 94 minutes; produced by Carlo Ponti and Dino De Laurentiis; written and directed by Federico Fellini; starring Giulietta Masina, Anthony Quinn and Richard Basehart. Although an Italian film, two of the strongest performances were by Americans Quinn and Basehart. The plot involves a triangle of love, jealousy and death among a circus strongman named Zampano (Quinn), his lover and servant Gelsomina (Masina) and Mario (Basehart), the clown she takes into her confidence. Although many critics found it to be the best performance of Quinn's career, only three years after a successful European run did the film find a United States distributor. The film received an Academy Award for best foreign film and an additional nomination for best screenplay. The movie was the basis of a 1969 Broadway musical, also named *La Strada*.

Let's Fall in Love

Columbia; 1934; black and white; 67 minutes; directed by David Burton; screenplay by Herbert Fields; starring Edmund Lowe and Ann Sothern. In a fluffy farce, a circus girl masquerades as an international film star under the guidance of a movie director.

The Lost Uncle

Mascot; 1934; 12-episode serial; black and white; directed by Armand Schaefer and David Howard; starring Clyde Beatty, Cecilia Parker, Syd Saylor and Mickey Rooney. In this serial adventure Beatty, as the exotic animal trainer, goes into the jungle to find his girlfriend's father.

Man on a Tightrope

20th Century-Fox; 1953; black and white; 105 minutes; produced by Robert L. Jacks; directed by Elia Kazan; screenplay by Robert Sherwood; starring Frederic March; Cameron Mitchell, Adolphe Menjou, Gloria Grahame and Richard Boone. In Czechoslovakia, a circus owner runs into trouble with the Communist party and attempts to flee the country.

The Men in Her Life

Columbia; 1941; black and white; 90 minutes; produced and directed by Gregory Ratoff; screenplay by Frederick Kohner, Michael Wilson and Paul Trivers, based on the novel *Ballerina* by Lady Eleanor Smith; starring Loretta Young, Conrad Veidt and Dean Jagger. An equestrienne star leaves the circus to enter the world of the ballet.

Merry Andrew

MGM and Sol C. Siegel; 1958; Metrocolor and Cinemascope; 103 minutes; directed and choreographed by Michael Kidd; screenplay by Isabel Lennart and I.A.L. Diamond from a Paul Gallico story; music by Saul Chaplin and lyrics by Johnny Mercer. Danny Kaye plays a supercilious professor who goes looking for an antique statue. Along the way, he joins a circus.

The Mighty Barnum

20th-Century Fox; 1934; black and white; 87 minutes; produced by Darryl F. Zanuck; screenplay by Gene Fowler and Bess Meredyth based on their stage play; music by Alfred Newman; starring Wallace Beery (Barnum), Virginia Bruce (his wife, "Nancy") and Adolphe Menjou (Barnum's aide, Mr. Walsh).

Although well intentioned, this film biography of the legendary showman has little historical accuracy. For instance, Barnum's wife throughout is called "Nancy," which *was* the first name of Barnum's second wife. They have live-in nieces, but no mention is made of their true-life daughters. Barnum is shown here as being completely surprised by the arrival of Jenny LIND; he subsequently falls in love with her and humiliates her. Barnum actually carefully calculated her coming, and there was never any hint of a romance between them. Perhaps the most unforgivable sin of the movie is that it shows Barnum as an agreeable nitwit, with his friend Walsh being the real brains behind the American Museum and other Barnum triumphs. At the movie's end, it is revealed that the real name of Mr. Walsh—the drunkard that the movie Barnum reformed—is supposedly none other than James A. BAILEY.

A Modern Hero

Warner; 1934; black and white; 70 minutes; directed by G.W. Pabst; screenplay by Gene Markey and Kathryn Scola from the Louis Bromfield novel; starring Richard Barthelmess and Jean Muir. A young circus equestrian gives up the ring to become an automobile magnate.

Octopussy

Eon/Danjaq; 1983; Technicolor and Panavision; 131 minutes; produced by Albert R. Broccoli; directed by John Glen, screenplay by George MacDonald, Richard Maibaum and Michael G. Wilson; starring Roger Moore, Maud Adams and Louis Jourdan. Long circus sequences form a major background for much of this standard Bond movie.

O'Shaughnessy's Boy

MGM; 1935; black and white; 88 minutes; directed by Richard Boleslawski; screenplay by Leonard Praskins and Otis Garrett; starring Wallace Beery, Jackie Cooper and Spanky McFarland. Beery and Cooper, reunited after *The Champ*, were moved from the prizefighter's arena to that of the circus. Unfortunately, this story of a Big Top performer who finds the son his wife took away in infancy was not as well received as their former film triumph.

Polly of the Circus

MGM; 1932; black and white; 72 minutes; produced by Paul Bern; directed by Alfred Santell; screenplay by Carey Wilson based on the Margaret Mayo play; starring Marion Davies, Clark Gable, C. Aubrey Smith and Ray Milland. A lady trapeze artist falls in love with a minister, but his bishop disapproves of the union. Although melodramatic on film, the plot is not farfetched: Even as late as 1932 local preachers were still warning their parishioners against the evils and sins to be found on circus grounds.

Ring of Fear

Warner/Wayne-Fellows; 1954; Warnercolor and Cinemascope; 88 minutes; produced by Robert M. Fellows; directed by James Edward Grant; screenplay by Paul Fix, Philip MacDonald and James Edward Grant; starring Clyde Beatty, Pat O'Brien and Mickey Spillane. Mysterious injuries and deaths occur all over the LOT when an insane ROUSTABOUT secretly returns to the circus from which he had been fired.

Sally of the Sawdust

Paramount/United Artists; 1925; black and white; silent; 78 minutes; directed by D.W. Griffith; screenplay by Forrest Halsey from the Dorothy Donnelly play *Poppy;* starring W.C. Fields, Carol Dempster and Alfred Lunt. Fields, as a circus juggler and con artist, tries to hide the fact from his daughter that she is adopted.

The Serpent's Egg

Rialto-Dino De Laurentiis, 1977; Eastmancolor; 120 minutes; direction and screenplay by Ingmar Bergman; starring David Carradine, Liv Ullmann, Gert Frobe, James Whitmore and Heinz Bennent. Carradine plays an American trapeze performer who has problems while performing in Hitler's Berlin.

Bergman's own 1953 Swedish circus film, *Sawdust and Tinsel,* was much more interesting. In that film a circus owner leaves his mistress to return to his wife. The manager is in turn challenged to a duel by the mistress's new lover.

Some Like it Hot

Paramount; 1939; black and white; 65 minutes; produced by William C. Thomas; directed by George Archainbaud; screenplay by Lewis R. Foster based on the play *The Great Magoo* by Wilkie C. Mahoney, Ben Hecht and Gene Fowler; starring Bob Hope, Shirely Ross, Una Merkel and Gene Krupa. (Not the classic Billy Wilder film with Tony Curtis, Jack Lemmon and Marilyn Monroe.) Hope plays a SIDE-SHOW owner who gets in comic mischief when his operation goes bankrupt.

Spell of the Circus

Universal; 1931; 10-episode serial; black and white; directed by Robert F. Hill; starring Francis X. Bushman, Jr., Alberta Baughn, Tom London and Walter Shumway. In a romantic triangle, a circus manager wants to marry the owner's daughter. She, unfortunately, is in love with the Wild West star of the show.

Street Angel

Fox; 1928; black and white; part silent, part sound; 101 minutes; directed by Frank Borzage; screenplay by Marion Orth based on Monckton Hoffe's play *Lady Cristallinda;* starring Janet Gaynor, Charles Farrell, Henry Armetta and Guido Trento.

Janet Gaynor, who has been forced by poverty to work as a prostitute, leaves the streets to become the female star of a circus.

The film won an Academy Award for Gaynor and one for Ernest Palmer as director of photography.

Three Ring Circus

Paramount; 1954; Technicolor and Vistavision; 103 minutes; produced by Hal B. Wallis; directed by Joseph Pevney; screenplay by Don McGuire and Joseph Pevney; starring Dean Martin and Jerry Lewis, Zsa Zsa Gabor and Elsa Lanchester.

Essentially a showcase for the clowning and mugging of the stars, *Three Ring Circus* has the comic duo as two ex-GIs who join a woman's circus as assistants to the trapeze artist and lion trainer.

A Tiger Walks

Walt Disney; 1963; Technicolor; 91 minutes; produced by Ron Miller; directed by Norman Tokar; screenplay by Lowell S. Hawley from the Ian Niall novel; starring Sabu, Brian Keith, Vera Miles and Una Merkel. A tiger escapes from a traveling circus and causes comic havoc in a small town in the West.

Toby Tyler

Walt Disney; 1959; Technicolor; 96 minutes; produced by Bill Walsh; directed by Charles Barton; screenplay by Bill Walsh and Lillie Hayward from the James Otis Kaler novel; starring Kevin Corcoran, Henry Calvin, Gene Sheldon, Bob Sweeney and James Drury. Set in 1910, an orphan boy joins a midwestern circus. Befriended by one of the chimpanzees with the show, Toby Tyler becomes the star of the circus.

Trapeze

United Artists/Hecht-Lancaster; 1956; DeLuxe Cinemascope; 105 minutes; produced by James Hill; directed by Carl Reed; screenplay by James R. Webb; starring Burt Lancaster, Tony Curtis and Gina Lollobrigida.

Trapeze was filmed almost entirely on location within the Big Top and on the grounds of a French winter circus. Lancaster and Curtis play two members of a flying trapeze troupe who begin to fight jealously when a third member, played by Lollobrigida, joins the act.

The Unholy Three

MGM; 1925; black and white; silent; 76 minutes; directed by Tod Browning; screenplay by Waldemar

Young from the Clarence Robbins novel; starring Lon Chaney, Harry Earles, Victor McLaglen, Mae Busch and Matt Moore. Murder is the result when a dwarf, a strongman and a ventriloquist set out on a crime spree.

Chaney did a remake in 1930, his only sound film, but he died before its release. Also for MGM, the 74-minute feature was directed by Jack Conway with a new screenplay by J.C. and Elliott Nugent. Harry Earles also returned from the original cast, complemented by Lila Lee, Ivan Linow, Elliott Nugent and John Miljan.

The Wagons Roll at Night

Warner; 1941; black and white; 83 minutes; produced by Harlan Thompson; directed by Ray Enright; screenplay by Fred Niblo, Jr., and Barry Trivers; starring Humphrey Bogart, Sylvia Sidney, Eddie Albert, Joan Leslie, Sig Rumann, Cliff Clark and Frank Wilcox. The girlfriend (Sidney) of a circus owner (Bogart) flirts with the new lion trainer (Albert) to disastrous ends.

You Can't Cheat an Honest Man

Universal; 1939; black and white; 79 minutes; produced by Lester Cowan; directed by George Marshall, screenplay by George Marion, Jr., Richard Mack and Everett Freeman from a story by Charles "W.C. Fields" Bogle; starring W.C. Fields, Edgar Bergen (with Charlie McCarthy and Mortimer Snerd), Constance Moore, Mary Forbes, Thurston Hall, Charles Coleman and Edward Brophy. Fields plays the owner of a small circus who gets into trouble with the law.

FINK   See LARRY.

FIRE-EATING   "Right inside the sideshow tent, ladies and gentlemen, see our fire-eater, the human blowtorch, the human salamander, the man who runs red-hot pokers up and down his body!" Thus the BALLY traditionally begins for one of the most unusual, misunderstood and dangerous of all circus skills.

One of the first historical records of fire-breathing was in 150 B.C. when a Syrian named Eunus was seen to emit flames as he supposedly talked with the gods. *A Book of Secrets*, attributed to Albertus Magnus, appeared in English for the first time in the year A.D. 1550 and contained a recipe for a fire-resistant lotion.

In his excellent book, *Learned Pigs & Fireproof Women*, author Ricky Jay chronicled a long line of itinerant showmen, court favorites and prevaudevillians who, for the next 350 years, amused and amazed the public with demonstrations of their ability to swallow fire and boiling oil, handle hot coals and, in effect, be burned alive. Over this same period, small publications appeared, many for the occult or magical trade, that purported to give the secret of fire resistance.

By the early 1900s, however, fire-eating had been reduced from an international reputation-maker to a staple of the carnival, fair and circus SIDESHOW. The fire-eater is still one of the most fascinating of circus artists, because he is, in the words of Penn Gillette (the talkative half of the comedy magic team Penn & Teller), "a self-made freak," one who deliberately mutilates his body or learns an exotic, dangerous skill to entertain the public.

Fire eating is one of the most common sideshow attractions. Baron Bill Unks, long time fire-eater with the CLYDE BEATTY-COLE BROS. CIRCUS, explained how most circus people learn to eat fire:

> When you get your first job, if you don't know anything they teach you to eat fire. They'll teach you how. Of course, I was real scared. I went into a show in Oakland and said I wanted a job. They said, "What are you? What do you do?" "I don't know," I said. "What do you want me to do?" They taught me to be a fire-eater.

The secret of fire-eating? Despite popular belief, no substance or fluid can coat the mouth and lips to prevent burning. If there were such a salve, every fire department in the country would be using it

Fire-eater Tom Davies on the bally platform as Charles W. "Doc" Boas gives the lecture on the Circus Kirk sideshow. (Photo courtesy of Charles A. DeWein)

and it would be in every first aid kit in the world. No—to eat fire you just *do* it.

The torches are usually made of cotton wicking one or two inches wide or rags sewn around some sort of metal rod, often with a decorative wood handle. The handle is also practical: The rod gets hot quickly and would soon become too hot to hold. The wicking from camping lanterns is ideal, and regular cotton thread holds up the longest. Wiring the rags to the rod only gives another hot metal to worry about; and waxed thread, although readily available on circuses for canvas mending, tends to melt and drip onto the tongue.

The completed torch is soaked in a flammable liquid. Many old-timers simply siphon gasoline from one of the nearby circus vehicles, cutting down their expenses; others feel lead-free gasoline or gasohol is less destructive to the body. Most of the younger generation of fire-eaters prefer lighter fluid. To the fire-eater's palate, the temperature of the flames is the same; but the different fluids do produce flames of different color and taste.

To actually eat the fire, the torch is removed from the liquid, and the excess is shaken off. The torch is lit. The fire-eater tilts the head back and up at about a 45-degree angle, opening the mouth in a wide O shape. The torch is held at the same angle and brought close to the face.

This is the moment of truth for the novice fire-eater. The intense heat must be ignored, and the torch is actually inserted into the mouth. The lips are closed around the stem of the torch without actually touching it, which would burn the lips instantly. The flame quickly consumes the oxygen in the mouth, and the flame goes out. Experienced fire-eaters can actually feel the minute "pop" as the fire snuffs. The performer must be certain that the fire is out: If the torch is removed before the flame is completely extinguished, the rush of oxygen will revive the fire quickly, burning—or at least terrifying—the performer.

Many variations on the single-torch consumption exist. By touching the hand or squeezing the tips of the fingers against a wet torch, the performer can have flames burn on the hand. Again, it is not the flesh but the fluid that burns. When the liquid is used up, the flame goes out. An experienced fire-eater can manually transfer flame from one torch to another or squeeze burning liquid onto the tongue to transfer the flame to another torch.

If the torch is held in the open mouth for a few seconds, the mouth cavity can continue to hold burning vapors even after the torch is removed. This flaming vapor can actually be puffed or "spit" to light a torch. The torch can also be clamped in the teeth, lips held wide open as the performer spreads the arms wide in an obvious applause cue.

The *pièce de résistance* in fire-eating has always been the HUMAN VOLCANO, or Big Blow-out. In this grand finale, the fire-eater takes liquid into the mouth and, holding the flaming torch at arm's length, spits the fluid at the fire. A huge ball of flame erupts.

Fire-eating has many real dangers. All of the flammable liquids used by fire-eaters are toxic, and there is no way to avoid swallowing or absorbing small amounts of the liquids through the walls of the mouth. Over a period of time, this can cause nausea, indigestion, diarrhea, bleeding gums, loss of teeth or even death. Baron Bill Unks would sometimes have to take off several months to allow his damaged liver to regenerate.

Fire burns! To repeat: fire burns! Every fire-eater has been burned often and, despite every precaution, will probably be burned again. If the flame does not go out, if wind (particularly during the Human Volcano) pushes the flame in the wrong direction, if the fluid is not used up quickly or drips onto a part of the body or clothes where it is not easily controlled or contained, the performer will get burned, perhaps seriously. The burns produce instantaneous third-degree blisters.

Kids—don't try this one at home!

FIRES, CIRCUS   Even more inevitable than a tent BLOWDOWN or a train wreck, the most feared tragedy on the circus LOT is the ever-present possibility of the circus TENTS catching fire.

In modern tents, the same liquids used for waterproofing also protect the canvas against fire. Such was not always the case: During World War II, when waterproofing materials were in demand for army tents, circus owners routinely coated their tops with paraffin wax. This, of course, created a disaster-in-waiting.

Surprisingly, only a few major incidents occurred. In one catastrophe, 39 animals died when the MENAGERIE tent on the RINGLING BROS. AND BARNUM & BAILEY CIRCUS caught fire on August 4, 1942, but fortunately no human life was lost. The most tragic circus fire began during the early minutes of the

July 6, 1944, matinee show of The GREATEST SHOW ON EARTH. The BIG TOP was engulfed in flames and within ten minutes had collapsed to the ground. Six thousand people attempted to evacuate the burning canvas; as cataclysmic as it was, only 168 persons—most of them children—perished. This, the HARTFORD FIRE, was the worst fire in American circus history.

These were far from the first, however. For that, historians most go back to the first American circus, Ricketts Circus. John Bill RICKETTS presented his performances in amphitheaters built expressly for circus performances in Philadelphia and New York in 1793. In 1799 both coliseums burned to the ground. Although there were no casualties in the fires, Ricketts was left penniless.

P.T. BARNUM was also plagued by circus fires. In fact, almost every major building Barnum ever owned was destroyed by flames. In 1857 IRANISTAN, his beloved mansion in BRIDGEPORT, CONNECTICUT, burned. His AMERICAN MUSEUM, with which he made his initial fame and fortune, burned in 1865; and its replacement was ravaged by flames just three years later. In 1872 his HIPPOTHEATRON, which housed his circus and MENAGERIE, burned. The cost of property and livestock lost reached $300,000. In 1887, just four years before his death, Barnum's circus WINTER QUARTERS in Bridgeport also burned down to a loss of $250,000.

A similar fire swept through the Rochester, Indiana, winter quarters of the COLE BROS. CIRCUS on February 20, 1940, reducing all of the main buildings housing the show to ash. Although there were no human casualties, two elephants, two zebras, two llamas, two tigers, two lions, two lionesses and their cubs, two leopards, two audads, a sacred Indian cow, a pygmy hippo and many monkeys were destroyed. The total loss was estimated at $150,000.

It is the memory of the horror of Ringling's catastrophe in Hartford and the loss of human life, however, that keeps the fear of circus fires fresh in the minds of all circus folk.

FIRST OF MAY

Circus jargon, highly derisive, for a first-season performer on a circus. Calling a person a "First of May," and usually preceding it with an expletive of one form or another, is the greatest insult you can call a novice or veteran performer on a show.

The term originates from when the early MUD SHOWS began their seasons on or around the first of May, after the winter snows and spring rains had cleared.

FLAGG & AYMAR'S INTERNATIONAL CIRCUS

Flagg & Aymar's International Circus was a new but unsuccessful show in 1856, the same year that John ROBINSON and Gilbert N. ELDRED split after an 11-year partnership.

Robinson used the money that he received from Eldred's purchase of his share of their show to obtain the Flagg & Aymar show. With the same personnel, he opened in Geneva, New York on September 1, 1856, under the name John Robinson's International Circus and Menagerie.

The show became so popular that even after Robinson's death his name was used in circus titles almost every year until 1930.

(See also JOHN ROBINSON CIRCUS; G.N. ELDRED'S GREAT ROTUNDA SOUTHERN CIRCUS AND MENAGERIE.)

FLAG'S UP

Circus jargon, "Flag's Up" is called across the BACK YARD of a circus LOT to inform the cast and crew that the COOKHOUSE is open and ready to serve meals. The cry is often accompanied by the raising of a small flag, usually red, over the top of the cookhouse TENT.

FLATFOOTS

Because both groups sought to control the ownership and exhibition of exotic animals in America in the 1830s, the Flatfoots syndicate and the ZOOLOGICAL INSTITUTE are often thought to have been the same organization. To further confuse the circus historian, many of the same MENAGERIE owners belonged to both alliances. Current scholarship, especially that of Stuart Thayer, shows that they were in fact separate entities.

The partners of the Zoological Institute, which was founded in 1835, became renowned for their stubbornness in business dealings. Because they were reported to have stated their terms and then add "On that I put my foot down flat," the term "flatfoots" was already being used to describe the Institute's practices by the time it officially disbanded on August 23, 1837.

Some of the Institute's members (notably founders Caleb S. ANGEVINE, John J. JUNE and Lewis B. TITUS) officially formed the Flatfoots. This latter organization was more openly dedicated to controlling the importation and display of exotic animals in the United States. The group lasted until 1842, when June, Titus, Angevine and Co. ceased operation.

Around 1863, a second association of businessmen formed a new coalition of Flatfoots, one active in full circus ownership. Prominent among them was George F. BAILEY, whose show was the last to be originated by the Flatfoot syndicate. Bailey called himself the Last of the Flatfoots, and he toured his George F. Bailey Circus until 1875. The Flatfoots did not disband, however, before having their own brush with the preeminent showman of the 1800s, P.T. BARNUM.

At the end of the 1875 circus season, Barnum broke with his partners W.C. COUP and Dan CASTELLO over the control of their show, BARNUM'S GREAT TRAVELING MUSEUM, MENAGERIE, CARAVAN, HIPPODROME AND CIRCUS. Barnum turned over the management to the Flatfoots, who handled the show—the last of their regular operations—from 1876 until at least 1878 or possibly 1880.

FLATTIES Circus jargon, not in current usage, for "people," on or off the LOT.

FLEA CIRCUS Although normally seen as a carnival MIDWAY or a seaside boardwalk attraction, a flea circus is at once a spoof and yet a fascinating realization of the circus in miniature. Working with the minuscule insects, the "trainer" is actually able to get the almost microscopic pests to juggle, foot balance, walk wires and mimic other skills performed by humans.

George Jean Nathan, American theater critic and essayist, claims that the flea circus originated with Professor Hupf in Coblentz, Germany, in 1885. Professor Leroy Heckler II, who exhibited the trained insects in Hubert's Museum (a New City emporium off a Times Square subway entrance as late as 1958) claimed "it was a woman in Germany in the seventeen hundreds invented flea circuses. The Kings of Prussia all had court flea trainers. The flea trainer was looked up to as one of the wise men of the court."

John C. Ruhl, one of America's pioneer flea-men, is credited with having brought the art to these shores. Working out of California, Ruhl died shortly after World War II.

Chuck Burnes examines the miniature Ferris wheel of Prof. Burnes' Great London Flea Circus.
(Jack D. Miller photo, courtesy of Bambi Burnes)

There are over 900 species of fleas in the world, subdivided into six major families. In North America alone there are 200 species and nearly 70 subspecies. As Heckler pointed out, "Flea Circuses are becoming extinct, but not because of the dearth of fleas."

The most common flea in America is the dog flea, or *Ctenocephalides canis;* but the best for training purposes due to its size, stamina and longevity is the so-called human flea, or European house flea, the *Pulex irritans.* The *Pulex* is shaped like a bee, brown or black in color, up to ⅛ of an inch in length and 1/20 to ⅕ of a grain in weight. It might be more clearly expressed this way: A human host could carry 5,000 fleas and add only one ounce of weight.

Professor Heckler selected his fleas carefully. Several were placed in a loosely covered jar that was set near a lighted bulb. Most of the fleas frantically dashed about to escape the heat and died of exhaustion. The smarter ones found the coolest part of the jug and remained there. These passed the first test.

They were then placed in individual test tubes. Fleas have a vertical jumping capacity of eight inches, so tiring them out taught them escape was impossible.

Tying the collars onto the fleas while the trainer controls the insects is probably the hardest part of the operation. Under a microscope, the flea-man ties a monofilament of copper wire around the neck of the insect, tight enough so it can't slip off, but not so tight that it will choke.

As with BULLS, female fleas are more responsive to training and are better performers than males. The females are larger and mild, but the males are too lethargic.

A flea will almost automatically wiggle an object placed on its foreleg; and, with a little imagination from the audience, this could easily be a baton, a flag, a spear or Emmett KELLY sweeping up a spotlight. A flea placed on its back, like a dung beetle or roach, will frantically wave its legs, trying to turn over. A small cotton ball placed on its six legs will be "juggled" in midair. Balance is innate to a flea, SO WIRE WALKING is a natural. Placed on miniature chariots, the insects can re-create the arena races around the HIPPOTHEATRON track of P.T. BARNUM.

Pulex irritans can live for 48 hours without blood. But, in order to give its best possible performance, the flea should be allowed to visit a human host briefly once or twice a day, for anywhere from 15 to 30 minutes at each feeding. Says Professor Heckler, "I have never become attached to the fleas like you would to a dog or cat. It's rather the other way around."

Author and mentalist T.A. Waters worked as the spieler for the Hubert's Museum in 1963 and remembers Professor Heckler saying he had been working at that location for over 40 years. Waters described the flea circus room as being able to accommodate only a few persons at a time. They would stand around a small, squarish table, approximately 18 inches by 36 inches, which was covered with what Waters was told was the largest magnifying lens created by Bausch & Lomb up until that time.

Waters, who gave the PITCH for the flea circus dozens of times a day, can still recall the GRIND:

Downstairs you'll meet Professor Roy Heckler's World-Famous Trained Flea Circus: Sixteen fleas, six principals and ten understudies, and they perform six different acts. As Act Number One you will see a flea juggle a ball while lying on its back. As Act Number Two, three fleas will hold a chariot race; and naturally the flea that hops the fastest will win the race. But the act, ladies and gentleman, that most people talk about, the one they bring their friends to see: Three tiny fleas are put in costumes and placed upon the ballroom floor and when the music is turned on, those fleas will dance. Now I know that sounds hard to believe, but may I remind you, that seeing is believing; and when you see Professor Heckler's World-Famous Trained Flea Circus it's something you will remember for the rest of your life. Downstairs, now.

CIRCUS REPORT, the publication that is the current bible of the circus industry, printed an article about the Alberti Flea Circus—the "Flea Ring Circus"—in April 1990. Jim Hobbs, the owner, said, "I learned about the management and presentation of the Alberti Flea Circus from my grandfather. It was he who taught me about the care and feeding of fleas, the method of training fleas, and most important, the secret of flea psychology." The Alberti Flea Circus, which has been in operation since the 1880s, is currently winter quartered in Winston-Salem, North Carolina, tours over 7,000 miles each season, playing to over 10,000 children and adults annually.

Although not currently in operation, the only other known true flea circus today is "Prof. Burnes' Great London Flea Circus," owned by Chuck Burnes of Anaheim, California. The apparatus was first toured as the "Great London Flea Circus," then retitled the "Coyote Gulch Flea Circus." As a youth, Burnes had been fascinated by the Hubert's Museum flea circus; and, when the opportunity came as an adult to purchase a real flea circus, he jumped at the chance. Once he acquired the miniature props Bob Matthew—the original owner who had exhibited the flea circus for years at Pacific Ocean Park—taught Burnes the secrets of raising, tying and training the fleas.

FLIP-FLAPS Circus jargon for an exciting equestrian trick. The bareback rider stands on the back of a moving horse and "flips" forward to a handstand, then "flaps" back to a standing position. The stunt can be repeated as often as desired for effect.

FLOATERS Circus jargon for the pieces of fake fruit, usually wax slices of lemons or oranges, that are dropped into the large dispenser of imitation JUICE served at the concessions wagon. Although neither the fruit nor the juice itself is real, the slices *do* seem to make the "lemonade" more appealing.

FLOATING PALACE Owned by circus managers Spalding and Rogers, the *Floating Palace* was a showboat that plied the waters of the Mississippi River. Originally pulled by a separate paddlewheel steamboat called the *North River* and the *James Raymond* beginning the following year, the *Palace* was in use from 1852 until 1865.

Designed by "Dr." Gilbert R. SPAULDING and his partner, the equestrian Charles J. Rogers (1817–95), the *Floating Palace,* built in Cincinnati by Edward M. Shield at a cost of about $42,000, was an amphitheater set onto a flat-bottomed barge that drew only 19 inches in the water and 25 inches when an audience was on board. It boasted a standard 42-foot circus ring, seating for 2,500 people and was decorated with mirrors and carved woodworks as well as velvet tapestries and carpets. Through his own innovation, Spalding lighted the theater with over 200 gas jets (rather than candles, common for the day). The towboat carried the MENAGERIE.

The *Floating Palace* opened in Pittsburgh in March of 1852; its success was no doubt in part responsible for Dan RICE's later decision to take his show on-board a steamboat as well. Steam heating in the theater (with the apparatus stowed on the *North River*) allowed a year-round season, and the *Palace* toured the Ohio and Mississippi rivers for 14 years, each winter making a long stand in New Orleans.

The *Floating Palace* was used to tour Spalding and Rogers's show only in 1852, 1853, 1857 and 1859. The remaining seasons it was leased and altered to accommodate VAN AMBURGH's Menagerie.

In the spring of 1865 an accidental fire completely destroyed the *Floating Palace* in New Albany, Indiana.

(See also DAN RICE CIRCUS.)

FLOATS Technically TABLEAU WAGONS, floats were miniature carriages used in the STREET PARADE. Usually based on simple themes or fairy tales, the floats were drawn by smaller horses and carried only a driver.

Among the many floats maintained by the CIRCUS WORLD MUSEUM in BARABOO, WISCONSIN are the 1885 "Old Lady in the Shoe Nursery Float," the 1885 "Mother Goose Float" and the "Cinderella Float."

Drawn by ponies, the Cinderella float was one of seven scenes based on fairy tales that were built in the 1880s for the BARNUM & BAILEY CIRCUS. The golden figures represent the kneeling prince fitting the slipper onto Cinderella's foot.

FLOTO DOG & PONY SHOW See DOG AND PONY SHOW; SELLS-FLOTO CIRCUS.

FLYERS Circus jargon for aerialists, especially those on the TRAPEZE. In common usage, "flyers" are those in a swinging trapeze act who actually jump from one bar to another or into the CATCHER's arms.

(See also FLYING TRAPEZE.)

FLYING CONCELLOS, THE Headed by Art and Antoinette CONCELLO, the Flying Concellos were the most outstanding and celebrated FLYING TRAPEZE team of the 1930s and 1940s.

Art Concello was performing with the Flying Wards on the HAGENBECK-WALLACE CIRCUS when he met Antoinette Comeau, then working on the SELLS-FLOTO CIRCUS. Shortly after the Flying Wards moved over to Sells-Floto, the young couple were married. In 1929 they made their professional debut as a team, the Flying Concellos.

In 1930 John RINGLING bought the AMERICAN CIRCUS CORPORATION, which owned both shows, and the Concellos moved onto The BIG ONE. Their act was performed in one of the side rings, since the CENTER RING was reserved for Ringling star flyer Alfredo CODONA. In 1933 Codona sprained a shoulder attempting a TRIPLE SOMERSAULT and retired from flying. The Concellos moved over to the center ring as the new featured attraction.

The Flying Concellos were noted for many technical innovations in equipment as well as for their remarkable skill. At their peak, up to six aerialists performed as part of the Flying Concellos in their six-minute act. Finally, in 1937, in Detroit Antoi-

The Flying Concellos.   (Author's collection)

nette Concello achieved the triple; this, coupled with her other aerial displays, made her known as the "Queen of the Flying Trapeze." By 1940 the Flying Concellos were unique in that every member of the act was able to execute the triple somersault in the same show.

In 1943 the original team of the Flying Concellos retired from the ring. Antoinette had suffered a shoulder injury, and Art moved into management in the Ringling offices. After six years, during which time their son was born, Antoinette briefly returned to flying; but she soon moved behind the scenes as Ringling's aerial coach.

FLYING CRANES, THE

The Flying Cranes have been the featured attraction of the MOSCOW CIRCUS with each American tour since the circus returned to the United States in 1988. Awesome in its conception, theatricality, production, and skill in execution, the Flying Cranes' routine is, arguably, the most critically acclaimed act of our time. Certainly it is the most internationally renowned FLYING TRAPEZE act working today.

The act, created by Petr Maestrenko in collaboration with artistic director Vilen Golovko, suggests that the soul of the dying Russian soldier soars upward, reborn in the form of the beautiful white crane. Performed to a mostly Wagnerian score, the balletic aerial act is based on a classic Russian ballad by poet Russal Gamzatov:

> Soldiers who fought for us in terrifying war
> They weren't simply buried in bloody fields of pain
> For their spirits flew up in the sky
> Where they could soar
> And they became all birds
> The Flying Cranes.
>
> That's maybe why when we look in the sky
> And unexpectedly see the beautiful white Cranes
> We talk to them and we can hear them cry
> And then they disappear
> Like time that goes by.

The act has three parts. In the first section, each Crane makes an appearance, with special attention given to one lone soldier. She prepares for battle, is killed and is carried skyward by her fellow Cranes. The second part is the most traditional in terms of the flying trapeze. The flyers perform, in addition to pirouettes and simple stunts, double, TRIPLE and even QUADRUPLE SOMERSAULTS. In fact, the Flying Cranes, the only act in the world other than the FLYING VAZQUEZ to regularly perform the quadruple somersault as part of their routine, never announces the trick for fear of breaking the mood of the piece. The third part of the act has the flyers returning to earth.

In addition to the regular apparatus employed by a flying act, Maestrenko devised a new concept for the aerial soaring. Each flyer is held by his own suspended cable that, when released, "flies" him upward.

Golovko had commissioned the act for his son, Willy, who was already an accomplished aerialist. Willy is the lead CATCHER and head of the act, giving all of the signals for the flyers; but the act is truly an ensemble piece. All of the flyers have been with the Cranes since its inception in 1981. Years in the making, the Flying Cranes did not make their public debut until 1985.

In the featured role of the female soldier is Willy Golovko's wife, Lena. After considering a career with the Bolshoi Ballet, Lena, at the age of 16, joined the circus where she met and later married Willy; they have one son. Petr Serdukov, who is the cast member who performs "the quad," was a Master of Sports before auditioning for the Cranes.

First seen by producer Steven E. Leber in 1987 as he was assembling acts for the historic return visit of the Moscow Circus to the United States, the Flying Cranes were instantly invited to be part of the troupe.

FLYING GAONAS, THE

One of the greatest TRAPEZE acts of all time, the Flying Gaonas is the only flying act ever to win the Gold Clown Award at the International Circus Festival of Monte Carlo.

The Gaonas of Mexico performed their family trampoline act for ten years. While working for the CLYDE BEATTY CIRCUS, brothers Armando (Manco) and Tito and their sister Chela went to see the Tony Curtis movie *Trapeze* (see FILMS, CIRCUS); the three, especially Tito, decided they wanted to learn to fly.

Their father, Victor, had been a circus performer from the age of three. As coach and CATCHER, he imparted to his sons the stamina and skills required of trapeze artists. He had particular hopes for 15-year-old son Tito. Victor felt that Tito had the ability to execute the TRIPLE SOMERSAULT, last performed by Antoinette CONCELLO in 1943.

In 1964 Tito Gaona performed his first triple at the age of 17. The next year the troupe was invited to join the RINGLING BROS. AND BARNUM & BAILEY CIRCUS. In 1979 they were joined by their younger brother, Ricardo. Since that time the Flying Gaonas have performed at numerous circuses, including The BIG APPLE CIRCUS.

As a baby, Ricardo played on the trampoline next to the trapeze. He held up his arms, wanting to join his siblings; by the age of four he could climb the ladder and jump into the net. At the tender age of five, he performed as, perhaps, the youngest flyer ever. His trick was swinging once, then dropping into the net. "The apparatus," he recalls, "was like a big swing set."

Armando Gaona, now the catcher, is the oldest of the Flying Gaonas. Although the flyers provide the flash, it is the catcher who has the most responsibility in the act. A master of timing, he makes the calls for the flyer's release. The catcher literally has seconds to decide if the flyer will arrive on time and at what angle. Armando doesn't miss flying, but he jokes, "Of course, I am no longer the center of attention. But if I want attention, I only have to drop one of my brothers. Then everyone looks at me."

In the act, Chela and Ricardo perform the PASSING LEAP. Chela is caught first, by the legs. Then, as she swings upside down on her return to catch the swinging bar, Ricardo releases the trapeze bar and passes up and over her into Armando's arms. Chela makes one swing back and Ricardo joins her; they return together to the platform.

Chela is quick to point out the risk involved in the trapeze. "Is it dangerous? Sure it's dangerous! . . . But I knew a flyer who killed himself walking down the stairs of his trailer." She explains that the net is welcome, but still risky. "People . . . don't realize how dangerous the net can be. You have to know how to fall; otherwise you can get badly hurt."

(See also FLYING TRAPEZE.)

FLYING SQUADRON

Circus jargon for the first group of a circus caravan to make the JUMP to the next LOT.

FLYING TRAPEZE

The trapeze bar as we know it today was invented in the early 1800s in the Toulouse section of France. Until the time of the young French aerialist Jules LÉOTARD, gymnasts worked on stationary bars, but Léotard fastened a shortened length between two ropes hung from the ceiling of his father's gym. At first his trapeze act consisted of gymnastic stunts performed on a still bar, then on a swinging apparatus. Soon Léotard was leaping from one swinging trapeze to another.

The first "man on the flying trapeze" made his debut with the new sensation at the Cirque Napoléon. Léotard became so renowned with the act that his gymnastic apparel, styled for ease of performance as well as to show off musculature, today bears his name.

By placing two trapeze bars next to each other, aerialists are able to swing from one bar and back again, performing twists and somersaults between the bars. As their acts mature, more members are added to the team, allowing one performer to specialize as a CATCHER. The catcher is responsible for pacing the leaps so that the aerialists have time to fly from one perch to another, meet the catcher's grasp and return, all with the confidence that a swinging trapeze bar will be there when needed. Precision and split-second timing are as important to the flyer as strength and stamina.

The Flying Gaonas, from left to right: catcher Manuel "Gordo" Zuniga, Chela Gaona, Tito Gaona and Armando Gaona. (Photo courtesy of Harry L. Graham)

An essential part of the early training of any flyer is the use of the safety net and learning to fall properly. A headfirst fall into the net almost always results in a broken neck. A belly flop causes severe rope burns and torn muscles. Landing feet first can result in broken ankles. When dropping from such a height, it is necessary to first fall onto the back, then bounce up and land on the feet. If this is not possible, the best alternative is to roll up into a ball and pray.

The net itself has undergone many changes. The first nets used in Europe were painted black, as if to suggest that they weren't there. The open net, of course, allows the audience visibility to see the flyers, but the cross-hatching of the net cannot be so broad that it allows the feet of a falling flyer to drop through. Nor can it be so close or tight that the net responds more as a flat screen than as an open-air spring. Its ideal position is nine feet from the ground. It covers the complete rectangular area within the flying bars' rigging and continues vertically on each side. This provides further protection should a flyer fall out of a long forward swing and overshoot the bottom net.

As the rigging and design of the apparatus improved, so did the skills of the flyers. The somersault, a midair forward roll, was a trick developed early on in flying. Another spectacular, if now standard, trick is the PASSING LEAP. In this stunt, the first flyer takes off from the swing bar. As he sails through the air and is grabbed by the catcher, another flyer takes hold of the swinging bar and makes

On the flying trapeze: The Montoyas on the Bentley Bros. Circus in Harrisburg, Pennsylvania in 1990. (Photo by Tom Ogden)

a take-off (known as a cutaway). As the first flyer returns to catch the swing bar, the second flyer releases hold and flies up and over the first flyer and into the arms of the catcher.

The initial quest for the TRIPLE SOMERSAULT assumed almost mythic proportions. Some accept the claim that a teenage orphan girl from Russia named Lena Jordan actually performed the feat in 1897, but that she grew too large to repeat the stunt after 1898.

In 1920 Alfredo CORDONA became the first flyer to perform the triple regularly. After climbing the rope ladder to the pedestal, Codona had to swing back and forth to develop a speed of over 60 miles an hour to be able to barrel over three times, coming out of the third spin into the arms of the catcher. Codona performed the trick for over a decade before having to retire from a shoulder injury incurred while attempting a triple in 1933.

The FLYING CONCELLOS were unique in the 1930s and 1940s in that every member of the troupe was able to perform the triple within the same six-minute act. Antoinette CONCELLO, who later became aerial director for Ringling, regularly performed the two-and-one-half somersault in her act and often did the triple in the same performance.

Soon flyers discovered that by raising the pedestal, or PERCH, during the cutaway for the triple, more speed and momentum were produced. The QUADRUPLE SOMERSAULT became the next challenge. Finally, the "impossible" trick was achieved by Miguel VAZQUEZ of the FLYING VAZQUEZ as he flew to catcher Juan Vazquez during a practice session on the RINGLING BROS. AND BARNUM & BAILEY CIRCUS at the Long Beach Arena in Long Beach, California on August 19, 1981.

On September 29, 1984 Miguel Vazquez also became the first to perform a triple somersault in a layout position with no turn to catcher Juan Vazquez at the Sports Arena in Los Angeles.

Although the quadruple has since been performed by others, the Vazquez Troupe and the

FLYING CRANES remain the only flyers to feature it as a regular part of their acts. The MOSCOW CIRCUS, however, has the distinction of being the only circus whose flyers often perform the quadruple without announcing the attempt or accomplishment of the feat.

In other trapeze records, Sarah Denu of the United States, at age 14, performed the most downward circles, or "muscle grinding," on the trapeze—1,350—in Madison, Wisconsin on May 21, 1983. Tom Robin Edelston performed the first triple-twisting double somersault to catcher John Zimmerman at CIRCUS WORLD in Florida on January 20, 1981. The first triple back somersault with one-and-a-half twists was accomplished by Terry Cavaretta Lemus (now Mrs. St. Jules) at CIRCUS CIRCUS in Las Vegas, Nevada in 1969.

"FLYING TRAPEZE, THE"

"The Flying Trapeze," the celebrated song also known as "The Man on the Flying Trapeze," was written by George Leybourne (music) and Gaston Lyle (lyrics) and published in New York City in 1868. It was popularized again in the early 1930s by Walter O'Keefe.

FLYING VAZQUEZ, THE

For at least five generations, the Vazquez family of Mexico has been a popular circus troupe. The father, Manuel Vazquez, born October 8, 1925 in San Felipe, Orizatlan, Mexico, performed the IRON JAW, PERCH and as a CLOWN. He has always been involved with music and has encouraged all of his children to become musicians. He personally plays drum and trumpet in circus bands whenever possible. His wife, born Reyna Rodriguez Rivas on January 6, 1930 in Irapuato, Guanajuato, Mexico, was accomplished on the low wire and perch act by the time they were married November 17, 1943 in Tijuana, B.C., Mexico. Together, they have nine children, almost all of whom have entered the world of the circus. In addition to the contemporary Vazquez fliers, the Vazquez children include Margarita Vazquez AYALA, the noted artist of the HAIR HANG.

Through 1975 or 1976, Juan Vazquez (b. February 28, 1949), his brother Felipe (b. November 3, 1954) and two uncles performed as gymnasts in a horizontal bar act. In the mid-1970s the two Vazquez brothers began to work out with FLYING TRAPEZE artists, and in 1977 they became the Flying Vazquez. Also in that first troupe was Juan's wife,

Patricia (b. Patricia Segrera Zamudio, December 20, 1977). A younger brother, Vinicio Vazquez (b. November 22, 1958) became a backup flyer, as did Miguel (b. December 6, 1964), the youngest brother.

Juan Vazquez began to keep meticulous notes of each trick he and his brothers achieved during performance. During the 1978 and 1979 seasons, the Flying Vazquez performed short runs on various shows. Since Miguel achieved his first TRIPLE SOMERSAULT in March 1978, they were noted as the only family in the world to have three brothers (Juan, Felipe and Miguel) who could perform the stunt. In 1980, the company moved onto the Hubert Castle Circus for 15 weeks.

The following season they opened as the flying act over Ring Three in the RINGLING BROS. AND BARNUM & BAILEY CIRCUS. Complementing them in Ring One were the Flying Farfans. Although many circus folk assumed that either Gino Farfan (17 years old) or Tato Farfan (12 years old) would be the first to accomplish the QUADRUPLE SOMERSAULT, that honor fell to Miguel VAZQUEZ.

In January 1981 the Vazquez Troupe began to work on the mythic trick. Miguel worked as the flyer and Juan as the CATCHER. They videotaped each attempt, and Juan continued to make extensive written observations of each try. Midway through the season, on August 19, 1981, the team achieved the quad in rehearsal, verified on tape, and eventually re-created it during a live performance on July 10, 1982 in Tucson, Arizona.

At the end of the 1985 season, Felipe left the Flying Vazquez. At the beginning of the following year, Milton Zamudio (b. 1968), a performer on the high wire and a cousin of Patricia, joined the troupe. Already able to throw a triple, he added a three-and-a-half somersault in 1987.

In 1992 the Flying Vazquez were the featured aerialists with the BIG APPLE CIRCUS during its spring and summer tour.

FOOT JUGGLING

A form of gyroscopic JUGGLING performed with the feet, this is technically known as "antipodism." Foot juggling dates back at least to the time of the Aztecs: The conqueror Cortez saw a foot juggler in the court of Montezuma and liked the act so much he took him back to Spain.

In its basic form, performers lie on their backs and raise their feet to a 90-degree angle, perpendicular to the floor. The hips and tail bones can be comfortably raised slightly with a pillow. A professional form of this, a cushioned mat that supports the lower back at about a 30-degree angle and has shoulder supports to keep the artist from sliding, is called a CRADLE.

An object is then placed across the soles of both feet and is kicked up, spun and twirled. The articles tossed vary considerably, which is part of the fascination of watching foot jugglers: Barrels, tables and umbrellas are among the most popular.

When the object supported and tossed is another human being, the foot-juggling performance is known as a RISLEY ACT.

FOREPAUGH, ADAM (1831–1890)   Forepaugh began his circus career as a candy BUTCHER in 1863 and had a show under his own name from 1866 through 1890. The ADAM FOREPAUGH CIRCUS was one of the major U.S. circuses, and for some years it was the largest in the country. The circus made its WINTER QUARTERS on an eight-acre plot off Lehigh Avenue in Philadelphia.

Among the many attractions Adam Forepaugh presented over the years in his two-ring show were Louise Montague, winner of a Forepaugh competition to find the most beautiful woman in America (1881) and BOLIVAR, an answer to P.T. BARNUM's exhibition of JUMBO (1883).

With the invention of the lithographic steam press, colored posters could finally be mass-produced cheaply. In addition to the ONE SHEETS, however, circuses engaged in the distribution of libelous brochures. Forepaugh, a flamboyant showman, issued a RAT SHEET in which Barnum was accused of "Fraud! Falsehood! and Downright Deceit!" because he claimed to carry 100 cages, 20 elephants and hundreds of performers in his STREET PARADE. Forepaugh countered that there were only 23 cages, 14 elephants and 25 entertainers. "Note the Discrepancy! A Gross Exaggeration Without a Single Word of Truth!" the sheet declared.

This was followed by a notorious 1884 campaign against Barnum's pachyderm Toung Taloung, in which Forepaugh claimed to have the nation's only true "WHITE ELEPHANT" on display. Forepaugh whitewashed one of his own BULLS for exhibition and distributed a rat sheet announcing that his pachyderm was "Too White For Barnum."

Like many of his era, Forepaugh was influenced by the enormous popularity of the new vogue in outdoor amusements ushered in by William Frederick CODY (Buffalo Bill)—the Wild West show. By the late 1880s, the "4 Paw Show," as it was often abbreviated in advertising posters, had added a Wild West CONCERT. The aftershow featured Captain Adam H. BOGARDUS, at the time the Champion Wing Shot of America. Bogardus had won the title in an 1871 match and had successfully defended it ever since.

Forepaugh still had many admirers, however. During his lifetime, Forepaugh frequently toured the state of Kansas; and, on January 30, 1890 the Topeka *State Journal* printed a moving editorial that stated, in part:

> *Adam Forepaugh, it is said, never smoked nor chewed tobacco nor drank intoxicating liquors. His success was due to thorough application to his business and to shrewd business methods. He was kind at heart—especially so to animals—rough in exterior, fond of a joke, haughty and brusque to his employees, except heads of departments, and he attended to the smallest detail himself. When all went well he used to go to his private car every night at 10 o'clock; at home this was his invariable hour of retiring. He always sat at the main entrance of the show, and his face was more familiar to the great mass of people, rich and poor, and in every state, than probably any living American.*

The veteran circus manager died in his home in Philadelphia on January 22, 1890 of pneumonia, after suffering for two weeks with influenza. At the time of his death, Forepaugh was believed to have been a millionaire. He was survived by a wife and his son, Adam, Jr.

FOREPAUGH-SELLS CIRCUS   See ADAM FOREPAUGH & SELLS BROS. CIRCUS.

FOX, CHARLES PHILIP "CHAPPIE" (1913–   )   Instrumental in the creation and one of the first directors (from 1960 through 1972) of the CIRCUS WORLD MUSEUM in BARABOO, WISCONSIN, "Chappie" Fox was also involved in originating the GREAT CIRCUS PARADE and the Great Circus Train.

A lifelong circus fan, collector, photographer and historian, Fox's books include *Circus Parades, Circus Trains, A Ticket to the Circus, A Pictorial History of Performing Horses* and, as co-author with Tom Parkinson, *The Circus in America* and *Billers, Banners &*

Bombast. He was an officer in the CIRCUS HISTORICAL SOCIETY and the Milwaukee County Zoological Society, as well as being one of the few American members admitted to the international *Union Des Historiens Du Cirque.* From 1973 until his retirement in 1983, Fox was also director of circus research for the RINGLING BROS. AND BARNUM & BAILEY CIRCUS.

FOX, GEORGE L. (1825–1877)

Considered by many to be America's answer to Joseph GRIMALDI, George L. Fox was the first great WHITEFACE CLOWN in the United States. While he spent his entire career on the theatrical stage rather than in a circus tent, his popularity and style had enormous influence on MUD SHOW clowns of his and later generations.

As a boy, Fox saw a French theatrical troupe in the 1830s, and he was no doubt impressed by the HARLEQUIN clown, the masked buffoon wearing the multicolor costume. When the Harlequin of a New York theater quit in 1850, Fox took his place. In 1856 he produced his own English-style pantomime, and two years later he moved it to the Old Bowery Theater. His career continued at peak popularity for the next 17 years.

Fox's contribution was to "Americanize" the Harlequin clown, by broadening the acrobatic athleticism of the French style while incorporating the British slapstick. His own shows tended to reflect the violent New York society in which he lived: Within his sketches, police were popped in ovens, babies were kidnapped and red-hot pokers were jabbed at derrieres. A turkey might come to life in a Thanksgiving scene, or a shaving brush might start to lather up the patron while the barber wasn't looking.

The tendency toward chaotic brutality set him apart from his English counterpart. Grimaldi may have used pratfalls and comic knockabout, but Fox's humor verged on the madly savage.

Late in his life, George Fox became unpredictable onstage with wide mood swings. Often his assistants would have to rush onstage to hurry him back to his dressing room. George Fox had a complete mental breakdown onstage after the first act of "Humpty Dumpty in Every Clime" in 1875; he was taken to a lunatic asylum, where he died two years later.

FRAMING A SHOW

Circus jargon, also in general usage in variety entertainment. Framing a show encompasses all of the planning and execution of building an act, including props and wardrobe, up to the point of rehearsal and performance. This does not include office and advance work, but only the look and physical layout of the grounds and show.

FRANCONI & ELDRED

See ELDRED, GILBERT N.; G.N. ELDRED'S GREAT ROTUNDA SOUTHERN CIRCUS AND MENAGERIE.

FRANCONI FAMILY

Natives of France, the Franconi family were already veteran circus performers when Philip ASTLEY visited their country with his troupe. The Franconis immediately adopted Astley's unique style of riding in their show.

Through experimentation, the Franconis perfected the dimensions of the circus ring, discovering the best possible diameter for their purposes. Soon they established the Franconi Hippodrome, the first open-air arena in France.

Of major importance, the Franconi family is credited with creating the SPEC, or opening parade and spectacular, that begins the circus performance.

FRANK A. ROBBINS CIRCUS

Frank A. Robbins's mentor was Adam FOREPAUGH. Robbins ran a railroad circus for a decade, beginning in 1881, but then the show failed. Robbins eventually recovered his losses and reopened the Frank A. Robbins Circus for another decade, 1905–15.

FRANK JAMES & COLE YOUNGER HISTORIC WILD WEST

The Buckskin Bill Wild West show traveled under this name for the 1903 season when two notorious outlaws, Frank James and Cole Younger, toured as part of the company.

FRANK KETROW SHOWS

From about 1906 until the 1940s, Frank Ketrow operated a long series of small shows under his own name, Kay and other titles.

FRANZEN BROTHERS CIRCUS

Opening on June 6, 1974, the Franzen Brothers Circus is owned and operated by Wayne Franzen (1947–   ). Originally a high school teacher and circus fan, Franzen enlisted his brother, Neil, and started a small show. Neil left after only three months on the road.

The first season the circus toured under a 40-by-60 foot tent, transported from town to town on a SPOOL WAGON made from a converted potato truck. The show included a "liberty goat" act (see LIBERTY HORSES) and a horse named "Tonto."

Fifteen years later the single-ring circus was touring under a TWO-CENTER POLE, BALE RING Scola vinyl top. Although the tent holds 1,000 when traditionally seated, Franzen often sets up the audience on only one side of the tent. WINTER QUARTERS are now in Florida with a northern office in Wapakoneta, Ohio. Thirteen trucks carry the Franzen Brothers Circus throughout the East and the Midwest.

As well as being the owner/manager, Wayne Franzen is also one of the main performers in the show. He opens the show with a six-tiger, two-lion caged CAT act, then later performs with Tonto and with his ELEPHANT. Franzen performs aerial LADDERS, but he is most recognized for his work with animals. Raised on a Wisconsin dairy farm, he likes to work with each animal individually before building the routines, believing the beasts work better after having been given personal attention.

FREAKS　The exhibition of freaks has always been a fascinating, if grotesque, part of the circus SIDE-SHOW tradition. Psychologists have discussed for decades the reasons people would want to view a "human oddity" such as a bearded lady or a midget. Some feel it is mankind's natural curiosity to want to experience the unique, the different or the unknown. Others theorize that spectators enjoy an unspoken sense of superiority over the bizarre humans on display.

The first recorded freak exhibited in America was a dwarf, Emma Leach. She could be seen in Boston in 1771 for one shilling a peek. Like animals before the introduction of the traveling MENAGERIE, a single freak would also be shown at a tavern or roadside inn. Soon several freaks banded together to form touring museums.

It was P.T. BARNUM, however, who popularized the display of freaks in large quantities at his AMERICAN MUSEUM in New York City. Among the attractions he offered were giants, fat ladies and SIAMESE TWINS.

It was in the sideshow tent on the circus MIDWAY, adjacent to the BIG TOP, that the exhibition of freaks really had its heyday. A poster heralding the side-show of the BARNUM & BAILEY CIRCUS as it toured England in 1898, for example, advertised 30 freaks, including: the Tatooed [sic] People, The Bearded Lady, What Is She?, The Human Skye Terrier, the Moss-Haired Girl, the Sword Swallower, The Double-Bodied Wonder, the Living Skeleton, the Egyptian Giant, the Armless Girl, the India Rubber Man, the Great Expansionist, the Human Pin Cushion and the Georgia Magnet.

This small list points out two very different types of freaks. The first is the congenital freak, one who was "born that way." The Egyptian Giant and Living Skeleton obviously fell in this category. At the turn of the century, people with deformed bodies, unusual growths or physical abnormalities may have been shunned in regular society, and so formed their own groups on the road. Their only employment opportunity may have been exhibiting themselves.

The other type of freak is what Penn Gillette (of the magical duo Penn & Teller) calls the "self-made freak," such as a sword swallower or tattooed person. "I find the self-made freaks the most fascinating," says Gillette, "because these people *chose* to learn these skills, or chose to mutilate their bodies, just to go on tour."

Bearded Ladies

Hirsute persons were always popular "anatomical wonders." Madame Josephine CLOFULLIA, a bearded lady who appeared at the American Museum, was taken to court when it was charged that she was not really a woman. She had a son, however—dubbed the Infant Esau—who was already growing a beard and body hair by the age of two. Jo Jo, the Dog-Faced Boy, was born Theodore Peteroff in Russia. First exhibited in the United States in 1885, he was sometimes billed as the Human Skye Terrier. Having long, soft hair on his cheeks, face and forehead, his face looked almost exactly like a canine Skye terrier.

The Seven Southerland Sisters were the daughters of a farmer from Lockport, New York. Essentially vaudeville performers who sang and played musical instruments, their floor-length hair was their "hook" or "gimmick." An early example of product endorsement, they earned a fortune by lending their name to a hair tonic. Grace, the last of the Southerland Sisters, died on January 19, 1946.

Krao, the Siamese Missing Link, had depressed cheekbones and no bones at all in her nose; and she was totally covered by hair. Despite her stage name, she was of normal intelligence and toured widely as an adult. Moung Phoset and his mother Mah Phoon, who traveled the States in the 1880s, were also covered from head to foot in wavy hair.

Midgets and Dwarfs

Whereas midgets are perfectly formed, only very tiny, dwarfs are achondroplastic (imperfectly proportioned), usually with a head, hands and feet that look too large for the rest of the body.

The smallest adult midget ever displayed was Lucia Zarate, who weighed five pounds and grew to only 20 inches. She had a 14-inch waist, an eight-inch arm and a two-and-a-half-inch forearm. Born in San Carlos, Mexico in 1864, she began to tour in the United States in 1876. Intelligent and outgoing, she died of exposure when the train in which she was traveling was caught in a blizzard in Truckee, California.

The most famous midget in the history of the American circus, of course, was Charles S. Stratton, whom Barnum renamed TOM THUMB. First exhibited in the American Museum, then sent out on a world tour, Tom Thumb was only 25 inches tall. Tom Thumb was so popular that he transcended the usual scorn accorded many midgets: He was never regulated to sideshow attraction status, nor was the word "freak" ever associated with his name. Other midgets who worked for Barnum included Lavinia WARREN, "Commodore" NUTT and Admiral Dot.

In the 1970s, Irvin FELD attempted to recapture the Tom Thumb mania when he hired MICHU, advertised as the smallest man alive, to tour as a star attraction on the RINGLING BROS. AND BARNUM & BAILEY CIRCUS.

Giants

Giants have always been crowd pleasers. Often giants were merely exceptionally tall people for their era, and their height seemed exaggerated by the cut of their clothes or their exhibition on a raised platform.

Indeed, giants exhibited by circuses and sideshows often have a clause in their contracts that they are not to be measured. Consequently, giants are almost invariably advertised as being taller than their actual heights.

Anna Hanen Swan (1846–1888), from Nova Scotia, was a seven-foot-5½-inch-tall giantess who was exhibited at Barnum's American Museum. On June 17, 1871, in London, she married Martin Bates (1845–1919), the seven-foot-2½-inch Kentucky Giant, also a Barnum attraction, making them the tallest couple ever married. They had a baby, born 30 inches long and 24 pounds, but it died when only a few days old. Swan survived both Museum fires, and she also appeared as Lady Macbeth on the New York legitimate stage. They retired and moved to their farm in Ohio in 1874. They built a "jumbo" house for themselves: The rooms had 14-foot ceilings, the doors were nine feet high, and all furniture was specially crafted. Their carriage had to be drawn by a pair of Clydesdale horses.

George Augur (1883–1922) was one of the most famous giants at the turn of the century. He stood just under eight feet and weighed 360 pounds; clothed, with high-heeled boots and a plumed hat, he looked to be over nine feet tall. Possibly the tallest giant on tour, he was also the most talented. He wrote and starred in his own vaudeville skit, "Jack the Giant Killer." Born in Cardiff, Wales, he signed with Barnum & Bailey in London. In 1902, he returned with the show to the United States where he spent the remainder of his life. For many years he was the sideshow's star attraction, billed as "Positively the Tallest Man on Earth." Augur died of acute indigestion on November 30, 1922 in New York City.

Some giants found a home in CLOWN ALLEY, where they used their extreme height for comic effect. One such clown is Buck Nolan, a popular JOEY on tour with such shows as the CLYDE BEATTY-COLE BROS. CIRCUS and on the ADVANCE for such shows as CARSON & BARNES CIRCUS.

One nonhuman giant also has a footnote in circus history. Purported to be a fossilized man, the CARDIFF GIANT was actually a granite hoax, unearthed in upstate New York in 1869 and displayed throughout the state, attracting the attention of such showmen as P.T. Barnum.

Other Large Freaks

Obesity was also displayed in the museums and sideshow tents. Although this human oddity has been shown to be caused by hormonal imbalances, not by over-eating, the condition has always fascinated the public. Vantile Mack was billed as "the Giant Baby! Weighs 257 pounds! 7 years old, measures 38 inches around the leg!!" Miss Jane Campbell, the "Connecticut Giantess," was one of the fattest women, weighing 628 pounds by the time she was 18. Carrie Akers of Virginia had the double attraction being both a fat lady and a dwarf. She was 35 inches tall, but weighed almost 300 pounds. All three were exhibited by Barnum in the American Museum, as were many others. In fact, when Barnum's second American Museum burned to the ground in 1868, Johnny Denham, a fireman, became a hero by carrying a 400-pound fat lady out of the blazing building.

Akin to the fat people were those freaks that had one or more enlarged extremity. In 1892 the Barnum & Bailey Circus was touring "the Big-Toed, Big-Fingered Boy." Over the years, many sideshows toured an "Elephant Boy," usually having overgrown legs. Perhaps victims of the little-known and less-understood disease commonly known as elephantiasis, these human wonders included Miss Fanny Mills, a beautiful blonde who, in 1885, wore size-30 shoes and was billed as having "the Biggest Feet on Earth."

Unique Deformities

Having *extra* limbs was an entirely different story, however. Francesco A. Lentini was born in Sicily in 1889 with an extra leg growing out of his hip. He actually used this third leg for walking up until the age of six. After that, his other legs outgrew it by two inches, so it merely dangled. The third leg could still be moved, however; and it retained enough strength to kick a football as part of Lentini's act. The extra leg accounted for about 15 pounds of Lentini's 165-pound weight, and he had to eat about 15 percent more food. Lentini married and fathered two boys and a girl. Among the many shows with which he traveled were BUFFALO BILL'S WILD WEST, the WALTER L. MAIN CIRCUS and The BIG ONE.

Myrtle Corbin had four legs, two of normal size and two smaller ones between them. According to an unauthenticated 1882 pamphlet, issued when she was first displayed, Corbin also had two sets of genitalia.

Along with freaks with body extrusions, such as Lentini and Corbin, the most peculiar and rare

abnormality exhibited were connected twins. As a result, they always earned the highest salaries, sometimes up to $1,000 per week.

The popularity of CHANG AND ENG, identical twin brothers inseparably joined at the chest, gave rise to a new term in the English language: SIAMESE TWINS. (They were, in fact, Chinese but had been born in Siam.) Millie and Christine were a black duo who sang (one was a soprano, the other a contralto), danced and played guitars. In the 1880s they were earning $600 per week. Born in 1851 as slaves in North Carolina, they were named the "Two-Headed Girl" by Barnum. They were actually joined at the back, sharing one set of intestines. They also shared a central nervous system, so that both girls felt the touch of any limb. Christine, the stronger of the two, could lift Millie. The girls were received by Queen Victoria in England, toured Europe twice and traveled the United States with the Barnum & Bailey Circus.

The Toccis Twins were born in Turin, Italy in 1875. They had normal parents and nine regular brothers and sisters. The twins were as close to a two-headed man as had ever been produced. Advertised as "the Greatest Human Phenomenon Ever Seen Alive," the twins had one pair of legs and one stomach; but above the waist they split, with two chest bones, four arms and two heads. One could eat enough for both, and one could sleep while the other was awake. Each brain controlled one leg, so they had difficulty walking. Manually they were ambidextrous. The Toccis Twins earned $1,000 per week while touring the United States.

Biologically, Siamese twins are caused by incomplete or arrested cell division of a fertilized egg, resulting in two linked fetuses rather than the development of separate identical twins in the womb. A more grotesque malformation occurs when the second twin never fully develops, but a portion of a body, a human-shape stump, is attached to the living individual after birth.

Such was the case of Jean and "Jacques" Libbera. Jean Libbera was born in Rome in 1884 and toured with the Barnum & Bailey show in 1907. Although his upper torso was normally developed, Liberra had a grotesque extrusion growing out of his stomach. The growth, whom Jean named Jacques, had arms, legs, hands and feet, both with growing nails, and a strong bone structure. The undeveloped stub of a head was buried within Jean's normal body. Jean could feel the touch of the extended flesh, and they shared blood circulation. Despite the aberration, Libbera married and fathered four normal children.

"Zip, What Is It?" was a cone-headed black man sporting a single tuft of hair. He was a happy imbecile with a continual grin who enjoyed being exhibited and meeting people. Born William H. Jackson in New Jersey in 1842, Zip was first displayed in 1859. He toured constantly for the next 67 years, longer than any other circus freak. It is said he believed he owned whatever circus he was on and had hired everyone WITH IT.

Plutano and Waino, "The Wild Men of Borneo" (the first to whom the phrase was applied), were not really "freaks" in the usual sense of the word, but they were exhibited as such. According to a Barnum circular, they were captured after a fierce struggle by sailors whose ship had anchored in Borneo looking for water. They were supposedly a new human species that had no oral language and spoke only in howls and gibberish. They were said to be ferocious enough to overpower tigers.

In fact, the " Wild Men" were Hiram W. (1825–1905) and Barney Davis (1827–1912), born on Long Island and in England respectively. Also of subnormal intelligence, the brothers traveled with their guardian, Hanaford A. Warner of Waltham, Massachusetts.

Such "wild human specimens" as "Krao, The Siamese Missing Link," "Zip, What Is It?" and "the Wild Men of Borneo" were always popular in sideshows. A new attraction around 1918 was almost contrived when a representative from the RINGLING BROS. AND BARNUM & BAILEY CIRCUS asked Louis "Pretty" Amberg (1898–1935) whether he would be interested in touring in the Ringling sideshow billed as "the Missing Link." Amberg had grown up in the Brownsville section of Brooklyn, New York; by the age of 20 he had a reputation for being not only mean but also the ugliest man on earth.

It is just as well that Amberg refused. Unknown to the sideshow agent from The Big One, Amberg was involved with Murder, Inc.; he was so ruthless that even other vicious murderers stayed clear of him. The Ringling agent was lucky that Amberg

didn't kill him at the time; but, in fact, the murderer used to like to brag about the job offer.

Self-Made Freaks
Most common were the self-made freaks. No sideshow was complete without the fire-eater, the sword swallower and the SNAKE CHARMER.

Worthy of special mention are those who indulge in self-mutilation, such as the tattooed man. Captain Georg Constantine (also seen as John Constantinos), a Greek Albanian displayed by Barnum in the 1870s, probably had more tattoos than any other person who ever lived to that time. Less than a quarter inch of his flesh was without a tattoo. Even his eyelids, genitals, the insides of his ears, his scalp and the skin between his fingers and toes were covered. He actually sported 388 symmetrical designs.

Constantine claimed to have been held captive in Burma for three months, during which time he received the tattoos by force. Experts concurred that the symbols looked Burmese, but thought it more likely that the captain paid a master artist to do the work with the intent of going on exhibition.

Most freaks never felt themselves to be outcasts, surely not monsters. Some considered themselves quite "special" or "touched by God." In the latter 20th century, however, public sympathies largely turned against the exhibition of the human eccentricities, and laws were passed in many states barring the display of humans. At the same time, many circuses were moving into arenas or, at the very least, abandoning their sideshows due to escalating costs. Although some indoor shows continued to carry a sideshow for a few years, by the time John Ringling NORTH made his historic 1956 announcement that the days of the tented circus were over, the heyday of the "freak show" was already a part of the circus's past.

FRONT DOOR Circus jargon for the entrance to the BIG TOP, usually located at the MARQUEE. When the Big Top is ready for the show and it is time for the front door to be opened, the call of DOORS! is given across the circus LOT.

FRONT YARD Circus jargon for the public area of the circus LOT located in front of the BIG TOP. Also known as the MIDWAY, the front yard is a wide

"To the Entrance"—Carson & Barnes's front yard in 1991. (Photo by Tom Ogden)

alleyway, bordered along on each side by PIT SHOWS, the SIDESHOW, concession TENTS and the wagons of the BUTCHERS. Typically, the front yard is bounded at one end by the ticket and office wagon—known as the RED WAGON due to its traditional color—and by the MARQUEE (or FRONT DOOR) entrance to the Big Top at the other end.

FUNAMBULIST
The technical term for a rope walker, the word "funambulist" is used equally to mean a tightrope walker, wire walker or slack wire walker. The word comes from the Latin *funis* (rope) and *ambulare* (to walk).

Among the great funambulists in circus history were BLONDIN, Philippe PETIT and Karl WALLENDA.

(See also WIRE WALKING.)

FUNNY ROPES
Circus jargon for extra ropes, usually added at angles to existing ropes, to give extra strength, stability and spread to a canvas top.

G

GAINESVILLE COMMUNITY CIRCUS   An annual event held by the residents of Gainesville, Texas, the Gainesville Community Circus began during the Depression years as a project to pay off debts incurred by the town's Little Theater.

This local circus has modern counterparts. Community circuses are sponsored each year in small towns all across the United States, including BARABOO, WISCONSIN; PERU, INDIANA; SARASOTA, FLORIDA (the SAILOR CIRCUS); and Wenatchee, Washington (the WENATCHEE YOUTH CIRCUS).

GALOP   Circus jargon for a fast tempo circus tune, usually used for entrances and exits. Among the more famous galops is "Fire Jump" galop, composed by Merle EVANS, longtime bandleader with the RINGLING BROS. AND BARNUM & BAILEY CIRCUS.

GAONA, TITO (1947–   )   Star of the sensational FLYING GAONAS, Tito Gaona is respected as one of the—if not *the*—greatest flyers and best all-around athletes currently working in the American circus.

At first a member of his family's trampoline act Gaona began trapeze work at the age of 15. In 1964 Tito Gaona achieved his first TRIPLE SOMERSAULT, becoming the first to accomplish the trick since Antoinette CONCELLO's final performances in 1943. By 1990 he had performed the triple somersault an estimated 13,000 times.

Gaona has gone on to create many spectacular stunts, including the double double (a double somersault with a double twist)—the most difficult in

his repertoire. On occasion he performs the triple blindfolded. "I usually do my most difficult tricks for my own satisfaction," he admits, "since most audiences don't understand what I'm doing."

Perhaps his flashiest trick is occasionally performed at the end of the act when he bounces into the net and back up into the air, landing in a sitting position in the catcher's swing. In practice sessions, Gaona is said to have accomplished the QUADRUPLE SOMERSAULT as well, but no documentation exists.

GARDEN BROS. CIRCUS   Operated in Canada with occasional forays into the United States, the Garden Bros. Circus is owned by William and Ian Garden. Founded by their father, the show usually tours as an indoor unit, but since 1957 it has often trouped under canvas as well.

GARGANTUA (1929?–1949)   A monster GORILLA for many years with the RINGLING BROS. AND BARNUM & BAILEY CIRCUS, Gargantua the Great was so terrifying because of his enormous size, his violent nature and the permanent snarl on his lips.

Gargantua was brought to the United States as a baby by Captain Arthur Phillips on his ship, the *West Key Bar*. He had been bought as a month-old orphan from a missionary couple in Africa for $400. Upon their arrival in Boston, a sailor on the vessel was fired by Phillips; after a few drinks, the sailor decided to seek revenge against the captain.

Knowing the value of the ape, the sailor sneaked on board and shot a fire extinguisher full of nitric acid into the gorilla's face. The acid burned the ape's hair, skin and muscles of the head and chest. The small, flat nostrils had almost been completely burned off, and a permanent scar drew up the left side of his mouth, exposing some teeth and curling the lips into a vicious sneer. The blatant act of cruelty turned the ape into a lifelong man-hater.

Captain Phillips sold the injured ape along with six or seven sick chimpanzees to Mrs. William Lintz of Brooklyn, New York for approximately $2,000. Born Gertrude Davies in England, Mrs. Lintz was an animal lover who had started to show St. Bernards in 1909. Her love of gorillas started in 1915 when she saw an ailing baby gorilla at the Ringling show in MADISON SQUARE GARDEN. By the time Phillips offered her the injured gorilla, Mrs. Lintz owned several primates, including one other young gorilla named Massa.

She slowly nursed the new baby back to health, naming him Buddha; but he was simply called Buddy during his six years in the Lintz household. At the time of his arrival, he was approximately 18 months old and weighed 22 pounds. Lintz oiled and massaged his skin and gave him the best in food and exercise to help him build his strength. In all of this work, she was helped by two able assistants, Tony Desimone and Richard Kroener (1890–1942). Kroener was an ex-butcher boy who became an expert in the kennel business. He loved animals and collected tropical fish and butterflies, grew prize-winning dahlias and was a bird watcher.

Mrs. Lintz often gathered her various animals into a small MENAGERIE and took them to shows, fairs and exhibitions, including the Chicago Century of Progress Exposition and Atlantic City's Steel Pier. In the fall of 1936 she had her animals, including Buddy, on display at the North Miami Zoo, under the direction of Guarling F. Sirman.

Lintz hired a drifter to help out around her cages, but when he didn't work out she fired him. In a repeat of the incident aboard the *West Key Bar,* the vagabond slipped back into the zoo and fed Buddy a bottle of chocolate syrup laced with disinfectant. The acid severely burned Buddy's stomach lining and intestines, and doctors could only give him a soft dissolved powder to try to ease the pain. Buddy lost 80 pounds, and it took five long weeks for Mrs. Lintz to nurse him back to health.

One night during a rainstorm, the 400-pound Buddy escaped from his basement cage and walked upstairs into Mrs. Lintz's bedroom. She awoke to a clap of thunder, only to find Buddy in bed beside her. Though she managed to lure the ape back down to his cage, she decided it was time to find Buddy a new home.

Lintz called John Ringling NORTH, whom she knew, and offered the gorilla along with two fairly common CHIMPANZEES for $10,000. At the time there were less than a dozen gorillas in captivity in the United States, and traveling shows had real difficulty in keeping them alive on the road. John and his brother, Henry Ringling North, agreed to buy the creature, accepting several of Mrs. Lintz's conditions of sale. Buddy had to be housed in a cage of her own design, and Richard (Dick) Kroener had to be hired to stay on with the ape as his keeper.

Mrs. Lintz wrote in her autobiography, *Animals Are My Hobby,* that

> *Dick was not only willing to go with Buddha, and take care of him as long as he lived, but he would have been wretched at any idea of separation. The two had one of the strangest relations that can be imagined. Though Buddy had cultivated his childish grudge against Dick until it became frozen into an attitude of waiting for the chance to kill him, he nevertheless trusted Dick implicitly.*

Gladwyn Hill, New York bureau chief of the Associated Press, got wind of the story; but the Norths asked him to sit on the story while they shipped the gorilla south. With a promise that he would be allowed to break the story when it was time, Hill agreed.

What the Norths wanted was time for their press agent, Roland BUTLER, to come up with a grand publicity campaign to present their newest sensation to the public. As the boxed ape was being sent incognito (and illegally) in the package car of a standard passenger train, Seaboard's *Orange Blossom Special,* Henry Ringling North was insisting the ape's name be changed.

Henry's nickname had always been "Buddy," and he certainly didn't want two Buddys—especially when one of them was a monstrous gorilla—on the grounds. The Yale-educated North suggested Gargantua, the name of the hero of *Gargantua and Pantagruel,* a 1534 epic poem by François Rabelais. In the ode,

Gargantua was a gigantic king known for his great physical prowess. On Sunday, December 12, 1937, Gargantua the Great arrived, shrouded in secrecy, in SARASOTA, FLORIDA.

Gargantua became increasingly unapproachable, even by Kroener, his longtime trainer. When he first arrived at the Ringling WINTER QUARTERS, Gargantua was housed in a deer cage, with bars eight to ten inches apart. Kroener once strayed too close to the bars, and the gorilla caught hold of him. Before Kroener beat him off with a metal rod, Gargantua had almost killed him.

Gargantua also grabbed John Ringling North once, but the circus magnate managed to struggle out of the sleeves of his leather jacket to get free. He did take a large bite out of North's arm, and the promotion-conscious Roland Butler sent out a press release saying North had been given "the most massive anti-tetanus shot ever administered to a human being."

To insure the spectators' safety, as well as for climate control and the health of the ape, Gargantua traveled on the road in a cage surrounded by two walls of glass with air between them; the living space was air-conditioned to a constant 78 degrees and 50% humidity. The ends were made of a ⅜-inch steel plate, and the cage had an oak floor with a main room measuring 20 feet by 7 feet, with a 6-foot sleeping area. The unique cage, designed by Mrs. Lintz, was built by Lemuel Bulware of the Carrier Corporation in Syracuse, New York.

A massive tire was placed in the cage by Butler because he sensed that Gargantua's bending it into a pretzel and figure eight would create dramatic photographs. The tire was left in the cage, suspended by a heavy chain; it became Gargantua's favorite plaything.

Butler sent out reams of copy and photos on the ape: "Most fiendishly ferocious brute that breathes!" "The world's most terrifying living creature!" and "Mightiest monster ever captured by man!" Gargantua's face appeared on posters, and the public lined up as never before to see the "Largest gorilla ever exhibited alive!" In his book *Center Ring*, Robert Taylor wrote that Gargantua was "as popular as Crosby and as temperamental as Garbo."

Despite a strike by the unionized ROUSTABOUTS, Gargantua made his debut at the 1938 Madison Square Garden date. He was introduced as part of a new $80,000 SPEC designed by Charles LeMaire and featuring Frank ("Bring 'Em Back Alive") Buck as the Maharajah of Nepal.

When labor difficulties forced the show to CLOSE AHEAD OF PAPER in Scranton, Pennsylvania, North moved many of the Ringling features over to the Al G. Barnes and Sells-Floto Circus, which the Ringling corporation also owned. It was in large part Gargantua's drawing power that enabled the Norths to stay in business, seeing a huge $400,000 profit for the season rather than the $40,000 a week the show was losing at the time of the Scranton strike.

In the winter of 1939 Gargantua was sent to London to appear with the Bertram Mills Circus at the Olympia Theatre. He created a sensation in England and returned to the States in 1940 to scare and amuse crowds throughout the season.

Although Gargantua had lost none of his appeal—in fact, the show folk had affectionately named the monster "Gargy"—John Ringling North was afraid that the attraction needed a new boost. Without mentioning his real publicity intentions, he flew to Havana, Cuba in late 1940 to negotiate the purchase of a 400-pound female gorilla, M'TOTO, from her owner, Mrs. E. Kenneth Hoyt. North never succeeded in purchasing her, but was able to negotiate a permanent lease.

The heavily published arrival of the new ape at Port Everglades in Ft. Lauderdale, Florida occurred in February 1941. By then the media was referring to the ape as Mlle. Toto or M'Toto for short. As soon as M'Toto arrived via train to the Ringling winter quarters, the circus announced a "wedding" between M'Toto and Gargantua, scheduled for February 22, Washington's birthday.

Mrs. Hoyt strongly disapproved of any such union, saying her baby was much too exhausted after the long journey. The day of the "wedding" she went into town to run errands, and Roland Butler quickly moved up the ceremony and assembled the newsmen. The two cages were butted end-to-end, and the panels between them were removed. Gargantua offered a stick of celery and a head of lettuce to M'Toto through the bars, but both gifts were refused. M'Toto sank back to a far corner of her cage and never again showed any interest in Gargantua, and vice versa. The North brothers decided never

Gargantua the Great as he appeared on April 4, 1938 at Madison Square Garden during his premier season with the Ringling Bros. and Barnum & Bailey Circus.
(Author's collection)

to put the gorillas into a cage together to avoid any possible fights or injury to their two prizes.

The outcome, though unexpected, was still less embarrassing than what the Philadelphia Zoo experienced some years before when it attempted to mate their gorilla Bamboo with a new ape, Massa. Newspapers wrote that Massa "coquettishly beat her chest with her strong hairy hands after tossing a few straws into Bamboo's cage." Bamboo rushed Massa in imitation. They tussled seven times over the next two hours, after each rollover moving to their own corners to catch their breath. It wasn't until after the ceremony was apparently consummated that zoo officials discovered that both Bamboo and Massa were males.

While the Gargantua-M'Toto affair was a bust from a news standpoint, it served well for the press

agents throughout the coming seasons. The apes were variously billed on posters and in advertising as "Mr. and Mrs. Gargantua the Great" and the "newly-married gorillas." Posters of the happy couple were used to help sell millions of dollars worth of war bonds during World War II.

Either Kroener (who died of cancer on May 11, 1942) or José Tomas (M'Toto's keeper, who subsequently took over Gargantua's care as well) was with the apes 24 hours a day, and Mrs. Hoyt was usually on the lot. Mrs. Lintz occasionally visited, but the journey was difficult for her. She wrote, "I went to see my Buddy as often as possible. As long as I can go to the back of the cage so that I can reach him through the bars, and hug his grotesque body . . . so long as Buddy knows there is one person who does not consider him a brute beast and killer."

One of the largest and oldest gorillas ever to tour America, Gargantua was advertised as weighing over 550 pounds. His strength was equal to that of dozens of men. On the Ringling show, he lived on a carefully balanced diet of chocolate, milk, water, every conceivable kind of fruit juice, all fruits, all vegetables, cooked liver, cod-liver oil and liver extract.

Gargantua's favorite foods were bananas and Coca-Cola. It was rumored that he was afraid of snakes, no matter how tiny, but his final trainer Tomas denied it. "He no afraid of snakes! He afraid of nothing! He only want to fight." His bedtime habits were also unique: Each night he was given a thick, fuzzy cotton blanket. He would spread this out on the floor and spend up to an hour smoothing out all of the wrinkles. Then he would lie down on it, curl up into a ball and go to sleep. Upon waking up, he would slowly and carefully tear the blanket to shreds.

In his last years, Gargantua visibly aged. Gray hairs filled his black coat, giving him a silver tinge. His eyes became sunken, and he slept or sat most of the day. When he was awake, he continued to entertain the audiences that still flocked to see him. In his last days, he was noticeably ailing, spending most of his day huddled in a corner. He made his final public appearance on the evening of Thursday, November 24, 1949. He died sometime during the night and was discovered at 8 A.M. the next morning, dead in his cage. He had passed away only one day short of the end of the season.

The Associated Press flashed "Gargantua Dead" across the wires—an honor held for only the most momentous stories, such as the death of Roosevelt or the bombing of Pearl Harbor. Within hours, all major services were making the death front-page news around the world. Bill ("Bojangles") Robinson, the famous black dancer, died the same day, as did J.C. Walton, a former governor of Oklahoma and noted Ku Klux Klan foe; but neither received the initial "flash" notice accorded Gargantua.

Despite his seeming docility at the end, Gargantua had still been too ferocious to treat medically. Although he had slowly lost strength, it was impossible to get close enough to him to diagnosis his disease. In fact, J.Y. "Doc" HENDERSON, chief veterinarian with the show, said,

He was his own worst enemy. . . . We would have stayed with him for months if there was anything we could do. . . . Gargantua died because of his distrust and viciousness. His outstanding characteristic prevented his friends from helping him, and eventually killed him. The real tragedy of a gorilla is that his diseases may be curable but the patient himself untreatable.

Gargantua's body was packed in dry ice and shipped to Johns Hopkins Hospital in Baltimore, where an autopsy was performed. The most savage animal ever to travel with a circus died of bilateral lobar pneumonia, complicated by a skin disease, a kidney disorder and poisoning by four impacted and rotting wisdom teeth. Although only 22 years old at the time of his death, half a gorilla's normal life span, this was still old for gorillas in captivity.

The skeleton was donated to the Peabody Museum at Yale University. Henry Ringling North, the Yale man who had named the ape, affectionately added, "Gargantua always was a Yale man."

For the record, Dr. S. Dillon Ripley, curator of vertebrate zoology at the Peabody, stated, "Gargantua was by no means the largest of the 23 gorillas in captivity. That was circus publicity. Nor was he the oldest. He was five feet seven and one-half inches tall, and weighed 312 pounds." He also noted that his foot would have worn a size 12 DDDD shoe and his hand would have taken a size 11 glove.

North attempted to recapture some of the gorilla fever by bringing two young gorillas, billed as "Mademoiselle Toto and Gargantua II," but the pair never captured the public's imagination.

Mrs. Gertrude Davies Lintz moved to a four-acre estate in Ojus, just north of Miami. Her death in a North Miami hospital on Labor Day 1968 was unreported in the press. Her husband, who died a few years later, would not allow the publicity. Marie Hoyt died as a result of an automobile accident in Vienna in 1969.

One of Gargantua's great legacies was his name. In his statement at the gorilla's death, John Ringling North said, "There was only one JUMBO and only one Gargantua." Jumbo the elephant added a new word to the English language. The name Gargantua was actually at least 400 years old; but its application to this modern beast brought it into the vernacular, so that now anything that is mammoth or mighty is said to be "gargantuan."

(See also MONKEYS AND APES.)

GATTI, "MAJOR" JOSEPH (1910–1991)

The founder of Circus Gatti, a popular show that tours primarily the western United States, Matthew Joseph Gatti retired from the air force after 26 years with the rank of major. For four of those years he held a welterweight boxing championship title. Throughout his circus career, Gatti enjoyed being referred to simply as "the Major."

He started as a PHONE PROMOTER for other shows, before beginning his own operation. Gatti died, following a stroke, on October 7, 1991. He was survived by his wife, Doris, and two daughters, Patricia and Carole.

Circus Gatti continues to tour annually with its operation managed on the road by Patricia Gatti and its home offices, located in Orange, California, managed by Carole Gatti.

GAUTIER, AXEL (1942–1993)

A premier animal trainer, Axel Gautier was celebrated as one of the top BULL HANDLERS on the RINGLING BROS. AND BARNUM & BAILEY CIRCUS. From Sweden, he was the head of the Gautier family of ELEPHANT trainers, and his command of the Ringling pachyderms on the Blue Unit was a mainstay attraction from 1959 through 1989. In addition to working with his wife Donna (a former Ringling WEB GIRL), Axel Gautier had two sons, Michael (1965–   ) and Kevin (1970–   ), who joined their father's act in 1976. The Gautiers remained in Florida for two seasons, working with the Ringling elephants. They returned to the road with The BIG ONE in 1992, with the sons leading their own BULLS in the end rings, complementing their father's CENTER RING display.

Axel Gautier was born in Breslau, Germany (later Wrocław, Poland) during World War II, the sixth generation of a circus family that had founded a small show in France after the French Revolution. Axel's father was a noted equestrian trainer, and his sister was part of a DRESSAGE act on the Ringling circus for many years.

Gautier joined The GREATEST SHOW ON EARTH in 1958 as an assistant to Hugo Schmidt, one of the top bull men in the country at the time. After Schmidt retired in 1970, Gautier replaced him on the Blue Unit. Many of the elephants he worked with were part of an entire herd of PUNK pachyderms that had been imported for Schmidt in 1955; the bulls are now over 30 years old.

"When an elephant is six months old," explained Gautier, "I can teach it basic maneuvers like TAIL UP and leg lifts. After the animal matures, it can learn more muscular stunts like leg stands and climbing. . . . But these elephants love the spotlight and music of the circus and are always anxious to perform. . . . Elephants are a lot like people."

Tragically, on the morning of May 5, 1993, Axel Gautier was killed while at the Ringling Elephant Farm in Wiliston, Florida. While videotaping the pachyderms and the compound in preparation for possible future training sessions, one of the bulls knocked him down and stomped him.

GEBEL-WILLIAMS, GUNTHER (1934–)

Born Gunther Gebel in the Silesian village of Schweidnitz in eastern Germany on September 12, 1934, the greatest animal trainer in the modern circus did not come from a circus family. His father, Max Gebel, a theatrical set designer, was forced into Germany's army during World War II and was sent to the Russian front. Captured, the elder Gebel was sent to the labor camps in Siberia.

Meanwhile, Gunther's mother, Elfriede, and older sister fled with the boy to West Germany, trying to escape the escalating war. In 1947, in Cologne, Mrs. Gebel joined Circus Williams as a seamstress. The older sister married and went off on her own. Gunther, then 13, went with his mother.

His mother left the show after two or three weeks, not enjoying the transient nature of the outdoor amusement business; but the 13-year-old boy stayed on. According to Gunther, "She signed a five-year contract [for me] with the Circus Williams and received a few dollars for me. At the end of that time, she didn't pick me up. At first, she wouldn't even answer my letters. Maybe after all she had been through, she wanted to start a new life."

Naturally inquisitive, Gunther learned every aspect of Circus Williams. The owner/director, Herr Harry Williams, was already training his daughter, Jeannette, to become a featured equestrienne. He took Gunther under his wing and began to teach him horsemanship as well.

One evening when Herr Williams was too sick to enter the ring, Gunther was asked to work the act alone. He displayed such skill and self-confidence that Williams expanded his training to the herd of ELEPHANTS. The pachyderms quickly became Gebel's favorite animals, partly because of their intelligence. "Elephants can be taught to listen, to do what you tell them," he once said. "I don't think it's necessary to push them or shove them around. All you have to do is work with them until they understand what's expected. Then you just remind them of their act and they do it." He didn't get to work his own herd of BULLS, though, for several years.

In 1951 Circus Williams traveled to England. While there, Harry Williams was mortally injured in the circus's staged chariot race. His wife, Carola, closed the show for a year, preparing to take over the business aspect of the circus. Gunther, meanwhile, worked for the Circus Althoff in Brussels, where once again he had an opportunity to work closely with elephants. It was upon his return to Circus Williams in 1953 that Gunther Gebel put together his own bull act.

Carola Williams asked Gunther—for all practical purposes her adopted son—to take over the technical side of the show. In 1956 the adoption was made official when the young man—at Carola's request—took the family name and became Gunther Gebel-Williams.

In 1960 he married Jeanette Williams; but by that time their relationship was actually more like that of a brother and sister. A two-year separation was followed by an amicable divorce in 1968. They have remained friends; at one point, Jeanette and Gunther's second wife (Sigrid) appeared simultaneously in opposite rings with The BIG ONE.

Gebel-Williams had become a major name among trainers and circus folk in Europe; and, in 1964, he won the Ernest Renke-Plaskett Award, a top European circus honor, for his horsemanship. He won this award an unprecedented two more times, the second time for his work with elephants and the third time as an all-around circus performer. At the same time, he was developing his talents with the big CATS, having purchased his first tiger for $1,000 in 1960.

In 1968 Gebel-Williams married a high-fashion model named Sigrid Neubauer, whom he had spotted in the audience. "I talk to many girls in the audience," he said at the time, "but I don't marry them." She brought a four-year old daughter, Tina, to the relationship from a previous marriage.

In February 1968 Irvin FELD made the startling announcement that he would be opening a second unit of the GREATEST SHOW ON EARTH the following season. He went to Europe to scout for new acts, and in March he first set eyes on Gunther Gebel-Williams, performing at the Circus Williams in Salerno, Italy.

John Ringling NORTH had reportedly also once attempted to bring Gebel-Williams to the United States, but at the time the European star did not want to leave the Continent. Feld, in a move reminiscent of John Ringling's acquisition of the AMERICAN CIRCUS CORPORATION, "bought" Circus Williams for $2 million.

In actual fact, Irvin Feld took a five-year lease on much of the Circus Williams property and many of its star performers, including Gunther, Sigrid (whom Gunther had trained as a bareback rider), Tina, Jeanette Williams, 13 elephants, 11 Bengal-Siberian tigers, 18 White Lippiazan stallions, four DRESSAGE horses and two ponies. Feld brought them to the States, along with one of Gebel-Williams's cousin's, Henri Schroer—who performed a macaw, cockatoo and pigeon act, Mrs. Ellen Bensalem and Papa Said (as an assistant to Gebel-Williams), plus other staff for a total company of 30 people.

Mrs. Williams retained the WINTER QUARTERS in Cologne, Germany and continued to do business with the remaining circus equipment and personnel in Europe. Despite his leaving for the United States and a new life, Gebel-Williams remained very close to his foster mother up until her death at age 84 in 1987. But his devotion to the show, and especially

his animals, was a higher priority. In fact, although Gebel-Williams's biological mother visited him in America several times, it was not until 1986—18 years after he had come to the States—that he felt he could leave his animals long enough to visit her back in Germany. And even then it was only because his own son was old enough to care for his charges.

With a personal five-year contract from Irvin Feld secured, Gunther Gebel-Williams made his debut appearance with THE RINGLING BROS. AND BARNUM & BAILEY CIRCUS. in their Venice, Florida pre-New York tryout as part of their 99th Edition.

In 1970 Feld offered Mrs. Williams an additional five-year contract on the lease of equipment; and, in the seventh year of the contract (1974), he negotiated to purchase of all of the acts, animals and equipment. By that time, the leopard act alone had grown to 18 cats.

Meanwhile, Gebel-Williams reportedly signed a personal ten-year contract for his services, beginning the first season at $1,000 a week. Jeanette Williams left the Ringling show in 1980.

Gebel-Williams quickly established himself as the greatest all-around animal trainer in circus history. He was equally at ease, and skilled, in the BIG CAGE with exotic cats, working with pachyderms (his favorites) or directing LIBERTY HORSES. He had even been trained as an ACROBAT, somersaulting backward from a TEETERBOARD onto the back of an elephant. (Another bull stepped on the other side of the teeterboard!) His sense of circus flair in his routines was astounding: standing astride a tiger perched on the back of an elephant; mixing horses, cats and elephants in the same act; rolling on the sawdust among 15 leopards, three panthers and two pumas; and his trademark pose of parading the big cage with a leopard draped around his neck and over his shoulders.

Gunther Gebel-Williams trained in the style of Karl HÄGENBACH, the great German animal dealer. His methods emphasized patience and reward rather than punishment to coax the desired responses from the animals.

Gebel-Williams was once asked why he gave all his commands to the animals in German. He is reputed to have answered, "Why, that's the only language the cats understand."

Gebel-Williams actually talked to his animals equally in German and English. He carried a trainer's whip when working with the cats. Rather than a gun, his holster held small chunks of meat for rewards. But, like all great trainers before him, Gebel-Williams emphasized, "No matter how long you work with an animal, how well you think you know him, there's always a chance that, one day, when you least expect it, he may revert to his natural instincts, and turn on you. A wild animal trainer who puts total trust in his animals is very foolish, very foolish." Although he has never been seriously mauled, Gebel-Williams's body is covered with over 500 scars.

Gunther adopted Tina in 1970; that same year he and Sigrid had a son, Mark Oliver, who was born in Houston, Texas. In 1973 Gebel-Williams won the "Outstanding Circus Performer of the Year" award from AGVA, the American Guild of Variety Artists. Gunther continued to include his family in his acts. Sigrid was already working a ring of horses herself in 1977 when Tina made her debut with the Ringling Bros. and Barnum & Bailey Circus, commanding three rings of liberty horses.

On December 21, 1979 Gunther Gebel-Williams became a citizen of the United States in a ceremony at the federal courthouse in Tampa, Florida. He has since donated his ELEPHANT HOOK, horse whip and elephant harness to the Smithsonian Institution as part of its History of American Entertainment Collection.

In 1980 Gunther introduced his son "Buffy," as he was nicknamed, as the world's first GIRAFFE jockey. Buffy rode in the SPEC for two years before making his own official ring debut in 1983, as Mark Oliver Gebel, with a trained goat act.

In 1989 Gunther Gebel-Williams began his farewell tour as part of the 119th Edition of the Ringling Bros. and Barnum & Bailey Circus. At the November 18, 1990 show at 5:30 P.M. in Pittsburgh, Pennsylvania, he made his final scheduled performance with the show for a total of 11,697 with The Big One.

Gunther Gebel-Williams has not completely retired from the circus, however. He has remained with the Ringling organization as vice president in charge of animal care. He still travels with the Red Unit and proudly watches as his son and daughter take full command of the rings in their respective acts. In March 1991 his autobiography, *Untamed: The Gunther Gebel-Williams Story,* was published by William Morrow.

GENERALLY USEFUL   A traditional phrase in all circus contracts, everyone in the company—crew and performers alike—are expected to be "generally useful" on the circus LOT. While the phrase was designed primarily for the workingmen's contracts to cover chores not specified in their main job descriptions, the expression also suggests to the entire cast and crew that in times of emergency or need, everyone associated with the show is expected to pitch in and help.

GENNIE   Circus jargon for the generator truck. Every MUD SHOW carries its own source for electricity, usually several diesel-run generators housed in a truck unit. The electrical department is kept busy all day, since the gennie is the first unit operational in the morning and the last piece of show equipment turned off at night. During the day, lines must be connected to each tent, show vehicle and living quarters that requires electricity. On some shows the gennie is run for a few hours even after TEAR DOWN as a courtesy to the performers and crew, to allow some time for rest and relaxation after the show.

GENTRY BROS. CIRCUS   In 1885 the Gentry Bros. Circus had its start when two farm boys in Bloomington, Indiana began giving afternoon performances featuring 20 dogs. Soon the circus was giving two shows daily; within four years one of the boys, Prof. H.B. Gentry, had increased his RING STOCK by eight ponies, making the Gentry Bros. Circus the first true DOG AND PONY SHOW. In 1891 the circus moved under canvas and toured on two railroad cars.

Gentry's brothers joined his operation, and in 1892 a second unit was started. They bought out a rival show that also had two units and continued to tour them separately; so there were, remarkably, four shows on the road, each bearing the Gentry Bros. Famous Shows name, traveling on 72 railcars. At one point, two of the units were "twins," carrying identical acts and matching BANDWAGONS, ticket wagons and CALLIOPES made by Sullivan & Eagles of PERU, INDIANA. All of the shows were successful, clean, family entertainments—SUNDAY SCHOOL SHOWS that catered to women and children with an emphasis on, literally, dog and pony acts rather than wild animals.

The number of units began to decline by 1905. In 1907 one of the shows was leased to the owner of Dan Patch, a famous harness horse of the era. From 1916 through the 1922 season the circus was operated by J. Ben Austin and J.D. Newman. Sold to a carnival owner in 1923, the show toured as Gentry Bros. & James Patterson Circus for two years. From 1926 until its failure following the 1929 Stock Market Crash, the King brothers, Floyd and Howard, owned and operated the Gentry title. Sam B. Dill used the name on an unauthorized motorized show in 1930.

In a last hurrah, the original Gentry brothers operated the show in its final years, 1931 through 1934.

(See also KING BROS. SHOWS.)

GEORGE F. BAILEY CIRCUS

See AARON TURNER CIRCUS; BAILEY, GEORGE F.; FLATFOOTS; TURNER, AARON.

GEORGE W. HALL SHOWS

Rather than operating one show, "Popcorn" George Hall ran a series of small circuses in and around Wisconsin, beginning in the 1880s. The shows were still continuing 40 years later when his grandchildren became managers in the 1930s.

GIANTS

See AMERICAN MUSEUM; FREAKS; GOSHEN AND BIHIN.

GIBSONTON, FLORIDA

Second only to SARASOTA, FLORIDA as a home to carnival and circus veterans, Gibsonton is fondly referred to as "Gibtown" by show folk. Originally settled primarily by carnival people, or "carnies," and many FREAKS, circus families began to spill over into Gibtown from the greater Sarasota area.

The two communities share so many friends and common experiences on tour that off the road they welcome each other's company. The town sports its own Showman's Club, where those who are and were WITH IT can sit around and cut up JACKPOTS day and night. Gibtown also sponsors an annual festival, held each January shortly after the close of the Sarasota International Circus Festival and Parade.

GILLY

See TOWNER.

GILLY WAGON

Circus jargon for a small trailer or cart used to carry lightweight pieces of show equipment around the LOT.

GIRAFFES

The term "giraffe" is circus and acrobatic slang for a very tall or high unicycle, one in which the unicycle has a particularly long pole between the wheel and seat so that the performer rides eight to ten feet off the ground.

To everyone else, the word "giraffe" refers to the popular and exotic animal often seen in a circus MENAGERIE. Giraffes are seldom used as ring performers. If seen in the BIG TOP at all, they are usually LEAD STOCK or SPEC animals.

Not an endangered species, giraffes are fast runners, able to bounce on every other foot as they try to flee their handlers. Despite the cliché "There is nothing worse than a giraffe with a sore throat," the animal is not especially prone to colds. Tuberculosis, however, is not uncommon among giraffes.

The major problem with giraffes on tour is shipping them from town to town. Although rail cars and special trucks have been built with a "sun roof" for the animals to stand upright, these have been mostly for publicity and show. Indeed, a sudden jerk or stop would do severe damage to a giraffe's neck stuck through a hole in the roof.

The usual animal wagon has a flat floor across the axles, but the giraffe wagon is underslung to about six inches off the ground, giving extra height to the interior of the car. The animal is then loaded with the neck tilted down to a 45- or 50-degree angle. This position is the same at which the giraffe eats, so it can remain quite comfortable this way for many hours.

This solution, of course, creates another problem: The specially built wagons, flatcars and truck beds must be unusually long.

G.N. ELDRED'S GREAT ROTUNDA SOUTHERN CIRCUS AND MENAGERIE

In 1858 G.N. Eldred's Great Rotunda Southern Circus and Menagerie, made up in part from apparatus and animals from ROBINSON & ELDRED'S GREAT SOUTHERN SHOW and the SANDS & QUICK'S MENAGERIE, opened under the management of veteran entrepreneur Gilbert N. ELDRED, but it was at least partially owned by Sands, Nathans & Co. Late that year it became one of the first American shows to visit Mexico. Retitled Franconi & Eldred in 1859, the show traveled to, and finally closed in, Cuba.

G.N. ELDRED'S GREAT SOUTHERN SHOW See ELDRED, GILBERT N.; ROBINSON, JOHN; ROBINSON & ELDRED'S GREAT SOUTHERN SHOW; SANDS & QUICK'S MENAGERIE.

GOLD UNIT, THE See FELD, KENNETH; RINGLING BROS. AND BARNUM & BAILEY CIRCUS.

GOLIATH In 1928 the main attraction in the MENAGERIE of the RINGLING BROS. AND BARNUM & BAILEY CIRCUS was a gigantic sea elephant named Goliath. Weighing in at three and a quarter tons, Goliath ate 150 pounds of fish every day and had to be carried in an immense water tank that occupied half a rail car.

Each day the behemoth had to be unloaded from the train and onto the WAGON that would carry him to the tent. There Goliath would be coaxed into the water tank that would be paraded in the SPEC.

Goliath was, in fact, one of a pair of sea elephants that John RINGLING had purchased from Hagenbeck's Zoo (see HÄGENBACH, Karl) in Hamburg, Germany. After the first creature's death, the second was put on tour in its place.

Dexter Fellows, press agent for the show, claimed that newspapers made more requests for photographs of Goliath than any other circus animal during his time with the show.

GOLLMAR BROS. CIRCUS The Gollmar brothers of BARABOO, WISCONSIN—Jacob, Charles A., Ben, Fred C. and Walter (known as Wallie)—were cousins to the RINGLING BROTHERS, but they ran their own circus for 20 seasons, on wagons from 1891 through 1902, then moving onto rails from 1903 through 1916.

Like the Ringlings, all five brothers took part in the operation of the show. Jacob was ADVANCE MAN, Fred was general manager, Charles was bandmaster, Ben was treasurer and Walter was the EQUESTRIAN DIRECTOR. They opened the first season of their 12-wagon circus in Mineral Point, Wisconsin on June 1, 1891. Shortly after opening, Fred Gollmar also went on the ADVANCE, and Charles became circus manager. Among the original company was another Ringling cousin, Henry Moeller, who was to travel with the Gollmar Bros. Circus for only one year before opening his MOELLER CARRIAGE AND WAGON WORKS.

In 1898 the Gollmar show added a second ring. In 1903 the circus moved onto rail, and five years later the show became a three-ring circus. By 1916 the Gollmar Bros. Circus was the fourth largest circus in the United States.

After a quarter of a century under direct operation by the Gollmar brothers, the circus title was sold to James Patterson (a Missouri carnival owner) at the end of the 1916 season. Part of the transfer agreement was that Patterson could use the Gollmar title the following year, so he toured the show as the Patterson-Gollmar Circus. Not used to operating a circus—a much different operation from a carnival—Patterson began to sell off apparatus and equipment in pieces at the end of the 1917 season.

In 1918 two of the brothers, Fred and Charles Gollmar, moved over to the HAGENBECK-WALLACE CIRCUS, becoming an advance man and manager, respectively. Many of the old Gollmar TROUPERS followed. Ed Ballard, later a partner in the AMERICAN CIRCUS CORPORATION, was taking an active interest and touring with the Hagenbeck-Wallace show at the time. In 1921 Ballard convinced the Gollmar brothers to lease their name to the corporation for five years.

In 1922 the Corporation repainted its Howe's Great London show and opened it in Montgomery, Alabama as the Gollmar Bros. Circus, with Fred Gollmar as general agent. In the company was a young Clyde BEATTY, who that year moved from CAGE BOY to Dorothy Asal's assistant trainer with her polar bear act.

The "new" Gollmar show was about the same size as the actual Gollmar Bros. Circus had been in 1916. For the southern swing of the 1922 tour, the American Circus Corporation added another popular name to the title; thus the show became the Gollmar Brothers-Yankee Robinson Combined Circuses.

The Gollmar title was not used in 1923. Instead the Corporation toured the equipment as the JOHN ROBINSON CIRCUS. The Gollmar name was resurrected one last time by the American Circus Corporation for use on a small, five-car rail show for the next two seasons.

GORILLAS Of all the animals exhibited in the circus MENAGERIE or SIDESHOW, the one most feared and considered most ferocious by the public is the go-

rilla. Often mistakenly called "monkeys" by laypeople, gorillas are actually apes and, like man, are biologically classified as in the Primate order.

Gorillas live and travel in polygamous families, with the male as the head. Baby gorillas are handled by the parents like human children, cradled in the mothers' arms or on their shoulders. The young stay with the parents until the age of two or three.

Gorillas move by day and sleep in a new location on the ground or in tree nests each night. Although occasionally carnivorous, gorillas primarily eat fruit and vegetables.

Adult male gorillas weigh about twice as much as the females, reaching a maximum of 600 pounds. Dian Fossey, one of the most noted observers of African mountain gorillas, stated that "A mature male may be six feet tall and weigh 400 pounds or more. His enormous arms can span eight feet."

Despite their imposing size, most gorillas are docile unless provoked, and they remain gentle throughout their lives. The unique drumming of the chest with cupped hands and accompanying roar is rare and is intended as a challenge, not an attack. Fossey witnessed very little true aggressive behavior during her studies. "These incidents were generally initiated by protective adults when their young approached me too closely. In all instances, the 'charges' proved to be bluff."

Gorillas have very good eyesight and hearing but have a poorly developed sense of smell. Like man, they seem to be psychologically complex, choosing their actions based on wants or interests rather than needs. Gorillas are also subject to most human diseases, such as measles, mumps, typhoid, cancer, pneumonia, appendicitis and syphilis.

Among the first to raise gorillas in this country were Mrs. William (Gertrude Davies) Lintz and Mrs. E. Kenneth (Marie) Hoyt, respective owners of the gorillas that were to become GARGANTUA and M'TOTO. At the time of John Ringling NORTH's purchase of "Buddy" from Mrs. Lintz, there were only 12 other gorillas in captivity in the United States.

(See also MONKEYS AND APES.)

GOSHEN AND BIHIN   Two giants, exhibited by P.T. BARNUM at the AMERICAN MUSEUM at the time of TOM THUMB's arrival in 1843.

GRAND ENTRY   Circus jargon for the opening parade of performers and the MENAGERIE around the hippodrome track of the BIG TOP.

During the heyday of the tented circus, many shows opened with an elaborately staged theatrical drama, or "Spectacular," only part of which was the grand entry and parade. Today the term "grand entry" is used interchangeably with the modern opening SPEC.

GREAT AMERICAN CIRCUS   See HILL, ALLAN C.; TUCKER, LEONARD BASIL "HOXIE."

GREAT CIRCUS BIM BOM, THE   Other Soviet circuses besides the MOSCOW CIRCUS have attempted to play the United States, but without much success. The Great Circus Bim Bom, with 126 performers and staff, came from Russia in 1990 after eight months of paperwork. Planned by International Showbusiness, Inc. of Hollywood, California (a rock-and-roll promotion company), the two-year "Peace and Goodwill Tour" was the organizer's first attempt at a circus venture. The route was to have included every major American city.

The first Circus Bim Bom was originated a century ago in Russia by two clowns, Bim and Bom. Although it had not performed continuously since then, it was restarted in 1980 by the clowns' grandchildren. The 1990 edition included 16 horses, nine bears, three lions, several monkeys, dogs—and a rooster! The two-and-a-half-hour show included a strongman juggler, a skateboarding chimpanzee, the Flying Stankeevs and bareback riders.

The show arrived in Wheeling, West Virginia in early April for three weeks of rehearsal. Traveling on a dozen tractor-trailers for the props and animals and three Silver Eagle buses for Soviet cast and another for the American crew, the Great Circus Bim Bom opened its tour to slow business in Hershey, Pennsylvania on a stand scheduled for April 25–29, 1990. Attendance was also small at Knoxville, Tennessee, and the itinerary was changed to take advantage of possible weekend crowds.

Meanwhile, the two main Kuwaiti investors withdrew, claiming they had obligated themselves only to the $300,000 in start-up costs. The show limped on to Johnson City, Tennessee but it never opened. The vehicles and support companies were leased out of Atlanta, so the artists and equipment were taken along to Georgia. The animals were taken to New Jersey instead, because the vehicles transporting them were leased out of there.

The stranded performers were comforted and aided by Atlanta residents and circus fans while new investors were sought. When none arrived, Steven E. Leber, the producer of the recent successful Moscow Circus tours, provided airfare and other costs to enable the performers to return to the Soviet Union in late August.

GREAT CIRCUS PARADE, THE Held each July, this weeklong celebration in Wisconsin re-creates the traditional piece of lost Americana known as the circus STREET PARADE.

The Great Circus Parade began in 1963 as the dream of CIRCUS WORLD MUSEUM founder Charles Philip "Chappie" FOX, and it was organized with the assistance of Robert Lewis PARKINSON and Ben Barkin, a museum trustee. The event begins when over 75 antique wagons are loaded by Percheron horses (a French breed) onto approximately 20 railroad flatcars a half-mile long at the Circus World Museum in BARABOO, WISCONSIN. Among the treasured wagons have been Twin Lions Telescoping Tableau, the Old Lady in the Shoe Nursery Float, the Mother Goose Nursery Float, the Pawnee Bill Bandwagon, the Columbia Bandwagon and, of course, the original TWO HEMISPHERES BANDWAGON.

The Great Circus Train travels for two days and 222 miles through 40 communities in southern Wisconsin and northern Illinois toward its final destination, Milwaukee, making major stops along the way at Madison, Wisconsin, an overnight at Janesville, and minor breaks at Arlington Heights, Illinois, and Kenosha, Racine and Cudahy in Wisconsin. Once in Milwaukee, the wagons are carefully unloaded and placed on display in Veterans Park for three days to allow visitors and circus fans to get close to them.

While on exhibition, the wagons encircle the MIDWAY—an area of nonstop circus-style acts—and climax with four performances a day by the ROYAL HANNEFORD CIRCUS.

On the last day, Sunday, the main procession begins as the wagons, bands and auxiliary units march through the streets of Milwaukee. An example of the spectacle is the Two Hemispheres wagon, which is pulled by a team of 40 Belgian horses, held in a double set of reins and 720 feet of leather.

The Great Circus Parade was first sponsored in 1963 by the former Jos. Schlitz Brewing Company, and it ran through 1973. It was revived again in 1985 under private foundation sponsorship and has been held annually ever since, managed by The Great Circus Parade Foundation, Inc. It is still presented and staged by the Circus World Museum. In addition, more than 2,500 volunteers and anonymous corporate sponsors take part in making the yearly event, a nostalgic visit to our nation's past, a reality.

GREAT INTER-OCEAN, THE A short-lived circus in the 1880s, the Great Inter-Ocean show claimed, as did all its competitors, to be the "Largest and Best Show on Earth." The Great Inter-Ocean claimed to have the rarest MENAGERIE on tour, including the "Great Egyptian Bovalapus." Pictured as a cross between a horse and a wild ox, there is no record of what the Bovalapus actually was—other than a fantastical name from an imaginative publicist.

Begun in 1883 by experienced showman John B. Doris, the Great Inter-Ocean actually had several very profitable seasons. In 1888 Doris took on John L. Sullivan, the heavyweight champion, as a partner. Sullivan, at the peak of his fame as a fighter and a drinker, was supposed to appear in a sparring match during each show. After several "lost weekends" in which Sullivan was unable to perform due to alcoholic binges, Doris gave up on the partnership and the show, having to CLOSE AHEAD OF PAPER midseason.

GREAT PAN-AMERICAN SHOW See LEMEN BROS. CIRCUS.

GREAT ROMAN HIPPODROME See P.T. BARNUM'S GREAT ROMAN HIPPODROME.

GREAT SYNDICATE SHOWS See WILLIE SELLS SHOWS.

GREAT WALLACE SHOW(S) The Great Wallace Show was started by a triumvirate consisting of Al G. Fields (who later became a major producer of minstrel shows), James Anderson and Ben Wallace. The show originated in 1884 in PERU, INDIANA. Starting out as a wagon show, the circus moved onto rails two years later.

In 1887 Wallace gained complete control of the show. Of the seven American circuses traveling by rail in 1891, the Great Wallace Show and the Ringling Bros. Circus were the smallest—each toured with only 20 cars. The show operated under a different title, the COOK & WHITBY CIRCUS, for the 1892–94 seasons; but it returned to the Great Wallace name in 1895.

In 1900 Wallace bought the J.H. LAPEARL CIRCUS and absorbed it into the Great Wallace Show.

At the end of the 1906 season, Ben Wallace purchased the Carl Hagenbeck Wild Animal Show; the two were combined into the formidable HAGENBECK-WALLACE CIRCUS in 1907.

GREAT WALLENDAS, THE   See WALLENDAS, THE.

GREATEST SHOW ON EARTH, THE   This title, linked forever with the name P.T. BARNUM, is the current moniker, or motto, of the RINGLING BROS. AND BARNUM & BAILEY CIRCUS.

The phrase was coined by Barnum personally and was first used in 1872 to promote his show, P.T. Barnum's Great Traveling Exposition and World's Fair. The exhibition was a new incarnation of BARNUM'S GREAT TRAVELING MUSEUM, MENAGERIE, CARAVAN, HIPPRODROME AND CIRCUS. From 1872 onward, Barnum used the motto in conjunction with every one of his shows.

When James A. BAILEY, in collaboration with James L. HUTCHINSON, joined forces with Barnum to create their new show, P.T. BARNUM'S GREATEST SHOW ON EARTH, HOWES' GREAT LONDON CIRCUS AND SANGER'S ROYAL BRITISH MENAGERIE, the advertising slogan came along as part of the package. The show lived up to its name, beginning its life with a CIRCUS parade that included hundreds of animals and performers down the streets of New York City on March 16, 1881.

Bailey temporarily withdrew from the arrangement, rejoining Barnum as sole partner and co-owner in 1887, this time as full manager as well. The BARNUM & BAILEY CIRCUS adopted the title "The Greatest Show on Earth" and often used it as part of its official name.

Up until its merger with the Barnum & Bailey Circus, the Ringling Bros. Circus used the slogan "World's Greatest Shows" in its advertising. Today, however, the combined Ringling Bros. and Barnum & Bailey Circus has adopted the more appropriate title "The Greatest Show on Earth" as its official, copyrighted trademark.

GREATEST SHOW ON EARTH, THE   See FILMS, CIRCUS; JACOBS, LOU; KELLY, EMMETT.

GRIEBLING, OTTO (1896–1972)   Otto Briebling was born in Colenz, Germany, the son of a tailor. His father died when the boy was 13. His mother came to America, leaving him behind as an apprentice to a bareback rider. Otto Griebling attempted to migrate to the United States at the age of 15 as a mess boy on a ship he thought was heading from Bremerhaven to America. His ship landed in Yokohama, Japan instead, so it was another nine months before the freighter finally reached New York. This comedy of errors seems almost fitting in the life of Griebling, who went on to portray a sad but lovable TRAMP CLOWN for years as a headliner on the RINGLING BROS. AND BARNUM & BAILEY CIRCUS.

When he finally arrived in the United States, Otto answered a newspaper ad for a circus bareback rider and was hired on as an apprentice with the Hodgini Riding act out of BARABOO, WISCONSIN. Sent into town by Albert Hodgini with five dollars to buy two loaves of bread and a quart of milk when the Ringling Bros. Circus played Madison, Wisconsin, Griebling decided to stay; becoming employed as a farmhand in nearby Sheldon, Wisconsin. Two years later, when the same circus came to town, Griebling returned to the LOT with the bread, milk and change and was rehired by Hodgini.

For ten years Griebling toured as an equestrian and was an excellent comic ROSINBACK rider, filling in at one point for "Poodles" HANNEFORD. Griebling toured with Tom MIX and had a series of fair dates with May WIRTH. Working for the SELLS-FLOTO CIRCUS, he took a bad fall in 1930 and decided to turn in his reins. His comedic skills came into play when he tried his hand at clowning; soon he was on his way to becoming one of the great physical comedians of his generation.

In 1932, while Griebling was a tramp clown on the HAGENBECK-WALLACE CIRCUS, Emmett KELLY signed on as a WHITEFACE CLOWN. The following year, Kelly switched to a tramp character as well. In the winter of 1934–35, they worked the annual Moslem Shrine Circus in Detroit and in 1935 performed together on the one-season COLE BROTHERS & CLYDE BEATTY CIRCUS. In 1939, Griebling worked with Mark ANTHONY on the COLE BROS. CIRCUS.

In 1951 (according to Fred BRADNA), Griebling began performing with the Ringling Bros. and Barnum & Bailey Circus, where he spent the remainder of his career.

As a producing clown, Griebling was the inventor of many classic CLOWN GAGS. In one routine, the little hobo carried a large block of ice around the ring; but by the time he thought he had found a buyer, to his puzzlement and sorrow, the ice had disappeared. During COME-IN he could always be seen JUGGLING metal pie pans, and throughout the show he had a running gag of trying to deliver a plant, package or that pesky block of ice.

In 1970 Otto Griebling's larynx was removed. During the last two years of his life, spent with the Ringling show, the pantomime he had brilliantly created for 40 years became a way of life both in and out of the ring. He died on April 19, 1972.

(See also CLOWNS.)

GRIFT   In reference to the American circus, grift was a catch-all phrase for the crooked games, short-change artists, pickpockets and other illegal cons on the circus LOT. Similarly, the person who ran the games or was engaged in the grift was known as a "grifter." Almost never seen on showgrounds today, grift was the rule rather than the exception on many circuses in the second half of the 19th century.

A "grift show" was a circus that, as a matter of policy, carried along people engaged in such activities. Three things were necessary for the grift on the grounds: the grifter, a gullible TOWNER and, of course, a circus operator who allowed it. Often the local authorities were also involved in a percentage of the "take." A "legal adjuster" traveled with every circus to "square" or smooth over problems, and on grift shows this "fixer" or "patch" would lay out cash as well as passes to take care of law enforcement officers in advance. No show had grift aboard unless there was a spoken or implied "go-ahead" from someone higher up in the chain of management and/or the local sheriff's office.

Many times in the late winter, when a circus inserted its "call" in the trade magazines for personnel needed for the next season, the show actually listed positions for grifters. Often the more genteel word "fakir" was used; but listings in some of the journals from the years 1890 to 1910 actually stated positions open for "Fakirs in all lines. Our people are waiting to be took."

There was big money to be taken in the con games, such as the three shell game (known as the "nuts" or "working the nuts") and three-card monte (known as "broad tossing" or "tossing the broads"). To make the games look easy to win, the grifters usually worked with several "shills" who would win large sums of money in front of the locals. The "broad mob," a hired group of shills who crowded the three-card monte game, would entice the townsfolk to join in on the possible winnings.

The circus management often exacted a PRIVILEGE from the "lucky boys" to allow them to work the games on the MIDWAY, or more often in the CONNECTION, the narrow alley bordered by SIDEWALL between the MENAGERIE and the BIG TOP. Some of these "connection workers" would pay to have the X, or exclusive right, to play their game in that area.

Ticket takers sometimes had their own way of making extra money. One way, of course, was shortchanging the customer as the money was counted into the patron's hand. This practice was also known as "duking." The money earned from shortchanging the "natives" was known as "short cake," and a person really skilled at the job was known as a "short cake artist." Some knowledgeable townspeople were aware that some ticket sellers were so good at this practice that they came to assume, often rightly so, that they were being "clipped" unless their change was counted onto the tabletop.

As a result, ticket stands were purposely built very high, so that buyers would often miss part of their change as they picked it up. Any currency or coins left behind were quickly swept into a waiting change trough built into the top of the ticket booth. Both the money and the people who didn't claim it were referred to as "walkaways." This was, in fact, the easiest way to "hype," or shortchange, a patron.

In the rush to buy tickets, people often stampeded the ticket booth. While the ticket seller would give change to one person, he would collect money from a second and ask "How many?" of a third. In such confusion and commotion, buyers had only a few seconds to receive the tickets and scoop up the change. If they later realized they had been short-changed, the mob was usually too large for them to complain. If a buyer did make a "beef," the smart ticket seller usually "squared" it instantly so as not to arouse suspicions among the next patrons in line. This was done as easily as handing back the correct money and saying, "I'm sorry. By the time I noticed, you had walked away. Thanks for coming back."

Some shows carried many more grifters than the con men seen on the showgrounds. A "booster" was a specialist in shoplifting. Back among the show folk, the grifter would take orders for any item, even a complete suit (down to color and size); and he would steal, or "cloat," it from a store in town. The term "cloat" was also occasionally used to mean shortchange; the artists in that particular scam also worked the town while doing legitimate shopping or exchanging large-denomination currency at the bank. Pickpockets worked the route during the STREET PARADE; and, often during the opening on the midway, the TALKER would warn the people standing on the midway to beware of pickpockets in the crowd. The men instinctively checked their wallets, and the thieves—who, indeed, *were* in the crowd—would be able to sight the more prosperous-looking gentlemen. An unbelievable number of confidence schemes—even extravagant offers to purchase whole herds of livestock and horses—were worked on gullible townsfolk.

Sometimes the sting of the grift from show day would be so strong that the circus could not return to the same town the next year. If so, the circus was said to have BURNED THE TERRITORY. Although the point has never been authenticated, this might explain in part why some early MUD SHOWS changed the names of their circuses from one year to the next without any change in management or performers.

Sometimes grift was overlooked by the townsfolk if the circus show itself was especially good. After all, reasoned those who had not lost any money, no one was forced to play the games.

On the other hand, if a circus had a terrible performance and also allowed an unforgivable amount of grift on the lot, circus folk referred to it as a "fireball," because the towns they played were "burned up." This also gave rise to the term "HEAT," for problems and fights with the towners. Because of the great risk of angry mobs literally tearing apart these operations, the equipment on "fireball outfits" was seldom first class.

The following review of the HAGENBECK-WALLACE CIRCUS, shows the sense of violation a community felt after a grift show blew through town. The review was printed in the Wausau, Wisconsin *Pilot* in 1908:

The circus employees while in the city were orderly and no robberies of houses were reported. But the show carried with it a bunch of grafters [sic] which is not a credit to any show management. Skin games were worked in the menagerie and sideshow tents and a great many soft ones lost sums ranging from $1 to $5. . . . Shortchange men, too, were in evidence and a number of people got caught on an old threadbare game.

Howes Great London Circus was also notorious for its grift, especially with its scam of selling horses. A circus boy would approach a prosperous local farmer and introduce himself as Mr. Howes. He would suggest that he had extra horses that he would be willing to part with at a very reasonable price. A second con man would accompany the farmer to the bank "as protection" and take him back to the lot. Once there, the farmer would pick out a horse, pay for it and start to lead it away by himself. A trainer would suddenly appear and stop him, asking for an explanation. The befuddled farmer would be led to the RED WAGON where the manager explained that the farmer had been swindled. A search was made of the area for the thieves, often with circus personnel helping, but the grifters were long gone—hiding or even dressed as clowns.

By the turn of the century, the tiny mud shows were starting to give way to larger, more-established shows with recognizable names and titles. These circuses began to build up regular clientele during repeat seasons; the money earned in ticket and concession sales far outweighed the money and extra problems caused by the grift. More and more circuses became SUNDAY SCHOOL SHOWS, keeping con men and grifters off their lot.

Many times the operators of Sunday School shows had to hire men to forcibly keep the grifters off their midways and from following the circus from town to town. By the early part of the 20th century, when the Ringling Bros. Circus proudly advertised itself as a grift-free, family show, the days of the true grift shows were already a thing of the past.

GRIMALDI, JOSEPH (1778–1837)

Born in London, England, Joseph Grimaldi was the son of a pantomime artist and dancer. By the age of nine, he had followed his father into the business.

"The Father of Clowning," Grimaldi moved the art of clowning from the HARLEQUIN era and look into today's conception of the slapstick comedian. At first he experimented with different costumes, wigs and characters. His first wardrobe was white with red and blue markings, and his blue wig was cut like a modern "Mohawk." At one time he also reportedly wore a skullcap with three antennae.

An early pantomime "clown" role was named "Guzzle," which he played opposite the actor Dubois, who portrayed "Gobble," the clown-in-residence at the Sadler Wells Theatre. Onstage, Guzzle drank prop "ale" while Gobble ate sausages. Each night it was a personal and professional contest to see who could consume the most and outmug the other to gain the audience's laughter.

Finally, at the age of 27, Grimaldi became an overnight success when he introduced the WHITE-FACE CLOWN, a clown with white-base makeup with colored cheeks and eyebrows and a red mouth. To pay homage to his redefinition of the art, the term "JOEY" is used in the circus world to mean any clown, whiteface, TRAMP or AUGUSTE.

As is so common with the comedian's life, Grimaldi's story was beset with tragedy. His only son and heir died an early violent death as an alcoholic. Grimaldi himself became crippled in his early 40s, probably aggravated by his heavy pratfalls, weighty costumes and manic performing schedule.

His last performance, a "benefit" for himself, was presented from a chair. He remained impoverished and in ill health, and he died about a year later. Joseph Grimaldi's grave, possibly in a potter's field, was neglected; the site has been lost to history.

(See also CLOWNS.)

GRIND In order to advertise the attractions in the SIDESHOW and convince people on the circus LOT to come inside, an OUTSIDE TALKER stands up on a raised platform to gain attention. The LECTURER gives a short talk, called a BALLY, describing the performers and exhibitions inside the tent.

This talking ends with the ticket boxes being opened and the first audiences streaming into the tent. What follows is the grind, a repetitive, droning narration that recounts over and over again the wonders to be seen inside. The purpose of the grind, of course, is to persuade the more reluctant patrons to part with their "fifty cents, half a dollar" and see the show.

Almost mechanical in nature, a good grind is also hypnotic. Filled with titillating promises and persuasive clichés, a grind should have even the most jaded and skeptical circusgoer eager to enter the tent. A typical sideshow grind would sound like this:

That's right. They're all inside. The Magician, the Ventriloquist, the Human Blockhead and the Human Volcano. They're in here. The Punch & Judy Show, Contortionist, the Human Pincushion. The Electric Lady and the Escape Artist. They're all here; they're all alive.

You go up one side and down the other. You go round and round like a merry-go-round. It's never out, and it's never over. You miss one part, you stay and see it again. It's all here on the inside.

That's right. You've heard about it; you've read about it; you've seen it on TV. Now's the time to see it in person, and it's on the inside.

Don't miss the Snake Charmer. She's on the inside too. You say you're afraid of snakes? Well, bring your boyfriend. Bring your girlfriend. Hold on real tight. But don't miss the Snake Charmer. She's on the inside.

Fifty cents, half a dollar. Where else can you see so much for so little today? Half a buck, less than the price of a hamburger downtown. Now's the time to see it.

Don't wait till tomorrow. Don't come back tomorrow saying you wish you had seen it. Tomorrow there'll be nothing left but wagon tracks and popcorn sacks. See it now, see it today.

The grind goes "round and round like a merry-go-round," repeating the catchphrases over and over, alternately giving reasons to go in and eliminating reasons to stay out. Finally the grind wears down the resistance of those waiting for the BIG TOP, and the patrons enter the sideshow.

Most PIT SHOWS also use a grind to draw in crowds, often without the use of a bally beforehand. Because there are no human attractions to bring out onto the bally platform, and there is no band on the inside, pit show bosses usually deliver a grind from the time customers wander onto the lot. In recent years, taped grinds have replaced live presentations. Although not nearly as effective to pull people in, the tape is often more cost-effective because the only personnel needed to "front the show," or stand out front to let passersby know the attraction is open, is a single ticket seller.

How to guy out a tent to the stake line. (Photo by Tom Ogden)

GROTESQUE Circus jargon for a particular style of character CLOWN. The grotesque usually wears an AUGUSTE CLOWN makeup, extremely exaggaerated wardrobe and makes use of wildly outrageous props.

GUMPERTZ, SAMUEL W. (1868–1952) When Samuel Gumpertz took control of the RINGLING BROS. AND BARNUM & BAILEY CIRCUS in 1929 as the head of ALLIED OWNERS, INC., he was no stranger to show business.

Early in his career, Samuel Gumpertz had been a cowboy rider in BUFFALO BILL'S WILD WEST. While there he met Flo Ziegfeld, whom he later assisted in the production of the first *Ziegfeld Follies*. Gumpertz oversaw the construction of the boardwalks and amusement centers at Brighton Beach, Long Beach and Coney Island's Dreamland on Long Island, New York. After its completion, Dreamland was also managed by Gumpertz until it was destroyed by fire on May 27, 1911.

When John RINGLING defaulted on payments to the AMERICAN CIRCUS CORPORATION, Gumpertz saw a unique opportunity. With the partnership of several New York investors and the encouragement of the widows of Charles and Richard Ringling (Alf T. Ringling's son), Gumpertz managed to buy up John Ringling's notes. Ironically, Gumpertz owned the Half Moon Hotel where Ringling was living at the time of the transfer of ownership.

Gumpertz managed the circus until, through court maneuvers and bank loans, John Ringling NORTH was able to buy out the Allied Owners, Inc. in 1938.

GUNSEL In circus jargon, a "gunsel" is a young man or a boy, usually a TOWNER, who helps set up the TENTS and performs other physical circus chores.

(See also KID WORKER; PUNK.)

GUY Circus jargon for the wires that are part of the rigging that supports the high wire and low wire, the aerial equipment. Guy wires usually hang loose until just before the act; the riggers then use large ratchet devices connected to the guys to pull the ropes taut, giving full tension to the lines. Guy ropes run from the canvas TOP and are stretched and tied to STAKES to make the TENT taut.

(See also GUY OUT; TENTS.)

GUY OUT   Circus jargon meaning to push down the ropes that have been tied onto the stakes until the canvas TOP becomes taut. To prevent a BLOWDOWN after the TENTS have been erected, a guy-out gang must check the ropes several times a day, especially in the case of high winds or rain, to make certain the lines are taut.

While the origin of its use in the circus is unknown, the term most likely has the same derivation as the tightened GUY wires that hold aerial apparatus into place.

GUY-OUT GANG   See GUY OUT.

HAGEN BROS. CIRCUS   Operated by Howard Suesz, the Hagen Bros. Circus was a motorized tent show beginning in the 1950 season.

HÄGENBACH, KARL (1844–1913)   A renowned German wild animal trainer, Karl Hägenbach—or Carl Hagenbeck, as the name became Americanized— also founded the Stellingen Zoo in Hamburg. Hägenbach first became interested in exotic livestock when his father, Gottfried Klaus Karl Hägenbach, a fish merchant, received six seals in payment for a debt. His father began to trade in zoo, circus and MENAGERIE animals; and in 1866 Hägenbach took over the business.

One of the major suppliers of exotic animals to circuses in the United States in the second half of the 19th century, Hägenbach's new humane methods of training animals, especially the big CATS, revolutionized the industry.

In his classic book, *Von Tieren und Menschen (Of Beasts and Men),* Hägenbach dismissed the notion that all carnivores are naturally savage and cruel. He wrote: "It is certainly a mistake to call them cruel. It is their nature in the wild state to hunt living prey, and they have to kill in order to live. . . . It is as reasonable to accuse mankind of cruelty . . . as it is to accuse carnivores."

Before Hägenbach's time, animal trainers felt that only fear of the trainer could keep control and force their charges to perform. The trainers poked at the animals with rods or whips and fired blank pistols close to their ears.

Hägenbach introduced a method of training based on reward for correct behavior, with no reward and mild rebuking for wrong behavior. He acknowledged that his method required more time and patience to train an animal than using what he called the "brute-force system"; but Hägenbach felt the animals remained healthier, stayed better trained and were less likely to turn on their masters.

(See also HAGENBECK-WALLACE CIRCUS.)

HAGENBECK-WALLACE & FOREPAUGH-SELLS BROS. CIRCUS   See ADAM FOREPAUGH & SELLS BROS. CIRCUS; HAGENBECK-WALLACE CIRCUS; SELLS BROTHERS CIRCUS.

HAGENBECK-WALLACE CIRCUS, THE   The Carl Hagenbeck Circus, named for the renowned German animal trainer and dealer Karl HÄGENBACH, toured in 1905 and 1906 under the ownership of John H. Havlin and Frank R. Tate. The 1906 season was not financially successful, and on December 4, 1906 Havlin and Tate signed a contract to consolidate with the RINGLING BROTHERS. Hägenbach would not relinquish title to his name, however, so the deal was never consummated.

On January 9, 1907 Benjamin Wallace, John O. Talbott and Jeremiah "Jerry" MUGIVAN did enter a partnership with Havlin and Tate. The plan was to form a new show: Wallace and Talbott combined their GREAT WALLACE SHOW with Havlin and Tate's circus, with each man receiving equal part-ownership of the newly formed show. Wallace sold any duplicate properties and split the proceeds among the partners.

Ten days later two loans were signed to Havlin and Tate, $30,000 from Wallace and $15,000 from Mugivan, with Havlin and Tate's interest in the new show as collateral. When Havlin and Tate defaulted on the loan, Wallace and Mugivan bought the Hagenbeck Circus for the $45,000 due them. Karl Hägenbach attempted a court injunction against the use of his name by the new owners, but Wallace and Mugivan won the suit. Hägenbach was hampered by the fact that he was in Germany and could not directly address the court with his complaints. Also, presumably because only his name but not personal property was involved in the exchange, the court injunction was denied.

Thus the Carl Hagenbeck and Great Wallace Circus, usually referred to as Hagenbeck-Wallace, was born. Its premier was in the spring of 1907, traveling by rails on 45 cars, with Ben E. Wallace listed as sole owner and general manager. Despite being plagued by bad weather and two train wrecks, the early seasons were successful; the press and public greatly admired the new show, which lived up to the expectations engendered by the combination of two such respected names in circusdom. It claimed as its TERRITORY the Midwest, touring mostly from the Appalachians to the Rockies. At times it was the second largest circus in the United States. Wallace continued operating the show until 1913, when it was sold to Edward Ballard.

Wallace's successors were still in charge when one of the great CIRCUS TRAIN wrecks in history occurred. On June 22, 1918 at least 86 people were killed and over 175 were injured when an empty troop train slammed into the back of the Hagenbeck-Wallace Circus train near Hammond, Indiana.

The Mugivan and Bowers combination took over the Hagenbeck-Wallace Circus in 1919 and toured it through the 1929 season. For the next six years, through 1935, the circus was made a Ringling subsidiary. By 1934, it was one of the most successful of all circuses of that period—in fact, that year it outgrossed its parent company, the RINGLING BROS. AND BARNUM & BAILEY CIRCUS.

In 1935 the show's name was changed to the Hagenbeck-Wallace & Forepaugh-Sells Bros. Circus, adding the other titles also owned by Ringling. The show never left WINTER QUARTERS in 1936, and

the following year it was leased to Howard Y. Bary. Bary toured the show for only two seasons, and 1938 was the last time the Hagenbeck-Wallace Circus was on the road.

Among the illustrious alumni of the Hagenbeck-Wallace show was legendary animal trainer Clyde BEATTY. While traveling with Hagenbeck-Wallace in the early 1920s, Beatty became the youngest wild animal trainer in the country when the regular trainer suffered a heart attack. Beatty left Hagenbeck-Wallace in 1934 to form his own show, the COLE BROTHERS & CLYDE BEATTY CIRCUS.

(See also WALTER L. MAIN CIRCUS.)

HAIGHT & DEHAVEN CIRCUS   The small DeHaven Circus toured from 1861 to 1865, when it was purchased by Andrew Haight. In 1866 Haight toured the show as the Haight & Chambers Circus; but the show lost money, putting Haight temporarily out of business.

In 1871 he returned, and the following year he started up a partnership with DeHaven. Together they owned the Great Eastern Circus through 1874, a year in which Haight independently operated the Great Southern Circus.

The next year Haight trouped a hippodrome show, the American Racing Association, under canvas; but after 1875 Haight gave up management and worked for other circuses.

HAIR HANG   The visual image of the hair hang is unbelievable. A beautiful woman with a long mane of braided hair is hooked to a long cable. She is pulled up into the air, attached to the rope only by her hair.

If circusgoers knew the secret of the hair hang, they might be even more astounded. This routine is almost a case of "what you see is what you get." The showgirl *does* hang from her real hair: A wig to withhold that pull could never be fastened to the scalp.

To prepare for the hair hang, the performer must have extremely long, heavy and thick hair. First, she wets her hair, then bends at the waist and tosses it down and forward. She then divides the hair into three or more sections and braids them into one length of hair. She also braids into each section of the ponytail a heavy, wet piece of twine or cord,

Princess LaKaChaNa performs the hair hang, seemingly suspended only from a knot tied in her braided hair.
(Photo courtesy of Bambi and Chuck Burnes)

such as a Venetian blind pull. (Some prefer to use just one stouter piece of twine.)

Next, the end of the braid is slipped through a small metal ring. The end of the braid is folded over and bent back on itself. If the braid is long enough, it can be threaded through the ring a second time and folded again. The ends of cords that are extending from the braid are then firmly tied to the metal ring. As the hair and twine dry, they become even more firmly attached to the metal ring.

When the act is performed, the ring is not visible to the audience, although there is no real attempt to hide it. A metal hook, attached to a cable, goes through the metal ring. The end of the cable stretches upward, through a pulley system and back down to ground, where it is manned by one or more people. When the rope is pulled, the performer flies up and "hangs" by her hair.

Usually as part of the act, the showgirl also juggles several items. Doing so is particularly difficult be-

cause of the circular motion that is inherent in hanging from a single pivot point.

Bambi Aurora, who toured as a Ringling showgirl, confided, "There's no magic to it. You really hang by your hair. And it hurts!"

(See also AYALA, MARGARITA VAZQUEZ.)

HALL, JOHN R. See HOXIE BROS. CIRCUS.

HALL, WILLIAM P. (fl. 1904–1935) Originally a horse and mule dealer from Lancaster, Missouri, William P. Hall made his mark in the outdoor amusement business by buying, selling or leasing used circus equipment, anything from old circus WAGONS or animal stock to a fully equipped show. His specialty MENAGERIE stock was ELEPHANTS.

Hall bought his first small show, the HARRIS NICKLE PLATE CIRCUS, in 1904. Also that year he bought the 25 railroad cars of equipment from the WALTER L. MAIN CIRCUS. His recycling of that and other apparatus gave rise to dozens of small circuses in the first third of the century. In 1935 Hall left the circus world by selling all of his remaining usable apparatus and pachyderms to the COLE BROS. CIRCUS.

(See also LEMEN BROS. CIRCUS.)

HAMID, GEORGE A. (1896?–1971) Born into a poor family in Broumana, Lebanon and christened on February 4, 1896, George A. Hamid moved to the United States in 1906. He performed as an acrobat with BUFFALO BILL'S WILD WEST, then later joined forces with Robert MORTON during the Depression to create one of the largest indoor circuses still touring today—the HAMID-MORTON CIRCUS.

In 1918 Morton brought the GENTRY BROS. CIRCUS indoors in Dallas, Texas under the sponsorship of a Shrine temple. Hamid also realized the potential for arena circuses under such local sponsors and began to book for Morton. He soon became a top-notch agent with a powerful route that included dates for the Shrine, police departments and other civic organizations in major cities all across the United States and Canada.

HAMID-MORTON CIRCUS One of the largest indoor circuses, the Hamid-Morton Circus is owned and operated by George Hamid, Jr. The show books a powerful route each year, usually opening each spring at the Roanoke (Virginia) Civic Center, and performs under the sponsorship of civic organizations such as Shrine temples and police departments, in major U.S. and Canadian cities.

The show's roots began in 1918, when Robert MORTON arranged for the GENTRY BROS. CIRCUS to perform an indoor date for the Shriners in Dallas, Texas. This was also the start of the sponsored circuses often referred to by show folk as "The TEXAS SHRINE DATES."

(See also HAMID, GEORGE A.; SHRINE CIRCUS.)

HANG PAPER

Circus jargon for the act of pasting up LITHOGRAPHS or posting WINDOW CARDS on poles.

Another circus use of the slang is giving a friend or another attraction a verbal buildup, as in the phrase "I'll impress the audience without your having to *hang paper* for me."

(See also ADVANCE MAN; BILLING CREW; PAPER; PRESS AGENT.)

HANNEFORD, EDWIN "POODLES" (1892–1967)

Edwin "Poodles" Hanneford was born in a circus wagon in Barnsley, Yorkshire, England. He was given his nickname by an aunt who said he looked like a fat poodle. As leader of the HANNEFORDS, one of the royal families of the American circus, he first moved to the United States in 1915.

Edwin was an expert horseman, but beginning around 1910 he chose to work as an equestrian CLOWN and was known as "the Riding Fool." Suiting the age-old PETE JENKINS ACT (originated by Charles Sherwood and popularized by Dan RICE) to his own style, Poodles Hanneford entered the ring wearing a long coonskin coat and carrying a cane. As if inebriated, he staggered around the ring, interrupting a liberty act (see LIBERTY HORSES) in the process. Before long, Poodles was clinging to a galloping horse; his coats and pants flew off as he circled the RING CURB. Finally Hanneford was revealed in leotards, and he finished his bareback act with professional flair.

He toured his troupe with the BARNUM & BAILEY CIRCUS, then the RINGLING BROS. AND BARNUM & BAILEY CIRCUS, for 15 years, from 1915 to 1930, before moving on to many other major circuses.

Poodles Hanneford holds a world's record for VAULTING, with 26 consecutive jumps on and off a running horse, performed on the Barnum & Bailey

Circus at MADISON SQUARE GARDEN in New York City in 1915.

In addition to his circus work, Hanneford appeared on the New York stage in *Circus Princess*, *Happy Days* and *Jumbo* (see THEATER.) His movie work included *The Golden Horde* and *The Circus Kid*. (See FILMS, CIRCUS.) He was also seen on such TELEVISION variety programs as "The Ed Sullivan Show" and "Hollywood Palace."

Although officially retired, he continued to work as a clown, appearing at Frontier Town in North Hudson, New York, through the summer of 1967. He died at his home in Kattskill Bay, New York, on December 9, 1967.

(See also HANNEFORD, TOMMY; HANNEFORDS, THE.)

HANNEFORD, TOMMY (1927–)

A descendant of the Hanneford troupe of equestrians, Tommy Hanneford is the owner/producer of the ROYAL HANNEFORD CIRCUS, which has played mostly Shrine dates since its first season in 1975. His wife, Struppi, is also active with Hanneford's circus and career.

Hanneford, a nephew of the famous equestrian clown Edwin "Poodles" HANNEFORD, was born September 18, 1927. He grew up with his brother George Jr. and sister Kay Frances on the old Downie Bros. Circus. He began performing in his father's ROSINBACK act as soon as he could walk. Billed as "the Riding Fool," Tommy Hanneford began his solo career as a clown and equestrian in the mid-1970s. He still serves as EQUESTRIAN DIRECTOR on his own show as well, and he has also led his own herd of trained ELEPHANTS for many years.

(See also HANNEFORDS, THE; SHRINE CIRCUS.)

HANNEFORDS, THE

One of the great families of the circus, the Hanneford dynasty began in 1621 when a young Irish showman, Michael Hanneford, traveled through England with a MENAGERIE. In 1777 a descendant, Ned Hanneford, competed against John Scott in a JUGGLING contest before King George III. For 113 years the showmen's families were rivals until Ned Hanneford IV married Elizabeth (Nana) Scott. Their son was Edwin "Poodles" HANNEFORD.

The Hanneford Riding Troupe first traveled to the United States from England in 1915. The head of the clan was Poodles Hanneford, who worked as an equestrian CLOWN. The original Hanneford

Troupe toured first with the Ringling-owned BARNUM & BAILEY CIRCUS, then with the RINGLING BROS. AND BARNUM & BAILEY CIRCUS to 1930, before moving on to many other major circuses. Members of the first American company included Percy Clarke, Poodles Hanneford, his mother, his sister, his wife Grace, Elizabeth Hanneford Clarke and her husband Ernest. Meanwhile, Edwin's brother George developed a separate bareback riding act with his children, George Jr., Kay Frances and TOMMY HANNEFORD.

Today the Hanneford dynasty continues, with Tommy and his wife, Struppi, producing the ROYAL HANNEFORD CIRCUS. George Jr. developed his own Cossack act and for a time owned and operated the Hanneford Family Circus. Today, he and his wife Vicky run the indoor Ft. Lauderdale Swap Meet Circus in Florida.

HANNIBAL Featured in the VAN AMBURGH CIRCUS in the 1830s, Hannibal was the largest ELEPHANT exhibited up until that time in the United States.

HAPPYTIME CIRCUS Owned and operated by Dave and Judy Twomey, the Happytime Circus is a small, tented one-ring circus that plays mostly MIDWAY and fair dates.

Under a 40-by-90-foot yellow BIG TOP, the show runs about an hour and features Dave Twomey as "Happy the Clown," working directly to the audience. Although there are no exotic animals, the show does display both bird and dogs acts.

HARLEQUIN Circus jargon for a CLOWN dressed in the original commedia dell'arte style, wearing a stereotypical black mask and white diamond-patterned wardrobe.

HARMON, LARRY See CLOWNS, TELEVISION.

HARRIS, THE REV. DR. L(LOYD) DAVID (1940–) AND TRUDY (1939–) Born April 28, 1940 in Wichita, Kansas, the Rev. Dr. L. David Harris is the founder of The CIRCUS KINGDOM, for which he finds sponsors, plans the route and performance and arranges music. He and his wife Trudy (born January 28, 1939 in Norristown, Pennsylvania) supervise the business affairs of the show as well as recruit and counsel its personnel.

David Harris first saw circuses as sponsored police dates when they played his hometown. A musician in high school, college and graduate school, Harris developed a deep love for circus music. During those years, he played with circus bands whenever possible, and tried his hand at clowning, animal handling, concessions and, finally, management and circus press agentry.

He actively assisted in the founding of Circus Noel and recommended church sponsorship to Dr. Charles W. BOAS for CIRCUS KIRK. He toured as chaplain with the Kirk in 1971, while Trudy was also WITH IT as nurse.

David became a correspondent for circus reports in *Amusement Business* and was a founder and board member of the National Congress of Animal Trainers and Breeders, an association that promotes the preservation of animal training and acts on circuses.

He has served in pastoral positions in the Midwest, Washington, D.C. and currently with the Calvary United Methodist Church in Pittsburgh. In 1989 the Rev. L. David Harris was awarded a doctorate of ministry (D. Min.) from his graduate school, Notre Dame. In 1991 he was entered in *Who's Who in American Religion*.

Along with her active work in civic and church activities, Trudy Harris is also a nurse at the Oakland Veterans Administration Medical Center in Pittsburgh. She received her R.N. in nursing from Bryn Mawr School of Nursing in 1959, plus a B.S. in nursing from the University of Pennsylvania in 1961. In 1981 and 1982 she completed graduate work on her master's degree in nursing from Wichita State University.

Throughout all of this, they coordinated and toured The Circus Kingdom for summer tours from 1973 through 1977, and again in the summers of 1988 through 1990, as well as two-week-long winter tours in Florida in 1991–92 and 1992–93 and a summer tour beginning May 20, 1993.

HARRIS NICKLE PLATE CIRCUS The Harris Nickle Plate Circus, started by a Chicago haberdasher in 1882, was one of the best-known of the small shows at the turn of century. The circus, which charged only 10 or 20 cents admission, was sold to William P. HALL in 1904.

HARTFORD FIRE The most tragic fire in circus history occurred on July 6, 1944 when the BIG TOP of the RINGLING BROS. AND BARNUM & BAILEY CIRCUS caught fire and collapsed, causing the death of 168 people, mostly children.

During World War II, waterproof and fireproof materials were scarce in the United States due to their high demand for use on army tents. To prevent water leaks during rainstorms, most circuses resorted to coating their canvas tops with paraffin wax.

That day the matinee crowd for The BIG ONE in Hartford, Connecticut, numbered over 6,000, primarily women and children. Only 20 minutes into the show, the SPEC had already been followed by Alfred COURT's famed CAT act. May Kovar, his assistant, was prompting the cats back down their chutes to their CAGE WAGONS. The WALLENDAS were in the middle of their incredible tightwire act.

Merle EVANS, the master bandleader, was one of the first to see a tiny flame heading up a roped seam of the Big Top. Immediately he switched to "The Stars and Stripes Forever," traditionally used on circuses to signal disaster and the need for an emergency evacuation of the tent. Panic ensued as heroic performers and ROUSTABOUTS stayed under the top, assisting as much as possible to get people out from under the burning cloth.

Somehow the Wallendas made it to the ground. Although their costumes were singed and a small piece of burning canvas fell on Helen Wallenda, the troupe escaped major injury. The BULL HANDLER in the background heard the change in tune and immediately yelled, "Tails! Tails!" forming the herd of 40 ELEPHANTS into a trunk-to-tail line. Not only were the pachyderms saved from danger, but no animals of any kind were lost in the firestorm.

The tent burned for only eight or nine minutes before the support for the CENTER POLES was gone and they came crashing down. The blanket of flames covered everyone still under its spread.

Despite the enormous tragedy, it is miraculous that so few perished. Two-thirds of the dead, however, were children, many of them trampled rather than burned to death; an additional 487 were injured.

Criminal charges were brought against the circus, which was fined $10,000; six Ringling officers were given prison terms for criminal negligence. The circus and its insurers paid $3.9 million in damage awards to survivors.

After the fire, the circus limped back to SARASOTA, FLORIDA for repairs; but in August it reopened, minus a top in the Rubber Bowl in Akron, Ohio. The show played arenas and stadiums for the remainder of the season, closing in New Orleans in October.

If any one story epitomizes the horror and suffering of that day, it is the story of Little Miss 1565. Among the many who had died in the flames was one "Jane Doe" whose story was different from those who had been burned. She had been trampled in the mass exodus from the tent and only slightly burned. With a bandaged arm and constant transfusions, she lived almost three hours in the hospital. Although her features were identifiable, her body was never claimed.

She was one of three children and three adults who were buried July 10, 1944 in Northwood Cemetery in Windsor, Connecticut. All were unidentified victims of the fire. A seventh unidentified victim, a dismembered infant, had been cremated at the hospital. It was the face of Little Miss 1565 that the policemen found so haunting, however; for years two detectives returned to the cemetery on the fire's anniversary to place flowers on her grave.

In 1983 Hartford Fire Chief Inspector Lt. Rick Davey, an amateur historian, attempted to reconstruct the tragedy of that day, reinvestigating the arson theory of the blaze. At the same time, he helped to uncover information that led to the identification of the Little Miss.

Davey took his evidence and photographs of the girl to Dr. H. Wayne Carver II, the state's chief medical examiner, and his deputy chief, Dr. Edward T. McDonough. On March 8, 1991 they officially issued an amended death certificate for Little Miss 1565 as being Eleanor Cook.

On July 6, 1944 Mrs. Mildred Cook, a claims adjuster and training supervisor at Liberty Mutual Insurance Co., left for the circus with her three children: Donald, nine; Eleanor, eight; and Edward, six. They sat on the top bleachers near the southwest corner of the tent.

After the fire, Mrs. Cook awoke in what was then Municipal Hospital in Hartford, entirely bandaged except for slits for her eyes. She held young Edward's hand until the doctors were forced to part them. The boy had died. She was told Eleanor was missing and presumed dead. Donald, who had become separated from the rest, managed to crawl under the SIDEWALL and escaped. He went home to a friend's house, and for a time it was hoped Eleanor had done the same.

Mildred Cook remained hospitalized for six months. She had been unable to attend her son Edward's funeral and burial in Center Cemetery in Southhampton, Massachusetts. His simple grave has a white marker inscribed: "Edward Parsons Cook. Feb. 26, 1938–July 7, 1944." Beside it was placed an identical tombstone marked "Eleanor Emily Cook. March 17, 1936–July 6, 1944." Her grave contained no body, but Mildred Cook planted flowers there to remember her daughter.

The pain of investigating to find the truth of her daughter's disappearance was too great to bear, and she came to accept her son Donald's notion that Little Miss 1565 was indeed little Eleanor. In 1991, 85-year-old Mildred Cook, living in Easthampton, Massachusetts, felt it was time for the truth to be known. Donald, now living in Iowa, matched the photographs of Little Miss 1565 to those of his sister Eleanor to certify identification.

Mildred Cook brought her daughter home for burial next to her little brother. "I'd like them to be together," she said. "And maybe have a little service and a hymn. Maybe 'Jesus Loves Me, That I Know'— something Eleanor would like." Eleanor Emily Cook, formerly Little Miss 1565, was finally laid to rest on June 22, 1991.

In May and June of 1950, while Robert Dale Segee was under suspicion for arson in Ohio, Deputy Fire Investigator R. Russell Smith went to Maine and New Hampshire where Segee had grown up. He discovered that in the years 1940 through 1946, there had been 28 major fires and 40 minor blazes within ten blocks of the Segee home in Portland, Maine. In June 1950 Robert Segee admitted having set at least 25, maybe 30 major fires in Portland between 1939 and 1946.

In Columbus, Ohio on June 26, 1950, nearly six years after the Hartford holocaust, Robert Dale Segee signed a written confession for having set the blaze. He had joined the circus when it played Portland on June 30, 1944. The muscular 14-year-old runaway became a roustabout. On that same day, a minor fire on the circus GUY OUT ropes was put out without injury or damage. The circus moved on to Providence, Rhode Island, where a tent flap

mysteriously caught fire. It too was extinguished without incident. The next stand was Hartford.

Segee's confession was compiled over three days and covered 33 single-spaced typewritten pages. It included interviews with his mother and sister, who revealed that he had set two fires inside their home. Constant nightmares about the Hartford fire prompted his coming to police. "I just see a big flash and a lot of people in the dark with just their faces showing and the flames coming up all around their faces," he told the detectives.

Segee told police that he often set a fire after a frustrating sexual encounter to "burn out a lot of bad memories." He said he had met and had "unsatisfactory" relations with a young girl near the showgrounds just before the 2 P.M. show.

Segee said that whenever he remembered lighting the match to start the blaze, he "blacked out," only to be awakened by a nightmarish "red man" with fangs, claws, red chest hair and flames coming out of his head. He said he had set the big fire in addition to the two minor ones the days before. He hoped the confession would make the nightmares go away.

The "Privileged and Confidential" file was sent to the Connecticut police but, remarkably, Segee was never questioned. Police held to the conclusions of their initial investigation released six months after the conflagration: A lit cigarette tossed from the bleachers accidentally set the fire.

In 1950, however, Robert Dale Segee was tried and convicted on two other counts of arson in Ohio. He was sentenced to a term of four to 40 years and was paroled after eight years. While serving time at the Ohio State Reformatory in Mansfield in November 1950, he recanted his confession to having set the Hartford fire. He was released in 1958 and arrested again on arson charges in 1960.

After nine years of work, Fire Lt. Rick Davey, using new investigative techniques and exhaustively reviewing decades-old documents, concluded the fire was deliberately set. In February 1991 a panel of federal arson investigators at the FBI Academy in Quantico, Virginia agreed. A cigarette could not have started the fire.

One of the FBI agents, Tim Huff, had proved in a 1970s California study that a smoldering cigarette dropped into dry grass could not ignite a fire if the relative humidity in the air was above 23%. At 2

P.M. on the afternoon of the Hartford fire, 20 minutes before the blaze began, the relative humidity was 43%.

As of this writing, the FBI officially has not ruled that the fire was arson, and the investigation is ongoing once more. Regardless, it is questionable whether Segee could be prosecuted today. There is no statute of limitations for murder charges, but prosecutors would have to prove that the boy had actually intended to kill people in the tent. Also, at the time arson murder was not a crime in the state; and all other criminal charges in Connecticut carry a statute of limitations of five years.

(See also FIRES, CIRCUS.)

HEAT   Circus jargon for problems, arguments or outright fights caused by friction between the circus folk and the TOWNERS.

Usually "heat" was caused by illegal gambling on the LOT, a very poor show for the money or unscrupulous business practices. The trouble might not even be the fault of the circus in town: It might be residual anger from the last show through the area.

A circus that causes too much "heat" and ruins a stand for itself or another show is said to BURN THE TERRITORY.

(See also GRIFT.)

HENDERSON, J.Y. "DOC" (1909–1991)   Beginning in 1941, Doc Henderson was the first chief veterinarian of the RINGLING BROS. AND BARNUM & BAILEY CIRCUS and remained so for more than two decades.

Born to a rancher in Kerrville, Texas, about 75 miles outside of San Antonio, J.Y. Henderson was surrounded by animals all of his life. As each child in the Henderson family was born, he was given a heifer by his father. When J.Y. became old enough, he was expected to take complete care of his own cow. By the age of five, he was riding a goat; and at ten he had his own horse.

Meanwhile, he attended a little one-room schoolhouse; after graduation at the age of 18 he wrote to Texas Agricultural and Mechanical College's veterinary school. So intimidated was he by the school's demands that Henderson enrolled in the engineering school instead.

During the Depression years, Henderson paid for his classes by training and riding horses for competition on the weekends. The dean of the school, Dr. R.P. Marstellar, noticed Henderson's love for horses and was instrumental in moving the student into the veterinary school.

It was during this time that Henderson developed a lifelong friendship with Tom Hogg, a wealthy rancher, who shared his passion for horses. When Henderson had to be hospitalized in 1933 for throat surgery, it was Hogg who helped with expenses. During his recovery he worked for the Magnolia Oil Company, and while on out-of-town expeditions with Hogg, Henderson discovered his interest in carpentry and hunting fossils.

After he was graduated from Texas A & M, Henderson entered practice with one of the best veterinary surgeons in the country, Dr. A.V. Young of Shreveport, Louisiana. It was in the middle of an anthrax epidemic in September 1941 that John Ringling NORTH offered Henderson a position with The GREATEST SHOW ON EARTH.

At first he didn't believe the call. Even then he never missed the circus when it came to town. Coming home from the show at the age of ten, Henderson had mused to his mother that when he grew up he was going to be a veterinarian with the Ringling Bros. Circus. Now he had a chance to fulfill the long-forgotten dream.

The North phone call was so unexpected that Henderson asked for one month to consider the offer. During that time he discovered that little was known about treating exotic animals and that the circus's main preoccupation was with its valuable and sizable collection of HORSES. The challenge of being a pioneer in the field of caring for wild animals was irresistible, and a month to the day of the phone call Henderson accepted the position.

From his very first day at WINTER QUARTERS, Henderson showed an uncanny aptitude for transferring the treatment of common farm animals to their exotic counterparts. He opened his clinic every morning at 6:30 A.M.; on the road he was assigned one rail car divided into stalls as a traveling hospital and, as an important member of the circus staff, his own Pullman car for a home.

His very first patient on the circus lot was Arvid, a black BEAR that had broken one of its claws. After lassoing and tying up the beast with the help of several animal handlers, Henderson was able to anesthetize the paw, amputate two broken toes, clean the infection and dress the wound. His hands-on work with wild animals had begun.

One of his first nontraditional treatments was for a broken jaw on one of Alfred COURT's lions. Henderson's first thought was to wire the jaws shut, the way he would for a dog. A docile dog can be fed milk through the corner of the mouth, but a lion would require much more milk during the healing weeks, if milk alone would sustain it. No handler would want to be near an irritable lion for that length of time. After putting the lion to sleep, Henderson drilled holes in the broken lower jaw bones and wired the pieces together. He then set two blocks of wood by the back molars and lashed the mouth partially closed. This incapacitated the jaws but allowed the lion to lap up milk for itself during the six weeks of perfect recuperation.

"Doc" Henderson was in charge of 700 animals, about half of them horses. Ever since Philip ASTLEY had developed the circus ring in London in the 1780s, horses have been the backbone of the circus. North hired Henderson primarily on his reputation as a horse veterinarian. The Ringling show had understandable pride in its horses, and it had one of the most valuable collections of steeds in the world. The show had even been known to assign as many as one groom for every three horses.

Henderson loved horses; in fact, shortly after moving to SARASOTA, FLORIDA he brought his own mare, Benny V., to the Ringling corral. Still, he believed horses were not the smartest creatures; when they became excited they had to be tended carefully so they didn't injure themselves or each other. Although they didn't take care of themselves very well, they could be groomed into beautiful animals. And of all the animals on the grounds, the horse was one of the hardest working and responded the most to human attention.

In October 1942 Helen and KARL WALLENDA introduced Henderson to Karl's first wife, Martha. After a season-long coy courtship, the couple decided to marry. When World War II intervened, Doc Henderson entered the army in February 1944 and served as a medic for two years. But on April 4, 1946, the day the circus opened at MADISON SQUARE GARDEN, the couple was married by a justice of the peace.

The perfect circus family needed a child; soon they "adopted" a small leopard, which they named Sweetheart and bottle-fed. Eventually, however, Sweetheart outgrew their home at quarters and was placed in the circus's MENAGERIE.

Henderson fully retired in 1982, but he maintained memberships in CIRCUS FANS ASSOCIATION OF AMERICA, Showfolks of Sarasota and the Florida Veterinary Association. He was honored by a plaque in the East Quadrant of the SARASOTA CIRCUS RING OF FAME. He died June 14, 1991 in a Sarasota hospital after suffering a heart attack.

HERALDS A type of handbill or small poster, heralds are circus advertisements, rectangular in shape, with printing on one or both sides. The earliest American heralds, dating from the 18th century, were printed on one side only, because they were supposed to be pasted onto a wall. As printing became less expensive, circus owners added text to the back side of the herald and began to hand them out on the street.

Usually five to 14 inches wide and one to four feet long, early heralds were generally not in color or very elaborate, but merely contained drawings and simple type. An industry standard for the size evolved, measuring 10 by 28 inches; this became known as a QUARTER SHEET.

Details in the advertisement included the factual (the circus's name and owners, the star performers and MIDWAY attractions) and the not-so-factual (colorful exaggerated descriptions of the show in general and the acts in particular).

Circuses began to use heralds on a wide scale by the beginning of the 19th century. Heralds could be produced cheaply, so even small circuses made use of them. Show printers carried stock artwork and layouts that DOG AND PONY SHOWS could afford, merely by adding their own names to the flyers. Other unusual heralds were printed for special occasions. Among these were excursion bills, printed to advertise the special trains that ran from far-flung communities to the circus town on show days.

By the mid-1840s, color LITHOGRAPHS were replacing heralds as the primary type of sheets posted by the ADVANCE MAN. Heralds continued to be used as handbills, however, and some color was added to almost all of them by the turn of the century. By the early 1900s heralds were displaying photographs in addition to the customary engravings and artwork.

HERO See ROGUE ELEPHANTS.

HERRIOTT, JOHN (1931–   ) One of the most important equestrians and ELEPHANT trainers of the second half of this century, John Herriott is a third-generation circus performer who, with his family, has appeared on almost every major American circus.

Herriott was born in St. Peter, Minnesota, the grandson of Pike Herriott, who had been a chef in the COOKHOUSE on the 101 RANCH WILD WEST. John's uncle, George Engesser, had toured with Shell Bros. Circus and Zellmar Bros. Circus, two small motorized shows of the 1920s and 1930s.

Milton Herriott (?–1962), John's father, was also a noted equestrian and trainer of sea lions and BULLS. Beginning around 1915, he toured with the MIGHTY HAAG CIRCUS, the SEILS-STERLING CIRCUS, the MILLS BROS. CIRCUS, the COLE BROS. CIRCUS and the AL G. KELLY & MILLER BROS. CIRCUS, among others. He was the last manager of the Cole show, involved with the National Zoo in Washington, D.C. and, after retirement in the 1950s, a trainer for the White Horse Mounted Patrol in Sioux City, Iowa.

During his school years, John traveled with his father during the summers, making his first appearance in the ring at the age of six. He proudly relates that he was the back end of Jargo (a clown act in which two men dress in a comic giraffe-horse costume to spoof a HIGH SCHOOL HORSE routine) behind Dime Wilson on the Barney Bros. Circus. At the age of 12, he fronted his first elephant act in an end ring on the Kelly-Miller Circus and also sold BANNERS in ADVANCE of the show. Herriott graduated from school in 1949 and entered the circus world full time.

In 1950 he traveled with the Cole Bros. Circus, then under the direction of Arthur Wirtz. The show opened playing open-air stadium and indoor arena dates, moving under canvas in July. Herriott presented eight LIBERTY HORSES in the circus, which featured Hopalong Cassidy as its headliner. At the end of the 1950 season, the Cole show had sold its animals to the KING BROS. CIRCUS, and John Herriott

and his father, who became manager, moved with them.

In 1951 and 1952 John Herriott worked with the White Horse Troupe and then toured with the combined King Bros.-Cristiani Circus. After a stint as a serviceman in Korea, Herriott matriculated at the Minnesota School of Business. In 1954 he returned to the WINTER QUARTERS of the King Bros. Circus.

It was while Herriott was performing at the Cleveland Groto Circus (a SHRINE CIRCUS under the direction of Orrin DAVENPORT) that the RINGMASTER, Col. Harry Thomas, introduced him to his future wife, Mary Ruth (1936–   ), then a high school senior. Following graduation, Mary Ruth and John Herriott married in a CENTER RING ceremony at the Ft. Worth Shrine Circus on Thanksgiving day, 1954. Mary Ruth, already an aerialist and showgirl, was soon performing her own educated poodle act.

In the summer of 1954, Herriott had traveled to California to assist in handling the Cole Bros. pachyderms used in the filming of *Jupiter's Daughter*. The following season the Herriotts were performing an act with three baby elephants on the Gil Gray Circus when they got word that Walt Disney was looking for animal acts to present in a Mickey Mouse Club Circus at his new Disneyland theme park. George Emerson, who had made a name for himself as a reliable animal trainer for the early Tarzan films, had befriended Herriott the previous year and recommended that Disney take a look at him. The staff flew to see the Gil Gray Circus in the Midwest and wound up taking the entire show to Disneyland, complete with Herriott's BULLS, CAMELS, llamas and ponies, and set them up at the end of Main Street USA. This exposure led to Herriott working an elephant on a 1955 episode of *The Millionaire*, along with various other TELEVISION and film appearances continuing to the present day.

Herriott stayed with the Gil Gray show six years, then moved onto the HUNT BROS. CIRCUS with a six-Arabian horse liberty act. The 1960 season saw Herriott taking over a golden retriever dog act for sports show dates, followed by a year with the CLYDE BROS. CIRCUS and two tours with the Mills Bros. Circus.

At the end of the 1962 season, John Herriott was selected to become assistant director to Charles Philip "Chappie" FOX at the CIRCUS WORLD MUSEUM in BARABOO, WISCONSIN. Herriott also maintained, trained and performed with the RING STOCK owned by the museum. The Herriotts remained with the Circus World Museum for seven years.

Irvin FELD became interested in Herriott in 1969 and traveled to Baraboo to meet the impressive trainer. The Museum was reluctant to lose Herriott and did not wish to keep its animals after the equestrian's departure. As a result, Feld not only hired Herriott for the RINGLING BROS. AND BARNUM & BAILEY CIRCUS, but he also purchased the museum's entire MENAGERIE.

Herriott stayed with Ringling two seasons, then moved to HOXIE BROS. CIRCUS in 1972. For the summer of 1973, the Herriotts were in residence at Storytown Park in New York state, presenting their own elephant, pony and dog show. When the park closed for the fall, the Herriotts returned to Hoxie for the remainder of the season.

Frank McCloskey invited the Herriotts to join the CLYDE BEATTY-COLE BROS. CIRCUS in 1974, where John performed his liberty and high school horse acts and Mary Ruth presented her dog and pony revue. The following year saw a return to Hoxie, after which they toured with the Diamond "S" Rodeo, a Wild West on which John Herriott was also arena director. In 1977 John Herriott returned to Ringling as the performance director of the Red Unit.

The next year Feld asked the Herriotts to move down to the troubled CIRCUS WORLD as part of a $3 million renovation. John became entertainment director, and the rest of the family worked in the various acts at the park. After a year Herriott went out with CIRCUS VARGAS for half a season, finishing up with bulls and horses in Mexico's Circo Atayde.

In 1980 the Herriotts returned as summer performers at the Circus World Museum, taking along three elephants on loan from D.R. "Dory" MILLER. That fall John Herriott toured as performance director for an indoor unit put out by the Clyde Beatty-Cole Bros. Circus. Following the failed half-year experiment, the Herriotts joined Beatty-Cole under canvas for the next season.

In 1982 they took their horses and dogs onto The BIG APPLE CIRCUS, then ended the year with Hoxie after Big Apple closed. That winter John Herriott trained a "Big and Little" horse act—a Clydesdale and a pony—for The Big Apple Circus, which was presented by his daughter Heidi the following season. The next year he stayed in residence at a miniature horse farm located in Pompano Beach, Florida.

From 1984 through 1989 the Herriotts toured their own small tented show, the Herriott Trained Animal Circus. The one-ring show appeared primarily as a free MIDWAY attraction on fair dates. Also over this period, Mary Ruth performed her act with a resident show the Herriotts placed into Kids World in Long Branch, New Jersey. They also put together a theme park circus show for the Power Plant, an inner harbor shopping mall in Baltimore, Maryland.

In 1988 John Herriott returned to Ringling, training and performing all the horse acts for the tented Gold Unit in Japan. The show opened in Sapparo in June, then spent two months in Tokyo before moving onto Osaka, where it closed for that year in October.

In 1989 the Herriotts took over management of the Land of Little Horses, a theme park that had been established 21 years earlier in Gettysburg, Pennsylvania. They have remained as owners and managers of the park ever since.

When not in residence at the Land of Little Horses, the Herriotts continued to free-lance as performers, appearing with Shrine shows, such as the TARZAN ZERBINI CIRCUS and the ROYAL HANNEFORD CIRCUS. Through the 1980s, Herriott was a prolific elephant trainer, and some of his bulls have also appeared, or are still traveling, in the herds on the George Hanneford show, Allan C. Hill's Great American Circus and the George Carden Shrine Circus.

John and Mary Ruth Herriott have four daughters (all of whom are circus aerialists and equestrians): Laura Herriott Caudill; Cindy Herriott; Heidi Koch; and Christine "Weiner" Plunkett.

HETH, JOICE (c. 1750–1836)

In 1835 Joice Heth became the first great attraction to be exhibited by the future master showman P.T. BARNUM. At the time Barnum was the owner of a small family grocery in New York City when he heard about Heth from a neighbor, Coley Bartram.

An aged black woman, Joice Heth claimed to be 161 years old and to have been George Washington's nursemaid. Her owners even had legal documents from 1727 to prove the assertions. She was blind, toothless and reportedly weighed only 46 pounds. Although partially paralyzed, she was still strong enough to engage in banter with an audience and to sing hymns.

On June 10, 1835 R.W. Lindsay, a Kentucky impresario, had entered into an agreement with Heth's owner, John S. Bowling (also of Kentucky), to become equal partners in touring her as an attraction for one year. Only five days later, Bowling sold his half-interest in the lease to Bartram, who sold it back to Lindsay on July 24.

Barnum traveled to Philadelphia, where Bartram had Heth on display, and was so convinced of her legitimacy and the authenticity of her papers—or else saw his first golden opportunity—that he sold his business, borrowed an additional $500 and returned on August 6 to assume Lindsay's lease for $1,000.

He put Heth on exhibition next to Niblo's Garden (a popular New York City cabaret of the time), perching her on a small table in a private room and dressing her in a Colonial-era gown. Barnum hired Levi Lyman to introduce the attraction and field questions from the audience. The crowds were so large to see this human oddity that ticket sales averaged $1,500 a week.

When initial receipts waned, Barnum took Heth "on tour" throughout New England. In Boston he spread the rumor that Heth was actually an automaton who spoke with the aid of a ventriloquist, and the exhibition was packed. Following another swing into New York, Heth returned to New England under the road management of Lyman. She became sick that autumn and was moved to the home of Barnum's half brother Philo in Bethel, Connecticut. Joice Heth died there on February 19, 1836.

Before her burial, Barnum allowed an autopsy by Dr. David L. Rogers, a well-respected New York physician. As was common in that period, the autopsy room was full of spectators, each of whom paid 50 cents apiece for the privilege. Rogers determined that Heth could not possibly have been over 80 at the time of death. The story was reported in the *New York Sun* by newsman Richard Adams Locke, who had been in attendance.

Lyman convinced James Gordon Bennett, the editor of the rival *New York Herald*, that some doctor had switched cadavers to humiliate Rogers. Heth, Lyman claimed, was still alive in Connecticut. Bennett dutifully printed these assertions; when he learned the truth of the swindle, he became a Barnum adversary for life.

The whole Heth incident turned out to have been Barnum's first major humbug. Whether Heth actually fooled Barnum is not known, but he claimed to the end that he had been completely convinced of her authenticity.

Regardless, the incident did persuade him that the public enjoyed harmless swindles. Barnum's final comment was that because doctors disagreed on Heth's age, the whole question "will probably always be shrouded in mystery."

Also according to Barnum, "the remains of Joice were removed to Bethel, and buried respectably." There is, however, no gravesite or record of Heth's remains there today.

HEY RUBE! Circus jargon. The yell of "Hey Rube!" across a circus LOT will immediately spring the troupe into action, because it is the traditional warning and call to arms of a fight between the circus folks and the townspeople.

HIGH SCHOOL HORSE A style of equestrian act, known in Europe as *haute école,* in which a horse performs without any apparent direction from its rider. The tricks might include dancing, walking sideways, waltzing, bowing, lowering down onto the knees, waving a flag, standing on the hind legs or even shaking hands with the bandleader.

Needless to say, invisible and precise directions are being given by the rider through slight pulls on the reins or pressure against the horse's flanks. It takes two to three years of continual work to train a high school horse well enough for performance.

(See also DRESSAGE; HORSES.)

HIGH WIRE See BLONDIN; PETIT, PHILIPPE; WALLENDA, KARL; WALLENDAS, THE; WIRE WALKING.

HILL, ALLAN C. (1948–) Born in Norfolk, Virginia on September 23, 1948, Allan C. Hill grew up in a circus family. His mother was a third-generation equestrienne and aerial performer; his father, Bill, was once BOSS CANVASMAN and general manager of the HOXIE BROS. CIRCUS.

"Like father, like son." Left: William Hill, longtime boss canvasman and manager of the Hoxie Bros. Circus. Right: his son, Allan C. Hill. The two stand on the lot of Allan C. Hill's Great American Circus in York, Pennsylvania in 1987. (Photo courtesy of Walter G. Heist, Jr.)

Hill began as a candy BUTCHER, selling peanuts, popcorn and COTTON CANDY under the BIG TOP. He left school after the eighth grade to pursue circus concession work full time.

In 1969 he enlisted in the U.S. Army 101st Airborne Division, serving 13 months in Vietnam. For his services he received a Bronze Star and the Army Commendation Medal.

Hill joined the Hoxie Bros. Circus in 1972, developing a telemarketing system for Leonard Basil "Hoxie" TUCKER to promote the show. By 1975 Hill was booking the Hoxie show on "buy-outs"—dates for which Hill paid the circus a flat fee for performances and then promoted for himself at his own risk. Also, with the new phone systems, the ticket sales quadrupled within three years. Hill was soon made Hoxie's manager in charge of promotion and daily operations. In 1983 Allan C. Hill bought the Hoxie Bros. Circus and Hoxie's Great American Circus.

Meanwhile, in the winter months, Hill promoted indoor dates, including a series of variety tours called the Pan-American Magic Shows, which began in the late 1970s. The shows, sold by PHONE PROMOTERS through local sponsors, played through the Northeast.

Hill now owns and operates his main show as Allan C. Hill's Great American Circus. Under a three-ring blue-and-white striped BIG TOP, the show contains approximately 20 displays. Playing the eastern half of the United States, the Great American Circus covers almost 250 towns over a 15,000-mile route each season. The show features several ELEPHANTS, a CAT and trained dogs as ring acts. Hill has also trouped a second unit under the title Circus USA, as well as continuing the Pan-American Magic Spectacular winter show.

Hill seldom travels with the show personally, concentrating his efforts on coordinating the phone rooms from his SARASOTA, FLORIDA offices.

In recent years, Allan C. Hill has become increasingly active in Sarasota community affairs, donating $10,000 to the Sarasota Boxing Club. Located in one of the town's drug-ridden neighborhoods, the club attempts to encourage children to develop their self-esteem and feeling of self-worth as they develop their bodies.

Now unmarried, Hill set a record—noted in the *Guinness Book of Records*—when two women "bought" him for $23,000 in the American Cancer Society's annual "Bid for Bachelors." As a result, Hill has also been featured in magazines such as *Glamour, Cosmopolitan,* and *Gulf Shore Life.* Hill has one daughter, Heather, from a previous marriage.

The circus remains Allan C. Hill's life.

It's in my blood. And when the weather is right, when the kids and their parents fill the big top, well, that's when there is no business like show business. On the other hand, when the show gets bogged down in rain or mud and business is not so good, that's when you wonder if it's all worth it. But as long as the good days outnumber the bad, I will—to use an old circus expression—be WITH IT and for it.

HIPPOTHEATRON   The Hippotheatron, located on 14th Street in New York City, was the winter performance site of BARNUM'S TRAVELING MUSEUM, MENAGERIE, CARAVAN, HIPPODROME AND CIRCUS for two years, until it was totally destroyed by fire in 1872. The Hippotheatron, which also housed P.T. BARNUM'S exotic MENAGERIE, was valued at $300,000.

HIT   Circus jargon for the space on the walls of buildings, stores, barns and fences where the BILLING CREW tacks or hangs—but does not paste—the HERALDS, cloth posters or WINDOW CARDS.

Although it is commonly used today to also mean the LOCATION to paste up LITHOGRAPHS, old-timers refer to a spot in which paste is used as a DAUB.

(See also HANG PAPER; PAPER; PRESS AGENT.)

HOFHEINZ, JUDGE ROY (1912–1982)   Born April 10, 1912 in Beaumont, Texas, Roy Hofheinz had a variety of careers throughout his life, including state legislator, county judge, sports and radio tycoon and circus owner.

Hofheinz, the son of a railroad man, first enrolled at Rice Institute in Houston and then transferred to Houston Junior College (now the University of Houston). Later he entered Houston Law School. In 1934 Hofheinz was elected to the Texas House of Representatives, serving one term. In 1938 he was elected county judge, at the time the youngest person ever to hold the office in a major U.S. city. Although he served for only eight years, he was known for the rest of his life as "Judge" Roy Hofheinz.

In 1944 he left public life temporarily, becoming involved in radio and real estate. In 1952 he became mayor of Houston, serving two terms.

In the early 1960s he became active in sports management, helping to form the Houston Sports Association. With the opening of the Houston Astrodome in 1965, he realized his dream of a resident baseball franchise (the Houston Astros).

In 1968, as part of a triumvirate that also included Irvin and Israel FELD, Judge Roy N. Hofheinz became one of the principal buyers of the RINGLING

Judge Roy Hofheinz balances clown Frankie Saluto on one knee and trapeze star Mary Gill of the Flying Waynes on the other.   (Author's collection)

BROS. AND BARNUM & BAILEY CIRCUS from John Ringling NORTH.

That same year, after opening the show's CLOWN COLLEGE, Irvin Feld created a second touring circus unit. The Blue Unit, as it became known, opened in Hofheinz's Astrodome to a great reception in 1969.

In 1969 Feld offered circus shares on the New York Stock Exchange for the first time. The next year Hofheinz suffered a stroke that paralyzed the left side of his body. Although able to walk after extensive therapy, due to his weight Hofheinz often preferred his wheelchair.

In 1971 Judge Hofheinz gave up his option to buy the controlling shares of stock. Irvin Feld sold his shares to Mattel Toys in exchange for an agreement to allow Hofheinz to remain as the chairman of the board of directors of Ringling (with Irvin as president and chief executive officer and Israel as accountant).

Judge Roy Hofheinz suffered a heart attack in his Houston home on November 21, 1982 and died at 11:25 P.M. later that evening at Twelve Oaks Hospital.

HOLD YOUR HORSES This slang expression, today simply meaning to "wait," had its origin in the days of the early American circus. In the 1800s, before the advent of the automobile, crowds would often travel to town on horseback or in carriages to see the free STREET PARADE. Patrons then followed the steam CALLIOPE, which brought up the rear of the parade, to the LOT for the matinee performance.

Circus owners were well aware that the noise and spectacle, as well as the exotic sight and smells of wild animals, bands and equine-drawn wagons, would cause even the tamest horse along the parade route to buck and become unmanageable. Mindful of lawsuits or ill will that might be engendered if a townsman's horse went out of control and caused injuries, many circus managers would have several employees run in front of and alongside the street parade to warn the locals to literally "hold your horses" as the circus came to town.

This call, of course, aroused a sense of expectation in the spectators. Over time, the phrase took on an idiomatic connotation akin to "Just wait until you see this!"

HOME RUN Circus jargon for the final JUMP of the season from the last show LOT back to WINTER QUARTERS.

(See also HOME SWEET HOME.)

HOME SWEET HOME Circus jargon for the last show date of the season. To mark the occasion, the bill posters traditionally paste one pack of posters upside down all over the town. To end the final show, many troupes also follow a tradition of gathering the entire company together in the CENTER RING to sing "Auld Lang Syne."

HOMY Circus jargon for "a man." A "bona homy" is slang for a good man. The slang is probably derived from the French *homme* (man) and *bon homme* (good man).

HOOVER, DAVE See CLYDE BEATTY-COLE BROS. CIRCUS.

HORSE Circus jargon meaning $1,000.

HORSE FEED Circus jargon for poor box office or poor sales due to bad business.

HORSE OPERY Circus jargon, not common. A horse opery is a jesting term and spelling for any circus. The phrase is probably related to "horse opera," which was a slang term for the shows in western frontier towns and saloons to which locals rode their horses or carriages to attend.

HORSES P.T. BARNUM may have said that "Elephants and clowns are the pegs to hang a circus on," but it is the horse and trainer that formed the basis of the circus as we know it today. The use of horse acts is so fundamental to the circus that one of the first terms used to describe the person in charge of the circus performance was EQUESTRIAN DIRECTOR.

Although he had predecessors as trick riders, most notably Thomas Johnson, Philip ASTLEY, a British soldier-turned-showman, made the discovery in 1766 or 1767 that centrifugal force would allow him to stand on a horse as it galloped around a ring. His addition of CLOWNS and gymnastic acts to his equestrian show resulted in the modern circus.

The first native American equestrian of note was Mr. Pool, who gave performances in his riding academy in Philadelphia in 1785 and in New York the following year. His act included an educated horse and a clown.

It was John Bill RICKETTS, however, who was to lay claim to the title of "the Father of the American Circus." A skilled English equestrian, Ricketts moved to the United States in 1793. His first show, which took place in his own amphitheater on April 3, 1793, is generally recognized to be the first performance of a complete American circus.

The circus was based on riding, of course, and it included Ricketts's feats with his speeding horse, CORNPLANTER. The show, however, was much more than just horsemanship and a clown: It also included rope walkers, tumblers, pantomime and dramatic recitations.

Horses continued to play an exciting part in the circus world throughout the 19th century. One of the most famous performers and circus owners, Dan RICE, started out working in a livery stable as a boy. From the age of ten until he was 17, Rice was a jockey.

Engaged in the circus world from 1844, in the 1850s Rice toured DAN RICE'S ONE-HORSE SHOW, an equestrian show featuring his famous horse EXCELSIOR.

Despite a 20th-century emphasis on exotic animals and clowns, the horse act remains the backbone of the American circus. Circuses carry three types of horses with them: performing stock, workhorses and DEADHEADS. Among the most popular breeds of performing horses are the Percherons, Clydesdales, Shires, Arabians and Lipizzaners.

Horses are excitable creatures and are not particularly intelligent. They are easily injured and do not groom themselves. They are, however, beautiful animals, especially when put through their carefully choreographed paces by an expert equestrian. Moreover, horses are hard workers, and they respond to human attention better than most other animals.

Geldings, or castrated males, are the best circus horses. Studs are often unreliable and quite excitable, while mares in heat are also likely to bite, kick and become wild.

Circuses do not want horses that are too gentle, however, at least not in the ring. High-strung and high-spirited horses, like people, make the best performers; but as a result, circus horses tend to be temperamental.

Equestrians have developed many different styles of acts; the main three categories are the HIGH SCHOOL HORSE, LIBERTY HORSES and ROSINBACK or BAREBACK RIDING.

The high school, or educated, horse is a saddled steed that performs seemingly without any verbal or physical command by the rider. DRESSAGE riding, as this is sometimes known, includes tricks such as bowing, standing on the hind legs, kneeling, walking sideways, dancing and waltzing. Of course, the rider does give imperceptible but definite commands, either by slight pulls on the reins, soft vocal cues or pressing the flanks of the horse. It takes two or three years of constant training for a high school horse to reach performance level.

Liberty horses perform unharnessed, without leads. The riderless horses respond to visual cues, a snapping whip or the sound of the voice; but the trainer, at least in performance, tries to make the signals as infrequent and unnoticeable as possible. The act demands visually stunning animals, and they are usually grouped by the same color. In a liberty act, one of the horses often seems to take it upon himself to be the "leader" and keeps the others in line.

Rosinback riders are so called because they perform on the bare back of the horse, without the benefit of a saddle. The name comes from the fact that the broad backs of the mounts as well as the riders' feet have been "powdered down" with rosin to provide a firmer footing.

Many troupes have become famous for their work as equestrians, among them the HANNEFORDS, the Justino Loyal Troupe and the LOYAL-REPENSKY TROUPE. Individual artists have become just as popular, including the Australian wonder, MAY WIRTH.

(See also CRISTIANI, LUCIO; CRISTIANIS, THE; DAVENPORT, ORRIN; HANNEFORD, EDWIN "POODLES"; HANNEFORD, TOMMY; HENDERSON, J.Y. "DOC"; HERRIOTT, JOHN; PAD RIDING; PAD ROOM; PETE JENKINS ACT; RING HORSE; RING STOCK; "TAILOR'S RIDE TO BRENTFORD, THE"; ZOPPE, ALBERTO; ZOPPE-ZAVATTA TROUPE, THE.)

HOTEL   Circus jargon for the COOKHOUSE and the tent in which meals are served. There are a few possible derivations of the unusual name "hotel." Some feel it is so called because mealtime is one of the few periods of the day when it is possible to relax and meet sociably with peers. Others feel that it earned its name because the interior of the cookhouse tent during the heyday of the giant American circus actually resembled a hotel dining room, complete with tablecloths and waiters.

Many historians feel the term "hotel" also has an economic basis. In the early days of the MUD SHOWS, circus operators used to pay for some employees to stay or eat at local hotels. When they quit the practice, they paid the employees an extra amount per day, which allowed them to buy meals at the cookhouse on the LOT. In a sense, the cookhouse on the showgrounds replaced the "hotel" where they had been eating; and thus the name became transferred to the on-site concession.

At one time, in order to operate the cookhouse and sell meals, cookhouse owners had to pay a PRIVILEGE back to the show. Thus employees had the convenience of eating on the lot among co-workers and away from TOWNERS, a cookhouse staff made money operating a circus-style restaurant and the manager saved money on per-diem expenses while earning back money on a privilege.

The practice of allowing the hotel as an individual concession did not last long, however, and soon the cookhouse had a hired staff. Many old-timers claim they ate better under the former system than they did after the show took over operation of the cookhouse.

HOWDAH   Also known in circus jargon as a "howdy," a howdah is a seat—often canopied—on the back of an ELEPHANT or CAMEL for a rider. Necessary when giving the public elephant rides, howdahs are lavishly decorated when used in a circus SPEC.

HOWES, NATHAN A(LVAH) (1796–1878)   Born April 22, 1796 in Brewster, Putnam County, New York, Howes was possibly the first American (around 1820) to put together a regular troupe of touring circus performers. With his later partner Aaron TURNER, Nathan A. Howes was also one of the first men in the United States to put a full show under a round-top canvas—helping to create the tradition of the tented circus in the States.

Howes and Turner were both influenced by the success of Hachaliah BAILEY of nearby SOMERS, NEW YORK.

(See also HOWES, SETH B.; MENAGERIE; TENTS.)

HOWES, SETH B. (1815–1901)   Fifteen years the junior of Nathan B. HOWES, a circus impresario, Seth joined his brother's show as an assistant at the age of 21. Soon Howes was buying interests in other circuses. An expert manager, Howes was brought in to manage the first season of the MABIE BROS. CIRCUS by owners Ed and Jere Mabie in 1840.

In 1857 with partner "Colonel" Joseph C. Cushing (1818–1884), he left for England with his own show, HOWES AND CUSHING. The show toured Great Britain until the breakup of the partnership in 1860.

Returning to the United States in 1864, Seth B. Howes first toured his show as Howes' European Circus and Menagerie, then as HOWES' GREAT LON-

DON CIRCUS AND SANGER'S ROYAL BRITISH MENAGERIE from 1864 through 1872. Having made millions of dollars as a showman, Seth B. Howes retired at the end of the 1872 season.

HOWES AND CUSHING   Although touring exclusively overseas, Howes and Cushing was owned and operated by two American circus showmen, Seth B. HOWES and "Colonel" Joseph Cushing (1818–1884).

The men became partners in 1856 for the express purpose of taking a new show, Howes and Cushing, to Great Britain. The circus, complete with performers, a group of Indians, TENTS, WAGONS and approximately 80 HORSES, left the United States on March 25, 1857. The circus entranced British audiences, performing at the London Alhambra and at least one royal performance for Queen Victoria.

The show was financially successful, so two units of Howes and Cushing toured the British provinces in 1858. A third company was added the following year.

On January 24, 1860 Cushing sold his interest in the Howes and Cushing circus back to Howes, ending the partnership. Although the two did join again briefly later that year to produce a small circus for a German tour that ran until autumn, the Howes and Cushing title ended when each man chose to operate his own show under different titles.

Cushing stayed in England with his own circus through the fall of 1862, then returned to the States. Howes returned to the United States two years later, retiring in 1872.

HOWES' GREAT LONDON CIRCUS AND SANGER'S ROYAL BRITISH MENAGERIE   When Seth B. HOWES returned to the United States in 1864 after eight years with his HOWES AND CUSHING circus in England, he reframed his show for American audiences.

Mindful that an international flavor to the show's name would make it a more attractive draw in the United States, Howes first toured his operation as Howes' European Circus and Menagerie. Within a year he changed the title to Howes' Great London Circus and Sanger's Royal British Menagerie.

Howes was a skilled businessman and had grown quite wealthy during his years as a showman. Seeking to retire in 1872, he sold (or turned over) the circus to his nephews, Egbert and Elbert Howes and James E. Kelley. The timing was unfortunate for the nephews, however, because the financial panic of 1873 and the depression that followed resulted in poor attendance.

The nephews sold the show at auction to James E. COOPER, James A. BAILEY and James L. HUTCHINSON. The COOPER & BAILEY CIRCUS absorbed the equipment and was expanded into Howes' Great London Circus and Sanger's Royal British Menagerie, and Cooper and Bailey's International Shows, also referred to as the International Allied Shows.

When P.T. BARNUM entered into the partnership in 1881, the resultant extravaganza toured as P.T. BARNUM'S GREATEST SHOW ON EARTH, HOWES' GREAT LONDON CIRCUS AND SANGER'S ROYAL BRITISH MENAGERIE, or the Barnum & London Circus. The show closed after the 1887 season, ending any direct link between the circus title and Seth B. Howes.

Although they had no authorization to use the famous name, other circus owners began to exploit the Howes title on smaller shows until 1908. That same year Jeremiah "Jerry" MUGIVAN and Bert BOWERS put the Howes' Great London Circus name onto one of their rail shows and toured it until 1921.

The name "Howes" had become so synonymous with circuses that the title remained in use for over a century, with independent shows using it as late as the mid-1950s.

HOXIE BROS. CIRCUS

One of the finest MUD SHOWS ever on the road, the Hoxie Bros. Circus was founded by Leonard Basil " Hoxie" TUCKER in 1952 when a friend, Harold J. Rumbaugh, convinced him to take over his ailing show, the Horne Bros. Circus. Hoxie renamed it, using the title "Bros." after his own name to make it sound like a "family" operation; and the Hoxie Bros. Circus opened in Greenville, Florida on November 17, 1952.

Hoxie Bros. Circus traveled by truck, starting out as a one-ring show under a 60-foot BIG TOP. Hoxie Tucker toured the show for only one season, then worked with Milton "Doc" Bartok's Medicine Company and in construction for the rest of the decade.

On April 8, 1961 Tucker reopened the Hoxie Bros. Circus in Adele, Georgia with his former boss, "Doc" Bartok, as the contracting agent. The show vehicles, which included three semi-trailers, were painted purple and lettered in red, a Hoxie trademark for years. The exotic painting had a practical as well as an artistic purpose. Tucker explained,

"When a truck is lost I can ask filling station owners and town people if they have seen a purple truck."

In 1962 Tucker and Bartok joined their two shows' equipment and formed the Hoxie and Bardex Bros. Circus, with its WINTER QUARTERS in Valdosta, Georgia. The show played from April 7 through October 27 with Col. Tim McCoy (see COL. TIM MCCOY WILD WEST SHOW) as the star CONCERT attraction. The tour was a financial success, but the two partners split at the end of the season end due to a conflict of personalities.

During the winter, Tucker completely reframed his show in his quarters, and the enlarged circus opened in Valdosta on April 12, 1963 and toured a 30-week season through November 2. Throughout the 1960s the Hoxie Bros. Circus continued to increase in size and stature in the circus community.

In the spring of 1966 John R. Hall became office manager of the Hoxie show. Hall had seen his first circus at the age of eight in his hometown of South Boston, Virginia. Following graduation from the University of Virginia in 1957, he received his master's degree from George Peabody College in Nashville, Tennessee and did further graduate studies at Southern Seminary in Louisville, Kentucky. After teaching high school for a few years in Nashville and Miami and Palm Beach in Florida, he joined the Hoxie circus. Hall moved up to business manager and press agent by 1968, and in 1970 he became the general manager.

In 1971 the Hoxie Bros. Circus grew to its largest size when it toured in 21 trucks, plus another on the ADVANCE.

On March 26, 1973 the circus moved under a revolutionary 3,000-seat circular TENT designed by Hall and constructed by Leaf Tent and Sail Co. of SARASOTA, FLORIDA. The 160-foot round canvas top had a single 55-foot CENTER POLE (redesigned at the end of the season to accommodate two poles) and two rows of QUARTER POLES. There were three rings and three stages clustered around the center pole. The BIG CAGE, located on the stage near the BACK DOOR and the bandstand, remained up throughout the entire show.

In August 1973 John Lewis and Jim Silverlake, the owners of the small tented LEWIS BROS. CIRCUS, split. Lewis asked Hoxie Tucker to become his new partner; and they moved the show to Tucker's winter quarters (which, by then, were in Miami, Florida). Lewis and Tucker trouped the reorganized show together for two seasons. In 1976 Tucker became sole owner and transformed the show into a second touring unit, Hoxie's Great American Circus.

That same year Hoxie Tucker toured a GORILLA on each unit. He purchased a nine-year-old male ape named Gory from Bobby Berosini for the Hoxie Bros. Circus. The gorilla, renamed Mongo, was toured in the original cage truck (leased from Bob and Mae Noel) that was built for GARGANTUA in 1938. For the Great American show, Tucker leased a second gorilla, Micky, from RINGLING BROS. AND BARNUM & BAILEY CIRCUS, dubbed him Kongo and toured him on the truck (also leased from the Noels) that had replaced Gargantua's original cage in 1965. For the next 20 years Tucker added and reduced equipment and personnel on both units according to the vicissitudes of the economy and need but always presented clean, family shows with good value for the price of admission.

Tucker was on Hoxie's Great American Circus show when he was stomped by Janet, one of his elephants, on June 5, 1983, in Geneva, New York. Due to his broken pelvis and advanced age, Hoxie Tucker chose to retire, selling the shows and titles to his then-manager, Allan C. HILL. The units were merged and evolved into Hill's current show, Allan C. Hill's Great American Circus.

HOXIE'S GREAT AMERICAN CIRCUS
See HILL, ALLAN C.; HOXIE BROS. CIRCUS; LEWIS BROS. CIRCUS; TUCKER, LEONARD BASIL "HOXIE."

HOYLE, GEOFF
See CIRQUE DU SOLEIL; PICKLE FAMILY CIRCUS, THE.

HUMAN CANNONBALL
A daredevil act that has been associated with circuses and outdoor amusements for over a century, the human cannonball remains a dangerous, if popular, attraction.

One of the primary forerunners of the modern cannonball act was LULU, who performed the act in the 1870s by being shot in the air by springs. The first actual cannon act performed in the United States was by George LOYAL, the "human projectile," in 1879. He was quickly followed by ZAZEL (born Rosa M. Richter) in England. Mademoiselle Zazel was introduced by P.T. BARNUM in 1880 in his BARNUM'S GREAT TRAVELING MUSEUM, MENAGERIE, CARAVAN, HIPPODROME AND CIRCUS.

Zazel was not actually exploded from the cannon by means of a regular powder charge. Nevertheless, the method was extremely dangerous. In an elaborate takeoff of Lulu's original act, Zazel stood on a small platform within the tube of the cannon. The bottom of the small circle was attached to a heavy spring, and as the tension of the spring was released, a light gunpowder charge was shot off. The landing was in a large net set up at the far end of the circus arena.

The first patent of the human cannonball apparatus (U.S. Patent No. 214,663) was granted to William Leonard Hunt on April 22, 1879. The technique, though refined, has basically remained the same to the present day.

The name most often associated with the term "human cannonball" is that of the man who perfected the stunt, its publicity and performance to a fine art: Hugo ZACCHINI. Since his first appearance with the RINGLING BROS. AND BARNUM & BAILEY CIRCUS in 1929, many members of the Zacchini family have entered the circus world. The original Zacchini cannon is on display at the CIRCUS WORLD MUSEUM in BARABOO, WISCONSIN.

The human cannonball act has become a permanent, if rarely seen, feature of the American circus. In the 1991 season, for instance, at least two shows, the BENTLEY BROS. CIRCUS and Ringling Red Unit, featured the stunt. On the Ringling show, Jon Weiss and Philip Peters appeared during the show's finale as human projectiles from a massive double-barreled cannon.

HUMAN VOLCANO
Usually reserved as a fire-eater's final trick, the human volcano is sometimes called the big blow-out. The volcano is the most impressive feat, and the most dangerous stunt in a fire-eater's repertoire.

The performer takes about a tablespoonful of flammable liquid, such as gasoline or lighter fluid, into the mouth without swallowing. Holding the burning torch at arm's length, the fire-eater "spits" the entire capful of liquid at the torch. A huge ball of flame erupts around the torch.

Besides the usual dangers of the FIRE-EATING act, the human volcano is particularly perilous because even a slight breeze can blow the burst of fire back into the fire-eater's face. Also, if the performer "dribbles" rather than forces out all the liquid at one time, the flame can follow the fluid and vapors back to the mouth and into the lungs. The audience is subjected to increased danger as well, because it is difficult for the performer to control the flame at such a distance.

HUNT, CHARLES T. (1873–1957)

Born in Rosendale, New York on August 7, 1873, Charles T. Hunt worked as a boy at his father's stables in nearby Kingston. At the age of 17, he joined the BARNUM & BAILEY CIRCUS.

In 1892 Hunt started his own show, Hunt's Vaudeville Circus, later taking his father (John Hunt) as a partner. After a succession of titles, the show was finally named the HUNT BROS. CIRCUS when Hunt turned over ownership to his sons, Charles J. and Harry T. Hunt, in the 1930s. He remained general supervisor of the show until his death.

Known as "Mr. Circus," Hunt was an expert animal trainer, especially of dogs and HORSES; occasionally he played the baritone horn in the circus band, and often he appeared as a CLOWN. Despite having lost sight in one eye as a result of a kick from a horse in 1919, he performed on the slack wire (see WIRE WALKING) until 1932.

Although suffering from asthma and heart trouble, he acted as RINGMASTER for the show's last performance of the 1957 season in Palisades Amusement Park in Palisade, New Jersey. Three days later, on September 11, he died of a heart attack at his WINTER QUARTERS home in Florence, New Jersey. In his 65 years of circus ownership, Hunt never missed a single performance of the show.

HUNT BROS. CIRCUS

The Hunt Bros. Circus was the longest-running circus in American history owned and operated under the same family management.

Originally entitled Hunt's Vaudeville Circus, the show was founded in 1892 by Charles T. HUNT, starting with just two WAGONS, four HORSES and five performers. Over the years, Hunt changed the title of the show to Hunt's Nickelplate Circus, Hunt's Three-Ring Circus and finally—upon turning over ownership in the 1930s to his sons, Charles J. and Harry T. Hunt—the Hunt Bros. Circus. Hunt re-

mained active with his show, however, appearing as RINGMASTER just three days before his death in 1957.

The Hunt Bros. Circus toured from April to October on a series of one-night stands up and down the East Coast, from Richmond, Virginia to Maine. A three-ring circus, the show's MIDWAY featured a combined SIDESHOW and MENAGERIE. One of the first shows to motorize, its equipment included 30 trucks, plus 50 horses, eight BULLS and six lions, a six-man band and 140 people in its cast and crew. At its peak in the mid-1950s it was performing its two-and-a-half-hour show under a 100-by-225-foot BIG TOP.

A SUNDAY SCHOOL SHOW from its inception, the Hunt Bros. Circus was welcomed back year after year by its local sponsors. Besides being a clean, family operation, the show was a real moneymaker and always active in its own promotion. It was the first circus to use a helicopter for publicity purposes. Among other innovations, the Hunt Bros. Circus was one of the first shows to use aluminum poles and flame-retardant canvas in its TENTS.

HUTCHINSON, JAMES L. (1846–1919)

James L. Hutchinson became a partner of James A. BAILEY and James E. COOPER when they expanded their COOPER & BAILEY CIRCUS into the International Allied Shows upon their purchase of the old Seth B. HOWES circus.

Their main competition by 1880 was the circus owned by P.T. BARNUM, then under the management of the FLATFOOTS. When Barnum suggested a merger of their circuses, James E. Cooper sold his interest, as did the Flatfoots. Hutchinson became the new partner of Barnum and James A. Bailey, and their revised show opened in New York City on March 18, 1881, following a torchlight procession through the center of town two nights earlier, as P.T. BARNUM'S GREATEST SHOW ON EARTH, HOWES' GREAT LONDON CIRCUS AND SANGER'S ROYAL BRITISH MENAGERIE.

Although Hutchinson was an equal business partner with Barnum and Bailey, he was not flamboyant and apparently preferred a behind-the-scenes position. Little has been noted about him historically, and he is not remembered as being an astute showman. The conservative Hutchinson was certainly an unlikely match for Barnum, the extravagant impresario. In late 1881, for instance, when Barnum was negotiating to purchase JUMBO for $10,000, Hutchinson is reported to have objected, "What is the difference between an elephant seven feet high and another 11 or 12 feet height? An elephant is an elephant."

During the next six years, Hutchinson and Barnum always remained partners, even as other members of the management team changed. In 1887 James A. Bailey returned from a health sabbatical and purchased Hutchinson's share of the show. Hutchinson retired from show business, and the remaining two partners renamed their show the BARNUM & BAILEY CIRCUS.

INSIDE TALKER   Circus jargon for the LECTURER who introduces the acts inside the SIDESHOW tent. The inside talker welcomes the audience and describes each act as he jumps from platform to platform. In fact, he may also double as a performer himself. He also turns the microphone over to the acts that want to do their own talks or have items to PITCH.

If a blade box is carried on the sideshow, the inside talker usually handles this final pitch. To perform the popular magical illusion, a young lady lies down in a horizontal box. The magician/talker pierces the box, and seemingly the girl, with a large number of swords, rods and broad blades. The talker assures the audience that the girl is not hurt but is a "female contortionist" who is able to wrap herself around the blades.

"Now the young lady receives no remuneration for this part of the program," he GRINDS. However, "for a small silver donation," audience members are allowed to come up onto the platform and look down through the open lid. Often, to make the offer more appealing, he feigns difficulty getting the last sword through the box. Only by his reaching in and apparently removing the girl's costume is there enough space for her to bend around the close blades.

(See also TALKER.)

INTERNATIONAL ALLIED SHOWS   See BAILEY, JAMES A.; BARNUM, P.T.; COOPER & BAILEY CIRCUS; HOWES, SETH B.; HOWES' GREAT LONDON CIRCUS AND SANGER'S ROYAL BRITISH MENAGERIE; HUTCHINSON, JAMES L.; P.T. BARNUM'S GREATEST SHOW ON EARTH, HOWES' GREAT LONDON CIRCUS AND SANGER'S ROYAL BRITISH MENAGERIE.

INTERNATIONAL CIRCUS HALL OF FAME, INC.   See PERU, INDIANA; WAGONS.

IRANISTAN   Located just outside BRIDGEPORT, CONNECTICUT, Iranistan was the ostentatious residence of P.T. BARNUM during his years as proprietor of the AMERICAN MUSEUM.

Built in 1848 and modeled after the original Oriental pavilion built for King George IV in Brighton, England, Iranistan was deliberately pretentious, with decorated spires, turrets and domes. The interior was filled with tapestries, Italian sculpture and floors of imported marble. Outside deer and elk roamed the 17-acre park on which Iranistan stood. The grounds were dotted with fountains and landscaped.

Iranistan was purposely built in view of the railroad tracks so that, according to Barnum, it "might serve as an advertisement of my various enterprises." It could be seen from a distance of three miles.

The palace cost Barnum $200,000 to build and furnish. Almost 1,000 guests attended his housewarming party, which was held on November 14, 1848.

In 1855, Barnum began to write his memoirs during his semiretirement at Iranistan. Following his bankruptcy due to a bad investment in the Jer-

Bambi Aurora performs the Iron Jaw, wardrobed as a human butterfly. (Photo by Bill Biggerstaff, courtesy of Bambi Burnes)

ome Clock Company in East Bridgeport, Barnum was forced to leave Iranistan and tour with TOM THUMB. Barnum returned to New York as manager of the American Museum, and while he was there in 1857 an accidental fire burned his beloved Iranistan to the ground.

IRON JAW The iron jaw is a classic circus act and is seemingly one of the most dangerous and impossible to perform. The aerialist performs the routine suspended at the end of a rope, held in place only by the teeth. The iron jaw is often a full act and at other times the BLOWOFF stunt of another AERIAL ACT.

The iron jaw mouthpiece is crucial to the performance of the act. The creation of the act is uncertain, but it dates back at least to the days of the early

MUD SHOWS. The first mouthpiece was simply several layers of leather sewn together to fit the contours of the inside of the performer's mouth. The semicircular leather pad was then attached to a swivel that hung from a suspended WEB. The performer simply bit as hard as possible into the leather while being drawn aloft.

With the introduction of modern plastic and nylon dental plates in the 1930s, it became possible to produce new and safer mouthpieces for the showgirls, who usually perform the routine. The artist has a cast made of the upper and lower teeth at a dental laboratory; then a full upper and lower set of plates, without teeth, is produced. A long leather strap, as wide as the performer's full bite, is folded in half; one plate is sewn (through holes drilled in the prothesis) onto each end of band.

Needless to say, this unique mouthpiece can be used only the showgirl for whom it was fitted. In performance, the artist still bites down against a leather band; but the plastic plates give an added safety factor by allowing a firm bite in the same place each performance.

One of the greatest dangers of the act is the possibility of gagging and choking. This first occurs when the apparatus, which fills the entire mouth cavity, is inserted. Also, when the performer hangs vertically, the tongue falls back toward the throat, a natural tendency that must be overcome with practice.

The mouthpiece also can chip or break during performance, which could result in a fall. Bambi Aurora, a showgirl who was taught the iron jaw by BARBETTE, had her mouthpiece plates made out of vitalium, a noncorrosive metal, to prevent just such a problem. To her knowledge, it is the only iron jaw mouthpiece currently made out of metal rather than the usual dental plastic.

One of the most famous iron jaw performers was Antoinette CONCELLO (née Comeau) who, after marrying Art CONCELLO, switched to the FLYING TRAPEZE and became the first female artist to perform the triple somersault.

J

JACKPOTS Circus jargon for stories and tall tales about the circus. When circus folk sit around and exchange anecdotes, they are said to be "cutting up jackpots."

JACKS AND STRINGERS Along with wooden planks for benches, jacks and stringers form the wooden bleacher-style seating found on MUD SHOWS that do not carry SEAT WAGONS. The invention of the 11-tier seating system is generally credited to "Dr." Gilbert R. SPALDING in the mid-1800s.

To manufacture a jack (also sometimes known as a "scissors jack"), two boards of the desired length are laid on top of each other. Halfway along the length of the boards, they are loosely bolted together. When stood up and spread, the boards form a large "X."

The stringer is a wooden 2 by 4, one side of which has been cut such that when the board is held at a 45-degree angle, it appears to be a miniature set of steps or stairs. One end of the stringer has a loop of iron attached to it so that a stake, driven through the ring and almost entirely into the ground, will hold the board down.

To set the seats, a jack is positioned near the SIDEWALL. A stringer is laid into the "X" with the steps on the stringer facing upward; the stringer is then staked into the ground. For safety, a STAKE COVER, usually a section of cut firehose, is placed over the head of the stake. After a series of these are set up, boards are placed across the notches of the stringers to form rows of seats. To prevent the planks from sliding sideways, they are lashed down to the stringers by criss-crossing ropes from top to bottom.

If the bleachers are very high and contain many rows, a smaller jack is often placed halfway down the length of the stringer and hammered into place. This second jack helps to support the weight of the spectators and to hold the bleachers into position.

A jack is also used during the LAY OUT and SET UP of the BIG TOP. After the CENTER POLE is positioned on a BALE RING tent, the upper end of the pole is raised off the ground and laid across a small jack. This allows the crew to set the bale ring and attach the necessary rigging to the pole before it is raised.

JACOBS, LOU (1903–1992) A fixture in the CLOWN ALLEY of the RINGLING BROS. AND BARNUM & BAILEY CIRCUS for over five decades, this AUGUSTE CLOWN began his professional career as a gymnast.

Born Jacob Ludwig in Wesermüde, Bremerhaven, Germany, Jacobs's first job in show business was the tail end in an alligator costume when he was seven. He saw his first clown act at the age of 11 and joined a small German circus as a clown that same year. Jacobs excelled as an acrobat and balancer by the age of 15 and appeared as a double contortionist with his partner/straight man, Michael Morris.

He first toured the United States in 1923, appearing at fairs and in a vaudeville tumbling act. While performing for a year with the Morris and Morris Circus in 1924, he was spotted by The GREAT-

EST SHOW ON EARTH; he moved to The BIG ONE in 1925 and stayed for the rest of his professional career.

Seen on many of Ringling's posters, Jacobs's clown character was instantly recognizable with his high arched eyebrows, elongated and pointed forehead and tiny hat; his makeup became the prototype for the flamboyant American auguste clown.

His most popular gag was the clown car: Jacobs, a 6-foot-1 inch-tall, gangly clown, would emerge from a rattling and backfiring minuscule 2-foot-by-3-foot automobile. He could perform this trademark stunt only because of his years as a contortionist. Jacobs first began working on the concept in 1944, finally introducing it in a 1946 Ringling SPEC.

His famous pet gags included a motorized bathtub or baby carriage, and carrying one of his live Chihuahuas (Knucklehead—who toured with Jacobs for 14 seasons—or Peewee) in a gigantic hot-dog roll.

In 1952, Jacobs appeared in Cecil B. De Mille's movie, "The Greatest Show on Earth." (See FILMS, CIRCUS.)

In 1953 Lou Jacobs married Jean Rockwell, a former circus performer. Both of his daughters, Lou Ann (Barrenda) and Dolly, entered the profession as aerialists, and Lou Ann toured as a showgirl with Ringling during Jacobs's last seasons.

Jacobs has been seen on millions of posters, T-shirts and other circus memorabilia, but his greatest honor was having his face appear on a 1966 postage stamp. Lou Jacobs officially retired from The Greatest Show on Earth in 1987, but he continued to occasionally teach clown techniques at the Ringling Bros. CLOWN COLLEGE in SARASOTA, FLORIDA where he lived.

In 1989 Jacobs was inducted into the Circus Hall of Fame and the CLOWN HALL OF FAME. He also received a Ringling Bros. and Barnum & Bailey Circus Lifetime Achievement Award.

Lou Jacobs died of heart failure in Sarasota Memorial Hospital on September 13, 1992.

(See also CLOWN GAGS; CLOWNS.)

JACOBS, CAPT. TERRELL (1903–1957)   One of the great trainers of big CATS, during the peak of his career in the 1930s and the 1940s Capt. Terrell M. Jacobs was second in popularity only to Clyde BEATTY. Working with black-maned African lions and black leopards, Jacobs was nicknamed "the Lion King."

Jacobs worked the largest cat act of all time—sometimes as many as 51 felines in a 50-foot cage. Eschewing the "great white hunter" look, he appeared in the ring dressed in a white jacket and a red cape. Over a 38-year career he appeared with various shows, including the RINGLING BROS. AND BARNUM & BAILEY CIRCUS in 1938 and 1939 and the COLE BROS. CIRCUS in 1950. For a time he operated his own circus.

For much of his lifetime Jacobs was a resident of PERU, INDIANA; and he died there in his home of a heart attack on December 24, 1957. His farm and training yards are maintained today under private ownership. His grandson, Capt. Terrell Jacobs III, was one of the founders and is a featured performer on the CULPEPPER-MERRIWEATHER GREAT COMBINED CIRCUS.

JAGUARS   See CATS.

JAMES, JIMMY (1940–   )   Popular RINGMASTER on the CLYDE BEATTY-COLE BROS. CIRCUS, Jimmy James was born on August 25, 1940 in Opelika, Alabama and raised in Columbus, Georgia. He saw his first circus, the RINGLING BROS. AND BARNUM & BAILEY CIRCUS, in the 1950s while it was still under canvas.

After graduation from high school, his first job in the entertainment field was as a country western and gospel music concert promoter for Martel Britt Enterprises out of Birmingham, Alabama. He also had the opportunity to promote several dates for the Ringling show.

James joined The GREATEST SHOW ON EARTH around 1960, hired to work in the transportation department, but immediately he transferred to the wardrobe department. When Art CONCELLO, who was manager of the Ringling show, bought shares in the Clyde Beatty-Cole Bros. Circus in 1965, James moved there. Concello sold his interest later that same season, but James remained with the tent show, becoming one of its featured WHITEFACE CLOWNS under producing clown Ken Dodd. In the 1970s James was elevated to producing clown, in charge of CLOWN ALLEY and the selection of the CLOWN GAGS.

Interviewed for WHITE TOPS Magazine, Jimmy James has very definite opinions on clowning. He loves "sight comedy gags" and "big clown production numbers with big props. . . . With a great payoff at the end!" Among his favorite gags are the firehouse sketch and the clown doctor routine.

It is a lot of work to be a whiteface clown. You have to remain immaculately clean; your wardrobe always must be perfect . . . It probably takes twice as long to make up. And twice as long to remove the makeup.

About TRAMP CLOWNS? I am a great believer that tramp clowns have to be older people. You've got to have mileage in your face.

Around 1980 James, the possessor of a deep, baritone voice, was asked to become the assistant or backup announcer in the BIG TOP. Eventually he was asked to announce full time. Dressed in the traditional red tails, black formal trousers and top hat ("Not to wear. Never to wear. I use it to direct more than anything else"), James considers Harold Ronk, the longtime singing ringmaster who retired from the Ringling show in 1981, to have been the greatest of all announcers.

Jimmy James holds definite views on the role of the ringmaster:

Announcements should be interesting . . . fascinating. You should use all kinds of tongue twisters, like "Mighty mobilization of ponderous performing pachyderms." . . . [And] a ringmaster can manufacture his own words.

A circus ringmaster should be someone of dignity . . . of excellence and class . . . But more than all that, I think a good ringmaster can be—and certain should be— the gold gingerbread trimming on the circus.

JAMES M. COLE CIRCUS   See COLE, JAMES M.

JANET   See ELEPHANTS; ROGUE ELEPHANTS.

J.H. ESCHMAN CIRCUS   Among the scores of small tented circuses that came and disappeared at the turn of the century was the J.H. Eschman Circus. Touring for about 15 years on rails, the show was abandoned after the 1917 season; its equipment was auctioned.

J.H. LAPEARL CIRCUS   The J.H. LaPearl Circus had its WINTER QUARTERS in Danville, Illinois in the 1890s and toured as its own operation for about a decade. In 1900, however, the equipment was purchased and merged into the Great Wallace Circus.

(See also GREAT WALLACE SHOWS.)

JILL   Circus jargon for "girl."

JOEY   Circus slang for a clown, named after Joseph GRIMALDI (1778–1837), a famous 18th-century English clown.

(See also CLOWN GAGS; CLOWNS.)

JOHN AND MABLE RINGLING MUSEUM OF ART, THE
Owned and operated by the state of Florida as a public museum, the John and Mable Ringling Museum encompasses a 68-acre estate, including all of the grounds, buildings and artwork acquired by John RINGLING—circus magnate—during his lifetime.

During his years as the owner of the RINGLING BROS. AND BARNUM & BAILEY CIRCUS, John Ringling was also a tycoon in railroads and real estate. In 1912 he moved his residence to Florida and bought a bayfront estate with an existing frame house in SARASOTA, FLORIDA, just south of Bradenton and the Manatee County line, as a winter vacation residence. After a number of years of real estate development in Sarasota County, Ringling began construction on his spectacular Venetian Gothic-style home, CA' D'ZAN ("House of John") in 1924.

During his travels around the world looking for new sensations for his circus, Ringling also amassed an enormous art collection. He collected some 600 paintings, numerous statues, decorative pieces and 27 tapestries between 1924 and 1931. Arguably, the most valuable portion of the collection are five tapestries by Peter Paul Rubens. The artwork also includes other important masterpieces; baroque paintings by Guercino, Poussin and Van Dyck; works by Cranach from the German late medieval era; the baroque-era realism of Hals; and the Renaissance work of Piero di Cosimo.

In 1927 John Ringling commissioned a building to serve as an art gallery for the collection, with the specific intention of eventually bequeathing both to the public. John H. Phillips designed the John and Mable Ringling Museum of Art—as the galleries alone were originally known—in an Italian Renaissance style. The halls consist of a 47,000-square-foot, U-shaped structure built with stucco walls on a stone base, enclosing a European-style formal courtyard. Twenty-one galleries are contained within the two wings joined by the large lobby area. The gardens within the courtyard exhibit reproductions of ancient and mannerist sculpture. Also part of the original museum building was the Asolo Theater, an 18th-century playhouse imported from Asolo, Italy.

The museum was completed in 1929 at a cost of approximately $4 million dollars. It was first opened to the public on March 30, 1930 and the entire estate—henceforth to be known as the John and Mable Ringling Museum of Art—was given to the state of Florida upon John Ringling's death on December 2, 1936.

The state accepted the grounds in 1946, making it the State Art Museum of Florida and providing funds toward its continued operation, including salaries for 96 staff members and funding for capital improvements. Two years later John Ringling's memory was honored by establishing a circus museum on the grounds. Ringling himself had not left any circus memorabilia as part of his legacy, so the museum acquired the extensive circus collection through donations and purchases. The Circus Galleries, housed in John Ringling's original garage—now renovated—include posters, photographs, costumes, props and rare circus wagons.

The museum's directors have also continued to acquire artwork. Including the Old Masters, the museum now owns approximately 750 paintings and more than 10,000 *objects d'art* from around the world. So extensive is the collection that it is now impossible to have it all on display at one time.

The Asolo State Theater, one of the nation's top regional theaters, is now located in the new $10 million Asolo Center for the Performing Arts, which also houses a laboratory theater for the Florida State University/Asolo Conservatory of Professional Actor Training, sound studios, classrooms and offices. The original Asolo Theater, still located on the Ringling grounds as an adjunct to the art galleries building, is used for the museum's educational programs and special presentations.

By the mid-1980s it became obvious that the facility was due for major renovation. Structural damage had been brought on by the hot, humid climate and the daily visits of hundreds of patrons. A ten-year, $20 million program was begun, commencing with emergency roofing in 1981.

Dr. Laurence J. Ruggiero, who became director in 1985, stated, "The restoration of this museum will be my first priority. I'm honored to be entrusted with the responsibility and the opportunity to bring this wonderful building and its collection to their rightful position in the art world."

Under his guidance, contractors installed proper state-of-the-art gallery lighting, climate controls and fire/safety and security systems. Ornamental moldings, ceilings and wainscoting were restored to their original grandeur. At the same time, every painting was examined and treated and its frame cleaned or replaced. A new entrance to the lobby was also added. The galleries were reopened to the public in January 1991.

Additional information on the John and Mable Ringling Museum of Art can be obtained by writing P.O. Box 1624, Sarasota, Florida 34230.

JOHN H. MURRAY CIRCUS   See STONE & MURRAY CIRCUS.

JOHN H. SPARKS OLD VIRGINIA SHOWS   See SPARKS CIRCUS.

JOHN ROBINSON   This call across a circus LOT creates an immediate stir of activity, because a "John Robinson" show is a hurried or abbreviated show, usually due to some imminent emergency.

The slang was originally aimed derisively at the circus entrepreneur John ROBINSON who was notorious for giving shortened, or briefer-than-advertised, performances without valid reasons. Because the public came away feeling cheated, the practice tended to BURN THE TERRITORY against other circuses.

In popular usage today, however, the stigma of bilking the public no longer exists. Indeed, a "John Robinson" is called only in the case of an impending disaster, such as a reported twister in the area, an accident or a violent gang threatening to disrupt the show. The word is given through BACK YARD word-of-mouth, and the RINGMASTER sometimes pages an imaginary "Mr. John Robinson" to the bandstand.

While none of the acts is canceled unless it is absolutely necessary to vacate the tent quickly, all acts are tightened to only their essential tricks and best stunts. In a well-effected John Robinson show, the audience is not aware that the acts are being sped up or that it is missing any part of the performance.

(See also HEY RUBE!; JOHN ROBINSON CIRCUS.)

JOHN ROBINSON CIRCUS Although the great circus owner John ROBINSON claimed to have started his show in 1824, the John Robinson Circus more probably began in the 1830s or 1840s. With its WINTER QUARTERS in Cincinnati, the John Robinson Circus toured in a variety of forms and in combination with other titles.

One of Robinson's first shows, Robinson & Foster, toured from 1842 to 1845. When a performer on that show, Gilbert N. ELDRED, became Robinson's new partner in 1846, the circus changed its name to ROBINSON & ELDRED'S GREAT SOUTHERN SHOW. The partnership came to an end on June 28, 1856 in Richmond, Virginia, when Eldred bought out his partner's share of the circus.

Robinson used the money to purchase a one-year-old, bankrupt show, FLAGG & AYMAR'S INTERNATIONAL CIRCUS. Merely retitling the operation John Robinson's International Circus and Menagerie, Robinson set out on tour in Geneva, New York on September 1, 1856.

Despite Robinson's Yankee ties, his circus was always the top-grossing show in the South both before and after the Civil War. In 1870 the elder John turned over management of his show to his grandson, John G. Robinson.

The Robinson show transferred to rails in 1881. Still undergoing name changes, the circus was one of the seven largest rail shows in the country, traveling on 35 cars by 1891. Ultimately, at the time of old John Robinson's death in 1888, it was known as John Robinson's Ten Big Shows. The show continued as a family operation, nevertheless. In the 1890s the circus was still able to boast of "three generations of circus kings," calling itself the "Greatest of All American Shows."

For the 1898 season, the RINGLING BROTHERS leased the show and set up Henry Ringling as manager. The Robinson family resumed ownership the following year and continued to tour with it through 1911. The show set idle through 1915, and it was purchased by Jeremiah "Jerry" MUGIVAN and Bert BOWERS for the 1916 season.

At season's end, Mugivan and Bowers sold all of the original Robinson equipment and kept only the title. Using new apparatus, they toured the John Robinson Circus through 1929.

John Ringling ran the original Robinson show for one last season in 1930. The title only was added to the SELLS-FLOTO CIRCUS name in 1932 and to the Al G. Barnes-Sells Floto Circus of 1938.

JOHN ROBINSON'S INTERNATIONAL CIRCUS AND MENAGERIE See JOHN ROBINSON CIRCUS; ROBINSON, JOHN.

JOHN ROBINSON'S TEN BIG SHOWS See JOHN ROBINSON CIRCUS; ROBINSON, JOHN.

JOHN STRONG CIRCUS See STRONG, "BIG" JOHN.

JOHNSON, FRED (1892–1990) A native of Chicago, Fred Johnson became one of the most renowned painters of sideshow BANNERS in the circus industry.

At the age of 14, Johnson began work with the U.S. Tent and Awning Co., a major tent and rag (i.e., painted canvas) BANNERLINE supplier, and he studied his craft under H.D. Cummings. Later he moved to O. Henry Tent & Awning Co., where he remained for 40 years.

In addition to his circus work, Fred Johnson also designed ads for the Century of Progress Exhibition, the 1933 Chicago World's Fair and other parks and amusement centers. He continued to paint clown pictures from his retirement in 1981 to his death in 1990.

Johnson's banners were used by almost every large and small circus, including the RINGLING BROS. AND BARNUM & BAILEY CIRCUS, the CLYDE BEATTY CIRCUS and CIRCUS KIRK. Considered true American folk art, examples of his work were exhibited in 1989 at the State of Illinois Art Center Gallery and are on display at the CIRCUS WORLD MUSEUM in BARABOO, WISCONSIN, and The JOHN AND MABLE RINGLING MUSEUM OF ART in SARASOTA, FLORIDA.

JOHNSON, RED See CULPEPPER AND MERRIWEATHER GREAT COMBINED CIRCUS; STRONG, "BIG" JOHN.

JOMAR After Alf T. Ringling's death in 1919, John RINGLING and Charles were the only two surviving founding brothers of the Ringling circus dynasty. John Ringling seldom visited the RINGLING BROS. AND BARNUM & BAILEY CIRCUS personally. When he did visit the show, John Ringling, by then one of the 20 wealthiest men in the world due to his speculation in oil, railroads and real estate, wanted to travel in style.

Around 1904 he had the Pullman Company design and build an eight-stateroom, 82-foot-long private railroad car, which he named the "Jomar," borrowing letters from the names John and Mable Ringling. the Jomar's interior was replete with Victorian splendor, and it was the longest Pullman car ever to travel on the nation's rails.

From the sitting room, a passageway connected to John Ringling's double stateroom, which in turn was connected to Mable's single stateroom by a bath. Both bedrooms had brass beds. Beyond them were the dining room, pantry, kitchen and servants' quarters. While in SARASOTA, FLORIDA, the Jomar was parked on a pier off Strawberry Avenue.

John Ringling used the car to entertain a host of dignitaries and stars that visited the circus, including General John Pershing, Thomas Edison, Senator Warren G. Harding and Queen Marie of Rumania.

After the death of "Uncle John," John Ringling NORTH removed much of the opulent interior and installed air conditioning. He used the Jomar as his office when visiting the circus and, like his uncle, to entertain important guests. Cecil B. DeMille used the Jomar as his home during preproduction of the film *The Greatest Show on Earth* (see FILMS, CIRCUS).

Eventually the car went on display at the Ringling WINTER QUARTERS, where guests could stand on an elevated platform to peer inside. For a time circus employees used it as a dormitory.

It moved with the circus quarters to Venice, Florida in 1961 and was put into storage, where it was vandalized. Although the Jomar was refurbished in 1973 and given a new roof, it was soon hauled to the Port Tampa yards of the Seaboard Railroad and stored with unremarkable circus rail cars. After that, the car seemed to have disappeared. Somehow it made its way to Louisiana where, in 1989, the Friends of Jomar Society located the rusting, historic car. They bought it and transported it back to Sarasota at a cost of $18,000, hoping eventually to restore it to its original beauty under John Ringling's ownership. "We figure it will take $300,000 or $400,000 to put Jomar back in original condition," says Don Hughes, treasurer of the not-for-profit society. "It's amazing the things that people have said they'd give us, things they'd gotten ahold of and stored away. We've been offered [the car's original] china and linens."

Meanwhile, the Jomar sits in the 1000 block of Central Avenue in Sarasota on a railroad siding donated by the Florida Mining & Materials Company.

JONAH'S LUCK   Circus jargon for unusually bad weather or mud. A storm or even heavy rains on a soft LOT can result in a BLOWDOWN.

JONES BROTHERS SHOWS   For more than four decades, J. Augustus Jones and his brother, Elmer Jones, toured a multitude of circuses and tented minstrel shows, often more than a half dozen different titles at a time. Augustus opened his first show in 1892, and Elmer closed their last show in 1936 before retiring to Pennsylvania.

Most of their operations were two-car railroad shows, which led to their nickname as the "Kings of the Two-Car Shows." Over the years their show titles included the Jones Bros. Circus, West & Wells, Great Eastern Hippodrome, Cole & Rogers, Cooper Bros., and King & Tucker. Three of their larger shows were Buffalo Ranch Wild West, Indian Bill's Wild West and, from the 1916 through the 1918 season, the COLE BROS. CIRCUS.

JUGGLING   The term "juggling" usually refers to keeping three or more items in the air simultaneously, catching each as it falls and tossing it back into the air. No great skill is required to "throw and catch" fewer than three items.

The most often used, or tossed, item in juggling is the ball. Each juggler finds balls that are easy to hold in the palm and are a comfortable weight. Many use common rubber balls from toy stores, tennis balls or, more often, lacrosse balls. The props of one manufacturer, the late Harry Moll of Denver, Colorado, were highly prized among professional jugglers for their weight, color and size; today "Moll" balls are collectors' items. Moll balls came in two sizes and shapes: a 2¼-inch white solid rubber ball and a 1¾-inch yellow solid rubber ball.

To perform the simplest of juggling "patterns," one ball is cupped in the left hand and two in the right hand (for right-handed performers). The right hand tosses, or "scoops," one of the balls upward and toward the left in an arc, with it peaking about eye level. As the ball starts to descend, the left hand tosses its ball in an arc up and toward the right. The first ball is caught by the left hand. Meanwhile, the right hand tosses up its second ball and, a split second later, catches the ball that was tossed by the left hand. The continuation of this series of tosses is the basis for all ball juggling.

There are, of course, myriad variations on the theme. The standard ball juggling assumes a criss-cross look to the spectators' eyes. The "shower," however, juggles all of the balls in the same direction, creating the image of a large circle. To perform the shower, the right hand tosses a ball up in the usual arc. The left hand, instead of tossing its ball up, tosses it horizontally directly into the right hand, replacing the first ball. A split second later, the first ball is caught by the left hand as the right hand throws up the third ball.

The "Fountain" is, in effect, a one-handed shower. The first ball is thrown straight upward. Before it is caught in the same hand, a second and third ball have already been tossed. Depending on the number of balls and the speed with which the juggler can perform this stunt, the fountain can literally look like water bubbling up and down. An ambidextrous juggler who can fountain with both hands simultaneously creates one of the prettiest juggling patterns possible.

"Clubs," sometimes called "pins," are the second most popular object that can be juggled. Formally called "Indian clubs," they resemble a sort of thin bowling pin. Professional jugglers often make their own clubs, adjusting the weight and shape to their own comfort and specific needs.

"Rings" are another commonly seen juggling object. A ring is made by cutting a circle approximately eight inches in diameter out of a sheet of wood or plastic. A concentric hole, approximately 6½-inches in diameter, is cut out of the center of the disc, thus forming a ring.

Of course, any object that can be lifted, balanced and caught can be juggled. Many jugglers toss varied items, such as a ball, club and apple, all at the same time. To increase the audience's thrill and suspense, many performers juggle truly dangerous items, such as flaming torches, butcher knives or battle axes. Throwing objects between two or more members of a juggling team is known as "passing."

A whole separate genre of the art is gyroscopic juggling, in which objects are not merely tossed and caught, but are also spun, twisted, twirled, swung or rotated in relation to the juggler's body. In essence, the object stays in a relatively stable position because it is spinning. Examples of gyroscopic juggling are antipodism (or FOOT JUGGLING), a RISLEY ACT, the DEVIL STICKS and spinning plates at the ends of sticks.

Although it is possible to learn to juggle from a book, such as John Cassidy and B.C. Rimbeaux's hilarious *Juggling for the Complete Klutz*, it is far easier to learn from another artist. One teacher renowned for the number of jugglers and circus performers he has gotten into the sawdust ring is Hovey BUR-GESS of New York City.

In Lorant and Carroll's book *The Pickle Family Circus,* Peggy Snider, co-founder of The PICKLE FAM-ILY CIRCUS, says that juggling has certain rules of etiquette, which can't be learned from a book.

> *One key to . . . our etiquette is that the responsibility for the pass is with the passer. You should not be required to catch any damn thing I throw your way; if you miss it, likely as not, I blew it. On the other hand, the responsibility for correcting the problem is with the person closest to the dropped club. It's up to them to figure out whether they can pick up the club while the act is still going on, or whether they should say, 'stop.'*

Both hobbyists and professionals are drawn to the ranks of the International Jugglers Association. The organization has local chapters, sponsors an annual convention that features competitions in many categories and publishes an official magazine, *Juggler's World.* Information on the International Jugglers Association can be obtained from Box 29, Kenmore, New York 14217.

(See also CYCLISTS; ROLA BOLA; ROLLING GLOBE.)

JUICE   Circus jargon for electrical current.

On the LOT, however, the more common usage of "juice" refers to the sweet imitation lemonade or orange juice that is sold out of a giant glass or plastic dispenser at the concessions wagon. The amount of sugar in the concoction helped earn its nickname "bug juice" because of the amount of flies and other insects it attracted. Also, the drink did little to quench the thirst: In fact, often it made the patron even *more* thirsty.

To make the imitation juice seem more palatable, a few slices of lemon or orange were often dropped into the top of the mixture. In pure circus humbug, these FLOATERS were often fakes too. The wax fruit did make the juice appear more inviting, however.

On the first MUD SHOWS, the drinks were made from powder using whatever water was available. Legend has it that the use of a bucket of water in which red long johns had been soaking led to the invention of PINK LEMONADE. Also, on the early circuses, before the days of disposable paper or plastic cups, the juice would be served in communal thick-bottomed glass tumblers. The drink would be served to one patron, drunk, then the glass refilled for the next customer. While today any of these practices would cause the Board of Health to close down an entire circus operation, there is no record of anyone ever having died as a result of any of these offenses.

JUMBO (1860–1885)

The most famous ELEPHANT ever exhibited and the largest of its time, Jumbo was the one of P.T. BARNUM's star attractions from 1882 to 1885.

When Barnum first heard of Jumbo, the pachyderm had been housed at the Royal Zoological Gardens in London for 18 years. Jumbo had been captured in Central Africa—most likely in Ethiopia—for the Paris Zoo and in 1865 was traded to the Gardens for a rhinoceros. The trade probably saved Jumbo's life; Parisians ate Castor and Pollux, two other young elephants, along with other zoo animals during the Prussians' siege of the city in 1871.

Although African elephants are reputed to be difficult to handle, Jumbo was naturally gentle and easily trainable; for 17 years he gave rides to children visiting the Gardens.

In 1882, however, Jumbo became uncharacteristically irritable and unmanagable. Barnum offered $10,000 for him and, despite the objections of the British people, the press and Queen Victoria, the zoo trustees sold the elephant to Barnum.

By the time Jumbo was to be moved, however, he was once again a docile beast; the pachyderm had to be tricked into entering a huge portable cage. In addition, Barnum had to hire Jumbo's keeper, Matthew Scott—who welcomed the continuation of his services—to get Jumbo to cooperate. Barnum transported the animal to the United States at a cost of $30,000; he arrived in New York on Easter Sunday, April 9, 1882 aboard the ship the *Assyrian Monarch*.

Jumbo and trainer Matthew Scott.
(Photo courtesy of The Historical Collections, Bridgeport Public Library)

Jumbo was immediately paraded through the streets of New York City in a giantic crate pulled by 16 horses and pushed by two elephants.

The furor had caused an international incident, and the resulting media uproar was more than even Barnum could have requested. The country went Jumbo-mad: In May the *Philadelphia Evening Star* announced that the new fashion-conscious color for the spring would be "jumbo gray." There were Jumbo cigars, hats, fans, pies and stew. Among Barnum's many publicity schemes for Jumbo was an unsuccessful 1883 attempt to have the elephant be the first "pedestrian" to cross the newly completed Brooklyn Bridge.

Jumbo became the star attraction of P.T. BARNUM's GREATEST SHOW ON EARTH, HOWE'S GREAT LONDON CIRCUS AND SANGER'S ROYAL BRITISH MENAGERIE. The elephant enjoyed handfuls of peanuts from his admirers and continued to give rides to children, just as he had done in London. During the circus performance, Jumbo was paraded into the CENTER RING, then he watched the remainder of the show from the sidelines. While being toured, the pachyderm was privileged to have his own railway car, Jumbo's Palace Car.

When Barnum bought him, Jumbo was the largest elephant in captivity. According to *Leslie's Illustrated News*, he stood 11 feet 6 inches high at the shoulder, spanned 15 feet across from ear to ear and weighed 6½ tons. His trunk was 27½ inches in circumference and 7 feet long, allowing him to reach to a height of 26 feet. His trainer fed Jumbo 200 pounds of hay daily, plus oats, vegetables, fruit and bread and an occasional bottle of whiskey.

James L. HUTCHINSON, Barnum's partner with the show, complained about the immense expense for Jumbo, claiming that one elephant was as good as another. The investment was repaid within two weeks, however, and by six weeks after his first appearance in the States, Jumbo had brought in $336,000. Jumbo was Barnum's major attraction for three and a half years; but at no time during the remainder of his life did he display the ill temper he exhibited in London.

On September 15, 1885, while the circus was setting up in St. Thomas, Ontario, Canada, Jumbo and a smaller elephant, Tom Thumb (named after Barnum's other famous miniature, the midget TOM THUMB), were walking along the railroad siding. An unscheduled train turned a bend and headed directly toward them. The engineer of the Grand Trunk locomotive blew his whistle and slammed on the brakes but was unable to avoid a collision. Tom Thumb was hit first and thrown into a ditch. Then the train smashed into Jumbo, slamming him against the circus cars. Although the small elephant only broke a leg, Jumbo suffered a fractured skull and internal injuries. He died a few minutes later. The engineer was also killed when his locomotive and two cars derailed.

Jumbo's skeleton was mounted and eventually sent to the American Museum of Natural History in New York City for display. The bones were last on public exhibition from 1969 to 1975 in the Biology of Mammals Hall (the "Whale Room") on the third floor of the museum. The skeleton is still kept in storage by the museum, preserved by the Department of Osteology. From January 22 to November 1993, it was put on display on the museum's main floor to help celebrate 200 years of the American circus.

The hide, weighing 1,538 pounds, was mounted by taxidermists from Ward's Natural Science Establishment in Rochester, New York. The carcass was toured with the BARNUM AND LONDON CIRCUS through 1887, then the BARNUM & BAILEY CIRCUS through 1890. It was then put on exhibition with other Barnum memorabilia at Tufts University in Medford, Massachusetts. Unfortunately, in 1975 fire swept through the small Barnum Museum on campus and the hide was destroyed.

Jumbo's heart, weighing more than 50 pounds, was reportedly sold to Cornell University for $40. Pieces of the original tusks that could not be mounted with the skeleton were given away as gifts by Barnum, and some pieces eventually made their way to the Smithsonian Institution.

For years it was assumed that the reason for Jumbo's violent disposition in London had been a condition known as a "musth," an occasional condition believed to affect sexually mature male elephants. In her 1971 book, *The Natural History of the African Elephant*, naturalist Silvia K. Sikes hypothesizes another theory. During its lifetime, an elephant goes through six sets of molar teeth, each set growing out as the exposed set of teeth is ground away through normal wear. Sikes believes that the period of Jumbo's distemper may have coincided with the appearance of his fifth set of molars.

In a 1991 article in *Natural History* Magazine, Richard G. Van Gelder, curator emeritus in the Department of Mammalogy at the American Museum of Natural History, tells of his own examination of Jumbo's upper jaw. Indeed, the fifth molars were distorted, having grown in sideways as the sixth molars pushed forward. In addition, Van Gelder noted that by 1883 Jumbo's health had begun to decline. The effects were noticeable enough for Barnum to secretly contract for taxidermy just in case Jumbo died suddenly. Jumbo was not eating properly and was having digestive problems, a sign in an aged pachyderm indicating that its sixth molars had worn away and it was unable to eat. In Jumbo's case, chewing was probably just too painful. Van Gelder's fascinating conclusion is that had the tragic accident not occurred in 1885, Jumbo would probably not have had much longer to live anyway due to his increasing inability to eat.

In 1985, on the 100th anniversary of Jumbo's death, a monument to his memory was erected in St. Thomas. The mighty statue, the work of sculptor Winston Bronnun, sets on a bluff overlooking the city. Nearby is a bright red Grand Trunk caboose car, which houses a souvenir stand; farther down the street is a museum that features a miniature circus created by Dr. Max Ryckman.

Although Jumbo the elephant is remembered over a century after his death, the greatest legacy is that his name has entered the English language to mean anything of an enormous, larger-than-usual size.

JUMBO   See THEATER.

JUMP   Also known as the "haul," a jump is circus slang for the distance traveled from one performance town to the next. The term is used as both a noun ("How long is the jump?") and a verb ("We only have to jump 50 miles tonight").

JUMP STAND   An extra ticket booth that is placed in the MIDWAY near the FRONT DOOR to the BIG TOP (or the SIDESHOW) to sell additional tickets on crowded days.

JUNE, JOHN J. (18??–1884)   From SOMERS, NEW YORK, the "Cradle of the American Circus," John J. June was one of the original members of the ZOO-LOGICAL INSTITUTE and later the FLATFOOTS organization. Spurred on by the success of Nathan A. HOWES of nearby Brewster, June was one of a number of successful farmers turned MENAGERIE owners who included Lewis B. TITUS and Caleb S. ANGEVINE.

(See also LENT, LEWIS B.)

JUNG, PAUL (1901–1965)   One of the best producing CLOWNS (the JOEY in charge of devising and choosing gags and sketches for the CLOWN ALLEY) of the 1940s and 1950s, Paul Jung began in vaudeville, performing an acrobatic act with his brother, Walter. The zenith of his stage career came in the late 1950s when the two were invited to "play the Palace" in New York City.

In 1916 Jung joined the BARNUM & BAILEY CIRCUS as a trapeze artist and stayed there for eight years. After another decade in vaudeville, Jung returned to the circus, joining RINGLING BROS. AND BARNUM & BAILEY CIRCUS in 1934 as a clown.

Paul Jung's makeup was unusual for a WHITEFACE CLOWN, because he used black greasepaint for contrast. He put a small half-circle under each eye, which, from a distance, appeared to be an enlarged pupil.

He graduated to producing clown, inventing new gags and reworking old routines. When he was not on tour with the show, he created props in his factory in Tampa, Florida; and, with his wife, Elsie—a retired wire walker from The BIG ONE—he provided gags for the Disney people as well as Ringling. He also produced performance troupes, hiring many LITTLE PEOPLE, including Prince Paul ALPERT, the famous midget clown.

Trading in on a newly topical gag of the era, Jung invented the "Adam Smasher" in 1946. He explained how some of the best clowning comes out of a performer's awareness of the world around him: "A clown is supposed to be a man with the mind of a child, so I figured that was the way a clown would see it: the atom as Adam, a man." In the routine, a full-size adult clown entered a box; a giant hammer then appeared to crunch down the top of the container. Out of doors on all sides ran four midgets, dressed identically to the large clown who had originally gone inside.

His work on the steam-roller gag shows his cartoonlike concepts at work. A stream roller runs over a clown, and a long, flat cloth clown comes out the back side of the vehicle. Clown medics appear with a stretcher to save the victim, but the steam roller goes berserk, knocking down and flattening everything in its way, including a street sweeper and a policeman. At the BLOWOFF—the big, final laugh-getter of the routine—the tractor knocks the head off a clown (a midget clown in a tall suit), and the headless clown chases the steam roller out of the ring.

Other clown props invented by Jung that have become "clown classics" are the shrinking washing machine, the reducing machine and the rocket gun.

Jung was well paid for his efforts. Traditionally, clowns are at the bottom of the wage-earners among BIG TOP performers. While most clowns were earning $40 a week in the 1940s, Jung was earning $125 a week. This was, of course, augmented by his outside prop work and occasional film and personal appearances. He was seen in the SPEC number of Cecil B. deMille's movie, *The Greatest Show on Earth* (see FILMS, CIRCUS), playing a barber on the clown float.

A gentle man, Paul Jung met a violent death, a victim of New York street crime. He was beaten to death during a robbery outside his hotel just a block from MADISON SQUARE GARDEN, where the Ringling show was playing.

(See also CLOWN GAGS; CLOWNS.)

JUSTINO LOYAL TROUPE, THE See LOYAL, GUISTINO; LOYAL-REPENSKY TROUPE, THE.

K

KAY, BOBBY (1908–1983)   Bobby Kay began his career as a WHITEFACE CLOWN on the Downey Bros. Circus in 1923. After touring with several different shows, he joined the CLOWN ALLEY of the RINGLING BROS. AND BARNUM & BAILEY CIRCUS. Soon he was appointed "goodwill ambassador" of the show, traveling as an ADVANCE CLOWN for the circus for many seasons.

In 1971 Kay joined the staff of the new CLOWN COLLEGE. Four years later he was put in charge of all makeup classes. He continued to be active with the touring show, however, producing many of the larger gags for the arena. He created a version of the classic "long shirt gag" in which the bottom of the tube of cloth turned out to be a gigantic American flag, so large that it required an entire ring and ten clowns to support it.

(See also CLOWN GAGS; CLOWNS.)

KAYE, PAUL V. (1930–   )   Born in Danbury, Connecticut, Paul V. Kaye was raised in nearby BRIDGEPORT, CONNECTICUT. He entered the circus world when he joined the HUNT BROS. CIRCUS as a clown in 1952.

After two seasons, he moved to the POLACK BROS. CIRCUS, a major SHRINE CIRCUS, and toured with them for four years. In 1958 he joined the Dobritch Circus and performed there for ten years.

In 1968 Kaye moved into production, providing circus acts or entire shows for circuses, spectaculars, film, television and nightclub revues. Along with Karl WALLENDA, Kaye helped put together the acts for Abe Pollin's CIRCUS AMERICA in 1974.

As executive director and producer of the Kaye Continental Circus (which celebrates its 25th anniversary in 1993), Paul V. Kaye works out of his offices in Hollywood, California. Kaye provides an average of six circuses a year for Shrine and police sponsors throughout the continental United States and is also active in the production of circus shows worldwide, including Hawaii and the Orient.

KEESHAN, BOB   See CLOWNS, TELEVISION.

KELLEY, JOHN M. (1873–1963)   Working for more than 15 years as the lawyer, then tax adjuster, for the RINGLING BROS. & BARNUM AND BAILEY CIRCUS, "Honest" John Kelley was the "creative accountant" who was the focus of the federal tax claims brought against the circus in the last years of John RINGLING's life.

Raised on a farm, Kelley was graduated from the University of Wisconsin law school in 1901. He set up an office in BARABOO, WISCONSIN and joined the Ringling show as a claims adjuster sometime in the early 1900s. His job was to smooth over possible legal claims against the circus before suits could be filed. Kelley was adept at his work: Many times he reportedly had patrons who had been injured on the LOT sign away claims against the show in exchange for nothing more than a pair of tickets to the following year's engagement.

In 1918, when the federal government income tax laws took effect, John Kelley assumed the major responsibility for filing the tax forms on Ringling's income. According to Kelley's books, from 1918 to 1932 the circus paid taxes on profits of $4 million—an amazing figure since various Ringling family members connected with the show reportedly received over $10 million during that period.

The Internal Revenue Service, under chief investigator Charles W. Clarke, estimated that the Ringling shows had grossed $53.4 million over those same 15 years, an average of $3.5 million per season. The government approximated expenses at $42 million, with net profits of $11,400,000. They claimed that the circus owed $2,826,000 in back taxes, with penalties and interest added for a grand total of $3.6 million.

To underestimate the net profits of the show, Kelley primarily misused allowances for depreciation. In 1918 the first inventory of circus assets valued them at $1.8 million. Kelley deliberately inflated the circus's holdings to $4 million by claiming ownership of nonexistent equipment. Using this figure as his standard, whenever the fictional tents, wagons, railroad cars and animals had been fully depreciated, he restocked the show with all-new imaginary equipment.

The depreciation ploy was particularly easy with the SPEC, the opening parade around the circus ring. One such themed spectacular, called "Joan of Arc," was declared a total loss in 1923 by Kelley, to the tune of $200,000. The only problem was that "Joan of Arc" had been built in 1911, and the props and costumes had disintegrated years before. Several Specs from the late 1890s were illegally depreciated in the 1920s.

Technically, if the entire cost of an item is to be depreciated in one year due to a complete loss, the legal term is "abandonment." Kelley was a master of this ploy: For three consecutive years he claimed the death of a $3,500 rhinoceros at $35,000 per year.

In 1927, when the circus moved its headquarters from BRIDGEPORT, CONNECTICUT, to SARASOTA, FLORIDA, Kelley claimed a full loss of acres of land, buildings and animals in Bridgeport. In a bold master stroke, Kelley claimed to have left behind, or set loose, a MENAGERIE of 23 CAMELS, 18 BEARS, 23 lions, 800 HORSES, hundreds of monkeys and 46 ELEPHANTS. The jury was informed, however, that the property in Bridgeport had only been rented, not owned. The circuit court judge at Kelley's appeal trial also stated that he had grown up in Bridgeport, and he was puzzled that he had never seen "abandoned" elephants wandering the streets of downtown.

During testimony at his trial, John Kelley claimed to have been working under orders from Charles Ringling, but the claim was never substantiated. In fact, the only foolish move on the part of any of the Ringling clan was signing blank tax forms for Kelley to fill out afterward. John Ringling, the last of the brothers, died before Kelley's final trial; but in his last years he fully cooperated with the government, turning over his own books and records and ordering the circus office to do the same.

Former circus employees were subpoened as witnesses. One carpenter swore that a parade wagon built in 1898 and reportedly depreciated for thousands of dollars had only cost $205. He explained, "I know what it cost in 1898 because I built it in 1898." An animal trainer gave evidence that Kelley had never purchased 45 expensive stallions for the show: "The show had a lot of mares, and if there'd been 45 stallions there wouldn't of been no circus."

On April 26, 1938 John Kelley was convicted of assisting and counseling in the filing of false and fraudulent federal income tax returns for the Ringlings. He received a two-year jail term and a fine of $10,000. Of the other five men indicted, two aides were also prosecuted and received jail sentences. The Ringlings—none of whom was ever involved or indicted in the scandal—received the largest fine: a bill for $3.6 million in back taxes, penalties and interest.

The Board of Tax Appeals reviewed the judgment. It determined that a forced sale of the circus would not bring anywhere near the $3 million owed the government. Equally out of the question was a suggestion that the government take over and run the circus until its fines were collected. (The government had once seized a smaller circus and lost money operating it.) As a result, the U.S. Government finally settled for a payment of $800,000.

In 1954 Kelley, by then long retired from Ringling, founded Circus World Museum, Inc., in BARABOO, WISCONSIN, as a corporate entity to create a circus museum and archive. On July 1, 1959 CIRCUS WORLD MUSEUM opened its door to the public.

John M. Kelley died on November 4, 1963.

KELLY, EMMETT (1899–1979)

Arguably the most famous modern American clown, Emmett Kelly's TRAMP CLOWN character "Weary Willie" has transcended the circus ring to enter the hearts of audiences of all ages. Similar to Charlie Chaplin's tramp character, Willie fought everyday obstacles as he brought comic understanding to his minor tragedies.

Kelly first visited a circus when it played his hometown of Sedan, Kansas, where his father was a foreman for the Missouri-Pacific Railroad. After moving to Texas County, Missouri, his father became a farmer. Emmett took a $25 correspondence course in cartooning as a teenager; it was in 1920 that Kelly first drew the hobo cartoon character that he would play for the rest of his life. Kelley actually created the pitiful character for a bread advertisement while working for the Adfilm Company. (Coincidentally, a fellow employee at the time was a beginner, Walt Disney.)

Emmett Kelly worked a variety of odd jobs before landing a position with Doc Grubb's Western Show Property Exchange. He painted carnival kewpie doll faces for six cents apiece, and when he had earned enough money he bought a trapeze and rigging. Joining Zieger's United Shows and the Frisco Exhibition Shows, Kelly painted carousels and sold tickets.

This led to work in small touring circuses as a trapeze artist and, occasionally, as a WHITEFACE CLOWN. He wished to introduce the sad tramp, but the circus owners felt the clown's unshaven hobo character was not in keeping with their show's image. Kelly gave up trying, and he continued to work as an aerialist with his first wife, Eva Moore, for the next nine years.

In 1932 Willie the tramp was finally accepted in Kokomo, Indiana, but not on a circus. During the winter, Kelly would tour nightclubs with a "chalk-talk" act, dressed as a hobo. In the routine, he would quickly sketch the scenery for short skits he performed or would draw comic pictures that changed when turned upside down.

In 1932 Kelly toured as a whiteface clown with Otto GRIEBLING on the HAGENBECK-WALLACE CIRCUS, but the following season on the show his tramp character made its circus debut. During the winter of 1934–35, Kelly performed with Griebling on the Moslem Shrine Circus in Detroit; and in 1935 they toured together on the one-season wonder, the COLE

Emmett Kelly, Jr., on the Cole All Star Circus in 1970. (Author's collection)

BROTHERS & CLYDE BEATTY CIRCUS. Weary Willie premiered to rave reviews at the New York Hippodrome in 1937.

Willie wore torn, disheveled black clothing, with a classic clown tramp face. A popular misconception is that Weary Willie wore an eternal frown. In fact, the white mouth was an almost perfectly shaped oval that, when combined with Kelly's facial dexterity, slumped shoulders and tired body language, gave the appearance of extreme sadness. As Larry Pisoni of the PICKLE FAMILY CIRCUS noted, "It was his body that was sad, not his makeup." To give a contrast to his dark costume, Weary Willie always wore bright Kelly green shirts. Emmett felt it gave a subliminal connection between his costume and his name.

In 1942 Kelly moved over to the RINGLING BROS. AND BARNUM & BAILEY CIRCUS. John Ringling NORTH personally extended the invitation after having seen Kelly perform at the Bertram Mills Olympia Circus in London.

Emmett Kelly was traveling with Ringling when the tragic fire in the BIG TOP occurred in HARTFORD, CONNECTICUT in 1944. A photo of Willie carrying a bucket of water and urging patrons to "keep moving" was published in newspapers the world over.

Besides touring with Ringling, Emmett Kelly appeared in other forms of entertainment. In the early 1940s he acted in several Broadway shows, including *Please Keep Off the Grass.* His first film was the 1950 *The Fat Man,* in which he played a villain dressed as a nontramp clown. His most notable film appearance was the next year in the Oscar-winning *The Greatest Show on Earth.* (See FILMS, CIRCUS.)

In 1956 he took a year's sabbatical from circuses, appearing—among other places—with the Brooklyn Dodgers baseball team, dressed as the little tramp with the red bulbous nose, cleaning the field. In 1957 he began working with the SHRINE CIRCUS.

Emmett Kelly was the first clown in modern circus history to be allowed to stay in the ring while others were performing. He was urged by both the Cristiani and Wallenda troupes to supply comic byplay to offset the drama of their acts.

Kelly is best remembered for his most famous skit, the shy, pathetic hobo, trying to sweep up the spotlight as if it were a spot of dirt on the arena floor. The solo routine was his version of a gag originated by Shorty Flemm, who had appeared as a clown on the Ringling Bros. Circus.

In Weary Willie's version, the spotlight acted as if it were alive, always moving away as he approached. Kelly varied the routine throughout his career, including having the spot follow him out of the ring. Sometimes the spot would shrink smaller and smaller, only to snap up to full size when he sneezed. Occasionally, as a finale, Kelly would get rid of the pesky spotlight by sweeping it under a rug. On a special television guest appearance on *The Carol Burnett Show,* Weary Willie swept the spot up into the dustpan of Burnett's Cleaning Lady character.

Emmett Kelly suffered a heart attack and died while emptying the trash outside his home in SARASOTA, FLORIDA on March 28, 1979. Although this was on the opening day of the 109th Edition of the Ringling show at MADISON SQUARE GARDEN, the humble humanity of his exit was more in keeping with his Weary Willie character than the spangle and glitter of the sawdust ring.

His eldest son, Emmett Kelly, Jr., continues to work as a tramp clown in his father's tradition.

(See also CLOWN GAGS; CLOWNS; TRAMP CLOWNS.)

KELLY-MILLER BROS. CIRCUS   See AL G. KELLY & MILLER BROS. CIRCUS.

KEN MAYNARD WILD WEST SHOW   By building his own show in 1936, cowboy film star Ken Maynard hoped to follow the success of other western movie stars who moved into the circus and Wild West arena.

However, good performers are not necessarily particularly good managers; in fact, most "personalities" that toured with circuses did so as featured attractions, not as part of the management team. Maynard's show was never properly financed to get beyond its California WINTER QUARTERS, but a few weekend performances were given there before the operation swiftly shuttered.

KICKING SAWDUST   Circus jargon for being a circus follower or part of the company.

KID WORKER   Each department in the circus during the railroad era of the tented shows had a man who recruited, hired, worked and supervised young boys from the town who were eager to work in exchange for free passes to the show. In circus jargon, this man was known as the "kid worker," also sometimes called the "punk pusher." During the heyday of the giant tent show, hiring workers for the day in each town was absolutely essential, as the circus could not support a traveling staff large enough to put up the tents every day without local help.

Each department was allowed to give out a certain number of passes each day. The boys in turn did every conceivable thing asked of them, from cleaning cages to helping set up tents.

The boys, while not manhandled, were not treated with a great deal of courtesy or respect, as evidenced by some of the other circus slang terms for them: GUNSEL and PUNK.

KIDSHOW   Circus jargon for any of the extra shows on the MIDWAY. The term is usually used to mean the main SIDESHOW that contains the performers such as the magician, the SNAKE CHARMER, the FREAKS and other human oddities.

KIESTER   Circus jargon for a wardrobe trunk.

KING, FLOYD See CRISTIANIS, THE; KING BROS. CIRCUS; KING BROS. SHOWS.

KING BROS. CIRCUS The King Bros. Circus was established by Floyd King (1888–1976) in 1946, and he toured it with various partners through 1951. For the 1952 season, it was on the road as the King Bros. & Cristiani Circus; but the show returned to its former title the following year. The circus had only one more successful season, however, in 1954.

At the end of the 1955 season, the King Bros. Circus showed a net loss of $125,000, and the Internal Revenue Service issued a tax claim of $100,000 against the show. The circus opened both its units, without much optimism, in the early spring. The first to fold was the western unit in May; the eastern unit followed a few weeks later, stranding its remaining equipment in Connecticut.

(See also CRISTIANIS, THE; KING BROS. SHOWS.)

KING BROS. SHOWS In 1919 brothers Floyd and Howard King left other circus jobs to become operators of their own two-railroad-car show, the Sanger Circus, the name taken from a famous British circus. The show switched titles to the Harris Bros. Circus for one season in 1924.

Through this period, the King brothers toured as a "car show," meaning that their rail stock consisted of baggage cars and sleepers. Wagons and other equipment were added when they changed to a flatcar operation in 1925. The second half of the decade was quite busy for the Kings, as they trouped the WALTER L. MAIN CIRCUS on ten or 15 cars from 1925 through 1928 and their GENTRY BROS. CIRCUS from 1926 through 1929. For two seasons, 1929 and 1930, Floyd and Howard King operated the COLE BROS. CIRCUS as well.

The Kings stayed active in outdoor amusements, although not in ownership of any major shows, until 1946 when Floyd King started up the KING BROS. CIRCUS. With various partners and under various titles, Floyd toured the show through 1955.

(See also CRISTIANIS, THE.)

KING TUSK (c. 1942–   ) A continuing feature of the SPEC on the RINGLING BROS. AND BARNUM & BAILEY CIRCUS, King Tusk is reputed to have the longest tusks of any pachyderm on tour.

First introduced to Ringling audiences on the Red Unit during the 1987 season, King Tusk is billed as "the largest living land mammal." True or not, King Tusk is certainly much more massive than Barnum's JUMBO (billed as "the largest brute on earth"). King Tusk has a 27-foot girth and weighs 14,762 pounds, compared to Jumbo's 13,000 pounds (or "six and one-half tons," as Barnum used to say). True, Jumbo—at 13 feet 4 inches—was taller than 12-foot-six King Tusk, but the latter brandishes uneven tusks that are six feet six and seven feet long.

King Tusk travels in a "royal car," advertised as "a 45 foot custom tractor trailer with appointments fit for royalty, complete with awning to shade the mastodonic mammal while he is not performing." His daily food consumption consists of 300 pounds of hay, 50 pounds of carrots, 50 pounds of apples, 25 pounds of grain and 100 gallons of water. He also has a hefty amount of clothing: His sparkling elephant blanket weighs 1,200 pounds—requiring 12 BULL HANDLERS to lift it—and the robe is covered with sequins, studs and mirrors.

King Tusk is still on the road with THE GREATEST SHOW ON EARTH. On October 9, 1992 the circus celebrated the pachyderm's 50th birthday.

King Tusk had toured as "Tommy" with many other circuses, such as the DAILEY BROS. CIRCUS in the late 1940s and Diano Bros. Circus in the early 1950s, before coming to the BIG ONE. Through clever promotion and circus hyperbole, however, the legend of the greatest mammal on earth was born.

KINKER Originally used only to refer to an acrobat, the term kinker has come to mean any circus performer. The jargon is perhaps derived from the artist's need to work kinks out of sore muscles.

KIT CARSON WILD WEST SHOW See WIEDEMANN BROS. BIG AMERICAN SHOWS.

L

L.A. CIRCUS, THE   Founded in June 1990, the L.A. Circus is a small but colorful, one-ring circus that appears under the auspices of local sponsors in the greater Los Angeles area. It is an open-air production, with its inflatable ring surrounded by bleacher seating (some on JACKS AND STRINGERS and some permanently set on a unique SEAT WAGON) and SIDEWALL. Beside the balloon arch FRONT DOOR, the show operates its own concessions stand of drinks, popcorn and snowcones.

For over a year before its premier performance, producer Tom Agostino, along with co-producer Wini McKay, marketing director Douglas Lyon and director Dick Monday worked to LAY OUT the show and its operation. Chester Cable came on board as production manager and designed the circus's seat wagon, bleachers and circus ring as well. Tiffany Riley has been performance director and choreographer since the show's inception.

The CLOWN ALLEY, led by Dick Monday, opens the performance. Chester Cable's FOOT JUGGLING act follows, in which Cable balances a six-foot cylinder, a wagon wheel and a 100-pound, ten-foot long table (the largest ever, according to the *Guinness Book of World Records*). The circus also features a Spanish WEB and Tai, the ELEPHANT, trained by Gary and Kari Johnson. A five-piece live circus band is led by musical director Bill Payne.

Tom Agostino is also the executive director of LAFFCA, an acronym for the Los Angeles Foundation for the Circus Arts. LAFFCA is a not-for-profit organization dedicated to the growth and support of circus arts in Los Angeles and southern California. Among its many activities, LAFFCA sponsors a weekly class in circus skills, a Hospital Clown Care unit and L.A. Circus Jr., a two-week educational program of circus workshops, classes and camps for children.

LAFFCA's offices are located at 21201 Victory Boulevard, Suite 135, Canoga Park, California 91303. The L.A. Circus can be reached at 22241 Ybarra Road, Woodland Hills, California 91364.

LACOMBE, DENIS   See CIRQUE DU SOLEIL.

LADDERS   Often called the "Roman ladders" or simply the "swinging ladders," this aerial act is often used as part of a display by all of the circus showgirls.

A Roman ladder is constructed by welding bars or tubes of rolled iron, steel or heavy aluminum into a rectangular frame approximately five feet by two feet. Three or four cross-bars, or "rungs," are added, giving the apparatus a ladderlike look. A metal ring is welded at each of the two upper corners, and a canvas hand-loop is usually attached to the middle of the top rung.

Two metal hooks, connected to pulley systems over adjacent poles, are attached to the ladder; the entire prop is raised upward, above the ring or hippodrome track. Several of these ladders can be hung around the perimeter of the tent or arena.

During the act, the showgirl climbs a WEB to get up to the ladder. The web is also used to start the ladder swinging back and forth; as it does so the

Ladders, sometimes called the Roman ladders, performed by Lois Washburn. (Photo courtesy of Charles A. DeWein)

BALLY BROAD strikes graceful poses, around and through the rungs of the ladder.

(See also AERIAL ACTS.)

LAILSON AND JAYMOND

In 1796 a troupe of French equestrians headed by Philip Lailson arrived in Boston. By year's end they were in New York. The following year Lailson and fellow rider Jaymond went to Philadelphia, opening a circus building on April 8, to give serious competition to John Bill RICKETTS and his NEW AMPHITHEATER.

Setting up at the corner of Fifth and Prune streets near Ricketts's amphitheater, Lailson and Jaymond presented the same type of show, even utilizing some of the same performers. Among them was Mr. Langley, the first American-born circus equestrian advertised by name.

Lailson also erected a circus on Greenwich Street in New York near Ricketts's arena, opening on De-cember 8, 1797. These are the first American examples where one circus would deliberately DAY AND DATE another, performing in the same town on the same date. According to circus historian Stuart Thayer, Lailson and Jaymond also introduced the first STREET PARADE in the United States.

In 1798 the brick dome of their Philadelphia arena collapsed under a heavy snow. They were financially unable to completely rebuild, and the building was put up for sale.

The next year the Lailson and Jaymond arena was the site of a benefit performance for their earlier rival, John Bill Ricketts, following the devastating fire at his amphitheaters. Shortly thereafter, the troupe departed for the West Indies, where their trail disappears.

LALIBERTÉ, GUY   See CIRQUE DU SOLEIL.

LALLA ROOKH

As unusual as it may seem, there were actually *two* Lalla Rookhs in American circus history—and they couldn't have been more different.

Named for the heroine of a Persian poem, the first Lalla Rookh was a rope-walking ELEPHANT, purchased in New York State in 1853 by Dan RICE from Seth B. Howes for $5,000. Lalla Rookh was a feature of DAN RICE'S ONE-HORSE SHOW, which had begun operation in 1850. Lalla Rookh's first public performance walking a tightrope (20 feet long, six inches in diameter and four feet off the ground) was in 1857. She died in Indiana in 1860.

In 1881, however, another Lalla Rookh appeared, this one billed as "Beauty's Tribute, the Handsomest Woman in America" and "The Lovely Oriental Princess." Louise Montague was the winner in a beauty competition, perhaps the first in the United States, organized by Adam FOREPAUGH. Montague was to win $10,000, in exchange for which she would tour with the show and lead the Forepaugh STREET PARADE, billed as "Lalla Rookh's Departure from Delhi." Montague trouped with the show for two seasons.

The contest, of course, was merely a publicity stunt and had been rigged from the start. Miss Montague never received the $10,000; rather, she was paid $100 per week. Nevertheless, the contest had received national publicity, and crowds lined the streets whenever the show came to town. In an attempt to get a glimpse of the woman purported to be the most beautiful in the world, a man fell out of a second-story window, breaking his neck; and a surging crowd smashed through the window of a Western Union office in Chicago.

Lalla Rookh helped to make Forepaugh a wealthy man. The show netted $240,000 in 1881 and $260,000 the following season.

LARIBLE, DAVID (1957–   )

A 1988 winner of the Silver Clown Award at the Monte Carlo International Circus Festival, David Larible (pronounced La-REE-Blay) first appeared in the United States on the Red Unit of the RINGLING BROS. BARNUM & BAILEY CIRCUS in 1991. He was born in Verona, Italy on June 23, 1957.

With a simple auguste face and floppy cap, Larible is a master pantomime clown. His is the first clown in the history of The BIG ONE to be given a full solo act in the CENTER RING.

Larible opens the show with a variation of the "Spotlight Gag" made famous by Emmett KELLY. At the end of the bit, he "catches" the spot in his cap and tosses it out over the arena; the light seems to break up into a mirror-ball swirl of a thousand points of light. This leads immediately into the grand SPEC opening.

Like famous Ringling CLOWNS before him, he interacts with other performers. He flirts with showgirls during the parade, and he "talks back" to the RINGMASTER. "The ringmaster is the power, the teacher, the mother, and the clown is the child—which, I think, is why children like clowns," Larible explained.

He is an integral part of his sister Vivian's act. As she perches high above him on the solo TRAPEZE, he commands attention between her tricks. He gives her a trumpet serenade of "Send in the Clowns" as she ascends, and they perform a bell-ringing duet during the routine. It is a classic example of "the clown and the showgirl" theme.

Larible's major spot comes in the second half of the show, when he brings audience members into the center ring to take part in a large comic production number. Like David Shiner's "silent movie" parody in 1991's CIRQUE DU SOLEIL, Larible fabricates an entire sketch around two young lovers and two men, one bald and one overweight. As they leave the ring, Larible gives each volunteer a lollipop.

"Being a clown is an artist packing two suitcases," David Larible once said. "In one, you have technique like the JUGGLING or music; and in the other, you have talent. To be a great clown, a terrific clown, you have to have both full."

(See also CLOWN GAGS.)

LARRY

Sometimes spelled "Larrie" and also known as a "Larry Cadota" or a "fink," this word is circus jargon for a broken toy or novelty that can't be fixed and is, therefore, worthless. It is, of course, still sold to the public.

Almost as an inside joke, candy BUTCHERS sometimes mention their wares as "Larry Cadota Toys," as if that increased their value. Often this actually helps to move the items.

LA STRADA

See FILMS, CIRCUS; THEATER.

LAUGH-MAKERS MAGAZINE

Begun in 1981, *Laugh-Makers Magazine* is a valuable resource of comic bits, sight gags, sketches and props for the hobbyist and professional clown. The magazine has been published since its inception by Bob Gibbons and is edited by his wife, Cathy Gibbons, both of Syracuse, New York.

Subscribed to by entertainers in every U.S. state, Canada and 35 other countries, each issue is approximately 50 pages of information, including tips on clowning, comedy magic, balloon sculpture, funny props, puppetry, ventriloquism, and juggling.

LAY OUT

This circus jargon refers to the position of the TENTS, WAGONS and other equipment on the LOT. The LAYOUT MAN, who is also often the BOSS CANVASMAN or lot Superintendent, positions all the equipment.

LAYOUT MAN

Circus jargon for the person who decides where the TENTS, trailers and other equipment should be located on the new LOT. The layout man is the one who actually paces out the lot, marking off the places to drop and unroll the canvas. The layout man's duties are sometimes performed by the BOSS CANVASMAN or lot superintendent, and the terms are often used interchangeably.

L.B. LENT'S NATIONAL CIRCUS

See LENT, LEWIS B.

LEAD STOCK   Circus jargon for any animals other than HORSES that are "led" by reins in parades, SPEC or performances. Common circus lead stock are CAMELS, llamas and zebras.

LEAMY LADIES   European trapeze act named after their American manager, Edward Leamy. The troupe originally consisted of Elinor Pelikan and her two sisters, but by the time the team toured the United States in 1910, it included Elinor's young daughter, Lillian LEITZEL. Though a great success in Europe, the Leamy Ladies were not well received and soon returned overseas. Leitzel remained behind, however, beginning a solo career that led to circus stardom.

LECTURER   Circus jargon for the person who performs the opening or BALLY outside the SIDESHOW tent. The term is also sometimes used for the person who introduces the acts inside the sideshow.

(See also TALKER.)

LEE, GENE (1920–   )   For 50 years, Gene Lee has worked as "Cousin Otto," a jolly, rotund clown billed as "America's Favorite Relative."

Lee was born in Milwaukee, Wisconsin to a family immersed in the stage, vaudeville, burlesque and the circus. Four uncles were involved in circuses, and his grandfather owned LEE BROS. CIRCUS until shortly after World War I.

Lee's father was a successful circus PRESS AGENT, and from the age of five Gene traveled on the road every summer. He was often asked to be a SHILL in the audience for the TALKER, the magician or other performers who needed a "plant" in the crowd.

Gene Lee's first experience as a CLOWN came as a result of an unusual "truth in advertising" on the part of a circus. His father, then handling the advance publicity for COLE BROS. CIRCUS, advertised that the show carried 50 clowns. He talked young Gene, then 15 years old, into joining CLOWN ALLEY to help fill up the ranks; on April 9, 1935 he became a JOEY.

After touring with Cole Bros., Lee also spent time in the alleys of the CLYDE BEATTY CIRCUS and the RINGLING BROS. AND BARNUM & BAILEY CIRCUS. In fact, his clown name, "Cousin Otto," was inspired by one of his peers on the Ringling show, Otto GRIEBLING.

Cousin Otto is a whiteface comedian, with a red mouth, a small red circle and a green star on his cheeks, and a green derby on a red wig. He wears red horn-rimmed glasses supported by a red bulbous nose.

Now living in Whitewater, Wisconsin, Gene Lee has been editor of *CLOWNING AROUND*, the official publication of the WORLD CLOWN ASSOCIATION, since 1982. He is publisher of "Three Ring News," the newsletter for the Midwest Clown Association, and he wrote three of the 20 chapters in the book *Creative Clowning.*

Currently on the board of directors for the CLOWN HALL OF FAME & RESEARCH CENTER in Delavan, Wisconsin, he is also their display director. As an instructor, Lee teaches clowning skills at CLOWN CAMP at the University of Wisconsin-La Crosse, Clown World in East Lansing, Michigan and the International School of Clown Performing Arts in Jacksonville, Florida. Summers he is also a stand-in clown at the CIRCUS WORLD MUSEUM in BARABOO, WISCONSIN.

Summing up his philosophy of clowning, Gene Lee has said, "You have to love it. You have to have it in your heart." Asked if he will ever retire, he conceded that Cousin Otto may only be around another decade. "Then I'll hang up my red nose and put away my floppy clown shoes. Well, maybe I won't."

LEE BROS. CIRCUS   The Lee Bros. Circus is a title that has been used by many different circus promoters over the years, including G.W. Christy, Robert Atterbury and Sam Dock.

The name has seldom been used for more than a year or two at a time by any operator, and usually there was no connection between two circuses bearing the same title. The origin of the "Lee Bros." name, therefore, remains one of the true circus conundrums.

During the history of the title, there was only one authenticated owner/operator that actually was named Lee. That unit toured until shortly after World War I, and one of the show wagons from that era is currently on display at the CIRCUS WORLD MUSEUM.

A grandson of that owner is Gene LEE, who toured as the clown "Cousin Otto" for a number of years.

(See ATTERBURY BROS. CIRCUS.)

LEITZEL, LILLIAN (1892?–1931) The undisputed queen of the aerialists in the first part of this century and for 12 years with The BIG ONE, Lillian Leitzel's early life is somewhat sketchy. She was born Leopoldina Altitza (Lillian Alize) Pelikan Eleanore in Breslau, Germany in 1882 or 1892. As a little girl she was nicknamed Leitzel, a tender sobriquet of Alize; years later she took this as her stage name.

Leitzel's father, a former Hungarian army officer, was a rigid disciplinarian and she rarely spoke of him. Her mother's side of the family was steeped in circus history: Her maternal grandmother was able to perform on the trapeze until the age of 84. Her mother, Elinor Pelikan, and two of her mother's sisters were trapeze artists, performing as the LEAMY LADIES. An uncle, Adolph Pelikan, originated the familiar clown stunt in which the JOEY enters the ring with a board balanced on his head, turns an about-face and continues walking with the plank in place.

Because Lillian's mother was often on tour, the young girl was sent to a girls' school in Breslau. She was a keen student, learning to speak five languages, and was such an accomplished musician that a career as a concert pianist was considered. Her dream was to become an aerialist, however, and by the age of nine she had taught herself tricks on a small trapeze. A few years later she joined the Leamy Ladies, toured Europe, and went with them to the United States in 1910. Though the others returned to Europe, Lillian stayed behind.

She hoped to be an immediate circus star, but Leitzel's first bookings were in vaudeville. Ironically, it was an accident soon after her first stage performance that helped catapult her to stardom. She took a fall—a presage to the one that was to claim her life years later—during a performance in New Jersey. Both of her legs were hurt, but she soon insisted on returning to work on crutches. Leitzel was carried to the WEB, the rope hanging from the ceiling, so that she could climb to her ROMAN RINGS. Her skill and determination won her audience acclaim, an increased salary and the billing "Lillian Leitzel, the World's Most Daring Aerial Star."

While appearing in a vaudeville show in South Bend, Indiana in 1915 she was spotted by a scout from the Ringling Bros. Circus. By the time of the 1919 merger of the Barnum & Bailey and Ringling

This monument commemorating Lillian Leitzel was commissioned by her husband, Alfredo Codona. The memorial is located in Inglewood Park Cemetery (Inglewood, California), where Leitzel, Codona and several members of the Codona family are interred. Note the detail of the snapped Roman ring beneath the statue. (Photo by Tom Ogden)

shows, Leitzel was a star performer and a CENTER RING attraction earning close to $300 per week.

At four feet nine inches tall and less than 100 pounds, the diminutive Leitzel was an audience darling. Her act was supposed to last eight minutes, but she would often lengthen it at whim if the audience seemed especially good—much to the consternation of other acts waiting to go on.

A giant dressed as a doorman would carry Leitzel to the ring where her personal maid, Mabel Clemings, would take her robe. Leitzel, bedecked in dazzling, jeweled costumes, would ascend the web by a series of "rollups," literally rolling her body up and over itself while holding onto the rope. After performing elaborate contortions on the Roman rings hung just below the peak of the BIG TOP, Lillian would glide back to the ground.

The second half of her act was even more incredible. Leitzel was hoisted upward by a second web; she then slipped her wrist into a padded rope loop attached to a swivel and ring. Throwing her body over head, she pivoted in the series of one-arm swings (known as a PLANGE) that was her trademark. With each plange accompanied by a roll of the drum, she would often perform over 100 pivots, with her record being an unbelievable 249 turns. Even late in her career Leitzel was able to perform up to 60 loops.

The one-arm planges were physically demanding. While the plange turns were not as graceful or beautiful as Leitzel's work on the Roman rings, the audience responded to the skill and stamina of the climax of her act. Each swing partially dislocated her right shoulder, which would then snap back into place. Despite different wrappings, her wrist was in constant pain; and, thinking the wrist unattractive, Leitzel went to great lengths to cover it. Otherwise very dainty, Lillian also displayed overdeveloped arms and shoulders, making her look almost gnome-like on close inspection.

Lillian Leitzel was adored by her public, and her fans treated her like a movie star. Her popularity was so great that she felt she could demand—and she received—her own private car on the CIRCUS TRAIN, the only performer at the time to be given this special consideration. Her mercurial temper and ego also seemed that of a diva, yet she was pursued by numerous handsome and wealthy suitors. At the height of her career in July 1928, while performing in Chicago, she married Alfredo CODONA, the "King of the Trapeze." His temperament matched hers, and many felt the marriage had been predestined.

Each year when the circus was in WINTER QUARTERS, Leitzel and Codona played theatrical dates in the United States and Europe. On Friday, February 13, 1931, while Lillian was performing the planges at the Valencia Music Hall in Copenhagen, Denmark, the swivel ring, fatigued by years of wear, snapped. Leitzel fell 20 feet to the ground, landing on her shoulders and back. Despite her attempt to go on, she was rushed to a hospital. Codona, who

was performing in Berlin, hurried to her side. Leitzel convinced him that her injuries were minor and that he must return to Berlin. As a result, Codona was not with his adored wife when on Sunday, February 15, 1931 she died of a concussion and complications from the fall.

Her husband returned her ashes to Inglewood, California, where they were interred on December 9, 1931 beneath an ornate monument, entitled "Reunion," that Codona had built in her memory. After his suicide in 1937, he joined the true love of his life beneath the marble stone.

LEMEN BROS. CIRCUS   Frank Lemen and his brothers first opened their show, the Lemen Bros. Circus, in 1887; but it was not until Martin Downs joined the partnership the following year that the circus really began to grow. Soon it was a 20-car railroad show.

For a few years around the turn of the century the circus was retitled the Great Pan-American Show, and in 1906 the circus's apparatus was used for the Hale's Firefighter's show. Eventually the entire circus inventory was bought by William P. HALL for resale.

LENT, LEWIS B. (1813–1887)   Lewis B. Lent, born in upstate New York, started his circus career as an agent for the FLATFOOTS syndicate in 1834. Having gained this invaluable experience, for the next five seasons he became a partner in his own BROWN & LENT CIRCUS, which traveled by riverboat.

Lent resumed his involvement with the Flatfoots through the 1842 season, then became a partner in a number of different shows, including the Rufus Welch National Circus, the Sands & Lent Circus and Van Amburgh's Menagerie. He teamed with circus personnel such as John J. JUNE, Lewis B. TITUS and Caleb S. ANGEVINE throughout the rest of the decade.

In the 1850s, Lent again went into business with "General" Rufus WELCH and Nathan A. HOWES and then opened his L.B. Lent's National Circus from 1857-to 1863. This show toured under many name variations during the following decade. The last show Lent owned and operated was the NEW YORK CIRCUS, which he toured from 1873 through 1874. In later years he became an agent or manager for a number of different shows. Lewis B. Lent tried unsuccessfully to revive the New York Circus in 1879 and retired shortly thereafter.

LEON W. WASHBURN SHOWS

Leon W. Washburn was the manager, then owner, of the Stetson Uncle Tom's Cabin shows. Moving from tented repertory, he organized a circus in 1881.

The Washburn show appeared under various titles until 1908, when Leon Washburn bought a theater. Occasionally, however, Washburn got the urge to travel, and he would take to the road with a circus, a carnival or another tour of *Uncle Tom's Cabin*. He continued to troupe until 1925.

LEOPARDS

See CATS.

LÉOTARD, JULES (1838–1869)

Generally credited with the invention of the act today known as the FLYING TRAPEZE, Jules Léotard was born in Toulouse, France on August 1, 1839. He graduated from gymnast to circus aerialist in his native France.

Jean Léotard, father of Jules and a teacher of physical education, operated a gymnasium in Toulouse in the 1850s. It was there that Jules began to practice on a single TRAPEZE, a short metal bar fixed horizontally at the ends of two vertical ropes hanging from the ceiling.

At some point in the mid-1850s, young Léotard developed the idea of hanging two trapezes several feet apart in the gymnasium. He perfected the ability of swinging from one bar, sailing through the air and catching the bar of the other trapeze.

His performance of this unique skill was seen by visiting circus performers, and he was invited to perform in Paris. There, on November 12, 1859, he made his debut—and the public debut of the flying trapeze—at the Cirque Napoléon (now known as the Cirque d'Hiver and the oldest permanent circus building in the world, in operation since December 11, 1852).

The act caused a sensation, and immediately circus aerialists attempted to duplicate his feats. Two English performers, James Leach and Richard Beri, were booked by an agent named Van Hare onto a circus bill at the Alhambra in London in 1860.

The following year Jean Léotard also performed at the Alhambra. By that time, however, the Leicester Square arena had been transformed into a music hall; Léotard performed his act over the heads of spectators seated at tables.

For its time, the tight-fitting body stockings that Jean Léotard developed and wore to show his musculature were quite shocking. While Léotard's contribution to the modern circus may not be commonly known today, the acrobatic world uses a similar style of athletic garment that still bears his name.

(See also AERIAL ACTS; CODONA, ALFREDO; COLLEANO, WINNIE; CONCELLO, ANTOINETTE; CONCELLO, ART; FLYING CONCELLOS, THE; FLYING CRANES, THE; GAONA, TITO; FLYING GAONAS, THE; FLYING VAZQUEZ, THE; VAZQUEZ, MIGUEL.)

LEWIS BROS. CIRCUS

Begun as a small tented show, the original Lewis Bros. Circus toured the eastern seaboard from 1932 through 1945. The show was motorized, moving on 25 trucks by 1941.

The title was resurrected by John Lewis and Jim Silverlake about two decades later. When their partnership ended in August 1973, Lewis brought in Leonard Basil "Hoxie" TUCKER. The reorganized show, featuring 37 animals and traveling on six trucks, opened the following spring under a modest 80-foot TENT with three 30-foot middles with seating for 1,800 people around the single ring.

By 1976 Lewis Bros. Circus was owned by Hoxie Tucker; and the show began life that season as Tucker's second unit, Hoxie's Great American Circus.

(See also HILL, ALLAN C.; HOXIE BROS. CIRCUS.)

LIBERTY HORSES

Liberty horses are trained to perform unharnessed, without leads or riders. As they are put through their paces, responding simply to the sound of a voice or the crack of a whip, the HORSES are said to be performing a "liberty act" or to be "at liberty."

LIFT

Circus jargon for the bounce or hop bareback riders make to jump from the ground up and onto the trotting horse.

LILLIE, MAJOR GORDON W. "PAWNEE BILL" (1860–1942)

By the early 1900s Major Gordon W. Lillie, nicknamed Pawnee Bill, was a chief rival of William F. CODY and his BUFFALO BILL'S WILD WEST. Like "Buffalo Bill," Pawnee Bill had also been a buffalo hunter; but rather than also being an Indian fighter, he had been an agent and interpreter for the Pawnee tribe of Oklahoma.

Ironically, Pawnee Bill first became interested in outdoor amusements when he supplied several Pawnee performers for the Cody show. In 1887 he formed PAWNEE BILL'S WILD WEST; it went on to tour the United States, Canada and Europe for a decade.

At the end of the 1907 season, Lillie sold his wagons and rail cars, and his Wild West spent the entire 1908 season at an amusement park.

Meanwhile, in 1906, one of Cody's partners, James A. BAILEY, died. In 1908 Lillie bought an interest in Buffalo Bill's Wild West. His investment temporarily eased money problems on the Wild West; it was hoped that their combined show, the BUFFALO BILL WILD WEST AND PAWNEE BILL GREAT FAR EAST SHOW (nicknamed the Two Bills Show), would prove to be a financial winner.

Unfortunately, the crowds did not pour in and 1911 was the worst year for the show. Even the following season, billed as the farewell tour, failed to bring in audiences. The show closed after the 1913 season.

Over the years Lillie tried to take several smaller shows back on the road, including a Wild West show on a carnival in the 1930s; but none of the circuses approached the magnificence of his original shows.

LIND, JENNY (1820–1887)

By 1850 P.T. BARNUM was unrivaled as a showman and presenter of curiosities. He was well aware of the overwhelming response that Jenny Lind, nicknamed "the Swedish Nightingale," was receiving in Europe. He began negotiations to bring the soprano to the United States; but Lind, also aware of Barnum's reputation, was hesitant to be presented as one of his "human oddities." Finally she was persuaded that his interests were genuinely cultural, and she agreed to tour under his management.

He also made her a lucrative offer: She would sing 150 concerts at $1,000 per performance, plus all expenses for her maid, butler and secretary, plus $25,000 for her musical director.

After a massive publicity campaign by Barnum, Jenny Lind arrived by ship to New York harbor on September 1, 1850, greeted by a mob of fans and admirers. She made her American debut at Castle Garden in New York on September 11, 1850 before a sold-out house of 7,000 people. New Yorkers paid

Jenny Lind as she appeared in 1850 during her tour under the auspices of P.T. Barnum.
(Photo courtesy of Ronald L. Lackmann)

more that $87,000 to see her first six concerts. In fact, Barnum had auctioned off tickets to her first concert in New York with the first ticket going for $225. For her Boston premiere, Ossian B. Dodge, the "Boston Vocalist," paid an unbelievable $625 for the first ticket. Public and critical accolades were almost unanimous. Songs were dedicated to her, and her name was lent to novelties and clothing.

Lind immediately set out with Barnum on a tour of 60 dates over the eastern seaboard and Cuba. Their temperaments were not well suited, however, and the diva displayed wide mood swings as her unhappiness grew.

After nine months, Barnum complied with Lind's request to get out of her contract. During her U.S. stay, ending in May 1852, she had performed 93 concerts, grossing a reported $712,161 of which

Lind earned almost $200,000. This, of course, meant that Barnum—in addition to gaining prestige as an impresario—also received a personal profit of over a quarter of a million dollars.

After returning to England, Jenny Lind married her German accompanist, raised three children and devoted her singing only to charitable causes for the rest of her life. She died in 1887 at the age of 67.

LINDEMANN BROS. CIRCUS See SEILS-STERLING CIRCUS.

LINE UP JOINT A ROUSTABOUT or another crew member who was so inclined usually had no problem meeting a potential lover somewhere in the village. More often the local "talent" came to them.

For many TOWNERS, the circus life was the ultimate in glamour: Before and shortly after the turn of the century, the scantily clad ladies and muscular men in leotards were certainly much more titillating than the temperance speakers who came through on the Chautauqua circuit. A bit of the sparkle and stardust fell off on even the sleaziest of the lice-laden louts working the show.

Many times a town girl would come onto the show grounds and take on all comers, often for a dollar a throw. A secluded, if somewhat impersonal and unsanitary, location had to be found; usually the back of one of the prop wagons was quite satisfactory. It was always easy to spot the "line up joint": There was a line of 15 or 20 men, of all shapes, sizes and colors, each with a hard-earned dollar bill clenched in his fist.

Management often "looked the other way"; after all, there were few single women traveling with the show and, depending on the show's customs, the girls may already have been taken on CHOOSING DAY. However, once the makeshift house of ill repute became common knowledge over the showgrounds, the front office was obliged to shut it down. The potential HEAT that could be generated by the bad press in the community had to be avoided at all costs.

One famous incident involving a line up joint occurred on the JOHN ROBINSON CIRCUS in Duluth, Minnesota around 1921. Four unfortunate black men happened to be in a young white lady's company when the joint was raided by the police. Her only defense was to claim rape. An angry mob lined up all of the black men on the show, and she picked out four at random. The crowd hanged the four

"rapists" from light poles on the showgrounds, even though it was certain at least two of the men had never even been in the line up joint. A final irony to the story: Jeremiah "Jerry" MUGIVAN initiated a lawsuit to claim damages against the town, and he eventually collected $2,000 for each of the dead men; although it is doubtful the money was ever passed on to the roustabouts' families.

LIONS See CATS.

LION TAMERS (TRAINERS) See BAUMANN, CHARLY; BEATTY, CLYDE; COURT, ALFRED; DHOTRE, DAMOO; GEBEL-WILLIAMS, GUNTHER; ROTH, LOUIS; STARK, MABEL; VAN AMBURGH, ISAAC; WHITE, PATRICIA.

LITHOGRAPHS When one thinks of circus posters, the first things that come to mind are the colorful lithographs that boldly give the circus's name, its show dates and, if the reader is lucky, some almost-factual information about what one might see in the show.

WINDOW CARDS are another small but important form of lithograph that is still in common use today. Printed on cardboard stock, the advertising pieces are usually placed in merchants' windows (in exchange for a few circus passes) or tacked on poles.

The word PAPER in circus jargon is a catch-all for all of the advertising lithos, HERALDS and window cards that are put up in a town. In fact, when a bill crewman posts the lithographs, he is said to HANG PAPER. Any spot where paper can be hung is known as a LOCATION. These include, in circus slang, a HIT, where window cards or cloth banners can be placed, or a DAUB, a spot to paste up a lithograph. Sometimes the lithograph paper itself is also called the daub. After all of the advertising was up, the circus referred to the complete papering in the town as the SHOWING.

During the heyday of the tented circus, three or four ADVANCE rail cars would hang 5,000–8,000 pieces of paper per day in a 20-mile radius of the show town. In 1915 the Ringling show used 10,000 lithos a day.

The basic unit of measure for a lithograph is called the ONE SHEET (approximately 28 inches by 42 inches), and all other size lithos are named in reference to it. Quarter sheets, half sheets, one sheets, two sheets, three sheets, four sheets and six sheets are usually printed on a single piece of paper. Larger

RINGLING BROS. & VAN AMBURGH'S UNITED MONSTER SHOWS

An 1889 one sheet lithograph of the single season of the Ringling Bros. & Van Amburgh's United Monster Shows. It was the last Ringling season as a wagon show; one year later the Ringling Bros. Circus moved onto rails.
(Photo courtesy of the John and Mable Ringling Museum of Art)

sizes, such as 12 sheets, 16 sheets, 20 sheets and 24 sheets, are printed on many sections of paper that, when assembled on the side of a building, made up a single picture. The average side of a barn was a 16-sheet hit. Some famous lithographs consisted of over 100 separate sheets to make up the single pictorial scene.

There is a subtle but essential difference between a litho that is "three sheets" and a THREE SHEET. The former would be made up of three separate lithographs pasted side by side to form one image. The latter refers to a single piece of advertising lithography.

The circus ordered all of the season's lithographs at one time and stored them at WINTER QUARTERS, cutting down on the cost of printing. If a STAND fell out or a town was added, it was much cheaper to print a small black-and-white strip to cover over the first date than to do a color run for a single one sheet. Each town's allocation with the correct dates was shipped to the BILLING CREW and other men on the ADVANCE a few weeks ahead of the scheduled date of performance.

Besides the colorful pictorials, there were specialty lithographs printed as well. One of these was the RAT SHEET, which unflatteringly described another circus that played the same TERRITORY. Rat sheets were more often heralds than posted paper, but the WAIT PAPER was definitely a one sheet.

Since one of the great joys of a bill-poster was to be able to cover up the OPPOSITION PAPER from another show, advance crew hoped that another

Lithograph for The Circus Kingdom. (Photo by Tom Ogden)

circus would not do the same to their own. Billing crews whose job was to double back and tear down—or, more efficiently, cover over—opposition paper were known as NIGHT RIDERS, because they usually did their work under the secrecy and safety of the dark.

Among the most famous manufacturers of lithographs were Enquirer Lithograph Company and Strobridge Lithographic Company (Cincinnati, Ohio), Courier Lithograph Company (Buffalo, New York) and Erie Lithographic and Printing Company (Erie, Pennsylvania). The business relationship between Strobridge and Ringling ended in 1939, but by then golden days of being able to cover an entire town with lithographs were over.

The art of creating the beautiful circus lithograph is not dead. It is carried on by such major circus

suppliers as Bill Biggerstaff at Graphics 2000 in Las Vegas. Custom posters are also created by Spotlight Graphics in SARASOTA, FLORIDA. Obstacles such as local laws against bill posting, the development of rural and vacant property and the economic impossibility of keeping a huge billing crew out on the road, however, have all signaled the end of the incredible barn-size, kaleidoscopic displays of elaborate lithographs.

LITTLE, GLEN "FROSTY" (1925–   ) Glen Little began his work as "Frosty the Clown" for a Denver, Colorado amusement park at the belated age of 29. After that he became involved for a number of years with a carnival.

A member of the first graduating class of CLOWN COLLEGE, he joined the Red Unit of the RINGLING BROS. AND BARNUM & BAILEY CIRCUS in 1968. Within two years he was "boss clown" of the unit. He held the position for a decade; and, in 1980, he was also named head clown of the Blue Unit as well as the director of all Ringling clown acts. In addition, Little has been a teacher at the Clown College for 20 years.

In 1983 Ringling management named Little a "Master Clown," the fourth to have received that honor.

As "Frosty," Glen Little has appeared on 12 network television shows, created more than 300 CLOWN GAGS and has also taught at the Japan Clown College. Little is now part of a "gag factory," named Felds' Creative Services, as a "producing clown."

In 1991 Little was inducted into the CLOWN HALL OF FAME. He has also recently announced the opening of his own clown school at his home in Rupert, Idaho. Up to three students per session partake of 24 hours of intensive personal instruction over three days of classes. (See also CLOWNS.)

LITTLE CIRCUS WAGON The monthly publication of the CIRCUS MODEL BUILDERS, INC., INTERNATIONAL, *Little Circus Wagon* contains a wealth of reference information on circus equipment details necessary for the hobbyist builder as well as club news.

LITTLE MADISON SQUARE GARDEN When the RINGLING BROS. AND BARNUM & BAILEY CIRCUS had its WINTER QUARTERS in SARASOTA, FLORIDA from 1927 to 1961, John RINGLING and later John Ringling

NORTH opened the grounds on Sunday afternoons as a tourist attraction.

Each week a Sunday matinee show was put on for the general public. Admission to the performance, including the huge MENAGERIE and the exhibition of floats and BANDWAGONS, was priced at around 90 cents for adults and 50 cents for children.

The "main show" took place in an open-air arena, nicknamed "Little Madison Square Garden" by show folk after the traditional opening site of the Ringling circus. The field itself contained three full-size rings, with aerial and ground rigging as needed; it was surrounded by a white fence to prevent spectators from wandering into the playing area. Audiences sat on folding wooden chairs that had been placed on the multitiered permanent bleachers located on three sides of the arena. The fourth side acted as the BACK DOOR of the missing BIG TOP, and a long low building for storage and dressing paralelled the track.

The Sunday matinee show was a perfect opportunity for performers to test new material before an appreciative crowd or to hone existing routines. Not only was it a great way to keep the act in shape for the following season, it was also undoubtedly a perfect showcase for those performers who were "between dates" and needed employment. This might be a reason why many of the Sunday acts were not Ringling performers at all but artists from other circuses as well as from carnivals, nightclubs and the variety stage.

LITTLE PEOPLE

Affectionate circus jargon for midgets and dwarfs. With their usual height of four foot six inches and under, most little people are relegated to the SIDESHOW with the other "human oddities" or join CLOWN ALLEY; occasionally, though, they are made stars of the BIG TOP. Two of the most famous little people ever to appear on circuses were TOM THUMB and, more recently, MICHU.

In popular usage, the term "midget" refers to perfectly formed, miniature men or women. Their condition is caused by an insufficient secretion of the hormone HGH from the pituitary gland. The word "dwarf" usually refers to misshapen small folk, usually with larger heads and extremities in proportion to the rest of their bodies; they are medically known as achondroplastics. Technically, however, all little people are dwarfs.

(See also ALPERT, "PRINCE" PAUL; FREAKS; NUTT, "COMMODORE" GEORGE WASHINGTON MORRISON; SALUTO, FRANKIE; WARREN, LAVINIA.)

LITTLE TOP

Circus jargon for the SIDESHOW tent. Even on shows where the MENAGERIE top happens to be larger, the sideshow is still referred to as the little top.

LIVING STATUES, THE

A holdover from the 1890s, the living statues is an unusual feature act still occasionally seen on circuses today.

Acrobatic performers wearing small wardrobe or leotards (to show the greatest amount of flesh that decency would allow) painted themselves gold and bronze or covered their bodies with clown white greasepaint. Occasionally similarly dusted animals would be added to the group. The company then formed a tableaux that the RINGMASTER announced as depicting a moral virtue, a historical moment or a biblical scene. Although the scenes were sometimes difficult to recognize—in fact, many times the displays were merely demonstrations of acrobatic strength and balance—the motionless golden-white human statues were always a crowd-pleaser, especially among the ladies.

LIVING UNICORN, THE

See FELD, KENNETH; RINGLING BROS. AND BARNUM & BAILEY CIRCUS.

LOCATION

In circus parlance, the location is the spot on which advertising PAPER can be tacked or pasted. Circus purists differentiate between two types of locations: DAUBS were places where LITHOGRAPHS were pasted up; HITS, however, were spots where HERALDS, WINDOW CARDS and cloth BANNERS were tacked or hung. Since paste is seldom used anymore to post circus paper, all locations are now commonly referred to as hits.

LOGAN, FRED (C. 1925–   )

One of the world's top BULL HANDLERS, Fred Logan has been in command of the herd of ELEPHANTS on the CLYDE BEATTY-COLE BROS. CIRCUS for 22 years.

Born in Brandon, Manitoba, Logan came to the United States in 1942 to work for Capt. Terrell JACOBS, the renowned lion trainer. Logan moved to the RINGLING BROS. AND BARNUM & BAILEY CIRCUS as an assistant to the famed BULL man Hugo Schmidt. In 1949 he went on the AL G. KELLY & MILLER BROS.

CIRCUS to work under elephant trainer Bill Woodcock, Sr. Finally, in 1970, he became the head bull handler on Beatty-Cole, where he still actively performs with a herd of at least ten elephants.

Among his many specialties, Logan is distinguished for his presentation of the walking LONG MOUNT, in which an entire line of pachyderms stand up on their back legs, rest their front legs on the elephants before them, then plod down the hippodrome track.

LONG MOUNT

The long mount is probably the circus-goer's favorite trick performed by the ELEPHANTS. The BULLS line up single file, trunk to tail. The second elephant in the row places her front feet on the back of the lead bull. The second pachyderm places her front feet on the back of the second bull, and so on.

An impressive sight, only increased by more elephants, the long mount is usually performed down one full side of the tent or arena track. Fred LOGAN, who commands a impressive herd of ten or more bulls on the CLYDE BEATTY-COLE BROS. CIRCUS, is renowned for his walking long mount, in which the elephants lumber forward, single file, while still standing in the long mount position.

LORD BYRON

Lord Byron was the celebrated educated pig owned by the early American clown Dan RICE and displayed by him throughout his career.

Lord Byron was first displayed by Rice when he worked with an itinerant puppet show in 1843 for $4 a week; but it was while touring for "Dr." Gilbert R. SPALDING of the NICHOLS CIRCUS (also known as the North American Circus) that Dan Rice truly developed his comic routines with the pig. Lord Byron would answer questions asked of him by scratching his paw the correct number of times in the dirt. Rice had discovered that pigs have an acute sense of hearing, and by snapping his fingers he could get Lord Byron to scrape the ground.

Lord Byron was also taught to select the American flag from a box of banners and wave it at the crowd.

Reportedly, due to the superstitious nature of the townsfolk at this time, some people (especially clergy) accused the pig—and Rice—of wicked if not supernatural powers.

LOST JUNGLE, THE

See BEATTY, CLYDE; FILMS, CIRCUS.

A boy and his pig, in the tradition of Dan Rice and Lord Byron. The chalk-faced comedian is Toby Sanders, author of *How to be a Compleat Clown*. The pig is Porkchop. (Photo courtesy of Charles A. DeWein)

LOT

In circus jargon, the lot is the field, open grounds or—in recent times—the paved parking lot where the circus TENTS, MIDWAY, BACK YARD and equipment are set up.

Needless to say, the condition of the lot is one of the primary concerns of the circus when it arrives. Ideally, the lot should be spacious enough to accommodate any design the LAYOUT MAN desires, so that the FRONT YARD can face toward the crowd's expected arrival. In related slang, if the lot is so small that all the equipment can barely fit on, it is said to be "tight." The lot should be flat and rut-free so that the springs and shocks on the trucks, the show equipment loaded on the semis and personal belongings in the coaches are not jostled too badly. (The opposite of a smooth lot is sometimes referred to as a "washboard lot.") A grassy lot is preferred, but circuses do not necessarily welcome football fields and ballparks. Problems with the property owners over STAKE holes and truck tracks quickly negate the benefits of a manicured lot.

The ground itself should be firm, but not hard. A sandy lot, especially if it has no "bottom," will not hold stakes in place, so instead tents must be tied down to trucks. Also, the lot should not be too wet (or worse, flooded) because vehicles would have to be pulled on and off by the ELEPHANTS—and, if that doesn't work, then by bulldozers.

LOT LICE   Disparaging circus jargon for bothersome townspeople on the showgrounds. While circus folk welcome visitors to the MIDWAY and inside the tents, they wish to have their privacy and their personal lives respected just like anyone else. Performers understand and tolerate the inquisitiveness of true circus fans but become understandably upset when TOWNERS wander indiscriminately throughout the BACK YARD and other nonpublic areas.

LOUIS, JOE (1914–1981)   Heavyweight champion of the world from 1937 through 1949, Joe Louis (born Joseph Louis Barrow) held the title longer than any other boxer (11 years, 8 months, 7 days). To this day, Louis holds the record for going the longest period without any "no decision" bouts—27 total, all heavyweight. He retired his belt on March 1, 1949, having defended his title a record 25 times.

In 1950 Louis became a featured circus attraction with the DAILEY BROS. CIRCUS during its final season, much as ex-boxing champion Jess WILLARD had on the 101 RANCH WILD WEST back in 1915. Louis's "performance" consisted of little more than making a CENTER RING appearance and accepting the spectators' acclaim. Years later, in a similar capacity, Louis became an official "greeter" at Caesar's Palace in Las Vegas.

LOW WIRE   See COLLEANO, CON; MILLMAN, BIRD; NAITTO, ALA; WIRE WALKING.

LOYAL, GEORGE (fl. 1875–1880s)   Billed as the "Human Projectile," George Loyal became the first HUMAN CANNONBALL to perform in the United States, probably with the YANKEE ROBINSON CIRCUS in 1875.

(See also LULU; ZACCHINI, HUGO; ZAZEL.)

Guistino Loyal rehearses an amazing equestrian stunt for his bareback act on The Big One in 1946. He leaps from the horse—jumping over the bridge formed by three assistants—and lands back on the galloping steed.   (Author's collection)

LOYAL, GUISTINO (c.1909–   )   Born August 2, 1909, and first appearing in this country in 1946, Guistino (also seen as Justino) Loyal became one of the premier equestrians of his generation.

Touring for years with The BIG ONE, the Guistino (or Justino) Loyal Troupe became known for flashy, dangerous tricks. One of the more incredible stunts was building an eight-person pyramid on top of five horses as they galloped abreast around the ring.

(See also LOYAL-REPENSKY TROUPE, THE.)

LOYAL-REPENSKY TROUPE, THE   The Loyal family is perhaps the oldest name in the circus world still active today. So revered is the name in France that the RINGMASTER, or EQUESTRIAN DIRECTOR, is known as "Monsieur Loyal."

The Loyal-Repensky troupe of equestrians moved to the United States from France in 1932 to join the RINGLING BROS. AND BARNUM & BAILEY CIRCUS. Jules Loyal was the patriarch of the clan, and Repensky (his mother's maiden name) was added for its impressive sound. Their act of ROMAN RIDING, which was subsequently seen on many circuses, featured a seven-man pyramid built on five horses galloping abreast. In the stunt, four performers stood astride the five horses while three acrobats/equestrians mounted their shoulders.

The Loyal-Repsenskys are an extended family. The Alfonso Loyal-Repensky troupe, featuring Mme. Luciana Loyal, currently rides with the CARSON & BARNES CIRCUS. Her most popular equestrienne routine is an adaptation of the old PETE JENKINS ACT. Her uncle, Guistino LOYAL, started his own troupe in 1945 and performed on his own with the Ringlings as well as with the CRISTIANIS. Other families include the Loyal-Suarez, featuring Guistino's son, Timi Loyal, who is able to perform four somersaults on horseback within one circle of the CENTER RING.

LULU (1855–?) A forerunner of the HUMAN CANNONBALL, Lulu performed in the 1870s. Born in the United States, Lulu was first fired from a Farini cannon at the Royal Cremorne Music Hall in London in 1871. Lulu was actually a man, Eddie Rivers, but he dressed as a woman because he correctly reasoned that, in his era, a woman would elicit more terror and concern from the audience.

Billed as "The Queen of Trapezists," in 1873 Lulu appeared at Niblo's Garden in New York City. Lulu stood on a small hidden square that was cut flush into the stage floor. The bottom of the trap was attached to heavy and tightly coiled springs. When the springs were released, Lulu flew up in the air 25 feet to catch a trapeze.

The spring platform apparatus was almost identical to that in the mouth of the wooden cannon used just a few years later by the most famous early human projectile—and a real woman—ZAZEL.

In 1875 lulu toured with HOWES AND CUSHING.

(See also LOYAL, GEORGE; ZACCHINI, HUGO.)

LUSBIE, BEN (fl. 1871–1890) Although little is known of him biographically, Ben Lusbie earned the title of "the quickest dispenser of show tickets in the world." Some of the shows on which he worked gave him equal billing to the performers in the BIG TOP and at least one (the ADAM FOREPAUGH CIRCUS) printed a lithograph of him.

Short, small, quick-tempered with a large mustache, Lusbie reportedly could sell tickets quicker than two ticket takers could take them. During his years with the circus operated by P.T. BARNUM and W.C. COUP, Lusbie was once clocked at selling 6,000 tickets in one hour. He later broke his own record, going through 6,153 tickets in an hour and three minutes on the 4 Paw Show. For this last stunt, the *National Police Gazette* named Ben Lusbie the champion ticket seller of the world.

MABIE BROS. CIRCUS   In 1840 Edmund Foster Mabie (1810–67) and Jeremiah Mabie (1812–67), from the vicinity of Patterson in upstate New York, founded their first Mabie Bros. Circus. Throughout their careers, the Mabie brothers toured their circus under a variety of names with a number of different partners and managers.

With circus maven Seth B. HOWES as a partner and manager in their first operation, The Howes & Mabie New York Circus toured throughout the East and into the Midwest. The brothers purchased 1,000 acres near Delavan, Wisconsin and moved the circus's WINTER QUARTERS there in 1847.

Howes left the partnership and retired, and the Mabie brothers became sole owners and managers. They renamed their show the Grand Olympic Arena and United States Circus. Edmund Mabie married in 1850 and also stopped touring with the circus. He did continue to manage the brothers' Wisconsin properties, however, and was active in Delavan civic affairs for the remainder of his life.

Jeremiah stayed on the road. By 1853 he added a MENAGERIE to the circus and retitled the show Herr Driesbach & Co.'s Menagerie Combined with Mabie & Co.'s U.S. Circus. P.A. Older was manager for the company. The wagon show traveled with 50 to 75 HORSES during the 1850s, playing throughout the Midwest.

Despite John ROBINSON's claim to have been the first to include a COOKHOUSE for his employees on the LOT, circus historians agree that it was most probably the Mabie brothers who made that innovation in 1857. Additionally, the Mabies were the first to offer an aftershow, or CONCERT, to their circus.

In 1861 the show underwent another name change to E.F. & J. Mabie's Circus and J.J. Nathans' American Circus Combined. The next year it became Mabie's Great Show, Circus and Menagerie. That winter the brothers operated a resident circus in Chicago called the Winter Garden, Zoological and Equestrian Entertainment. Among the company were Dan RICE with EXCELSIOR (billed as a blind trained horse) and Dan CASTELLO as a CLOWN and performing acrobatic VAULTING.

Jeremiah Mabie's health deteriorated in the 1860s, and the last show closed in 1864. The equipment was dispersed: The menagerie, for instance, was transferred to Adam FOREPAUGH in Chicago. Both of the Mabie brothers died just three years later.

MADISON SQUARE GARDEN   The traditional site of the annual opening engagement of the RINGLING BROS. AND BARNUM & BAILEY CIRCUS, Madison Square Garden is located in New York City, bounded by 31st and 33rd streets between 7th and 8th avenues. Owned by Paramount, its parent company, the Madison Square Garden Corporation operates its own television network and sports franchise in addition to the arena facilities. When the circus is in residence, seating is configured to accommodate 15,000 spectators.

Madison Square Garden first became associated with circuses when Richard SANDS and associates built the New York Hipprodome at Madison Square (Broadway and 23rd Street in Manhattan) in 1846. When not on tour, his circus appeared there through November 1853.

Later, following the destruction of his museums, P.T. BARNUM entered a partnership with W.C. COUP and Dan CASTELLO to tour a circus, one that Barnum was to call The Greatest Show On Earth. The show opened in Brooklyn under canvas on April 10, 1871, and it traveled for three successful seasons.

In the winter, Barnum produced his shows in the HIPPOTHEATRON on 14th Street in New York; but the building burned to the ground in 1872. At the end of 1873 season, Coup leased the property at Madison Square, located between 26th and 27th Street and Fourth and Madison avenues. Since Barnum was in Europe at the time, there is some controversy as to whether he was ever consulted.

Regardless, P.T. BARNUM'S GREAT ROMAN HIPPO-DROME moved into the giant arena on the site of what was later to be called Madison Square Garden. Ten thousand people attended the first performance in April 1874. The show featured a SPEC, the "Congress of Nations," which "required nearly 1,000 persons, several hundred HORSES, besides llamas, CAMELS, ostriches, etc." Next came chariot races around the track, followed by the regular circus performance. As would happen years later with THE BIG ONE, after the winter run the Hippodrome show went on the road.

When the original Madison Square Garden closed and a colosseum was built adjoining Penn Station, the Garden name moved over and uptown, and the Ringling circus moved with it. Although the Garden is used for sporting events and other entertainment attractions such as rock concerts, the Ringling show is the only circus to perform there.

Although the thought of opening in Manhattan seems exciting to the layman, many circus folk today dislike the Garden date. In Florida the circus has rehearsed for weeks in an open area the size of the average arena. The line-up for the spec and other entrances has been assigned assuming there is adequate "backstage" space. This area doesn't exist at the Garden, and performers must wait in narrow corridors; the animals must wait in the basement. Sometimes, right before the Spec begins, the long parade must continue down the hall and out onto the street. Those entering the arena and those leaving must squeeze through the same hallways up and down the ramp to the subterranean level.

Also, the circus hits New York in the beginning of April when the city is cold, snowy, rainy and sleety. The performers and animals, having just finished up weeks of rehearsal in sunny Florida, immediately fall victim to colds and other illnesses during their five-week stay.

In addition to the outside weather, the Garden itself is not exactly conducive to strong health. The main arena is steam-heated; but the basement, where most of the props and animals wait, is open and drafty, as are the hallways leading up and down to the almost overheated arena. In addition, the basement is often badly ventilated and usually humid.

Despite these BACK YARD limitations, the Madison Square Garden arena itself remains the ideal location to stage and to view the GREATEST SHOW ON EARTH. In addition to—or perhaps because of—the freshness of the acts, the wardrobe, choreography, music and other spectacular elements of the show, there is a special excitement to the opening stand, among both the performers and the audiences.

MAIN GUY Circus jargon for the guy rope that holds up the CENTER POLE of the BIG TOP.

MAKE✳A✳CIRCUS Founded in San Francisco, California in 1976 by Peter Frankham, MAKE✳A✳CIRCUS performs open-air audience participation programs that are free to the public.

Its history reaches back to the streets of London in 1970, where Frankham and several friends performed circus-style sketches in vacant neighborhood lots. In 1974 Frankham brought his "circus with a purpose" across the ocean, finding an American audience in the Bay area.

MAKE✳A✳CIRCUS appears on Summer Festival Day in a local city park under area sponsorship—usually the City Parks and Recreation Department, a major corporation or foundation. Neighborhoods are selected to provide audiences (sometimes as many as 1,000 per show) of low-income, minority children and families who otherwise might not have the opportunity to see a circus.

The main show consists of a scripted children's theater piece that utilizes circus skills, backed by a

Make∗A∗Circus in 1990 during a Los Angeles area park appearance.   (Photo by Tom Ogden)

live four-piece jazz band. Immediately following the hour-long performance, the actor/circus performers hold "hands-on" workshops in circus skills for the children. Classes are devised for all age and skill levels, and enthusiastic kids are taught everything from JUGGLING and STILT WALKING to basic body movement. Finally, there is the "Community Show," in which workshop participants get to actually perform. This second piece is completely different from the first show and is loosely scripted to bring in whatever that day's audience provides—from a troupe of beginner gymnasts to a covey of three-year-old CLOWNS.

A typical MAKE∗A∗CIRCUS main performance was the 1990 show, "The Mouth That Roared." It told the story of a bunch of students trying to outflip, outjuggle, outclown and outtumble each other in competition for the "Crown of Coolness" bestowed by the town's most popular D.J., "Big

Mouth." An hour later the workshop participants took part in a second show, "Feelers."

With WINTER QUARTERS at Fort Mason Center in San Francisco, MAKE∗A∗CIRCUS provides educational training throughout the year in clowning and circus skills to disabled adults, emotionally disturbed children and people with a multitude of disabilities. Approximately 300 disabled children and adults annually take part in seminars at recreational facilities and in conjunction with physical therapy staffs, as part of an outreach program to bolster self-esteem and develop motor skills.

In its unprecedented Teen Apprentice Program (TAP), MAKE∗A∗CIRCUS actively seeks out disadvantaged youths who are interested in the performing arts and provides a ten-week training course that also focuses on confidence-building, leadership and cooperation. Upon completion of the course, qualified participants are offered salaried positions on the MAKE∗A∗CIRCUS Summer Festival Day tour. Working closely with the San Francisco mayor's office, teen advocacy organizations, high schools and social welfare agencies, approximately 20 teens enter TAP each year.

"MAN ON THE FLYING TRAPEZE, THE"   See "FLYING TRAPEZE, THE."

MARCH, THE   Circus jargon for the daily STREET PARADE.

MARQUEE   Circus jargon for the small canvas-topped entranceway to the BIG TOP. The marquee is located at the end of the MIDWAY often at the FRONT DOOR to the main show.

The front of the marquee sometimes has the name of the circus colorfully painted on it, but often it is just emblazoned with the words "To The Circus." The ticket takers stand underneath the marquee.

On circuses where the MENAGERIE is not contained within the SIDESHOW, the animal tent is located between the marquee and the entrance to the Big Top. Sometimes a wall of canvas runs from each side of the marquee to the Big Top, directing the patrons to the menagerie; at other times the marquee acts as the entrance to the menagerie.

MCBRYDE, LEON "BUTTONS" (1943–   )   From the time he was seven years old, Leon McBryde only wanted to be a clown. Literally a "giant" in his field, McBryde grew to be 6 feet 7 inches tall, one of the tallest CLOWNS ever to tour with The BIG ONE.

As an AUGUSTE CLOWN named "Buttons," Leon McBryde toured for only one season with the RINGLING BROS. AND BARNUM & BAILEY CIRCUS before being selected as its "Goodwill Ambassador." As an

Marquee and ticket wagon of the five-ring Carson & Barnes Circus—known as the "Biggest Big Top on Earth"—in Ojai, California in 1991.   (Photo by Tom Ogden)

advance publicity clown, he showed his mettle as a PRESS AGENT, devising many new promotional concepts. Back in Florida, he spent five years as part of the CLOWN COLLEGE staff.

Leon "Buttons" McBryde was the first Ringling clown to be inducted into the Clown Hall of Fame in Delavan, Wisconsin.

MCPHEE, ANDREW DOWNIE   See DOWNIE, ANDREW.

MECHANIC
Circus jargon for a leather safety harness that is worn by acrobats or aerialists during rehearsals and some performances in case of a fall. The mechanic is connected to wires ("lunge ropes") that run through a pulley system and are held by "spotters" on the ground. The persons holding onto the lunge ropes must regulate the slack in the wire so that the performer has enough freedom to perform the stunt, but will not hit the ground in the event of a missed trick.

On the very early circuses where the CENTER POLE was positioned in the center of the ring, the pulley for the mechanic was attached to one end of a long horizontal pole. The other end of the "arm" had a metal hoop that went over the pin at the top of the center pole, thus allowing the arm to circle the ring over the performer. In modern tents and arenas, the mechanic is usually attached to the CRANE BAR or other rigging immediately over the ring.

Almost every acrobatic, aerial and equestrian performer has been trained with the use of a mechanic. During the more dangerous stunts, mechanics are used today even in performance for insurance as well as safety reasons. Besides, the mechanic in no way assists the artist in completing a trick; and audiences are aware that it is the performer and not the mechanic that provides the skill.

MENAGERIE
Technically any collection of animals, in the circus world a "menagerie" is a group of unusual or rare beasts—a sort of traveling zoo—taken on tour for exhibition.

The first exotic animals seen in the United States were not part of an organized circus or even part of a touring show. The earliest form of a traveling menagerie was most probably a lone pioneer or trapper who brought a tamed BEAR out of the forest, or a sailor who came to port with a monkey perched on his shoulder.

The first deliberate importations of wild animals for exhibition occurred in Boston. A lion arrived by ship in 1716, a CAMEL in 1721 and a polar bear in 1733.

In the 1700s and early 1800s, single animals were still being toured for display. One of the first to carry an exotic animal on the road was Hachaliah BAILEY of SOMERS, NEW YORK who exhibited OLD BET, the second ELEPHANT to reach America. Soon, however, full traveling zoos were being trouped.

In effect, the menagerie was born and blossomed as an entertainment separate from the circus. In fact, while the early American circuses—such as the first arena show of John Bill RICKETTS—always included performing animal acts, exotic animals were not part of the presentation.

At least 30 menageries, many of them originating out of the Somers group influenced by Bailey, trouped across the United States in the early 1820s, from Maine to Alabama and as far west as the Appalachian Mountains. Most of the "traveling museums," as they often billed themselves, were two- or three-wagon affairs. The ZOOLOGICAL INSTITUTE, begun in 1835, was a syndicate made up of independent menagerie owners, with many members from the Somers group. Located in a building in the Bowery district of Manhattan, the Institute controlled importation and leased its animals to touring shows for many years, creating a virtual monopoly on the menagerie business.

Over the years the menagerie and the equestrian circus combined. At first, a trained animal would be added to create a "show" in a static menagerie exhibition; or a few cages of African beasts were carried with the circus caravan as a special attraction. So successful were such unions that soon all circuses were being judged by the size and diversity of their menagerie—both their nonperforming as well as their performing stock.

Exhibition of the mobile ZOO was so important that during the heyday of the railroad show, the wild animals were housed in a separate top, also called the menagerie. In time, the menagerie tent grew to be the second-largest top on the LOT, smaller only than the BIG TOP.

Admission to the menagerie was included in the ticket price to the main show; in fact, it could not be visited separately. Passing through the MARQUEE, the circus-goer moved directly into the menagerie

Inside the combined menagerie and sideshow tent of the Clyde Beatty-Cole Bros. Circus in 1975.   (Author's collection)

and, after viewing the rare beasts, moved on to seating in the Big Top.

Smaller menageries with separate admissions are still often seen on the midway, even if the main stock is enclosed within a SIDESHOW or a menagerie top. These shows might be themed, such as a reptile show, or may exhibit a unique animal, such as a rare white rhino or a miniature pony.

(See also BULLS; CATS; GARGANTUA; GIRAFFES; GO-LIATH; GORILLAS; HORSES; MONKEYS AND APES; M'TOTO.)

MICHU (1941–   ) In 1971 Irvin and Kenneth FELD got word that an incredible midget lived in Hungary; and, in February 1973 the father-and-son team tracked him down to a tiny village, Lilliput Faly, outside Budapest, Hungary.

At the end of the search, however, was Michu. He stood 33 inches tall, weighed 25 pounds and was already trained in circus skills. Both parents, each about 40 inches tall, were members of Budapest's Lilliputian Theatre, a children's theater company made up entirely of LITTLE PEOPLE.

Michu was born Mihaly Mezaros, weighing only 2½ pounds. As a child he studied at a state-run school teaching circus arts. After graduation, he traveled for 15 years with a tented Hungarian circus, the Liebel Circus, as a CLOWN, announcer, unicyclist and dancer.

Upon Michu's joining the RINGLING BROS. AND BARNUM & BAILEY CIRCUS, Irvin Feld advertised him as "Seven inches shorter than P.T. Barnum's Tom Thumb." Although it had been 136 years since BARNUM had introduced Charles Stratton to an admiring public as General TOM THUMB, the American public instantly understood the analogy.

It is interesting to note that Irvin Feld was using a bit of his own Barnum-style "humbuggery." Michu was, indeed, seven inches shorter than Tom Thumb; but he was not shorter than the 25 inches that Tom Thumb stood when he was touring for Barnum. By the end of his life, Tom Thumb had grown an additional 15 inches; it was this height that Feld compared to Michu's.

Michu was such an asset to the Ringling Bros. and Barnum & Bailey Circus that the Felds took out a $2 million insurance policy on him with Lloyds of London against additional growth. The policy seemed secure, since Michu hadn't grown an inch in over 26 years.

While Michu was small in size, he was a full-grown man in temperament. He enjoyed the proverbial "wine, women and song". His language was frequently sprinkled with vulgarities in both English and Hungarian.

Much as Tom Thumb had found a mate in Lavinia Warren, Feld hoped to find a "wife" for Michu—if not in actuality, then at least for a ceremony in the show. Feld hired Juliana, another midget from Hungary, for The BIG ONE; but, despite Michu's attempts to woo her, Juliana never fell in love and was reportedly shocked by much of Michu's behavior.

Regardless, for two seasons (1976 and 1977), The GREATEST SHOW ON EARTH staged a "circus marriage," complete with an invitation enclosed in the souvenir program. For each performance a local boy and girl were chosen to be ring bearer and flower girl, respectively; dozens of others got to ride in the wedding procession. After the two years were over—with her contract completed—Juliana left the Ringling circus.

Michu continued with the show. He traveled in his own railroad car with all of the furnishings built to his scale. In one of his acts, Michu rushed into a telephone booth to become a miniature Man of Steel. In another he engaged in a slapstick battle with the largest clown on the circus.

By the 112th edition of the show in 1982, Michu was performing two animal acts: A Liberty pony act (see LIBERTY HORSES) with Elizabeth and Sandor Raski—also midgets with whom Michu had studied at the Hungarian circus school—and a comedy poodle and terrier act with an assist by Hungarian trainer Bela Tabak. In the latter, Michu performed a spoof version of a bareback equestrian act, using the poodles as if they were his HORSES.

(See also FREAKS.)

MIDGETS
See ALPERT, "PRINCE" PAUL; AMERICAN MUSEUM; BARNUM, P(HINEAS) T(AYLOR); BARNUM MU-SEUM, THE; FREAKS; LITTLE PEOPLE; MICHU; NUTT, "COMMODORE" GEORGE WASHINGTON MORRISON; P.T. BARNUM'S GREAT ASIATIC CARAVAN, MUSEUM AND ME-NAGERIE; SALUTO, FRANKIE; TOM THUMB; WARREN, LAVINIA.

MIDWAY
Approaching the main gate and FRONT DOOR to the BIG TOP, the circus-goer must pass through the FRONT YARD, or midway. This is the area near the main entrance that is lined on both sides by the SIDESHOW, PIT SHOWS, MENAGERIE, ticket wagon, souvenir stands, food stands and other attractions. Some MUD SHOWS have also begun to carry kiddie rides or a MOON BOUNCE on the midway. As opposed to a carnival, however, no games of chance will be found on a modern circus.

(See also TENTS.)

MIGHTY BARNUM, THE
See FILMS, CIRCUS.

MIGHTY HAAG CIRCUS
The Mighty Haag Circus started as a small wagon show in the 1890s in Louisiana, continuing to tour southern cities for almost 50 years.

Growing steadily, it became a railroad show in 1909. The circus had outgrown its roots, however, and lost money in the larger towns serviced by rail. The show returned to wagons after the 1914 season.

In 1918 the show became motorized and bought its first trucks. The last of the original Mighty Haag Circus wagons was replaced in 1919.

Like most of the circuses on the road, it was forced to close at the end of the 1938 season due to recessionary times.

MILLER, DORY "D.R." (1916–   )
Born July 27, 1916, Dory Miller is the producer and co-owner of the CARSON & BARNES CIRCUS and the Kelly-Miller Bros. Circus.

D.R. first entered the circus of his father, Obert Miller (1886–1969), in 1924, when he was only eight years old. He worked as a SIDESHOW performer, trick rider and CALLIOPE driver. Eventually he became known for his WIRE WALKING act.

In 1938 Obert Miller formed a small DOG AND PONY SHOW, the Miller Bros. Circus, which grew into the AL G. KELLY & MILLER BROS. CIRCUS. Dory and his brother Kelly (1930–60) became actively involved in the family operation. At the request of local businessmen and circus fans, the show's WINTER QUARTERS were moved to Hugo, Oklahoma in 1942. Even during World War II, the show prospered. While D.R. was away from the States, his wife Isla and Kelly's wife, Dale, kept the show operational.

With Kelly Miller's death in 1959, much of the day-to-day operation of the circus fell on D.R.'s shoulders. Gradually he modernized and enlarged the show. Meanwhile, he had become a part owner of the FAMOUS COLE CIRCUS and the CARSON & BARNES CIRCUS, the latter under the management of Jack Moore.

Obert Miller, feeling that "smaller is better," started a new operation, the Fairyland Circus, which lasted from about 1962 to 1965. When Jack Moore died in 1969, D.R. took complete control of the Carson & Barnes show. After his father's death, D.R. retired the Kelly-Miller title and concentrated on building the Carson & Barnes Circus into the largest show under canvas.

D.R. was also involved in the resurrection of the Kelly-Miller title a decade later. "Big" John STRONG sold his circus in the fall of 1983, and Miller bought the entire operation. The nucleus of the show was put under the management of David E. Rawls; and, with partners D.R. Miller and Jess Jessen, the Al G. Kelly-Miller Bros. Circus—soon shortened in name to the Kelly-Miller Circus—opened in the spring of 1984.

D.R. Miller still travels intermittently with Carson and Barnes—with five full rings the largest tented show in the world—as well as with the Kelly-Miller show. He remains totally involved with both circuses, helping to plan the routes and working with the general agents from his winter quarters.

Isla was born August 9, 1917 on a small family farm in Smith Center, Kansas. Referred to by friends and admirers as the "First lady of the Circus," Isla continues as a full partner in D.R.'s circuses and his life. She keeps her eye on the accounting side of the business and assists in interviewing new employees. Each year she also helps to plan the annual themes and the coordinated wardrobe for the shows.

Their daughter, Barbara, is also a director and co-owner of both shows. She is married to Geary Byrd, the president and co-owner of Carson & Barnes and co-owner of Kelly-Miller. Together they have two daughters, Traci and Kristin.

If ever there was a living legend in circus, it is D.R. Miller. He and his wife, Isla, celebrated 50 years in circusdom in 1986. D.R. has been involved in over 25,000 performances and has launched the careers of innumerable circus families and luminaries.

MILLER, OBERT   See AL G. KELLY & MILLER BROS. CIRCUS; MILLER, DORY "D.R."

MILLER BROS. 101 RANCH WILD WEST   See 101 RANCH WILD WEST.

MILLMAN, BIRD (1888–1940)   Featured on the RINGLING BROS. AND BARNUM & BAILEY CIRCUS in the 1920s, Bird Millman was the first American female circus star to perform on a loosened tightwire known as the slack wire. The nickname "Bird" was given to this tiny performer because of the small, birdlike steps she would take as she crossed the wire.

Millman was also the first American wire walker to perform without an umbrella or pole for balance. Clutching a child's balloon as she held her arms out in balance, Millman sang songs backed by a chorus as she danced across the cord.

Millman's parents were TRAPEZE and wire artists on a small circus. Born in Canon City, Colorado, Bird joined the circus and gave her first performance at the age of six. In a typical show-must-go-on story, Bird Millman first performed on the wire when her father was injured and her mother rushed with him to the hospital. The circus owner rushed Bird onto the "silver strand."

By the age of 12, she was an accomplished wire walker, and the family toured Europe for the next two years. In 1914 she returned to the United States as a CENTER RING star attraction for John RINGLING and later with The BIG ONE. During the winter seasons, she performed in vaudeville and posh supper clubs, such as the Ziegfeld Roof in New York City.

It was after a performance at the Greenwich Village Follies that she met Joseph O'Day. At the height of her career, she gave it all up to become Mrs. O'Day. She lived a quiet, happy life with him in Boston until his death in 1931. She returned to Canon City, where she stayed until her own death on August 5, 1940.

(See also WIRE WALKING.)

MILLS BROS. CIRCUS

In the spring of 1940, Jack Mills purchased the Richard Bros. Circus, a ten-truck operation. In partnership with his two brothers, he moved the show to new WINTER QUARTERS in Berea, Ohio. The show opened in mid-April the following year as the Mills Bros. Circus. In later years the quarters were moved to the fairgrounds at Circleville, Ohio.

All three Mills brothers were circus men with previous experience. Jack Mills was manager, Jake Mills was producer and Harry Mills was concessions manager. Their motorized show grew quickly, becoming one of the most popular family shows in the United States.

Their TERRITORY went from Illinois, east to New York and down the eastern seaboard to Florida. They were among the first to develop the system of using local sponsors to ensure blocks of ticket sales. The Mills Bros. Circus was always a SUNDAY SCHOOL SHOW and, appropriately, never performed on a Sunday.

Except for the RINGLING BROS. AND BARNUM & BAILEY CIRCUS, the Mills Bros. Circus had more production numbers than any other show. It was also second only to Ringling in the importation of foreign acts and performers.

The Mills Bros. Circus opened with a "herd" of one BULL, Big Burma. Formerly named Virginia, she was probably the best-known elephant in the 1950s. Big Burma appeared at many Republican functions and was seen in the presidential parades for Eisenhower in 1953 and 1957. In 1950 Big Burma was joined by more pachyderms, with numbers varying from four to eight over the years; the bulls were handled by such veterans as Hugo Schmitt and Virgil Sagraves.

After 27 seasons, the Mills Bros. Circus closed its tent flaps following the 1966 tour. The show's equipment and animals were sold, but the name was merely retired. As late as 1990—with Harry Mills still surviving—there was talk in the circus industry of the Mills title being revived.

MILT HOLLAND INDOOR CIRCUS

See POLACK BROS. CIRCUS.

MIX, TOM (1880–1940)

A performer in several Wild West shows, Tom Mix entered movies in 1918 when he was signed by William Fox and became a major star in western films. He appeared in almost 400 films, most of them silent, as a movie cowboy; and he starred in the original *Destry Rides Again* in 1932. Prior to that, however, Mix had served in the Spanish-American War, was a Texas ranger, a western sheriff, an army scout, a U.S. marshal and a rodeo champion. Like many cowboy film stars, he was attracted to the outdoor amusement industry. In 1929 he was featured in the SELLS-FLOTO CIRCUS for the first of three seasons before starting his own show.

Mix became part owner of the Sam B. Dill Circus & Tom Mix Wild West in 1934. That same season they reorganized and Mix became the sole owner, retitling the show the Tom Mix Circus. A truck show with a cast of 150, the circus starred Mix with his horse, Tony, Jr.

In 1936 the Tom Mix Circus made circus history by becoming the first truck show to tour from coast to coast. The show trouped until 1938, the worst year economically for outdoor amusements in the United States. That year it—like most circuses on the road—folded.

M.L. CLARK CIRCUS

Beginning humbly as a wagon show in the 1890s, the M.L. Clark Circus toured primarily in the South until the advent of World War I. After it ceased operation, the circus's name was included in the title of other rail and truck shows for many years.

MOELLER CARRIAGE AND WAGON WORKS

Operated in the last quarter of the 19th century and the first decades of the 20th, the Moeller Carriage and Wagon Works was located in BARABOO, WISCONSIN. Its owners were Henry C. and Corwin G. Moeller, cousins of the Gollmar brothers and the RINGLING BROTHERS. Needless to say, most of the wagons that the Ringling Bros. Circus used in its STREET PARADES were made at the Moeller yards.

In addition to building regular farm wagons and buggies, the Moeller Brothers Wagon Works also produced some of the most famous circus WAGONS in the United States. The artistic craftsmanship of the heavy-duty wagons made them some of the most prized in the American circus of the time.

(See also BANDWAGON; CAGE WAGON; TABLEAU WAGON; TWO HEMISPHERES BANDWAGON.)

MOLLIE BAILEY CIRCUS, THE

When James Augustus "Gus" BAILEY became too ill to tour with the BAILEY CONCERT AND CIRCUS SHOW, his wife, Mollie, reorganized and renamed the company "The Mollie Bailey Show." Thus Mollie BAILEY became the first woman to own and operate her own circus in the United States.

The show grew as it toured from 1885 until 1920. A clean family circus, the Mollie Bailey Circus was welcomed back to the same Texas towns year after year. As the cast increased, the show moved from wagons onto rail in 1907, performing in larger cities.

The circus was loved as much for the warm, generous owner as for the show itself. Mollie owned property in about 150 small Texas towns and used her own land as the showgrounds each year. In between show dates, she allowed the towns to use her property free of charge for civic functions.

In 1915, three years before Mollie's death, her four sons took over day-to-day operation of the show. They moved the show onto trucks in 1919, but without the charismatic Mollie to guide the circus, the Mollie Bailey Circus closed the following year.

MONEY WAGON   See RED WAGON.

MONKEYS AND APES

Monkeys and apes are among the average spectator's favorite animals. Almost every circus has lots of them—from the great apes (GORILLAS, CHIMPANZEES, orangutans) to the small rhesus monkeys that ride on the backs of ponies in the CENTER RING. The great apes are the largest of the Primate order, which includes monkeys and man.

Although lay people often incorrectly and generically use to word "monkey" to mean either monkeys or apes, the animals are of different families. The major noticeable physical difference is that monkeys have tails, whereas apes—like man—develop a jointed tail in the embryo stage that shrinks to a dimple at the end of the spine before birth.

(See also GARGANTUA; M'TOTO.)

MONTGOMERY QUEEN CIRCUS

The Montgomery Queen Circus bought its equipment from Adam FOREPAUGH in 1873. The show successfully toured the western United States for five seasons, selling its holdings after the 1878 season.

MOON BOUNCE

Originally designed as a carnival and amusement park attraction, a moon bounce is a large inflated plastic-and-rubber pillow, or cushion, usually walled on three sides. By jumping up and down on the surface of the mat, children (and children at heart) can bound trampoline-style. The name "moon bounce" comes from the notion that hopping on the air cushion resembles the slow leaps of the astronauts on the moon's surface.

As economics force circuses to eliminate the SIDESHOW, many shows have placed a moon bounce on one side of the MIDWAY.

MOON BROS. CIRCUS   See NEWTON, LUCKY BILL.

MORTON, ROBERT (1894–1956)

Born on June 1, 1894, Robert morton was a pioneer of the sponsored indoor circus. He produced his first show by hiring the GENTRY BROS. CIRCUS to appear for the Shriners in Dallas, Texas in 1918.

This, in effect, was the first of the "TEXAS SHRINE DATES." Today, each fall and winter the Shrine temples sponsor a series of major circuses in the Lone Star State. This has grown into a string of indoor dates for circus artists throughout the country during the off-season.

The Bob Morton Fraternal Circus, which operated by selling tickets to benefit local charities or civic organizations, grew from Morton's first show in 1918. When business fell during the depression, George A. HAMID—a former acrobat with BUFFALO BILL'S WILD WEST—became his partner. With Hamid's ability as a booking agent, the two built the HAMID-MORTON CIRCUS into one of the greatest of the indoor circuses.

Robert Morton died on September 16, 1956.

MOSCOW CIRCUS

The Moscow Circus, the official circus of the old Soviet Union, was not a single circus but a collective title for any one of the many state-run circus units that performed throughout the former Soviet Union. The country had over 4,000 performers, who might be assigned to any of the units that performed in the more than 70 permanent circus buildings or 30 tent circuses. In addition, the Soviet Union had developed circus arts and supported their work through a network of circus and gymnastic schools all over the country, including the Moscow Circus School. An estimated 50 to 70 million people visited the circus annually in the Soviet Union.

The official beginning of the entertainment tradition began when the circus was introduced into the court of Catherine the Great in 1793 by Englishman Charles Hughes. Hughes had been a fellow cavalryman with Sergeant Major Philip ASTLEY, who went on to found his own riding school and become the "Father of the Circus."

The first permanent circus building in Russia was opened in St. Petersburg in 1877 on land donated by the czar to the Italian showman Gaetano Ceniselli. Soon other permanent circus "tents" were constructed in Kiev, Odessa and Moscow. Many of these, such as the Old Circus Building in downtown Moscow and the Leningrad Circus building, have been renovated and are still in use. Others, such as the new state-of-the-art concrete "top" that stands on Lenin Hills in Moscow, have been built to accommodate the demand for tickets.

The circus was nationalized in 1919 when Soyuzgocirck—the organization that oversaw all aspects of the circus, from the selection of artists to the planning of itineraries—came into existence. Soyuzgocirck also founded the circus school in the late 1920s to help train artists for its many shows. Prospective performers trained for four years and then, with the help of trainers, choreographers, composers and directors, framed their acts. Upon audition, if the act was accepted by Soyuzgocirck, a professional career was virtually guaranteed.

Until the time of *perestroika,* the Moscow Circus made only limited appearances in the United States, mostly because of economic and political reasons. Transporting a circus in the United States is expensive enough for a native show, whose managers are familiar with the arenas, unions, press and management. The costs of an international venture multiply. Also, the Soviet Union feared losing its artists through defection.

Moscow Circus acts tended to be traditional, if spectacular, with a heavy concentration on trained HORSES and BEARS, as well as CLOWNS. The most famous of these clowns was the celebrated Popov. The show appeared in a single ring format. During the tours in the mid-1970s, the entire second half of the program was given over to the Soviet Union's greatest illusionist, Kio. In one of his routines, he made a horse-drawn carriage full of people disappear; and, during a funeral pyre–cremation trick, the accompanying flames and fireworks could be felt in the uppermost balconies of the arena.

In 1988 the Moscow Circus returned to the United States after a ten-year absence, produced by Steven E. Leber. The most renowned act was The FLYING CRANES, which premiered with the show in 1985. It is one of only two troupes (the other being The FLYING VAZQUEZ) that regularly performs the QUADRUPLE SOMERSAULT as part of its act.

In the autumn of 1991, under a different producer, a smaller-scale edition of the show, Moscow Circus-Cirk Valentin, attempted to invade Broadway itself by booking into the Gershwin Theater.

"We don't want people to confuse us with other shows—like, for instance, the Moscow Circus that played Radio City Music Hall—but we have to use the umbrella title of Moscow Circus," director Valentin Gneushev explained to *Playbill* magazine. "However, Cirk Valentin is a completely different thing from all the other Moscow Circuses that have come and gone."

Perhaps in an attempt to emulate CIRQUE DU SOLEIL, Cirk Valentin relied on acrobatic, aerial and clown acts, but had no animals—one of the Soviet circus's traditional strengths. "We believe we don't have the right to make the animals suffer as they do in many circuses," Gneushev claimed. "People ask me why I don't have animals in my show, and I always say, 'When I invite an artist to work with me, he has the option either to agree or to disagree and not work with me. Animals don't have that choice; they are forced to work.' "

Reviews for the Moscow Circus-Cirk Valentin were mixed to bad; New York audiences, in recessionary times, did not come. The show, already scheduled for a limited run, had to CLOSE AHEAD OF PAPER. "This is a complicated time, especially for Soviet artists," Gneushev said.

With the breakup of the Soviet Union and the beginning of the Commonwealth of Independent States, the future of the Moscow Circus as a state-supported institution remains in question, especially with regard to interrepublic cooperation and international touring.

M'TOTO (1931–1968)

In 1941 trainer José Tomas brought M'Toto, a giant female GORILLA, to the RINGLING BROS. AND BARNUM & BAILEY CIRCUS to be a mate for GARGANTUA.

Mrs. E. Kenneth (Marie) Hoyt had raised the gorilla from a baby. She and her husband had received the gorilla from a chieftain in the French Congo in February 1932 when it weighed only nine pounds. Because the ape was approximately three months old, the couple named her "Toto," which meant "Baby" in Swahili. They brought Toto to New York via Paris; and, after Mr. Hoyt's death, Marie moved with Toto to Havana, Cuba. There she hired Tomas to be the gorilla's keeper.

Tomas had emigrated to Cuba from Barcelona, Spain, and was working at the time at a primate colony owned by Madame Rosalia Abreau. Tomas, his wife, Emilia, and Mrs. Hoyt became close friends, and all cared for the young gorilla, making her their constant companion.

John Ringling North traveled to Cuba and convinced Hoyt to give him a perpetual lease on Toto. She agreed, with the following stipulations: that Toto be given a cage identical to Gargantua's; that Tomas continue as her trainer; and that she be allowed to visit the gorilla any time, day or night.

Toto—whom the newspapers named Mademoiselle Toto or Mlle. Toto and M'Toto for short—arrived in SARASOTA, FLORIDA in February 1941. Despite a much-ballyhooed "gorilla wedding," M'Toto and Gargantua did not take to one another. Nevertheless, they were displayed in the circus MENAGERIE in separate, side-by-side cages and were advertised as "Mr. and Mrs. Gargantua the Great."

M'Toto's personality was completely opposite that of Gargantua. Although technically dangerous due to her size and strength, she was always gentle. One time M'Toto accidentally swatted Tomas with the back of her hand, sending him flying, unconscious, across the cage. M'Toto cradled him in her arms, kissing and cooing over him; she would not let him go until he had awakened.

In his broken English, Tomas told circus historian Gene Plowden, "Toto always gentle. The female always more gentle than male. Toto never caged in

M'Toto (or Mademoiselle Toto), the 350-pound gorilla, stands on the roof of Mrs. Kenneth Hoyt's estate in Havana, Cuba before being brought to the Ringling show as Gargantua's "wife." (Author's collection)

Cuba, never; loose all time. She play with cats, dogs—anything. I taught her to count on fingers and toes. She do anything! She throw me kisses. She loved people look at her."

After Gargantua died in 1949, M'Toto—who had trouped with the giant ape for nine seasons—appeared depressed and detached. Tomas said, "Toto was never turned loose in the cage with him, but they were neighbors. She was very grieved, very sad. When Gargantua died, she was all alone."

From that time, M'Toto was exhibited only at the MADISON SQUARE GARDEN opening date, spending the rest of the season in WINTER QUARTERS. When the show moved to Venice, Florida in 1959, M'Toto went along; she died there on July 17, 1968.

The circus was on tour at the time, so little space was given to her passing in the newspapers. She had not been ill and did not refuse food until the morning of her death. José Tomas describes her final morning: "I went into her cage. She didn't want her milk—nothing. She looked very sleepy. It was then about ten o'clock, and she would not eat. I tried again at eleven o'clock. This time she was more sleepy than before. She died in my arms—died of old age—just went to sleep in my arms." At the time of her death, M'Toto was about 36 and weighed 575 pounds.

Mrs. Hoyt and Tomas mourned heavily. Hoyt buried M'Toto in a Sarasota pet cemetery; she arranged for fresh flowers on the grave every day up until her death in an automobile accident in Vienna in 1969.

(See also MONKEYS AND APES.)

MUD SHOWS

A slang term today for any show—particularly a tented one—that sets up on dirt lots, which could become muddy during inclement weather. Circus purists, however, use the term "mud show" to mean only the original circuses that moved by wagon. To the technical historian, railroad circuses and truck or motorized shows are not considered mud shows, even if they set up outdoors.

Indeed, the origin of the term refers to the circus's mode of transportation as well, because the first traveling troupes toured in Conestoga-style wagons, then later in regular horse-drawn wagons over dirt country roads. During rainstorms, the wagons often floundered or were stuck in the mud. The phrase persisted even after the advent of macadam highways and truck transport, because the heavily loaded vehicles could also become bogged down in the circus's playing fields.

"MURDEROUS" MARY

See ELEPHANTS; ROGUE ELEPHANTS.

MUGIVAN, JEREMIAH "JERRY" (1873–1930)

With his partners Bert Bowers and Ed Ballard, Jeremiah Mugivan built his circus empire, the AMERICAN CIRCUS CORPORATION, beginning in 1921.

Mugivan was a ticket seller on the Sanger & Lent Circus when he met co-worker Bowers in 1893. Together, they moved to the Ben Wallace Circus in 1900. Four years later, and without authorization, they adopted the name Van Amburgh Circus for the first of their shows.

The small rail show had no connection to the Van Amburg Circus started by the famous animal trainer, or with Hyatt Frost, the manager of that show from 1846 through 1885. Their Van Amburgh Circus toured through midseason 1908, when Mugivan and Bowers changed the name of the show to Howes' Great London Circus. Again, the circus had no connection to any of the previous shows bearing the Howes name. They toured the new show until 1921, during which time the Van Amburgh title was used briefly as a subtitle, then dropped completely.

Also that year Mugivan purchased the SELLS-FLOTO CIRCUS, which had started life as the Floto Dog & Pony Show in 1902. The show had toured under many titles, including the Sells Floto-Buffalo Bill Circus, before its purchase by the American Circus Corporation.

In 1928 Mugivan bought the AL G. BARNES CIRCUS, a 30-car rail show, for the Corporation. The circus had been started by trainer Al G. Barnes two decades earlier.

That year Mugivan also acquired the SPARKS CIRCUS. Charles Sparks, then the owner/manager, claimed he did not know the identity of the real purchaser.

In 1929 John RINGLING lost his bid to take the RINGLING BROS. AND BARNUM & BAILEY CIRCUS into its usual MADISON SQUARE GARDEN stand when a dispute arose over the Friday night spot. The Garden awarded its contract to the American Circus Corporation, and Mugivan placed his Sells-Floto show in the arena.

Infuriated, Ringling bought the American Circus Corporation from Mugivan and his partners for a reported $2 million. The Corporation was disbanded, but Ringling defaulted on his payments following the stock market crash of 1929.

MUSIC, CIRCUS

Music was an integral part of the American circus from its very beginning. The earliest performances were accompanied by string orchestras, but brass bands came into fashion by the start of the 19th century.

During the heyday of the tented circus show, local band concerts and high school bands were the exception rather than the rule. The music that accompanied the circus was seen as an event, and the bands and the number of musicians on the show were often featured in the newspaper advertising. Some circuses, such as The BAILEY CONCERT AND

CIRCUS SHOW, realized that music was so integral to the performance that they made it part of their title.

Every "Circus Day" began with a STREET PARADE through the center of town. While bands on the smaller shows might occasionally march in the procession, the larger circuses always had them perched on specially designed BANDWAGONS. It was not uncommon for more than one band to appear in the parade, and later in the circus. The SIDESHOW and MENAGERIE, for instance, often had their own bands inside the tents. Often a secondary band was made up of all black members, perhaps a link to the then-popular minstrel shows.

The last vehicle in the street parade was always the CALLIOPE, the unique-sounding steam-powered musical instrument that beckoned the townsfolk to follow the parade back to the circus LOT.

Circuses that did not parade often gave a free concert in town to help advertise the show, with the band usually playing in the city park, public square or on the front lawn of the courthouse.

Back on the showgrounds, the band sometimes played on the MIDWAY in front of the MARQUEE to announce the beginning of the sideshow. As soon as the ticket boxes were opened, music coming from within the tent also drew people inside. The same custom often had the BIG TOP band playing an additional concert in the CENTER RING before the main show began.

The director of the Big Top's circus band must select, or in some cases write, appropriate music to accompany every action in the show. This involves dozens of pieces of music, from waltzes to quick-step GALOPS, and literally hundreds of cues each performance.

As show costs escalate and union wages rise, the circus band has shrunk in size or disappeared completely. At its peak, the RINGLING BROS. AND BARNUM & BAILEY CIRCUS band—under the direction of Merle EVANS—had more than 25 musicians on the stand. It is not uncommon today to see a small circus band of only two to four members. Even some major circuses have been financially forced to drop their live bands in favor of taped recordings. CIRCUS VARGAS has reached an interesting compromise: For the first few weeks of each annual tour, the show carries a live band. Once the show and routines are set, the live band is recorded and the tapes are used for the remainder of the season.

WINDJAMMERS UNLIMITED, INC. is one fraternal organization dedicated to the love and preservation of the traditional sound of the circus brass band.

(See also *CIRCUS FANFARE*; DOUBLING IN BRASS; MARCH, THE; ORCHESTMELOCHOR; TWO HEMISPHERES BANDWAGON; WAGONS; WINDJAMMER.)

MUSICALS, CIRCUS   See THEATER.

N

NAITTO, ALA (1925–) Known as the "female Colleano" when she was touring with the RINGLING BROS. AND BARNUM & BAILEY CIRCUS in the early 1920s and 1930s, Ala Naitto was the only woman who was able to perform the forward somersault on the low wire. This stunt was invented by Con COLLEANO, and it is much more difficult to achieve than the backward somersault: When spinning forward the performer cannot see his or her feet until they actually touch the wire.

Ala Naitto juggled hoops as she balanced herself on her sister Nio's shoulders. Later in the act, Ala performed a head stand on her sister's head as Nio walked up a set of stairs, across a tightrope and down steps on the other side.

NANTY Rarely used circus jargon meaning "nothing."

NEW AMPHITHEATER Following the success of his first road tour, John Bill RICKETTS returned to Philadelphia where he replaced his original open-air arena with a permanent structure, Ricketts' New Amphitheater (also seen as the Pantheon).

The new building was winterized, boasted artificial lighting and a figure of the Roman messenger god Mercury on the roof. The arena had a circus ring, a stage and seating for 1,200 people. The ring was used for traditional circus acts, and the performance was followed by stage presentations and pantomimes, which foreshadowed the innovation of the aftershow or CONCERT.

The amphitheater's shows were so popular that during the period from October 10, 1796 to February 23, 1797, 48 circus performances were given. During that time 20 new aftershows and 13 repeated numbers appeared.

In 1799 Ricketts New Amphitheater burned to the ground. Although the livestock inside was saved, Ricketts was ruined financially.

NEW UNITED MONSTER SHOWS Begun in 1879, the New United Monster Shows was a travelling exhibition and museum headed by circus legend W.C. COUP.

Following the breakup of his partnership with P.T. BARNUM in 1874, Coup took a two-year hiatus, then opened the New York Aquarium and the EQUESCURRICULUM.

Coup's next venture was the New United Monster Shows. Like similar touring exhibitions of its time—such as Barnum's Traveling World's Fair, which was operated by the FLATFOOTS—the Monster Shows had a variety of unusual attractions. There was a Japanese Art Gallery, a White Whale, a Lightning Zouave Drill and the purported Imperial Barouche of Napoleon III.

The 1882 edition had a tribe of Zulus in response to those on the Traveling World's Fair. Coup also added wax statues depicting the assassination of President Garfield and its aftermath.

One of the show's strangest displays was billed as a "Gigantic Devil Fish, 39½ feet including head, body and the longest tentacles. . . . Preserved in pure alcohol." Coup offered $50,000 to anyone who could produce another. Mademoiselle Rinehart, "the only female lion tamer, who enters a massive den of living wild lions and leopards and performs them like kittens," was one of the live entertainers, and Coup offered $10,000 to anyone who could equal her skill.

A tragic train wreck forced Coup to close the New United Monster Shows. Despite several attempts, Coup was never able to make a successful return to the road.

NEW YORK CIRCUS

Touring from 1873–1874, the New York Circus was the last major show put out by circus owner and manager Lewis B. LENT.

After a varied circus career beginning in 1834, Lent took out his own show, L.B. Lent's National Circus, from 1857 through 1863. While the show toured under different titles for an additional decade, the National Circus was finally replaced by the New York Circus.

Lent acted as agent or manager for other shows for five more years after the end of the New York Circus run. He tried one last unsuccessful tour of the New York Circus in 1879 before retiring.

NEWTON, HONEST BILL

See NEWTON, LUCKY BILL.

NEWTON, LUCKY BILL (1859–1937)

Born October 1, 1859, William Newton was the first of three generations of circus owners. Lucky Bill Newton, as he was known, was a colorful manager. Active primarily in the Midwest, he toured Lucky Bill's Big 25 Cent Show (also seen as Lucky Bill's Big Wagon Shows and Lucky Bill's 25¢ Tent Show).

Newton settled into Quenemo, Kansas for his circus's WINTER QUARTERS following a performance there on October 24, 1903. He immediately became one of the town's leading citizens, investing heavily in local real estate. From two marriages (the first having ended in divorce), Newton had five sons (William Jr., LeRoy, Henry, Eddie and Jesse) and a daughter, Della.

In 1909 William Newton Jr., known as Honest Bill Newton, premiered his first show, Honest Bill's America's Greatest 25 Cent Shows (also seen as Honest Bill's America's Best Shows). Also operating out of Quenemo, Honest Bill worked in partnership with W.L. Casten for his first season.

In 1910 Lucky Bill purchased his first ELEPHANT, Hero. Also that year, the father and son's shows made a combined appearance for the first time, a regular occurrence until Lucky Bill's retirement. For instance, in 1912 the shows toured as The Two Bill's Big Combined Shows (not to be confused with the *other* Two Bills Show, the BUFFALO BILL WILD WEST AND PAWNEE BILL GREAT FAR EAST SHOW.)

The following year Henry Newton, nicknamed Happy, formed his own show that toured one season. Happy Bill's Big Wagon Show premiered as part of a combined show with his father and brother on May 3, 1913. Nine days later Baby Hamburg, a young elephant, was added to the show. The BULL had been purchased from the Hagenbeck zoo (see HÄGENBACH, KARL) and had been shipped via Hamburg, Germany—hence the pachyderm's name. Happy Bill's circus toured on its own until its final performance in Stiedman, Oklahoma on September 13, 1913.

In 1915 Lucky Bill Newton joined a growing list of circus pioneers by adding a COOKHOUSE to his BACK YARD. The next year he sold his elephant Hero, which was becoming increasingly unmanageable, to the ORTON BROS. CIRCUS for $4,500. (The sale was timely, because shortly thereafter Hero turned into a ROGUE ELEPHANT. After overturning several railroad flatcars in Elkton, South Dakota, Hero was executed—with a reported 2,000 shots required to kill the bull.)

On April 2, 1917 Honest Bill purchased a biplane to use as a free attraction to publicize his show. The pilot, W.T. Wilkins, crashed the plane in May and a new one was obtained. On February 24, 1918 the second was also wrecked. By this time Lucky Bill Newton had an 11-piece brass band with his show, which was fully motorized with a dozen trucks.

Meanwhile, with the United States involved in World War I, Honest Bill was commissioned as an army second lieutenant. He was stationed in Newport News, Virginia from November 1, 1917 to November 16, 1918.

Following his 1919 tour, Honest Bill did not return his show to Quenemo. Instead, he wintered in Ada, Oklahoma.

On October 21, 1921 Lucky Bill Newton retired from active touring. He sold his show and equipment to Honest Bill, who promptly moved it all to Ada.

By 1925 Honest Bill had two additional circuses on the road: Orange Bros. Circus and Moon Brothers Big Consolidated Shows. His son, Clyde, entered the business, helping to manage the shows.

The next year Honest Bill moved all his holdings back to Quenemo. His two circuses were combined into one large show in 1926, but Moon Bros. Circus toured independently in 1927 under Clyde's management. The show closed for good in May 1928.

Together Honest Bill and Clyde Newton continued to operate the Newton Bros. Circus, the Honest Bill Circus and other small shows until 1937. Although in later years they held interests in other minor circuses, in 1937 Honest Bill became the manager and part owner of the WALTER L. MAIN CIRCUS.

On June 1, 1937, Lucky Bill was visiting the Main show when he injured his ankle near the FRONT DOOR. Strep poisoning set in, and he died ten days later. His estate was valued at $2,000, including 24 city lots and 23,000 square feet of farmland. Today none of the original buildings owned by Lucky Bill Newton still stand in Quenemo, Kansas.

NICHOLS CIRCUS

One of the earliest traveling circuses—the Nichols Circus was touring the Northeast in 1843 when it was first visited by Dan RICE, then a general helper in a livery stable.

Rice made friends with and learned from the equestrians and the strongman. It was here that Rice learned to throw cannon balls from his shoulders, earning him the nickname of "Young Hercules."

Rice next met up with the Nichols Circus in Pittsburgh, but by then it was called the North American Circus and was operated by impresario "Dr." Gilbert R. SPALDING.

The Nichols Circus was originally owned by Samuel H. Nichols, the former minstrel who introduced the famous song "Jim Crow." During the winter, the show performed in S.H. Nichols' Amphitheatre in Albany, New York.

Although the nature of Nichols's debt to Spalding is unknown (some historians feel it was for the purchase of paint from Spalding's dry goods store), Spalding foreclosed on Nichols in 1843. Shows continued to play in Albany through February 17, 1844.

On March 25, 1844, Spalding tried to reopen the Amphitheatre "for a short season," but by April 11,

1844, he was on tour with the circus. Spalding occasionally returned to the Amphitheatre for winter shows, but the last performance there took place on February 2, 1847.

NIGHT RIDERS

Circus jargon for the BILLING CREW that tears down or, more often, merely covers up OPPOSITION PAPER with their own LITHOGRAPHS. Although the bill-posters were generally a fearless bunch, the slang probably comes from the assumption that their crafty—if not sleazy—job could be more productively and safely done under the cover of darkness.

NORRIS & ROWE CIRCUS

Norris & Rowe had a humble beginning as a DOG AND PONY SHOW around 1900, but it quickly grew to a rail show of 20 to 25 cars.

The circus toured Mexico as well as the western United States before folding right after the opening of its 1910 season.

NORTH, HENRY RINGLING

See GARGANTUA; NORTH, JOHN RINGLING; RINGLING, JOHN; RINGLING BROS. AND BARNUM & BAILEY CIRCUS.

NORTH, JOHN RINGLING (1903–1985)

John Ringling North, the nephew of the five founders of RINGLING BROTHERS, was owner/manager of the RINGLING BROTHERS AND BARNUM & BAILEY CIRCUS from 1938 until 1942 and then again from 1947 to 1968.

Born on August 17, 1903, North had grown up in BARABOO, WISCONSIN, the son of Ida Ringling and Henry W. North, a railroad tycoon. After attending the University of Wisconsin, then Yale University for two years (in the class of 1916), John Ringling North began working for a New York stock brokerage firm in 1924. Two years later he joined the real estate company of his uncle, John RINGLING. In 1929 North returned to New York as a broker and stayed until 1936 when he returned to Florida as co-executor (with his mother) of uncle John Ringling's complicated will.

A codicil limited Ida's inheritance to $5,000 a year and cut John out of the will completely, but John Ringling North was determined to fight for the circus. He managed to refinance the circus, which had been under outside ownership for five years, and regained ownership for the Ringling clan. Immediately other heirs started fighting over control of the circus and the $22,366,000 Ringling fortune. A clan of three rival factions almost immediately clashed over ownership.

Meanwhile, North had a circus to run. Unfortunately, 1938 was the most disastrous year economically for circuses in the United States. Bad business and union troubles forced North to close the Ringling show on June 22 in Scranton, Pennsylvania.

After the successful 1939 season, John turned his attention back to the estate. Knowing that the artwork and galleries of the JOHN AND MABLE RINGLING MUSEUM OF ART were the estate's greatest assets, he had them appraised for $12 million. North took a working vacation to Europe; when he returned he had been elected president—with his brother Henry Ringling North (1909–   ) as secretary-treasurer—of the Rembrandt Corporation, the subsidiary that controlled the museum.

After five harried years of warring family factions, John Ringling North relinquished the presidency of the circus to his cousin, Robert Ringling. It was under Robert Ringling's management that the HARTFORD FIRE occurred in 1944.

The Ringling estate was finally settled in 1946, and John Ringling North was reelected president of the Ringling corporation one year later. He immediately appointed his brother Henry as vice-president and Art CONCELLO as general manager.

Although circus people were pleased with Concello's appointment, North was still criticized by the circus fans. North was producing the show with Broadway-style artistic designs and streamlining the circus with many of Concello's cost-saving innovations; but many fans felt the circus was starting to look like a grade-B Broadway revue. North had also discontinued outdoor advertising, meaning fans would no longer see roadside barns and buildings plastered with sheets of colorful posters. In a final coup d'etat, North replaced many long-term staff members with new personnel who had never been WITH IT.

Like his uncle John, North had a keen eye for discovering talent. Every summer he would travel overseas, meet with his European agent Umberto Bedini in Paris, then take a whirlwind tour of the continental circuses. During the trip he would usually see about 50 circuses, variety shows and revues,

making offers to about 20 performers to come to the United States to join THE BIG ONE.

Once again in 1956, labor disputes caused the early closing of the show. Union pickets at the MADISON SQUARE GARDEN date cooled attendance, and the show fought union-caused rail and labor holdups all over the East Coast.

On July 15, in Alliance, Ohio, John Ringling North joined the show in his private Pullman car. The following morning, in Pittsburgh, he announced that due to ever-increasing costs the circus would close after that evening's performance. Almost as an aside, he said, "The tented circus as it now exists is in my opinion a thing of the past."

That night the Ringling Bros. and Barnum & Bailey Circus dropped its canvas for the last time. As always, North opened the new season on April 3, 1957 at Madison Square Garden; but the circus had become an arena show forever. Although the show was becoming highly profitable and was reflecting modern 20th-century values, the diehard traditional circus folk never forgave North for taking away their beloved tents and trains.

In the early 1960s, John and Henry Ringling North became Irish citizens. Henry had purchased the ancestral home of their father in County Galway, Ireland.

In 1968 a triumvirate including Irvin FELD, Israel S. FELD and Judge Roy N. HOFHEINZ bought the Ringling Bros. and Barnum & Bailey Circus from John Ringling North, ending the Ringling family's ownership.

North died June 4, 1985, of a stroke in his hotel suite at the Hilton in Brussels, Belgium.

NORTH, LEVI J. (1814–1884)   Billed variously as the "North Star" and "The Apollo on Horseback," Levi J. North was the premier horseman of his time and later a circus owner. Born in Newton, Long Island, New York on June 14, 1814, he was handsome and dark-skinned at five and a half feet tall, with long blond hair.

Following his father's death in 1826, North began to work under Jeremiah P. Fogg, a co-owner (with Isaac Quick) of the Washington Circus. North immediately began riding lessons, and he made his first appearance as an equestrian that same year in Camden, South Carolina.

In 1828 North moved with his mentor to Fogg & Stickney's Circus and stayed there, still as an apprentice, until 1831. He then worked for J. Purdy BROWN through the 1837 season. Not only was he an accomplished bareback rider by this time, but North also excelled in acrobatics. From 1831 to 1835, his salary increased from $14 to $25 a week in 1835.

During a trip to England in 1838 North defeated a famous British ACROBAT, James Price, in a one-on-one springboard VAULTING contest at Astley's Amphitheatre. In 1839 while touring with Batty's Circus in Great Britain, he became the first man to perform a full standing forward somersault on the back of a moving horse, and the following year he repeated the stunt for the first time in the United States.

At the peak of his career, 1841, he was being paid $350 week—thus making him the highest-paid performer in the American circus at the time.

North left the Welch and Mann Circus in 1841, and the next year he went back to England. There he married Sophia West, and they had three children over 12 years. For 1843 and 1844 North formed a performing partnership with Price, his former opponent. North returned to the United States the following year.

His career, both on his own and with others' shows, spanned nearly 40 years. He retired, still a star at age 52, while performing with Lent's NEW YORK CIRCUS in 1864. He also served a single term as a Chicago alderman, beginning in 1857. He died on July 6, 1884.

NOYES, CHARLES   See THAYER & NOYES CIRCUS.

NUMBERING THE WAGONS   Every wagon on a MUD SHOW, every truck and trailer on a motorized show or every circus train car on a rail show is assigned a number to keep track of the vehicles, or rolling stock. Traditionally, however, there are few (if any) single-digit vehicles; numbers are usually skipped and randomly assigned to make it appear as if the show has many more pieces of equipment than it actually does.

NUT   Circus jargon, shared with the theatrical trade, meaning the amount of income required daily to

break even on expenses. The daily operating expenses would include performers' salaries, the cost of food for the acts and livestock, fuel and traveling costs, as well as prorated annual expenses such as insurance, maintenance, home office and WINTER QUARTERS expenses. The expression "crack the nut" means to meet the daily expenses.

NUTT, "COMMODORE" GEORGE WASHINGTON MORRISON (1848–1881)   George Nutt, a midget who exhibited with P.T. BARNUM at the AMERICAN MUSEUM in the 1860s, was a contemporary of both General TOM THUMB and Lavinia WARREN. He is chiefly remembered today as a suitor for Warren's hand and as a romantic rival of the General.

According to Barnum's autobiography, Nutt was "a most remarkable dwarf, who was a sharp, intelligent little fellow, with a deal of drollery and wit." He further wrote that Nutt visited him in the museum offices in December 1861, where he was so engaged that he immediately hired Nutt. Barnum had neither "discovered" Nutt nor was he the first to exhibit him.

George Nutt was born April Fool's Day, 1848, the son of Major Rodnia Nutt, a gentleman farmer from Manchester, New Hampshire. When Barnum first heard of the midget, Nutt was being exhibited throughout New England by a showman named Lillie. A poor manager, Lillie was charging as little as a nickel for admission to see the young man.

Barnum hired B.P. Cilley, a lawyer and neighbor of Rodnia Nutt, to convince the father that, if a full five-year contract could be secured, Barnum promised to "take every pains [sic] to have him *properly educated* and *trained* so that he shall become a genteel, accomplished, and *attractive* little man, the same as I made Genl. Tom Thumb."

Although Barnum offered more money than Lillie, he asked that Cilley withhold his name during negotiations until the last possible moment. He knew that whenever his name was involved, prices escalated accordingly. Instead of completing negotiations on Barnum's behalf, Cilley became Nutt's lawyer. Nevertheless, a contract was concluded on December 12, 1861.

The contract called for Barnum to engage not only the 29-inch, 25-pound George, but also his

Line-up of replica wagons from the International Circus Hall of Fame showing the numbering of the wagons. They were exhibited at Knott's Berry Farm during the summer of 1991. In the foreground is a ¾-scale replica of a 1930 Cole Bros. Circus cage wagon.   (Photo by Tom Ogden)

older brother and traveling companion, Rodnia, Jr., who, at 21 years of age, was only 49 inches tall. The boys were to be fed, clothed and have medical, travel and educational expenses paid. The salary was $12 per week, plus 10% of all souvenir sales against a $260 annual guarantee. Each of the remaining four years, the salary was to increase to $14, $18, $23 and $30 dollars, with souvenir sales also increasing to a guarantee of $440.

Barnum started his publicity machine without revealing that he already had the boys under contract. Soon circus impresario Joseph Cushing offered the father $5,000 a year for George's employment. June, Howes, Quick & Co. offered $16,000 for three years. Barnum, through an agent, Parson Hitchcock, "leaked" a telegraph to the press that said, "Rather than fail in getting [Nutt], you may offer him or his father *thirty thousand dollars* for the privilege of ex-

hibiting him. . . ." The newspapers quickly dubbed the midget "the $30,000 Nutt."

Barnum, in a typical flair of showmanship, gave Nutt the unofficial title of "Commodore." Barnum immediately ordered a new wardrobe, miniature ponies and an English walnut–shaped carriage for his new attraction. Partly because he was, in fact, "new" and partly because Tom Thumb was on an extended out-of-town tour throughout the South and the West, Nutt attracted enormous attention in the museum.

In 1862 Nutt was presented to President Abraham Lincoln and members of his Cabinet. When the President quipped to the Commodore that "when you are in command of your fleet, if you find yourself in danger of being taken prisoner, I advise you to wade ashore," Nutt retorted, "I guess, Mr. President, you could do that better than I could."

Many people, including some of Tom Thumb's acquaintances in BRIDGEPORT, CONNECTICUT, began to believe that Nutt was, in fact, the General in disguise. Despite the fact that Tom Thumb was considerably older and, by this time, rotund, Nutt—only four inches taller than his peer—did bear an uncanny resemblance to the Tom Thumb of a decade earlier.

Barnum immediately sensed a business opportunity and convinced Tom Thumb to cut his western tour short and return to New York for a four-week engagement at the museum beginning August 11, 1862. Announcements heralding "The Two Dromios" and the "Two Smallest Men, and Greatest Curiosities Living" brought hordes of people to the palace to see for themselves if Nutt was, indeed, a different sensation.

That same year Barnum hired the dwarf, Lavinia Warren, for exhibition at the museum. Although she was several years his senior, Nutt fell in love with Warren. Warren added fuel to the fire when she gave Nutt a diamond and emerald ring (that Barnum had given her) as a token of friendship.

That autumn, however, General Tom Thumb visited the museum, met Miss Warren and announced, in confidence, to his friend and mentor Barnum that it was "love at first sight." Nutt was no fool, and he immediately sensed a challenger for the lady's affection. When Nutt discovered that Warren was planning a weekend visit to Barnum at his home, he casually but firmly invited himself to Bridgeport as well. Had Nutt been aware that Tom Thumb had already arranged to meet Warren there, he might not have waited until the late Saturday train to travel. When he arrived at Barnum's home at 11 P.M., he discovered the couple alone in the downstairs parlor. The following week he was gently informed by Warren and Barnum that the older midgets were engaged.

Barnum suggested that Lavinia's younger sister, Minnie, was actually a better match for Nutt. Nutt declared, "I would not marry the best woman living. I don't believe in women, anyway." Barnum further pressed Nutt to attend the wedding as Tom Thumb's best man with Minnie as bridesmaid, but Nutt refused. Later, Tom Thumb personally asked Nutt to so honor him, and Nutt consented. Nutt told Barnum, "It was not your business to ask me. When the proper person invited me I accepted." Indeed, at the wedding of Lavinia and Tom Thumb in Grace Church, New York City, on February 10, 1863, Nutt served as the groom's best man.

Following a few European tours, Barnum asked Nutt why he had not yet married. "Sir, my fruit is plucked," he answered. "I have concluded not to marry until I am thirty." Nutt added that he was not concerned about the height of a mate, but he would "prefer marrying a good, green country girl, to anyone else."

It was rumored—and even announced four times in the newspapers—that Nutt and Minnie Warren were married; but, while remaining close friends, such an event never took place. Minnie, in fact, married a short person (although not a dwarf) named "Major" Edward Newell who performed a song-and-dance act on roller skates.

In the 1870s Commodore Nutt toured on his own, eventually marrying a Miss Elston of Redwood City, California. Only slightly smaller than normal height, she referred to her husband as her "dear little boy." Commodore Nutt died of Bright's disease in 1881.

(See also LITTLE PEOPLE.)

O

OAKLEY, ANNIE (1860–1926) Born in a log cabin in Darke County, Ohio, on August 13, 1860, Phoebe Anne Oakley Moses (called Mozee) learned to shoot a rifle before she was ten years old. Her skill as a marksman grew; and after her father's early death when she was 12, she became the main support of her family by her hunting and trapping.

At the age of 15 she entered a contest against professional sharpshooters at the Cincinnati Opera House and won. She fell in love with the man she beat, Frank E. BUTLER, and they were married a year later. They began to work as a team, playing vaudeville and variety shows, and the young woman adopted the stage name of Annie Oakley. Partly because of her sex but mostly because of her skill, Annie always received top billing in the act.

In 1884 Annie Oakley and Frank Butler joined the SELLS BROTHERS CIRCUS for a short tour. It was during this period that today's image of Annie Oakley, dressed in a cowgirl hat, pleated skirt and leggings, was born. As Annie galloped on horseback, she would shoot colored glass balls thrown into the air by Butler.

Oakley met William F. CODY when the Sells Brothers Circus "DAY AND DATED" BUFFALO BILL'S WILD WEST in New Orleans. Anxious for a change from the Sells show where they were not particularly happy, Butler retired from the ring and became Oakley's manager. Annie asked Buffalo Bill if she could join his Wild West and he brought on "Little Missy" (as Cody nicknamed her) in Lexington, Kentucky in 1885, the day that the famous Bogardus family of sharpshooters, headed by Captain Adam H. BOGARDUS, left his show.

For the next 17 years, Annie Oakley followed the opening SPEC on the Wild West. Cody wanted Oakley to work near the beginning of the show, figuring that her presence would calm any ladies who might be in attendance. Annie soon became a favorite of the audiences as well as the company. Chief Sitting Bull, the famous warrior who had returned from Canada to join his ex-enemy's show, made Annie an honorary Sioux and tagged her "Little Sure Shot."

Her skill was remarkable. At one performance she hit 4,772 out of 5,000 glass balls tossed into the air. She developed the trick of hitting the edge of a playing card from 90 feet, then puncturing the card with several more holes before it hit the ground. These cards, known as "ANNIE OAKLEYS," became prized souvenirs by the townsfolk.

Even overseas, with the Wild West tour under the management of Nathan SALSBURY, Annie Oakley garnered praise. In 1887, on the first of three European tours, she made the first of two appearances before Queen Victoria at a royal command performance during the royal Golden Jubilee. On the continent she was received by Princess Alexandria and beat the Grand Duke Michael of Russia in a shooting match arranged by the Prince of Wales, who offered her a medal and exchanged photographs. Perhaps with a bit of jealousy of her reception, Cody felt that Oakley's manners around royalty were more rude than rustic. Nevertheless, society women sought shooting lessons and adopted her style of dress as fashionable.

The company returned to the United States in 1892, spending the entire winter in preparation for its appearance at the Chicago World's Fair of 1893. Because of the inclusion of an international host of horsemen, Cody renamed his show BUFFALO BILL'S WILD WEST AND CONGRESS OF ROUGH RIDERS OF THE WORLD. Oakley was still the show's star attraction, however, and remained so until her farewell tour.

The show's final tour of Europe began in 1902 and lasted four years. When the show played Germany in 1906, at the request of the Crown Prince Wilhelm, Annie agreed to perform her famous trick of shooting a lit cigar out of his mouth. Years later, when the prince had become Kaiser Wilhelm II and the architect of World War I, Annie Oakley is reported to have said, "I wish I'd missed that day."

A train crash during the tour severely injured her, and in 1911 she was further hurt in an automobile accident. She had recovered enough by the time of World War I, however, to come out of retirement to entertain at army camps.

Annie Oakley, loved and honored in her own time and later immortalized in film and on stage, died peacefully in her sleep in Dayton, Ohio in November 1926. Her dedicated and caring husband Frank died 18 days later.

OAKLEY, FRANK "SLIVERS" (1871–1916)

The most popular CLOWN of his generation, Frank Oakley was a master mime and comedian. Born in Sweden, both of Oakley's parents were concert singers. At the age of 14, he began to practice as a contortionist and at 16 he joined his first circus. His parents convinced him to enroll at the University of Michigan, but two years later Oakley was back under the BIG TOP.

His first show was Andrew MacDonald's Circus, but he joined the Ringling Bros. Circus in 1897. Before the turn of the century Oakley performed with the BARNUM & BAILEY CIRCUS, followed by three seasons with the ADAM FOREPAUGH & SELLS BROS. CIRCUS (1900–2). Oakley returned to the Barnum & Bailey Circus for four seasons (1903–7), where he reportedly received up to $1,000 a week.

Slivers Oakley always worked alone. His featured ring sketch was a one-man baseball game in which he played all the positions of both teams. Among his classic CLOWN WALKAROUND items was a gag in which he rode two giant lobsters around the arena.

He went on to perform with other circuses and vaudeville. He married a vaudeville singer, Nellie Dunbar, in 1902, and they had one daughter, Ruth.

When he tried to return to Ringling, he was offered only $75 per week. On March 8, 1916 he committed suicide, dying by gas asphyxiation in a boardinghouse on West 71st Street in New York City. Some colleagues conjecture that the cause was disappointment in love: He reportedly had been romantically involved with but refused marriage by a woman who was sentenced to Bedford Reformatory in 1914. A more probable reason was depression over the loss of his career or general dissipation.

(See also CLOWN GAGS.)

O'BRIEN, JOHN V. "POGEY" (1836–1889)

John O'Brien entered the world of outdoor amusements by renting horses to a small show as it passed through his hometown in 1861. He first became a circus owner in 1862 by buying a one-third interest in the Gardner & Hemming Circus.

Immediately showing great skill as a circus owner, O'Brien had four units of his show running simultaneously. During the same years he was variously in charge of the DAN RICE CIRCUS, a partner with Adam FOREPAUGH and a shareholder in P.T. Barnum's Great Traveling World's Fair.

Unfortunately, what success he and his shows enjoyed was a result of O'Brien's open approval and employment of excessive GRIFT on the LOT. Perhaps it was his tendency to BURN THE TERRITORY that explains his owning or operating approximately two dozen differently titled shows in his last 27 years as a circus manager.

Because of his blatant dishonesty, not all showmen were great admirers of O'Brien; W.C. COUP considered him particularly disreputable. In fact, it was O'Brien's use of P.T. BARNUM's name in association with his own show that caused Coup to drop his partnership in BARNUM'S GREAT TRAVELING MUSEUM, MENAGERIE, CARAVAN, HIPPODROME AND CIRCUS.

In his last years, waning finances forced O'Brien to cut the size of his shows; but he continued to tour up until his death (in poverty) in September 1889.

OLD BET (1792–1816)   Old Bet was not the first ELEPHANT to reach the shores of the United States. A nameless pachyderm that was brought to this country by Captain Jacob CROWNINSHIELD in 1796 owns that honor.

Old Bet, the *second* elephant to come to the United States and the first one known by a name, was much more important to circus history. The four-year-old female African elephant arrived in Boston on June 25, 1804. Her first owner was Edward Savage, who exhibited Old Bet in 1805 before selling her to Hachaliah BAILEY for a reported $10,000.

In 1808 Bailey sold a two-thirds interest in Old Bet to George Brunn and Benjamin Lent; but he later reacquired the shares. While remaining Old Bet's sole owner, Bailey leased her to others for exhibition for the rest of her life. When Old Bet appeared briefly with the Cayetano and Company circus in New York City, beginning on June 25, 1812, she became the first elephant to appear on a circus program in the United States. Old Bet was displayed for years, earning an enormous profit, until she was shot down in Shapleiegh, Maine on July 26, 1816 by an irate farmer named Daniel Davis. In his defense, he claimed the showmen were taking away money that should be spent locally. Bailey erected a monument in her memory in front of his ELEPHANT HOTEL in SOMERS, NEW YORK.

Old Bet's skeleton was mounted, and it was exhibited after April 5, 1817 in New York City. The display was later acquired by P.T. BARNUM for his AMERICAN MUSEUM.

ON THE SHOW   Circus jargon for all performers and crew connected with the circus.

101 RANCH WILD WEST   Always pronounced as the "One-Oh-One" Ranch Wild West, the show was originally known as the Miller Bros. 101 Ranch Wild West. This 16-rail-car Wild West was formed in 1908 when Edward Arlington, a circus man, became partners with Joseph, Zack and George Miller, a family of Oklahoma ranchers. It grew out of a Wild West show the Miller cowboys had put on at the James Exposition the year before.

The 101 Ranch itself was founded during the opening of the Cherokee Strip on September 16, 1893. Joe Miller went to claim the land that formed the ranch—a purported 101,000 acres (hence the name) in Ponca, Oklahoma. Miller was later made a chief of the Ponca Indian tribe, an honor accorded to few white men; and he was considered to be second in stature only to Chief White Eagle.

The 101 Ranch Wild West, sometimes combined with the Miller or Arlington title, continued to grow through 1915 when its star attraction was famed boxer Jess WILLARD. The following year the legendary William F. CODY himself became a member of the troupe.

Taking advantage of its new star's name, the show changed its title to the BUFFALO BILL & 101 RANCH WILD WEST. At 70 years of age, the innovator who had created the genre of the Wild West show ended his circus career working for the 101, giving his last performance on November 11, 1916.

At the end of the 1916 season, Arlington bought out the Millers. Soon after, on January 10, 1917, Buffalo Bill died. Nevertheless, Arlington combined forces with Jess Willard and retitled their show the BUFFALO BILL WILD WEST & JESS WILLARD SHOW. Willard took full ownership of the show at season's end, but that year—perhaps over doubts about the impending war—the show failed.

The show closed in 1917 at the request of the U.S. government, which wanted to use the Millers' 110,000-acre ranch to supply mules and horses to the army during World War I.

In 1925 the Millers reentered show business with a new 30-car Wild West show, once again using the 101 Ranch title. The show had a profitable run of six years, but was never as strong as its prewar days when it netted over $800,000 per year. The 101 Ranch Wild West finally folded in 1931. The name was used one last time on a small show during the 1945–46 outdoor amusement season.

The ranch went bankrupt in the 1930s and was auctioned off in parcels. The old ranch store burned in 1987, and fire also destroyed the blacksmith shop in September 1991. Only the old elephant barn and the dairy barn of the original 101 Ranch still stand.

ONE SHEET   A term used both as a noun and as an adjective, a one sheet is the basic unit of measurement for circus advertising LITHOGRAPHS. Related

One sheet lithograph for Circus Kirk.   (Photo by Tom Ogden)

advertising pieces, WINDOW CARDS and single-piece HERALDS are not usually called one sheets.

The one sheet is about 28 inches by 42 inches, although some pictorial one sheets were specially printed an inch or two smaller all the way around. Thus any lithograph smaller than that standard size might be a "half sheet" or even a QUARTER SHEET. Larger sizes might be two sheets or six sheets, for example.

One sheets come in "uprights" (printed on one side with a vertical design) or "flats" (printed with a horizontal picture). Thus, two vertical one sheets posted with one directly above the other would be a "two sheet upright streamer."

(See also ADVANCE MAN; BILLING CREW; DAUB; HIT; LOCATION; NIGHT RIDERS; OPPOSITION PAPER; PAPER; RAT SHEET; THREE SHEET; WAIT PAPER.)

OPENING   See BALLY; BALLY BROAD; SIDESHOW.

OPPOSITION PAPER   Circus jargon for posters and advertising HERALDS pasted up by competing circuses.

ORANGE BROS. CIRCUS   See NEWTON, LUCKY BILL.

ORCHESTMELOCHOR   A form of WAGON-transported musical instrument, "the Gigantic Orchestmelochor" was on the road with P.T. BARNUM's Great Traveling World's Fair in the late 1870s. Barnum described the instrument as being "of such immense volume and power that its melodious strains can be heard for a distance of over five miles, giving the effect of a full orchestra."

ORRIN DAVENPORT CIRCUS   Orrin Davenport was a featured bareback rider with the Ringling Bros. Circus in 1906 when he started producing indoor shows during the winter off-season for SHRINE CIRCUS sponsors.

He and his family continued their riding act for several years as his own circus's route grew. In 1937 he left the ring to devote his full time to the management of the Orrin Davenport Circus.

The circus appeared under a different sponsor's name in each city, touring mainly in Michigan, Ohio, Minnesota, the Dakotas and Canada.

ORTON BROS. CIRCUS Hiram Orton, a sailor on the Great Lakes, opened his first wagon show in 1854, becoming the patriarch of a clan of circus owners and performers including W.W. "Chilly Billy" COLE. When Hiram retired in 1862, his son Miles continued to operate the Orton Bros. Circus alone until 1895. That year Miles's brother, R.Z. Orton, joined on as a full partner; together they ran the show for three more years.

In 1898 they split the show into two units; one or both toured until Miles's death in 1903. R.Z. Orton continued to run a small circus, experimenting as a rail operation in 1916. The change was not lucrative, and the Orton Bros. Circus switched back to wagons the following year.

In the 1920s the show became motorized and traveled by truck from then until the early 1930s, establishing itself as one of the major small shows in the United States. After the close of the Orton Bros. Circus, several family members continued in the business, moving on to other shows.

OUTSIDE TALKER Circus jargon for the LECTURER who performs the BALLY outside the SIDESHOW tent.

(See also GRIND; INSIDE TALKER; SPIEL; TALKER.)

P

PACHYDERMS See BULLS; ELEPHANTS.

PAD RIDING A form of acrobatic horsemanship, "pad riding" is when the equestrian covers the back of the horse with a thick carpet, or "pad." The blanket cushions the blows of the bouncing rider's feet and gives the equestrian some traction while performing.

Working without the pad, James ROBINSON probably did more to popularize "bareback riding," than any other equestrian in the middle of the 19th century. "The Man Who Rides" was so popular that during his lifetime, pad riders all but disappeared from the American circus. However, pad riding is still seen today.

(See also HORSES.)

PAD ROOM Circus jargon for the performers' dressing room, usually one of the TENTS in the BACK YARD. The term comes from equestrians hanging their "pads" (cloths and equipment) there between acts and while getting into wardrobe.

Usually the pad room is a combination dressing room/equipment room. Sometimes, however, the riding equipment is housed in a separate tent.

PALLENBERG, EMIL (fl. 1914–1930) A BEAR trainer from Germany, Emil Pallenberg and his wife, Catherine, moved to the United States in 1914 to join the RINGLING BROS. AND BARNUM & BAILEY CIRCUS.

Pallenberg's bears were of huge Russian stock. He worked on a platform ring without a cage separating the wild beasts from the audience. In addition, he trained his animals to roller-skate and ride bicycles—a new novelty for the public. Pallenberg developed several tricks that are now standards in bear acts, including teaching the bears to play musical instruments and walk on a tightrope.

The Pallenbergs stayed with The BIG ONE for 13 consecutive seasons and, at the same time, owned three other touring bear acts. During World War I, when imported talent was the exception rather than the norm, they were the highest paid performers on the Ringling LOT. Their years with the Ringling show, more than anything else, created the modern image of the "Russian dancing bear" in the American psyche.

PAN-AMERICAN MAGIC SPECTACULAR Originally begun as a small winter variety show under the title Pan-American Magic Show, this indoor revue of Allan C. HILL comes to town with a local sponsor, engaging PHONE PROMOTERS to assist in selling tickets. Its main TERRITORY is the northeastern United States.

PANTHERS See CATS.

PAPER Circus jargon for all advertising sheets put up in a show town, from LITHOGRAPHS to WINDOW CARDS and HERALDS. For instance, one of the BILLING CREW would be said to HANG PAPER or to "paper a town."

The word is sometimes used to mean free passes as well, as in the phrase "to paper the house." This is more often a theatrical term for giving away complimentary seats to fill up a house and make the show look prosperous.

(See also ADVANCE MAN; ANNIE OAKLEYS; PRESS AGENT.)

PARIS PAVILION
Throughout the long career of Dan RICE, America's first famous clown, "Dr." Gilbert R. SPALDING—another circus manager and entrepreneur—was variously competitor, co-worker, friend and nemesis.

In 1868 Spalding approached Rice following the latter's unsuccessful presidential bid concerning the purchase of his newest creation—a portable, canvas-topped, wooden amphitheater. The Paris Pavilion, as it was called, was to travel the Mississippi by steamboat, stopping to set up in towns along the river.

Rice had traveled along the Mississippi River before, in 1848, on the *Allegheny Mail,* until a bout with yellow fever forced him to cancel his tour. Eager to reenter show business, Rice purchased the Pavilion from Spalding. In the North, Rice toured the Pavilion in wagons; but on the Mississippi River he toured the amphitheater by steamboat, setting up on land in river towns. The *Will S. Hays,* a 340-ton steamboat built in 1865, was only one of many river boats to carry the DAN RICE CIRCUS. Unfortunately, large audiences did not materialize for Rice's tours with the Pavilion, and Rice soon lost the show to creditors.

PARKER & WATTS CIRCUS
Parker & Watts traveled as a small truck show for two seasons in 1938 and 1939.

PARKINSON, ROBERT LEWIS (1923–1991)
A noted circus historian and collector, Robert Lewis Parkinson was the original librarian of the CIRCUS WORLD MUSEUM archives in BARABOO, WISCONSIN.

Born in Decatur, Illinois, Parkinson saw his first MUD SHOW, the HAGENBECK-WALLACE CIRCUS, on May 16, 1934 when it played his hometown. Robert began his collection with a RINGLING BROS. AND BARNUM & BAILEY CIRCUS program from its 1936 Decatur appearance. Encouraged by circus historians John Grace, Charles Bernard and especially Bill Wood-

cock, Sr., Robert Parkinson and his brother Tom became fascinated with circus lore.

Robert Parkinson graduated from Millikin University in 1946, and he was soon working as an insurance adjuster in Cambridge, Illinois. During this time he continued to follow circuses and add to his collection. Among his holdings was the finest privately assembled compilation of newspaper circus ads.

In December 1964 Chappie FOX—director of the five-year-old Circus World Museum—asked Parkinson to create a library and head the archives. With his family's support, Parkinson readily agreed.

Parkinson began at the museum on March 15, 1965. As a circus fan with organizational skills, he was the perfect man for the job. Parkinson overcame meager supplies and funding in the early years to create a world-famous library. He added his own circus collection to those of the museum and the State Historical Society; soon the library started attracting gifts from other notable collections. In 1970 the archives were moved from their humble backroom beginnings to a 15,000 square foot, temperature/humidity–controlled building adjacent to the museum grounds.

In addition to his work with the library, Parkinson assisted Fox in the organization of the Schlitz circus parades (see GREAT CIRCUS PARADE, THE) in the 1960s and 1970s, heading the parade in 1973. He managed eight marches in Baraboo, Chicago and Milwaukee from 1980 through 1988. From July 1984 until February 1985 he also served as acting director of the museum. Having joined the CIRCUS HISTORICAL SOCIETY in 1944, Parkinson served as president in 1966 and 1967.

For many years Robert Lewis Parkinson suffered from heart disease, having survived a heart attack in 1965. In February 1991 he recovered from open heart surgery; but one month later he died as a result of complications from emergency follow-up surgery.

As a fitting tribute to his 26 years of service, the archives at the Circus World Museum have now been named the Robert L. Parkinson Library.

PARLARI
Obscure term for circus people talking together.

(See also JACKPOTS.)

The Flying Cavarettas perform the "passing leap" at Circus Circus in Las Vegas. Terry Cavaretta St. Jules (front) is acclaimed as the world's greatest living female flyer; brother Jimmy and sister Maureen (left) have been winners at the International Circus Festival in Monte Carlo and London's Circus World Championship. (Photo courtesy of Circus Circus)

PASSING LEAP

One of the most spectacular, if now-standard, tricks in the aerialist's repertoire on the FLYING TRAPEZE.

One FLYER takes off from his perch, then releases his hold on the swinging TRAPEZE. While he is still sailing toward the arms of the CATCHER, a second flyer grabs the swing bar and makes his cutaway. As the first flyer returns to catch the swing bar, the second flyer soars over his head toward the catcher.

The first flyer does not immediately return to the pedestal, but waits for the second flyer to join him on a second swing. Together they mount the perch and release the swing bar.

PAUL SILVERBURG CIRCUS

See SELLS BROTHERS CIRCUS.

PAWNEE BILL

See LILLIE, MAJOR GORDON W.

PAWNEE BILL'S WILD WEST

Imitative of the popular Wild West show pioneered by William F. "Buffalo Bill" CODY, Pawnee Bill's Wild West was owned and operated by Major Gordon W. LILLIE.

Pawnee Bill was a buffalo hunter as well as an agent and interpreter for the Pawnee Indian tribe in Oklahoma. Ironically, Pawnee Bill became interested in the possibility of building his own Wild West after supplying several Pawnee braves to BUFFALO BILL'S WILD WEST.

Pawnee Bill's Wild West opened in 1887 and toured Europe, Canada and the United States for over a decade. It settled into American tours only after the turn of the century. Following the 1907 season, Pawnee Bill sold all of the show wagons and rail cars to other circuses and spent the entire 1908 season working at an amusement park.

The next year Lillie became partners with his old rival, William Cody, and for the 1909 through 1913 seasons they toured together in a combined BUFFALO BILL WILD WEST AND PAWNEE BILL GREAT FAR EAST SHOW. Also known as the Two Bills Show, it folded in 1913.

Pawnee Bill made several attempts to return to the road. Many of his planned shows never materialized, and those that did quickly vanished. He did revive a short-lived Wild West show on a carnival in the 1930s, but none of his late-career circuses ever reached the splendor of Pawnee Bills's Wild West or the Two Bills Show.

PERCH

A "perch act," first introduced under canvas in 1853, is any circus routine in which an artist performs on a long rod known as a perch pole. One end of the pole, today made of aluminum, is balanced on the shoulders, head, forehead, stomach, hands or feet of a BOTTOM MAN or "understander." With one performer in the air—clinging to the metal rod—and the other gymnast firmly on the ground—a perch act combines the skills of acrobatics and balancing.

The "artist" on the top of the perch need not be a human, of course. For instance, a perch has been used as a novelty trick in many dog acts.

(See also ACROBATS; AERIAL ACTS; AERIAL PERCH.)

Perch pole act by the Great Olveras on the Clyde Beatty Trained Wild Animal Circus in 1946.

(Photo courtesy of the *Herald Examiner* collection/Los Angeles Public Library)

PERFORMANCE DIRECTOR

See EQUESTRIAN DIRECTOR; RINGMASTER.

PERU, INDIANA

Peru served as the WINTER QUARTERS for the AMERICAN CIRCUS CORPORATION as well as its many shows. In the 1920s this small town was the "circus capital of the world," quartering five of the largest circuses in the United States.

Today, Peru (pronounced "PEE-ROO" by circus folk) is still an active circus community and each summer the town sponsors its own youth circus. Since 1960, every year it has sponsored the Festival Circus (sometimes called the Circus City Circus), an amateur circus starring about 200 children from Miami County. The show is performed in a permanent circus building that also houses a small circus museum.

In 1989 the International Circus Hall of Fame, Inc. opened its doors in Peru. At the center of its collection are 1,000 artifacts and 23 original circus wagons that it acquired from the bankrupt Circus Hall of Fame in SARASOTA, FLORIDA. In 1991 the International Circus Hall of Fame re-created ten wagons in three-quarters scale for daily STREET PARADES through the amusement park at Knott's Berry Farm.

Also preserved by private owners in Peru, Indiana is the farm of Capt. Terrell JACOBS—the trainer who had worked with the largest CAT act of all time. Across town stand several of the old white barns that had housed the American Circus Corporation.

Information on the town's annual Circus City Festival, Inc. can be obtained through 154 N. Broadway, Peru, Indiana 46970.

PETE JENKINS ACT

Also known as the "Pete Jenkins from Mud Corners" act, the origination of this comic equestrian routine in the 1850s is variously credited to Charles Sherwood or Dan RICE. Regardless of the true creator, it was primarily Rice who developed the act for his DAN RICE'S ONE-HORSE SHOW.

The feature of the act was EXCELSIOR, Rice's pride HORSE. Originally Excelsior had been trained only to walk up and down a small set of stairs. Added to this was a baggy-pants CLOWN trying in various unsuccessful ways to mount the steed. Each time the clown tripped, a piece of costume would fall off. Eventually a vibrant, colorful wardrobe was revealed under the tramp clothing, and the equestrian triumphantly rode the horse out of the ring.

Many historians believe that the circus described by Samuel "Mark Twain" Clemens in his *Adventures of Huckleberry Finn* was based on what he saw at the DAN RICE CIRCUS during one of its stops in Hannibal, Missouri. Regardless, no better contemporary description of the act could be given than Twain's own:

> By and by a drunken man tried to get into the ring— said he wanted to ride; said he could ride as well as anybody that ever was. They argued and tried to keep him out, but he wouldn't listen, and the whole show come to a standstill. Then the people begun to holler at him and make fun of him, and that made him mad, and he begun to rip and tear; so that stirred up the people, and a lot of men begun to pile down off of the benches and swarm toward the ring, saying, "Knock him down! throw him out!" and one or two women begun to scream. So, then, the ringmaster he made a little speech, and said he hoped there wouldn't be no disturbance, and if the man would

Five young funambulists form a human pyramid as part of the annual Circus City Circus in Peru, Indiana.
(Photo courtesy of Betty and Tom Hodgini)

promise he wouldn't make no more trouble he would let him ride if he thought he could stay on the horse. So everybody laughed and said all right, and the man got on. The minute he was on, the horse begun to rip and tear and jump and cavort around, with two circus men hanging on to his bridle trying to hold him, and the drunken man hanging on to his neck, and his heels flying in the air every jump, and the whole crowd of people standing up shouting and laughing till tears rolled down. And at last, sure enough, all the circus men could do, the horse broke loose, and away he went like the very nation, round and round the ring, with that sot laying down on him and hanging to his neck, with first one leg hanging most to the ground on one side, and then t'other one on t'other side, and the people just crazy. It warn't funny to me, though; I was all of a tremble to see his danger. But pretty soon he struggled up astraddle and grabbed the bridle, a-reeling this way and that; and the next minute he sprung up and dropped the bridle and stood! and the horse a-going like a house afire, too. He just stood up there, a-sailing around as easy and comfortable as if he warn't ever drunk in his life—and then he began to pull off his clothes and sling them. He shed them so thick they kind of clogged up the air, and altogether he shed seventeen suits. And, then, there he was, slim and handsome, and dressed the gaudiest and prettiest you ever saw, and he lit into that horse with his whip and made him fairly hum— and finally skipped off, and made his bow and danced off to the dressing room, and everybody just a-howling with pleasure and astonishment.

"PETE JENKINS FROM MUD CORNERS"   See PETE JENKINS ACT.

PETIT, PHILIPPE (1949–   )   Already established as a wire walker in his native France, Philippe Petit created a sensation in 1974 by walking a tightwire that he stretched between the twin towers of the World Trade Center in New York City.

Philippe Petit was born on August 13, 1949 in Nemours, France. The son of an army officer, he began to walk on wire at the age of seventeen. Two

Rosinback rider during the comic opening of the Pete Jenkins from Mud Corners act. (Author's Collection)

years later he wrote, directed and starred in a play about WIRE WALKING entitled *L'IF,* which was performed at the Théâtre de l'Amicale in St. Germain-en-Laye.

In the autumn of 1969, he crossed the Seine River and continued on to the Eiffel Tower on a tightrope. For three hours he again startled Paris as he performed on a wire that he had secretly strung between the 226-foot tall towers of Notre Dame Cathedral. He made a similar death-defying walk over the span of the Sydney Harbour Bridge in Australia. In 1971, to celebrate the 90th birthday of Pablo Picasso, Petit walked a wire in Vallauris, France. Meanwhile, he was earning a living as a street performer, entertaining with JUGGLING and magic.

He planned the World Trade Center walk for ten months, visiting the spot dressed as a construction worker or a tourist, then finally smuggling his equipment to an upper floor of one of the towers. He rigged the wire by shooting it from one tower to the other using a bow and arrow. Then, on August 7, 1974 at 7 A.M., he took the 200-foot walk, 1,350 feet in the air (still the world's record for height). He was, of course, arrested and did not contest. He was

sentenced to put on a free show for the children of New York, climbing an incline cable to the top of Belvedere Castle in Central Park.

Philippe Petit made his debut with the GREATEST SHOW ON EARTH in Venice, Florida on January 3, 1975. Four days later during a rehearsal at the Bayfront Center in St. Petersburg, he slipped because he did not properly ROSIN his slippers before descending the incline from the high wire to the floor. His chest hit the wire; although he caught the cable with his hands, he couldn't hold on. He fell 25 feet to the cement, breaking a rib, a wrist and suffering internal injuries. He was not sufficiently healed to make the opening at MADISON SQUARE GARDEN on March 25, but he did eventually join the show on May 8 while it was still in New York.

During his single season with the Ringling show, Petit also set the record for the longest indoor tightrope walk by crossing a 700-foot-long, 200-foot-high wire six times in a row under the cover of the Louisiana Superdome in New Orleans during its opening celebration.

Unfortunately, while Petit's bravery makes him a daredevil, he is not a traditional circus performer. Perhaps Petit's facility made his work seem too easy, or perhaps his pure white wardrobe was not "flashy" enough for the crowds' expectations. In any event, audiences seemed to be more impressed with the more flamboyant aerialists that same season.

In a 1979 interview in the *New York Times,* Philippe Petit said, "What makes me different from other wire walkers is that they . . . try to sell the act. They think they have to show it's dangerous. . . . I think the courage of a high walker is beautiful if he can hide it. I'm trying to get rid of all the equipment . . . even the balancing pole. I want . . . to make it more pure and simple, almost forgetting the wire is there."

In 1977 Petit had assisted his friend Paul BINDER during the initial setup of the BIG APPLE CIRCUS. The tent contractors had missewn the canvas, and it was Petit's expertise that allowed the crew to rerig the tent on the spot. In 1981 he joined the cast of the intimate, one-ring circus for one season, walking barefoot on a slender, steel cord.

(See SKYWALK.)

PHONE PROMOTER   Today most circuses in the United States do not merely send out a 24-HOUR MAN, poster up a town and arrive without a huge advance sale. Because of the huge daily expense, or NUT, required simply to keep a show open, the circus looks for some guarantee of financial success before setting out on the road.

Thus was born the "sponsored" date, where the circus operates under the auspices of a local group that can arrange the LOT or arena, aid in securing area permits and, most important, assist with advance ticket sales. Over the years, all sorts of civic groups have sponsored circuses into town, from chambers of commerce to churches. One of the most active and supportive sponsors has been the Shriners.

Often the local group does not have any idea how to do a widespread ticket sale or simply does not want to go through the trouble. In this case it hires what has become a "necessary evil" in the circus industry—professional telephone solicitors known as phone promoters. Many times the circus can provide the callers. The solicitors keep a large percentage of the sales in exchange for providing their services; by handling the phones for the sponsor, the circus can gross more in each city.

The hours are long and thankless, if profitable, for the telephone solicitor. The sales team holes up in one or more hotel rooms, sets up its own outside telephone lines and begins to canvas the community.

The first calls go out to companies, since it is assumed that businesses have more cash available than families to buy tickets. The salespeople try to convince local leaders to buy books of tickets to use as gifts, incentives, perks, rewards for their employees or as giveaways for their customers. Another part of the phone crew calls individuals, selling them "family packs" of tickets.

The call usually goes something like this: "Hello, I'm calling today on behalf of the local Shriners. We need your help to continue our fine job right here in our community. From January 3rd to the 6th we are holding our 20th annual Shrine Circus, and we are offering books of tickets to families just like your own. A portion of every ticket sold goes to help crippled children at our Shriners Children's Hospital."

Although telephone solicitation is certainly a respectable and time-honored way of raising money, some salespeople—as in any profession—become greedy and ruin the reputation for everyone in the field. Phone men have been known occasionally to misrepresent themselves to the public regarding their legitimate sponsors, to collect funds without any intention of providing a show or to skim large sums of monies off the top before reporting sales to the civic group.

Certainly such conduct is illegal and unethical. Perhaps because these shady dealings give the impression of having taken place in dark, backroom hideouts, the notorious use of telephone sales has become known as a BOILER ROOM operation. This phrase may also be derived from the high pressure that the crew sometimes applies to close a sale.

(See also SHRINE CIRCUS; TEXAS SHRINE DATES, THE.)

PICKET LINE   Circus slang for the loose chain that is strung in front of a row of animals to keep people from getting too close to them. This is seen most often in the MENAGERIE, both in front of the uncaged animals and the WAGONS themselves.

PICKLE FAMILY CIRCUS, THE   Based in San Francisco, the Pickle Family Circus was begun in 1974 by Peggy Snider, Larry Pisoni and Cecil MacKinnon as the first "new wave" circus in the Western Hemisphere. Its style of combining theater, comedy, dance and nontraditional circus music in a one-ring format was unique in the United States at the time of the circus's inception. After 19 years, the Pickle Family Circus ceased continuous operation in May 1993.

Until 1991, Executive Director Peggy Snider was the only continuing staff member to have been WITH IT since the beginning. She was born in New York City and acquired her bachelor of arts degree from Bennington College in 1965. Three years later she began working with the San Francisco Mime Troupe, a gritty, antiestablishment theater troupe that also managed to be comedic and accessible; she remained associated with them until 1976.

While working with that troupe, she met Larry Pisoni, who joined as a teacher and performer in 1971. Pisoni was also born in New York City, and he had studied circus techniques there with Hovey BURGESS and performer Judy Finelli. In 1970 Pisoni moved to San Francisco to form his own group. Instead, he became associated with the San Francisco Mime Troupe the following year and toured with them through 1974.

Pisoni taught Snider the skills he had learned in New York; the two worked well together and decided to form their own group of jugglers. Pisoni introduced Snider to Cecil MacKinnon, who had also learned from Burgess and Finelli. MacKinnon was born in Chicago, had obtained a master of fine arts degree from New York University and worked in New York theater before moving to the Bay area.

The three co-founded the Pickle Family Jugglers in San Francisco. According to Snider, "The Pickle Family Jugglers went everywhere. We performed in the parks and on college campuses; we performed at corporate Christmas parties with some lame orchestra behind us that was playing our music about ten times too slow. We even juggled on the radio. Don't ask."

Before long the trio conceived of a show that combined the politics of the mime troupe and the skills of the jugglers with the theatrics of a circus. The Pickle Family Circus was born.

From the start, they decided to avoid animal acts, BALLY BROADS and a low-paid crew of working ROUS-TABOUTS. Everyone on the show performed, and everyone helped set up and TEAR DOWN. The show worked hard at operating as a cooperative; and, in policy-making decisions, everyone had one vote. Salaries were established on the assumption that all jobs were equal in value. In the beginning, the base salary for everyone was only $250 per week.

In its first seasons Pisoni was artistic director, juggler, CLOWN (as Lorenzo Pickle), ACROBAT, wire walker, tuba player and truck driver. Snider was technical director, juggler, costume designer and company manager. When she joined as a touring member in 1976 (through 1979), MacKinnon was a juggler, acrobat and actress.

The first show, in May 1975, took place in the gymnasium of John O'Connell School in the Mission district of San Francisco. To this day the Pickle Family Circus has never been performed under a BIG TOP. Shows take place in indoor auditoriums or surrounded by a SIDEWALL IN OPEN PARKS.

Among the cast in its first season were two performers, Geoff Hoyle and Bill Irwin, who first established their now-internationally known clown characters with the Pickle Family Circus.

Geoff Hoyle was born in Hull, England, and received a bachelor of arts degree in English and drama from Birmingham University. He continued his studies with Ecole de Mime Etienne Decroux before moving to the United States and joining the circus. He created a unique clown, Mr. Sniff, who sports a trademark elongated, sausage-shaped red

nose. Hoyle toured with the Pickle Family Circus through 1981 before beginning independent work. In 1991 he appeared as the featured clown on the American tour of the CIRQUE DU SOLEIL.

Bill Irwin was born in Santa Monica, California, and received a bachelor of arts degree from Oberlin College in 1973. He came out of Ringling CLOWN COLLEGE and toured with the Pickle Family Circus through 1980, creating his memorable inquisitive and put-upon WHITE-FACED CLOWN character, Willy the Clown. Since that time, his best-known theater piece, "In Regard of Flight," developed with Doug Skinner and Michael O'Connor, allowed him to show a pratfall comedian/clown without makeup; the show has appeared Off Broadway and on television. In 1984 he was named a Guggenheim Fellow and was awarded a five-year MacArthur ("Genius") Fellowship. After acting in numerous plays in New York, Irwin appeared again on Broadway in 1989 as a bewildered clown in his own piece, *Largely New York*. In 1993 he appeared on Broadway in *Fool Moon*.

The first major outside funding for the Pickle Family Circus came in part through the federal Comprehensive Employment and Training Act (CETA) program. Although 50% of the show's revenues come from ticket sales, grants have been accepted from the National Endowment for the Arts, the California Arts Council and many more.

Joanne Sonn, who worked with the circus from 1978 through 1984 as business manager, booker and fund raiser, explained, "We never tailored our schedule or our shows to please funders. We said, here's what we are, here's how we work, we're worthy; we'd like your support.

"We were always fiscal conservatives. We never overspent . . . if we didn't have it, we didn't spend it. If we needed a truck, we'd ask a corporate donor for the money to buy a truck, or bleachers or whatever."

In addition, the circus relied on the volunteer work, contributions and generosity of its home neighborhood, Potrero Hill. Numerous grants allowed the Pickle Family Circus to make a five-weekend tour in 1976, traveling to small northern California towns, such as Ferndale, where the show was scheduled around farmers' milking time. During the weekdays, the troupe set up sleeping tents in camp sites.

In 1977 Oregon was added to the route, followed by Washington, Nevada and Arizona in subsequent seasons. An Alaskan stand highlighted the 1979 season only. Zoë Leader, who was with the circus from 1975 to 1984 as business manager, publicist, graphic designer, juggler and roustabout, says her favorite on-the-road experience took place in Gold Beach, Oregon: "The show had been packed the first evening. When Larry [Pisoni] was doing his closing remarks, it was almost like a conversation between friends. He says, 'Now I want you to go home and tell everybody you know to come and see the Pickle Family Circus for themselves.' And a little girl who was sitting right up by the ring yelled, 'But this *is* everybody we know!'"

The "cooperative" concept of the company was strongly tested in 1980 when the show was set to play Portland, Oregon immediately following the eruption of Mount St. Helens. Pisoni said, "We had a giant debate inside the company about whether or not to cancel. . . . it got real heated, as a lot of Pickle debates tended to get, with one side saying 'We've never done that before, cancel a show on account of a volcano, it would be a bad precedent,' and the other side saying they weren't prepared to die for the Pickle Family Circus." They decided to make their date.

In 1981 the three Pickle clowns, Pisoni, Hoyle and Irwin, produced a noncircus theatrical show entitled *Three High* at the Marine's Memorial Theater in San Francisco. Then, during the Christmas season of 1981, the entire Pickle Family Circus performed for six weeks at the Round House in London.

In 1982 Judy Finelli joined the troupe. Born in New York City, she had received her bachelor of arts degree from New York University. A juggler, clown, actress, circus historian and critic, Finelli was a past president of the International Jugglers Association. She had worked with Hovey Burgess on his book *Circus techniques.* Leaving the touring company after the 1983 season, Finelli stayed on as the co-director of the Pickle Family Circus School and was artistic director of the circus through 1990.

By the end of its first decade, the Pickle Family Circus was touring annually from San Diego to Seattle, traditionally ending its season in San Francisco with a December holiday run of self-produced indoor shows.

In 1984 the circus inaugurated the Pickle Family Circus School, teaching classes in the general circus arts to children ages five through 12 on Saturdays. With the first generation of students graduated,

current instructors Wendy Parkman and Hannah Kahn began to teach intermediate and advanced classes in circus skills, assisted by Lu Yi, artistic director of the Nanjing Acrobatics Troupe of China. On February 18, 1993 the school was incorporated separately as the San Francisco School of Circus Arts to ensure its continued operation in the face of the circus's increasing financial problems.

Skill acts on the show included WIRE WALKING, acrobatics and the FLYING TRAPEZE. A basic tenet of the show, however, was the elimination of risk for risk's sake. The trainers acknowledged that accidents happen in life. The Pickle acts played up the art of the performer rather than the daredevil. Larry Pisoni put it this way:

> I'm not particularly interested in watching people risk their lives. Life is much too precious. . . . If he dies, what do I get? I've seen people fall from a high wire; I've seen people fall from a trapeze. I didn't get a good feeling when they hit the ground. What I am interested in is seeing people make beautiful images and project them and demonstrate the power of a human being.

The Pickle Family Circus was one of the first shows to break tradition and use a completely modern sound to back its performance—in their case, jazz music. The size of the band varied from season to season but usually counted between five and ten. Preshow music was often by known composers such as Fats Waller and Herbie Hancock, but the music that accompanied the acts was specially written each season by the show's composer or the entire band.

Jeffrey Gaetto, one of the show composers, explained, "It's often impossible to have a final version of the music . . . because the acts aren't finished by the time the music has to be composed. I find myself more and more working with images of the type of movement that will be going on." He often saw acrobats in a six-eight meter; the trapeze is a three-four time for the swinging, with an occasional break to four-four.

The Pickle Family Circus remained true to its principles of concern and community. One of the circus's original mandates was to perform nonprofit work and to institute an outreach program to minority audiences and shut-ins. On its commercial venues, the circus shared box office profits with sponsors. Once a group agreed to bring the show into town, the local liaisons had primary responsibility for ticket sales; they earned one dollar from each advance ticket sold, plus the proceeds from any MIDWAY attractions or concessions they set up.

Ticket prices were kept down to make the show available to low-income audiences. The Pickles also gave several benefit shows during the year for community sponsors who provided a minimum guarantee for the performance. In 1985, for instance, the daily minimum expenses, or NUT, for the show was between $12,000 and $14,000; but the guarantee to buy out a weekend day for a benefit performance was a reasonable $5,000, and the fee was $3,000 for a midweek day. The circus provided the show, all publicity, advance work and a much-imitated sponsor workbook detailing advice to the local committee.

A forerunner of the new look of American one-ring circuses, the Pickle Family Circus influenced modern shows from CIRCUS OZ and The BIG APPLE CIRCUS to CIRQUE DU SOLEIL. Ironically since its first appearance in the Bay area, Cirque du Soleil had a major impact on the style of the Pickle Family Circus. By Pickle's 1990's "La La Luna Sea" show, the attempt to incorporate a theme, plot and structure had overtaken much of the simplicity of the earlier athletically oriented productions.

Larry Pisoni, who had left the Pickle show in 1987 to pursue an independent career with other shows, returned to direct the 1991 Christmas production. When he attempted to stay on as artistic director, however, the board of directors voted not to renew his contract.

Pisoni commented:

They told me they didn't share my vision of where the circus was going, and they didn't like my administrative style. They want me to make the Pickles move like Cirque du Soleil, to do circus theater, with plot and narrative. I believe the elements in each circus act are expressive in and of themselves, that the poetry of each act is where the value of circus lies. To impose a plot and character on the circus is like trying to turn a piece of sculpture into a symphony.

Board member Marc Snyder, who had been with the Pickle Family Circus for 15 years, confirmed that Pisoni's vision "is more of a traditional variety style circus. . . . We're interested in exploring the connections with circus, theater and dance. We have to find new directions instead of doing the same old thing."

Peggy Snider resigned in 1991, as did business manager Bill Baer. The company, which operated with a $1.2 million annual budget, ended up its 1991 season with a deficit of $100,000.

The Pickle Family Circus opened its fall 1992 season in southern California, followed by a visit to Canada, a December holiday return to San Francisco, a month-long run in Cleveland, Ohio and a national tour until May 1993. The new edition entitled "Tossing and Turning," described as a clown comedy, was co-directed by current artistic director Tandy Beal and Lu Yi. The show's theme involved sleep and the waking dream world, interspersed with the circus's usual gymnastic acts, clowns and spectacle.

It was announced in April 1993 that at the end of the spring season the Pickle Family Circus would go into Chapter 7 bankruptcy protection, and papers were filed in late May 1993.

PICTURE GALLERY   Circus jargon for a tattooed man or lady.

(See also FREAKS.)

PIE CAR   Circus jargon on a rail show for the car that served snacks and drinks as well as provided gambling for the cast and crew. For many, especially the ROUSTABOUTS who were usually low-paid unskilled laborers, the pie car was the place where the showmen inadvertently returned their wages back to the show. The car was sometimes handled by the COOKHOUSE and sometimes operated as a separate concession.

On today's truck shows, the term is also used for the trailer that serves the cast in the same capacity after the show. For some, it is the center for rest, relaxation and company in the late evenings, a place to "cut up JACKPOTS."

PINK LEMONADE   Circus legend has it that pink lemonade was created on a small circus touring Texas in the 1880s. The weather was dry and hot and, due to a drought, water was scarce. The concessions wagon, or "JUICE joint," had used up its allowance of water for the day; so, when circus-goers demanded more refreshments, one of the BUTCHERS rushed around the LOT, looking for any water he could find.

He located a full bucket, but unfortunately a clown (or other performer) had just finished washing his red costume or tights in it. That, of course, didn't stop the "juice man," who mixed his powders in with the precious liquid, giving it its famous pink coloration.

The drink was a hit and soon had the cowboys clamoring, "Give me some more of that there pink lemonade!" Thus a circus tradition was born.

Noted circus author and historian Joe KcKennon wrote, "Having run a 'juice joint' myself for a few months on Hagenbeck-Wallace, I am inclined to believe the story is true."

PISONI, LARRY   See BURGESS, HOVEY; CIRCUS FLORA; JUGGLING; PICKLE FAMILY CIRCUS, THE.

PIT SHOWS   Located on the MIDWAY or FRONT YARD, pit shows are found in small TENTS, often 10 by 10 feet or less, that contain extra, unusual attractions not found in the SIDESHOW, MENAGERIE or BIG TOP.

Technically, the pit show is so called because the inside attraction, often human, sat in a dirt pit, dug a few inches to one or two feet down into the ground. Spectators stood around the four sides of the pit and looked down. This type of pit show, which often displayed reptiles or other animals, FREAKS or "geeks" (people who ate raw chickens or snakes) disappeared from circus LOTS by the mid-20th century. Today such pit shows are seen only on carnivals, and then rarely.

As a result, some now use the term "pit show" in a more generic sense to mean any small exhibit on the midway, such as "The Pygmy Horse" or "Mongo, the Gorilla" or a themed display, such as "Reptilerama." Each pit show carries its own BANNERLINE and ticket seller; and, although an OUTSIDE TALKER may give an occasional BALLY, a GRIND tape is usually set to expound on the marvel to be found within the tent.

PITCH   Circus jargon for a "sales talk." A pitch could take many forms, including the opening or BALLY out front of the SIDESHOW and the RINGMASTER selling boxes of candy or coloring books from the CENTER RING.

Those who do the SPIEL are, of course, known as pitchmen.

(See also CANDY PITCH; COLORING BOOK PITCH.)

PITCHMEN   See PITCH.

PLANGE   An aerial stunt requiring both strength and stamina. After climbing a WEB high into the air, the performer slips a wrist into a padded rope loop that is attached to a swivel and ring. By swinging upward, body over head, the performer makes a complete circle.

The one-arm plange is particularly grueling because during the swing-over, the shoulder is partially dislocated before it snaps back into place. It also causes great wear on the wrist and extreme disproportionate upper body development.

Aerialist Lillian LEITZEL was famous for performing the one-arm plange during the early part of the century, often completing more than 100 revolutions; her record was 249. While performing in Denmark on February 13, 1931, the swivel ring, crystallized from repeated heating and cooling during performances, snapped in two and Leitzel fell 20 feet. She died of complications two days later.

(See also AERIAL ACTS.)

PLAYS, CIRCUS   See THEATER.

POLACK BROS. CIRCUS   The Polack brothers operated major railroad carnivals throughout the United States from the 1920s until the Great Depression forced their closure.

One of the brothers, I.J. Polack, then became general agent for the Milt Holland Indoor Circus. Since Holland operated only in the winter months, Polack and Louis Stern leased the show to tour in the summer as the Eastern States Circus.

This show evolved into the Polack Bros. Circus and continued to play only indoor sponsored dates. By World War II the show had more offers for show dates than it could fill, so a second unit was formed.

The circus remains active today playing "sponsored dates." The Polack Bros. Circus does not have a single roster of talent or book its own route. Rather, the management seeks out local organizations, often police associations, Mason or Shriner groups, and shows frequently appear under their name or title rather than as the Polack Bros. Circus.

For instance, telephone solicitors (PHONE PROMOTERS) might sell blocks of tickets to merchants and families for the SHRINE CIRCUS, mentioning that

During an appearance with the Polack Bros. Circus, Jose and Lalo Palacios come out of a "passing leap." Jose is returning to the "fly bar," while Lalo is about to be caught by the hands of the third brother, Raul.   (Author's collection)

a portion of the proceeds is going to a worthy cause. Indeed, in such cases the Shriners are involved in name and act as a local liaison, but the Polack Bros. Circus actually provides the show. After paying the minimal expenses for advertising and talent, the major portion of the monies collected goes to the promoter—or organizer of the circus itself—with a significantly smaller portion going to the sponsor.

The Polack Bros. Circus enjoys an immaculate reputation, always giving the audience members their monies' worth for the ticket prices. Since the shows are framed to be able to play indoors or outdoors, in theaters, auditoriums, stadiums or ballparks without a full-season cast, the owners can select from the best available talent in every performance category to create a powerhouse show for each specific show date.

POLAKOV, MICHAEL "COCO" (1923–   )   Born in the Soviet Union, Michael Polakov became a third-generation circus CLOWN. His clown character, "Coco,"

was developed in England, where he parents had moved while he was still a child.

Although wearing the same style nose and clothing as his ancestors, Polakov's AUGUSTE CLOWN face is completely different. He began work with the Bertram Mills Circus and the Billy Smart Circus in England, also appearing briefly in Poland, Germany and back in the Soviet Union.

In 1953 he first traveled to the United States to work with the MILLS BROS. CIRCUS. He quickly returned to England, but visited the United States again in 1958. During that time, Polakov brought two classic gags, the "Busy Bee" and the "Painters and Decorators."

He worked for eight seasons with the RINGLING BROS. AND BARNUM & BAILEY CIRCUS as an ADVANCE CLOWN and as "goodwill ambassador." Since leaving The BIG ONE, Michael Polakov has worked as an advance clown for smaller MUD SHOWS and independently as "Coco" on promotional dates.

(See also CLOWN GAGS.)

POLLIN, ABE   See CIRCUS AMERICA; FELD, IRVIN; KAYE, PAUL V.; RINGLING BROS. AND BARNUM & BAILEY CIRCUS.

PONGER   Circus jargon, in disuse, for an ACROBAT.

POOL, THOMAS (fl. 1770–1790)   According to his own HERALDS and circulars, Mr. Thomas Pool was the first American-born circus equestrian. More likely, however, he was English-born, having traveled to the colonies as early as the 1770s with other British equestrians (including M. F. Foulks and Jacob Bates in Philadelphia and New York and John Sharp in Boston). He claimed American birth in order to take advantage of the patriotism of the new nation.

Pool gave performances at his Philadelphia riding academy in 1785, moving his act to New York the following year. Although not yet a full circus—merely a display of trick riding—the show did include a CLOWN and concluded with Philip ASTLEY's famous act, "The TAILOR'S RIDE TO BRENTFORD."

(See also DIBDEN AND HUGHES.)

POSSUM BELLY   Circus jargon for a storage box underneath a truck, work wagon or railroad car. So that ROUSTABOUTS do not have to lift them high during loading, heavy pieces of small equipment are usually placed into the possum belly of the appropriate truck.

STAKES, for instance, might be carried in a possum belly under the pole wagon. That way, as the truck pulls along the LAY OUT pins to unload the canvas and poles, the crew has to lift or carry the stakes a minimum distance.

PRESS AGENT

As opposed to the PUBLICITY or public relations department in the home office of the circus, the press agent is an ADVANCE MAN, one of the crew who travels several weeks ahead of the circus, facilitating the show's arrival into town.

Although their duties may occasionally overlap, usually two types of press agents are on the road for a show of any size. The first, known as the "contracting press agent," is the advance man who distributes press releases and arranges for newspaper space, radio slots and television time. This would include the paid advertising as well as the stories and interviews that appear free of charge under the category of news.

An "advance press agent" spends one or more days in a town immediately before the show arrives for last-minute follow-up on publicity needs for the show. The agent then doubles back to the circus on show day to deal with the journalists on the LOT and to expedite the day-of-show interviews. Needless to say, a circus may employ several press agents at any one time, some specializing in the various media.

PRIVILEGE

In order to be granted the right to be the only vendor on the circus LOT selling a specific product or service, the cast or crew member must pay a "privilege" to the circus management. Popular services that often require the payment of a privilege include being the sole act selling a souvenir item in the SIDESHOW or being the only electrician allowed to hook up the acts' travel vans to the generator.

The amount paid for the privilege depends entirely on the potential income that the unique service might earn the vendor and the demand from others to be accorded the "X," or the exclusive right, to it. Since the monies received are usually in the form of cash, this amount is difficult to verify. The privilege, therefore, is usually paid each week to the RED WAGON in the form of a flat fee.

The term "privilege" never carries the underlying connotation of a bribe, commission or kickback. It has always been considered by show folk as a standard way of doing business—an aboveboard, agreed-in-advance fee for the privilege of being allowed to provide a unique service.

P.T. BARNUM'S GREAT ASIATIC CARAVAN, MUSEUM AND MENAGERIE

In 1851, a few months before the arrival of Jenny LIND in New York, P.T. BARNUM sent a ship to India to collect animals for his AMERICAN MUSEUM. His partners in the venture were the renowned circus impresario Seth B. HOWES and Sherwood Stratton, TOM THUMB's father.

Instead of placing the beasts into the museum's MENAGERIE, however, the men opened a canvas show that became known as P.T. Barnum's Great Asiatic Caravan, Museum and Menagerie (technically, "Barnum's Asiatic Caravan, Museum and Menagerie" in 1851 and 1852 and "P.T. Barnum's Grand Colossal Museum and Menagerie" in 1853 and 1854). Appearing under a 110-foot canvas top, the caravan had no ring acts and did not advertise itself as a circus.

The traveling museum featured ELEPHANTS; wax statues of the presidents; Tom Thumb; Mr. Nellis (an armless man); Mr. Alviza Pierce (a lion trainer) and, according to Barnum, a "fine military band" and more "wonderful objects of nature and art." Admission was 25 cents, half price for children. The show toured for four years until the partnership broke up.

The first season was spent completely in New England and New York. In 1852 the show traveled into Canada, Michigan and Ohio. The following year manager Lewis B. Lent led the Caravan into Kentucky, Tennessee, Illinois and Wisconsin. He also raised the admission price—50 cents in the South, 30 cents in the North.

The last season was spent in Pennsylvania, Maryland and New Jersey. Lion trainer Pierce was replaced by Elijah Lengel, but otherwise the troupe remained the same. Also in 1854 the show stopped advertising the herd of elephants as having ten BULLS—a number that had been true only in its inaugural parade and never on tour. The season ended in Brooklyn, New York on October 20, and an auction of all the animals and apparatus was held in New York City on November 15.

For all four years that it toured, the Caravan received unanimous bad press for its shabbiness and

"Barnum's Mammoth Tent" on P.T. Barnum's Great Asiatic Caravan, Museum and Menagerie, sometime between 1854 and 1881. (Photo courtesy of Ronald W. Lackmann)

for not living up to its advertising. Nevertheless, the tour was a financial success: The initial investment had been only $109,000, but the net profit for the 1852 season alone had been $71,000.

P.T. BARNUM'S GREAT ROMAN HIPPODROME Site of the original MADISON SQUARE GARDEN, P.T. Barnum's Great Roman Hippodrome opened in April 1874 as the first indoor home of BARNUM'S GREAT TRAVELING MUSEUM, MENAGERIE, CARAVAN, HIPPODROME AND CIRCUS.

W.C. COUP, a former SIDESHOW manager, and Dan CASTELLO, a former CLOWN, asked P.T. BARNUM to join them in founding a new circus. Coup management, coupled with Barnum's name and financial backing, made a formidable team; on April 10, 1871 the Great Traveling Museum opened in Brooklyn. This was the first time P.T. Barnum, then 61, had owned and managed a circus.

The Traveling Museum toured under three acres

of canvas and grossed $400,000 in the first of its five highly successful seasons. In 1872 Coup moved the show onto rails, and the show grossed $1 million in six months. For the 1872 season, the show's title was officially changed to "P.T. Barnum's Great Traveling Exposition and World's Fair" and for the first time Barnum used the slogan The "GREATEST SHOW ON EARTH" to describe one of his shows. Another innovation that season was the introduction of a second ring under the BIG TOP.

At the end of the 1872 season, the show was divided, with some of the company moving south and the larger group setting up in New York City's HIPPOTHEATRON, which Barnum had leased from Lewis B. LENT. On the morning of December 24, the building burned to the ground, destroying all of the equipment, the performers' personal and professional effects and most of the MENAGERIE animals.

The show managed to regroup, and the even

larger 1873 circus toured with a daily expense, or NUT, of $5,000. That autumn, while Barnum was in Europe purchasing animals, Coup leased the property at Madison Square between 26th and 27th streets and Fourth and Madison avenues to move their giant show into an arena setting. They named the building P.T. Barnum's Great Roman Hippodrome, although Barnum himself did not see the structure until his return to the United States on April 30, 1874, several days after the colosseum had already been open.

In later years Barnum claimed that he was consulted and approved of the plan. Coup denied this, sometimes saying that Barnum was never told and other times declaring that Barnum was advised but turned down the plan.

Regardless of the true facts, the largest crowd ever assembled in a New York structure up to that time (10,000 people) gathered to see the Hippodrome's first performance. The show began with an incredible SPEC entitled the "Congress of Nations," which, according to Barnum, "required nearly 1,000 persons, several hundred HORSES, besides llamas, CAMELS, ostriches, etc." The GRAND ENTRY was followed by chariot races around the track and the rest of the usual circus performance.

A company from the Hippodrome show soon went on the road, again touring as "Barnum's Great Traveling World's Fair." It was during a BALLOON ASCENSION in Chicago, on July 15, 1874 that the pilot Professor Washington H. Donaldson and a reporter went aloft from the showgrounds and were swept out and lost over Lake Michigan.

That month the show incorporated as "The Barnum Universal Exposition Company" with outside stockholders, including John V. "Pogey" O'BRIEN. By the end of the 1875 season, with receipts stretched among the Hippodrome show, the touring circus and a third unit owned by O'Brien, the company's revenue was overextended and the corporation officially and amicably dissolved.

P.T. BARNUM'S GREATEST SHOW ON EARTH, HOWES' GREAT LONDON CIRCUS AND SANGER'S ROYAL BRITISH MENAGERIE

When P.T. BARNUM purportedly approached James A. BAILEY, James E. COOPER and James L. HUTCHINSON—co-owners of the International Allied Shows—about selling Columbia, the first baby elephant born in captivity in the United

States, the offer was refused. It did, however, start the men talking; when Cooper dropped from the partnership, Barnum suggested the other two join him in a new venture.

Using all of the circus titles they owned, the merger was known as P.T. Barnum's Greatest Show on Earth, Howes' Great London Circus and Sanger's Royal British Menagerie, or the BARNUM & LONDON CIRCUS for short. Barnum consolidated the two shows at a new single WINTER QUARTERS in BRIDGEPORT, CONNECTICUT.

To celebrate the new confabulation, a huge spectacle featuring 350 HORSES, 20 ELEPHANTS, 14 CAMELS, four brass bands and 300 performers paraded down the streets of New York City on March 16, 1881. When the show moved into MADISON SQUARE GARDEN, it featured an innovation that became a staple of American entertainment: the three-ring circus.

Indeed, Barnum never claimed to have invented the three-ring circus. The British showman George Sanger had experimented with the format as early as 1860. But it was the popularity of the Barnum & London Circus that allowed it to spread throughout the American circus.

The Barnum & London Circus continued the COOPER & BAILEY CIRCUS improvement of using arc (or electric) illumination instead of gas lighting. The SIDESHOW section of the show included the original FEEJEE MERMAID, General TOM THUMB and his wife, Lavinia WARREN.

After the Garden spot, the show moved onto rails. Although their tour was successful, their greatest competition came from the ADAM FOREPAUGH CIRCUS. The Barnum & London owners signed a secret agreement with Adam FOREPAUGH not to DAY AND DATE for the 1882 and 1883 seasons; but the following year, the cutthroat rivalry, complete with RAT SHEETS and all sorts of OPPOSITION PAPER, broke out anew.

On February 2, 1882 one of the Barnum & London show's elephants, "Queen," gave birth to a baby (the second born in captivity in the United States), which Barnum proudly named "Bridgeport."

On Easter Sunday, 1882, Barnum brought the mighty JUMBO to the Barnum & London Circus. Jumbo continued to tour on and off with the circus until his death. After that his mounted hide was carried in the show's MENAGERIE.

Another famous elephant Toung Taloung, a "sacred white elephant," was toured on the circus during this period.

In 1885 Bailey retired from the corporation due to ill health. On November 20 a devastating fire all but leveled the Bridgeport quarters, killing all of the menagerie except a single lion and most of the elephants, including Toung Taloung.

The quarters and show were immediately rebuilt, however, and Bailey was succeeded by W.W. "Chilly Billy" COLE and James E. Cooper as the new partners of Hutchinson and Barnum. With profits having to be split among four owners, Barnum realized belatedly that this meant he was no longer a controlling partner. The show traveled for two more seasons, though not as successfully as during Bailey's tenure; the Barnum & London Circus was dissolved after the 1887 season.

When James A. Bailey—in restored health—formed the Barnum & Bailey Circus with P.T. Barnum in 1887, it was as a sole equal partner.

PUBLICITY   Circus publicity claims have always been prone to exaggeration and overstatement. Nothing is "ordinary" or "mere" about a circus performance. Consider a Ringling Brothers Circus program description of their SPEC: "a mighty moving panoramic display of opulence, grandeur, magnificence and splendor, presented by the new invincible monarch of the circus world."

It was the duty of the PRESS AGENT to ensure that the local media—newspapers, radio and television—not only got the message the circus was selling but also to accept it as fact. This was not always easy, as in the case of the FRANK A. ROBBINS CIRCUS, which promised "the most marvelous, magnificent and interesting consolidation of attractions the world has ever seen." A 1889 review by the Hays City, Kansas *Sentinel* of that same show reported, "If anything was presented as advertised the audience failed to recognize it. The best way to dismiss the subject is to say that the whole business was a fraud."

While circus advertising has always been given to hyperbole, often the performances more than live up to the show's exuberant publicity. After all, few areas of show business have such flamboyant, unusual and often unique acts and performers to present to the press. Circuses will always take advantage of the fact that they have the "Biggest," the "Best" and the "Greatest" to entertain their audiences.

(See also ADVANCE MAN.)

PUGH, JOHN W. "JOHNNY" (1938–   )   Long associated with the CLYDE BEATTY-COLE BROS. CIRCUS, Johnny Pugh has been the show's owner and manager since 1982.

The son of "Digger" Pugh, a British variety show and theatrical producer, Johnny Pugh has been in and around show business his entire life. He got his first stage contract when he was less than one year old.

He moved to the United States in 1942 to appear with the COLE BROS. CIRCUS, but he returned to England to be with his family during World War II. When he returned to the Cole show in 1948, he was part of a CENTER RING trampoline act with Otto GRIEBLING.

A three-year run with the MILLS BROS. CIRCUS followed, and then he returned to England once more to work in television and film. Although he wound up on the cutting-room floor, he was Richard Burton's double during the filming of *Cleopatra* and also worked the BULLS during the shoot. His stage work included an appearance on the Palladium with comedian Benny Hill.

He returned to the United States in 1961, joining up with the Beatty-Cole show, and he has been WITH IT ever since. In 1964 he broke his leg while working the trampoline act, so he moved to the front office. By 1966 he was manager under a triumvirate of owners, and he continued to learn every aspect of the circus.

In 1982 he had the opportunity to purchase the show himself. Although the circus was heavily in debt, Pugh jumped at the chance to make the show successful on his own. The following year he invited E. Douglas Holwadel to become a co-owner. With Pugh's knowledge of circus and Holwadel's Wall Street expertise, the operation was scaled down and made into an efficient, solvent modern tent show.

PUGH, PAUL   See WENATCHEE YOUTH CIRCUS.

PUNK   In circus jargon, the term "punk" has a variety of unrelated meanings. Usually it refers to a child or an very immature young person. However, the term can also mean a young animal. Others have used the word to mean bread or as slang for a sexual pervert.

PUNK PUSHER   See KID WORKER; PUNK.

PUSH POLE   Circus jargon for one method of raising a circus tent. In a push pole tent, the canvas is spread out and, if multisectioned, laced. Next, the canvas is tied down to the STAKES, and the SIDEPOLES are raised. Finally, the CENTER POLE is slid under the canvas. If electrical or other rigging is required, it is attached to the top of the center pole under the canvas at this time. The tip of the pole is slipped through a large hole in the middle of the canvas, and a flag is attached to the top of the pole from the topside of the canvas. Finally, the ROUSTABOUTS—often with the help of local town boys (or, on larger TENTS, the ELEPHANTS)—literally push the pole forward and up, vertically into position.

Even a tent with more than one center pole can be a push pole top. A push pole tent is usually easier and quicker to tear down than a BALE RING tent, but the extreme canvas weight and size of some mammoth tents require the latter design.

Q

QUADRUPLE SOMERSAULT After the TRIPLE SOMERSAULT was perfected in the early part of this century, many circus folk considered the quadruple to be the "impossible quest." On July 10, 1982, however, the feat was first attained in performance by Miguel VAZQUEZ of the FLYING VAZQUEZ during the evening show of the RINGLING BROS. AND BARNUM & BAILEY CIRCUS in Tucson, Arizona.

Miguel Vazquez actually achieved his first quad (authenticated by videotape) around 11 P.M. on August 19, 1981 during a postperformance rehearsal while appearing in the Ringling show at the Long Beach Arena in Long Beach, California. He often repeated his first quad in rehearsal before finally accomplishing it in performance the following summer.

In his autobiography *Born to Fly,* Tito GAONA claims to have thrown his first quadruple somersault—caught by his older brother Armando—during a rehearsal at 11:10 P.M. on January 24, 1981 in Tunja, Colombia. Although there were reportedly witnesses among the cast and crew at the circus where they were performing, no formal verification or videotape exists to substantiate his success.

The quadruple somersault has been performed by other aerialists since Miguel Vazquez, but the Vazquez Troupe remains the only group of FLYERS regularly appearing in the United States to make it a standard feature of their act. The FLYING CRANES with the MOSCOW CIRCUS are the only flyers who perform the quadruple without ever announcing the feat.

QUARTER POLE Smaller TENTS just require SIDE-POLES (which hold up the sides of the canvas) and CENTER POLES (which hold up the top). Tents over 110 feet wide, however, require more support due to the weight of the canvas. One or two rows of quarter poles are placed midway between the center and side poles and help hold the top as well as take up slack in the canvas. On still larger tents, a second row of quarter poles is sometimes added. The invention of the quarter pole is generally credited to "Dr." Gilbert R. SPALDING and they were probably introduced in 1848.

QUARTER SHEET Circus jargon for a particular standard size of circus HERALD or LITHOGRAPH. Rectangular in shape and measuring ten inches wide by 28 inches long, the quarter sheet was the most popular size for a herald between 1810 and 1820.

(See also ONE SHEET.)

QUEEN See ROGUE ELEPHANTS.

R

RAILROAD   See CIRCUS TRAIN.

RAISING THE BLUES   See BLUES.

RAT SHEET   Circus jargon for an advance HERALD, LITHOGRAPH or handbill that contains negative comments about a competing circus.

One of the most famous exchanges of rat sheets occurred in 1884 between P.T. BARNUM and Adam FOREPAUGH. Competing for the same TERRITORY, the two circus giants were not content to plaster every available wall with colorful posters touting their own shows. Barnum issued a rat sheet that showed his head on an ox, trying to warn Forepaugh—whose head was shown on a frog—not to try to blow himself up to Barnum's size or he would "go bust." Forepaugh responded with a rat sheet in which he showed himself towering above Barnum and his partners.

In the WHITE ELEPHANT war with Barnum, Forepaugh sent out a rat sheet that claimed his own pachyderm, the "Light of Asia," was "Too White for Barnum" and "Proved by the Highest Scientific Authority to be Genuine and Barnum's 'Sacred White' Elephant and All Its Surroundings a Rank Fraud."

RAZORBACKS   Circus jargon for the labor crew that loads and unloads the railway cars.

Two stories circulate regarding the origin of the term. The first involves the way in which the men loaded the short, slim cages that were used on many circuses. The CAGE WAGONS were end-loaded and pulled along the length of the train as usual; however, once they were in position, they could be lifted by four men and turned, in effect, sideways. Because of their narrow width, each wagon turned this way would give an extra three or four feet of loading space per flatcar.

When the wagon was to be turned, one man would get under each of the four corners. On a verbal command from a lead man, they would lift the tiny wagon up onto their backs, swing it sideways and drop it back onto the flatcar. The traditional phrase used as a signal to lift was "Raise 'er back, let 'er go."

Another possible explanation is that once the wagons were all roped in place, their silhouette resembled an Arkansas razorback hog.

READ THE LOT   Circus jargon for checking the LOT for STAKES, rigging or other apparatus that may have been left behind after the show has been torn down and packed away. This prevents the loss of equipment, and ensures that the show leaves the grounds as clean as possible to keep the sponsors and local authorities happy.

REBO THE CLOWN   See CLOWNS, TELEVISION.

RED-LIGHTING   Circus jargon—left over from the days when shows traveled by rail—referring to the unsavory practice of literally tossing an unwanted member of the show off the back end of the circus train while it was in motion. The ejected showman, looking up from the tracks, would see nothing in the dark but the red lights of the caboose fading off into the darkness. Those who were "let go" in this unethical and dangerous way were always injured, if not killed.

Circus personnel and managers defended the practice (or looked aside), claiming it was the only way to "fire" or to permanently get rid of true undesirables, often drifters who had signed on as ROUSTABOUTS. They claimed the men would otherwise linger, never leave the grounds, follow the show from town to town and eventually cause trouble.

Red-lighting was not reserved solely for the vagrant types, however. Charles T. Tinney, a bandleader on many shows in the early 1900s, would "dismiss" band members in this manner for even the smallest infraction. Many times red-lighting was the result of arguments among the cast and crew, when one member wanted another to leave the show or to be killed "accidentally".

One of the most famous incidents of red-lighting involved Fred Buchanan following the close of his ROBBINS BROS. CIRCUS on September 12, 1931. The roustabouts were each given $1 and told that there was no more pay coming. Those who objected were thrown off the back of the circus train about 14 miles from Mobile, Alabama as the train was traveling on the Mobile & Ohio Railroad line enroute to WINTER QUARTERS in Lancaster, Missouri. Several workers were seriously hurt and one died in the Mobile City Hospital on October 17 as a result of his injuries. Buchanan, the owner of the circus, was indicted for the death; but the case was never brought to trial.

RED UNIT, THE   See FELD, IRVIN; RINGLING BROS. AND BARNUM & BAILEY CIRCUS.

RED WAGON   Circus jargon for the ticket wagon or box office, sometimes also called the "money wagon." Usually placed at the front end or beginning of the MIDWAY, the box office is often painted red so that it is easy for circusgoers to locate.

RICE, DAN (1823–1900)   The first great CLOWN in the United States, Dan Rice was born Daniel McLaren, Jr. in New York City on January 23, 1823. His father was a law student who became a grocer;

his mother Elizabeth Crum was the daughter of a Methodist minister. The couple had eloped because the bride's parents disapproved of the union. Following the newlyweds' return from a honeymoon, the parents sought and obtained an annulment of the marriage. Only then did Elizabeth discover she was carrying a child, whom she later named after the father.

When Daniel was two years old, his mother married Hugh Manahan, a dairyman who had a great love of horses. This affection was passed along to Daniel who, being a small boy, became a jockey at the age of ten, riding as Dan Rice. Until he was 17—when he became too heavy to ride—Dan Rice remained a jockey, but in 1840 he moved to Pittsburgh to work at a livery stable. The origin of Rice's professional or stage name is uncertain. One source suggests that Manahan recommended he take the name Dan Rice after an Irish clown. Another states it was the name of his maternal grandfather. According to a third, the boy adopted the surname because he liked rice pudding.

Rice's first contact with the circus may have been the NICHOLS CIRCUS. When the show performed near the stables, Rice picked up several equestrian tricks as well as the ability to juggle cannonballs, gaining him the nickname of "Young Hercules." Not long thereafter, Rice earned another name, "Yankee Dan," when he entertained Senator Henry Clay with his dancing and a song he had composed, "Hard Times."

In 1843 an itinerant puppet show paid Rice $4 a week to exhibit his educated pig, LORD BYRON; but Rice didn't give his first true circus performance until 1844. When the Nicols Circus returned to town it had a new owner, "Dr." Gilbert R. SPALDING, and a new name, Spalding's North American Circus. The manager easily convinced Rice to join his show where, in addition to his skits with Lord Byron, Dan Rice acted as a clown and a strong man.

Feeling underappreciated, Dan Rice left Spalding in 1845 to briefly join the Philadelphia winter run of the Nathan A. Howes Circus as a strongman, catching cannonballs on the back of his neck. This was followed by a stint with the Rufus Welch Company. In May 1848 Rice organized his own DAN RICE CIRCUS. Probably financed by Spalding, Rice's show traveled for a time on the *Allegheny Mail* steamboat.

Combination red wagon and air calliope on the Campa Bros. Circus in 1951. (John Heckman photo from the Bakner collection)

Billing himself as "America's Favorite Clown," Rice became known as "the modern Shakespeare jester." He would answer questions with quotes from the Bard; and, later, he would retell *Romeo and Juliet* in backwoods venacular as part of his act. Another regular part of his routine was exchanging jokes and barbs with the RINGMASTER.

By this time, Rice was dressed in quite an eccentric manner, a stars-and-stripes costume, with blue leotards and red-and-white trunks, a top hat and the ever-present gray chin beard. His famous look was immortalized when Thomas Nast caricatured it for *Harper's Weekly* as "Uncle Sam."

Among his friends and admirers in those pre-Civil War days were Abraham Lincoln, Jefferson Davis and Robert E. Lee. So many of his political associates came to his benefit performance in Washington, D.C. in 1850 that Congress adjourned for the day.

Later that year a bout with yellow fever forced Rice to cancel his tour. While recuperating in a New Orleans hospital, he met presidential aspirant General Zachary Taylor. Once Rice was back on the road, he became an active supporter of Taylor, beginning each performance with a campaign speech. Once Taylor was elected, he thanked Rice by giving the honorary title of "Colonel."

Over the next few years, boosted by a renewed popularity from the presidential attention, Rice enjoyed a series of short-term mergers with a number of circus owners, including his old boss, Dr. Spalding. This time the parting with Spalding was not as congenial, and in 1850 Rice was jailed for slander. While in prison, Rice composed "Blue Eagle Jail," a song that became a much-requested part of his act after he was released.

Undaunted by his brief stay behind bars, Rice quickly reentered the circus world with DAN RICE'S

The Famous Circus Bartok ticket wagon in Mont Alto, Pennsylvania in 1970.   (Photo courtesy of Andy Bakner)

ONE-HORSE SHOW, featuring his steed Aroostook, then later his famous horse EXCELSIOR. During this period Rice—a generous if egomaniacal maestro—often gave special matinee performances for charity groups and orphanages.

Even as Dan Rice's fortunes were peaking in the late 1850s and early 1860s, he was attracting critics due to his pointed political songs and his outspoken opinions. As the Civil War progressed, Rice was forced to play only indoors in the larger cities; President Lincoln himself is reported to have visited the show when it played the capital. At this point in his career, Rice was, in fact, earning a higher salary than the president. Nevertheless, circus attendance was down: Audiences had more on their minds than simple entertainment.

Also, because of Rice's friendship in the South with Jefferson Davis and Robert E. Lee, some Northern towns accused him of siding with the Confederacy, and near riots erupted during the

1861 and 1862 tours of the Dan Rice Circus. Regardless of the reasons, Rice soon went bankrupt. He was divorced, but remarried within two years.

In 1862 Spalding reappeared, offering Rice the astronomical salary of $1,000 a week to go into partnership with him. Rice refused, preferring to work on his own. Following the Civil War, Rice had bounced back enough to offer his second wife's hometown $35,000 to build a monument to its fallen soldiers. Unfortunately, he soon entered a disastrous association with Adam FOREPAUGH and was again ruined financially.

In 1866 Rice's old interest in politics resurfaced. Two years later (the same year P.T. BARNUM temporarily left the entertainment world for a life in politics), Rice was nominated by a Pennsylvania soldier's delegation as a candidate for Congress and the presidency. Campaign posters read "Rice for Pudding and President." Unlike Barnum, however, Rice lost his bid for the legislature. Some citizens must have assumed it would be unseemly to have an actor/entertainer in the White House. It was also during the mid-1860s period that Rice, depending on his financial circumstances, would operate his own show, star in another circus or lease out his show's title and appear as the featured performer. Adam Forepaugh, for example, owned and managed the Dan Rice Circus during the 1865 and 1866 seasons.

In 1868 Dr. Spalding sold Rice the PARIS PAVILION. For one year Rice toured his circus in the wooden amphitheater, which was carried to towns along the Mississippi River by steamboat. During the following winter, Rice appeared in Rice's Amphitheatre—located on Charles Street in New Orleans—which had been built for him by his friends and admirers.

Large audiences never materialized for the show. Rice, a broken man, soon lost the Pavilion and turned to drink. Potential partners disappeared, and Rice was never again to own or operate a circus.

At the end of his life, through great self-control, Rice overcame alcoholism and turned to the lectern as a temperance speaker. Dan Rice, the premier clown of his generation, officially retired from the ring in 1887 and died just three years later, on February 22, of Bright's disease in Long Branch, New Jersey. The *New York Times* gave the once-famous clown only a two-paragraph obituary.

The popular Rice name continued on, however, and it appeared on unauthorized shows for over 50 more years: There was a Dan Rice Circus in 1901; the Rice Bros. Circus, 1909–14; various "Rice" shows in 1923, 1934–37 and 1945; and a Dan Rice Circus carnival unit as late as 1954 and 1955.

(See also PETE JENKINS ACT.)

RICKETTS, JOHN BILL (c. 1760–1800)

Acknowledged as the presenter of the first complete American circus, John Bill Ricketts was a Scottish equestrian who moved to the United States in 1793 after serving an apprenticeship at the London riding school of Charles Hughes. Although roving bands of entertainers and exotic animal exhibitions had previously appeared in the colonies, it was Ricketts who established the first true circus, which opened most probably in Philadelphia on April 3, 1793.

Located at the equestrian's riding school at Twelfth and Market streets in Philadelphia, the show offered Ricketts's dangerous feat of leaping from his horse,

CORNPLANTER, "over a riband [sic] suspended 12 feet high and at the same time through a cane held in both hands with the horse in full gallop," landing back on the saddle. In fact, Cornplanter was trained to leap over the back of another horse. Ricketts's trademark was assuming the pose of the Roman messenger god Mercury on bareback, sometimes with another performer on his shoulders. The show also included rope walkers, tumblers, pantomime and dramatic recitations and Tom SULLY, a British CLOWN. Later the show would feature John Durang, thought to be the first native American clown. Ricketts is recognized as the first circus owner in the United States largely because he added variety acts to his equestrian exhibition, built amphitheaters expressly for his shows, advertised them specifically as circuses and kept the company together as a recognizable troupe when it traveled to New York.

On April 22 and 24 of that first year, the performances were attended by President George and Mrs. Martha Washington, who shared Ricketts's love of horsemanship. Word of Washington's visits to the show assured its success; soon Ricketts was able to take his circus to New York, first performing there on August 7, 1793 and moving to a larger venue on Broadway on November 19, 1794. He moved on to Boston and Hartford in 1795, then Charleston, finally opening a permanent amphitheater on Greenwich Street in New York on March 16, 1797. On October 21 President John Adams visited the circus there.

Ricketts returned to Philadelphia, replacing his original open-air arena with Ricketts's NEW AMPHITHEATER (also seen as the Pantheon), an enclosed building with artificial lighting and a figure of Mercury on the roof. The amphitheater, located at Sixth and Chesnut streets, had a stage as well as an arena and could seat 1,200 people.

The show's format was that of a traditional circus, followed by stage presentations and pantomimes. Although there was no additional charge for patrons to stay for the stage pieces, their incorporation into the circus also made Ricketts the first circus manager to utilize an aftershow or CONCERT. By changing the postcircus theatrical plays, Ricketts gained repeat business.

On January 24, 1797 Washington visited Ricketts's circus again. Two days later Washington sold the showman Jack, the horse the general had ridden during the Revolutionary War, for $150. Despite the horse's advanced age, its publicity value made it more than worth its selling price.

Tragedy soon struck both of Ricketts's amphitheaters: First, the New York arena burned to the ground in 1799; on December 17 that year his Philadelphia academy also burned down. Ricketts opened a new season on April 3, 1800, but the rent for the building was too high. He took part of his crew and set sail for the West Indies. When part of his company became ill, Ricketts sold his HORSES and set sail for England. The ship was lost at sea.

RICKETTS CIRCUS   See CORNPLANTER; NEW AMPHITHEATER; RICKETTS, JOHN BILL; SULLY, TOM.

RIG   Circus jargon for putting up the aerial apparatus and the GUY wires and ropes that support it. The apparatus itself, including the guys, is known as the "rigging". The work crew members who put the paraphernalia into place are the RIGGERS.

(See also TENTS.)

RIGGERS   Circus jargon for the men who set, or RIG, the wires, nets and mechanical apparatus for the aerial acts. Their work is more specified and skilled than that of the ROUSTABOUTS, who are considered to be more GENERALLY USEFUL laborers.

(See also TENTS.)

RIGGING   See RIG; RIGGERS.

RING BANK   On the first American circuses in the 18th century, the performing area was separated from the audience and defined by a large circular ridge of dirt known as a ring bank.

Skilled ring makers were part of the regular circus troupe. At each location, they would level the ground, then build up a bank of dirt to form a circular ring 42 feet in diameter.

According to circus legend, the ring bank was sometimes used as quick, effective and undetectable burial spots for the TOWNERS who "disappeared" after fights with the ROUSTABOUTS or for the victims of feuds among the circus crew. This may be the reason that circus superstition warns people against sleeping overnight under a raised BIG TOP: The Roustabout might be approached in the dark by a

spirit, or he might be in danger of becoming a ghost himself if he has a few enemies on the show.

As circuses began to forgo long stands and travel more frequently, building a new ring bank in each town became impractical. This gave way to the use of ropes or canvas to mark out the ring and, eventually, to the evolution of the RING CURB.

RING BARN   Circus jargon for a building in WINTER QUARTERS that contains a regulation-size RING CURB for rehearsals and training sessions.

RING BROS. CIRCUS   Owned by Franco Richards in the 1950s, the Ring Bros. Circus mostly played small towns in the East and the South.

RING CURB   On the first circuses, a raised circle of earth known as the RING BANK designated the performance area. As the shows began to travel more frequently, constructing a ring bank increasingly became too time-consuming for the BIG TOP crew.

The ring curb was a logical invention by the early equestrian-laden circuses. The banking enforces a strict circle for the horse to gallop within as the rider performs feats on bareback.

The first portable ring curb was probably made of rope—or possibly canvas—sections. The demarcation evolved into today's traditional ring curb, a wooden circle approximately 18 inches high and 12 inches wide encompassing the 42-foot-diameter performing area. The curb is built into curved sections approximately five feet long for easier transportation. Also, sections of the curb can be left out, allowing an entrance and exit for performers and low-stepping animal artists.

The area within the ring curb is usually sprinkled with sawdust for animal acts. The ground may be covered with mats for acrobats; a wooden flooring for a unicycle or a ROLLING GLOBE might be used if the ground is not level or is pitted with holes.

Today some ring curbs are padded, made of lightweight wood or have electrical lights set within them. There are even inflatable curbs, such as those manufactured by Chester Cable, that are portable and practical for indoor shows or for any shows where the acts do not have to stand on the curb.

(See also RING CURB MEETING.)

RING CURB MEETING   As in any organization, sometimes it is necessary to get a consensus opinion of the company, to air grievances or just to distribute information efficiently. On smaller MUD SHOWS, one of the easiest methods of doing this is to call the troupe to the CENTER RING for a ring curb meeting, sometimes simply referred to as a "ring curb" (named after the wooden circle encompassing the performing area). The term is still used even if the cast is too large and must meet in a section of the stands rather than sitting on, or gathering around, the actual RING CURB.

RING HORSE   Circus jargon for a HORSE that has been trained to perform in a ring rather than in an open arena.

(See also RING STOCK.)

RING OF FAME   See SARASOTA CIRCUS RING OF FAME.

RING STOCK   Circus jargon for all of the circus animals that perform or appear in the main show, including HORSES, ponies, CATS, dogs and ELEPHANTS.

(See also RING HORSE.)

RINGLING, AL   See RINGLING BROTHERS, THE; RINGLING BROS. AND BARNUM & BAILEY CIRCUS.

RINGLING, ALF T.   See RINGLING BROTHERS, THE; RINGLING BROS. AND BARNUM & BAILEY CIRCUS.

RINGLING, CHARLES   See RINGLING BROTHERS, THE; RINGLING BROS. AND BARNUM & BAILEY CIRCUS.

RINGLING, GUS   See RINGLING BROTHERS, THE; RINGLING BROS. AND BARNUM & BAILEY CIRCUS.

RINGLING, HENRY   See RINGLING BROTHERS, THE; RINGLING BROS. AND BARNUM & BAILEY CIRCUS.

RINGLING, IDA   See RINGLING BROTHERS, THE, RINGLING BROS. AND BARNUM & BAILEY CIRCUS.

RINGLING, JOHN (1866–1936)   One of seven sons of August and Marie Salome Rüngleling, John was one of the youngest siblings to play a part in the creation of the greatest dynasty in American circusdom, the RINGLING BROTHERS. He was born Johann Ringling on May 30, 1866 in McGregor, Iowa.

Although his older brothers, Al, Alf T. and Otto, took a more active role in the early years of their various circuses, John was involved from their first variety shows in BARABOO, WISCONSIN in 1882 and 1883. He was the last living brother of the original five founding brothers to be involved with the circus.

As he matured, John became more active in management. It was he who negotiated the purchase of the BARNUM & BAILEY CIRCUS in 1907. Traveling the world to discover the best circus talent, John was responsible for bringing most of the early stars associated with the Ringling circus to the United States. For example, it was John who visited the Wirth Brothers Circus in Australia in 1912 and saw 16-year-old May WIRTH, equestrienne, who went on to star in the Ringling show.

By 1919 John and Charles were the only surviving Ringling brothers. Charles stayed actively involved and traveled with the show, but John was really the driving managerial force. That year John made the decision to combine the Ringling Brothers Circus and the Barnum and Bailey Circus and consolidate their WINTER QUARTERS in BRIDGEPORT, CONNECTICUT.

Charles became increasingly critical of his "big brother" for his reckless spending. There may have been a touch of envy there, as John had become a prosperous speculator in oil, railroads and Florida land, amassing a fortune of $100 million by 1925.

One of the 20 richest men in the world at the time, John built a dream estate on Sarasota Bay in SARASOTA, FLORIDA, which he called CA' D'ZAN (House of John). With Charles's death in 1926, "Mr. John"— as he was known on the LOT—was in total control of the circus. The next year he moved the circus headquarters from Bridgeport to Sarasota.

During a dispute with MADISON SQUARE GARDEN over Friday night performances (the Garden wanted to reserve them for prize-fighting), Ringling lost the lease option to his greatest competition, the AMERICAN CIRCUS CORPORATION. On September 6, 1929, in prideful retaliation, John purchased the circus syndicate for $2 million. As a result of the Stock Market Crash a month later, Ringling became overextended financially and defaulted on his payments for the American Circus Corporation.

In 1932, Sam W. GUMPERTZ was made general manager under the new owners, the ALLIED OWNERS, INC., but John remained nominal president. That same year, Ringling suffered a blood clot; and at about the same time, divorce proceedings (from second wife Emily) and tax litigations were begun against him. In an argument during the 1936 Garden opening, Gumpertz ordered Ringling off the lot, telling John he no longer belonged with the show.

The last Ringling brother died in his Park Avenue home in New York City of bronchial pneumonia at 3 A.M. on December 2, 1936, but due to a bizarre set of circumstances he was not finally laid to rest until 1990. John Ringling had said that he wanted to be buried on the grounds of his Sarasota estate and had built a large cryptlike facility for that purpose. He never completed the building, perhaps because of its expense. After his death, his body was placed in a temporary vault in New Jersey next to that of his first wife, Mable (née Burton, 1875–1929).

In 1958 John Ringling North (Ringling's nephew) had them buried in a cemetery close to their New Jersey summer home while he began legal attempts to accede to what he believed were his uncle's wishes. He tried to take their remains back to Florida, but both Ringling relatives and the state of Florida—which by then owned the JOHN AND MABLE RINGLING MUSEUM OF ART—refused to allow burial on the property. The problem was further exacerbated by North's desire also to bury his mother, John's sister Ida, near Ca' d'Zan.

When John Ringling North died in 1987, his brother Henry became legal next of kin. Without consulting other relatives, he had John and Mable Ringling's bodies secretly disinterred from their New Jersey vault and transferred to Florida, where they were stored in an unmarked crypt at Restlawn Memorial Gardens in Port Charlotte. Ida's remains, meanwhile, were still in a Sarasota funeral home, where they had been stored since 1950.

After years of legal battles, the museum finally granted permission in 1990 to Henry Ringling North (who currently lives in Switzerland) to entomb John, Mable and Ida Ringling on the grounds of Ca' d'Zan. They were buried on June 4, 1991 in a small grassy area enclosed by a black chain-link fence just north of Ca' d'Zan. The gravesites will be marked with small broze plaques on tilted marble bases, with all expenses for the memorial to be paid by North. No signs or walkways direct tourists to the 50 by 70 foot site lying north of a spot Mable Ringling had always referred to as her "secret garden."

RINGLING, OTTO See RINGLING BROTHERS, THE; RINGLING BROS. AND BARNUM & BAILEY CIRCUS.

RINGLING BROS. AND BARNUM & BAILEY CIRCUS

The story of the Ringling Bros. and Barnum & Bailey Circus is really that of the 20th-century, American circus. The circus has moved from wagon, to rail, to truck and back to rail. It has appeared under canvas, in the open air and in arenas. While celebrating its triumphant seasons, the show has weathered its share of disasters, including train wrecks, fires and union strikes. Almost every major circus artist and personality passed through the ranks of at least one of the Ringling-owned shows during his or her career. The many circuses that the Ringling Bros. and Barnum & Bailey Combined Shows owns or claims title to include Ringling Bros. and Barnum & Bailey Circus; Barnum & Bailey Greatest Show on Earth; Ringling Bros. World's Greatest Shows; SELLS-FLOTO CIRCUS; SPARKS CIRCUS; JOHN ROBINSON CIRCUS; AL G. BARNES CIRCUS; BUFFALO BILL'S WILD WEST, ADAM FOREPAUGH CIRCUS, ADAM FOREPAUGH & SELLS BROS. CIRCUS; and SELLS BROS. CIRCUS.

The Ringling Bros. and Barnum & Bailey Circus has its roots in the two largest tent shows of the turn of the century. The Ringling Bros. Circus grew out of variety shows and small circuses (including the Yankee Robinson and Ringling Brothers Great Double Shows, Circus and Caravan) owned and operated by the RINGLING BROTHERS out of BARABOO, WISCONSIN in the 1880s. Meanwhile, the BARNUM & BAILEY CIRCUS was started by veteran showmen P.T. BARNUM and James A. BAILEY in 1888.

In 1905 the Ringlings bought a half interest in the Forepaugh-Sells Circus from Bailey. When Bailey died the following year, John RINGLING negotiated the purchase of the Barnum & Bailey Circus. The history-making deal was concluded on October 22, 1907.

The Ringling Bros. Circus and the Barnum & Bailey Circus toured separately for 13 years. In 1919 John decided to combine the two shows into one to form the Ringling Bros. and Barnum & Bailey Circus. The WINTER QUARTERS were also merged at the Barnum & Bailey headquarters in BRIDGEPORT, CONNECTICUT.

When Charles Ringling died in 1926, John was left in complete control of the circus. The following year he moved the show from Bridgeport to SARA-

SOTA, FLORIDA. Meanwhile, he traveled around the world to scout for new talent.

Many circus people refer to this period as the golden era of the American circus. Ringling accepted only the best performers in his show. Lillian LEITZEL was among the great aerialists on the circus, and May WIRTH and the HANNEFORDS were among the top equestrians who were on the circus in the 1920s.

In 1929 John Ringling purchased the AMERICAN CIRCUS CORPORATION, giving him title to all of the major rail shows in the United States at the time. Following the Stock Market Crash, he defaulted on payments; and, in 1932, the ALLIED OWNERS, INC. gained management control of the show. On December 2, 1936 the last of the five founding Ringling brothers died.

John Ringling's long and complicated will, drawn up on May 9, 1934, included the following provisions: (1) His estranged wife, Emily, was to receive the sum of $1. (2) CA' D'ZAN and the art museum and grounds of the Ringling estate were to be turned over to the state of Florida, along with half of the remainder of the estate to be set up as a trust for its management. (3) The remaining half of the estate was to go to Ida, his sister. (4) Executors of the estate were to be Ida Ringling North and John Ringling NORTH. (5) Trustees for the estate were to be John and Henry Ringling North, along with their brother-in-law, H.L. Wadsworth.

Because the North family had disapproved of John Ringling's choice of lawyers in trying to gain back the circus from the Allied Owners, Ringling had made a codicil in 1935 that left Ida with only an annual $5,000 stipend and nothing for her two sons, John and Henry.

Control of the Ringling stock was divided among Edith Conway Ringling (Charles's widow), 30%; Aubrey Ringling Haley (widow of Alf T.'s son Richard), 30%; the John Ringling Estate (John Ringling North, voting executor), 30%; treasury stock, 10%. Since Ringling had forgotten to change executors or trustees in his codicil, the stage was set for the fight over control of the circus and the $22,366,000 Ringling fortune.

With a loan from Manufacturers Trust, John Ringling North managed to refinance the circus—purchasing the outstanding notes of Allied Owners, Inc.—and regained ownership for the Ringling clan in 1938. He was elected as president and managing director of the Ringling Bros. and Barnum & Bailey Circus for a five-year term.

Ironically, 1938 was the worst year economically in the history of the American circus, with only one rail show (the Ringling-owned Al G. Barnes-Sells Floto Circus) making it through the entire season. Even the Ringling show had to CLOSE AHEAD OF PAPER, folding in Scranton, Pennsylvania on June 22, 1938 due to bad business and union troubles.

In 1932 Samuel W. GUMPERTZ, then executive vice president and general manager, had signed a five-year contract for the workingmen, or ROUSTABOUTS, with the American Federation of Actors, which was associated with the American Federation of Labor. According to the agreement, the minimum-wage pay scale for winter quarters was to be carried through the MADISON SQUARE GARDEN and Boston dates, doubling when the show went under canvas.

When the show moved to New York in 1938, the union demanded North honor Gumpertz's earlier contract and immediately place the promised higher wage in effect. North refused. All of the workers except the executive staff, performers and sideshow personnel went on strike. Staff and volunteers attempted to fill in, even managing to get GARGAN-TUA—making his debut with the show—onto the track for the opening SPEC. Also among the many difficulties for the inexperienced, temporary labor was North's decision to reverse John Ringling's 1926 ban on wild animal acts in the show.

The labor troubles were resolved on April 30 when the Garden date ended. The Boston date, May 2–7, also went on without incident; but pickets went up again for the five Brooklyn dates beginning on May 9 and for the following two days in Washington, D.C. Problems escalated in Baltimore, Philadelphia, Newark, Trenton and Wilmington.

Besides the continual labor disputes, the bad economy was also causing bad houses; following small crowds in Reading, Harrisburg and Pittsburgh, the Cleveland date was canceled. The show dragged through Wheeling, Columbus, Dayton, Lima, Sandusky and one-night stands in Fort Wayne, Toledo and Erie. By the time the show reached Scranton, John Ringling North claimed it was losing $40,000 a day.

At matinee time, workers went on strike. Shows were canceled for two days and nights as the circus sat on the Scranton lot, often without food or water being delivered to the showgrounds. Finally, North ordered the show home; nonstriking workers managed to load the circus train for Sarasota.

With Henry Ringling North in charge, many of the top acts and equipment were moved from The BIG ONE over to the Al G. Barnes-Sells Floto Circus, also owned by Ringling and at that time playing without difficulties in the Midwest. They joined the show in Redfield, South Dakota on July 11, 1938.

The new advertising read "Al G. Barnes and Sells-Floto Circus, presenting Ringling Bros. and Barnum & Bailey Stupendous New Features." Those "features" included Mabel STARK, "the Queen of the Jungle, presenting a notable congress of the earth's most ferocious performing lions and tigers," several flying acts, Roman chariot races and Gargantua the Great.

The tour, ending on November 27, was the last for the Al G. Barnes and Sells-Floto Circus; but its revenue probably allowed the Ringling corporation to continue. John Ringling North reported a profit of $400,000 for the 1938 season.

The next season's opening canvas date sported a new, oval BIG TOP that featured four—rather than the usual six—CENTER POLES. The tent was deep blue at the top, shading to a light blue at the bottom. The center poles were painted gold and the QUARTER POLES were silver. Gold stars decorated the ring carpets and the poles. Giant fans were placed by the entrance flaps to circulate air during the hot summer days.

The 1939 season showed a $650,000 gross at the April 5–20 Garden stand. When the show closed in Tampa, Florida on October 30, the tour that had included Canada, Washington, Oregon, California and Texas in addition to the usual dates had grossed $2,635,000.

In 1940 the circus had no major difficulties with labor, fire or storms, and the show opened as usual in the Garden on April 5. It moved to Boston on May 2, then went under canvas in Baltimore on May 13. A route that included Maine, the Dakotas and Nebraska, Texas and the East Coast ended in Sarasota on November 18. One of the highlights of the 1941 season was the exhibition of "Mr. and Mrs. Gargantua the Great" in the MENAGERIE. Gargantua had "married" M'TOTO on February 22, 1941 before the show left quarters. During the next four years, the couple's picture on posters

helped to sell millions of dollars' worth of war bonds.

There was some question as to whether the circus would tour following the U.S. entry into World War II. Many of the essentials of running a circus—food, building materials, transportation and personnel—were almost impossible to come by. North managed to convince members of the government that a bit of joy and normalcy back home were essential to the American way of life. Thus he was able to send out the following bulletin:

> *The Management of Ringling Brothers-Barnum and Bailey Circus thinks it timely and fitting to state its policies and hopes for the future at this critical period in our national history. Through letters from many individuals, wide editorial comment . . . and direct expressions from the country's Army, Navy, and political leaders, it has been made clear that the public wants The Greatest Show on Earth to carry on during wartime. . . . President Roosevelt personally has expressed his appreciation of that fact that the Show is Going On.*

Disaster did hit The Big One that year, however. On the morning of August 4, 1942 in Cleveland, Ohio, the paraffin-and-benzene coated menagerie top suddenly burst into flames. Sixty-five animals were killed in a conflagration that lasted only minutes. Fortunately, no people were injured. (See FIRES, CIRCUS.)

At the end of the season, North's contract with the circus was over. Despite the fact that the circus showed a steady profit during his five years in office, North faced the opposition of Robert Ringling (Charles Ringling's son), Edith Ringling (Robert's mother and Charles Ringling's widow) and Aubrey Ringling (Haley). North suggested placing the circus under the sponsorship of the federal government during wartime, but his proposal was turned down at the January 1943 board of directors meeting. North resigned and, with Henry away at war, Robert Ringling took control.

The show, with a smaller train and a more traditional format, enjoyed a profitable 1943 season. The following year also opened well. Robert Ringling left early in the season for health reasons and Jim Haley, Aubrey Ringling's new husband, took charge. The most infamous and heartbreaking tragedy surrounding the Ringling show occurred under his management while the circus was in Hartford, Connecticut.

During the July 6, 1944 matinee show in Hartford, Connecticut, the Big One suffered the most disastrous fire in circus history. Over 6,000 people, most of them women and children, were in the tent when the Big Top burst into flames only 20 minutes into the show. In the melee, 168 people died—two-thirds of them children—while another 487 were injured.

In the spring of 1945, the circus opened as usual at Madison Square Garden. It preceded its stand by staging a traditional STREET PARADE, the first New York had seen in 25 years. For the occasion, the show refurbished many of its old circus WAGONS, including three ornate BANDWAGONS. Once on the road, the Ringling Bros. and Barnum & Bailey Circus was back under canvas, this one properly flame-proofed.

John Ringling North had not given up his dream of recovering his circus and taking over complete ownership. Following his release from a year in jail (following the negligence conviction stemming from the HARTFORD FIRE), Jim Haley offered to help North in his plans if Haley were allowed one more year as president of the corporation. North assented.

Henry Ringling North described the 1946 stockholder's meeting:

Aubrey was ill—either really or diplomatically—and was not present. Jim Haley, holding her proxy, voted her stock with Brother John. What an unholy row ensued! Robert and Edith in outraged voices demanded that the stock be voted in accordance with the Ladies' Agreement (which the women had, apparently, made before the meeting began). The arbitrator, Carl Loos, ruled that this must be done. Jim Haley told Loos where to go and voted with John. A new board of directors was elected, which named Haley president and John Ringling North executive vice-president of Ringling Brothers-Barnum and Bailey Combined Shows.

The following year, John Ringling North succeeded in buying up 51% of the stock. Now firmly in command as president, his brother Henry was voted in as vice-president.

Among North's first appointments was Art CONCELLO, the former Ringling flyer, as general manager. It was with the considerable influence and financial help of Art and Antoinette CONCELLO that

North was able to regain his control of the Ringling show.

Concello was an excellent manager and was also widely respected by the performers. In time, however, he became a thorn in North's side; Concello constantly pushed North to economize and streamline the size of the show. Finally, in 1953, the Concellos left.

The year 1956 was a watershed year for the Ringling show. Despite pickets by the Teamsters Union and the American Guild of Variety Artists, the traditional Madison Square Garden run started with brisk business. By the end of the run, however, sales slacked off. During the next stand, in a deliberate attempt to DAY AND DATE the Big One, the unions put on their own circus in Boston's 7,200-seat arena. To further undercut Ringling, the unions charged only $1.50 a ticket—with kids free—compared to Ringling's price of $4.

On May 22 the show traveled to Baltimore for the first tented stand of the season, but with inexperienced, nonunion roustabouts the SET UP was slow-moving. Bobby Hassen, the sideshow TALKER, had the unenviable task of telling the crowds waiting on the MIDWAY that the usual 2:15 matinee would be delayed. This trend went on to occur in every town, often causing delays of up to four hours.

Rather than cross picket lines, more than a dozen performers—including Emmett KELLY, Felix ADLER and Otto GRIEBLING—left the show. The unions caused rail delays, and the Ringling show limped up the East Coast. Word soon spread about the delays and shortened matinees, and business dropped significantly.

On July 15, in Alliance, Ohio, John Ringling North joined the show in his private rail car. Rumors ran rampant that the circus was going to cut short its season. The next day North made a short announcement to the press that, due to ever-escalating costs, the show would close after that evening's show. Almost as an afterthought he added, "The tented circus as it now exists is in my opinion a thing of the past."

The show, after all, carried 1,300 people in its cast and crew, plus 30 to 50 BULLS among its animals, all traveling in 90 to 100 rail cars. Its Big Top alone covered the area of two football fields, seating 12,000 spectators, yet the circus was still expected to travel to a new city and perform every day.

The news, while shocking to most, was not unexpected by many. In 1955, despite attempts at modernization and streamlining, the show grossed $5 million but lost $1 million. By July 1 of its 1956 tour, the circus had already lost an additional $1 million.

On the parking lot at the Heidelberg Raceway outside Pittsburgh, Pennsylvania, the Ringling Bros. and Barnum & Bailey Circus Big Top was raised for the last time. Performers watched their final matinee from the BACK DOOR in stunned disbelief. Circus fans quickly gathered in Pittsburgh, and that night a STRAWHOUSE of 10,000 people saw the final performance of The Big One under canvas.

When it was near midnight, the crowd filed out of the tent as the band played its traditional end-of-season tune, "Auld Lang Syne"; a few minutes later the roustabouts began to lower the top. It took three days for the circus train to slowly make its way back to Sarasota. Hundreds of townspeople met the train, and a band welcomed the passengers home. The question on everyone's lips was: "Would the Ringling show ever reopen?"

Art Concello resurfaced and made a proposal to North. He would manage the show as executive director for a half-interest in the circus, and Antoinette would return as aerial director. Partly because of Concello's expertise in management and partly because of financial need, North and the other Ringling executives eventually consented to his suggestions.

North opened the new season on April 3, 1957, as usual, at Madison Square Garden. In addition to the fact that Ringling had become an arena show, the circus had undergone another noticeable transformation. The show now traveled north on 15 trucks (three sleepers, eight flats, four stock cars) rather than on its 60 railroad cars. For the first time in 86 years the circus season began without a single show on rails. Although the Ringling show did return partially to rails in 1964, beginning with 19 cars, the heyday of the railroad circus had also become "a thing of the past."

Circus folk were somewhat mollified by seeing the return of Concello. His appointment was a marked improvement over his relatively inexperienced predecessor, Michael Burke. Despite this, North continued to receive enormous criticism by circus fans. Many felt that his attempts to modernize the look of the circus was turning it into a bad Broadway revue. He had discontinued outdoor advertising, and he had replaced key long-term staff members with new noncircus people.

In 1957, the group of Ringling minority stockholders (nicknamed the Forty-niners), headed by Hester Sanford (Charles Ringling's daughter) and Stuart Lancaster, her son from a previous marriage, sued John Ringling North, Henry Ringling North and Art Concello for $20 million for mismanagement of the circus. After three years of inconvenience to the defendants, the suit was dropped. It was during this period, in 1958, that Henry resigned as vice president of the organization.

In 1961 the circus moved its winter quarters from its location adjacent to the Ringling estate to nearby Venice, Florida.

In 1968 Judge Roy HOFHEINZ, Israel S. FELD and Irvin FELD purchased the Ringling Bros. and Barnum & Bailey Combined Circus from John Ringling North. The final papers consummating the sale were signed in the COLOSSEUM in Rome. With Judge Hofheinz increasingly involved in his own project (the Houston Astrodome) and Israel content in a background role as Ringling accountant, Irvin had a clear path to mold the flagship American circus to his own vision.

When Feld realized that the Ringling show was unable to fill all of its possible dates, he created a second touring unit. The "Blue Unit," which opened in Hofheinz's Astrodome, was created to cover the new dates while the "Red Unit" continued to tour the usual route. The units switched routes each year.

In 1969 Feld offered shares of Ringling circus stock to the general public on the New York Stock Exchange for the first time. In 1971 Hofheinz gave up his option to buy the controlling shares of stock in the circus, and Irvin Feld sold his $8 million investment to Mattel Toys for a reported $47 million. As part of the deal, Hofheinz remained the chairman of the board of directors of Ringling, Israel stayed on as accountant (until his death in 1973) and Irvin Feld became president and chief executive officer (CEO).

Under Feld, the circus cast was filled with European acts, including the remarkable animal trainer Gunther GEBEL-WILLIAMS. While Feld relied on smaller casts, he increased the number and size of the SPECS and parades.

On March 17, 1982 Irvin and Kenneth FELD bought

back the controlling shares of stock from Mattel, Inc. Since his father's death in 1984, Kenneth Feld has been president, chief executive officer and producer of the Ringling Bros. and Barnum & Bailey Circus.

Into the 1990s, Kenneth Feld's stamp is just beginning to be felt on the show. He has maintained his father's vision of the sparkling and spectacular, mingled with a bit of humbug (such as the 1985 tour which featured the Living Unicorn). In June 1988 Feld mounted a brief return to Ringling under canvas, opening a "Gold Unit" in Sapparo, Japan, then moving on to Tokyo for two months and Osaka, where it closed in October. The 1989 tour of Japan was not financially successful and closed midseason. In the 1991 edition of the Red Unit, there was a new emphasis on traditional circus acts, including the clown: European circus star David LARIBLE became the first clown ever to appear in a solo spot on the show. The Blue Unit, touring in 1992, carried a rock-and-roll band, N/Motion, which appeared in the many production numbers. KING TUSK was there, plus other pachyderms under the direction of Axel GAUTIER. The show had few AERIAL ACTS, but featured artists from the Mongolian State Circus. Climaxing the show, those artists performed folk dances, gymnastics and Cossack riding.

At the end of the 1992 season, due to the deterioration of the rail line between Sarasota and Venice (the estimated cost of repairs was approximately $1.5 million), the Ringling Red Unit did not return to its Venice winter quarters. The Ringling quarters were moved, at least temporarily, to the Florida State Fairgrounds in Tampa. Ironically, the Ringling Bros. and Barnum & Bailey Circus spent 32 years at both its Sarasota and Venice winter quarters.

(See also ALPERT, "PRINCE" PAUL; ALZANA, HAROLD; ANTHONY, MARK "TONY"; AYALA, MARGARITA VAZQUEZ; BALLY BROAD; BARBETTE; BAUMANN, CHARLY; BEATTY, CLYDE; BRADNA, ELLA; BRADNA, FRED; BUTLER, ROLAND; CASTLE, HUBERT; CIRCUS AMERICA; CIRCUS CAMPS; CIRCUS WORLD; CLARKE, CHARLES AND ERNEST; CLOWN COLLEGE; CODONA, ALFREDO; COLLEANO, CON; COLLEANO, WINNIE; COURT, ALFRED; CRISTIANI, LUCIO; CRISTIANIS, THE; DHOTRE, DAMOO; EVANS, MERLE; FLYING CONCELLOS, THE; FLYING GAONAS, THE; FLYING VAZQUEZ, THE; GAONA, TITO; GOLIATH; HANNEFORD, EDWIN "POODLES"; HENDERSON, J.Y. "DOC"; JACOBS, LOU; JACOBS, CAPT. TERRELL; JOHN AND MABLE RINGLING MUSEUM OF ART, THE; JOMAR; JUNG, PAUL; KAY, BOBBY; KELLEY, JOHN M.; LITTLE, GLEN "FROSTY"; LITTLE MADISON SQUARE GARDEN; LIVING STATUES, THE; LOYAL, GUISTINO; LOYAL-REPENSKY TROUPE, THE; MCBRYDE, LEON "BUTTONS"; MILLMAN, BIRD; MOELLER CARRIAGE AND WAGON WORKS; NAITTO, ALA; OAKLEY, FRANK "SLIVERS"; PALLENBERG, EMIL; PETIT, PHILIPPE; POLAKOV, MICHAEL "COCO"; ROBINSON, YANKEE; SALUTO, FRANKIE; SUNDAY SCHOOL SHOW; TOGNI, FLAVIO; UBANGIS; UNUS; VALDO, PAT; VAZQUEZ, MIGUEL; WALLENDA, KARL; WALLENDAS, THE; ZACCHINI, HUGO; ZOPPE-ZAVATTA TROUPE, THE.)

RINGLING BROS. AND BARNUM & BAILEY CIRCUS CAMP   See CIRCUS CAMPS.

RINGLING BROS. CIRCUS   See RINGLING, JOHN; RINGLING BROS. AND BARNUM & BAILEY CIRCUS.

RINGLING BROTHERS, THE   Of all families connected with outdoor amusements in the United States no other name connotes "circus" more than "Ringling." Born of August (d. 1898) and Marie Salomé Juliar (d. 1907) Rüngeling from Germany, seven brothers—Albrecht C., called Al (1852–1916); August G., called Gus (1854–1907); Otto (1857–1911); Alf T. (c. 1863–1919); Charles Edward (1864–1926); John (1866–1936); and Henry (1868–1918)—and one sister—Ida (1874–1950)—all played a part in the creation of The BIG ONE.

The children were raised in the Midwest, first in BARABOO, WISCONSIN; then McGregor, Iowa; next Stillwater, Minnesota; and last, a return to Baraboo. Although only Ida finished high school, all of the brothers were intelligent and musically gifted.

Only five of the brothers (Al, Alf T., Otto, Charles and John RINGLING)—usually regarded as the "five founding brothers"—played a significant role in the building of the circus dynasty, although Gus and Henry did join them on the road within two years of their first tour. The seed to put on a circus was probably planted in the boys' minds in McGregor in 1868 or 1869 when they saw Dan RICE's great PARIS PAVILION, a circus traveling the Mississippi River by steamboat. The boys' father, a harness worker who had moved to the United States in the 1820s, had received passes in exchange for leather work done for a circus performer.

Their first youthful attempt at a circus was in 1870, when they sewed scraps of muslin and blankets for a tent. Besides the versatile boys, the show featured a trained goat named Billy Rainbow. Albert (Al), the oldest son, was RINGMASTER. The show grossed $8.37.

Around 1880, the Ringling brothers began performing variety shows in the Baraboo area, with the boys taking all the roles—as musicians, jugglers, CLOWNS, ACROBATS and dramatic actors, as well as being bookers and publicists. Al, for instance, was an accomplished strongman, juggler, tightrope walker and TRAPEZE artist.

Their first road show, in 1882, was titled The Ringling Bros. Classic and Comic Concert Company. It was billed as their "Fourth Season," but that exaggeration no doubt took into account their earlier variety hall experience. On May 19, 1884 the show opened as Ringling Brothers' Great Carnival of Fun. It performed in a homemade tent and traveled in nine farm wagons. Star billing in that show went to brother John who, as a clown called "The Emperor of Dutch Comedians," performed "Dutch songs, positions, jokes, sayings, hibdy-dibdy fazes, and his roaring song and dance in big wooden shoes."

The Ringling brothers were successful with their small show. They had credit—and about $1,000 in savings—to finance the leap to a full circus; the only thing they lacked was a name. During 1883, however, Al had met circus legend Yankee ROBINSON and convinced the elderly veteran to lend his name and presence to their new show. On May 19, 1884 the first Ringling circus—the Yankee Robinson and Ringling Brothers Great Double Shows, Circus and Caravan—opened in Baraboo.

During the first season, Robinson himself took the ring before each show and prophetically introduced the Ringling brothers as "the future showmen of America." Although the show toured on less than a dozen farm wagons, it still managed to turn a profit.

Robinson died before the next season was to begin, but the Ringlings carried on. During the winter months, they toured the show as a concert known as the Carnival of Fun, building the size of the circus for the following season. By 1887 the show was being carried in wagons specially built by the MOELLER CARRIAGE AND WAGON WORKS and pulled by 60 horses.

The name of the show grew as well: It was variously titled "The Ringling Brothers Great Double Shows, Circus and Caravan and Trained Animal Exposition" or "Ringling Brothers United Monster Shows, Great Double Circus, Royal European Menagerie, Museum, Caravan and Congress of Trained Animals."

Two ELEPHANTS were added in 1888, and they toured under the more modest name of the Ringling Brothers Greatest Show. The season was disappointing, but the show moved onto rails in 1890 with 18 cars and 54 artists, performing under a 170-foot rounded BIG TOP.

The Ringlings were now in the "big leagues," heading up against well-known shows such as the BARNUM & BAILEY CIRCUS and the SELLS BROTHERS CIRCUS. As the show gained more performers, the brothers themselves moved into management: Al remained EQUESTRIAN DIRECTOR, but was also producer and director of the show; Charles was general manager and in charge of logistics; Otto headed the box office and finances; Alf T. ran concessions and was the public relations director; John routed the show; Gus became the ADVANCE MAN for the show for 18 years; and Henry was in charge of the FRONT DOOR.

In 1892 the show, traveling in 28 rail cars, survived bad weather and three train wrecks; and, in 1893, the brothers began their tour with a three-week stand in Tattersall's horse arena in Chicago rather than with the traditional opening in Baraboo.

By then the Ringling circus was the main competition to the Barnum and Bailey show (owned solely by James Bailey, Barnum having died in 1891), even though the shows had an unwritten agreement to avoid each other's routes. In 1898 Bailey took The GREATEST SHOW ON EARTH to Europe for five years, during which time the Ringling show became the primary circus in the United States.

When Bailey returned, he was up against a Ringling show of 300 circus performers, 400 HORSES, a huge MENAGERIE and an incredible SIDESHOW. Bailey countered with his magnificent 1903 STREET PARADE, featuring the TWO HEMISPHERES BANDWAGON.

In 1905 the Ringlings bought half interest in Bailey's Forepaugh-Sells Circus. Henry Ringling became manager and made sure the three shows stuck to exclusive routes.

James Bailey died in April 1906, and John Ringling—the best negotiator of the brothers—offered to purchase the Barnum and Bailey show and title. When the deal was consummated on October 22, 1907 for $410,000—a sum recouped within a year—the Ringlings became the undisputed kings of the American circus.

They also bought the remaining shares of the Forepaugh-Sells show and toured it through the 1907 season. Meanwhile, the brothers separately toured the Barnum and Bailey Circus (with John as general manager, assisted by Alf T. and Otto) and the Ringling show (with Charles and Al in charge).

By 1910, "The World's Greatest Show," as their Ringling unit was known, was the largest on the road—85 rail cars compared to the average 30 of other shows and 1,000 people on tour. It was also the cleanest run. Following honest, midwestern ethics instilled by their mother, Marie, the Ringling brothers always put on the show as advertised (barring emergencies), and kept pickpockets, hustlers and other GRIFT off the LOT. They even stationed a man near the ticket wagon to remind patrons to count their change. These and similar rules, including their usual avoidance of Sunday performances, gained the Ringling show the nickname of a SUNDAY SCHOOL SHOW.

By 1919 only two of the seven brothers were still living. Gus had died in 1907; Otto had died on March 31, 1911; Al had died on January 1, 1916; followed by Henry in 1918 and Alf T. in Oak Ridge, New Jersey, on October 31, 1919. Meanwhile, around 1900, Ida had married Henry W. North. She added two sons, John Ringling NORTH and Henry Ringling North, to the extended family.

In 1919 John decided to combine their two shows into the RINGLING BROTHERS AND BARNUM & BAILEY CIRCUS. To cut down on postwar costs, the WINTER QUARTERS were also combined; all of the Ringling equipment was moved from Baraboo to the Barnum & Bailey quarters in BRIDGEPORT, CONNECTICUT.

When Charles Ringling died on December 3, 1926, John—known as "Mr. John"—was in complete control of the circus. In part to protect his own investments in Florida real estate, he moved the circus headquarters from Bridgeport to SARASOTA, FLORIDA in 1927.

Under John Ringling's leadership, the 1920s were the golden years for the Ringling show, featuring such talent as May WIRTH, Lillian LEITZEL, the HANNEFORDS, the WALLENDAS and the beginning of Merle EVANS's remarkable career.

In 1932, as a result of bad business transactions by John Ringling, the Ringling Bros. and Barnum & Bailey Circus fell out of the hands of an actual Ringling brother forever. The last of the five founding Ringlings died on December 2, 1936.

RINGLING CLOWN COLLEGE   See CLOWN COLLEGE.

RINGLING MUSEUM   See JOHN AND MABLE RINGLING MUSEUM OF ART, THE.

RINGMASTER   The ringmaster in the modern circus is actually a hybrid of three separate jobs: the announcer, the EQUESTRIAN DIRECTOR and the actual ringmaster.

There are at least two possible origins for the term itself. One obvious explanation is that he is literally the "master of the ring." This would seem to harken back to the time of the original one-ring circuses, however, before the term "ringmaster" was in common use. With the introduction of several rings under the BIG TOP, each animal act had its own "ring master-trainer." This newer derivation would coincide with the word's more common usage.

In the one-ring circuses and even in some of the smaller multiring shows, the ringmaster frequently interacted with the performers during their acts, most often exchanging banter with the CLOWNS. This tradition has continued and could be seen in the patter between the ringmaster and featured clown David LARIBLE during his first season with the RINGLING BROS. AND BARNUM & BAILEY CIRCUS in 1991.

Of course, the early circus tradition was based on horsemanship. It was the director of the equestrians who governed the pacing and length of the individual acts and often of the entire show. Although they were usually capable of performing the tasks, equestrian directors did not necessarily have to be riders or trainers during the performance itself.

During the show, the equestrian director indicated each new act by the use of a sharp whistle saying, in effect, "Listen up! Here's something worth seeing!" The only other person to use a whistle in the circus is the LIBERTY HORSE trainer who signals the charges by audio and visual clues alone.

On many early shows, instead of a ringmaster a separate announcer called the acts. He never blew a whistle, and he was never really considered a ringmaster. Nevertheless, before the days of amplified sound, this was a very special position. Eventually the ringmaster assumed his duties.

Needless to say, the distinctions among the duties of the ringmaster, the equestrian director and the announcer are very blurred. Today the titles are—for all practical purposes—interchangeable to the 'layman.

The traditional ringmaster's wardrobe is derived from that of the formal British riding schools: tall black riding boots, white jodhpurs, red swallowtail coat, white shirt, black bow tie and black top hat. The modern costume might add some sequins and a few extra colors, but the outfit remains essentially the same.

While today's ringmaster must have an excellent speaking voice, some are also called on to sing, especially during the SPEC and other production numbers. During the show, the ringmaster's duties include making announcements, focusing attention on certain acts or individual stunts within a routine and coordinating the endings of the acts in a multiring circus. He must also be alert to any emergencies that might require his ordering a change in the usual flow of the program. Once the show has begun, the ringmaster is, in essence, the final decision maker and the person in charge of the performance.

(See also BRADNA, FRED; JAMES, JIMMY.)

RISLEY ACT

An unusual combination of acrobatics, balancing and JUGGLING, a risley act in essence is one ACROBAT, lying on his back, FOOT JUGGLING another person, usually a small boy. Technically known as icarianism, the skill dates back at least to the time of the Aztecs, as evidenced by ancient stone carvings.

One acrobat lies on his back either on the ground or on a low table, with the lower back often supported by a pillow or CRADLE, and holds the legs together perpendicular to the torso. When balancing another performer, the second acrobat—or top-mounter—sits or lies on the soles of the partner's feet. The BOTTOM MAN, or understander, twirls, twists, somersaults and tosses the airborne balancer. With a several-member company, acrobats can be thrown from one gymnast to another.

The name of the act is purported to have come from a 19th-century circus performer, Richard Risley Carlisle (1814–74). He first appeared on a circus in 1841 before touring Tasmania, Australia and Europe. He first performed the act in the United States around 1843. Though American, Carlisle performed mostly in England and Europe. It was at the Theatre Royal in Edinburgh, Scotland in February 1844 that Carlisle and his son performed the first back somersault from a feet-to-feet position. Carlisle traveled the world with his own circus, bringing back many acrobatic acts from Asia to perform in Europe and the United States. In 1864 he was the first to introduce the western-style circus to Japan. He died in an insane asylum in 1874.

R'IZHII

The r'izhii was a particular style of CLOWN in the Russian and Eastern European circus in the 19th century. R'izhii clowns were identifiable by their pink and red face markings, red wigs and knockabout style of comedy.

It is generally believed that the r'izhii inspired the development of the modern AUGUSTE CLOWN.

(See also CHARACTER CLOWNS.)

ROBBINS BROS. CIRCUS

In 1924 Fred Buchanan's World Bros. Circus of 1923 was retitled the Robbins Bros. Circus. The circus, still owned by Buchanan, operated on rails until 1931.

During the Great Depression, various truck shows used the name, and in 1938 a railroad show took its title. The Robbins Bros. Circus was last seen as a motorized show in 1949.

ROBERTS BROTHERS CIRCUS

A family-run show, the Roberts Brothers Circus is operated by Doris Earl and her sons Robert T. and Jeff. Robert is the president, staying in the Florida office throughout the season. Jeff, the vice president and secretary, manages the show on the road. Doris, who is treasurer, is frequently seen as a BUTCHER when she is on the LOT.

Doris Earl was a featured aerialist with the show when it was started as the Robert G. Earl Circus by her late husband around 1964. Their two boys literally grew up under the BIG TOP.

Their 70-×-210 top now plays up to 200 shows between March and October each year, from Florida to Maine and back. Traveling on around 20 vehicles, they spend three months of each season in Pennsylvania. The show does not feature CATS, but each year presents trained ponies, llamas, dogs and Baby Lisa—the elephant they have leased from Dory "D.R." MILLER since the show's inception.

ROBINSON, DAN (fl. 1910–1913)

A circus owner, Dan Robinson operated the FAMOUS ROBINSON CIRCUS from 1910 through 1913. At the end of that season, Jeremiah "Jerry" MUGIVAN and Bert BOWERS bought the name to compete in the same territory with the more famous JOHN ROBINSON CIRCUS.

Mugivan and Bowers repainted their Sanger Circus over a weekend and rechristened it with the Robinson title. They toured the show for two season's under Dan Robinson's name. In 1916, however, they succeeded in purchasing the original John Robinson Circus, and the Famous Robinson show was retired.

(See also SANGER'S GREAT EUROPEAN CIRCUS.)

ROBINSON, JAMES (1835–1917)

Born James Michael Fitzgerald in Boston, James Robinson was the master equestrian of his day. For years he was billed simply as "The Man Who Rides."

James was adopted by John ROBINSON, the famous circus owner, who taught the boy how to ride. From the start, it was obvious the lad was built to be an equestrian. He was five feet five inches tall, muscular and agile with small feet.

Acrobatic riding was not unknown before his time, of course; but until Robinson began riding bareback, most equestrians rode "pad"—that is, with a pad covering the horse's back. His own acrobatic skills did more to popularize bareback riding than those of any other performer. During his lifetime pad riders all but disappeared from the circus repertoire.

Beginning his career in the 1850s, Robinson always rode bareback on his gray horse, Bull. In 1856, while touring with the SPALDING & ROGERS CIRCUS, Robinson performed his greatest feat and a still-standing world's record, turning 23 consecutive backward and forward somersaults over four-foot-wide banners as Bull trotted around the ring. Robinson's backward somersault was a specialty: He stood on the rump of the horse, facing the tail. He would then vault with his feet over his head, ending by standing facing forward on the horse's back.

Charles W. Fish, another great rider of the era, almost matched Robinson in skill, but Robinson defeated him and others in competition, winning trophies. Robinson retired from the ring in 1889.

(See also PAD RIDING.)

ROBINSON, JOHN (1802–1888)

A performer as well as circus owner, John Robinson was born on July 22, 1802 in upstate New York. Variously described by his contemporaries as "impulsive, strong-headed, but after all, kindly-hearted" he was also "blunt, laconic and outspoken."

His JOHN ROBINSON CIRCUS, with its WINTER QUARTERS in Cincinnati, was connected with various titles and partners. The show became so popular throughout the South that during his lifetime, and for decades after, John Robinson was a household name. In fact, his name has entered circus jargon: Due to his disreputable practice of cutting shows short on whim, an abbreviated performance—for whatever reason, emergency or not—is still referred to as a JOHN ROBINSON.

Robinson took over a small WAGON SHOW, called it Robinson & Foster and toured it from 1842 to 1845. One of the performers on that show, Gilbert N. ELDRED, became his new partner in 1846. For 11 successful years Robinson and Eldred were partners and owners of ROBINSON & ELDRED'S GREAT SOUTHERN SHOW.

Sometime during the 1850s Robinson adopted a boy, James Michael Fitzgerald, who had run away from his home in Boston to join Robinson's circus. Fitzgerald took his mentor's name, becoming James ROBINSON (1835–1917).

The partnership between John Robinson and Eldred came to an end on June 28, 1856 in Richmond, Virginia. The clash between two such strong personalities was perhaps inevitable and reasons for the split accumulated over the years. It was apparently Robinson's cruelty—even to his wife—however, that finally caused Eldred to buy out his partner's share of the show. The *Chester Standard* of Chester, South Carolina reported on June 25, 1857 that "the separation took place on account of the barbarous cruelty of R, which he extended even to the wife of his bosom."

Robinson used that money to purchase a year-old bankrupt venture, FLAGG & AYMAR'S INTERNATIONAL CIRCUS. Keeping the same cast and crew, he retitled the show John Robinson's International Circus and Menagerie and set out on tour in Geneva, New York on September 1, 1856.

Robinson developed the show into a huge moneymaker and continued to tour it in the 1860s with his sons, John F. and Gil Robinson. Finally, in 1870, he retired from active participation in the circus and turned over management of his show to his grandson, John G. Robinson.

John Robinson died a very wealthy man in 1888. The Robinson title—in some variation—was on the road almost every year until 1938.

ROBINSON, YANKEE (1818–1884)

Born Fayette Lodawick Robinson, Yankee Robinson owned one of the most popular circuses in the Midwest in the 1870s. Early in his career, Robinson had been an actor, CLOWN and dancer; these talents served him in good stead when he became a circus entrepreneur.

His first YANKEE ROBINSON CIRCUS opened in 1854, and some form of the show toured each season through 1876. For the next seven years, Robinson sporadically toured a tented repertory theater.

In 1883 Yankee was invited by Al Ringling (see the RINGLING BROTHERS)—who had worked one summer for Robinson—to join his family's fledgling show. Al correctly surmised that, although the Ringlings could bankroll a circus, they needed a "name" to attract an audience.

Well into his 60s, Robinson still sat on a lead wagon in the circus parade of the Yankee Robinson and Ringling Brothers Great Double Show, Circus and Caravan, whose season began in BARABOO, WISCONSIN on May 19, 1884. Before each show, Robinson would take the ring himself, extolling the virtues and future of the young Ringling brothers:

Ladies and gentlemen, I am an old, old man. For 40 years I have rested my head on a stranger's pillow. I have traveled in every state in the Union, and have been associated with every showman of prominence in America.

I will soon pass to the arena of life that knows no ending; and when I do, I want to die in harness and connected with these boys. If I could have a dying wish granted, it would be that my name should remain associated with that of the Ringling Brothers; for I tell you the Ringling Brothers are the future showmen of America; they are the coming men.

Yankee Robinson was, indeed, prophetic. He died at the age of 66 at season's end and was buried in Jefferson, Iowa. The Ringlings went on to see their names become synonymous with the circus in the United States.

ROBINSON & ELDRED'S GREAT SOUTHERN SHOW

One of the longest partnerships of the American circus had its start on John ROBINSON's first show, Robinson & Foster, when Gilbert N. ELDRED toured with him from 1842 to 1845. Eldred, who had started on his brother's show as a CLOWN in 1834, moved onto Robinson's show as a trick rider and "ceiling walker."

Robinson and Eldred formed their own show in 1846, and for 11 years toured Robinson & Eldred's Great Southern Show. They chose the South as their main territory, venturing north of the Mason-Dixie line only one or two months each season. Their annual returns to towns created a loyal following, and they were always greeted enthusiastically. In fact, it was largely due to their kind reception from the southern press and public that they named their show The Great Southern Circus in 1851. For years Robinson and Eldred advertised the show as "Southern Men, Southern Horses and Southern Enterprise against the World."

Robinson & Eldred's Great Southern Show performed almost continually. There is no evidence that they returned to any WINTER QUARTERS between 1844 and 1854—a perhaps an unequaled record of 11 years of uninterrupted performances. During the winter months, the show would book one- and two-month stands into a great southern city, such as Savannah or Charleston. It was there that tents would be mended, props repaired and changes in personnel made.

In 1852 the show traveled uncharacteristically far north. While touring south from Maine, it leased or purchased SANDS & QUICK'S MENAGERIE. It is uncertain exactly when the new animals were added, but the first existing advertising of the combined MENAGER-

IES appeared in Raleigh, North Carolina on December 9, 1852.

The Robinson and Eldred partnership ended on June 28, 1856. Eldred bought out Robinson and kept the circus's title. When Robinson left the show, however, so did the performers. Eldred soon managed to replace the cast and continued the season south to Florida under the name G.N. Eldred's Great Southern Circus.

(See also JOHN ROBINSON CIRCUS.)

ROBINSON & FOSTER See ELDRED, GILBERT N.; JOHN ROBINSON CIRCUS; ROBINSON, JOHN.

ROGERS, CHARLES J. See *FLOATING PALACE;* RICE, DAN; SPALDING, "DR." GILBERT R.; SPALDING & ROGERS CIRCUS.

ROGUE ELEPHANTS True instances of a ELEPHANT "going bad" are few and far between; but animals, like people, have individual personalities affected by stress, pain or discomfort. In addition, any animal worker readily concedes that a wild animal can only be "trained," not "tamed."

Although some elephants may be difficult to train or handle, a BULL is not really considered a rogue until it becomes a threat to the safety of either the trainer or the public. Unfortunately, the life-endangering behavior is often sudden and unexpected. Some trainers insist that the axiom "an elephant never forgets" is true—that a pachyderm can actually hold a grudge against another animal or person for years, waiting for the ideal opportunity to strike back.

P.T. BARNUM scored one of his greatest successes when he was able to purchase JUMBO because the elephant has been labeled a rogue by his keepers at the Royal Zoological Gardens in London. Jumbo, for years a peaceful pachyderm, developed a brief mean and unmanageable disposition in 1882. Keepers at the time suggested that Jumbo might be undergoing "musth," a violent temper characteristic of some sexually mature male elephants. By the time the sale was consummated, Jumbo was once again docile and never again gave his handlers difficulty. An inspection of the skeleton after Jumbo's accidental death suggested that his temporary temper was more likely caused by the outbreak or impacting of his sixth set of molars.

A sentimental, if unlikely, handling of a rogue elephant is seen in the Walt Disney film *Dumbo* (see FILMS, CIRCUS). In the animated feature the mother pachyderm is isolated in a separate circus wagon so that she can't hurt any of the public or the circus personnel.

Tops

Unlikely as such incidents seem today, several bizarre elephant executions have been recorded. Tops, a vicious and uncontrollable pachyderm, had killed three men, the first being her trainer in Waco, Texas in 1900. Later that year she killed her new trainer in Paris, Texas. On May 22, 1902 Tops killed a young circus follower in Ft. Wayne, Indiana when he put a lighted cigarette into her mouth.

Although valued at $6,000, Tops, 28 years old, was scheduled to be killed on January 4, 1903 at Luna Park, Coney Island, New York. The execution was witnessed by a huge crowd, many of whom had been invited. Others scaled the fence to see the six-ton elephant die, even though guards were supposed to keep out the morbidly curious. Troublesome to the end, Tops refused to mount the platform from which she was to have been hanged and was instead shot with 6000 volts of electricity. She died within 22 seconds of the current being turned on.

Queen (aka "Mary")

According to those who knew her, "Queen" was one of the most vicious bulls ever to tour. On the original ADAM FOREPAUGH CIRCUS, she wrapped her trunk around her keeper's neck and choked him to death. She was sold to the John O'Brien Circus, where she was billed "Empress, the War Elephant." During her stay, she killed at least five men.

Her name was changed to "Mary" when she was bought by the W.H. HARRIS NICKLE PLATE CIRCUS. While the show was playing on a LOT on Robey Street in Chicago, she killed her keeper who was known as "Jimmy the Bum." She was condemned to death, but Col. George ("Pop Corn George") W. Hall secured her stay of execution. It almost cost him his life. Hall was feeding a peanut to Palm—a baby elephant standing next to Queen in the MENAGERIE—when the older pachyderm went jealously berserk. Barney ("Elephant Fat") Shea, their new keeper, diverted Queen by sticking his thumb in her eye; but the beast had already slammed Hall to the ground and was about to crush him. Hall's hip was broken in two places and, despite a long hospital recovery, he was crippled for life.

Queen was leased to GOLLMAR BROS. CIRCUS, then sold to the Sells & Downs Circus. A former bull man with the Forepaugh show, John ("Blue Jay") Durham bought out Sells's interest in the circus. Queen remembered Durham and was very peaceful under his command. When Durham sold out his part of the show to Martin J. Downs in the spring of 1906, the title of the circus was changed to the Cole Bros. World Toured Shows. Queen missed Durham and ran away from the LOT whenever possible; otherwise she remained calm that season.

Even before the show left the Harbour Creek, Pennsylvania WINTER QUARTERS the next year, Queen attempted to kill her keeper, Archie Dunlap. Only a short foot chain held her back. When a spring snow snapped the QUARTER POLE in her top, she broke her chains and demolished several cages and most of the menagerie before being brought under control. Luckily, no one from the public was in the top at the time.

Later that season, a small boy darted in front of her during the STREET PARADE in Buffalo, New York. She knocked him down and knelt on him, crushing him instantly. At the end of the season in Columbia, South Carolina, Queen killed an assistant BOSS CANVASMAN named Gordon. He had been repairing the SIDEWALL on the outside of the menagerie, when a gust of wind blew it upward. He was revealed to Queen, who instantly knocked him down and crushed him. He died of his injuries in the hospital the following day, thus becoming Queen's 13th victim.

The elephant was kept securely chained until the sale of the show upon Martin Downs's death in 1909. Queen was finally sold to the FRANK A. ROBBINS CIRCUS, but she was so unruly that Robbins decided to have her killed. An admission fee was charged to watch her electrocution at Tattersall's Pavilion in Chicago. In a coup for the ANIMAL ACTIVISTS, the Humane Society managed to hold up the execution. She was sold to the HAGENBECK-WALLACE CIRCUS, where her trail of killings finally ended.

"Murderous" Mary

A notorious "lynching" took place in Erwin, Tennessee on September 13, 1916 when "Murderous" Mary—a pachyderm with the Sparks-World Famous Shows—was hanged from a railroad derrick.

Performing as part of a quintette at the time of her death, Mary was 30 years old (half of her life expectancy) and was valued at $20,000. One or two days before the execution, Mary had killed her trainer, Walter "Red" Eldridge of St. Paul, following a matinee in Kingsport, Tennessee. There are different accounts of the apparently bloody attack: One suggests Mary became violent when Eldridge refused her a piece of watermelon she wanted; another says Mary became enraged when she was treated cruelly; and a third purports that the violent outburst was caused by Mary's suffering from abscessed teeth.

Although no other cases were documented during the 15 years she toured with the SPARKS CIRCUS as the "Largest Living Land Animal on Earth," rumors spread that Murderous Mary had actually killed from three to 18 people over the years. Nevertheless, whether fearing for its own safety or the loss of box office receipts, the circus bowed to public sentiment and agreed to execute the pachyderm. It is uncertain who actually condemned Mary to death, but plans were made to hang her because one gun was not enough to bring her down quickly.

On the day of the execution, Mary was kept with the other elephants so she did not sense anything out of the ordinary. BULL HANDLERS lured Mary into place in the yards of the CC&O Railroad where a $7/8$-inch chain was wrapped around her neck. Mary was hoisted by a crane only five or six feet into the air when the chain snapped, and she fell to the ground. In a stupor, Mary offered no resistance as another chain was secured. She was hoisted a second time, gave a twist and a sigh and died.

Mary reportedly had enormous tusks, which were sawed off either at the time of her burial or later that same night by unknown persons. Her carcass was moved by a steam shovel to a gravesite that has been disputed. Most local residents maintain that she was buried south of the old roundhouse and below the tracks.

Hero

In 1916, Lucky Bill NEWTON sold his elephant, Hero, that he had purchased six years earlier, to the ORTON BROS. CIRCUS for $4,500. Although not yet a rogue, Hero had become increasingly uncontrollable on Lucky Bill's Big 25 Cent Show.

Soon after moving over to the new circus, Hero went berserk in Elkton, South Dakota, overturning several railroad flatcars. Although there was no loss of life, the decision was made to shoot the elephant. During the execution, reportedly more than 2,000 rounds were required to kill Hero.

Black Diamond

On October 12, 1929 Black Diamond, a long-tusked elephant with the AL G. BARNES CIRCUS, went berserk and crushed a woman to death, destroyed a car and injured two trainers. John RINGLING, who had recently purchased the show as part of his takeover of the AMERICAN CIRCUS CORPORATION, sent a telegram to the show's manager advising him to "Kill Diamond in some humane way."

Black Diamond was led into a forest clearing where he was chained to three trees. Five riflemen shot from a distance of about 18 feet. The first round of fire hit Diamond behind the ears. He merely turned, puzzled. The second volley had no effect; but on the third round he jumped spastically and fell. The executioners shot more than 50 bullets from all directions until Black Diamond was finally killed.

Janet

Incidents of rogue elephants still occur in contemporary times. On February 1, 1992 at 4:43 P.M. in Palm Bay, Florida, just outside Titusville, Janet—a 27-year-old, 8,000-pound Indian elephant with the Great American Circus—suddenly became excited and began to charge her way out of the Big Top. Unfortunately, she was giving five children and a woman, Kathy Lawler, an "elephant ride" on her back at the time.

Janet smashed a cage around the CENTER RING, grabbed a rope and yanked at the tent. The trainer was tossed to the ground, and the elephant ran from the tent. By that time, Cpl. Blayne Doyle, an officer with the Palm Bay Police Department, had arrived. He attempted to rescue the riders and was also knocked down. Another trainer on a second pachyderm rode next to Janet and removed the children, then Lawler, one at a time. Doyle, having recovered, was asked by Tim Frisco, the general manager and elephant trainer, to shoot Janet. After receiving authorization from headquarters, he opened fire; despite being mortally wounded, Janet ran back toward the tent as patrons ran from the scene. She dropped, then died at 5:01 P.M.: The entire traumatic incident had lasted less than 20 minutes. Xan Rawls of the Brevard County Animal Control ex-

amined Janet and declared that any clues as to the reason for her unpredictable, unusual behavior had been destroyed by the 40 rounds of police gunshots to the head.

Because of a bull's great value, a circus owner would go to almost any lengths to avoid having to eliminate a rogue elephant. There is an apocryphal story about a British circus that was having difficulty with one of its favorite Indian elephants. When it was decided that the pachyderm was too dangerous to handle, tickets were actually sold to the beast's execution. Before the show, a well-respected author who had traveled in the Far East asked to see the creature. Because of his reputation, the man was permitted to go close to the cage; but the authorities were surprised when the man boldly walked straight up to the supposedly wild beast. The man spoke a few quiet words of gibberish to the elephant, and the creature immediately calmed down. So radical was the transformation that the execution was postponed, then canceled when the animal never again exhibited a temper. When asked what he had said to the elephant, the writer said, "I just spoke some words to her in Hindu. I thought she might be homesick." That man was Rudyard Kipling.

ROLA BOLA   The apparatus for a particular genre of balancing act, a rola bola simply consists of a cylinder and a board. The cylinder is placed on the ground or on an elevated platform, and the board is laid across it. Acrobats balance as they place their feet on the board, slightly straddling the cylinder below it.

By laws of physics, the apparatus has only two possible motions. It can teeter like a fulcrum or seesaw, or it can roll side to side with the board parallel to the floor. The mastery of a combination of these two movements makes balancing possible.

A rola bola act, of course, is much more complicated. It almost always involves some form of JUGGLING while on the board and often holding another acrobat on the shoulders. Some "daredevil" rola bola artists build a stack of cylinders and boards—each set crossways at 90 degrees to the one below it—and balance on top of all of them.

ROLLING GLOBE   Just as it sounds, the rolling globe is simply a large sphere—usually about 2–3 feet in

Acrobats perform on the rola bola—a classic piece of balancing apparatus—at the Garden date on the Ringling Bros. and Barnum & Bailey Circus in 1940. (Author's collection)

Lalage, billed as "The High Priestess of Rhythm Aloft," performs a split on the Roman rings during the Madison Square Garden engagement of the Ringling Bros. and Barnum & Bailey Circus in 1946. (Author's collection)

diameter—on which the acrobat tries to balance or walk. Humans as well as animals (especially BEARS and seals) have been trained to walk on the rolling globe.

The gymnast hops up onto the ball and gains his balance, often by holding the arms out to the sides. The globe can be moved forward (while maintaining balance) by slight side-to-side movements.

Tricks in a rolling globe act might include JUG-GLING while on the sphere or moving up and over a TEETERBOARD. Like the CYCLIST Leonati, early daredevil rolling globe artists were known to climb lengthy straight or spiral ramps, take their applause at a brief stop at the upper platform, then slowly work back down the ramp.

ROLL-UPS   Circus jargon synonymous with aerial PLANGES.

(See also AERIAL ACTS; LEITZEL, LILLIAN.)

ROMAN RIDING   Also known as Roman post riding, Roman riding is circus jargon for an equestrian stunt in which the rider stands astride two HORSES, one foot on each steed, as they gallop around the ring.

ROMAN RINGS   A piece of circus apparatus, derived from ancient Greek and Roman gymnastics. Two large rings hanging from ropes rigged from the top of the tent are held by the aerialist as he or she performs swings, twists and contortions. Lillian LEITZEL was among the famous circus stars who performed on the Roman rings.

Because each ring hangs from an individual WEB from the CRANE BAR, the Roman rings are not stationary. When they are used to swing, the act is often referred to as the "flying rings." Flying Roman rings was a competitive gymnastic event for men from 1885 to 1962 and for women from 1933 to 1957.

ROOKH, LALLA See LALLA ROOKH.

ROPER Circus jargon for a cowboy in a Wild West show.

ROSIN Rosin is a dry, hard product made of resin that has been distilled from the sticky pitch or sap of trees. It is dark amber and looks like glass when in crystal or rock form, but it appears almost pure white when powdered.

Rosin is used by gymnasts, aerialists and equestrians to dust hands, feet or any part of the body that needs a firm extra grip to another person, animal or piece of apparatus.

In the circus, rosin is often placed in a drawstring cotton bag. Like the CLOWN's makeup powder sock, the rosin bag can be conveniently carried or hung from rigging ready for use.

(See also ROSINBACK.)

ROSINBACK Circus jargon for bareback riding as well as for the HORSES used in the act.

Rosinback horses are aptly named because ROSIN is sprinkled on their backs to help keep the standing performer's feet from slipping during the act.

Rosinback riding is usually performed on Percherons, a favorite breed of horse, or on some other draft horse. Draft horses, the big-boned animals kin to the to the work horses that pull plows in farmers' fields, are used in 95% of all bareback act.

Among the most famous rosinback riders on the America circus have been Lucio CRISTIANI, Edwin "Poodles" HANNEFORD, Tommy HANNEFORD, Guistino LOYAL, May WIRTH and Alberto ZOPPE.

(See also CRISTIANIS, THE; LOYAL-REPENSKY TROUPE, THE; VAULTING; ZOPPE-ZAVATTA TROUPE, THE.)

ROTH, LOUIS (18??–1949) In the fall of 1909, Al G. Barnes brought Hungarian animal trainer Captain Louis Roth to the United States to perform in his AL G. BARNES CIRCUS. Often working with BEARS and CATS, Roth presented several animals in various combinations in the BIG CAGE. He was made head trainer and superintendent of the MENAGERIE and remained in that position for a decade.

Roth took on pupils only reluctantly. His star pupil on the Barnes show was Mabel STARK. In 1921 he became mentor to Clyde BEATTY when the boy joined Howes' Great London Circus, where Roth was boss of the menagerie.

In 1945 Roth was still working an act with two one-year-old black-maned African lions and a mixed act of five tigers and four lions. He broke his last act at his home in Thousand Oaks, California before taking it out as a free act on the West Coast shows and as a feature at Harry Chipman's animal park. Roth died at his small ranch near Yakima, Washington in 1949.

ROUSTABOUTS Circus jargon for the unskilled laborers and workmen on the show. Roustabouts are those who travel with the circus and do not include the laborers who are employed each day locally to augment the crew.

Signed on as being GENERALLY USEFUL, the roustabouts perform duties such as setting up the TENTS, carrying props in and out of the ring and helping to clean up after the animals during the performance. Some skilled roustabouts, known as RIGGERS, help to set the mechanical apparatus for the wire walkers and aerialists.

Except for apprentices—who sign on to learn performance skills from a particular artist—roustabouts are the lowest-paid workers on the LOT. Compensation consists of only a few dollars more than room and board, most of which often disappears in the PIE CAR when the performance is not taking place.

ROUTE BOOK The first known route book, a type of permanent record of the year on the road produced at season's end, was published by the ZOOLOGICAL INSTITUTE in 1835. A small booklet, it literally printed the route of one of its units, Branch Number 7, Noell E. Waring, manager.

During the heyday of the tented circus, many shows produced a souvenir route book (also seen as "routebook") at season's end that detailed the cast, show vehicles, MENAGERIE, program and itinerary. Route books ranged from cheaply produced mimeographed, side-stapled albums to expensive publications that included photographs. The books were made available to the cast and crew as well as to circus fans.

Few circuses today carry on the luxurious tradition of putting together a route book after returning to WINTER QUARTERS. A superior example of the route book and the most complete volume currently being produced each year is for the CARSON & BARNES CIRCUS, edited by James K. Judkins, the show's vice president and general manager.

ROUTE CARDS The itinerary of a show is given out to the cast and company of a circus in the form of a series of route cards throughout the run of the season. Each card lists a number of stands, usually about three weeks at a time.

The route card supplies the town's name, the date it will be played and the distance of the JUMP from the previous day's town. The new card is given out at the beginning of the second week of the last card so that copies can be forwarded to families and friends. This way mail can be sent directly to the show in care of General Delivery, where the show's mail agent can pick it up. Otherwise, personal mail would have to go through the main office in WINTER QUARTERS, delaying its delivery by a week or more.

The company does not release the entire season's route for several reasons. Some shows—especially ones that are doing poor business or have a vendetta against another show or owner—will reroute their circus to deliberately DAY AND DATE another if they know where the competing show is playing. The motive might be to attract turnaway business or to hurt the other show's possibility of success. A second show might also try to book itself into the town ahead of the already-booked show to try to steal its business in advance.

Also, a town might be dropped from the schedule for any number of reasons. The ADVANCE MAN might find the LOT to be unsuitable; a town's permits might be withheld; ANIMAL ACTIVISTS might be causing problems.

Many times the entire season has not been fully booked by opening day, so the complete route cannot be released in advance. In recessionary times, there is one more sad possibility: The circus withholds the route cards rather than announce dates that it may not stay open long enough to play.

Circus programs regularly state "Due to the hazardous nature of circus acts, the program is subject to change without notice." Much the same thing can be said about a circus's route. As a result, to prevent any problems with misdirected mail or deliveries, route cards are released detailing only a few weeks at a time.

Route cards, like baseball cards, have become popular collectors' items among circus fans. While most route cards are simply a plain listing of the itinerary, some—such as those designed by Roland BUTLER—had bold multicolored decorative mastheads that made them true pieces of circus art.

ROWE, JOSEPH A. (1819–1887) At the age of ten, Joseph A. Rowe ran away to join a circus playing in his native Kingston, North Carolina. Later Rowe toured the West Indies and South America with various troupes. By the 1840s he had become an accomplished equestrian; he was playing Lima, Peru with his own circus when the California Gold Rush began.

After boarding the sailing ship *Tasso*, Rowe and his company arrived in San Francisco on October 12, 1849. Seventeen days later California saw its first circus at a theater on Kearney Street.

Rowe's Olympic Circus played to 1,500 people and featured Mrs. Rowe as an equestrian, a riding clown, two wire walkers, and Rowe himself as a trick rider on Adonis, his educated HIGH SCHOOL HORSE. General admission was $3 and box seats were $5. (These were, of course, gold rush prices: In the East, circus shows were 50 cents. Inflation was such a problem that Folley, Rowe's clown, quit the show because he couldn't live on his $1,200-a-month salary.)

After playing in San Francisco for a year, Rowe set off for Australia, where he netted over $100,000. In the South Seas, the show played under various titles, such as Rowe's Olympic Circus, Rowe & Co.'s Pioneer Circus, Rowe and Smith's Circus and (in Australia) Rowe's American Circus.

He retired in 1854 but reopened in 1856 to tour the inland California mining towns. The gold boom went bust, however, and admission dropped to only 50 cents. The average day's gross fell to only $250.

Rowe's solution was to augment his show. With a company of 33 and a large BANDWAGON, he toured the interior of the California territory in 1857. It was a ruinous season, as was his next year's tour in Australia. The show closed and Rowe was forced to work for other circuses in a variety of capacities, including MENAGERIE manager, RINGMASTER, ADVANCE MAN and horse trainer. His death on November 3, 1887 went largely unnoticed in the circus world.

ROWE'S OLYMPIC CIRCUS   See ROWE, JOSEPH A.

ROYAL HANNEFORD CIRCUS   An indoor arena circus, the Royal Hanneford Circus was created in 1975 by Tommy HANNEFORD and his wife, Struppi.

When the Irish clan of Edwin "Poodles" HANNEFORD was touring England, they posed as Canadians to avoid the wrath of the British citizenry. It was then that the word "royal" first came to be part of their billing as the "Royal Canadian Hannefords." Today the word is still used in the circus title, but their colleagues also consider the Hannefords—descended from a line of circus performers dating back at least to 1621—to be a "royal family" by circus industry standards.

Today's Royal Hanneford Circus has its WINTER QUARTERS in Osprey, Florida, just south of SARASOTA. The show makes 80% of its appearances as a SHRINE CIRCUS, working a "sponsored date" under the auspices of a local Temple and bearing the Shrine name. The circus can be split into two units, if required; occasionally plans include taking at least one of them under canvas.

The Royal Hanneford Show is a family affair. Besides acting as owner/manager, Tommy Hanneford continues to act as RINGMASTER and perform in the ring with his herd of ELEPHANTS. Struppi, who was a famous equestrienne and worked a tiger act, also appeared on the TRAPEZE as "Tajana, Goddess of Flight" before moving into every phase of production with her husband.

Each July, the Royal Hanneford Circus is seen under canvas as part of the weeklong celebration surrounding the GREAT CIRCUS PARADE in Milwaukee, Wisconsin.

R.T. RICHARDS CIRCUS   In 1917 the R.T. Richards Circus operated out of WAGONS but was, in fact, a motorized show: The wagons were hauled from LOT to lot by trucks. The circus was titled by reversing the name of its owner, Richard T. Ringling, the son of Alf T. Ringling. Although the full name was never used, the abbreviated "R" in the title actually stood for Ringling, not Richard.

See also RINGLING BROTHERS, THE.

RUBBERMAN   Circus jargon for a novelties salesperson who sells balloons.

See also BUTCHER.

RUFUS WELCH NATIONAL CIRCUS   See DAN RICE CIRCUS; LENT, LEWIS B.; RICE, DAN; WELCH, "GENERAL" RUFUS.

RUSSELL BROS. CIRCUS   The original Russell Bros. Circus was operated by Mr. and Mrs. C.W. Webb beginning in the 1920s. Throughout the 1930s the show grew into a large motorized circus.

Russell Bros. Circus performed throughout the Midwest until 1941 when its WINTER QUARTERS and most of its route was transferred to California. The show opened in Los Angeles in 1942 and was sold to Art CONCELLO for the 1943 season.

In 1944 a merger transformed the show into the CLYDE BEATTY & RUSSELL BROS. CIRCUS. It was moved onto rails the following year as the Russell Bros. Pan-Pacific Circus. In 1946 the operation was bought out by Clyde BEATTY.

RUSSELL BROS. PAN-PACIFIC CIRCUS   See RUSSELL BROS. CIRCUS.

S

SAFETY LOOP Attached to the WEB, the safety loop is the canvas-covered loop into which the artist places a hand while performing the aerial ballet. After the wrist is placed through the loop itself, a small strap is slipped against the wrist to keep the hand from accidentally falling out.

Such a loop may, of course, also be used on an ankle or, with great care, the neck. A safety loop is also commonly seen on pieces of other aerial apparatus such as the Roman ladders.

(See also AERIAL ACTS.)

SAILOR CIRCUS The Sailor Circus of SARASOTA, FLORIDA is an annual event, open to all students from Sarasota County who maintain a grade of C or better in their scholastic work. William D. Lee, the circus's director, describes the Sailor Circus as an extension of the same "pursuit of excellence" to be found in the classroom.

The circus was founded in 1950 under the direction of Bill Rutland. At first it was a coeducational tumbling and acrobatics demonstration and was part of the school system's physical education program. Five hundred people crammed the small gymnasium to see the first performance.

The Sailor Circus now maintains its own rehearsal building; training begins there as early as October of each year. By the end of March, approximately 60 students are selected to take part in the circus. The show itself is performed under canvas. By 1973 it was performed under a tent that covered 28,320 square feet and seated 2,250 people.

Because the community is very much aware of its circus traditions—in fact, many of the performers belong to circus families—the level of performance is exceptionally high for an amateur student show. The RINGLING BROS. AND BARNUM & BAILEY CIRCUS also gives its blessing to the show, allowing the Sailor Circus to paraphrase its trademarked motto and call itself "The Greatest Little Show on Earth."

SALSBURY, NATHAN (1846–1903) In 1882 William F. CODY met with Nathan Salsbury, an actor-turned-promoter, in Brooklyn, New York, to discuss the possibility of FRAMING A SHOW to trade on Buffalo Bill's fame as an Indian fighter. Some sources suggest that it was actually Salsbury who conceived the idea for a Wild West.

It was not until after Cody's final European tour, however, that Salsbury joined forces in the management of BUFFALO BILL'S WILD WEST. In 1894 they were joined by James A. BAILEY.

Salsbury remained a partner when, following Bailey's death in 1906, Major Gordon W. "Pawnee Bill" LILLIE bought out the Bailey interest. The show was renamed BUFFALO BILL WILD WEST AND PAWNEE BILL GREAT FAR EAST SHOW.

SALUTO, FRANKIE (1906–1982) Frankie Saluto, one of the LITTLE PEOPLE, was a longtime WHITEFACE CLOWN with the RINGLING BROS. AND BARNUM & BAILEY CIRCUS.

A dwarf, Saluto began clowning in 1928. One of his favorite routines was his uncanny impression of a miniature Charlie Chaplin. In Lou JACOBS's famous clown car sketch, Saluto played the bewildered gas station attendant. He was best known for his CLOWN WALKAROUND gag with a live rabbit that was almost as large as he was. The rabbit went through a long string of names before Saluto finally settled on "Buns."

CLOWNS—natural pranksters—frequently play gags on each other as well. One famous practical joke involved the others in CLOWN ALLEY telling Frankie that there was a fatal epidemic passing among rabbits. The telltale symptom was the rabbit's feet turning black. Needless to say, they dyed Buns's paws black. Saluto was so distressed that the rabbit was quickly "cured" by the other clowns and returned to his "healthy" pure white.

Saluto was a member of the Ringling Giants, a baseball team made up of the Ringling little people, who played exhibition games for publicity and charity causes. In his will, John RINGLING bequeathed a diamond stickpin to the one clown chosen "most popular" by his peers in the clown alley; Saluto won the honor.

Frankie Saluto retired in 1974 after 46 years in the circus ring.

(See also CLOWN GAGS.)

SAM B. DILL CIRCUS & TOM MIX WILD WEST   See MIX, TOM.

SAM DOCK CIRCUS   Sam Dock, born in Pennsylvania, toured various shows throughout the East Coast—usually under his name—beginning with the original Sam Dock Circus around 1887. In 1951 he was on his grandson's small unit, also titled the Sam Dock Circus.

(See also A.F. WHEELER SHOWS.)

SANDS, RICHARD (1814–1861)   After performing as a CLOWN and trick rider with the AARON TURNER CIRCUS in 1831, Richard Sands was hired to manage shows owned by Nathan A. HOWES and Seth B. HOWES and eventually became a co-owner of several small circuses.

In 1842 he became a partner of Lewis B. LENT in the R. Sands & Co.'s Circus. By performing in England from 1843 through 1845, his show became the first indigenous American show to perform overseas. The show returned to the United States

and toured as an arena and tent show for ten years. Lent left the company, and John J. Nathans (1814–1891), a veteran equestrian and circus manager, took over his shares.

With Nathans, Seth B. Howes, Avery Smith and other minor partners, Sands build a permanent circus building at the northwest corner of Broadway and 23rd Street, also known as Madison Square, in New York City. The New York Hippodrome, modeled after the stadium owned by the FRANCONI FAMILY in Paris, held 4,000 spectators and contained a 700-foot arena track. In fact, the Franconis were brought to the United States to perform in the inaugural Hippodrome season.

There the "hippodrome track," as the wide area between the rings and the seating came to be known, was introduced to the American circus. It was this broad track fully surrounding the rings for the entire circumference of the arena that allowed the GRAND ENTRY at the start of the circus show to evolve into the true spectacular, or SPEC.

Following a three-week resident show, Sands, Nathans & Co. took their Hippodrome circus on the road. The major expenses incurred in trying to make the road company as glamorous as the indoor Hippodrome made the tour unprofitable. After smaller indoor and tented engagements, the company returned to New York, where shows continued in the Hippodrome until late November 1853.

The company stayed in operation until Richard Sands died in Havana, Cuba on February 24, 1861. As with so many other popular showmen, his death did not deter other unauthorized circuses from using the Sands title long afterward.

(See also MADISON SQUARE GARDEN; P.T. BARNUM'S GREAT ROMAN HIPPODROME.)

SANDS & LENT CIRCUS   See LENT, LEWIS B.

SANDS & QUICK'S MENAGERIE   The Sands & Quick's Menagerie was formed by the Richard SANDS group, which already owned another circus MENAGERIE. By 1852 both were overstocked with animals that had recently been imported from England.

Sometime during the 1850s ROBINSON & ELDRED'S GREAT SOUTHERN SHOW—on a northern swing—either leased or purchased the menagerie, with the first existing advertising for its inclusion in the circus dated December 9, 1852 in Raleigh, North Carolina.

A more precise date of the menagerie's leaving the show *is* known. On June 28, 1856 in Richmond, Virginia, the Robinson-Eldred 11-year partnership collapsed and Eldred bought Robinson's half of the show. Eldred was unable to keep up payments and on October 21, 1857 a lien was placed on the renamed G.N. Eldred's Great Southern Show by Sands, Nathans, Quick and Avery Smith in Medina, Ohio.

(See also ELDRED, GILBERT N.)

SANGER CIRCUS   See SANGER'S GREAT EUROPEAN CIRCUS.

SANGER'S GREAT EUROPEAN CIRCUS   Although the name originated with Lord George Sanger in England, the Sanger title initially reached the United States as part of Seth B. HOWES's circus, HOWE'S GREAT LONDON CIRCUS AND SANGER'S ROYAL BRITISH MENAGERIE. The title later became part of the circus owned by P.T. BARNUM, James A. BAILEY and James L. HUTCHINSON. The other American shows that used the title were not in any way associated with the British operation. The first recorded unauthorized use of the name in the United States was by Jeremiah "Jerry" MUGIVAN and Bert BOWERS. When they purchased the Dide Fisk Circus, they called it the Sanger Circus for the 1911–13 seasons.

To compete with the JOHN ROBINSON CIRCUS, Mugivan and Bowers bought Dan ROBINSON's name in 1913. Over a weekend, they painted over the "Sanger" name on the WAGONS and rechristened the show the FAMOUS ROBINSON CIRCUS.

(See also P.T. BARNUM'S GREATEST SHOW ON EARTH, HOWES' GREAT LONDON CIRCUS AND SANGER'S ROYAL BRITISH MENAGERIE.)

SARASOTA, FLORIDA   Sarasota's association with the circus world began when John RINGLING, a speculator in Florida real estate, built his "dream house"—which he called CA' D'ZAN (House of John)—on his property there. Resembling a Venetian palace, the mansion cost nearly $1.5 million, which included the seawall, swimming pool and adjoining buildings. Construction lasted from 1924 to 1926. In 1927, perhaps to increase the value of his own property and the worth of Florida land in general, John moved the headquarters of the RINGLING BROS. AND BARNUM & BAILEY CIRCUS from BRIDGEPORT, CONNECTICUT to Sarasota. Located on the west coast of Florida, just south of Tampa and St. Petersburg, Sarasota was the circus's home for 34 years before John Ringling NORTH moved it to Venice, Florida in 1961.

To this day Sarasota is considered a "circus city," serving as the permanent residence of many retired show folk; even more return to trailer parks each winter during the circus's hiatus. English is definitely the second language among the European and South American circus artists living in these parks, where a cacophony of native tongues can always be heard. Today, the population of Sarasota is over 52,000; but the number swells to twice that during the winter months, due in large part to the many off-season circus performers.

During the years The BIG ONE quartered in Sarasota, the city was a constant hubbub of circus activity. The Ringling quarters took up 200 acres and was open year-round as a tourist attraction. On Sunday visitors could enjoy two matinee performances, a big MENAGERIE and a display of floats and WAGONS. The weekly show took place in an open-air arena nicknamed the LITTLE MADISON SQUARE GARDEN by show people, where newcomers showcased their talents and veterans kept their old acts fresh and tried out new routines.

In the winter of 1925, the first Mennonite family moved to Sarasota from the North, and friends and family soon followed to help farm celery. Soon more than 100 families were living in Sarasota. Not as strict in their religious beliefs as their more orthodox brethren the Amish, the Mennonites socialized and quickly became true circus fans. Perhaps the greatest dichotomy seen in the circus city were the number of Mennonite visitors to the quarters—the plain people standing amid the tinsel, sparkle and glitter of the costumed showgirls.

During the winter months, not just on the circus grounds but in backyards all over the city, artists practiced their acts and worked on new routines. Meanwhile, on the quarters, painters, carpenters and mechanics readied the equipment for a new season.

Until John Ringling North took the show out from under canvas in 1956, the grounds housed a huge tent factory, nicknamed the "sail loft," where new tents were created for the following year and old tents were repaired. During the heyday of the tented Ringling show, a new BIG TOP was introduced every year.

Winter in Sarasota, Florida means rehearsal for the new season. A group of young boys watch the female aerialists practice in March of 1940. The backyard rigging looks much the same today.   (Author's collection)

Sarasota did not play host to just the Ringling show. Less than a mile from the Ringling grounds were the winter quarters of the Cristiani Brothers Circus. In the 1950s the show moved its quarters to Sarasota from Macon, Georgia.

Sarasota has been the site of many other circus attractions over the years, including the Florida state-owned Museum of the American Circus and the privately owned Circus Hall of Fame, both now closed. In addition, each year Sarasota plays host to many circus festivals and celebrations, not the least of which is Sarasota High School's SAILOR CIRCUS, an all-student youth circus that plays for several weeks in a tent adjoining the school. Other circus-related spots that may be visited are the JOHN AND MABLE RINGLING MUSEUM OF ART (which includes Ca' d'Zan, the Ringling art galleries and a circus museum on the grounds) and the SARASOTA CIRCUS RING OF FAME.

The first week of January each year, the city hosts the Sarasota International Circus Festival and Pa-

rade. Open daily from noon, the festival features band concerts, a children's circus show, magic shows, circus competitions and a gala dance. There are aerial acts, pony/camel/elephant rides, circus art and photography exhibits, model builder shows, plus many crafts for sale. The last day is reserved for the massive STREET PARADE that includes floats, bands and circus artists from around the world.

SARASOTA CIRCUS RING OF FAME   Located in St. Armands Circle across Sarasota Bay from downtown SARASOTA, FLORIDA, at the intersection of John Ringling Boulevard and the Boulevard of Presidents, the Sarasota Circus Ring of Fame honors many of the greatest performers ever to appear in the American circus. Each year in the late spring or early summer, a citizen committee made up of former circus performers, owners, managers and fans choose the artists who are then inducted into the Circus Ring of Fame the following winter.

The community project was started in 1988 in recognition of the many circuses, related activities and show folk who live in and around Sarasota. The site was selected because St. Armands Circle is round (like a circus ring) and was originally designed along with the rest of St. Armands Key by John RINGLING.

Sarasota artist Frank Hopper created the unique Ring of Fame, an authentic replica of a circus wagon wheel in bronze. In addition to the large statuary in the center of the circle, individual wheels accompanied by brass plaques salute the artists or troupes that have been selected.

In the North Quadrant of the Circle, Clyde BEATTY, Merle EVANS, John Ringling NORTH, Lou JACOBS, the Wallenda Troupe (see WALLENDAS, THE), the RINGLING BROTHERS, the Hanneford Family (see HANNEFORDS, THE), P.T. BARNUM and Felix ADLER are currently honored. The East Quadrant recognizes Fay Alexander (an aerialist on the FLYING TRAPEZE), Harold ALZANA, J.Y. ' 'Doc" HENDERSON, May WIRTH and the Zacchinis (see ZACCHINI, Hugo). Artists noted in the West Quadrant are Elly Ardelty (aerialist), James A. BAILEY, Otto GRIEBLING, the LOYAL-REPENSKY TROUPE and Gunther GEBEL-WILLIAMS. The South Quadrant pays tribute to the Cristiani Family (see CRISTIANIS, THE), Emmett KELLY, Lillian LEITZEL, La Norma (TRAPEZE artist), Franz UNUS, Antoinette CONCELLO, the Clarke Family (equestrians and aerialists; see CLARKE, CHARLES AND ERNEST), the Nelson

Family (ACROBATS and RISLEY ACT) and Wilson F. STOREY. These last four inductees, the most recent, were all added to the South Quadrant in a ceremony on December 30, 1992.

SCHLEENTZ, OSBORN R. "OZZIE" (1925–1991) A longtime circus veteran and ADVANCE MAN, Ozzie Schleentz was associated with the HUNT BROS. CIRCUS; the MILLS BROS. CIRCUS; the CARSON & BARNES CIRCUS; the Great American Circus; the Lewis Bros. Circus; the ROBERTS BROTHERS CIRCUS and the Allen Bros. Circus.

Schleentz was once a circus owner himself, having operated the Royal Ranch Wild West Circus. Born in Lakewood, New Jersey, he lived in Valdosta, Georgia, for the last 20 years of his life. After a long illness in a nursing home there, Ozzie Schleentz died on September 8, 1991.

SCRIBNER & SMITH CIRCUS See WALTER L. MAIN CIRCUS.

SEAT WAGONS In 1947, while traveling as manager for the RINGLING BROS. AND BARNUM & BAILEY CIRCUS, Art CONCELLO perfected and patented the modern seat wagon, a form of portable metal grandstand (35-feet long and holding 200 seats). Concello held U.S. Patent No. 2,635,889, granted on April 21, 1953, for the design of his wagons, first used on the road in 1948.

The concept of foldaway seats permanently mounted onto a truck bed is actually credited to William H. "Cap" Curtis , then on the HAGENBECK-WALLACE CIRCUS. His U.S. Patent No. 1,301,107 was granted on April 22, 1919. (As a side note, "Cap" Curtis went on to become Ringling's BOSS CANVASMAN under John Ringling NORTH's ownership and Concello's management. He also held the patent for the spool truck (see SPOOL WAGON).)

Concello, however, found a way to make his seat wagons more sturdy, durable and safe. He added stairways onto the sides of the folding steel seats so that patrons wouldn't trip while climbing over the bleacher-style seating to their locations. The new arrangement also prevented grandstand seats from collapsing due to too much weight or loose rigging.

So ingenious was the design that it has changed little since it was introduced on the tented Ringling Bros. and Barnum and Bailey Circus. Once the top is up, each wagon can be pulled into place and set within 45 minutes. Before seat wagons were invented, it took men up to four hours to set up wooden bleachers for the show and almost as long to strike them down.

A bonus of the motorized seat wagon is that the space behind, between and under the bleachers is all available to the performers as waiting areas and makeshift dressing rooms for quick changes.

SEILS-STERLING CIRCUS Growing out of the Lindemann Bros. Circus of the 1920s, the Seils-Sterling Circus was a large motorized circus in the 1930s. The show went out of business and the equipment was disbursed in 1938.

SELLS & GRAY See WILLIE SELLS SHOWS.

SELLS BROTHERS CIRCUS The four Sells brothers—Ephraim (1834–1898), Lewis (1841–1907), Peter Sells, Jr. (1845–1904) and, briefly, William "Ad" Allen (1836–1894)—of Columbus, Ohio owned and operated their first circus under the title the Paul Silverburg Mammoth Quadruple Alliance, Museum, Menagerie, Caravan and Circus in 1872. In 1875 the show was using the Sells name.

The show continued to grow; and by 1878, when the show moved from wagons onto rail, it was already touring as the Sells Bros. Circus. That same year the Sells brothers purchased much of the MONTGOMERY QUEEN CIRCUS equipment and moved it onto rails as a second unit. By 1884 the original rail show had retitled itself the Sells Bros. 50-Cage 4-Ring Circus; it was this edition of the Sells Bros. Circus that was joined by Frank BUTLER and Annie OAKLEY.

In 1885 one show had reached a 45-rail car length; the other unit carried 44 cars. In the 1880s the second unit was managed by S.H. Barrett, a nephew; and in 1889 and 1890 his name was added to the show's title and was seen in advertising and on posters. Among the circus's star performers was Billy Burke, a clown and father of actress Billie Burke.

In 1887 the Sells show had what was probably the longest official title in circus history: Sells Brothers' World Conquering and All-Overshadowing 3-Ring Circus, Real Roman Hippodrome, Grand Firemen's Tournament, Indian Village and Museum, Five Continent Menagerie and Pawnee Bill's Famous

Original Wild West. In 1888 the units were merged into the Sells Bros. and Barrett's Colossal United Shows; the following year the official name became the Sells Bros. Circus.

With 42 rail cars, the Sells Bros. Circus was only the third largest show in the country by 1891, bested by the BARNUM & BAILEY CIRCUS and the ADAM FOREPAUGH CIRCUS. The show made an unprofitable tour of Australia that year and returned to San Francisco on June 9, 1892.

In 1896, the two surviving Sells brothers joined with James A. BAILEY in creating the ADAM FOREPAUGH & SELLS BROS. CIRCUS out of the old Sells Bros. Circus equipment. Nine years later Bailey acquired full ownership of the show and immediately sold a half interest to the RINGLING BROTHERS. They continued touring the show as a separate entity through 1908 and again in 1910 and 1911. Although an entirely different show, the title was used for legal purposes one last time in 1935 on the Ringling-owned Hagenbeck-Wallace & Forepaugh-Sells Bros. Circus.

SELLS FLOTO-BUFFALO BILL CIRCUS See SELLS-FLOTO CIRCUS.

SELLS-FLOTO CIRCUS In 1902 H.H. Tammen and F.G. Bonfils, the owners of the Denver *Post*, operated a small circus, the FLOTO DOG & PONY SHOW. The show was named after Otto Floto, the newspaper's sports reporter. By 1906 the show had grown such that it needed a more marketable name; thus the owners brought Willie Sells (1865–1908), a nephew of the Sells brothers, into the company as "director general." The name of the show was changed to the more respectable Sells-Floto Circus. Although Sells left after one season, the title was maintained.

By this time, however, the SELLS BROTHERS CIRCUS title was owned by the RINGLING BROTHERS. So circusgoers would not confuse the two operations, the Ringlings sued the Sells-Floto show in 1909, ordering it not to use photos of the original Sells brothers in its advertising.

Four years later the BUFFALO BILL WILD WEST AND PAWNEE BILL GREAT FAR EAST SHOW went bankrupt. Tammen and Bonfils hired Buffalo Bill and, in 1914 and 1915, toured their show as the Sells Floto-Buffalo Bill Circus, with William F. CODY (Buffalo Bill) as one of the main attractions.

The following year Cody joined the 101 Ranch company, and their circus was retitled the BUFFALO BILL & 101 RANCH WILD WEST. The Sells-Floto Circus, meanwhile, returned to touring under its old name.

In 1916, with the departure of Cody, the circus was retitled The Sells-Floto Champion Shows, featuring boxing champ Jess WILLARD and wrestler Frank Gotch for the season. The following year the circus was managed by Henry B. Gentry, one of the owners of the defunct GENTRY BROS. CIRCUS. At the end of the 1920 tour, the Sells-Floto Circus was sold to the AMERICAN CIRCUS CORPORATION, which operated it from 1921 through 1929. It was the Sells-Floto Circus that the Corporation placed into the regular Ringling date in MADISON SQUARE GARDEN in 1929. When John RINGLING bought the corporation, the Sells-Floto show became his property and title. Ringling toured it as a separate unit from 1930 through 1932.

In a final hurrah, the title was added onto the AL G. BARNES CIRCUS, making a last appearance in the 1937 and 1938 seasons.

SET UP Circus jargon for the operation of erecting the circus, from LAY OUT at dawn until all of the TENTS are in the air. Although the set up is a daily ritual for the tented caravan, it requires a master of management abilities. In a few short hours an entire community can be built on a LOT that was empty the day before.

The set up begins with the first rays of daylight when the LAYOUT MAN walks the lot and decides where to position the many tents, vehicles and pieces of show equipment. The lay out man must consider the direction from which the patrons will be arriving, any unmovable or unchangeable hazards (such as tree stumps, boulders, trenches, swampy areas) on the lot and the ability for all of the show units to squeeze onto the field. He paces the lot and marks the positions for the various tents, poles and vehicles by driving long, thin white metal rods, or "pins," into the ground.

After the lot has been pinned, the BOSS CANVASMAN (sometimes the same person as the lay out man) signals the show vehicles to drop their piles of canvas, poles and STAKES and other paraphernalia at the appropriately marked locations. While the boss canvasman usually assumes duties on the BIG TOP, each tent has its own canvas man and crew as well.

These crews—augmented by town boys hired by the local sponsor in exchange for free circus passes—begin the set up within an hour of the show's arrival on the lot.

The canvas is spread and the SLEDGE GANG begins to drive in the stakes around the tarp. Once the tents are in the air, rigging is set inside the arenas while the BANNERLINES, MARQUEE and ticket boxes are set outside.

Meanwhile, the BACK YARD comes to life. The COOKHOUSE dining tent goes up first, feeding the hungry, tired workers and performers in shifts. Artists help set their rigging and tend to their animals, while others prepare their small dressing tents.

Finally, by midmorning, everything is set and everyone awaits the call of DOORS! to open the BIG TOP for the matinee performance.

SHANTY Circus jargon for the electrician who operates the lights. Sometimes he is also known as the "chandelier."

SHILL Although more common as a carnival term, "shill" refers to someone who pretends to be part of the public or townsfolk but is really paid by the show.

One of the major differences between the carnival and the circus is that circuses operate clean, family entertainment and today do not operate games—especially crooked ones—on the MIDWAY.

On a GRIFT show, however, shills would play games and operators would let them win. The game would look easy to beat, so the locals would gather to play and soon lose money.

Even on a SUNDAY SCHOOL show a shill might be employed by the SIDESHOW to help draw a crowd, or TIP, to the BALLY platform as the TALKER begins the PITCH. Many times even eager patrons are hesitant to start lines to buy tickets; thus, when the box office opens to the sideshow, the shill is the first up to the ticket box. To help make the show look busy, he might also be seen holding souvenirs or refreshments or even standing in line by the RED WAGON, or box office.

SHINER, DAVID See CIRQUE DU SOLEIL.

SHOWING Circus jargon for the total amount of advertising displayed in the complete papering of a town and its surrounding communities. This includes all of the LITHOGRAPHS, HERALDS, WINDOW CARDS and banners in place.

It does not, however, refer to any single display, no matter how spectacular it might be. A TROUPER would never say "Isn't that side of a barn covered by 24 sheets a remarkable showing?" Instead he would remark, "That town's showing really brought in the business!"

(See also BILLING CREW; DAUB; HANG PAPER; HIT; LOCATION.)

SHOWMEN'S REST Located in the Mount Olive Cemetery in Hugo, Oklahoma, Showmen's Rest is the burial spot of many of America's premier circus showmen, such as Obert Miller, "Big" John STRONG and Herbie WEBER.

Information on the site can be obtained by contacting P.O. Box 310, Hugo, OK 74743.

SHRINE CIRCUS In today's circus world, most circuses on the road operate under local auspices, working in conjunction with an area sponsor to increase ticket sales.

For the smaller MUD SHOWS, this might be a chamber of commerce or other civic organization. The most active group to enter into the arena of sponsored shows is the Masonic order known as the Shriners.

The Shrine name and goodwill is so important to the sale of tickets that many times the actual name of the circus playing a date need not be given: It is merely the "Shrine Circus" that has come to town. Some circuses, such as the HAMID-MORTON CIRCUS and POLACK BROS. CIRCUS, specialize in filling Shrine dates, the oldest in the country being the Detroit Shrine Circus. For other Shrine venues, a circus booker or promotor, such as Paul V. KAYE, will put together a balanced show of available talent specifically for that run. Today there are more than 500 Shrine circuses appearing each year in the United States.

Usually a local Shrine outfit contracts with a particular circus or agent for a single run of shows; but several clubs may go together to arrange a "tour" for the circus, increasing the profits to both the show (they can get artists and materials cheaper because expenses can be distributed over many weeks of work) and to the Shrine (because the circus is grossing more on the whole tour, it can charge each individual club less for its services). This sort of block booking has resulted in amenable arrangements such as the TEXAS SHRINE DATES.

Generally, the Shrine provides the hall, undertakes advance sales and provides local permits. In addition to the show, the circus provides advertising and promotional backup. Some agreed-upon fixed costs are deducted from the gross income, and the net profit is split between the circus management and the Shrine on a sliding scale; as the show grosses more, the Shrine earns a higher percentage.

(See also BOILER ROOM; HAMID, GEORGE A.; MORTON, ROBERT; PHONE PROMOTER.)

SIAMESE TWINS   A sideshow staple, the term "Siamese Twins" refers to siblings of either sex who are inseparately linked at birth at some part of their bodies.

The phrase had its origin with CHANG AND ENG, the famous cojoined twins exhibited by P.T. BARNUM. Although the pair had Chinese parents, they were born in Siam. Hence they were dubbed Siamese Twins and the term has been used to describe similar human oddities ever since.

(See also FREAKS.)

SIDEPOLE   Circus jargon for the poles—wooden or aluminum—that surround the TENTS, holding up the canvas top.

On a PUSH POLE tent, sidepoles are erected before the top. The canvas is laid out, laced if there are multiple sections and tied to STAKES. The crew then works its way around the top, lifting each sidepole into place. As it does, the crew will also GUY OUT the tent, adjusting the tension of each rope. The CENTER POLE is slid into position and raised after all of the sidepoles are in place.

On a BALE RING tent, the center poles are erected first. The canvas is then unrolled, laced and connected to the bale rings. Then the sidepoles are raised, followed by the canvas being hauled up the center poles.

Larger tents sometimes require the support of a second ring of poles halfway between the outer sidepoles and the center poles. These inner sidepoles are known as QUARTER POLES.

Two small animal sideshows line the midway on the 1991 season of the Carson & Barnes Circus in Ojai, California. (Photos by Tom Ogden)

SIDESHOW   Housed under a tent nicknamed the LITTLE TOP, the sideshow is the largest canvas on the circus MIDWAY. Performing inside the "sideshow and annex of human wonders" are acts such as the sword swallower, the human pincushion, the fat lady, the electric lady and the contortionist.

Outside the tent is the bally platform, usually a 4-by-8 foot piece of plywood on workhorses that is draped with a canvas drop cloth. On each side of the platform is a ticket booth; if business is expected to be heavy, an extra ticket booth (or JUMP STAND) might be placed in the center of midway.

Along the front side of the tent itself is the BANNERLINE, a line of pictures painted onto heavy cloth, tarp or canvas, hauled up by ropes on pulleys between upright poles. Instead of using a "rag bannerline," some modern circuses park the tractor trailers that haul the tent and equipment in its place. Colorful illustrations on the sides of the trucks take the place of the banners. Some shows, such as the current Kelly-Miller Bros. Circus, have used a truck bannerline with additional rag banners at either end.

After the TALKER has given his BALLY to bring the TOWNERS into the tent, he calls for the salesmen to open the ticket boxes. He then breaks into a repetitious GRIND. As patrons file into the tent, DUCAT GRABBERS take their tickets.

Surrounding the inside SIDEWALLS of the tent are numerous platforms, each holding a different attraction. The performers range from fire-eaters to midgets. Once enough people have gotten inside, an INSIDE TALKER goes from platform to platform—or from performer to performer—explaining what the viewer is seeing. Sometimes artists take the microphone themselves to give their talks especially if they are going to give a PITCH for a postcard, magic packet or other souvenir.

After the talker has described the last act, spectators are given a few minutes to walk around and look again at those "human oddities" that remain on their platform. When the talker senses there has been a big enough "turnover" in his crowd, he starts a new show at the first platform. As the man outside has said, "It's never out; it's never over. They go round and round like a merry-go-round." The acts are repeated again and again until it is time for the main show to begin.

By the 1950s, most motorized shows had scaled back their operations. The MENAGERIE was often included within the sideshow top, with live performers lining one long wall and the cage wagons and standing animals against the opposite side. In the 1990s, few circuses carry a menagerie, a sideshow or a combined menagerie-sideshow. The only complete traditional circus sideshow currently touring is on the Kelly-Miller Bros. Circus.

Technically, any tented attraction on the front end (or FRONT YARD) that requires an additional admission is a sideshow. Another type of sideshow more often seen on the modern circus midway than the traditional large show of variety artists and FREAKS is a "single-o," a small tent that exhibits one attraction, such as the "World's Smallest Horse" or a themed display, such as a snake show "Reptilerama." A PIT SHOW is a very specific type of a single-o attraction, not technically called a sideshow and most often seen today on carnival rather than circus LOTS.

The true pit show gets its name because the exhibition, usually a human "geek," is set in a shallow trench or pit dug out under the top.

SIDEWALL Circus jargon for the lengths of canvas that stretch around the perimeter of the TENTS to enclose the attractions inside. The sidewall is one of the last pieces of canvas affixed to the tent, added after all of the SIDEPOLES are in place and the top is raised.

The sidewall is connected in one of two ways. Usually the top has a metal ring on the underside of the fringe near each grommet hole for the sidepole. A cord attached to the sidewall is passed through the ring, the sidewall is drawn up, and the rope is tied to the nearest sidepole. Sometimes, however, the underside of the canvas top has a cord running around the circumference to which the sidewall is clipped.

In the event of a storm, ROUSTABOUTS and all circus personnel who are not otherwise involved might be asked to "sit sidewall"—that is, literally stand or sit on the bottom edge of the sidewall to keep high winds from gusting under the walls of the tent and lifting the TOP. An emergency chore like sitting sidewall is a good example of the need for the "GENERALLY USEFUL" clause in most circus contracts.

SIG SAUTELLE CIRCUS Beginning his career as a ventriloquist, Sig Sautelle opened a small wagon circus in 1885. It moved onto rails in 1902 and remained so through the 1905 season. The Sig Sautelle Circus switched back and forth between wagon and rail for the next several seasons, finally folding in 1919.

SKELTON, RICHARD "RED" (1913–   ) The creator of one of the most memorable TRAMP CLOWN characters in American history, Red Skelton was born Richard Skelton on July 18, 1913 in Vincennes, Indiana.

His father, a clown with the HAGENBECK-WALLACE CIRCUS, died two months before Skelton was born. Richard's bright red hair as a youth gained him the nickname of "Red," which stuck with him throughout his career.

Before he was 16 Skelton joined the same show as his father. Although he left touring circuses by his 20s, the skills he developed in CLOWN ALLEY have served him since as his career diverged to include singing, acting and dancing in minstrel shows, medicine shows and later vaudeville, radio, television and films. Today his original oil paintings and lithographs of CLOWNS are in high demand, and Red Skelton remains a beloved entertainer whose concerts are sellouts whenever he performs.

SKY BOARDS Circus jargon for the illustrated boards trimming the top of the CAGE WAGONS used in STREET PARADES.

(See also SPLASH BOARDS.)

SKYWALK A skywalk is a daredevil feat of WIRE WALKING in which the height or length of the cable exceeds that of a normal high wire act (approximately 30 feet high and 35 feet long).

(See also BLONDIN; PETIT, PHILIPPE; WALLENDA, KARL.)

SLACK WIRE See COLLEANO, CON; MILLMAN, BIRD; WIRE WALKING.

SLANGER Circus jargon—uncommonly heard—for a lion or tiger trainer.

SLEDGE GANG Circus jargon for the work crew that pounds in the tent STAKES each morning. Several people form a circle around a stake. Many times to a repeated chant, each man would hit the top of the stake with a sledgehammer in turn until it is driven far enough into the ground.

An efficient sledge gang is truly amazing and beautiful to watch—arms and hammers are all continually in motion, each member of the gang tied to the motions of the person next to him.

SNAKE CHARMER A standard SIDESHOW act in the tented circus, the snake charmer was usually a woman, often scantily clad, who did little more than hold up a variety of nonvenomous reptiles for display as the INSIDE TALKER described them. During the act, the snake charmer almost always wrapped at least one giant boa constrictor around her neck or body.

Many times the vipers were not owned by the snake charmer, but were cared for by one of the regular animal trainers. One of the BALLY BROADS or perhaps the wife or girlfriend of one of the other

performers on the LOT would offer to handle the reptiles as an extra source of weekly income.

Snakes were not seen only in the sideshow. Many times a separate PIT SHOW on the other side of the MIDWAY offered the townsfolk an opportunity to see the rare giant jungle serpents.

(See also BALLY.)

SOFT LOT Circus jargon for a wet or muddy lot. The LAYOUT MAN needs particular skill on a soft lot, because he must place the heaviest vehicles where they will sink the least.

Also, it is courteous—and good business—to place the MIDWAY in an area where townsfolk will not have to walk through thick mud to reach the BIG TOP. Patrons will not freely move about from concession to concession in the mud and may cluster too close to the FRONT DOOR to be drawn back to the SIDESHOW during the BALLY. Also, potential visitors who don't already have tickets might turn back from a midway that is too muddy.

One cosmetic solution to this problem is to spread hay thickly over the mud on the midway.

SOMERS, NEW YORK Often referred to as the "Cradle of the American Circus," Somers is located approximately 50 miles north of New York City. It was there in 1815 that a local entrepreneur, Hachaliah BAILEY, bought OLD BET, the second elephant to reach and be exhibited in the United States.

Many area residents were influenced by Bailey's success and also entered the MENAGERIE business. Several became famous names in the annals of the American circus, including Aaron TURNER, John J. JUNE, Lewis B. TITUS, Caleb S. ANGEVINE and the Howes and Crane families.

Today in Somers an obelisk built to Old Bet's memory can be seen in front of Bailey's ELEPHANT HOTEL. It was in this hotel that 128 menagerie owners and businessmen met in January 1835 to form the ZOOLOGICAL INSTITUTE.

SPALDING, "DR." GILBERT R. (1812–1880) Gilbert R. "Doc" Spalding owned and operated a drugstore (where he obtained his nickname for selling patent medicines) near Albany, New York until 1843, when he became infatuated with show business when he foreclosed on S.H. Nichols's Amphitheatre. By April 11, 1844, Spalding was on tour in Troy, New York, with his new show, the North American Circus (formerly NICHOLS CIRCUS.

Spalding was intelligent and creative: He invented the QUARTER POLE, a SIDEPOLE that is placed midway between the CENTER POLES and the SIDEWALL to take up the slack in the canvas top and increase stability. He also invented the JACKS AND STRINGER system of 11-tiered bleacher seating, which has remained a standard for setting the BLUES in the general admission section of the BIG TOP on a MUD SHOW. Both were probably introduced in 1848. In 1850, Spalding was also the first to use "lime light" lanterns rather than candles to illuminate the tents during night performances.

In 1848, Spalding became the first circus operator to purchase his own steamboat (the *Allegheny Mail*) to tour his show.

Spalding is often credited with being the first to take a circus onto rails, although he did not do so exclusively or on a regular basis. In 1853, Spalding was probably responsible for his brother-in-law, W.T.B. Van Orden, briefly taking the "Railroad Circus & Crystal Amhitheatre" onto rails. In 1854 he started the Great Western Railroad Circus, toured the Spalding & Rogers New Railroad Circus in 1856 and in the mid-1860s he ordered special rail cars adaptable for different gauges of rail.

For years, much of Spalding's career entwined with the most famous circus clown of his time, Dan RICE. Spalding was the owner of the North American Circus when it was visited for a second time by Rice in Pittsburgh. Spalding was immediately impressed by the talent and charisma of Rice and invited him to join the show.

Spalding was to become a lifelong savior and nemesis for Rice. In 1848 Rice left Spalding. Despite the split, some historians believe Spalding had a part in financing and organizing Rice's first solo outing, the DAN RICE CIRCUS on the *Allegheny Mail* in May 1848.

That same year, Charles J. Rogers became the star equestrian on the North American Circus. At season's end, he bought an interest in the show which was renamed Spalding & Rogers North American Circus, or the SPALDING & ROGERS CIRCUS.

It has been documented that when Spalding next met with Rice in 1849, the famous clown was near the peak of his popularity but physically drained from a recent bout with yellow fever. Rice accepted Spalding's invitation to join him in a new show. The union was short-lived, however, and a bitter division followed. The artists battled whenever they played near one another, and in 1850 Rice was jailed for slander against Spalding and his partner.

In 1852 with his partner Charles J. Rogers, Spalding created his masterpiece for which he is most often remembered, the *FLOATING PALACE.* Idle only during the most dangerous periods of the Civil War, the *Palace* accidentally burned to the waterline in New Albany, Indiana in the spring of 1865.

Meanwhile, Dan Rice had lost his famous circus, DAN RICE'S ONE-HORSE SHOW, due to the economics of the Civil War. Once again Spalding surfaced, this time to offer Rice the princely sum of $1,000 per week to tour with him. Rice refused.

In the end, Spalding was perhaps responsible for Rice's final failure. In 1868 Spalding approached him with the offer to sell his newest creation, a portable canvas-topped wooden amphitheater that he had named the PARIS PAVILION. Rice borrowed heavily to purchase the Pavilion, but the tours were not economically successful, forcing Rice into bankruptcy.

Spalding died in New Orleans on April 16, 1880.

SPALDING & ROGERS CIRCUS In 1848 Charles J. Rogers (1817–1895), a star equestrian, joined the North American Circus owned by "Dr." Gilbert R. SPALDING, coming from the Rufus WELCH show. Rogers had arrived in the United States in 1821 with William West's English circus. At the end of the season, Rogers, an apt student in circus entrepreneurship, bought an interest in the show, which was renamed Spalding & Rogers' North American Circus in 1849.

It was on the Spalding & Rogers Circus around 1848 that Spalding first introduced QUARTER POLES and JACKS AND STRINGERS. Spalding also replaced the commonly used candles with "lime light" lamps under the canvas for night performances at about this same time. The circus performed year-round, appearing in southern theaters during the winter months. In 1851, they had a second troupe on the road, Spalding, Rogers & Van Orden's People's Circus.

In March 1852 their river circus arena, the *FLOATING PALACE,* was christened in Pittsburgh, Pennsylvania. As the *Floating Palace* plied the Ohio and

Mississippi rivers, pulled by the steamboat *North River,* Spalding and Rogers continued touring their wagon show as the North American Circus. During the winter the steamer show performed next to the DAN RICE CIRCUS in New Orleans.

On October 15, 1853 the *James Raymond* replaced the *North River* in Cincinnati, Ohio. The Van Amburgh & Raymond Menagerie was purchased and added to the show the next year.

The year 1855 was one of diversification for Spalding and Rogers. They replaced the *Floating Palace* circus show with a touring museum of oddities. The wagon show, which had continued to tour, was either split or duplicated, with each partner touring a separate show. Spalding's unit, which was probably known at the time as The Railroad Circus, traveled at least part of the season on railroad cars. On October 24, 1855 they purchased a second steamboat, *Banjo,* which presented minstrel and variety shows beginning the following season.

In 1856, in addition to all their other endeavors, they sent out two units of the Spalding & Rogers New Railroad Circus on nine railroad cars each that they had specially built to accommodate the shows. Also that year they toured a wagon show, Spalding & Rogers Two Circuses Combined. In December they combined their shows as the "Three Consolidated Circuses" in Mobile, Alabama. Spalding and Rogers purchased the Pelikan Theater in New Orleans for their winter performances and renamed it the Amphitheatre. When they moved their "Three Circuses in One" there at year's end, James ROBINSON was among the show's 30 performers.

Only the *Floating Palace* and *Banjo* minstrel shows toured in 1857, beginning their seasons on the first of March. In December and through January 1858, the owners called their Amphitheatre show Spalding & Rogers' New Orleans Circus. In the cast were two new clowns, Dan CASTELLO and "Dr." James L. Thayer (see THAYER & NOYES CIRCUS). Spalding and Rogers's outdoor amusement activities are uncertain for the 1858 season, but their show returned to the Amphitheatre as usual that December.

They toured a circus (probably Spalding & Rogers European Circus) up the Mississippi River beginning on March 14, 1859 and returned to New Orleans for a winter season through February 6, 1860. The show began upriver again on March 14, 1860, but this time it never returned. Keeping ahead of the Civil War hostilities, the circus moved north and eastward, finally opening in the Bowery Amphitheatre in New York City on November 5, 1860 and appearing through January 28, 1861. Dan Castello—listed as an acrobat—and Levi J. NORTH were in the company.

With their *Floating Palace* moored in New Albany, Indiana, Spalding and Rogers attempted to escape the Civil War conflicts by taking their circus to South America from 1862 until April 1864. Following a four-week stand at New York City's HIPPOTHEATRON, they toured west with the Ocean Circus, a wagon MUD SHOW.

From January 2 to February 19, 1865, the Ocean Circus ended its tour with an indoor date at the New Orleans Academy of Museum. Before the *Floating Palace* was able to return to traveling the river following the end of the war, it burned to the waterline in the spring of 1865. The circus owners took out one last wagon show that summer, following it in early autumn with Spalding, Rogers & Hanlon's Grand Combination, an indoor exhibition of AERIAL ACTS by the Hanlon brothers, in Chicago. Spalding and Rogers ended their 17-year partnership around October 8, 1865. Charles J. Rogers died on April 3, 1895.

SPANISH WEB   See WEB; WEB GIRL; WEB SITTER.

SPARKS, CHARLES   See SPARKS CIRCUS.

SPARKS CIRCUS   The Sparks Circus started as the John H. Sparks Old Virginia Shows in 1889. Only a two-car show in 1900, the circus was traveling on seven railroad cars by 1909. By 1916 Charles Sparks, the adopted son of John H. Sparks, was managing a show of 15 rail cars.

Work rapidly spread among show folk that the Sparks Circus was a perfect organization and Charles was a model manager, which earned the show the nickname the "circus man's circus." The show, best known in New England, continued to grow, and through the 1920s the circus toured on 20 cars. After the 1928 season Sparks sold the show, unaware that the true buyer was the AMERICAN CIRCUS CORPORATION.

The corporation toured the show in 1929 before selling it—along with the rest of its holdings—to John RINGLING. Ringling sent the Sparks Circus out as a separate unit in 1930 and 1931. John Ringling NORTH, head of the RINGLING BROS. AND BARNUM & BAILEY CIRCUS, leased the Sparks title to a motorized show in 1946. It moved onto rails one year later. The show folded at the end of the 1947 season in Washington state. Much of the equipment, including a BIG TOP with 120 rounds and 50-foot middles (see TENTS), was bought by Clyde BEATTY.

In the meantime, Charles Sparks had purchased the Downie Bros. Circus in 1930 and trouped it through 1938.

SPEC   Short for "spectacle," the term "Spec" is circus jargon for any major procession, parade or pageant in a circus show. Originally the grand opening of the circus, some shows (such as recent editions of the RINGLING BROS. AND BARNUM & BAILEY CIRCUS) now present the Spec directly before intermission.

The modern version of the Spec—a glorified parade around the hippodrome track of the performers and some of the MENAGERIE, all dressed in glittery wardrobe—bears little resemblance to the glorified spectacles during the heyday of the American tented circus.

At the turn of the century almost up until the Depression days, the Spec was presented in the form of a play or giant pageant. With a plot and story, the Spec could take up as much as the first half hour of the circus. Most of the themes were from the Bible, mythology or fairy tales; the show employed almost everyone involved on the show, including the bands, CLOWNS, animals and even the ROUSTABOUTS.

Performed on the arena track and in all three rings, some of the more famous Ringling Bros. Circus Specs were "Solomon and the Queen of Sheba," "Nero or the Burning of Rome" and "Joan of Arc." One of the earliest specs, "Cleopatra," was first produced by the BARNUM & BAILEY CIRCUS in 1895. The cast of 1,250 included 300 SPEC GIRLS,

"Bulls" become "swans" for the 1952 spec of the Ringling Bros. and Barnum & Bailey Circus.
(John Heckman photo from the Bakner collection)

500 mounted Roman soldiers, 500 Roman soldiers on horseback, 200 foot soldiers, 22 actors and the entire Barnum & Bailey menagerie. In the 1912 edition, the Spec used a giant stage that covered the seats on one whole side of the BIG TOP.

For the 1913 Ringling Bros. Circus production of "Joan of Arc" the show used a cast of 1,200 people, including 650 mounted soldiers plus 40 elephants. Their 1916 "Cinderella" used—in addition to the elaborate scenery—735 horses, all 1,310 performers plus all 60 clowns and "five herd of ELEPHANTS."

The last true "Spectacular" with special stages set up at end of the Big Top was "Aladdin and His Wonderful Lamp," performed on the 1917 and 1918 seasons of the Barnum & Bailey Circus.

The early Specs were true wonders to the eye, but because of their cost and slow action, they were soon dropped from the standard circus repertoire and were replaced by the up-tempo spangled grand entry at the beginning of the show that is today known as the Spec.

SPEC GIRLS   Circus jargon for the showgirls who appear in the grand pageant, or SPEC.

(See also BALLY BROAD.)

SPIEL   Circus jargon for an opening, PITCH or GRIND. The TALKER is sometimes known as the "spieler."

SPIELER   See SPIEL.

SPLASH BOARDS   Circus jargon for the decorated bottom border of CAGE WAGONS used in circus STREET PARADES.

(See also SKY BOARDS.)

SPOOL WAGON   Today standard equipment on any major show, the spool truck was virtually unknown during the days of the early MUD SHOW. The first experimentation with mounting gasoline-driven giant spools onto the back of circus WAGONS for the purposes of rolling and hauling canvas occurred in the 1920s. Until that time, canvas was folded and rolled on the ground by hand and then lifted by the ROUSTABOUTS onto the wagons. William H. Curtis, BOSS CANVASMAN on the SELLS-FLOTO CIRCUS, was granted U.S. Patent No. 1,184,672 for the first practical circus application of the spool principle.

Most historians credit Wayne C. Saguin and/or Kelly H. Miller with its adaptation to the motorized spool truck, the first major modification to the spool wagon. The two-spool truck was described in U.S. Patent No. 2,536,571, granted on January 2, 1951. The modern spool truck was first introduced on Kelly's family-owned AL G. KELLY & MILLER BROS. CIRCUS in 1949.

Like its wagon counterpart, the spool truck carried one or more spools—giant replicas of those that sewing thread comes on—permanently mounted on the back of the trailer. Each piece of the tent top is folded into a long strip of canvas in preparation for loading.

One of the principal changes in design from the spool wagon to the spool truck is the method of winding and unwinding the canvas. The horse-drawn spool wagon dragged the tent across the ground toward the spool, often causing great damage as the canvas was pulled across the LOT; the spool truck backs up toward the canvas as it rolls up onto the spool.

In the morning during SET UP, the spool truck slowly drives the length of the LAY OUT—away from the canvas—unwinding the tent according to the boss canvasman's desired placement.

ST. LOUIS   Circus jargon for seconds or a double helping of food at the COOKHOUSE.

The term originated because of the common circus practice of playing St. Louis in two sections on consecutive days, one on each side of the Mississippi.

STAKE BITE   Circus slang for a cut or gash in the leg caused by running into an unprotected metal stake. To prevent such an occurrence, a STAKE COVER—usually a section of a cut-off fire hose—is dropped over the exposed portion of the stake.

STAKE COVER   As the name suggests, the exposed end of each metal STAKE is covered to prevent the performers and the public from running into it and suffering accidental injury. While any canvas or padded material can be used, the most common stake cover is a section of cut-off fire hose slipped over the end of the stake.

To manufacture the stake cover, a small block of wood is positioned in one end of the section of hose. The end is nailed shut, through the canvas-covered

A descendant of the spool wagon is this modern spool truck, which was used on Allan C. Hill's Great American Circus in Hershey Pennsylvania in 1991. (Photo courtesy of Walter G. Heist, Jr.)

rubber hosing and into the block of wood. This closes off one end of the hose, which can then be placed over the end of the stake without its dropping to the ground.

(See also STAKE BITE.)

STAKES The SIDEPOLES on all TENTS are held in place by ropes that are tied to stakes driven in the ground. A MUD SHOW carries two types of stakes—metal and wooden—often in a rack nicknamed the POSSUM BELLY underneath the bed of the truck. Each type of stake has advantages and disadvantages.

Although sizes vary, metal stakes—commonly known in circus jargon as "irons" but made of steel—are usually about two feet in length and one inch in diameter. Cut from rods of steel, metal stakes can be made out of broken axle rods as well.

Metal stakes are more easily driven and removed from the ground than wooden stakes. Unless they hit a rock or are being used on macadam, metal stakes are almost impossible to break or bend. Ropes

tied to them will remain secure, and it is easy to GUY OUT on metal stakes.

The same properties of surface tension that make them easy to use can cause problems in bad weather. In wind, the ropes can easily slide up the smooth shaft of a metal stake; and, with less "grip," the stakes can be pulled out of the ground if a strong wind lifts the canvas top. In the rain, it is also possible for the stake hole to become flooded; causing the metal stake to lean or wash out of the ground.

Wooden stakes are about the same length as metal ones but are much broader, usually about four inches in diameter. Hewn from soft but durable wood and carved to a blunt point, a wooden stake has a ring of metal attached around the circumference of the top to prevent splitting.

Wooden stakes are more difficult to drive into the ground than metal stakes, but they provide extra safety and security because they are also more difficult to remove. Ropes will also remain guyed out

Minnie helps pull stakes during tear down on the Carson & Barnes Circus. Note how she has been trained to use her leg as leverage to lift the stake with little effort. (Photo by Tom Ogden)

longer on wooden stakes. Both are important considerations in wind or rain storms. Wooden stakes are bulky and heavy, and they can become almost impossible to pull out in muddy or damp ground.

One of the more fascinating sights on the old tent show LOT was the stake crew—known as the SLEDGE GANG—who drove in the stakes. Also of great interest to the circus fan is the removal of stakes at night. The crew works over the lot, tapping the side of each stake to loosen it from the ground. The stakes are then removed manually or by the ELEPHANTS led over the lot by the BULL HANDLERS.

More recently, the crews have been replaced by portable gas-driven stake-drivers, pulled behind cars or small trucks. The first gasoline-powered stake driver, a miniature "pile driver" mounted on the back of a wagon, was devised by George H. Heiser and introduced on the Ringling Bros. Circus in 1904. Still, stakes must be hand-driven in locations where stake-drivers cannot be taken, such as inside the tents or close to posts and equipment.

STAND   Circus jargon for the town in which a circus performs. Except when performing in the largest cities, most circuses appear in a new town every day. This practice has given rise to the phrase in the popular language of the "one-night stand."

STAR BACKS   Circus jargon for the more expensive "reserved section" seats; usually these are folding chairs with backs rather than bleacher seating.

STARK, MABEL (1889–1968)   Although there have been other female animal trainers before and since, no tamer of wild CATS has caught the imagination of the American circus public as much as Mabel Stark.

Born in Toronto, Canada, the young Stark was

Mabel Stark, the premiere female cat trainer of her generation, as she appeared in 1938.
(Photo courtesy of the *Herald Examiner* collection/Los Angeles Public Library)

raised on a tobacco farm in Kentucky. An attractive blonde, she trained as a nurse, but a breakdown following graduation sent her to California for recuperation. While there in 1911, she visited the Selig Zoo in Los Angeles, where she saw a stuntman wrestle a tiger. She bought the creature for $350 and began to train it herself.

She joined the AL G. BARNES CIRCUS as a horse groomer and became an equestrienne in 1911 or in 1912. She also had a pet tiger with her and wanted to perform a cat act. Barnes himself was a great lover and promoter of animal acts; he asked his noted cat trainer, Louis ROTH, to work with her. Roth reluctantly agreed, and Stark was an apt pupil.

In 1916 she became known as "the tiger lady" when she debuted her own arena-full of tigers. At the time, she was the only female to have broken, trained and performed with tigers, often with as many as an unprecedented 16 cats in the cage at one time.

Stark taught the exotic felines to wrestle with her, and one of her trademark stunts was a wrestling match that included rolling over an adult Bengal tiger. She finished her act by sticking her face in the tiger's mouth, a trick first conceived by Isaac VAN AMBURGH.

Part of her mystique was that she always appeared in the ring unarmed—no gun, whip or chair. Although she was, as a result, mauled and bitten several times throughout her long career, her fearlessness matched by her femininity made her a legend in circus history.

She toured with numerous shows throughout her more than 50 years in the BIG CAGE. In 1922 she moved to the RINGLING BROS. AND BARNUM & BAILEY CIRCUS. At her MADISON SQUARE GARDEN opening in an end ring, one of her panthers caused her great trouble. It took several minutes to get him under control; but her cool management that was in such contrast to the fascinated horror of the audience drew magnificent reviews in the *New York Times.* Stark was moved to the CENTER RING, where she stayed until 1925 when the circus dropped all cat acts from its show.

She toured for a year in Europe, worked the JOHN ROBINSON CIRCUS in 1929, then returned to the Al G. Barnes Circus. She stayed through 1936, then worked smaller circuses and independent dates. In the 1950s, she toured Japan and performed at the World Jungle Compound at Thousand Oaks, California.

In her autobiography, *Hold that Tiger,* she wrote that working with the tigers was "a matchless thrill, and life without it is not worth living." They were prophetic words. Mabel Stark left the ring for the last time in 1967; four months after her retirement—on April 20, 1968—she was dead.

STILT WALKING

Also seen as "stiltwalking," the use of stilts, not limited to the circus world, can trace its ancestry back to ancient times. Prehistoric drawings seem to indicate the use of stilts in ritualistic magic and religion. Today they are used theatrically as well as recreationally. In some areas they even have practical uses: In Les Landes—a marshy region of France—and on the Marquesas Islands in the South Pacific, stilts are used just to locomote over wet land. Some painters, fruit pickers and brick layers use aluminum stilts instead of ladders.

Stilts, however, are still associated primarily with the circus and with CLOWNS in particular. When first learning, the student uses short stilts with steps or foot rests attached to the sides of the poles. The walker holds onto the stilts and leans slightly forward as he moves. Gravity assists the balancer in taking small—then larger—steps. As the performer improves, the height of the stilts is increased.

Eventually the accomplished stilt walker will graduate to the professional aluminum strap-on stilts that literally attach directly onto the bottom of the feet and are supported along the sides of the shin. If long pants cover the stilts, the performer or clown appears, of course, to be ten to 20 feet tall. Some acrobats with tumbling and TEETERBOARD acts also wear the strap-on stilts outside their wardrobe and perform difficult and incredibly dangerous somersaults.

STODDARD, JOSHUA C. (1814–18??)

Joshua C. Stoddard of Worcester, Massachusetts is given credit for the invention of the steam CALLIOPE (pronounced "COW-lee-ope" by circus folk).

On October 9, 1855 he was granted U.S. Patent No. 13,668 for the "new musical instrument to be played by the agency of steam or highly compressed air." The calliope was, in fact, a much-improved version of an earlier nonsteam musical instrument.

Although the word "calliope" is based on two Greek words that mean "beautiful voice," the inconstant steam pressure that produces the sounds through whistles causes quite unharmonious sounds. Nevertheless, the calliope quickly became a mainstay of the American STREET PARADE and always headed up the rear of the march, leading patrons to the circus LOT.

STONE & MURRAY CIRCUS

Den [sic] Stone was already an accomplished clown and trick rider when he decided to move into the management of his own show. The partnership resulted in the Stone, Rosston & Co. Circus.

In 1864 John H. Murray joined their ranks and the show title was changed to include his name. The next year the Stone, Rosston & Murray Circus became the first show to make a complete tour of the South following the Civil War.

Rosston sold his interest at the end of the season. The show toured as the Stone & Murray Circus from 1866 through 1875.

That year Stone himself retired. The sole remaining partner toured the show as the John H. Murray Circus for three more seasons, through 1878.

STOREY, WILSON F. (1904–1992)

Wilson F. Storey was born on March 24, 1904 in Beziers, France, while his parents were touring with Circus Pinder. His father, trained as an acrobat, was performing at the time as Bolero, a clown.

When Storey was six years old, his father died. He and a younger brother began school in Montauban while their mother continued with Circus Pinder as a wardrobe mistress. She too settled in Montauban in 1914 when World War I made circus travel difficult. Eight years later she married Eugene Vasserot, a horse trainer with Alfred COURT's Zoo Circus.

In 1923 Wilson Storey joined Zoo Circus as a trainer of LIBERTY HORSES. He also assisted with setting up the horse tent and saw to their care and feeding.

Vasserot's sister, Renee, was Court's wife; and Alfred Court took an interest in his new nephew. He recommended that Storey learn the administrative end of the circus business, and by 1926 Storey was working in the office wagon. The following year Court placed Storey and his brother in charge of a second unit, a position Wilson Storey held for six years.

In 1933 the financial depression preceding World War II caused Court to close his shows. Through 1939, Storey supervised the training and international leasing of Court's wild animal acts.

One of those contracts took Court's leopard act to Blackpool, England. On September 15, 1940 John Ringling NORTH wired Court to join the RINGLING BROS. AND BARNUM & BAILEY CIRCUS. Storey, as contract agent, accepted the proposal, and he and Court joined the Ringling operation for the next five years. In 1946 North bought Court's animals; Storey remained WITH IT to manage the cat acts.

Also that year, Storey married Dorothy Webster, a ballerina. He left the Ringling operation, opting to manage a circus traveling in Latin America for two years. At the end of the 1947 seasons he returned home on doctor's orders.

Storey opened his own booking agency, Wilson F. Storey Entertainment Enterprises, booking circus acts into shows in the United States, South America and Mexico. For many years he served as artistic director for Jimmy Harrington's Gran Circo Panamericano.

An association with Jerry Collins and Walter Kernan led to Storey's becoming the talent agent for the CLYDE BEATTY CIRCUS and later the CLYDE BEATTY-COLE BROS. CIRCUS. The last of his contracted acts with the Beatty show was in 1989.

Meanwhile, he had moved onto the Sells & Gray Circus, managing the show from 1968 for ten years.

Following the 1978 season, he became comptroller for the Beatty-Cole show, where he remained through 1988 when he retired from the road.

Wilson F. Storey died on September 5, 1992.

STRATTON, CHARLES S.   See TOM THUMB.

STRAWHOUSE   Also written as straw house, this term is circus jargon for a sold-out or oversold performance. Before fire laws prevented the practice, circuses would spread straw or hay on the ground in front of the reserved seats—right against the arena track—for patrons to sit on when the tent was overcrowded.

Many audience members enjoyed sitting on the ground: The hay hid the dirt and mud, and the straw somehow made the ground look softer. In addition, the circusgoers got very close to the action and felt more a part of the show.

For the circus, this was a practical solution: By accommodating the extra spectators in this way, the circus did not have to perform an extra show and pay the performers additional salary, or CHERRY PIE.

At one time, circus managers could judge the maximum potential size of the audience from the size of the town being played. As more and more shows began to rely on phone promotions and BOILER ROOM sales techniques, however, performances were frequently oversold.

Although statistics show that only a small fraction of the tickets sold to businesses by phone promoters are ever distributed or used, occasionally all of them do get into the hands of actual circusgoers. Coupled with regular advance sales and day-of-show ticket purchases, a circus may find itself in a standing-room only, or strawhouse, situation.

Of course, insurance and fire regulators have long since caused circuses to cut out the practice of scattering straw under the circus BIG TOP. Today the term remains only as a reminder of the golden days of the circus.

STREET PARADE   The first circus parade was probably a motley collection of WAGONS, passing through the dust-filled streets of a town on their way to the circus LOT. As small boys and townsfolk followed the procession to find out what all the commotion was about, it must have become obvious to the early circus entrepreneurs that the circus parade was an excellent form of advertisement for their show.

Soon wagons and chariots were being built specifically for the street parade. Among the first to exploit the street parade in a major fashion was Isaac VAN AMBURGH. The great BANDWAGON that toured with his 1846 show, for instance—billed as "the largest ever seen on the continent"—was over 20 feet long and 17 feet high. It was topped with a canopy that had to be lowered when passing under bridges.

Before long the street parade was one of the most anticipated events of Circus Day. The excitement would begin when a "crier"—an 1870–1880's term for a TALKER—would be pressed into service to precede the march, warning citizens to "Hold your hosses [sic]; the elephants are coming!" After the procession, still more would walk the parade route, urging the viewers to follow the parade to the show grounds for the big, free exhibition about to take place on the lot.

The move to rail travel enabled circuses to expand their street parades. Just as the number of cars on the CIRCUS TRAIN was an indication of a circus's status in the entertainment industry, so was the number and variety of wagons, animals and bands in the circus parade. Bigger and more elaborate wagons could be transported by rail; the largest and costliest in history, the TWO HEMISPHERES BANDWAGON, was 28 feet long and originally valued at $40,000. Eight- and ten-horse teams were used to pull the wagons; sometimes 12- and 24-hitch teams were employed just for effect. At one time, a dozen circuses used 40-team horses on their number one bandwagons.

Besides bandwagons, the procession would also include CAGE WAGONS, TABLEAU WAGONS and, of course, the CALLIOPE at parade's end. Each had a distinct purpose: the cage wagons, of course, carried part of the MENAGERIE; the tableau wagons, although primarily ornamental, might also carry circus personnel, including a clown or sideshow band. Interspersed among the wagons would be CLOWNS, acrobats, ELEPHANTS, CAMELS and other performers.

The participants in the street parade had several rules of conduct. Parade rules from the 1904 WALTER L. MAIN CIRCUS include the following:

Drivers watch your teams; If any vehicle breaks down in parade, pull to one side and after fixed up, get in anywhere, but do not stop parade; Every employee that is not in parade and is not active on the lot, must be stationed along the line of parade telling people to look out for their horses; Drivers must be cleanshaven and have their boots blackened when time permits; no smoking or chewing.

Perhaps the most elaborate—certainly the most celebrated—single street parade in the history of the American circus was the one staged by the BARNUM & BAILEY CIRCUS in 1903 in New York upon its return from a European tour. It was at this parade that the incredible Two Hemispheres Bandwagon was unveiled.

Reportedly, the ostentatious parade was a celebration of its triumphant five-year tour abroad. However, it is probable that Barnum and Bailey had lost ground to the RINGLING BROTHERS during their absence and wanted to signal other circus owners and the public that they were back in town.

By the 1920s automobile traffic jammed small city streets. The costs of manufacturing and carrying extra parade wagons became prohibitive to many circuses, and it actually seemed that many otherwise-potential patrons did not attend the shows because they felt they had seen it all at the parade. A rapid decline in the number of street parades resulted; smaller circuses held the last of the regular street parades in 1939.

From time to time, some circuses have tried to revive the street parade as a special feature, usually for press purposes at an important show date; but the days of the regular parade are over. In 1965 Charles Philip "Chappie" FOX and the CIRCUS WORLD MUSEUM organized the GREAT CIRCUS PARADE, now an annual event that features meticulously restored wagons of the bygone era. For one week each July, a procession of wagons is hauled by rail from BARABOO to Milwaukee, Wisconsin, then paraded through the streets of downtown. Now run by an independent organization but still closely coordinated with the Circus World Museum, the Great Circus Street Parade is a nostalgic reminder of one more indelible piece of Americana that is gone forever.

(See also HOLD YOUR HORSES; MOELLER CARRIAGE AND WAGON WORKS.)

STRINGERS See JACKS AND STRINGERS.

STRONG, "BIG" JOHN (1920–1992) Known as "the man with more friends than Santa Claus" and "the king of the High Grass Country," John Strong was one of the last of a breed of circus owners that had come up through the ranks—from performer, to announcer, to promoter and, finally, to producer.

Born in Jamestown, New York on August 14, 1920, John August Strong II was the son of a vaudevillian and a juggler. At the age of five, John began filling circus scrapbooks; by eight he was selling balloons around the route of the STREET PARADE. One of his preteen jobs was painting house numbers on curbs, helping to support his family at the age of 12. It allowed him to buy his first car (which he was too young to drive), so he hired a chauffeur to drive him and his family.

At the tender age of 15 he produced, directed and promoted his first circus. He advertised it in his high school newspaper, where he was president of both the senior class and the debating team.

Also in 1935, he began to work for his uncle, driving a truck to deliver mattresses. Whenever he dropped one off, he would, on his own initiative, sell mattresses throughout the neighborhood. He was so successful that demand was bigger than the supply. While the company stopped sales for the factory to catch up, Strong was given a vacation as a reward.

John Strong chose to go on holiday in Hollywood. Upon his arrival there, he looked up a former Jamestown resident and old friend, Lucille Ball, who helped him get into films. *The Canterville Ghost* was one of his first credits.

As he was not a studio contract player, Strong had to find other work. He started a new business selling maps to the stars' homes and offered personally guided tours as well. He is generally credited with starting what is now a major portion of the tourist industry in Hollywood.

In 1948, remembering his early dab at circus production back in high school, Strong began to offer special backyard circuses for friends such as Errol Flynn. From those early private circus shows grew the Big John Strong 3-Ring Circus that toured from 1946 to 1983.

In 1955 he bought a tent and traveled beyond California into Nevada and Utah. Later he toured as far north as Canada and as far east as the Atlantic. His first ELEPHANT was added to the show in 1962. Soon it took three tractor trailers to haul the circus.

Strong always kept the one-ring format to stay close to the audience. He was famous for his seating: No seat was higher than 27 inches off the ground. Because all of the spectators could keep their feet on the ground, Strong regularly avoided hassles by the state safety inspectors.

Strong saw to it that his circus was always run as a SUNDAY SCHOOL SHOW—standards he highly valued. As a result, he had an impeccable reputation in the industry; his word was his bond. He was able to book, hold and play dates on the strength of a phone call or a handshake. A family man, he respected young talent and encouraged new professionals.

Increased government regulations, the escalating costs of touring and personal health problems all caused Strong to consider giving up the tented circus in the early 1980s. Then one of his performers, a clown, was accidentally killed in a show vehicle while under contract to Strong. The legal claims made by the young man's relatives—who had been estranged from the performer up until that time—were paid in full by Big John Strong; but the lengthy litigation perhaps tipped the scale.

In 1983 he sold his BIG TOP and all of the equipment of the John Strong Circus to Dory "D.R." MILLER in Hugo, Oklahoma. Much of the gear became the nucleus of the resurrected AL G. KELLY & MILLER BROS. CIRCUS—known simply as the Kelly-Miller Bros. Circus—which resumed touring the following spring.

John Strong, not one to admit defeat or to enter gracefully into retirement, bounced back as a producer of indoor circus variety shows. At times he had up to seven units on the road. He was still booking stage shows out of his home in Yucaipa, California at the time of his death.

After a long bout with cancer, Big John Strong passed away on January 6, 1992. The rosary was recited for him at the Hughes Mortuary on January 8, with the funeral mass taking place in Frances X Cabrini Catholic Church, both in Yucaipa. After a graveside service and a eulogy by Red Johnson (owner of the CULPEPPER-MERRIWEATHER GREAT COMBINED CIRCUS) Big John Strong was interred in the SHOWMEN'S REST section of the Mount Olive Cemetery in Hugo, Oklahoma on January 11, 1992.

STYLE Circus jargon for the "ta da" pose, in lieu of a bow, that a circus performer assumes as an applause cue following the execution of a difficult or dangerous stunt. Showgirls (or BALLY BROADS, as they are unflatteringly called) are especially trained in the ability "to style."

While there is not a standard or uniform fashion of "styling" an act, the pose must point up the performer as well as the feat. One sample posture might be to stand facing the audience, feet together, with the left arm pointed toward the artist while the right arm points straight up in the air. A sharp stabbing motion with both hands signals that now is the time to applaud.

SULLIVAN, JOHN L(AWRENCE) (1858–1918)

In 1888 John B. Doris, owner of the GREAT INTER-OCEAN show, started an unusual tradition by inviting London boxing champion John Sullivan to tour as the star performer of a circus. Doris reasoned that Sullivan, at the height of his fame, would be a major draw and competition to other circuses on the road.

Sullivan had won his first "heavyweight championship" in bare-knuckle fighting in 1882. The Queensberry rules of boxing had been formulated in 1867 for John Sholto Douglas—the eighth Marquess of Queensberry—but were not in universal use until the end of the century.

On August 19, 1885 Sullivan defended his title in six rounds under Queensberry rules against Dominick F. McCaffey in Chester Park, Cincinnati, Ohio with both boxers wearing gloves. The referee, Billy Tait, left the ring without reaching a verdict, but two days later he admitted that Sullivan had won the bout.

Sullivan was at the peak of his popularity when he traded the boxing ring for the circus ring. His only duty was to stage a sparring bout with a local citizen in each show. Unfortunately, Sullivan was also a very heavy drinker; often he was physically unable to appear in the performance. Disgusted and angry, Doris closed his show midseason.

After his tenure with the Great-Inter Ocean, Sullivan returned to boxing, where he defended and retained his title in the last bare-knuckle heavyweight championship fight, held in Richburg, Mississippi on July 8, 1889.

In what has long been acknowledged to be the first true heavyweight title fight under Queensberry rules, with gloves and three-minute rounds, "Gentleman" James John Corbett beat John L. Sullivan in 21 rounds in New Orleans, Louisiana on September 7, 1892.

Sullivan went back to performing exhibition boxing matches in vaudeville with a sparring partner, Jake Kilrain. He wrote a letter to the Ringling Bros. Circus, offering to join the troupe for either a salary or a percentage. He described his act as "very en-

tertaining, and as a box office attraction it has no equal, appealing to ladies and giving them the opportunity of seeing me, such as they never had before." In his eight-to-ten-minute act he would appear "with a black gymnasium shirt and white flannel trousers, presenting an appearance such as any athlete would do in any club room or public church entertainment."

The RINGLING BROTHERS offered Sullivan the job on November 4, 1908 for a salary of $100 a week, which would be "all clear profit, all usual expenses being paid by us."

Sullivan had second thoughts. He rejected the offer in a letter written November 19, 1908:

I did not like the idea on account of the one night stands. Another thing is, I don't know as that I could get the proper food unless I stopped at the hotel—and my health is worth more to me than anything else in the world. . . . While I am no better than anyone else, it is unpleasant to be compelled to walk on the streets and have a lot of people following you, trying to tear the buttons off your coat for a souvenir.

In travelling with your company everybody would have a friend that they would want to introduce, and this could only be avoided by my being in some separate apartment by myself . . . [I] would not mind if I had to stand in mud six inches deep, but I do detest being followed around and not being able to seek some seclusion.

While I have never been with the circus, I can judge pretty near what the mob would try to do to me.

Thus the union of two of the most famous entities in entertainment never occurred.

SULLY, TOM (fl. 1790s)

Tom Sully was a British CLOWN imported by John Bill RICKETTS to perform as part of his Ricketts Circus in 1793. Although he was not born in America, Sully is the first clown known by name to be working in the United States and, by virtue of his association with Ricketts, the first to perform in an American circus. Sully's trademark song was "Four and Twenty Perriwigs."

SUN BROS. CIRCUS

Three brothers, George, Peter and Gus Sun, opened the Sun Bros. Circus in 1892. The show, traveling on nine rail cars through most of its 26 years, toured mainly in the East and the Southeast.

Around the turn of the century, Gus Sun left the triumvirate to start his own minstrel show, another

Sunburst wheel.   (Photo by Tom Ogden)

circus and then finally a theater that resulted in a chain of vaudeville houses known as the Sun circuit.

George and Peter Sun successfully continued the circus operation until they sold the show in 1918.

SUNBURST WHEELS   Popular on TABLEAU WAGONS and BANDWAGONS during the era of the circus STREET PARADE, these wheels had their spokes painted in a particular style to resemble a "sunburst" effect. The center of the rim was painted red, softening into orange and then yellow closest to the outside of the wheel. As the wheel moved, it gave the impression of a red sun giving off yellow rays.

(See also WAGONS.)

SUNDAY SCHOOL SHOW   Circus jargon, part derisive and part laudatory, for a show that is noted for clean family entertainment, giving good value for the admission price and forbidding con games, short-change artists and pickpockets and other GRIFT on the LOT.

Early in their careers, the RINGLING BROTHERS were noted for running a Sunday school show. They were so adamant that the ticket sellers not swindle the public that the brothers stationed a man by the window to remind patrons to pick up their change. The boys' mother, Marie, was influential in discouraging them from booking Sunday performances.

The Ringling brothers went so far as to print 50 specific rules for their employees to read. Some of them included:

1. Be clean and neat in dress and avoid loud display.
2. No smoking in cars at any time.
3. Do not bring liquor or intoxicants into the dressing rooms.
4. Do not take strangers or friends into dressing rooms without permission.
5. Do not chew gum while taking part in spectacle.
6. Male performers are not to visit with ballet girls. The excuse of "accidental" meetings on Sunday, in parks, at picture shows, etc., will not be accepted.
7. Do not sit cross-legged on floats or tableaux wagons.

With the women, they were even more strict. Additional rules for single women included:

1. Do not dress in a flashy, loud style.
2. You are required to be in the sleeping car and register your name not later than 11 P.M. and not to leave car after registering.
3. Girls must not stop at hotels at any time.
4. You are not permitted to talk with male members of the Show Company, excepting the management, and under no circumstances with residents of the cities visited.
5. The excuse of "accidental" meetings will not be accepted.

The opposite of a Sunday school show was known as a grift show. By the early part of the 20th century, the major circuses discovered that their good names and the ability to repeat major towns was more important than the monies they received from con men who paid for the PRIVILEGE of operating on the lot.

SUNNY   See THEATER.

SWAN, ANNA   See AMERICAN MUSEUM; BARNUM, P(HINEAS) T(AYLOR); FREAKS.

SWAN BROS. CIRCUS   Owned and operated by Andy and Mike Swan out of North Highland, California, the Swan Bros. Circus is a recently formed small, tented one-ring circus that plays mostly fairgrounds as a free midway attraction.

The 60-minute show consists of Andy as "Zipper," Mike as "Hi-Tops," plus CLOWNS, JUGGLING, FOOT JUGGLING and cunning canines. The finale of the show often takes place outside the TOP: a solo TRAPEZE act requires rigging that is too tall for their small top. Billing itself as the "Almost World Famous Circus," the Swan Bros. Circus is family entertainment on an intimate scale.

SWAY POLE   One of the most difficult and dangerous circus acts, a sway pole resembles a giant flag-pole. The act dates back to early Roman times, and the first poles were actually wooden ship masts. Today the sway pole is made of metal, usually aluminum, so it has much give and take although it is firmly grounded.

At the turn of this century, many of the German sway pole performers were costumed in naval wardrobe. Some circus historians have suggested that Karl WALLENDA may have worked on a high wire strung between two sway poles in Germany, giving rise to The Great Wallendas' dressing in sailor suits throughout their career as a troupe.

In the act the performer climbs, or is lifted to, the top of the pole and holds on with the aid of a hand or foot canvas loop. By force of body weight, the aerialist is able to make the pole sway in large arcs as he or she performs tricks high in the sky or arena dome. Two or more poles may be set in close proximity, and at a given signal the

Outside the Swan Bros. Circus top, an aerialist performs a foot catch on the solo trapeze in Orange County Fairground, Costa Mesa, California in 1990.   (Photo by Tom Ogden)

artists can switch staffs, leaping from one to the other.

Besides the risk of falling from the great height of the poles, performing on the sway pole is quite dangerous because the pole itself has a tendency to break or snap suddenly. Unfortunately, microscopic cracks develop in poles during their use; it is only a matter of guess and estimation as to when it these very expensive poles should be repaired or replaced.

SWORD SWALLOWING
If fire-eating is dangerous, then sword swallowing is just plain stupid! Do not try this, even at home in the privacy of your own room.

An ancient art, no one knows where or when the practice of sword swallowing began. Regularly seen from the days of the AMERICAN MUSEUM to the modern MUD SHOWS, sword swallowing was a staple of the circus SIDESHOW. And, regardless what anyone may think, the swords are real. They do *not* fold up into the handle. On the PBS television special "Penn & Teller Go Public," comic magician Penn Gillette said, "You really do gag, and you really do choke, because you're sticking metal down your throat. And I tell you this because when you look at a sideshow performer, you shouldn't be thinking about *how* [they're] doing it: You should be thinking about *why.*"

Sword swallowing is actually a two-part process. The blade of the knife, bayonet or sword is first placed down the throat, then retrieved.

Albert A. Hopkins describes the typical sword-swallowing act in 1897 in his book *Magic: Stage Illusions and Scientific Diversions:*

> *Taking a flat saber whose blade and hilt have been cut of the same sheet of metal, the blade being from 55 to 60 centimeters in length, he introduces its extremity into his throat, taps the hilt gently, and the blade at length entirely disappears. He then repeats the experiment at a single gulp. Subsequently, after swallowing and disgorging two of the same swords, he causes one to penetrate up to its guard, a second not quite so far, a third a little less still, and a fourth to about half its length. . . .*
>
> *Pressing now on the hilts, he swallows the four blades at a gulp and then takes them out leisurely, one by one. The effect is quite surprising. After swallowing several different swords and sabers, he takes an old musket armed with a triangular bayonet, and swallows the latter, the gun remaining vertical over his head. Finally he borrows a large saber from a dragoon who is present for the purpose*

> *and causes two-thirds of it to disappear. As a trick, on being encored, the sword swallower borrows a cane from a person in the audience and swallows it almost entirely.*

The first recorded American-born circus sword swallower worked at the beginning of the 19th century under the name Cliquot. He claimed to be French-Canadian, but he was in fact Fred McLand, born in Chicago. He joined an unknown circus on its way to South America and learned his new art from a Buenos Aires performer.

Popular primarily in London music halls, Cliquot was one of the first to swallow an electric light bulb, which was connected to an eight-volt battery on-stage. He performed at least one engagement in New York, during which a disbelieving doctor yanked 14 nine-inch swords sticking out of Cliquot's mouth, causing serious throat injuries and a long period of recuperation.

One of Cliquot's students was Delno [sic] Fritz, a popular British music hall vaudevillian; he, in turn, passed the art along to 15-year old Edith Clifford of England. She joined the BARNUM & BAILEY CIRCUS in Vienna in 1901 and traveled with the circus sideshow for many seasons. Her act included gulping razor blades, a huge pair of scissors and a saw blade. For her 1919 finale, she placed the tip of a bayonet blade in her mouth and lowered the hilt into the barrel of a small hand-held cannon. The recoil from the blast jammed the blade down her throat.

Perhaps the first—and certainly one of the very few—"how-to" books was purportedly written by Miss Victorina and her husband Joe Van Victorina, a sword swallower and a magician, respectively. In fact, the husband, who worked as Kar-Mi, was really Joseph B. Hallworth, a native American born in 1872; his wife was Kitty Fisher. Their book, *A Text Book on the Art of Sword Swallowing, Explaining How to Do It Sixteen Different Ways,* was a complete farce. The techniques included learning by hypnosis, starting with a silver chain or a feather, swallowing a rubber tube first as a sort of "scabbard" for the real sword, the "Chinese way" (eating opium first to dull the senses) and using various trick swords (including one that was made of licorice).

William "the Baron" Unks of San Francisco is a veteran sword swallower, who began at about the age of 18:

A couple of years ago in Chicago a girl came onto the show, wanted to be more than just a bally girl. She said, 'Teach me how to swallow swords.' I told her what to do, how to stand. She practiced day and night and she got 'em down. In a week, she was pretty good.

You can do one sitting, but you have to be sitting—or standing—straight. Just follow your tongue, right on around and all the way down. Just push it when you start to gag.

According to the Baron, sword swallowing isn't unsanitary, even though he does wipe down the blade first. "Why use Listerine? The dirtiest part of your body is from your tongue to your stomach."

The real "trick" to sword swallowing is having the ability to control the gag reflex, caused by touching the pharynx muscles at the top of the esophagus. Because the act is really a one-trick stunt, sword swallowers attempt to outdo each other with the styles, widths and lengths of the swords swallowed. Of these, length is perhaps the most dangerous. If the blade is longer than the tract of the esophagus, the sword can actually pass into the stomach and puncture the bowels.

When one sword becomes too easy, swords swallowers may take more than one at a time. The Baron likes to swallow three at one time to make what he calls a "sword sandwich." Because people are so skeptical about the rigidity of the blades, performers have begun to swallow objects besides swords—screwdrivers, pipes or, the most dangerous, neon tubes. Once the tube is ingested, it can be lit, showing a luminescent glow through the skin. More than one sword swallower has been the victim of the fluorescent tube breaking while inside: The shattered glass is one of the most painful and slow causes of death imaginable.

Edward "Count Desmond" Benjamin (1941–   ) of Binghamton, New York holds the record for the most and longest swords ever swallowed: 13 23-inch-long blades. The swords passed below his xiphisternum—the lowermost point of the breastbone—and he was injured in the process.

T

TABLEAU WAGON Shortened to "tab wagon" by circus folk, the tableau WAGONS were ornate wood-carved carriages in the STREET PARADE that had little utilitarian use beyond elaborate display. The intricate designs represented nursery rhymes, mythology or nations of the world. Performers, musicians and clowns, dressed in appropriate garb, would ride on the tops of the wagons for additional impact.

Some of the tableau wagons were "telescoping wagons." A hidden platform could be lifted into view by a windlass to create awe along the parade route. An example of a famous TELESCOPING TABLEAU WAGON is the Lion and Mirror Bandwagon, which carried a replica of St. George slaying the Dragon. Built for the ADAM FOREPAUGH CIRCUS, the allegorical statues were removed when it was converted to a BANDWAGON by the Ringling Bros. Circus in 1894. Today the Lion and Mirror Bandwagon is maintained by the CIRCUS WORLD MUSEUM in BARABOO, WISCONSIN.

The Continent wagons were a renowned set of tableau wagons, bearing bas-relief replicas of designs seen on the Prince Albert Memorial in London. Each wagon displayed the giant letters of the continent on its side. Carvings representing the different countries of each continent circled the top of the carriage, and heads of the nations were sculpted below. Both the Asian and the American wagons were smaller than their counterparts, and the American wagon was later converted to a CALLIOPE for the COLE BROS. CIRCUS.

Among the other coaches maintained by the Circus World Museum are the 1865 Twin Lion Telescoping Tableau Wagon, the 1885 Barnum and Bailey Tableau Den, the 1920 Elephant Tableau Wagon, the 1914 Seashell Tableau, the 1890 Star Tableau and the 1903 Asia Tableau Wagon.

TACK SPITTERS See BILLING CREW.

TAIL UP This phrase is a command by an elephant trainer or the BULL HANDLERS for the ELEPHANTS to follow in line.

"TAILOR'S RIDE TO BRENTFORD, THE" Also seen as "The Taylor Riding to Brentford," this comic act was devised by Philip ASTLEY and performed in his ampthitheatre shows. It was already a staple equestrian act among showmen in the United States by the time John Bill RICKETTS opened his first circus.

The first documented appearances of the act in the United States actually occurred at Thomas POOL's Philadelphia riding school in 1785 and the next year when he took his show to New York. It was most probably introduced to America, however, in 1773 by Jacob Bates when he toured the colonies with several other British horsemen, including Pool, Charles Hughes, John Sharp and M.F. Foulkes.

The act was a comic parody of a reportedly true incident in England, in which various misfortunes befell John Gilpin, a tailor, trying to ride his horse to vote in a special election in Brentford. In the act,

The Tarzan Zerbini Circus appears in Gaithersburg, Maryland in 1987. Floats line up outside the back door in preparation for the Spec. (Photo courtesy of Walter G. Heist, Jr.)

the CLOWN equestrian would first have difficulty getting onto the horse. Next the horse wouldn't move. Then the nag wouldn't go fast enough; then it galloped at high speed. The rider would have trouble staying on the horse, seguing into the usual trick riding that proved the equestrian's skill.

(See also DIBDEN AND HUGHES.)

TALKER   Also known as the LECTURER, this is the person who speaks directly to the crowd on the MIDWAY. The talker is the one who gives the SPIEL or BALLY to try to lure people (a TIP) into the SIDESHOW; and, once the doors are open to the LITTLE TOP, he is usually the one who continues the GRIND.

The main sideshow often has two different talkers—the OUTSIDE TALKER who does the opening and the INSIDE TALKER who describes the acts within the tent as he travels from platform to platform.

TANBARK   A word forever associated with the tented circus, tanbark is actually the shredded bark from trees from which tannin has been extracted. The tanbark is spread as a cover on the arena floor and inside the ring.

TARZAN ZERBINI CIRCUS   Begun in the late 1970s by John "Tarzan" Zerbini, the Tarzan Zerbini Circus has three units, two indoor and one under canvas.

John Zerbini was born into a circus family in France, and he moved to the United States as a CAT trainer in the 1950s to tour with the MILLS BROS. CIRCUS. In the 1960s he developed his persona as "Tarzan Zerbini, Lord of the Jungle" in his wild animal act. Dressed only in a loincloth and riding the back of an ELEPHANT, he stampeded into the BIG TOP, grabbed a "monkey vine" web and swung into the BIG CAGE.

He later went on to work for the Dobritch show and the top SHRINE CIRCUS dates in the country. Zerbini gave up the loincloth for a tuxedo and the elephant for a pink Cadillac, but the nickname remained.

He mounted his own show by buying out Hubert Castle's International 3-Ring Circus and set up WINTER QUARTERS in Webb City, Missouri. His two three-ring indoor units, known as the "Blue" and "Gold" units, both of which he tours under the title "Tarzan Zerbini International 3-Ring Circus," play the East and West coasts, respectively. Zerbini also often tours a third, single-ring European-style circus under canvas. The round Canobio tent can hold 3,000 spectators, and the unit travels on a fleet of 15 tractor trailers.

Tarzan Zerbini does not perform regularly anymore. He and his wife, Elizabeth, are involved in the management of the three units and supervise them personally. The shows have remained family affairs: Elizabeth Zerbini's father, Joseph Bauer—once a top PERCH pole artist and now a circus producer—works with the show; her brother, Joseph Dominic Bauer, performs as RINGMASTER and as an aerialist on the "Giant Space Wheel"; and Sylvia Zerbini, Tarzan and Elizabeth's daughter and thus a ninth-generation circus performer, is featured on the WEB and single TRAPEZE.

TEAR DOWN   Circus jargon for packing the TENTS and apparatus after the evening's performance and either returning to the CIRCUS TRAIN on a rail show or shutting down the LOT for the night on a motorized unit.

The tear down usually begins as soon as the final BIG TOP performance begins. Some attractions on the MIDWAY, such as the SIDESHOW or PIT SHOWS, try to capture customers on the way out of the Big Top during the BLOWOFF. The other crews drop their tents and pack their equipment in the circus WAGONS or show trucks. If business was slow that night or a night JUMP is planned, all of the concessions on the FRONT YARD may be packed by the time the main show is over; visitors to the circus thus come out of the Big Top to an empty field.

The generator truck—or GENNIE—that has provided electricity for all the tents and show units during the day now provides work lights. The ROUSTABOUTS, ELEPHANTS and town boys drop the Big Top, unlace and roll the canvas and pack the poles and other gear. Finally, the workers "walk the lot" to double-check for small odds and ends—especially dropped STAKES—that may have been left behind. Besides making sure all the apparatus is accounted for, leaving a clean lot is a keen booking tool for the following season.

When the circus vehicles leave the lot, the show grounds have magically returned to an empty field. Just hours before, an entire city of canvas stood where now, as the old circus saying goes, "There is nothing left but wagon tracks and popcorn sacks."

TEETERBOARD   A standard piece of apparatus for many circus acrobatic and gymnastic acts, a teeterboard resembles a large seesaw from a children's playground in both appearance and construction.

A person standing on the lower end can be catapulted into the air when a partner jumps on the high end. In essence, it is used as a springboard, except that the support is in the middle rather than at the end.

The name comes from the fact that when someone jumps onto the upper end of the board, the wood will bend slightly, teeter and spring because of its innate flexibility.

In a two-person act, the person thrust upward might somersault in midair or perform rolls when hitting the ground. The partner might also run around and catch the first person on his shoulders, creating what is known as a TWO HIGH. More common, however, is a multiperson troupe in which the top-mounters build taller and taller towers.

A "five high" is not performed on a regular basis. It has been achieved by starting with a base of more than one BOTTOM MAN, but this is not a true single column.

One of the riskiest uses of the teeterboard involves the acrobat wearing strap-on stilts on the lower end of the board. When vaulted upward, he performs a full single or double somersault, landing once again on the stilts. One of the first acts to perform the stunt in this country was the Dovyeko troupe during the 1963 visit of the MOSCOW CIRCUS.

(See also ACROBATS; STILT WALKING.)

During tear down, roustabouts unlace the Big Top canvas sections on the Carson & Barnes Circus in 1991. (Photo by Tom Ogden)

TELESCOPING TABLEAU WAGON In a STREET PA-RADE, a telescoping tableau wagon was a special type of TABLEAU WAGON in which a hidden platform or figures were lifted occasionally for additional effect.

(See also BANDWAGON; WAGONS.)

TELEVISION From its beginnings, television has had a symbiotic relationship with the circus. Especially in the early days of television—when there was little rehearsal time and when acts had to be performed live—variety acts were a mainstay of the new, visual medium.

Circus-theme Television Series

In the black-and-white days of television, several series with circus stories actually made it to the small screen. *The Buick Circus Hour* had a most unusual history. Although it ran from October 7, 1952 through June 16, 1953 on NBC, it only appeared every fourth week, in the spot normally held by *Milton Berle's Texaco Star Theatre*. With the story set

on a circus, an aging CLOWN (Joe E. Brown) tries to help the career of a young singer (Dolores Gray) who has joined the show to be near the larger-than-life owner, Bill Sothern (John Raitt). The other series regular was Frank Gallop as the RINGMASTER. Musical numbers as well as real circus acts were interpolated into the live production out of New York City.

Circus Boy premiered on NBC on September 23, 1956 and ran for one year. On September 19, 1957 the show moved to ABC and appeared weekly through September 11, 1958. Reruns continued on Saturday mornings until September 1960. The show, a Screen Gems production, told stories of life on the sawdust trail for Corky (played by Mike Braddock), a young boy whose parents had been killed in a high wire accident. Corky had a guardian, Big Tim Champion (played by Robert Lowery) who was the new owner of the circus. Some of the other cast members included Noah Beery, Jr. as Uncle Joey (a clown); Billy Barty as Little Tom (the midget); and

Guinn Williams as Pete (a ROUSTABOUT). Braddock, whose real name was Mickey Dolenz, later went on to become one of the four leading roles in the successful television hit *The Monkees.*

Frontier Circus was a hybrid between a circus drama and a western, airing for one season on CBS from October 5, 1961 through September 20, 1962. With Ben Travis (John Derek) as the boss of the roustabouts and Tony Gentry (Richard Jaeckel) as the ADVANCE MAN, Col. Casey Thompson (Chill Wills) operated the T&T Circus—a small MUD SHOW owned by Thompson and Travis—throughout the American Southwest in the late 1800s.

The Greatest Show on Earth first appeared on September 17, 1963 and lasted through September 8, 1964 as a behind-the-scenes circus drama, with local color and backup acts supplied by the RINGLING BROS. AND BARNUM & BAILEY CIRCUS. Jack Palance played Johnny Slate, the workingmen's boss, and Stu Erwin played Otto King, the paymaster. Each week's story centered around the problems of one genre of performers, such as clowns, ACROBATS or equestrians. Richard Rodgers supplied the show's theme music, "March of the Clowns."

Circus/Variety Format Shows

Most of the circus talent that has been seen on television, however, has been used in the variety show format. The ground-breaking CBS program, *The Ed Sullivan Show* (lasting from June 20, 1948 through June 6, 1971) regularly showcased circus performers. Even Clyde BEATTY once appeared on Ed Sullivan's Sunday night extravaganza; Sullivan was visibly shaken when the CATS did not wish to end their act on cue. Not wishing to cut to commercial lest the home audience think there was an off-screen tragedy, he walked into the audience to introduce his weekly "drop-in" guests. The roars of the lions and the cracks of the whip continued quite audibly in the background until Sullivan suddenly turned back to the camera to announce everything was under control.

Other variety shows emulated the Sullivan show in its use of circus acts. *Big Top* aired on CBS each Saturday evening from July 1, 1950 through January 6, 1951. Each week saw a full hour of live circus acts performed in the Camden, New Jersey Convention Hall. Jack Sterling was the series ringmaster, Ed McMahon (later the sidekick of Johnny Carson

on *The Tonight Show*) and Chris Keegan were the regular clowns, and Dan Lurie was seen each episode as the strongman. At least six different acts were seen each week, from trained animals to acrobats. After its six-month nighttime run, the show moved to a Saturday afternoon slot, where it remained for seven years.

From October 4, 1956 until June 27, 1957, *Circus Time* appeared as a Thursday night, hour-long show on ABC that featured circus novelty acts. The program was hosted by ventriloquist Paul Winchell and his pals, Jerry Mahoney and Knucklehead Smith.

From September 15, 1961 through September 10, 1965, NBC aired the one-hour *International Showtime* each Friday night. Hosted by Don Ameche, the program presented European circus acts. Some episodes focused on a specific talent, such as clowns or daredevils. Ameche would introduce each act, then sit down in the audience to enjoy the show. He traveled all over Europe with the producers and was actually present when each act was taped.

The Hollywood Palace premiered on January 4, 1964 on ABC as a highly touted variety show in the Ed Sullivan style but featuring a different host each week. The show remained on the air for three seasons, but circus acts were seen less often in the later years. *The Hollywood Palace* was last aired on February 7, 1970.

Continental Showcase was a Saturday night summer replacement show that lasted from June 11 through September 10, 1966. Host Jim Backus toured Europe, presenting some of the top variety acts, including many circus stars.

Hippodrome was a circus variety show that was filmed in England. It aired on CBS television as a summer replacement for *The Red Skelton Hour* (see SKELTON, RICHARD "RED") from July 5 through September 6, 1966. Guest hosts included singer/comedian Allan Sherman, Woody Allen and Merv Griffin.

Coliseum, airing Thursdays on CBS from January 26 through June 1, 1967, also traveled around the world to film circus programs, such as the MOSCOW CIRCUS, in addition to providing a showcase for circus and other variety performers out of New York.

Beginning in the fall of 1971, Bert Parks hosted a syndicated half-hour series called *Circus!* The show followed the same format as *International Showtime,* which had been originated by the same producers.

European circus acts were filmed on location for 52 episodes between 1971 and 1973.

Monday Night Special, seen on ABC from January 10, 1972 through August 14, 1972, had a different topic each week. On several occasions, circuses were featured. Similarly, *The DuPont Show of the Week* aired a documentary-style show with a different topic each week on NBC from September 17, 1961 through September 6, 1964. One of the most celebrated episodes was Emmett KELLY's discussion on the universal love for the circus.

Made-for-TV Movies

The high cost of shooting and the supposed limited audience appeal has prevented studios from producing more first-run theatrical films with circus themes. On a tighter budget, made-for-television movies dealing with circus personalities are much more common. As with most film "biops," great dramatic license is taken with actual events.

The Great Wallendas was a 1978 movie telling of the famous family of aerialists, the troupe's tragic 1962 fall as well as their psychological turmoil in its aftermath. The movie also celebrated the family's determination to return to the wire and eventually re-create, if only briefly, the seven-person pyramid on the tightwire. The Daniel Wilson Productions film for CBS-TV included Lloyd Bridges (Karl WAL-LENDA), Britt Ekland (Jenny Wallenda), Taina Elg (Helen Wallenda), John Van Dreelen (Herman Wallenda) and Cathy Rigby (Jana Schmidt). Karl Wallenda was technical advisor on the film, and the then-current Wallenda troupe doubled in the WIRE WALKING sequences.

In 1987 Robert Halmi Productions produced *Barnum* with Burt Lancaster portraying the legendary showman. Although a few incidents and characters were changed for dramatic purposes, the Michael Norell screenplay was quite accurate historically, closely following Barnum's autobiography. The film also employed the interesting device of having Barnum occasionally break from the action and talk directly to the camera.

Circus Specials

Each year a multitude of circus "specials" appear on television. *Circus of the Stars* has been an annual television special on CBS for two decades. Professionals spend weeks training television and film stars as well as other celebrities to perform actual circus acts for the taping. These routines range from the simplest (riding an ELEPHANT) to the difficult (the FLYING TRAPEZE) and the dangerous (working with lions and tigers in the BIG CAGE). Beginning in 1955, the Ringling Bros. and Barnum & Bailey Circus has presented highlights of its new edition on an annual special that closely coincides with its MADISON SQUARE GARDEN opening.

Cable stations and public broadcasting have also gotten into the act with specials based on various circuses. HBO, for example, has broadcast a special on the BIG APPLE CIRCUS, and PBS has produced documentaries on CIRQUE DU SOLEIL, the Great Circus Train (see GREAT CIRCUS PARADE, THE) and the circus competitions in Monte Carlo.

Television is the most powerful advertising medium ever created, and one 30-second national spot has the potential to reach more people than all the PAPER ever posted by every BILLING CREW since the dawn of the American circus. By working together effectively, circus and television can continue to create the demand to experience "live and in person" the greatest shows on earth.

(See also CLOWNS, TELEVISION; FILMS, CIRCUS.)

TENTS   One way to trace the history of the American circus is by the periods in which different structures were used to house the performances. The first of these, inaugurated by John Bill RICKETTS in 1793, marked the era of the outdoor amphitheater or enclosed coliseum.

The second era—which to some extent continues to this day—was that of the tented circus. Most often credited as the first men in the United States to set up a full equestrian show under a round-top canvas—thereby creating the first tented circus—were partners Nathan A. HOWES and Aaron TURNER. Current scholarship suggests, however, that J. Purdy BROWN probably deserves that honor.

The third and most current trend is the indoor arena show. For all practical purposes, the new age began on July 16, 1956 when John Ringling NORTH—burdened by the spiraling costs of rail transportation, insurance and maintenance of an outdoor show—announced in Pittsburgh, Pennsylvania that the era of the tented circus was finished. The BIG ONE had to CLOSE AHEAD OF PAPER midseason. It opened the following season indoors in MADISON SQUARE GARDEN.

During the heyday of the tented circus, however, the circus LOT was a wonder to behold. On circus day, the show grounds sported over a dozen TENTS of various shapes and sizes, all positioned during the LAY OUT of the LOT by the BOSS CANVASMAN or the LAYOUT MAN. As visitors first approached the circus FRONT YARD they saw several small tents on the MIDWAY. The smallest sold souvenirs and concessions. (Refreshments would also be available on the midway, but these were usually housed in a wagon rather than under canvas.) The front yard might also contain a number of PIT SHOWS, housing special attractions such as "The Worlds Smallest Pony" or "The World's Largest Python," with each little tent having its own BANNERLINE, ticket box and GRIND. The largest tent on the midway, located closest to the MARQUEE top, was the SIDESHOW or LITTLE TOP.

Passing under the marquee, itself a small canvas top, patrons traveled between two walls of canvas to reach the MENAGERIE. There, on the way to the main show spectators viewed exotic caged animals and some of the performing stock close at hand with no additional charge. In the second half of the 20th century, however, many circuses dispensed with a separate menagerie top, combining it with the sideshow attractions under one larger tent on the midway. Finally, leaving the menagerie, visitors passed between walls of canvas directly into the largest tent on the show grounds—the BIG TOP—where the main show was held.

Behind the Big Top, in the BACK YARD, were still more tents—those reserved for the cast and crew. These included the COOKHOUSE (dining tent); a baggage-stock tent (for working horses); and a RING STOCK tent, sometimes called the PAD ROOM (for performing horses). There was always a large dressing tent (often combined with the pad room for convenience); but some star performers had private wardrobe tents of their own. On the largest shows, skilled craftsmen such as blacksmiths and physicians had tents on the lot. The CLOWNS usually dressed under their own canvas, nicknamed CLOWN ALLEY.

To this day, the types of tents vary not only according to size but also according the way in which they are erected. Some smaller tops, such as the concession and pit show tents, are one rectangular or round piece of canvas. These tops are the easiest to put up. The top is laid out flat on the ground; STAKES are driven around the tent, about a yard from the canvas and with a foot or more of the shaft of the stake sticking out of the ground. Ropes that are sewn around the perimeter of the top are stretched out and loosely tied to the stakes. At the point where each rope meets the top, the ROUSTABOUT finds a grommeted hole, pushes the pin at the end of a SIDEPOLE through it and lifts the sidepole upright. Workers quickly make their way around the top to GUY OUT or tighten the tension on the ropes by sliding the knots down the shafts of the stakes. When all of the sidepoles are in place and the ropes are tight, the CENTER POLE is pushed under the canvas and through the large hole in the center of the top. At this point light fixtures or any special rigging is placed on the top of the pole. With a lot of muscle—and sometimes the assistance of an ELEPHANT or two, the center pole is pushed upright into a vertical position. SIDEWALL canvas is clipped or raised all around the top to hide the attraction inside and a bannerline is set up out front, along with ticket boxes and BALLY or grind platforms. This type of top is known as a PUSH POLE tent, named after the way in which the center pole is raised.

If the tent is large enough, the top breaks down into multiple sections. This is done for two reasons: It reduces stress on the canvas top and the smaller sections are easier to lift and transport. Every morning the sections must be laid out and laced together.

When a tent comes in sections, the dimensions of the top are given according to the size of the sections. This can best be explained by examining an imaginary giant Big Top that measures 510 feet long and 210 feet wide. This top, suitable for a five-ring circus, would have five rectangular sections, each 210 feet by 60 feet. When laced together, this would make a huge piece of canvas, 300 feet by 210 feet. At each end of this enormous rectangle a semicircle of canvas would be laced, each with a diameter of 210 feet. In circus terms, this is a "210 round with five 60-foot middles." This hypothetical top would take six, or perhaps four, center poles—in this case, 62 feet high, each weighing about one ton and costing close to $2,000. A tent this size would require not only a row of sidepoles along the canvas wall but also one or two rows of longer sidepoles—sometimes called QUARTER POLES—midway between the wall of the top and the center poles.

Due to the extreme weight and size of its canvas, this type of top would almost certainly be set up as a BALE RING tent rather than as a push pole top. In a bale ring operation, the center poles are raised first. The sections of canvas are spread around the poles and laced together, then tied to the steel bale rings around the bottoms of the poles. When the bale rings are pulled to the top of the poles by a pulley system, the canvas is raised as well. As the sidewall is attached, the SEAT WAGONS are driven into place or bleacher-style seats with JACKS AND STRINGERS are set up. Meanwhile, the RIGGERS set the wires, steel bars and other mechanical apparatus for the TRAPEZE and other aerial acts.

By midmorning the miracle of the traveling city is complete: A city of canvas has appeared—for one day only—as if by magic.

During the period when the RINGLING BROS. AND BARNUM & BAILEY CIRCUS maintained its WINTER QUARTERS in SARASOTA, FLORIDA, the Ringling show kept its own tent factory, or "sail loft," on the grounds.

Each winter until 1956 the skilled craftspeople sewed more than 30 tents for the following season, including a new Big Top each year. The last Ringling top was designed by Leif Osmundson in 14 pieces—each weighing just under a ton—for a combined weight of 28,000 pounds dry (and twice that wet). Laced together and raised, the Big Top was 406 feet long and 206 feet wide.

The previous two years' tops were kept in quarters. One was used as a rehearsal tent; the other was placed in storage, kept at the ready in case an emergency on the road required all or part of it to be rushed to the touring company.

Today circuses that travel "under canvas" purchase their tops from major tent manufacturers. Two longtime reliable circus suppliers are A-1 Tents, Inc. of Sarasota and Anchor Industries, Inc. of Bradenton, Florida. Except for the tents used by CIRCUS WORLD MUSEUM and the ROYAL HANNEFORD CIRCUS, the big tops of all major circuses are currently made of polyvinyl rather than canvas.

TERRITORY   As the actual definition of the word suggests, "territory" is circus slang for an "area"—

in this case, the area that a particular circus plays most often.

Early circuses were known to route themselves primarily within one section of the country; circuses protectively guarded their towns and sponsors. Crossing into another circus's territory often was an unofficial declaration of war, causing competing BILLING CREWS to tear down the circus's LITHOGRAPHS, or OPPOSITION PAPER, or distribute unflattering HERALDS, or RAT SHEETS, about the other show. At the very least, they would post WAIT PAPER, circus posters suggesting that the people in the town hold off going to the circus until their show came to town.

(See also BURN THE TERRITORY.)

TEXAS SHRINE DATES, THE   One of the pioneers of the indoor sponsored circus was Robert Morton who, in 1918, leased the GENTRY BROS. CIRCUS to play for the Shriners in Dallas, Texas. Later, in conjunction with his partner George A. HAMID, Morton made their HAMID-MORTON CIRCUS one of the first to always appear indoors under the auspices of an area sponsor, varying its show content for local tastes or available talent.

The "sponsored date" was an entirely new concept in financing the circus operation. By working under the sponsorship of a local charity or civic organization, the circus adds legitimacy to its show while boosting ticket sales. Since profitable sales depend on moving large blocks of tickets to merchants or individuals, the circus tries to tie in with the most "beneficial" charity (such as the police or firefighters) or an influential organization (such as the Shriners or Masons).

A series of dates in Texas, all sponsored by Shrine temples, takes place in the late fall and throughout the winter; circus promoters compete heavily for the lucrative contracts to provide the shows. Likewise, since many circus acts are on hiatus from their regular shows during these times, the Texas Shrine Dates—as they are known—are highly prized.

(See also SHRINE CIRCUS.)

THAYER, "DR." JAMES L.   See SPALDING, "DR." GILBERT R.; THAYER & NOYES CIRCUS.

THAYER & NOYES CIRCUS Both "Dr." James L. Thayer (1830–1892), a CLOWN, and Charles Noyes (1832–1885), a skilled animal trainer, had toured successfully on various small circuses before meeting in about 1860 when they toured with the DAN RICE CIRCUS.

In 1861 Noyes leased the title and operated the Rice show. Meanwhile, Thayer left the circus, opting to open his own tiny tent show. In 1862 they teamed up to form the Thayer & Noyes Circus, which toured successfully through the 1868 season.

The year 1869 was one of the most devastating economic seasons in circus history. Only six of the 28 shows touring that year finished out the season and survived to reopen in 1870. Thayer & Noyes was among the casualties, and the circus was sold at auction.

Noyes immediately opened his own show, the C.W. Noyes Crescent City Circus and trouped with it through 1874. Thayer managed P.T. BARNUM's interests on the show Barnum had leased to John V. "Pogey" O'BRIEN. In 1877 and 1879 Thayer took out two last small shows of his own.

(See also SPALDING, "DR." GILBERT R.)

THEATER While not having the in-home intimacy of TELEVISION or the big-screen spectacle of CIRCUS FILMS, the live performances of the stage are closest in feel to the circus: Circus Is Theater.

Broadway has long presented plays and musicals that have dealt, in whole or part, with the life on the circus.

Annie Get Your Gun

Musical about BUFFALO BILL'S WILD WEST. Music and lyrics by Irving Berlin; book by Dorothy and Herbert Fields; directed by Josh Logan; and produced by Richard Rodgers and Oscar Hammerstein II. Premiering at New York's Imperial Theatre on May 16, 1946, *Annie Get Your Gun* had an initial run of 1,147 performances.

This is the story of sharpshooter Annie OAKLEY, a role created on Broadway by Ethel Merman. The plot traces her rise from hillbilly to star of Buffalo Bill's Wild West and how she tops the fame of the show's main attraction, marksman Frank BUTLER. A rivalry, and finally romance, blossoms between Oakley and Butler, with the finale culminating in the show business standard, "There's No Business Like Show Business."

In *Annie Get Your Gun* Irving Berlin gave the musical theater such other classic songs as "Doin' What Comes Naturally," "The Girl That I Marry," "You Can't Get a Man with a Gun," "They Say It's Wonderful," "I Got Lost in His Arms," "I Got the Sun in the Morning," "Anything You Can Do" and, in a 1966 New York revival, also starring Merman, "An Old Fashioned Wedding."

Barnum

The musical comedy *Barnum* opened on April 30, 1980 on Broadway at the St. James Theatre to much fanfare and expectation, not only because of the rumors of the extravagant nature of the show, but because it also marked the first time that "traditional" theater creators joined forces with a circus production team to stage a show.

Barnum was co-produced by Broadway veterans Judy Gordon, Maurice and Lois F. Rosenfeld and Cy Coleman; but the insight necessary for a true circus-style production may have come from their collaboration with their associate producers, Irvin and Kenneth FELD, the producers of the RINGLING BROS. AND BARNUM & BAILEY CIRCUS. With music by Cy Coleman, lyrics by Michael Stewart and a book by Mark Bramble, director Joe Layton infused every scene of *Barnum* with the sparkle and glitter of a circus arena show. Each production number was filled with the reminder that this was the story of "The Greatest Showman on Earth," as the stage overflowed with CLOWNS, jugglers, ACROBATS, wirewalkers, TRAPEZE artists, stilt walkers and even a RINGMASTER.

To experience *Barnum* fully, one had to come early to the theater because the entertainment began outside, where a street magician began to BALLY for a full half hour before curtain. Once inside, patrons could take tours through "The Exhibition of Wonders" that displayed rare, original P.T. BARNUM memorabilia.

Barnum is loosely based on biographical details of the life of P.T. Barnum between the years 1835, when he first exhibited Joice HETH, and 1880, the year he partnered with James A. BAILEY to form The GREATEST SHOW ON EARTH. Among the names and places out of Barnum's life covered in the musical are the AMERICAN MUSEUM; JUMBO; TOM THUMB;

Jenny LIND; and BRIDGEPORT, CONNECTICUT. The show begins as Phineas Taylor Barnum announces, "Barnum's the name. P.T. Barnum. And I want to tell you that tonight you are going to see, bar none, every sight, wonder and miracle that the name stands for!"

Jim Dale, who created the role of Barnum, learned to juggle and walk a tightwire expressly for the play. Also notable in the original cast was Glenn Close as Mrs. Barnum. Many of the other actors brought their own circus skills to the roles. Some were gradúates of the Ringling CLOWN COLLEGE. In addition to the 23 speaking and singing characters listed, the program also boasted, in true circus-program style, "Clowns, Bricklayers, Acrobats, Tumblers, Gymnasts, Jugglers, The Bridgeport Pageant Choir, Bands of Every Size, Shape and Description, the Mob in general, and Characters too numerous to mention."

Barnum was nominated for ten Tony awards, including Best Musical, Best Director (Joe Layton), Best Book (Mark Bramble), Best Score (Cy Coleman, music; Michael Stewart, lyrics), Best Lighting Design (Craig Miller), Best Choreography (Joe Layton) and Best Featured Actress in a Musical (Glenn Close). It won three, for Best Actor in a Musical (Jim Dale), Best Scenic Design (David Mitchell) and Best Costume Design (Theoni V. Aldredge). In addition, *Barnum* won the 1980 Outer Critics' Circle Outstanding Musical Award. Jim Dale was the recipient of a Drama Desk Award, and a Theatre World Award went to Marianne Taum for her portrayal of Jenny Lind.

Carnival

Broadway musical. Music and lyrics by Bob Merrill; book by Michael Stewart; produced by David Merrick; directed and choreographed by Gower Champion; based on the film *Lili* by Helen Deutsch; adapted from a story by Paul Gallico.

Premiering in New York on April 13, 1961, *Carnival* ran for 719 performances. The first Broadway musical to be adapted from a screen musical, *Carnival* effectively created the backstage atmosphere of a small down-and-out European circus in an American idiom. In addition to showcasing various individual circus acts, the show featured several circus ensemble pieces, including the opening in which ROUSTABOUTS set up the tents and the closing number, in which the tent packs up to move on.

The story involves an orphan girl (created by Anna Maria Alberghetti) who falls in love with the circus magician, Marco (James Mitchell). She befriends the puppets in a MIDWAY and finally realizes her true love is for the lame puppeteer, Paul (Jerry Orbach). *Carnival* introduced the standard song "Love Makes the World Go Round."

Jumbo

Musical. Music by Richard Rodgers; lyrics by Lorenz Hart; book by Ben Hecht and Charles MacArthur; produced by Billy Rose; and directed by John Murray Anderson and George Abbott.

Jumbo, a sensational combination of musical comedy and circus, opened at the Hippodrome theater in New York City on November 16, 1935 for the then-record cost of $340,000.

After an 11-week postponement due to the troubles in coordinating the book, circus acts and songs, *Jumbo* opened to enthusiastic reviews. The high production costs, however, caused the show to close after only five months and 233 performances.

The story, Hecht and MacArthur's only team musical, was a sawdust ring *Romeo and Juliet*, with two rival circus families brought together by the love of the daughter and son of the feuding families. The show, starring Jimmy Durante and Edwin "Poodles" HANNEFORD, introduced such songs as "The Circus Is on Parade," "The Song of the Roustabouts" and the standard "The Most Beautiful Girl in the World."

Pachyderms were not common performers on the Broadway stage. During one 1936 performance, Tuffy the ELEPHANT was onstage when he forgot he was housebroken. Durante got the biggest laugh of the evening when he dead-panned, "Hey, Tuffy, no ad-libbing!"

In 1962 a film version (known mainly as *Billy Rose's Jumbo*) was produced by Joe Pasternak and Martin Melcher for MGM in Metrocolor and Panavision.

La Strada

Based on Federico Fellini's 1954 film of the same name, *La Strada* was a major Broadway musical flop of the 1969 season, lasting only one performance on December 14 at the Lunt-Fontanne Theatre. Its story centered around Zampano, an Italian circus strongman who buys the naive Gelsomina to be his latest assistant and lover. Gelsomina actually falls in love with the brutal Zampano, and she shares her confidences with an acrobatic clown, Mario. The jealous Zampano kills Mario and leaves the grieving Gelsomina to die on the road as the circus moves on.

La Strada was produced by Charles K. Peck, Jr.; Alan Schneider directed; Alvin Ailey was the choreographer; and Lionel *(Oliver!)* Bart was composer-lyricist. A young unknown, Bernadette Peters, played the unfortunate Gelsomina; Larry Kert (Tony in *West Side Story*) played Mario; and Zampano was performed by Vincent Beck, who was replaced on the road by Stephen Pearlman. Also during pre-Broadway tryouts, most of Bart's music was dropped (only three numbers remained by opening night), and Martin Charnin and Elliott Lawrence were called in to "doctor" the show with additional music.

The story, however, was unswervingly tragic with a tone more suited to the opera house than to musical theater. Despite the show's few good songs, notably "Seagull, Starfish, Pebble" (written by Charnin in the Bart style for Peters) and "Sooner or Later" (written by Lawrence for Kert), the reviews were uniformly negative. *La Strada* lost its entire $650,000 investment.

Sunny

Broadway musical which opened at the New Amsterdam Theatre in New York on September 22, 1925 and ran for 517 performances. Music by Jerome Kern; lyrics and book by Otto Harbach and Oscar Hammerstein II; presented by Charles B. Dillingham and directed by Hassard Short.

The show tells the story of Sunny (originated by actress Marilyn Miller), an English circus bareback rider. To avoid marrying the circus owner, Harold Harcourt Wendell-Wendell (Clifton Webb), Sunny stows away on a ship bound for New York. Although she loves someone else, Sunny marries a rich man—Jim Deming—onboard to be allowed to disembark in the United States. After a divorce, Sunny discovers she loves Jim after all and they remarry.

The musical prompted two film versions, one in 1939 for Warner and another in 1941 for RKO.

As long as the American theater continues to contribute songs such as Stephen Sondheim's "Send in the Clowns" and Irving Berlin's "There's No Business Like Show Business" to the popular culture, it seems likely that the arts of the circus and of the live theater will continue to be inextricably linked.

THREE HIGH Circus jargon for a vertical tower of three ACROBATS. One person, the BOTTOM MAN or "understander," is on the ground. On his shoulders balances a second performer, also in a standing position; a third performer tops them both.

(See also TEETERBOARD.)

THREE SHEET A three sheet was a one-piece LITHOGRAPH, 42 inches by 84 inches, which contained three horizontal images on one piece of paper.

One advantage of using a three sheet was that it was much easier to paste up than three separate pieces of paper. In addition, the three sheet looked much different from a lithograph that would be sized as "three sheets." The term "one sheet" was used as a measurement, not referring to how many images were on the poster. Thus, a "three sheets"-size litho would also be 42 by 84 inches, but it would have one large overall picture or pictorial image. A "three sheet," on the other hand, would appear to be three separate rectangular posters, each 28 inches by 42 inches.

For the most striking appearance, the three pictorials were often of the same illustration. If they were different, one of the sections might give the show date or other information regarding the upcoming circus appearance.

The bold appearance of the three sheet may have given rise to such circus expressions as "He is three sheeting again," "He three sheets all over town" and "He is a real three sheeter" to mean the person is a braggart or a self-promoter.

THUMB, TOM See TOM THUMB.

TICKET WAGON See RED WAGON.

TIGERS See CATS.

TIGHTROPE See ALZANA, HAROLD; BLONDIN; FUNAMBULIST; NAITTO, ALA; PETIT, PHILIPPE; WALLENDA, KARL; WALLENDAS, THE; WIRE WALKING.

TIP Circus jargon for the crowd that must be drawn into an attraction, usually the SIDESHOW. The tip may be gathered by a BALLY—also called an opening—or drawn in by a GRIND, or a combination of the two. The action of bringing the crowd into the tent is referred to as "turning the tip."

TITUS, LEWIS B. (1800?–1870) Lewis B. Titus, from Somers, New York, was one of the original members of the ZOOLOGICAL INSTITUTE and later the FLATFOOTS organization. Spurred on by the success of Nathan A. HOWES of nearby Brewster, Titus was one of a number of farmers-turned-MENAGERIE owners.

TOGNI, FLAVIO (1960–   ) In a move reminiscent of his father's lease and eventual purchase of Circus Williams, Kenneth FELD bought the entire renowned Italian Circo Americano in 1989. He merged the show's equipment and animals into the Blue Unit of the RINGLING BROS. AND BARNUM & BAILEY CIRCUS and added the Circo Americano's stars to the Ringling roster.

Foremost among these were Flavio Togni and his family, the fourth generation of one of Europe's greatest circus families and twice winners of the Golden Clown award in competition at the International Festival du Cirque de Monte Carlo. Performing his own mixed act of HORSES and ELEPHANTS, Flavio Togni became the youngest performer with an elephant display ever to win the Silver Clown award at the festival. In the act, re-created on the Ringling show, four perfectly matched Palomino stallions "danced" with four Asian BULLS, directed by Togni's voice alone.

Togni grew up in the circus, and there was never any question as to his future career. Speaking fluent Italian, Spanish, German, French and English, he was at home wherever he traveled. Flavio Togni is quick to credit his family for his circus success: "From my grandfather, I began to learn about horses. From my Uncle Bruno I learned how to train and how to treat animals, to be gentle, to be calm." And from his father, Enis Togni, he learned the cooperative nature necessary to be part of a traveling city: "From my father, I learned how to be a man."

Flavio Togni first began to work with horses, learning to ride in a DRESSAGE act. Although Togni still enjoys training horses the most, he also likes to perform with elephants "because you can play and joke, you can be a showman." Flavio Togni gives a nod to Gunther GEBEL-WILLIAMS; it was from Gebel-

Williams that he "learned how to present with style, how to perform with energy."

A master animal trainer, Flavio Togni's CENTER RING acts include his horse and elephant act, a separate display of elephants and a mixed caged MENAGERIE of panthers, leopards and a great white rhinoceros named "Thor." During the LIBERTY HORSES, in ring one, Flavio displays eight Arabian horses; in ring two, sister Daniele Togni leads 12 Palominos; and, in ring three, cousin Walter Forgione directs seven Lipizzaners. In his dressage act, Flavio Togni and four other riders, including family members Andrea, Daniele and Silvana Togni, take their Andalusian stallions through the synchronized display. A descendant of the type of riding popularized by the Spanish Riding School in the 18th century, the Togni HIGH SCHOOL HORSES presented in the 120th edition of the Ringling show was the first dressage act seen there in 20 years.

TOM MIX CIRCUS See MIX, TOM.

TOM PACKS CIRCUS Tom Packs began his career as a successful sports promoter of boxing and wrestling matches. Then he moved into rodeos in St. Louis; it was through his promotion of cowboy and western film stars that Packs naturally became interested in Wild West shows and circuses.

In 1937 he presented the first edition of the Tom Packs Circus as an open-air show in front of grandstands and on baseball fields. The popular show, efficiently run by an expert publicist, quickly became a sure-fire sponsored date for local organizations. Soon the Tom Packs Circus was playing indoor arenas as well as outdoor stadiums and ballparks throughout the East and the Midwest. In 1956 a second unit was added to play the western United States.

TOM THUMB (1838–1883) Born Charles Sherwood Stratton on January 4, 1838, Stratton was best known as General Tom Thumb—possibly the most famous attraction ever exhibited by P.T. BARNUM.

Born of normal-size parents, Charles had stopped growing at the height of 25 inches when he was just seven months old. Although he did grow ten more inches by his mid-20s, he remained a true midget— perfectly proportioned in all ways—throughout his life.

Barnum first heard of Stratton in 1843. He quickly sent his brother Philo to BRIDGEPORT, CONNECTICUT to talk to the boy's parents about bringing Charles to New York. Barnum not only saw the financial potential of the boy's exhibition but also seemed to genuinely like him. Mr. and Mrs. Sherwood Stratton consented to allow their boy to be the star of the already-famous AMERICAN MUSEUM.

Barnum changed the boy's name to General Tom Thumb, reportedly after a character in a King Arthur story. According to biographer Irving Wallace, Barnum "reached back into history and found the legend of the original Sir Tom Thumb, one of King Arthur's knights, who dwelt in a tiny golden palace with a door one inch wide and rode in a coach drawn by six white mice and was killed in a duel with a spider." To compound the absurdity, Barnum tagged on the military title of "General." He also claimed Tom Thumb came from England and changed the boy's birth date to January 4, 1832. As a result, when it was advertised that young Tom Thumb measured 30½ inches at the age of 18 he was really only twelve.

Barnum taught the boy songs, rhyming jokes and impersonations of Napoleon and Cupid. Barnum also wrote Tom Thumb an introduction that the boy recited at the beginning of every performance: "Good Evening, Ladies and Gentlemen. I'm only a 'thumb' but a good 'hand' in a 'general' way at amusing you."

Finally, Tom Thumb made his debut at the American Museum on December 8, 1842. At this time the American Museum was also displaying variety acts as well as FREAKS, but it was Tom Thumb that drew crowds of people. In his first 14 months at the museum over 80,000 people came to see him. Because of Tom Thumb, the museum's average "take" soared to $500 per day, a percentage of which was split with Tom Thumb's parents.

Tom Thumb overcame his initial shyness and became not only gentlemanly on stage but also a true theatrical trouper. Barnum took him on a successful East Coast tour, then, before leaving for Europe, advertised the "Last Chance to See General Tom Thumb Before He Leaves on His Great Journey." Again, visitors packed the American Museum.

In 1844 an entourage of Barnum's family and Mr. and Mrs. Stratton traveled with Tom Thumb

General Tom Thumb.
(Photo courtesy of The Barnum Museum, Bridgeport, CT)

to Europe. More than 80,000 people lined the streets of Manhattan to see them off. England discovered Tom Thumb to be charming and intelligent, and the first of what was to be three command performances was arranged for Queen Victoria. A special general's costume with plumed hat and sword was prepared for his audience with the Queen.

One of the more amusing incidents of the tour occurred when Tom Thumb had to withdraw from the Queen's presence. Tom Thumb had been told that one never turns his back to the Queen; but he found it difficult to walk backward the long distance from the throne to the door. He solved the problem by making a deep bow, turning and running a few steps, again facing the Queen, taking another bow, another sprint, until he finally reached the door. The series of comic bows so entranced the Queen that he repeated them at many of his performances from then on.

Also in England, Barnum made Tom Thumb the gift of a miniature carriage only 39 inches high and 19 inches wide, pulled by four white ponies.

In France, Tom Thumb was presented as Le Général Tom Pouce to King Louis-Phillippe. The European tour lasted three years, including two more audiences with Queen Victoria, before the travelers returned home from this, the first of Tom Thumb's several overseas tours. By the time they returned to the States, Barnum had secured a lifetime contract with Tom Thumb.

In all, his first tour abroad lasted four years, with additional stops in Spain and Belgium. Tom Thumb's impression of Napoleon was especially welcomed in England. As Tom Thumb paced in character one day, the Duke of Wellington asked what he was pondering. "The loss of Waterloo," Tom deadpanned. According to Barnum's autobiography, Tom Thumb "left America a diffident, uncultivated little boy. He came back an educated, accomplished little man."

While Tom Thumb was touring abroad, Barnum discovered a female midget, 22 years old and 32 inches tall. Her name was Mercy Lavinia Warren Bump, which Barnum shortened to Lavinia WARREN. Upon his return from Europe, Tom Thumb fell in love with her; but another midget in Barnum's employ, "Commodore" George Washington Morrison NUTT, was a rival for her attentions.

Once again Tom Thumb's personality won out, and he and Lavinia were married on February 10, 1863 in New York's Grace Episcopal Church when he was 25 years old. Commodore Nutt was the gracious best man. Two thousand people attended the ceremony; at the reception held in New York the couple stood on top of the grand piano to greet well-wishers, then later cut a wedding cake that weighed more than both of them put together. Another ornate reception was held in Philadelphia, but the most distinguished reception was held at the White House by President and Mrs. Abraham Lincoln. When shaking hands with the groom, the President—a humorist at heart—said, "General, here we have the long and the short of it."

The couple was happily married for 20 years but had no children. A few years after their marriage, Barnum arranged a hoax in which a baby girl was supposedly born to them. It was a borrowed baby, photographed with the "mother" for publicity purposes.

Near the end of his life, Tom Thumb—a lover of fine wine and food—grew a goatee and ballooned to 70 pounds, despite his 3 feet 4 inch height. When he died of apoplexy at the age of 45 on July 15, 1883, over 10,000 people attended his funeral in Bridgeport, Connecticut. Because of his expensive tastes in life, Tom Thumb left little in the way of an estate for his wife Lavinia.

(See also FREAKS; LITTLE PEOPLE).

TOOT UP Circus jargon for playing the CALLIOPE to get the attention of the crowd.

TOP Circus jargon for a canvas TENT. Each tent has its own nickname: the dressing room or PAD ROOM is the "dressing top"; the main show is performed in the BIG TOP, and the SIDESHOW is performed in the LITTLE TOP.

TOPS See ELEPHANTS; ROGUE ELEPHANTS.

TOUNG TALOUNG See ELEPHANTS; WHITE ELEPHANT.

TOWNER Circus jargon for someone from town and not part of the troupe or, more generally, any outsider. Also sometimes called a "townie" or "gilly."

TRAIN See CIRCUS TRAIN.

TRAIN WRECKS See CIRCUS TRAIN.

TRAMP CLOWN One of the major types of CHARACTER CLOWNS, the tramp clown usually dresses in dark, rumpled clothing, often with a broken top hat. The face sports a perpetual "five o'clock shadow" blackened onto the cheeks and chin. Surrounding the mouth is a white oval, sometimes with the ends turned down into a frown. Occasionally a large red bulbous nose or accented eyes complete the makeup. White greasepaint is not used above the beard; the face remains flesh-toned above the stubble. Often tramp clowns use their own hair, but a wig and false nose could be part of the makeup design.

The tramp character is most probably adapted from the minstrel show era. One of the earliest

A clown using fingers to apply black makeup for his tramp clown character. (Photo by Tom Ogden)

theatrical tramp acts was "Alexander and Hennery," played on the vaudeville stage by Tom Heath and Jim McIntyre from 1874 to 1924. They wore the traditional minstrel "blackface"; but instead of playing their characters as servants or freed slaves, they made them hobos.

In the minstrel era, before the introduction of greasepaint and modern makeup, actors used to darken their faces using burnt cork, often from recently emptied wine bottles. The expression "cork up" is still sometimes used in theatrical circles to refer to getting into a blackface makeup.

Tramp clowns usually work as CARPET CLOWNS, doing side bits and CLOWN GAGS of their own as well as accenting other performers' acts. Rarely are they made characters in a sketch involving the entire CLOWN ALLEY; and, if they are, they still remain sad, bungling, aloof misfits off to one side of the ring.

At first glance, tramp characters would seem to be the easiest to play, because performers get to choose their own gags, work alone and do not have to conform to many of the restraints put on the other clowns. In reality, however, they are perhaps the most challenging and difficult characters because they require the acting ability not only to make the audience laugh but to make it feel empathy as well.

As with the other types of makeup, performers must employ white, red and black greasepaint, flesh paint and perhaps a gray stick, liners, brushes and a powder sock or two (made by placing talcum powder in a men's stocking and tying it with a knot).

The face must be dry and clean-shaven. Even though a beard is going to be painted on, it is unprofessional to allow people to see real stubble showing through the makeup.

Because of the amount of dark makeup that will be used, the white greasepaint should be applied first. That way, if a mistake is made, it can more easily be covered with the black paint. White is often used to outline the eyelids and eyebrows, and to surround the mouth. It is applied using a brush, stick or, preferably, the fingers.

As in all clown makeup, the shape of the designs is critical. White around the eyes gives a bleary-eyed look and an expression of surprise. Some clowns like to paint on a permanent white frown. It should be noted, however, that Emmett KELLY—perhaps the most famous of all tramp circus clowns—merely painted a white oval for the mouth. He expressed his emotions with body language and facial expression, not a permanent mask of sadness.

The white paint should not be "powdered down" at this point, because it is not "set" until later. Instead, flesh-colored greasepaint is applied next as a full face base, including over the ears and throat.

The black greasepaint is then applied along the chin line, over the cheeks, partway down the throat and, if desired, as a small mustache. The most difficult part of the makeup, which usually takes years to master, is "feather edging" the black, white and flesh makeup together. This gives the appearance of stubble, a "shadow" and real hair, not a straight line between the beard and flesh.

The entire makeup is then powdered and set: This prevents it from smearing and smooths out the entire appearance. The excess powder should be brushed away. Liner pencils are used to highlight expressions; it is then that accent marks—perhaps a red-tipped nose or red-rimmed eyes—are added.

Although a tramp clown is an attention-getting character, it is possible to have more than one hobo in an alley. Another of the most famous tramp clowns in history, Otto GRIEBLING, appeared with the RINGLING BROS. AND BARNUM & BAILEY CIRCUS for many years in the same show as Emmett Kelly.

(See also CLOWN GAGS; CLOWNS.)

TRAPEZE To many, the trapeze is the most glamorous of the AERIAL ACTS. Many have seen it as a metaphor for Man's desire to fly. The single crossbar, held in midair by two cloth-covered ropes hanging from the top of the TENT, form a platform from which the artist can display feats of dexterity, grace and beauty. It is little wonder that songs such as "The Man on the Flying Trapeze" have been written to celebrate the story of the dauntless souls who dare to fly through the sky.

An early star of the trapeze was the French performer Jules LÉOTARD, whose costuming—erotic for its time—still bears his name. More modern aerialists include BARBETTE, Charles and Ernest CLARKE, Alfredo CODONA, Winnie COLLEANO, Art and Antoinette CONCELLO, Tito GAONA and Miguel VAZQUEZ.

The trapeze may be performed either still or swinging. In one variation, the CLOUD SWING, a piece of padded length of canvas takes the place of the trapeze bar.

Two or more swinging trapeze bars gave rise to leaping from one to the next, hence the origin of the FLYING TRAPEZE. Flyers leave an elevated platform, holding onto a bar as they swing across space. They let go and "fly" into the arms of a CATCHER who waits, hanging upside-down from another distant trapeze bar.

(See also FLYERS; FLYING CONCELLOS, THE; FLYING CRANES, THE; FLYING GAONAS, THE; FLYING VAZQUEZ, THE; QUADRUPLE SOMERSAULT; TRIPLE SOMERSAULT.)

TRIPLE SOMERSAULT First achieved in 1897 in Sydney, Australia by Lena Jordan, a Latvian woman, into the hands of CATCHER Lew Jordan, her adopted American father, the triple back somersault was considered, in its time, the ultimate trick possible to be performed by an artist on the FLYING TRAPEZE. Starting in 1909, Ernest CLARKE also was able to achieve "the triple"; but it was Alfredo CODONA's ability to consistently throw the triple somersault, beginning in 1920, that won him accolades as the "King of the Flying Trapeze."

In order to perform the stunt, the flyer who is about to somersault has to swing back and forth until achieving a forward velocity of over 60 miles an hour, which allows the performer to roll over three times before coming out of a spin and meeting the hands of the catcher. As rigging was improved, it was discovered that additional speed could be achieved by raising the pedestal higher before taking off from the perch; but the trick still requires split-second timing.

Now a staple in most flying acts, Codona performed the precise and exhausting trick until a shoulder injury forced his retirement in 1933. During the 1930s and '40s, every member of The FLYING CONCELLOS was able to perform the triple within the course of the act.

(See also AERIAL ACTS; QUADRUPLE SOMERSAULT; TRAPEZE.)

TROUPER Circus jargon for a performer or one who travels with a circus. The highest compliment one can be paid on a show is be called "a real trouper." The opposite of a trouper would be a "FIRST OF MAY."

TRUNK UP Circus jargon used by BULL HANDLERS and trainers as a command for the ELEPHANTS to put up their trunks in a salute to the audience.

TUBS, ELEPHANT Elephant tubs are large circular stools on which ELEPHANTS can sit up, or step up onto, during their acts.

Made of welded steel, the base of each tub is a metal ring approximately four feet in diameter. The top of the tub is a metal-lined circular platform made of thick wood about three feet in diameter. The tub is usually not a solid drum or cylinder; rather, the two are joined by steel rods spaced around the circumference of the two rings.

Although the tubs are very heavy to withstand the weight of the pachyderms, the open latticework makes them more manageable. Even so, the BULL HANDLER must tilt the unwieldy tubs on their sides and roll them in and out of the performance area.

TUCKER, LEONARD BASIL "HOXIE" (1910–) Leonard Basil Tucker was born August 7, 1910 in Somerset, Kentucky. His father's nickname was "Big Hox"; so when the boy went into show business and joined the Redpath Chautauqua as a prop boy at the age of 15, he added an "ie" to the name. In addition to honoring his father's name, the boy felt this had a glamorous connotation to the movies: Cowboy star Jack Hoxie was playing "Deadeye Dick" in a string of serials.

Thunderous tons of ponderous pachyderms sit on bull tubs, touring with the Clyde Beatty-Cole Bros. Circus. (Author's collection)

He stayed on the circuit for 12 years, then joined the Heffner Venson (also seen as Vernon) Stock Co., a tented dramatic troupe. He started as a popcorn BUTCHER and helped put up the BIG TOP, eventually winding up BOSS CANVASMAN.

It was on that show that he met his wife, Betty, who had joined the cast at the age of 15. She was a member of the Noble Sisters, an acrobatic dance troupe that toured with the show. Four years later Hoxie and Betty were married. They left the stock company, and for one winter Hoxie toured a Hawaiian show. The next spring he became assistant manager for the Billroy Comedians, starring singer Gene Austin, then general manager for 1939 and 1940.

Upon settling in Nashville, Tennessee, Tucker became involved with the Grand Ole Opry. He began to book country music stars out on the "kerosene circuit," playing backwoods towns under canvas to the light of kerosene lanterns. He often chartered airplanes to get the acts to the Opry for their regular Saturday night performances, then back to their personal appearances. One of his many attractions was Eddy Arnold with the Pee Wee King band.

In 1952 a friend convinced Tucker to take over his failing circus. Tucker named it HOXIE BROS. CIRCUS. Of course, there were no brothers, but ever since the RINGLING BROTHERS had come onto the circus scene, the word "Brothers"—indicating a clean, family SUNDAY SCHOOL SHOW—was frequently seen in circus titles.

The first Hoxie Bros. Circus trouped only one season. In 1953 Tucker continued to use the circus equipment, but toured it as a Grand Old Opery tent show. From 1954 throughout 1957 he worked as an agent, boss canvasman and electrician for Milton "Doc" Bartok's Bardex Medicine Company, a medicine show. The following year Tucker stayed in Miami, where he worked in construction through 1960.

In 1961 he reopened the Hoxie Bros. Circus, with Bartok as agent. For the next season only, they became partners with a combined show, the Hoxie and Bardex Bros. Circus. For the next 20 years, Tucker was the sole owner of the Hoxie Bros. Circus.

Each year he sought to improve the show, adding extra rings and ELEPHANTS as soon as possible. A wise manager, however, Tucker let the size and "NUT," or daily operating expenses, vary from year to year, depending on the vicissitudes of circus economics.

Tucker was an excellent manager, some feel the "king of the mud show" (see MUD SHOWS), because he understood his audiences' wants and knew how to deliver them while keeping his operation solvent. He understood every aspect of the circus world from top to bottom, from the correct way to GUY a rope to how to drive the semi-trailers.

He realized his place was in the realm of the small to medium-size tent show, and he gave the best show of that size that could be found. Hoxie was not a performer himself, and he preferred to employ full circus families—especially ones that could, with a change of wardrobe, supply a variety of acts.

Because he was always actively and anxiously involved, however, Tucker suffered three heart attacks over the years. At one point he had a nervous breakdown that laid him up in a hospital for three weeks.

Late in his career, Hoxie Tucker opened up a second unit, which he called the Great American Circus. It was on this show that on June 5, 1983, in Geneva, New York, Hoxie Tucker was stepped on by Janet, one of his BULLS, breaking his pelvis and bruising his back. Unable to oversee the circus personally, he sold the operation—along with a four-year right to the title—to his manager, Allan C. HILL on September 22, 1983. Among the items for sale was the African elephant "Hoxie" that Tucker had named after himself.

Betty Tucker died on September 22, 1985. Leonard Tucker officially retired in 1987, as had his namesake elephant the year before, but his 40 years in the business have made him a living legend. The Orlando, Florida chapter of the CIRCUS FANS ASSOCIATION OF AMERICA named their group after him: the Hoxie Tucker Tent #137. Hoxie Tucker currently resides in Miami.

TURNAWAY

Circus jargon for a full house or sold-out show where, as the lingo suggests, potential audience members must be turned away.

(See also STRAWHOUSE.)

TURNER, AARON (c. 1790–1854)

Aaron Turner was born the son of Mercy Hony in Fairfield, Connecticut; but around 1799 he was put under the guardianship of another Fairfield resident, Dorcas Osborn. He was apprenticed to a shoemaker and married in 1815.

Turner had three children, two sons, Napoleon B. (1816–18??) and Timothy (1820–1858), and a daughter. Whether Aaron or Napoleon, the older son, entered the circus profession first is unknown; but Aaron was first mentioned in an 1823 HERALD as a trick rider. It is certain that by 1826 Aaron Turner was a partner with Nathan A. HOWES and Sylvester Reynolds in an equestrian show. Seth B. HOWES, Nathan's younger brother, was a member of troupe.

Records of his circus are scant, but Turner had parted company with Howes and Reynolds by 1828 when he took out his own "Columbian Circus." His Aaron Turner Circus, with its WINTER QUARTERS in Danbury, Connecticut, was on the road by at least 1836 when P.T. BARNUM and George F. BAILEY were touring with the operation.

By 1838 Turner had left active management of his show; he completely retired from the road in the 1840s.

TURNING THE TIP   See TIP.

24-HOUR MAN

Circus jargon for the ADVANCE MAN who travels just one day ahead of the circus to check out final details. From the turn of the century to shortly after World War II when rail shows took up 30 or more cars, many of the shows had two 24-hour men, who worked alternate days ahead of the show. At one point, the RINGLING BROS. AND BARNUM & BAILEY CIRCUS had three men working every third stand.

Since he is the last person with the show into town before the circus actually arrives, the 24-hour man has one of the most important jobs of the entire operation. After confirming all permits, the 24-hour man must clear up last-minute details with the press and sponsors. In the days of the railroad circus, he had to check with the yard superintendent to make sure the appropriate crossings and sidings would be clear.

He checks the condition of the LOT, arranging for dirt or straw to be spread if it is muddy or full of ruts. Often the 24-hour man makes a tentative LAY OUT for the benefit of the LAYOUT MAN and BOSS CANVASMAN. Among his last preparations are providing for water to be delivered to the lot as well as straw and hay for the animals. Finally he calls back to the show and gives a status report to the office manager.

On some MUD SHOWS, the 24-hour man also must act as the ARROW MAN, posting paper ARROWS and chalking telephone poles to mark the route the circus is to take to the next town.

TWO BILLS SHOW   See BUFFALO BILL WILD WEST AND PAWNEE BILL GREAT FAR EAST SHOW.

TWO HEMISPHERES BANDWAGON   Manufactured in 1903 by the Sebastian Wagon Works of New York at the cost of $40,000, the Two Hemispheres Bandwagon is the world's largest show wagon. The wagon was created specifically for the BARNUM & BAILEY CIRCUS to commemorate its return from a five-year tour of Europe and to head its 1903 STREET PARADE.

Like the popular Columbus-John Smith Bandwagon, also created by Sebastian, the Two Hemispheres Bandwagon had the distinction of being different on each side; one is carved to represent the Eastern Hemisphere and the other the Western. The wagon measures 28 feet long, almost 8 feet wide and 10½ feet high. Barnum & Bailey later sold the wagon to the Ringling Bros. Circus, which sold it to the ROBBINS BROS. CIRCUS.

Maintained for years by the Circus Hall of Fame in SARASOTA, FLORIDA, it is now privately owned by John Zweifel of Sarasota. As of this writing, the Two Hemispheres Bandwagon is on loan to the CIRCUS WORLD MUSEUM in BARABOO, WISCONSIN, where it is on display.

TWO HIGH   Circus jargon for one person balanced in a standing position on top of another gymnast's shoulders. The performer standing on the ground is known as the "understander" or BOTTOM MAN.

(See also ACROBATS; TEETERBOARD.)

U

UBANGIS The Ubangi tribe was arguably the most popular SIDESHOW attraction ever to travel with the RINGLING BROS. AND BARNUM & BAILEY CIRCUS. The 13 saucer-lipped women, including Queen Guetika, and two men toured with the BIG ONE in 1930 and 1932.

Brought out of French West Africa by Dr. Ludwig Bergonnier, the Ubangis were a huge draw to the LITTLE TOP and commanded a salary of $1,500 per week. Most of the money, of course, was kept by their "manager."

The public's fascination with them was the huge size and, by western standards, the deformity of the women's lips. In their culture, however, women were judged beautiful by the length of their lips. The stretching was started in infancy, when the girls' lips were slit open and small disks were inserted. As the children grew, the size of the disks was also increased.

Among their unusual habits to western eyes, the Ubangis ate raw whole fish and unpeeled bananas. Purportedly, one of the women fell in unrequited love with bandleader Merle EVANS.

UNICYCLE See CYCLISTS.

UNUS (c. 1907–   ) Born Franz Furtner in Vienna, Austria, Unus was a superb balancer whose solo CENTER RING act climaxed with his creation and trademark, the "one finger stand." John Ringling NORTH spotted Unus in a Barcelona, Spain nightclub in 1946, and brought him to the United States to perform with the RINGLING BROS. AND BARNUM & BAILEY CIRCUS. Unus's American debut in 1948 was advertised as the "Upside-down, gravity-defying, equilibristic wonder of the world."

Working in tails, top hat and white gloves, Unus stepped onto a small raised table on which sat a lit globe, made for him by General Electric. At the finale of his routine, Unus extended the forefinger of his right hand and balanced it on the ball. He then threw himself up into a "handstand"—at first using his cane for assistance in balancing, then using only his forefinger for support.

Before performing the one-finger stand, Unus would always deliberately remove his gloves and show that his hands were empty of special devices. He always replaced his gloves before proceeding into the finale. Although Unus's detractors dismissed the ending because of the possibility of a metal brace concealed in the glove, the stunt was still an impressive feat; the act had a great audience impact during his 13 years on the Ringling show in the late 1940s and early 1950s.

After seeing Unus perform, Ernest Hemingway wrote, "In your dreams you watch Unus standing on one finger and you think, 'Look at such a fine, intelligent and excellent man making his living standing on one finger when most of us can't even stand on our feet.' "

V

VALDO, PAT (1881–1970) Pat Valdo was born Patrick Francis Fitzgerald in Binghamton, New York. Because his father, William J. Fitzgerald, owned the largest union cigar factory in the city, it was assumed that the young man would follow in the trade.

As a youth, however, Pat was fascinated with show business, assisting touring repertory companies and sneaking into circuses. He learned to juggle from a traveling vaudevillian. Eventually he quit school in tenth grade to go on the road.

His first professional touring was as a candy BUTCHER with the WALTER L. MAIN CIRCUS. Just a few months later he signed onto the JOHN ROBINSON CIRCUS as an apprentice CLOWN for $10 a week. Soon he had developed his trademark character as a WHITEFACE CLOWN, accenting the face with broad red lips and black eyebrows. It was also there that a veteran JOEY in CLOWN ALLEY recommended Fitzgerald change his surname to Valdo.

In 1904 he was hired away by the Ringling Bros. Circus. During the off-season, he toured the vaudeville circuit, sometimes appearing as an equestrian clown with the Orrin DAVENPORT troupe.

As a producing clown on Ringling, Valdo was a master at creating CLOWN GAGS. Among his best known were the midget clown firehouse gag and his red whirling wig. In the tradition of Dan RICE, Valdo comically interacted with the EQUESTRIAN DIRECTOR as well as with other performers.

Perhaps Valdo's most remembered gag was dressing up his pet dog as a miniature elephant. After performing several stunts, the tiny "elephant" would jump into Valdo's pants. The gag created a sensation, and Valdo even did the bit as an actor in the Broadway play, *Polly of the Circus*—later made into one of the first movies with a circus theme (see FILMS, CIRCUS). To this day, an elephant-dog is still a popular CLOWN WALKAROUND.

Valdo moved from Ringling to the BARNUM & BAILEY CIRCUS and briefly onto The HAGENBECK-WALLACE CIRCUS. Back on the 1910 Barnum & Bailey show he met Laura Meers, who was performing with her brother as a wire walker. After marrying her in 1914, Valdo joined their act.

In 1923 Valdo's career changed direction when Charles Ringling made him an assistant to Fred BRADNA, the RINGMASTER on The BIG ONE. In 1929 John RINGLING promoted Valdo to supervisor of performance and director of personnel, a position he fulfilled for the rest of his professional career. Three years later Valdo made his first European tour as a talent scout for new acts for the RINGLING BROS. AND BARNUM & BAILEY CIRCUS.

About his new management role of working with the cast and crew, Valdo said:

It's one big family of children. We take care of them. I listen to their gripes, calm down their artistic outbursts, feed them, help them save their money, take care of their insurance and doctor's bills, send their children to school. We're a league of nations, learn each other's language.

In 1969 Pat Valdo was made the Ringling circus's first director emeritus. He died in SARASOTA, FLORIDA on November 7, 1970.

VAN AMBURGH, ISAAC (1808–1865)

Isaac Van Amburgh was the first lion trainer of major note in the United States and the most famous in the 19th century. Among his many feats, he is credited with being the first to stick his head into a lion's mouth. That this is a dangerous and fool-hardy stunt is self-evident; what is not often considered is the fact that lions—because they are carnivores—have incredibly bad breath! He is also often credited with being the first American trainer to enter a cage of lions. According to his biographer, O.J. Ferguson (*Biographical Sketch of I.A. Van Amburgh,* Booth & Co., 1865), Van Amburgh first performed the daring stunt in public on the stage of the Richmond Hill Theatre in New York in 1833.

Born in Fishkill, New York in 1808, Van Amburgh started in the MENAGERIE business in 1829 as a CAGE BOY for June, Titus, Angevine & Co., who were operating as part of the ZOOLOGICAL INSTITUTE. Working in the 1830s and 1840s in the pre-Karl HÄGENBACH era of humane treatment of trained animals, Van Amburgh employed the "brute force" method, often using an iron bar to enforce his will. In striking contrast, he became the first trainer of the big CATS to display the proverbial lion and the lamb in the same cage—an attempt to counter conservative religious prejudice against circuses and menageries. Later he added a child to the enclosure to show that all of God's creatures could live in peaceful harmony together.

On January 8, 1834 he began performances at the Bowery Theatre in New York City as Constantius, a Greek, in *The Lion Lord,* a play that interpolated his act with two lions. During his regular routine Van Amburgh, dressed in a Roman toga, entered four different cages, holding two tigers, two leopards, hyenas, and a lion and lioness, respectively.

The following summer he went on tour with June, Titus, Angevine & Co. and stayed with them through the 1837 season. In June 1938 he returned (with his animals) to the New York stage in *Bluebeard* at Wallack's National Theatre. On July 7, 1838 he left for a European tour under the auspices of Lewis B. Titus, and the circuit lasted seven years. He made his London debut at Astley's Amphitheatre (see ASTLEY, Philip) on August 27, 1838. While in England, he made several command performances before Queen Victoria and he was painted by famed portrait artist Sir Edward Landseer. Van Amburgh returned, triumphant and famous, in 1845.

Titus, John J. June, along with other partners (variously over the years, Caleb S. Angevine, Avery Smith and Gerard Crane) named one of their new menageries—now under the FLATFOOTS organization for their star performer—Van Amburgh & Co. The show performed at the Bowery Amphitheatre in New York from December 18, 1845 through April 4, 1846 before beginning a road tour under canvas. Besides the band members, Van Amburgh was the only human performer. Among the menagerie holdings were two elephants (including HANNIBAL, the largest BULL exhibited up to that time), 100 HORSES and 60 assorted exotic beasts. Earning over $400 per week, Van Amburgh toured with the menagerie, although he only rarely performed after 1847. The show title was sold to James Raymond after the 1849 season.

A wealthy man, Isaac Van Amburgh retired around 1856. He died of a heart attack in his own bed in Philadelphia on November 29, 1865. The lion trainer's name was to be associated with other menageries and circuses, even after his death, until 1921.

VAN AMBURGH CIRCUS

Isaac VAN AMBURGH, the first important wild animal trainer in the United States first appeared as a featured performer with the ZOOLOGICAL INSTITUTE and FLATFOOTS shows. Later he started his own circus and the Van Amburgh Menagerie.

From 1846 through 1883, Hyatt Frost was the manager of the Van Amburgh Circus (also originally known as Van Amburgh's Menagerie); it was he who continued its successful tours after Van Amburgh's death in 1865. Despite Frost's otherwise astute direction, the circus was one of the last shows to make the switch from wagons to rail.

Frost resurrected the Van Amburgh title in 1885, then leased the name to the Ringling Bros. Circus as a subtitle in 1889. Soon other shows picked up the name and used it without permission.

In 1904 Jeremiah "Jerry" MUGIVAN and Bert BOWERS started their circus empire, which culminated in the 1921 charter of the AMERICAN CIRCUS CORPORATION. Among the corporation's holding was a small rail show they called the Van Amburgh Circus. It toured until mid-season 1908. At that time, they changed the name to the more recognizable Howes'

Great London Circus. The Van Amburgh name was once again moved to a subtitle until finally, it was dropped.

VAN AMBURGH'S MENAGERIE See LENT, LEWIS B.; VAN AMBURGH, ISAAC; VAN AMBURGH CIRCUS.

VARGAS, CLIFFORD E. "CLIFF" (1924–1989)
Starting with three trucks and eight animals, Cliff Vargas built his own circus—CIRCUS VARGAS—into an immense three-ring circus and the only major circus to have its WINTER QUARTERS on the West Coast.

Cliff Vargas, born December 7, 1924, was not part of a circus family; but his father, a farmer, did take him and his older brothers to the circus when it came to town.

Vargas began his show business career as a PHONE PROMOTER for the Rudy Jacobi show in northern California. "I came in and immediately outperformed a lot of the veteran salesmen," he said in *The Executive* magazine. "I've always been very good at everything I've done because I've always been willing to make that extra effort. I'd call up a prospect and if the wife answered and said, 'Ernie's away on a fishing trip,' I'd ask, 'When will he back?' I'd make a note and I'd call again and say, 'Is that Ernie? How was your fishing trip?' Things like that make the difference."

About a year after the phone jobs, he went on the road with the Miller Johnson Circus. The police inspectors would not allow the small stadium show to open in Palo Alto because of dangerously antiquated electrical equipment. When the circus owner explained that he couldn't afford to buy new equipment—even though his wife was in Europe and they were leaving for a cruise thereafter—Vargas realized that the man was skimming profits while compromising both the show and the safety of the patrons.

Vargas left the show, sold his house in San Francisco and bought equipment for his own show's first season. Rather than rely on phone sales, Cliff Vargas was one of the first to promote tie-ins with shopping centers. The circus would set up on the mall's parking lot; merchants would promote the show with sales and ticket giveaways; and the location would generate family customers.

Vargas, with his ever-present cigarette, was a nervous, energetic and likable man. A bachelor and self-proclaimed workaholic, he was tireless in mak-

Clifford E. Vargas and "Colonel Joe."
(Photo courtesy of Bill Biggerstaff)

ing his show a success, keeping a 60-hour work week—and more when he was on the show LOT—up until the time of his death.

Vargas knew the show from top to bottom. He was admired as a "hands-on" operator who claimed, "I've never asked anyone to do something I would not do." In one instance, Vargas complained to his drivers that they were taking too long on the JUMP. They countered that he just didn't understand how difficult it was to move a big rig. He approached Wally Ross, one of his animal men, and asked him for instructions on how to drive an 18-wheeler.

"A week later, we were leaving for Dallas, Texas, to open the season," Vargas recalled. "The first hill I'm on in this big truck loaded with semis, I lose my gears going to downshift and I thought, 'Oh my God!' But I survived and I learned and I didn't have any problems with my drivers after that because I was one of them. See, circus people will never accept a boss who's just a manager."

To keep his trained personnel and ROUSTABOUTS from one season to the next, Vargas improved working conditions, such as providing a superior COOK-HOUSE and installing showers in the workingmen's living quarters, or "sleepers." As many as 70% of his crew returned each year after the winter hiatus.

On the other side of the coin, Vargas did not sign his performers to multiyear contracts. "If I sign them up for the following year too soon, the edge goes off their performances," he reasoned.

Vargas once said that, had he known what he was getting into, he might not have started his own circus. While he knew the odds of success were small, he also saw tremendous grosses on the large shows. He soon discovered that being on the road with the show was essential. Vargas explained:

> When Ringling was running, they had a lot of fat. They had been there for years and years. In those days, the business was different. They had people inside the tent hyping the better seats and customers had to walk around inside the tent before getting to general admission. Well, a lot of that money never got back to that office.
>
> Then they had purchasing agents on the road, negotiating for animal feed and provisions for the cookhouse. The thing was, some of those agents would make deals. If the bill was $50, they'd write it as $150 and split it with the suppliers. In my operation, I'm the sole owner. I watch everything. When I started, I slept in the trucks to save money. I think that's made the difference.

After a heart attack and bypass surgery in the mid-1980s, Vargas no longer traveled full seasons with the show, leaving his friend, Joe Muscarello, to manage the circus. Until his death on September 4, 1989, he did continue to make frequent spot visits to his namesake show.

Cliff Vargas derived great fulfillment in carrying on the tradition of the tented circus. "The real satisfaction is that time and time again, I'll go out and take tickets . . . or people from the audience who recognize me will come up and say, 'We never realized this still existed. I saw the circus as a kid and it's wonderful—it's still available for *my* kids.'"

VAULTING

Also known by the French *voltige*, the term "vaulting" is used in both acrobatics and equestrian riding. In gymnastics, vaulting is the act of acrobatic leaping or jumping, whether by springboard, TEETERBOARD, swinging from a bar or being thrown into the air by another person.

If no apparatus is used in the act, the second acrobat is able to give an extra boost or thrust that would not be possible for the leaper to achieve using the legs alone. The ACROBAT or vaulter who is being thrown is sometimes referred to as the *voltigeur*, while those who do the lifting are known as cavaliers, pitchers, swingers or throwers. If a vaulter is boosted primarily in a vertical direction (as a springboard might), the action is called a lift or pitch. A looped motion analogous to a fly bar is called a swing.

The equestrian world can trace its use of vaulting as far back as the ancient bull-leaping exhibitions on the island of Crete. It was an unknown Roman cavalry officer who adapted the leapers' movements to teach cavalry riders how to safely fall from the backs of their moving HORSES.

It was a logical next step to combine gymnastic vaulting with being able to leap onto and balance on a trotting, or preferably cantering, steed. According to Lilly Walters, a degreed Horse Master and competitive coach, vaulting is an internationally recognized sport outside of circus venues. In 1920 vaulting even appeared as a demonstration (noncompetitive) event at the 1920 summer Olympics in Antwerp, Belgium. The routine is performed in an open arena; and the horse moves in a 42-foot-diameter circle, controlled by a lunge line held by the trainer, or lunger.

Although the word *voltige* is occasionally seen, the term "ROSINBACK" or "bareback riding" (rather than vaulting) is used in the circus arena to describe this style of act. One significant difference is that the horses move freely around the ring; trainers do not hold reins or lunge lines as the acts are performed.

VAZQUEZ, MIGUEL (1964–   )

Born Miguel Angel Vazquez Rodriguez on December 6, 1964 in Autlan, Jalisco, Mexico, Miguel Vazquez became the first flyer in history to achieve the QUADRUPLE SOMERSAULT.

Born into a circus family, Vazquez was performing on the trampoline by the age of six. By nine he was a gymnast on the horizontal bars, and he began his career on the FLYING TRAPEZE at the age of 13.

Although his older brothers were touring in the United States as the FLYING VAZQUEZ, most of Miguel's childhood was spent in Mexico City where he performed in a cousin's small circus. His brothers encouraged him to become a serious flyer, and he joined the family troupe after the 1977 season.

Vazquez attained his first TRIPLE SOMERSAULT in March 1978 in Toledo, Ohio.

Although he was already a superb athlete and an accomplished gymnast, Vazquez's technique as a flyer was inconsistent. Among his supposed "errors" was his tendency to swing too high while somersaulting into the triple. It was this natural inclination, however, that was the key to his perfecting the quad.

He began to practice the quadruple somersault while performing with the RINGLING BROS. AND BARNUM & BAILEY CIRCUS in January 1981. The practice sessions were videotaped and studied after each attempt. At first, the challenge was to perfect the somersaults themselves. The catch and return would come later. The brothers raised the cross bars holding up the TRAPEZE rigging, allowing Miguel to gain even more height and speed.

On August 19, 1981, during a practice session following a Ringling performance at the Long Beach Arena in Long Beach, California, all of the elements connected. Miguel Vazquez threw a perfect quad and was caught by his brother Juan.

On opening night at MADISON SQUARE GARDEN the following season, Irving FELD announced that The Flying Vazquez would be attempting the elusive quadruple somersault. Miguel Vazquez finally achieved it in performance at the 7,000-seat Tucson Community Center in Tucson, Arizona on July 10, 1982.

VIDBEL'S OLDE TYME CIRCUS A small three-ring circus under canvas, the Old Tyme Circus was started in 1984 by veteran animal trainers Alfred and Joyce Vidbel. With WINTER QUARTERS in the Catskill Mountains of New York, Vidbel's Olde Tyme Circus advertises itself as "America's Finest Family Entertainment." Their TERRITORY is the central East Coast.

VIRGIN CAR Circus slang on the old rail shows for the single women's sleeper cars. Each "virgin car" did have a matron—usually one of the dressers or wardrobe mistresses—who looked out for the girls and reported unseemly behavior to the front office.

See also BALLY BROAD; CHOOSING DAY.

VOLTIGE See ACROBATS; VAULTING.

VON BROS. CIRCUS Henry Vonderheid owned and operated this small circus in the early 1900s, touring mainly the eastern seaboard.

WAGONS Before the advent of the truck show, all circuses were transported in circus wagons. The early American circuses toured in heavy, functional nonornamental wagons that carried stock, baggage, personnel and equipment.

It was circus manager W.C. COUP who revolutionized the industry: He is generally credited with inventing the method of end-loading packed wagons onto railroad flatcars, allowing the heyday of the railroad show to begin with his first rail tour around 1872. Even during the years of the railroad shows, therefore, circuses still traveled, in essence, by wagon.

Wagons in parades had their origins back to the chariot processions in the Roman COLOSSEUM. During the Renaissance, painted wagons traveled the streets during festival times. Many historians feel that the rush to hold circus STREET PARADES really began after Seth B. HOWES brought back decorated wagons from a European tour in the late 1800s.

As the street parade became not only a fixture but an essential part of a circus, elaborate wagons were developed just for that purpose. These wagons fell into the categories of TABLEAU WAGONS, BANDWAGONS, CAGE WAGONS and the CALLIOPE. Of course, the circus also carried simple, unadorned but sturdy work wagons for hauling equipment, but they were not usually seen in the street parade. On the LOT, the bandwagons often doubled as baggage wagons.

The decoration of circus wagons reflects a distinct style of folk art indigenous to the United States. Many of the early wood-carvers were of European descent, and they carved the first American circus wagons with biblical and landscape scenes with bas-relief designs. The first RINGLING BROTHERS wagon, for instance, was a work cart made over with an eagle and tin mirrors on either side by a Ringling cousin, Henry Moeller, at his MOELLER CARRIAGE AND WAGON WORKS.

The Moeller name became one of a select few famous for their artwork on circus wagons, including: the Bode Wagon Works of Cincinnati; the Sullivan and Eagles Company of PERU, INDIANA; and the Fielding Brothers Company and the Sebastian Wagon Works, both of New York.

The circus would give the craftsmen an idea of the artwork they wanted, and the finished panels were shipped to WINTER QUARTERS for assembly onto a circus wagon. One show, the GOLLMAR BROS. CIRCUS, hired its own artisans on staff to build the wagons and decorate them.

The wagons themselves were oak, maple or hickory. Red was the dominant color on most wagons, and gold-leafing was frequently employed. Many wagons rolled on SUNBURST WHEELS, a dazzling effect created by painting the spokes in many colors. Like CLOWN faces, no two wagons were alike; each had a specific place in the parade. All of the wagons were numbered, although not consecutively. As a subtle ruse, circuses routinely gave the impression of carrying more wagons than they actually did by assigning very high numbers to some carts.

By the 1920s logistical and economic realities made the street parade a thing of the past. With the end of the last regular street parades, wagon-building

Three replica wagons in three-quarter size, built by the International Circus Hall of Fame and exhibited at Knott's Berry Farm, Buena Park, California in 1991. Inspired by a classic Albert M. Wetter Circus Ibex Tableau Wagon, this style of parade/baggage wagon would have been seen in the late 1800s (top); a near duplicate of a Gollmar Bros. Circus tableau wagon, circa 1910 (middle); an almost exact duplication of an early 1900s cage wagon from the Gentry Bros. Circus (bottom).   (Photos by Tom Ogden)

and decoration also became a lost art. Collectors and historians keep the tradition alive, however, beautifully restoring the antique wagons whenever they are found. A large collection at the CIRCUS WORLD MUSEUM in BARABOO, WISCONSIN, includes the famous TWO HEMISPHERES BANDWAGON. Each summer "for one day only" the GREAT CIRCUS PARADE—sporting some of the premier wagons of the bygone age—makes its appearance in downtown Milwaukee.

Replicas are also a constant reminder of this grand tradition. In 1991 Knott's Berry Farm amusement park in Buena Park, California commissioned the International Circus Hall of Fame in Peru, Indiana to create ten authentic, historically accurate three-quarter scale reproductions. The wagons were a summer feature in 1991, as twice daily a circus street parade rode through the park.

Hall of Fame circus historian Tom Dunwoody researched the wagons to be built with design assistance from Fanning Howey & Associates. John Fugate of the Hall of Fame supervised the project in which skilled Amish and Mennonite craftspeople fabricated the wagons. Miller Carriage Company of Shipshewana, Indiana built the undergear, while Troyer Carriage Company made the remainder of the wagons by hand.

The ten reconstructed wagons include replicas of the Albert M. Wetter's Big 3 Shows bandwagon (c. 1888); three tableau wagons (after those of The HAGENBECK-WALLACE CIRCUS and the Gollmar Bros. Circus); four cage wagons (one suggested by JOHN ROBINSON CIRCUS cages); and two small tableau wagons (inspired by the Wetter Circus parade/baggage wagons.) At summer's end, the reproductions returned to Peru, Indiana for permanent display at the Circus Hall of Fame.

WAIT BROTHERS SHOW   A joking nickname for RINGLING BROS. AND BARNUM & BAILEY CIRCUS referring to their early posters, which read "Wait for the Big Show."

WAIT PAPER   Circus jargon for the advertising LITHOGRAPHS, usually ONE SHEETS, that have the word "wait" on them. They were posted by the BILLING CREW of a second show coming into town, warning the townsfolk to wait for the bigger and/or better circus.

Sometimes the wait paper merely declared "WAIT" and was posted next to pictorials. In some cases it might have a short phrase, telling the TOWNERS which show to expect. Many of the larger shows carried a particular wait paper slogan. The BARNUM & BAILEY CIRCUS, for instance, pasted up "Wait for Barnum" as its wait paper. After the show was combined with the Ringling Bros. Circus into Big Bertha, the wait paper read "Wait for The Big One."

WALKAROUND   See CLOWN GAGS; CLOWN WALKA-ROUND.

WALLENDA, KARL (1905–1978)   Karl Wallenda was born in Magdeburg, Germany into a circus family from Austria-Hungary. His great-grandfather was the leader of a company of jugglers and tumblers, his grandfather trained animals, his grandmother was an ACROBAT and his mother was a TRAPEZE artist.

Wallenda naturally became interested in acrobatics as a boy. After World War I, he answered a newspaper ad for a "handstander" and wound up as an apprentice to the famous German wire walker Louis Weitzman. At 16, Karl Wallenda was performing handstands on the shoulders of Weitzman 40 feet in the air.

After a year, Wallenda formed his own troupe with his brother Herman and two other acrobats. His new company, The Flying Wallendas—as they were then known—made its debut in Milan, Italy in 1922, causing a sensation as the first wire walkers to stand on each other's shoulders to create a human pyramid. The following year, to promote the group, Karl Wallenda made a solo walk on a cord stretched across the Danube River.

The WALLENDAS were performing in Havana in 1927 when they were seen by John RINGLING, who immediately signed them to his show. The next year, when as The Great Wallendas, they premiered with the Ringling show at MADISON SQUARE GARDEN, their pyramid drew a 15-minute standing ovation. In 1930 Karl married a Munich-born acrobat, Helen (b. December 11, 1910–   ), who performed with the troupe until 1959.

Karl had been wary of safety nets ever since the accidental death of his brother Willy in a fall in Sweden in 1933. The back wheel of Willy's bicycle fell off while he was riding on the wire; but Willy

A 1949 baggage wagon pulled by a pair of work horses on the Ringling Bros. and Barnum & Bailey back yard.
(John Heckman photo from the Bakner collection)

did manage to fall into the net. On the rebound, however, he struck a wall and died soon after. From that time on, Karl felt that the nets were dangerous: If the performer fell, every piece of apparatus—such as poles, chairs, bicycles, shoulder bars—would fall on top of the artist as well.

With the Great Wallendas, Karl had his share of luck as well as misfortune. When the troupe's pyramid collapsed in Akron, Ohio in 1934, Karl was able to catch Helen with his legs. During the Wallendas' tragic fall in 1962, Karl suffered only a cracked pelvis. His indomitable spirit forced him back up onto the wire the following evening.

In July 1970 Karl Wallenda, at the age of 65, achieved the incredible feat of a SKYWALK on a 997-foot-long cable stretched across Tallulah Gorge in Tallulah, Georgia. Spectators were reminded of BLONDIN's early feats over Niagara Falls. Seven hundred fifty feet high above the bottom of the gorge on a wire 1½ inches in diameter, Karl Wallenda celebrated his 50th year in show business. He received $10,000 for the 17-minute walk.

In 1974 Wallenda set a new world's distance record by walking 1,800 feet at a height of 60 feet over King's Island in Ohio. Although he still performed occasionally at ballparks, stadiums or natural gorges, he only had two more major televised walks, the second ending in his death. On January 31, 1977 he walked 720 feet between the Fontainebleau and Eden Roc hotels in Miami Beach. After it was finished, he told an interviewer, "It was a very dangerous walk. It was pitch black. I couldn't see anything and it was very windy. But I had to do it. The whole United States was waiting. When you chicken out, you're not a showman anymore."

The following year he made his final walk on the wire. Karl Wallenda was in Puerto Rico, making an appearance at the Pan American Circus with his 17-year-old granddaughter, Rietta, where they crossed a 50-foot high wire every night. To promote the show, the senior Wallenda agreed to a televised walk in new San Juan.

On March 22, 1978—the same day as the Garden opening of the 108th Edition of the Ringling Show—he started his cross of a 750-foot tightwire that had been strung ten stories high between the Condado Holiday Inn and the Flamboyan Hotel. Wallenda was only partway across when a gust of wind unbalanced him. At the age of 73, he no longer had the strength to control the pole. Nor did he have the quick reflexes to drop the pole and catch the wire, as he had done in the 1934 collapse of the Wallenda pyramid. He fell 100 feet into the parking lot, bouncing off a car, and dying on the scene as family members and hundreds of spectators watched what was perhaps the inevitable end for the greatest wire walker of his generation.

(See also WIRE WALKING.)

WALLENDAS, THE   After a season of working with German wire walker Louis Weitzman, 17-year-old Karl WALLENDA joined with his brother Herman and two other acrobats to form a tightwire act. Making their debut in Milan, Italy in 1922, the Wallenda troupe was the first high wire act in which performers stood on each other's shoulders to form a human pyramid.

While performing in Havana, Cuba in 1927, the Wallendas were spotted by John RINGLING, who signed them for his circus. The next season the Great Wallendas (Herman, Joe, Carl and Helen), joined the BIG ONE at MADISON SQUARE GARDEN. They were a spectacular sight, dressed in matching sailor-suit wardrobe, possibly based on those worn by German SWAY POLE artists. (In addition to their trademark wardrobe, the Great Wallendas occasionally wore Spanish toreador-style suits, blue with yellow stockings and red trim.) The American premier of their human pyramid, performed 40 feet in the air without a safety net, drew a 15-minute standing ovation from the audience.

Over the years, the troupe changed personnel. As the pyramid grew from two-high to three-high, the act had as many as nine people on the wire at one time. The Wallendas stayed with the RINGLING BROS. AND BARNUM & BAILEY CIRCUS until 1946.

While the Wallendas were performing in Akron, Ohio in 1934, Helen Wallenda, at the peak of the pyramid, lost her balance when a guy wire became loose. Karl held onto the wire and, amazingly, caught Helen with his legs. She was dropped into a makeshift net, and the rest of the company worked its way hand-over-hand off the cable.

They were also on the wire when fire broke out under the BIG TOP in Hartford, Connecticut on July 6, 1944. Their costumes were singed and a piece of burning canvas landed on Helen, but none of the Wallendas was seriously hurt. They also escaped injury when an earthquake struck as they were on the wire in Nicaragua.

Their good fortune, however, finally ended as they were performing at a SHRINE CIRCUS at the Detroit Coliseum on January 30, 1962. Six thousand spectators were watching as the Wallendas walked, as usual, almost 40 feet in the air without a net in a seven-person pyramid. In this arrangement, two men balanced on poles attached to the shoulders of four men on the wire. Atop the pyramid was 17-year-old Jana Schepp, one of Karl's nieces brought from East Germany after World War II. Jana's brother, Dieter Schepp, was leading the four-man group on the wire.

Dieter lost his grip on his balance pole. He hollered, "Ich kann nicht mehr halten!" meaning "I can't hold any longer." He fell and, with the pyramid attachments on their shoulders, most of the troupe followed him.

Jana was caught by Karl and Gunther, a cousin. They dropped her into an improvised net and worked hand-over-hand to the cable perch. Dieter Schepp and Richard Faughnan, Karl's son-in-law, both died in the fall onto the concrete floor; and Mario Wallenda, Karl's adopted son, broke his back and was partially paralyzed for life. Karl suffered a cracked pelvis and related injuries, but he insisted on returning to the tightrope the following night; two days later, the act was back in place with replacements. After the accident, the Wallendas eliminated the seven-person pyramid from the act, replacing it with a four-person pyramid (two on the wire, one on the shoulders and a girl sitting on a chair on top).

The 1962 tragedy was not their last, however. The following year Helen's sister, "Miss Rietta," fell from a 50-foot high wire in Omaha, Nebraska.

Since Karl's death from a fall in San Juan, Puerto Rico in 1978, several members of the Wallenda clan have continued as wire walkers. Among them, grandson Tino and family perform as the "Flying Wallendas," grandson Enrico and wife Debbie appear as the "Great Wallendas" and grandnephew Steven Gregory and wife Angel work as "The Incomparable Wallendas." Perhaps most remarkable, Angel Wallenda performs her high wire feats despite having an artificial leg—the only person ever to accomplish the feat. After hundreds of hours of struggle, she returned to the wire after losing her right limb in a bout with cancer in August 1987.

(See WIRE WALKING.)

WALTER L. MAIN CIRCUS   Walter L. Main founded his show in 1885 with only seven horses, but it was a 90-horse operation when it was sold to the Scribner & Smith Circus only four years later.

Main began touring a new wagon show in 1890. The next year he moved it onto rails and toured the show on 27 cars. In 1893 the Main show was involved in one of the circus world's worst train wrecks, but the unit was soon rebuilt. The show toured for six more seasons before selling out at the end of 1899.

Two years later Main was back again; but in 1904 the Walter L. Main Circus made its last tour under Main's personal management. Its 25 railroad cars of equipment were sold to William P. HALL, and the horses were leased to Karl HÄGENBACH's associates to build their new show.

In the ensuing two decades, Main leased his popular name to other circus operators. Andrew DOWNIE toured his Walter L. Main Circus from 1918 through 1924; Floyd King and Howard King trouped with the title 1925 through 1928; and various other managers operated the circus from 1930 until 1937.

(See also CIRCUS TRAIN; KING BROS. CIRCUS.)

WARREN, LAVINIA (1841–1919)   First appearing at the AMERICAN MUSEUM in 1863, Mercy Lavinia Warren Bump was a 29-pound, 32-inch-tall midget and former Middleboro, Massachusetts schoolteacher. Although she had already toured on a Mississippi River showboat, P.T. BARNUM announced her as his newest discovery, shortening her name to Lavinia Warren. She became the most famous female midget ever to be exhibited by Barnum.

Lavinia Warren had stopped growing at the age of ten. Both of her parents were tall, and she had two sisters and four brothers of normal height. One younger sister, Minnie, was also a midget, however, and even smaller than Lavinia. Minnie later toured as Lavinia's traveling companion, but she never exhibited as a separate attraction.

TOM THUMB had been on a European tour when Warren was hired. When he first set eyes on her at the museum, he immediately fell in love. A short courtship ensued, and Tom Thumb succeeded in winning her hand. In what was popularly called a "Fairy Wedding," they were married in Grace Church in New York City on February 10, 1863. A rival for Warren's hand, midget "Commodore" George Washington Morrison NUTT, was best man, and Minnie Warren, served as maid of honor. Receptions, attended by thousands, were held in New York and Philadelphia. A ceremony was also given by President and Mrs. Abraham Lincoln at the White House in Washington, D.C.

Lavinia and Tom Thumb were married for 20 happy years until his early death in 1883. During that time, they exhibited in Europe from 1864 to 1867, then again from 1869 to 1872. Although the couple had earned millions of dollars during Tom Thumb's lifetime, his lavish style of living left Lavinia an estate of only $16,000, a few securities and some small pieces of property in Brooklyn, New York.

Lavinia Warren began to troupe again only three months after her husband's death, this time with Count Primo Magri, eight years her junior, and his brother. Lavinia and the three-foot-nine-inch-tall Count married in 1885. Together they took out an opera company of midgets, then later appeared in vaudeville and four early silent film comedies.

When they briefly made their home in Marion, Ohio, the couple opened their house, filled with miniature furniture, as a tourist attraction. They appeared at Coney Island and ran a dry goods store back in Lavinia's hometown of Middleboro. Late in

Helaine, upside down on the web.   (Author's collection)

life, Lavinia Warren became a Christian Scientist and a member of the Daughters of the American Revolution and the Eastern Star.

Before her death on November 25, 1919, Lavinia requested to be buried beside her beloved General Tom Thumb. To the end of her life she wore a picture of him in a locket around her neck. She asked that her simple stone next to Tom Thumb's monument in the Bridgeport cemetery be engraved with the single word "Wife."

(See also LITTLE PEOPLE; FREAKS.)

W.C. COUP SHOWS   See W.C. COUP.

WEB
In circus jargon, a web is technically just a single cable or flat "webbing" hanging from an attached aerial point, such as the ropes holding up a TRAPEZE bar. Today, however, the term "web" generally refers to a canvas-covered rope, stuffed with cotton, that is hung on swivels from the CRANE BAR tent rigging from high in the air down to the ground.

Also known as the Spanish web or Spinning web, the rope is round with an unbraided cotton core and has foot and hand loops attached to it. Used as part of an aerial ballet, the web is climbed by the performer who then places a hand into a loop that has been attached partway up the rope. The web is swung from the ground in a large circle as the aerialist—usually a woman—performs graceful stunts and poses.

(See also WEB SITTER.)

WEB GIRL
Circus jargon for the showgirl who performs on the WEB in an aerial ballet.

(See also BALLY BROAD; WEB SITTER.)

WEB SITTER
Circus jargon for the person on the ground who accompanies the WEB GIRL into the arena, helps her begin her climb up the WEB (or hanging rope) and holds the rope during the act.

For the majority of the spinning web ballet, the web sitter on the ground holds the rope taut as the aerialist performs various gymnastic stunts and strikes stylish poses. As the finale to the routine, the aerialist secures her wrist in a SAFETY LOOP attached to the web; the web sitter swings the rope in a large circle, controlling the speed and the duration of the spin.

(See also BALLY BROAD.)

WEBER, HERBIE (1914–1991)
One of the most renowned wire walkers in the business, Herbie Weber was born May 17, 1914 in Ney, Ohio. He began his 60-year career at the age of 17, billing himself as "The Great Huberto."

His agility on the wire was often followed by a sensational backward "Slide for Life" down the incline wire. Over the years, he was featured on most of the large tented circuses, including the Ringling Bros. Circus, the AL G. BARNES CIRCUS, the CLYDE BEATTY CIRCUS, the COLE BROS. CIRCUS and others. He also appeared on the major SHRINE CIRCUSES and filled in winter dates by performing in vaudeville. His TELEVISION work included appearances on *The Ed Sullivan Show*.

On December 27, 1987 he married his performing partner for the previous 24 years, Maricela Sanchez Hernandes. Together they worked as "Los Latinos."

Weber died in 1991. Services were held in Hugo, Oklahoma, followed by internment in SHOWMEN'S REST. Mrs. Weber donated his "slide boots" to the CIRCUS WORLD MUSEUM in BARABOO, WISCONSIN; his wire walking shoes went into the vaudeville collection of the Smithsonian Institution in Washington, D.C.

(See also WIRE WALKING.)

WELCH, "GENERAL" RUFUS (1801–1856)

Born in upstate New York, Rufus Welch was one of the first great American showmen, an exhibitor of a traveling MENAGERIE of exotic animals. He took his own circus to the West Indies in 1829. During the next decade, Welch traveled to Africa; he returned to the United States with the largest collection of wild beasts ever assembled up to that time.

In the early 1830s, he teamed up with a variety of partners to tour several menageries, including Handy and Welch (1830); Purdy, Welch, Finch & Wright (1832); Purdy, Welch & Co. (1833); Purdy, Welch, Macomber & Co. (1833) and Macomber, Welch & Co. (1834). In 1835 most, if not all, of Welch's menagerie holdings and units were toured under the auspices of the new ZOOLOGICAL INSTITUTE. In 1837 he imported three GIRAFFES, the first ever seen in the United States.

Rufus Welch died on November 28, 1856, leaving only a modest estate.

WELSH BROS. CIRCUS

In 1890 the Welsh family of Lancaster, Pennsylvania briefly toured a small circus called Welsh Bros. Circus "Combined with Dock's Carnival," with Sam Dock as superintendent. They operated independently as the Welsh Bros. Circus from around 1890 through 1904 and again from 1909. In 1898 and 1899 the novice escape artist Harry Houdini was among its cast. In 1914 or 1915 the Welsh Bros. Circus was sold to Al F. Wheeler.

(See also A.F. WHEELER SHOWS; SAM DOCK CIRCUS.)

WENATCHEE YOUTH CIRCUS

In 1992 the Wenatchee Youth Circus, the "Biggest Little Circus in the World," celebrated its 40th year in operation. The origin of the show was a tumbling unit formed in 1952 by Paul Pugh, then a junior high school teacher, at his hometown YMCA in Wenatchee, Washington. The first public performance of the extracurricular tumbling group made up of students at the junior-high level was given in 1953, and soon they were performing at basketball game half-times, civic organizations and other public events. In 1954 the group was expanded into the Wenatchee YMCA Circus; and it remained under YMCA affiliation until 1962.

Pugh's love affair with the circus began when he saw the AL G. BARNES CIRCUS in 1933. Even after he became the principal of Orchard Middle School in Wenatchee, Pugh continued to train youngsters (up to college age) to take part in his show. Having performed every role himself from chief RIGGER to band director, Paul Pugh often joined in the show as a CARPET CLOWN, "Guppo" or "Gup," during COME-IN, or occasionally appeared as the CATCHER in the FLYING TRAPEZE act. Now retired from education, Pugh runs a travel agency when the circus is off the road.

With a cast of about 65 performers, all high school age or younger, and a dozen or more adult supervisors (usually parents), the Wenatchee Youth Circus sometimes tours up to 10,000 miles annually. By the early 1960s the circus was routed throughout Washington, Oregon and northern California, playing a series of minitours of a week to ten days in length each summer. Today the circus tours all of June, July and August and occasionally weekends in September and December (indoors). Although most of its show dates are still in Washington, the circus plays a few spots in Oregon, Idaho and British Columbia, Canada each year and has traveled as far afield as Anchorage, Alaska, San Diego, California and El Paso, Texas. Usually the routing allows the circus to pass through Wenatchee once a week, which allows mail pickup and an exchange of chaperons.

Although the performers rehearse indoors beginning in October and throughout the winter—and perform some dates indoors—all of the rigging for the Wenatchee Youth Circus is designed for open-air, rather than under-canvas, use. The circus, which usually performs two shows a day, sets up primarily on athletic fields and in rodeo arenas, with seats, water, access to showers and night lighting (if needed) supplied by local sponsors.

Travel is scheduled to allow time to set up the night before the first show in a new town. This allows performers to have a chance to rehearse on location and rest up before the first performance. Immediately following the last performance, the show will TEAR DOWN, except for two sleeping/dressing tents and the COOKHOUSE, which are packed in the morning before making the JUMP to the next town.

All of the equipment of the one-ring circus is carried in five custom-built "circus wagons" (each 8 feet by 7 feet by 6 feet) that, in turn, are loaded onto the 45-foot flatbed of a tractor trailer. The show's other semi-trailer is a 35-foot cookhouse truck. As opposed to the circus tradition of NUMBERING THE WAGONS with misleading high figures, Wenatchee Youth Circus's first trailer, bought for the 1954 tour, was stenciled "No. 1"; and all vehicles have been numbered consecutively ever since.

The show is heavy on gymnastics, including tumbling and trampoline, WIRE WALKING (high, low and incline), JUGGLING and CLOWNS. Apparatus includes aerial rigging for four swinging LADDERS and WEBS as well as a 28-foot RING CURB. The circus also carries a 12-piece band. The show does not use animals, but on rare occasions a DRESSAGE or other equestrian act has appeared on the bill. In addition to the two 20-by-40 dressing tents and the cookhouse top, the canvas includes 14 sections of 20-foot-long, 10-foot-high red-and-white striped SIDEWALL.

The tours have become family affairs, with many parents accompanying the circus and staying in tents and recreational vehicles in campgrounds along the way. The board of directors of the not-for-profit circus consists of ten parents elected for two-year terms.

Many of the show's performers have gone on to other circuses during its 40-year history, including Australia's Ashton Circus, CIRCUS KIRK, the RINGLING BROS. AND BARNUM & BAILEY CIRCUS, CIRCUS VARGAS, the original AL G. KELLY & MILLER BROS. CIRCUS and the Big John Strong Circus.

The Wenatchee Youth Circus and Paul Pugh can be contacted at P.O. Box 1733, Wenatchee, Washington 98807-1733.

WHEELER, AL F.   See A.F. WHEELER SHOWS.

WHEELER BROS. CIRCUS   See A.F. WHEELER SHOWS.

WHITE, PATRICIA (1955–   )   With waist-length, taffy-blond hair, Patricia White traveled for 12 years on the CARSON & BARNES CIRCUS as one of the few female CAT trainers ever to grace a circus's CENTER RING. She worked in a cage with a mixed MENAGERIE of Nubian lions and Siberian tigers.

Patricia White placing her head into the mouth of a 500-plus-pound Nubian lion of the Carson & Barnes Circus. (Photo courtesy of Carson & Barnes Circus)

Born in Michigan, Patricia White had no circus family background. "When I was younger," she explained, "I had no idea what I wanted to do except go into the theater. After my freshman year at Western Michigan University, I got a summer job working in an amusement park. I spent my breaks watching the park's animal acts and became totally in love with the big cats."

She claims it took her only three days to decide to quit college and pursue a career training lions and tigers. "I said to myself that I didn't want to go back to English and chemistry. There's more to life than college."

The difficult part, of course, was getting experience. She began by working as a CAGE BOY, cleaning and feeding another trainer's animals. Soon she was working with cats, HORSES, ponies and ELEPHANTS. Her true love, however, remained the cats. She describes her work as a psychological game:

I have to bluff them into thinking I'm tougher than they are. I have to insist on mutual respect. Even though I raised each cat from the time it was young, and I know and love each cat, I cannot treat them as pets. They are not and never will be tame; and if I forget they're wild, that's when it's dangerous.

The art of training animals does not mean making the animals do unnatural acts. It means training them to do natural acts, sitting up, leaping, rolling over on cue. When a cat is young I observe its play time, watch what that cat enjoys doing and adapt that action into the act as the cat matures. The problem in the ring is choreographing all of these tricks into a complete act, while keeping the various cats from clashing.

Although she escaped serious injury during her career, White carries several scars from clawings. One of the features of her act was placing her head into the mouth of Rex, one of her prized lions, recreating a stunt first performed by early American animal trainer Isaac VAN AMBURGH.

After her retirement from the circus at the end of the 1990 season, Patricia White trained Andrea Jewell, who succeeded her on the Carson & Barnes show. White has since made guest circus appearances, including a 1993 tour of Japan. Today she lives in Cody, Wyoming where she produces original bronze sculptures with circus themes.

WHITE ELEPHANT In 1884 P.T. BARNUM planned a new feature, "The Grand Congress of Nations," as part of his GREATEST SHOW ON EARTH. The exhibition was to display a sort of human ZOO—people of every ethnic background from around the world.

Along with this great scheme he decided to present a never-before-seen sensation: a white elephant! For many years, Barnum had been attempting to capture or purchase such a beast from the Far East. In November 1884 one of his agents, J.B. Gaylord, succeeded in purchasing Toung Taloung from King Theebau of Burma. Barnum bought the pachyderm sight unseen, just on the word of its description. The "Royal Sacred White Elephant" was heavily advertised for the following season.

The press scoffed at the possibility of such a creature. In Barnum's reply to the *Maine Farmer* he claimed, "This is written . . . to assure you that although your editor seems a little dubious in regard to the statement published concerning him, it is *terribly true!* If the 'crittur' lives to reach this continent, everybody will be convinced that it is an achievement unparalleled in the history of public shows."

Toung Taloung arrived in New York City by ship on March 28, 1884. The elephant was certainly not white, but rather merely a light gray with pink eyes and covered here and there with pink patches. This did not, of course, prevent the great showman from exhibiting the pachyderm as heralded.

Despite the obvious humbuggery involved, the "white elephant" generated significant press wherever the show traveled. The greatest rival of the Barnum circus at that time was Adam FOREPAUGH, who had his WINTER QUARTERS in Philadelphia. Forepaugh announced an albino elephant of his own, the "Light of Asia," which drew crowds even after it was revealed by an investigative reporter to be nothing more than a whitewashed pachyderm. Barnum's retort was to parade a noticeably bleached BULL named Tip as the "Light of America" through the streets of Philadelphia.

The press had a field day with the "White Elephant War" and, as a result, the public naturally believed that all white elephants were hoaxes. The term "white elephant" came to mean any item reduced in price because no one wanted it.

The White Elephant War ended on November 20, 1887, when Toung Taloung perished in a fire at the winter quarters of the new BARNUM & BAILEY CIRCUS. Although never entering into the Barnum-Forepaugh feud, the Ringling Bros. Circus purchased its own Burmese pachyderm, Keddah, and toured her as "The Royal White Elephant of Siam" in 1887 and 1888. In October 1888 Keddah died of severe burns after her railroad car caught fire.

(See also ELEPHANTS; P.T. BARNUM'S GREATEST SHOW ON EARTH, HOWES' GREAT LONDON CIRCUS AND SANGER'S ROYAL BRITISH MENAGERIE.)

WHITE TOPS, THE *The White Tops*, founded in 1927 by Karl Kae Knecht, is the official publication of the CIRCUS FANS ASSOCIATION OF AMERICA (CFA). In this bimonthly magazine, *The White Tops* gives club news, book reviews and product notices as well as informative historical articles on the history of the American circus.

Subscriptions are free to members of CFA but are also available to nonmembers. Information is available through the offices at P.O. Box 59710, Potomac, Maryland 20859-9710.

WHITEFACE CLOWN One of the major types of CLOWNS, the whiteface clown is not only the most commonly seen in the United States but is also the style American audiences usually associate with the word "clown."

The most probable origin of the whiteface style of makeup goes back to the Commedia dell' Arte and English pantomime. In the Italian Commedia dell' Arte, two of the "zanni," or comic servants, were named Harlequin and Pedrolino. When the plays moved to France, the Pedrolino character evolved from a victim of pranks into the romantic lead and his name was changed to Pierrot.

Pierrot always wore a decorative, baggy white costume. While most characters in the Commedia dell' Arte wore half masks, the actor playing Pierrot powdered his face white—perhaps the start of the whiteface clown tradition.

Meanwhile, the English pantomime had adopted many of the Commedia dell' Arte characters; but in December 1800 James Byrne changed the wardrobe of the silent Harlequin to white silk tights covered with colorful diamond-shaped patches and spangles.

As Harlequin became a more sophisticated character, the slapstick, knockabout role was given to the "clown." One of the first to play the role in British pantomime was Joseph GRIMALDI. After experimenting with other forms of makeup, including a face similar to the modern AUGUSTE CLOWN with a blue wig and motley wardrobe, Grimaldi synthesized the characteristics of the comic Commedia dell' Arte and pantomime clowns into his JOEY character.

Today's chalkfaced comedians are all descendants of the popular "Joey," with his white painted face and "pretty" costume. Grimaldi's distillation of the makeup, wardrobe and comic antics of the theater clown into the whiteface clown seen on circuses today earned him the title of the "Father of Clowning."

To apply whiteface makeup, the performer needs these basic materials: white greasepaint (water-based paints are available and easier to remove but not as dark and "full" as oil-based ones); colored greasepaints (usually red, blue and black); broad pencil liners, powder socks (ordinary cotton men's stockings, tied off at the end, with about a cupful of white talcum powder in each); and makeup brushes.

Ideally, the subject should be clean-shaven, with no stubble and a dry face. Some like to apply a base

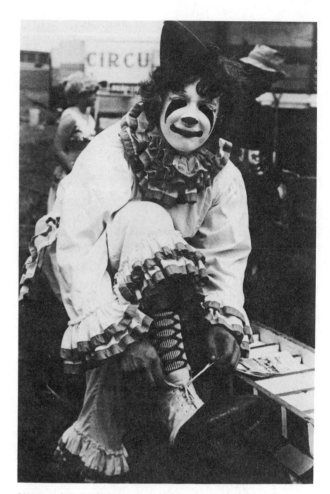

Classic whiteface clown, Lou Hyland, with Circus Kirk in 1972. (Photo courtesy of Charles A. DeWein)

of cold cream to fill the pores so that the makeup is easier to remove later. The first item that is applied is the white greasepaint. While some performers may use a damp sponge, the easiest and preferred method is to apply the paint in wide swipes with four fingers of the hand. The neck and ears must also be covered.

When first applied, the greasepaint will be streaky and uneven. It is smoothed out by "slapping" or "patting out." This is done exactly as the term suggests: The palms of the hands are used to gently slap over all of the painted areas. This helps to remove the finger streaks and distribute the heavier clumps of makeup onto lighter areas.

The paint will look greasy and shiny at this point and can easily be smeared, so it is essential to "powder down." The powder sock is beaten gently against the face, like a huge powder puff. Enough talc will seep through the holes in the cotton weave to take the shine off the makeup and "set" it. At this point—and this point only—it is better to use too much rather than too little powder: If the base greasepaint moves, everything painted on top of it will smear away as well. The powder should be smoothed out and any excess brushed away by using either a nylon makeup brush or a very soft sable paintbrush three or four inches wide.

After deciding on the colors, designs and lines that are to be added, the clown starts at the top of the face and works down. This allows the performer to rest his cheek or chin on his other hand as he draws on the paints. Most subjects use a forefinger to stroke on the color, but some use the greasepaint stick itself. Still others use a fine brush or a lining stick.

After all of the colors are applied, the face must be powdered down again using a talc sock. This should be a different stocking from the one used for the white greasepaint, or colors may splash onto the white base during the next makeup sessions. Some clowns keep a different sock for each color and powder down after applying each individual color. Powdering after the color application should be thorough but very light. A gentle brushing will again remove excess powder, while it sets and brings out the colors. Powdering or brushing too hard at this point smears the colors on the base and ruins the makeup.

Finally, lines are applied to help separate the colors from the white base and enhance their contrast. The lines, usually applied with a black liner pen, which is less greasy than the paint, should not be powdered. The outlines must appear strong and crisp.

A painted or character nose (made of sponge, putty or rubber), plus a wig or skull cap, wardrobe and possibly a hat are added. White gloves complete the look of the whiteface clown: Flesh-colored hands would spoil the illusion created by the rest of the makeup and wardrobe.

Like actors, clowns use various cold creams and oils to remove makeup after performing; each artist swears by a personal favorite. The easiest and cheapest way to remove makeup is to splash a generous amount of baby oil in each hand. Using both hands, the clown massages the painted areas of the face, throat and ears until the makeup is swimming in a colored, greasy mess. This is quickly wiped off with disposable paper towels or rags, followed by washing the face with soap and water.

WIEDEMANN BROS. BIG AMERICAN SHOWS The Big American Shows was a small tented circus owned and operated by Tom Wiedemann from 1908 through 1910. Wiedemann went on to manage the Kit Carson Wild West Show from 1911 through 1914 and the Barton & Bailey Circus in 1915.

WILLARD, JESS (1882–1968) As Joe LOUIS would do after him, Jess Willard was a boxing champion who entered the world of outdoor amusements as a star circus attraction. As opposed to Louis, however, Willard toured with the Wild West shows while he still held his heavyweight crown.

On April 15, 1915 Willard won his belt in Havana, Cuba, after knocking out Jack Johnson in the 26th round. Willard held the title until July 4, 1919, when he was knocked out in the third round by Jack Dempsey.

Willard joined the 101 RANCH WILD WEST in 1915. He also toured with it in 1916 when the show was renamed the BUFFALO BILL & 101 RANCH WILD WEST to celebrate William F. CODY's becoming a member of its troupe.

At the end of that season, Edward ARLINGTON bought out the shares of the show's co-owners, the Millers, and brought in Willard as a partner. Cody died while the show was in WINTER QUARTERS, but when the revamped circus came out in 1917 it was nevertheless retitled the BUFFALO BILL WILD WEST & JESS WILLARD SHOW.

Willard bought out the show from Arlington the following year. Unfortunately, the heyday of the Wild West show was over and the circus quickly folded.

WILLIAM P. HALL SHOWS See HALL, WILLIAM P.

WILLIE SELLS SHOWS Willie Sells, an adopted son of one of the Sells brothers, was first a performer in the SELLS BROTHERS CIRCUS, then later a part owner.

His other partnerships include: Sells & Andress (1889); Sells & Renfew (1892–1894); the Great Syndicate Shows (1895–96); Sells & Gray (1900–1); Sells & Downs (1902–5) and SELLS-FLOTO CIRCUS (1906).

WINDJAMMER Circus jargon for a member of a circus band. The oldest reference to "windjammer" in print is from 1904, as a theatrical expression meaning "a musician who plays a wind instrument." At the turn of the century, the word was also slang for any long-winded, talkative person.

Merle EVANS, longtime bandleader with the RINGLING BROS. AND BARNUM & BAILEY CIRCUS, named his own concert circus show band "The Windjammers." The band made several of the earliest recordings of circus music.

(See also WINDJAMMERS UNLIMITED, INC.)

WINDJAMMERS UNLIMITED, INC. The official fraternal group dedicated to the preservation of traditional circus music, Windjammers Unlimited, Inc. was founded in 1971 by Arthur Stensvad of North Platte, Nebraska and Charles Bennett, Jr. of Wichita, Kansas. Although most of its members are former or current musicians in circus bands, membership is open to anyone who loves the unique sound of the circus band.

The society is registered as a not-for-profit corporation in the state of Ohio. It is operated by a 16-member board of trustees and four corporate officers who govern over eight regional territories.

Each January its members hold a convention in SARASOTA, FLORIDA, where many of its members perform in the "Windjammers Circus Concert Band." Its first concert was a ten-piece band in 1973. In 1983 it boasted a 90-piece band, and by 1989 it had grown to 140 musicians. Two of the members of the original band, Ward Stauth (secretary-treasurer of the Windjammers) and Charles Schlarbaum (noted circus band director), still play today in the concert at the annual conclave. "Regional meets" are also held throughout the year.

The bimonthly publication of the Windjammers is *CIRCUS FANFARE*. Enrollment in the organization as well as a subscription to the magazine may be obtained through its offices at 2500 Old Forest Road, Corydon, Indiana 47112.

WINDOW CARDS Window cards are advertising LITHOGRAPH posters printed on light cardboard for displaying in windows or posting on poles. Distrib-

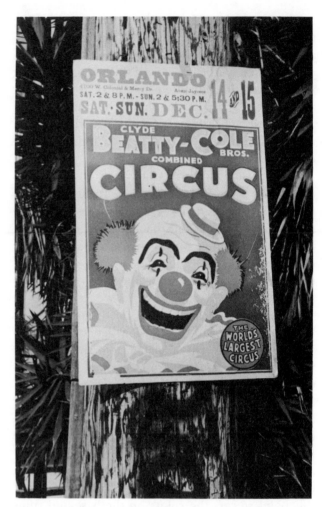

WINDOW CARD FOR THE CLYDE BEATTY-COLE BROS. CIRCUS. (Photo by Tom Ogden)

uted by the BILLING CREW, the ADVANCE MAN and the PRESS AGENT—in fact, by anyone in advance of the show—the posters are usually displayed by merchants in exchange for a pair or two of free passes to the show.

The standard size for a window card is 14 inches by 22 inches, slightly smaller than a ONE SHEET.

WINTER QUARTERS Sometimes shortened to "quarters," this is circus jargon for the location where a circus is housed when not on tour. The term developed because almost all early MUD SHOWS ceased travel during wintry weather. Even today, those shows that no longer work under canvas or have their off-season headquarters in warm climates use the expression for their homes when not on the road.

One of the entrance gates to the Ringling Bros. and Barnum & Bailey winter quarters, Sarasota, Florida in 1949.
(John Heckman photo from the Bakner collection)

In the early part of the 1800s, most circuses kept their winter quarters in the North. This kept them close to the larger cities, allowing easy access to maintenance materials that might be needed to restock and rebuild the show. Also, because most shows play their strongest routes early in the season (to ensure that they will meet their annual operating expenses, or NUT, and end the season "in the black"), circuses would quarter as close as possible to the large population centers.

As the cities grew and became more industrialized in the South, circuses began to take advantage of the better winter weather. Moving their quarters to a southern climate allowed the circuses more weeks to repair and refurbish their shows before the opening of the following season.

Even after the circuses' flood of moves to Florida (especially into the Orlando-Tampa-Sarasota area), several northern cities are still fondly remembered and identified as circus towns because of the great shows that were quartered there. These include: BARABOO, WISCONSIN; BRIDGEPORT, CONNECTICUT; and PERU, INDIANA.

WIRE WALKING   "Walking the tightrope," a cliché that has its source in the world of the circus, has come to mean any dangerous, risky or anxiety-ridden activity. Besides the tightrope, however, there are many other types of wire walking acts, and each has its own unique apparatus and circus jargon. In addition to the ability to balance, all types of wire walking require that the artist consider variables such as heat, wind and the height and tension of the wire itself.

The word "tightrope" is frequently used by lay people instead of "tightwire"; but once reliable cable became readily available about the turn of the century, circus performers began to change their rigging to use steel wire instead of rope or cloth cord.

Los Posos, wire walkers from Colombia, South America, perform on the open-air high wire on the Bentley Bros. Circus in 1990. Note the height of their tightrope in relation to the center poles behind them. (Photo by Tom Ogden)

Today circus folk refer to "tightrope walkers" by the more technically correct term "tightwire walkers."

The high wire, also often seen as "highwire," is the act that noncircus people most often think of as wire walking. The standard high wire runs approximately 35 feet in length and is set about 30 feet off the ground. On some special occasions or exhibitions, wire walkers have been known to cross significantly longer spans, such as Philippe PETIT's cross between the twin towers of Manhattan's World Trade Center. This type of daredevil stunt is aptly known as a SKYWALK.

Circus people never use the phrase "wire act" to mean the high wire. Instead, the term refers to a type of wire walking act performed closer to the ground. The most common of these is the low wire, with a 15- to 20-foot length of taut wire set about six feet off the arena floor and strung between two pieces of upright triangular framework. The artist, who does not have to fear a major fall from a great height, can concentrate on more entertaining stunts while performing closer to the audience.

The slack wire rigging is similar to the low wire apparatus, but the wire itself is not pulled tight. Because the performer must control the side-to-side swaying while maintaining vertical balance, the slack wire is often used for comic effect. Many performers feel that the slack wire is much more difficult than a standard low wire because every bit of swing or shakiness by the artist is multiplied several times over.

Some contemporary performers prefer the flex or "give" of cloth cord rather than wire. If they use actual rope in their rigging, the act is known as a slack rope act. Another type of "low wire" act that uses cord is called the bounding rope. The rope is pulled taut, but it is connected to the rigging by a hard spring at one or both ends. This allows an extra bounce when the performer climbs, sits on or walks the rope, often resulting in increased laughter by the audience.

The history of tightrope walking dates back at least as far as the times of the Roman emperors, as evidenced by early frescoes. The earliest written records of rope walking were around 1385, however, when M. Froissart, a Parisian, described a FUNAMBULIST at the celebration of Charles VI's wedding to Isabel of Bavaria. Rope walkers were also staples of country fairs and jubilees in 16th- and 17th-century England.

The first slack rope walker to be seen in New York was Anthony J. Dugee in 1753. Wire walking was not introduced into the American circus until John Bill RICKETTS included a rope walker as part of his show in 1793. Wire walking had been raised to a fine art by the time BLONDIN made his first famous walk on rope stretched across Niagara Falls on June 30, 1859.

Sando Counts, wire walker with the PICKLE FAMILY CIRCUS from 1977 through 1980, claims it's easier than it looks:

> When you're on the rope, there's really a lot of surface area to stand on, your foot curves around and touches a lot of rope. But your foot doesn't curve that much, and when it tries to keep curving . . . well, that's why people are shaky on the rope at first.
>
> There's one great secret of wire-walking. . . . and I'll tell you what it is: Keep your ass over the rope. That was always my rule; that was always what I thought about first, last and always. Keep your ass over the rope. There's a trick I did . . . sitting on a chair on the rope. It's a very, very hard balance. And the secret is . . . well, you know.

The United States has had its share of beauty on the wire, such as the graceful Bird MILLMAN. But perhaps the wire walker who most captured the audience's imagination is the name now synonymous with wire walking: Karl WALLENDA of The WALLENDAS.

(See also ALZANA, HAROLD; COLLEANO, CON; NAITTO, ALA; PETIT, PHILIPPE; WEBER HERBIE.)

WIRTH, MAY (1896–1978)

Born in Queensland, Australia, May Wirth (occasionally seen as Mae Wirth in early circus posters) came from a family of circus performers and riders. She was a five-year old orphan when she began performing with a contortion act on Australia's popular Wirth Brothers Circus. The following year she was adopted by two of the show's owners, Maricles Wirth Martin, an accomplished equestrienne, and her husband John. Mrs. Martin trained May and her sister in the art of bareback riding in her youth. By her teens, she was performing as an equestrienne.

John Ringling saw Wirth in Australia and invited her to join his show. In 1911, accompanied by Mrs. Martin, May Wirth moved to the United States. In 1912 Wirth made her American debut in the CENTER RING of the BARNUM & BAILEY CIRCUS in MADISON SQUARE GARDEN when she was only 17 years old. By the time the show merged with the RINGLING BROS. CIRCUS in 1919, May Wirth was already an established star, billed as "The Greatest Bareback Rider That Ever Lived."

Critics were ecstatic in their praise. The critic for the *New York Clipper,* for instance, wrote, "Pretty of face and finely formed, she is the acme of ease and grace. But she does not rely upon her physical attractions for her success. She is an equestrienne in all that the word implies."

May Wirth was known for thrilling tricks on bareback, all performed with incredible grace. She could already perform a flawless forward somersault (even from a kneeling position) when Orrin DAVENPORT, the well-known American rider, taught her the backward somersault—making her the first woman to accomplish this feat. (This trick, which begins with the performer standing on the horse facing away from the head, was also a stunt in the repertoire of famed rider James ROBINSON.) Wirth soon added a half twist to this stunt, so that she faced in the opposite direction as she landed. She could also perform a double backward somersault from one horse to another galloping behind it, even while blindfolded.

From Australian rider John Cooke, May Wirth learned the "flip-flap" trick: Standing on horseback, she would drop to a handstand, then push herself back to an upright position. She repeated this several times as the horse cantered around the ring. Despite her short stature compared to the horse, Wirth was such a master of VAULTING onto the back of a moving horse that she often wore wicker baskets over her feet to make the trick more challenging.

During her 26 years in the ring, Wirth had only one serious accident. On April 22, 1913, in Brooklyn, New York she was lying on a horse's back with her foot in a loop stirrup. The horse shied, and she slipped from its back. Still held by the stirrup, she was dragged five full circles around the ring, with her head bumping the RING CURB. Although she was knocked unconscious and suffered a concussion, she soon returned to the ring.

May Wirth appeared with the RINGLING BROTHERS AND BARNUM & BAILEY CIRCUS from 1916 until 1929. When the show was in WINTER QUARTERS she toured on the Keith and Orpheum vaudeville circuits. Her performances were seen by American presidents Wilson and Harding, and her shows overseas were attended by royalty such as King Edward VII and Queen Alexandra.

After leaving Ringling, Wirth continued to play longer fair and variety dates until she retired in 1938. With her husband Frank (who, like Fred BRADNA, had taken his famous wife's last name) she opened a talent booking agency, which she operated until her death in 1978. May Wirth is still recognized as the greatest woman bareback rider the American circus has ever seen. Fred Bradna, the RINGMASTER during most of her tenure on the Ringling show, put it quite simply when he wrote: "Her like will never be seen again."

WITH IT

Circus jargon meaning that a member of the company has loyalty to the show. Different from ON THE SHOW, which indicates that the person is one of the troupe, "with it" or "with it and for it" suggests a deeper dedication to a greater good for the show.

WORLD CLOWN ASSOCIATION

The World Clown Association is one of the largest fraternal clubs dedicated to the art of clowning. As of June 1990, the association's membership numbered 2,288 members.

Besides sponsoring a major one-week international clown convention each summer, the association also publishes a monthly magazine, *CLOWNING AROUND*, edited by Gene LEE. Each issue features performance tips, advertisements of clown supplies and news of clowning.

The association's motto is "We Clown Around the World." Offices are located at World Clown Associan, P.O. Box 273, Grandview, Missouri 64030.

W.W. COLE CIRCUS See COLE, W(ILLIAM) W(ASHINGTON) "CHILLY BILLY".

X, THE In circus jargon, having the "X" means possessing the "exclusive" right to sell a particular product or service on the circus LOT. For instance, if one of the FREAKS was the only performer allowed to hawk souvenir postcards of himself in the SIDE-SHOW, he would have the "X" on picture sales. A BUTCHER might have the "X" on COTTON CANDY or inflated balloons.

Circus management, of course, expects payment of a PRIVILEGE from the cast member to be accorded the "X." The amount of the privilege varies depending on the demand for the "X" and its income potential; it is usually paid weekly in the form of a flat sum because a commission on sales would be difficult, if not impossible, to ascertain and collect.

YANKEE DOODLE CIRCUS   A new one-ring indoor show, the Yankee Doodle Circus is owned and operated by Mike Naughton. Performing mostly in the area surrounding its WINTER QUARTERS in New York State, the show plays in front of a colorful red-and-white striped backdrop.

In addition to the full show, there are also novelties and concessions BUTCHERS.

YANKEE ROBINSON AND RINGLING BROTHERS GREAT DOUBLE SHOWS, CIRCUS AND CARAVAN   See RINGLING BROTHERS, THE; ROBINSON, YANKEE; YANKEE ROBINSON CIRCUS.

YANKEE ROBINSON CIRCUS   The first Yankee Robinson Circus was begun by impresario Yankee ROBINSON in 1854. In the early years, the show gave matinees only, using the BIG TOP for dramatic performances of *Uncle Tom's Cabin*. Thus Robinson became the first of hundreds of tented repertory shows to enact theatrical versions of the famous Harriet Beecher Stowe novel.

Robinson had two units on the road by 1858. On the second unit he became one of the first circus owners to house and feed all of the show personnel on the LOT rather than putting them up in hotels.

In 1859 the name "Yankee" Robinson infuriated southerners in the Carolinas. The show folk had to flee a lynch mob, leaving behind all their equipment.

Yankee Robinson rallied and the show made a comeback during the Civil War years, from 1860 to 1864. For the next four years after the war, the Yankee Robinson Circus was one of the largest wagon shows on tour. By 1869 it was outgrossing every other circus on the road. The success was short-lived, however; Robinson put out a second unit again in 1870, but this time both units lost money. By 1876 the circus had gone bankrupt.

Yankee Robinson died in 1884 at the age of 66 after operating a tented theater for seven years and a tour with the young RINGLING BROTHERS. His name was not used on a circus again until Fred Buchanan toured a Yankee Robinson Circus from 1905 through 1920. Buchanan then sold his show and title to the AMERICAN CIRCUS CORPORATION, and the name was added to the GOLLMAR BROS. CIRCUS of 1922.

YI, LU (1939–   )   Born in the Jiangsu Province of China in 1939, Lu Yi has been variously a consultant, director and trainer for CIRCUS OZ, the BIG APPLE CIRCUS and the PICKLE FAMILY CIRCUS.

Having studied with the famous acrobat Pan Ying in 1952, Yi began performing two years later. Beginning in the Shanghai Red Acrobatic Troupe, his acts included plate spinning, martial arts and the pagoda of bowls. In 1957 he moved on to the Nanjing Acrobatic Troupe and was elected a star performer in the Nanjing Art Festival two years later. From 1963 to 1976 he performed hand balancing, worked on the TEETERBOARD and the unicycle.

During the 1980s he trained performers with the Circus Oz in Australia, then directed performances for the Big Apple Circus in New York in 1988 and 1989.

In 1991 Yi become Master Trainer for the Pickle Family Circus; and from the time he arrived in San Francisco on March 21, his work was clearly seen in that year's production, "La La Luna Sea." Yi also assisted in teaching the intermediate and advanced classes of the Pickle Family Circus School.

Lu Yi is president, artistic director and chairman of the Artists Jury in Nanjing, vice-chairman of the All-China Acrobatics Association, a member of the China Culture Union Committee and chairman of the Jiangsu Acrobatic Artists Associations.

YOUNG BUFFALO BILL WILD WEST SHOW   The show, operated 1910 through 1914, was one of several Wild Wests that shamelessly traded on the name of Buffalo Bill. It had no connection with the BUFFALO BILL WILD WEST AND PAWNEE BILL GREAT FAR EAST SHOW that was touring at the same time.

Z

ZACCHINI, HUGO (1898–1975) Although he had predecessors, the name Hugo Zacchini is synonymous with the term "HUMAN CANNONBALL."

Zacchini conceived the modern form of the classic act while serving with the Italian artillery in World War I. In 1922 he first performed the human cannonball act on the island of Malta while appearing on his father's show, the Zacchini Bros. Circus. The chrome cannon, developed in Italy by his father, Ildebrano, and brother, Edmondo, and valued at $35,000, was permanently mounted on the back of a truck.

Rather than relying on spring tension, Zacchini's cannon used compressed air to hurl him at a reported speed of 80 miles per hour, 75 feet into the air and 150 feet horizontally into a net. The rush of air, accompanied by a small powder charge for cosmetic effect, gave a huge, thunderous clap.

In 1929 John RINGLING saw the act in Copenhagen, Denmark and immediately invited Zacchini to join the RINGLING BROS. AND BARNUM & BAILEY CIRCUS.

During Zacchini's 40-year career, he toured with many circuses and performed for special events. He returned to the Ringling show in 1934 when he and his brother, Mario, were shot from a double-barreled cannon. Five years later Zacchini appeared at the New York World's Fair. Hugo Zacchini continued to actively perform through the 1950s, including a tour on the Cristiani Bros. Circus.

Zacchini once described the sensation of being shot from a cannon to an interviewer:

Oh, I used to be frightened. Now it's nothing. When I am shot out, the jar knocks the breath from my lungs. It comes back on the way to the net. And when I hit the net, it is knocked out again. It is nothing.

Hugo Zacchini left the circus ring in 1961. His original cannon is on display at the CIRCUS WORLD MUSEUM in BARABOO, WISCONSIN. His son, Hugo A. Zacchini, and nephew, Hugo Zacchini II (Edmondo's son), most actively continued to re-create the act; but over the years five Zacchini brothers and eight of their children have performed as human cannonballs. During World War II, for instance, while the Zacchini men were serving in the armed forces, they were replaced by the Zacchini women. Of them all, only Hugo Zacchini II still performs as a human cannonball today.

Besides being a master at his circus craft, Zacchini was also an accomplished oil painter. He had graduated from the Rome Art Academy in 1919, and art remained his lifelong passion. In fact, he confided to friends that he would much rather have been "another Michelangelo or Rembrandt than a mere bullet." He once told a reporter backstage at a MADISON SQUARE GARDEN performance, "Do not forget that it is as a painter, as an artist, that it is my ambition to be known. My cannon cannot give me the thrills that I can get with my brush." After his retirement to Fontana, California Hugo Zacchini taught art classes at Chaffey College in nearby Alta Loma.

He died of a stroke in San Bernardino, California on October 20, 1975.

(See also LOYAL, GEORGE; LULU; ZAZEL.)

ZANIES Circus jargon for CLOWNS.

ZAZEL (1865–1919) Born Rosa M. Richter in England, Zazel was the first great HUMAN CANNONBALL. She was first shot from a cannon, landing in a net, in 1877.

P.T. BARNUM had known about Zazel for years. In an August 15, 1878 letter to Schuyler Colfax (the vice president under Ulysses S. Grant) Barnum wrote, "I have *seen* the woman shot from the cannon and have been trying for a year to get her. Hope to succeed." Barnum introduced Mademoiselle Zazel to American audiences in 1880 in BARNUM'S GREAT TRAVELING MUSEUM, MENAGERIE, CARAVAN, HIPPODROME AND CIRCUS.

Wearing pink tights, Zazel climbed into the mouth of the wooden cannon and was "fired bodily from a cannon, flying with violent velocity through the air for a distance of over 75 feet and falling upon a net." Over the years, Zazel was a feature on many circuses. During that period several other human cannonballs "borrowed" her name. Her career ended suddenly and tragically when she missed the net during a performance and broke her back. She was confined in a steel corset until her death on November 25, 1919.

(See also LOYAL, GEORGE; LULU; ZACCHINI, HUGO.)

ZERBINI, JOHN "TARZAN" See TARZAN ZERBINI CIRCUS.

ZOOLOGICAL INSTITUTE Following the success of Hachaliah BAILEY's exhibition of OLD BET in and around SOMERS, NEW YORK, many of his farmer-neighbors in Brewster turned showmen, among them Nathan A. HOWES, his partner AARON TURNER and Nathan's brother, Seth B. HOWES, who made his circus fortune primarily in Europe.

These and most of the other major American MENAGERIE owners met on January 14, 1835 at the ELEPHANT HOTEL in Somers and formed a syndicate, the Zoological Institute. While its stated purpose was "to more generally diffuse and promote the knowledge of natural history and gratify rational curiosity," the institute's true purpose was probably to attempt to control the exhibition of menagerie animals in the United States.

With their separate and collectively owned shows, John J. JUNE, Lewis B. TITUS, Caleb S. ANGEVINE, Lewis B. LENT, Gerard Crane and others attempted to control first the exhibition of wild animals, then many of the routes, and therefore the business, of circuses in the eastern United States.

With 128 shareholders, not all of them showmen, the Zoological Institute set up its menagerie and new headquarters in the Bowery district of New York City. The Institute owned most of the imported wild and exotic animals in the country at the time, so it was able to lease them out on their own terms. Those circuses not working with the syndicate were often mysteriously wrecked or burned.

The Zoological Institute disbanded as a corporation on August 23, 1837, but many of its zealous, monopolistic practices were carried on by the FLATFOOTS.

ZOPPE, ALBERTO (1922–   ) A fourth-generation equestrian, Alberto Zoppe's great-grandfather started the first Zoppe riding troupe and circus (Circo Zoppe) in Italy in 1842. A cousin to Secondo Zoppe and Aurelia Zavatta of The ZOPPE-ZAVATTA FAMILY, Alberto Zoppe was born January 4, 1922 in Vittorio Veneto, Italy. He arrived in the United States in 1948 and opened on the RINGLING BROS. AND BARNUM & BAILEY CIRCUS the following year. His troupe included his sister Ruggera and their 38-inch-tall cousin, Cucciolo. The Zoppes were among the Ringling acts Cecil B. De Mille shot in the winter of 1949–50 as background performers for his 1952 circus film *The Greatest Show on Earth* (see FILMS, CIRCUS).

When Zoppe left The BIG ONE and began to work independently, he solved the logistical problem of shipping his HORSES around the world by training two sets of RING STOCK. By sending a group of horses ahead to a second venue, Zoppe was able to double the number of dates played each season.

Eventually Alberto Zoppe opened his own shows, first Circus Italia, then the under-canvas Circus Fantasy and currently the Circus Europa. His routines expanded to include mixed CATS and horses. In 1977 his ten-year-old son, Giovanni, became the youngest circus performer to complete a full feet-to-feet somersault in a ROSINBACK act. Carla Zoppe-Emerson, Alberto's daughter, performs in her own troupe, the Zoppe Riders, for the CIRCUS WORLD MUSEUM.

ZOPPE-ZAVATTA TROUPE, THE   This large family of equestrians, led by Secondo Zoppe and his half sister, Aurelia Zavatta, first came to the United States in 1936 as the Aurelia Troupe to perform with the COLE BROS. CIRCUS. Their cousin, Alberto ZOPPE, followed 12 years later, opening on The GREATEST SHOW ON EARTH in 1949. Separate from Alberto Zoppe's activities, the Zoppe-Zavatta side of the family has created many different routines over the years, with such exotic titles as the "Original Indian Spectacular" and the "Bedouin Riders." The newest performing generation of the family includes James Zoppe, Secondo Zoppe's grandson, who started his own troupe in 1978. Acknowledged as a master equestrian, he appeared with The BIG APPLE CIRCUS in 1984 and 1985 and CIRCUS FLORA in 1988.

"Here Today; Gone Tomorrow. Tomorrow there will be nothing left but wagon tracks and popcorn sacks."   (Photo by Tom Ogden)

BIBLIOGRAPHY

BOOKS

American Circus Posters in Full Color. Edited by Charles Philip Fox. New York: Dover Publications, 1978.

American Heritage. *Great Days of the Circus.* New York: American Heritage Publishing Co., 1962.

Antekeier, Kristopher, and Greg Aunapu. *Ringmaster! My Year on the Road with "The Greatest Show on Earth."* New York: E. P. Dutton, 1989.

Ballantine, Bill. *Wild Tigers & Tame Fleas.* New York: Rinehart & Company, 1958.

Barnum, P.T. *Struggles and Triumphs: Or, Forty Years' Recollection of P.T. Barnum.* 1855. Reprint, edited and abridged with introduction by Carl Bode. New York: Penguin Books, 1981.

———. *Life of P.T. Barnum.* Buffalo: Courier Company, 1888.

———. *Selected Letters of P.T. Barnum.* Edited by A. H. Saxon. New York: Columbia University Press, 1983.

Baumann, Charly, and Leonard A. Stevens. *TIGER TIGER: My 25 Years with the Big Cats.* Chicago: Playboy Press, 1975; distributed by Simon & Schuster.

Beatty, Clyde, and Edward Anthony. *Facing the Big Cats: My World of Lions and Tigers.* Garden City, NY: Doubleday & Co., 1965.

Bergan, Ronald. *The Great Theatres of London.* London: Admiral Books, 1987.

Bradna, Fred, and Hartzell Spence. *The Big Top: My 40 Years with The Greatest Show on Earth.* New York: Simon and Schuster, 1952.

Brooks, Tim, and Earle Marsh. *The Complete Directory to Prime Time Network TV Shows, 1946–present,* rev. ed. New York: Ballantine Books, 1981.

Burgess, Hovey. *Circus techniques.* New York: Thomas Y. Crowell Company, 1977.

Cassidy, John, and B. C. Rimbeaux. *Juggling for the Complete Klutz,* 2nd ed. Stanford, CA: Klutz Press, 1977.

Clausen, Connie. *I Love You Honey, But the Season's Over.* New York: Holt, Rinehart and Winston, 1961.

Clement, Herbert, and Dominique Jando. *The Great Circus Parade.* Milwaukee: Gareth Stevens Publishing, 1989.

Coxe, Antony Hippisley. *A Seat at the Circus.* London: Evans Brothers, 1951.

———. *A Seat at the Circus,* rev. ed. Hamden, CT: Archon Books, 1980.

Culhane, John. *The American Circus: An Illustrated History.* New York: Henry Holt and Company, 1990.

Dickens, Charles. *Memoirs of Joseph Grimaldi.* Annotated and edited by Arichard Findlater. New York: Stein and Day, 1968.

Drimmer, Frederick. *Very Special People.* New York: Amjon Publishers, 1973.

Durant, John, and Alice Durant. *Pictoral History of the American Circus.* South Brunswick, NJ: A.S. Barnes and Company, 1957.

Eckley, Wilton. *The American Circus.* Boston: Twayne Publishers, 1984.

Faith, Nicholas. *The World the Railways Made*. New York: Carroll & Graf, 1990.

Fellows, Dexter W., and Andrew A. Freeman. *This Way to the Big Show: The Life of Dexter Fellows*. New York: Viking Press, 1936.

Fowler, Gene, and Bess Meredyth. *The Mighty Barnum: A Screen Play*. New York: Couici-Friede, 1934.

Fox, Charles Philip. *A Ticket to the Circus*. New York: Bramhall House in association with Superior Publishing Co., 1959.

———. *A Pictoral History of Performing Horses*. New York: Bramhall House in association with Superior Publishing Co., 1960.

Fox, Charles Philip, and Tom Parkinson. *The Circus in America*. Waukesha, WI: Country Beautiful, 1969.

Gaona, Tito with Harry L. Graham. *Born to Fly: The Story of Tito Gaona*. Los Angeles: Wild Rose, 1984.

Gebel-Williams, Gunther with Toni Reinhold. *Untamed: The Autobiography of the Circus' Greatest Animal Trainer*. New York: William Morrow, 1990.

Gianolo, Luigi. *Horses and Horsemanship Through the Ages*. Translated by Iris Brooks. New York: Crown Publishers, 1969.

Goldsmith, Lynn. *Circus Dreams*. New York: Rizzoli International Publications, 1991.

Gollmar, Robert H. *My Father Owned a Circus*. Caldwell, ID: Caxton Printers, 1965.

Green, Stanley. *Encyclopedia of the Musical Theatre*. New York: Da Capo Press, 1976.

The Guinness Book of World Records 1991. Edited by Donald McFarlan. New York: Bantam Books, 1991.

The Guinness Book of Records 1993. Edited by Peter Matthews. New York: Facts On File, 1992.

Hall, Ward. *Struggles and Triumphs of a Modern Day Showman: An Autobiography*. Sarasota, FL: Carnival Publishers, 1981.

Halliwell, Leslie. *Halliwell's Film Guide*, 7th ed. New York: Harper & Row, 1989.

Hamid, George A., as told to his son George A. Hamid, Jr. *Circus*. New York: Sterling Publishing Co., 1950.

Hammarstrom, David Lewis. *Behind the Big Top*. South Brunswick, NJ: A. S. Barnes and Company, 1980.

———. *Big Top Boss: John Ringling North and the Circus*. Urbana, IL: University of Illinois Press, 1992.

Harris, Neil. *Humbug: The Art of P.T. Barnum*. Boston: Little, Brown and Company, 1973.

Henderson, J.Y., and Richard Taplinger. *Circus Doctor*. Boston: Little, Brown and Company, 1951.

Hill, Charlie. *First of May*. Sarasota, FL: Carnival Publishers, 1978.

Hoh, LaVahn, and William H. Rough. *Step Right Up! The Adventure of Circus in America*. White Hall, VA: Betterway Publications, 1990.

Hubler, Richard. *The Cristianis*. Boston: Little, Brown and Company, 1966.

Hunt, Charles T., Sr., and John C. Cloutman. *The Story of "Mister Circus."* Rochester, NH: Record Press, 1954.

Irey, Elmer L., with William J. Slocum. "Abandon All Beasts!" from *The Tax Dodgers*, 1948. In *Grand Deception,* ed. by Alexander Klein. Philadelphia, J. B. Lippincott Co., 1955.

Kelly, Emmett with F. Beverly Kelley. *Clown*. New York: Prentice-Hall, 1954.

Kirk, Rhina. *Circus Heroes and Heroines*. Maplewood, NJ: Hammond Incorporated, 1972.

Jay, Ricky. *Learned Pigs & Fireproof Women*. New York: Villard Books, 1986.

Jamieson, David, and Sandy Davidson. *The Colorful World of the Circus*. London: Octopus Books, 1980.

Keeshan, Bob. *Growing Up Happy: Captain Kangaroo Tells Yesterday's Children How to Nurture Their Own*. New York: Doubleday, 1989.

Kunzog, John C. *The One-Horse Show: The Life and Times of Dan Rice, Circus Jester and Philanthropist; A Chronicle of Early Circus Days*. Jamestown, NY: John C. Kunzog, 1962.

———. *Tanbark and Tinsel: A Galaxy of Glittering Gems from the Dazzling Diadem of Circus History*. Jamestown, NY: John C. Kunzog, 1970.

Lorant, Terry, and Jon Carroll. *The Pickle Family Circus*. San Francisco: Pickle Press, 1986.

Machotka, Hana. *The Magic Ring: A Year with the Big Apple Circus*. New York: William Morrow & Company, 1988.

Mandelbaum, Ken. *Not Since CARRIE: Forty Years of Broadway Musical Flops*. New York: St. Martin's Press, 1991.

May, Earl Chapin. *The Circus from Rome to Ringling*. New York: Duffield & Green, 1932. Reprint. New York: Dover Publications, 1963.

McKennon, Joe. *Horse Dung Trail: Saga of the American Circus*. Sarasota, FL: Carnival Publishers, 1975.

———. *Logistics of the American Circus: Written by a Man Who Was There.* Sarasota, FL: Carnival Publishers, 1977.

———. *Horse Dung Trail: Saga of the American Circus. Index.* Sarasota, FL: Carnival Publishers, 1979.

———. *Circus Lingo: Written by a Man Who Was There.* Sarasota, FL: Carnival Publishers, 1980.

———. *Logistics of the American Circus: Ringling Brothers and Barnum & Bailey Supplement; Written by a Man Who Was There.* Sarasota, FL: Carnival Publishers, 1984.

———. *Rape of an Estate.* Sarasota, FL: Joe McKennon, 1986.

———. *The Back Yard Scene.* Sarasota, FL: Joe McKennon, 1990.

McKennon, Marian. *Tent Show.* New York: Exposition Press, 1964.

McNeil, Alex. *Total Television: A Comprehensive Guide to Programming from 1948 to the Present,* 2nd ed. New York: Penguin Books, 1984.

Miller, Art "Doc." *Little Ol' Show.* Art "Doc" Miller, 1982.

Murray, Marian. *Circus! From Rome to Ringling.* New York: Appleton-Century-Crofts, 1956.

Nash, Jay Robert, and Stanley Ralph Ross. *The Motion Picture Guide, 1927–1983.* Chicago: Cinebooks, 1987.

North, Henry R., and Alden Hatch. *The Circus Kings: Our Ringling Family Story.* Garden City, NY: Doubleday & Company, 1960.

Novosti Press Agency Publishing House. *Tonight and Every Night: The Soviet Circus Is 70 Years Old.* Novosti Press Agency Publishing House, 1989.

Parkinson, Tom, and Charles Philip Fox. *The Circus Moves by Rail.* Boulder, CO: Pruett Publishing Company, 1978.

Partridge, Eric. *A Dictionary of Slang and Unconventional English.* New York: Macmillan, 1961.

Plowden, Gene. *Those Amazing Ringlings and Their Circus.* New York: Bonanza Books, 1967.

———. *Gargantua: Circus Star of the Century.* New York: Bonanza Books, 1977.

———. *Singing Wheels and Circus Wagons.* Caldwell, ID: Caxton Printers, 1977.

———. *Circus Press Agent: The Life and Times of Roland Butler.* Caldwell, ID: Caxton Printers, 1984.

Powledge, Fred. *Mud Show: A Circus Season.* New York: Harcourt Brace Jovanovich, 1975.

Ragan, David. *Who's Who in Hollywood.* New York: Facts On File, 1992.

Rennert, Jack, and The Circus World Museum. *American Circus Posters* (auction book). Baraboo, WI: Circus World Museum, 1984.

Sanders, Toby. *How to Be a Compleat Clown.* New York: Stein and Day, 1978.

Saxon, A.H. *P.T. Barnum: The Legend and the Man.* New York: Columbia University Press, 1989.

Sifakis, Carl. *The Encyclopedia of American Crime.* New York: Facts On File, 1982.

———. *The Mafia Encyclopedia.* New York: Facts On File, 1987.

Simon, Peter Angelo. *Big Apple Circus.* New York: Penguin Books, 1978.

Speaight, George. *A History of the Circus.* San Diego: A.S. Barnes and Company, 1980.

Sutton, Felix. *The Big Show: A History of the Circus.* Garden City, NY: Doubleday & Company, 1971.

Taylor, Robert Lewis. *Center Ring: The People of the Circus.* Garden City, NY: Doubleday & Company, 1956.

Thayer, Stuart. *Annals of the American Circus. Volume II. 1830–1847.* Seattle: Peanut Butter Publishing, 1986.

———. *Annals of the American Circus. Volume III. 1848–1860.* Seattle: Dauven & Thayer, 1992.

Tompert, Ann. *The Greatest Showman on Earth: A Biography of P.T. Barnum.* Minneapolis, MN: Dillon Press, 1987.

Tully, Jim. *Circus Parade.* New York: Albert & Charles Boni, 1927.

Twain, Mark. *Adventures of Huckleberry Finn.* New York: Signet Classic, 1959.

Uehling, Carl T. *Blood Sweat & Love.* Philadelphia: Fortress Press, 1970.

Vail, R.W.G. *Random Notes on the History of the Early American Circus.* Worcester, MA: American Antiquarian Society, 1933; The Davis Press, 1934.

Verney, Peter. *Here Comes the Circus.* New York: Paddington Press, 1978.

Wallace, Irving. *The Fabulous Showman: The Life and Times of P.T. Barnum.* New York: Alfred A. Knopf, 1959.

Wallace, Irving, and Amy Wallace. *The Two.* New York: Simon and Schuster, 1978.

Walters, T.A. *The Encyclopedia of Magic and Magicians.* New York: Facts On File, 1988.

Wilson, Mark. *Mark Wilson Course in Magic.* North Hollywood, CA: Mark Wilson Publications, 1975.

NEWSPAPERS AND MAGAZINES

Allen, Stan. "Tihany, Coming to America." *Inside Magic* (August 1989).

Andre, Mila. "Moscow Circus Onstage." *Playbill* (December 1991):8, 10.

Barber, Matthew. "No Illusions: Cirque du Soleil." *San Francisco Independent,* 1991.

Barnes, Harold. "Ring of Fame." *Circus Report,* 25 January 1993, 23–25.

Barton, Billy. *Circus Report* (14 December 1992):21.

Billboard. 9 December 1911, p. 22, quoted by Stuart Thayer, "A Parting of the Ways," *Bandwagon* (January–February 1991):45.

———. "Slivers Oakley" (obit.), 10 March 1916.

Brattle, Blue. "About Clowns International." *Clowning Around* (February 1991):8.

Buchalter, Gail. "The Circus Taught Him Love." *Parade Magazine,* 18 August 1991, 18–19.

Burnes, Chuck. "From So. Calif." *Circus Report* (17 August 1992):14.

Bygrave, Michael. "Circus Vargas." *The Executive* (February 1986):38–40.

Cain, Frank. "Capt. Louis Roth." *Circus Report* (8 March 1993):25.

Chandler, Betty B. "Hanging of the Elephant Keeping Erwin on the map." *The Erwin Record,* 2 October 1991, 8A.

Chester Standard, Chester, South Carolina, June 25, 1857, quoted by Stuart Thayer, "A Parting of the Ways," *Bandwagon* (January–February 1991):46.

Circus Report. "Elephant Killed." 7 October 1991, 22.

Clowning Around. June 1990–March 1991, double issue May–June 1991, July 1991–December 1991. Monthly.

———. November 1992. Cover.

Cobblestone 3, no. 8 (August 1982).

Collins, Glenn. "Daring the Impossible." *New York Times Magazine,* 30 December 1990.

———. "Under the Small Top in the Big Apple." *New York Times,* 26 October 1990.

Countryside. "Circus Flora." (Spring 1993:100–105).

Davis, Robert. "Berserk Elephant Gunned Down." *USA TODAY,* 3 February 1992, 3A.

Dean, Chuck. "Join the Circus." *Special Report: Personalities* (May–July 1990):67.

Dean, Paul. "Under the Small Top." *Los Angeles Times* ("View," 14, June 1992).

Disend, Michael. "When Red Horses Die." *Special Report: Personalities* (May–July 1990):24–33.

Drake, Sylvie. "*Quelle* 'Experience.'" *Los Angeles Times,* 13 October 1990, pp. F1, F7.

Fairbanks, Donald A. "40 Years Young, Wenatchee Youth Circus Is Thriving." *The White Tops* (November–December 1992):76–81.

Graham, Harry L. "The Tragic Fall of Aerial Queen Margarita Vazquez Ayala." *Circus Report* (Printed in four weekly installments, October 1, 8, 15, 22, 1990).

Hay, Peter. "Gone to the Dogs." *Performing Arts* (May 1991):54.

Hoffman, Neil. "Las Vegas Desert Spiel." *Drama-Logue,* 14–20 November 1991, 27.

Horsman, Paul. "James M. Cole, Ingenious Showman and Friend." *The White Tops* (March/April 1993):44–45.

Hurt, Henry. "An Angel on High." *Reader's Digest* (March 1991):191–224.

Jackler, Rosaline. "Judge Roy Hofheinz." *Houston Post,* 23 November 1982.

James, Jimmy. "Jimmy James, voice of the big top" (as told to Gordon Taylor). *The White Tops* (November–December 1992):18–21.

Johnson, Bruce. "The Spotlight Classic Routines." *Clowning Around* (December 1990):12.

———. "Educationally Speaking." *Clowning Around* (July 1991):2–3.

———. "Educationally Speaking." *Clowning Around* (August 1991):3.

———. "Educationally Speaking." *Clowning Around* (September 1991):3–4.

Johnston, Bill. "African Elephants with American Circuses 1804–1936." *Bandwagon* (May–June 1992):24.

King, Orin Copple. "The Only Triple-Horned Unicorn, Chapter 4, Part Two: The Gates of Wonderland Thrown Wide Apart." *Bandwagon* 35, no. 4 (July–August 1991):38–46.

———. "The Big 25 Cent Wagon Show or The Times & Troubles of Lucky Bill Newton." *Bandwagon* (November–December 1992):4–12.

Los Angeles Times. "Morning Report," 30 October 1991, F2.

———. "Lou Jacobs" (obit.), 16 September, 1992, A20.

Lyke, Mary Lynn. "Strutting Peacock Turns into Graceful Eagle for the Cirque." *Post Intelligencer,* 29 June 1990.

———. "Cirque du Soleil." *Post Intelligencer,* C1, C3.

MacDonald, Amy. "Lord of the Rings." *Special Report: Personalities* (May–July 1990):63.

Meeks, Virginia. "Clowns Worth Knowing." *Clowning Around* (November 1990):12–13.

———. "Clowns Worth Knowing." *Clowning Around* (February 1991):28.

———. "Clowns Worth Knowing." *Clowning Around* (March 1991):22–23.

Mesic, Penelope. "The Great Circus Train." *Town and Country* (July 1991).

New York Clipper. 18 December 1858, p. 26, quoted by Stuart Thayer, "A Parting of the Ways," *Bandwagon* (January–February 1991):45.

New York Times. "Charles T. Hunt" (obit.), 12 September 1957, 31.

———. "Ella Bradna" (obit.), 13 November 1957, 32.

———. "Terrell Jacobs" (obit.), 26 December 1957, 19.

———. "Edwin Hanneford" (obit.), 11 December 1967, 47.

———. "Pat Valdo" (obit.), 12 November 1970, 46.

———. "Israel S. Feld" (obit.), 16 December 1972, 34.

———. "Hugo Zacchini" (obit.), 21 October 1975, 40.

———. "John Ringling North" (obit.), 6 June 1985, 18.

———. "Lou Jacobs" (obit.), 15 September 1992, A17.

Special Report: Personalities (May–July 1990).

Pfening, Fred D., Jr. "The Hoxie Tucker Story, Part One." *Bandwagon* (September–October 1992):4–16.

———. "The Hoxie Tucker Story, Part Two." *Bandwagon* (November–December 1992):16–32.

Pfening, Fred D. III. "Robert Lewis Parkinson 1923–1991." *Bandwagon* (March–April 1991):17–18.

Shettel, James W. "The 1st Elephant." *Circus Report* (9 November 1992):2–3.

State Journal, Topeka, Kansas. 30 January 1890. Quoted by Orin Copple King, "The Only Triple-Horned Unicorn, Chapter 4, Part Two: The Gates of Wonderland Thrown Wide Apart," *Bandwagon* 35, no. 4 (July–August 1991):45.

Thayer, Stuart. "The First Cookhouse." *Bandwagon* (July–August 1992):25.

———. "Bad Press, Big Crowds: The Barnum Caravan of 1851–1854." *Bandwagon* (September–October 1992):32–33.

Tuohy, Lynne. "Mystery of Girl Solved 47 Years After Fatal Fire." *Los Angeles Times,* 24 March 1991, A2, A26, from *The Hartford Courant.*

———. "Probe Reignites 1944 Circus Fire Arson Theory." *Los Angeles Times,* 24 March 1991, A2, A27, from *The Hartford Courant.*

———. " 'Red Man' Haunted Suspected Firebug." *Los Angeles Times,* 24 March 1991, A27, from *The Hartford Courant.*

USA Today. "Stores that Clown Around," 14 June 1991.

Van Gelder, Richard G. "A Big Pain." *Natural History* (March 1991):22–27.

Variety. "Cirque Du Soleil: Nouvelle Experience," 15 October 1990.

Wiley, Ed P. "A Bad Elephant." *Circus Report,* 9 October 1989, 29–30.

PRESS KITS

The Barnum Museum, 1991; Big Apple Circus, 1990, 1992; Carson & Barnes Circus, 1991; Circus Circus, 1991; Circus Vargas, 1991; Cirque Du Soleil, 1991, 1992; The Pickle Family Circus, 1990, 1992; Ringling Bros. and Barnum & Bailey Circus, 1990, 1991; Moscow Circus, 1991.

CIRCUS PROGRAMS

Bentley Bros. Circus, 1990; Big Apple Circus, 1990, 1992; Carson & Barnes Circus, 1989, 1991; The Circus Kingdom, 1989–92; Circus Kirk, 1970–76; Circus Vargas, 1990–1991; Circus World Museum, 1991; Cirque Du Soleil, 1989, 1991; Clyde Beatty-Cole Bros. Circus, 1970, 1971, 1974; Hoxie Bros. Circus, 1975, 1976; Kelly-Miller Bros. Circus, 1991–92; Mills Bros. Circus, 1966; Moscow Circus, 1991; Polack Bros. (Shrine) Circus, 1974, 1975; Ringling Bros. and Barnum & Bailey Circus, 1943, 1972, 1989–91; Sailor Circus, 1973; Tommy Scott's Country Music Circus, Stage Show and Wild West, 1990; Walt Disney's World on Ice, 1991; Wenatchee Youth Circus, 1975, 1976.

CIRCUS ROUTE BOOKS

Boas Bros. Circus, 1973; Circus Kirk, 1972, 1973; Carson & Barnes Circus, 1988, 1990, 1991, 1992;

Kelly-Miller Bros. Circus, 1992; Mills Bros. Circus, 1958.

VIDEOTAPES

All New Circus of the Stars & Side Show. Proctor & Gamble Prods., 1991.

The American Experience: Barnum's Big Top. WGBH Educational Foundation and WNET/Thirteen, 1991.

The American Experience: Coney Island. WGBH Educational Foundation, WNET/Thirteen and The Coney Island Film Project, 1991.

Barnum. Robert Halmi, Inc. 1986.

Circus: A Living Tradition. Spectral Films, 1987.

The Circus Kingdom: Highlights. Circus Kingdom, 1990.

Circus Kirk 20th Anniversary Reunion Video. 1989.

Circus of the Stars. 1991.

Circus Vargas. View Communication Group, 1989.

Cirque du Soleil: We Reinvent the Circus. Telemagic Prods., 1989.

Elephants: A National Geographic Special. The National Geographic Society, 1989.

Elephants and Cherry Pie. Diana Gerba, prod., 1988.

Great Circuses of the World. 1991.

The Greatest Show on Earth. Paramount, 1952.

The Great Wallendas. Daniel Wilson Prods. 1978.

It's Howdy Doody Time: A 40-Year Celebration. Fries Entertainment, 1987.

I Witness Video. National Broadcasting Company, 1992.

Learned Pigs & Fireproof Women. The Solt Egan Co.-Ricky Jay, 1989.

The Mighty Barnum. Twentieth Century, 1934.

Mister Rogers' Neighborhood. Family Communication, 1987.

The Most Death-Defying Circus Acts of All Times. Irvin Feld & Kenneth Feld Prods., 1987.

Penn & Teller Go Public. Community Television of Southern California, 1985.

Ringling Bros. and Barnum & Bailey Circus: 115th Edition Video Program Book. Irvin Feld & Kenneth Feld Prods., 1987.

Ringling Bros. and Barnum & Bailey Circus: 119th Edition Video Program Book. Ringling Bros. and Barnum & Bailey Combined Shows, 1989.

Ringling Bros. and Barnum & Bailey Circus: 120th Edition Video Program Book. Ringling Bros. and Barnum & Bailey Combined Shows, 1990.

Ringling Bros. and Barnum & Bailey Circus: 121st Edition Video Program Book. Ringling Bros. and Barnum & Bailey Combined Shows, 1991.

Ringling Bros. and Barnum & Bailey Circus Camp. Advanced Video Systems, 1991.

7 Wonders of the Circus World. Joe Cates Prods.

Strange, Odd and Curious. David Fulton, 1976.

INDEX

Boldface page numbers indicate main headings;
italic page numbers indicate illustrations or captions.